SPIRIT LIFE

The New Covenant Believer's Guide to Living and Walking in the Spirit

Vincent Boateng

(Apostle of Jesus Christ)

Spirit Life by Apostle Vincent Boateng
Published by Faithful & True Gospel Publications,
Vincent Boateng Ministries
Book cover designed by www.jdandj.com ©2017

Unless otherwise noted, all Scripture quotations are from the New King James Version of the Bible. Copyright ©1982 Thomas Nelson. All rights reserved.

All emphasis (i.e. capitalizations, boldface font, italics, bracketed information) in all Scripture quotations are the author's, unless otherwise noted.

Scripture quotations marked KJV are from the King James Version of the Bible.

Scripture quotations marked NIV are from the Holy Bible, New International Version. Copyright ©1984, International Bible Society.

Scripture Quotations marked NLT are from the Holy Bible, New Living Translation. Copyright 1996, 2004, 2007 by Tyndale House Foundation. All rights reserved.

Scripture quotations marked AMP are from the Amplified(R) Bible. ©2015 by the Lockman Foundation, La Habra, CA 90631. All rights reserved.

Scripture quotations marked ASV are from the Holy Bible, American Standard Version. Copyright ©1901 by Thomas Nelson & Sons.

Scripture Quotations marked ESV are from The Holy Bible, English Standard Version® (ESV®), Copyright © 2001 by Crossway, a publishing ministry of Good News Publishers. All rights reserved.

Scripture quotations marked NASB are from the New American Standard Bible. © 1960, 1962, 1963, 1968, 1971, 1972, 1973, 1975, 1977, 1995 by The Lockman Foundation. All rights reserved.

Hebrew and Greek word definitions marked "STRONG'S DEFINITIONS" are from:

Strong, J. (1890). Strong's exhaustive concordance of the Bible. Abingdon Press; &The New Strong's Exhaustive Concordance of the Bible, 1984, Thomas Nelson Publishers, New York.

Copyright ©2016 by Vincent Boateng & Vincent Boateng Ministries. All rights reserved.

For information about permission to reproduce selections from this book, email vincentboatengministries@gmail.com

Published in the USA by Faithful & True Gospel Publications, Virginia.

ISBN-13: 978-1-387-17118-7

"Behold, a door standing open in heaven." (see Revelation 4:1).

You're invited to enter the door before it is closed. Jesus said, "I am the door. If anyone enters by Me, he will be SAVED, and will go in and out and find pasture." (John 10:9).

**Dedicated to the Body of Christ,
with Love**

This is more than a book; it is life.

"I thank you, Father, Lord of Heaven and Earth, that You have hidden these things from the wise and prudent and revealed them to babes. Even so, Father, for so it seemed good in Your sight."

Contents

Introduction: As New Creations in Christ, We Were Created to Live and Walk in the Spirit, and Not in the Flesh xi

Chapter 1: The Biblical Truth About the First or Old Creation Headed By Adam. 1

Chapter 2: Adam's Fall and How God Came To The Rescue of Mankind .. 31

Chapter 3: Grace Was Given To Us in Christ Jesus Before Time Began ... 51

Chapter 4: The Evolution of God's Everlasting Covenant With Abraham and His Descendants 79

Chapter 5: The Law Was Given Through Moses 103

Chapter 6: Jesus the Spiritual Man Brought and Established the Spiritual Life 135

Chapter 7: Jesus' Walk of Faith 159

Chapter 8: Jesus' Faith Worked Through Love 205

Chapter 9: Jesus Our Sacrificial Lamb and Substitute 233

Chapter 10: Love Still Won 253

Chapter 11: Jesus Our Ransom 281

Chapter 12: The Death, Burial and Resurrection of Jesus Christ and How it Changed the Destiny of Man Forever 311

Chapter 13: He is Risen: The Power of the Resurrection of Jesus Christ . 345

Chapter 14: New Creation Realities 391

Chapter 15: The Spirit Walk: A Walk of Faith 421

Chapter 16: The Spirit Walk: A Walk in the Truth or in the Word of God 447

Chapter 17: The Spirit Walk: A Walk in Love 479

Chapter 18: The Spirit Walk: A Walk in the Light or in the Newness of Life 515

Chapter 19: The Spirit Walk: Being Led By the Spirit of God 565

Chapter 20: Unleash the Spiritual Man Inside of You 645

About the Author 665

Introduction

As New Creations in Christ, We Were Created to Live and Walk in the Spirit, and Not in the Flesh

"But you are not in the flesh but in the Spirit, if indeed the Spirit of God dwells in you…" (Romans 8:9). "If we live in the Spirit, let us also walk in the Spirit." (Galatians 5:25). "For if you live according to the flesh YOU WILL DIE; but if BY THE Spirit you put to death the deeds of the body, YOU WILL LIVE." (Romans 8:13).

FOR MANY PEOPLE, "How to walk in the Spirit" has become an all-too-familiar conundrum. There are many Christians today who are asking: "What does it mean to live and walk in the Spirit, and how do I live by walking in the Spirit as instructed by the Bible? How do I, BY THE SPIRIT, put to death the deeds of the body, so that I will LIVE, and not DIE?" This is an urgent question; it demands an immediate answer, because it is a matter of LIFE and DEATH. And yet, there is no major book until now that authoritatively and definitively offers a practical, Scriptural answer. The Bible says, "He has made everything beautiful in its time." (see Ecclesiastes 3:11). "Spirit Life," prophetic in its timing, offers the much-needed answer to the aforementioned conundrum. It is the first book to present the believer's walk in the Spirit as an all-encompassing lifestyle that comprises walking in love (see Ephesians 5:2), walking by faith and not by sight (2 Corinthians 5:7), walking in the Word of God or in the truth (see 3 John 1:3-4; Matthew 4:4; Ezekiel 36:27), walking in the light (see 1 John 1:7), walking in newness of life (see Romans 6:4), and walking in Christ (see Colossians 2:6). It also offers practical advice and guidance on how to accomplish each.

Beloved in Christ, you were created anew or born again to live and walk in the Spirit (or Spirit realm), and not in the flesh (or the natural or Sense realm). Therefore, in order to live effectively as a new creation, you need to fully understand what it means to live and walk in the Spirit. And in order to understand and appreciate the necessity of walking in the Spirit, you need to understand the differences between the New Creation (which you are now), and the first or Old Creation (which you used to be). There is so much to say about this subject, hence the birth of this book. Indeed this is a pioneering book, and I proclaim to the glory of God that it contains life-transforming revelations. If you are not a new creation (or a Christian), this book is for you also, and I can guarantee that by the time you finish reading it, you will understand why you must be born again in order to enter the Kingdom of God, and you will know how to receive the new birth experience and thus become a child of the Most High God. You will also understand why no born-again person should walk according to the flesh, and yes, you will know how you can walk in the Spirit consistently and demonstrate the Spirit and power of God.

My conscience bears me witness in the Holy Spirit that I didn't just set off to write this book; the Spirit dropped the idea in my spirit.

At the beginning I thought it was just going to be a 3-part series of teachings, so I started writing and sharing on my Ministry Page on Facebook. But toward the third part of the series, the Spirit told me to remove the limitation that I had put on the series, in terms of how many parts it was going to be, which I did. And it turned out to be a 20-Part series of teachings, which is now the basis for this book. I received many glorious testimonies from those who followed the teachings in the series on my page, about how much it blessed them. There were some who wanted to have personal copies of the entire series, as well as copies to share with friends and family. Therefore, moved by the Spirit, I decided to expound on the teachings and publish it as a book for the benefit of the entire humanity, and especially for the Body of Christ. I have no doubt that the revelation in this book is a gift from the Holy Spirit to our generation. This is indeed an anointed book for an anointed generation.

Before we launch into the first chapter, let me alert you also that a lot of the things you're going to learn here in this book would be new to you. I have personally not read or heard anyone preach some of these truths before, which is why I call it a pioneering book, but if you have, praise God! Most of the things you will read here will shake the very foundation of what "Vain Religion" has taught you to believe about Adam and the Old Creation he heads. It will also shake the very foundation of what "Vain Religion" has taught you about the New Creation which is headed by Jesus Christ. And this is mainly because I don't teach or preach an idea or doctrine just because it is popular, just because somebody else or even everybody else is teaching and preaching it; I only preach and teach what the Bible teaches, as the Holy Spirit reveals it to me, and so you will notice that everything I say, no matter how insignificant it may seem, is substantiated with a specific verse if not verses of Scripture. And trust me, all the Bible verses are easy to understand, because they mean exactly what they say. The prophecies of Scripture have no hidden or private meaning. (see 2 Peter 1:20-21). In fact, rather than add the Scriptural references as notes in the back matter to keep you going back and forth through the pages to look them up, I have inserted them in the main text of the book (and even in the middle of individual sentences where necessary) to make it easier for you to verify the accuracy of the teachings without turning a page — a sacrifice of the smooth flow of the sentences (in some cases) which I can assure you was worth making. For it is important to the Holy Spirit and to me that you read this book with your Bible in tow, and like the Berean Jews, examine the Scriptures to see if the things I'm saying are true.

To those of you who might question my teaching authority, I have nothing to tell you except the same words Jesus told those who questioned His teaching authority in the Temple: "My teaching is NOT MY OWN. IT COMES FROM THE ONE WHO SENT ME. Anyone who chooses to do the will of God will find out whether my teaching comes from God or whether I speak on my own. WHOEVER SPEAKS ON THEIR OWN DOES SO TO GAIN PERSONAL GLORY, but HE WHO SEEKS THE GLORY OF THE ONE WHO SENT HIM is a man of truth; there is nothing false about him." (John 7:16-18 NIV).

When God called me into active ministry as an overseer to shepherd the Church of God which He purchased with His own blood (see Acts 20:28), He gave me a very specific office as an apostle and minister of the New Covenant. And He said that my ultimate mission is to make His glory and power known to the world through the preaching and teaching of THE FAITHFUL AND TRUE GOSPEL

OF CHRIST, and the healing of the sick. In fact, He emphasized that I should know my mission. Therefore, just like the apostle Paul, I am appointed for the defense of the gospel (see Philippians 1:17, with Jude 1:3); the unveiling and proclamation of the truth of the gospel to the nations is my priestly duty (see Romans 15:16) as well as my mission; and it is this mission that I seek to further in this book. I pray that you will read this book with humility and with an open heart and mind, and allow the Spirit of truth to speak to you. May the Lord open your heart to heed the message you are about to hear, and be blessed. Amen.

Now, grab your Bible and let us begin.

Chapter 1

The Biblical Truth About the First or Old Creation Headed By Adam

What "Vain Religion" Never Taught You and Never Will

THE OLD CREATION is headed by Adam — God's first created man — and thus every member of the Old Creation has the blood of Adam and bears the image and likeness of Adam. (see Acts 17:26-28, with Genesis 5:3). The Bible says that Adam was created on the earth (and lived in the flesh or natural realm — see 1 Corinthians 15:45-48); and thus every man born of Adam's blood was also born in his image to dwell on the face of the earth. (see Acts 17:26-28). Adam and his offspring were not created (or made) to dwell in the Spirit but in the earth (or Sense realm). The earth was their natural dwelling or habitat (see Genesis 1:28), so they were earthly-minded. And thus the Bible says that Adam was earthy (or natural), he was of the earth; and so were all those born of him (see 1 Corinthians 15:47-48 KJV). You see, many people have been erroneously taught to believe that God created Adam as His son; but if that were so, Adam would've been born of God just like Jesus Christ and all of us who believe in Him, and Adam would've lived in the Spirit and in Heaven with God, instead of on Earth, because Heaven is where God lives (see Isaiah 66:1; Acts 7:49;

1 Kings 8:27; Matthew 5:45; Matthew 6:9), and Heaven is where God's sons come from. (see 1 Corinthians 15:47-48; Philippians 3:20; John 8:23).

Why Did God Create Adam?

Obviously, God had a different reason for creating Adam; He created Adam to take care of His creation and rule over it (see Genesis 1:26-28). He created Adam for His own pleasure, just like all of His creation. (see Revelation 4:11 KJV). Adam, then, was never a son of God, even though he could be called a son of God **in a generic sense**, just like everyone God ever created. In a generic sense, all of mankind are the offspring of God. (see Acts 17:28-29). God is the Father of all creation (see 1 Corinthians 8:6; Malachi 2:10), and He is the Father of all mankind. (see Isaiah 64:8; Malachi 2:10). But **in an exclusive sense**, God has only one begotten Son, Jesus Christ (see John 3:16), who is equal with God and existed with God even before the foundation of the earth, and long before Adam was created. (see John 17:5; John 1:2-3; Colossians 1:16-17; John 3:13; 6:33, 38, 62; John 8:23; John 16:28; Hebrews 1:2; Philippians 2:5-8). God also chose us (that is, believers; and mind you, Adam was not a believer); He chose us IN CHRIST "before the foundation of the world, that we should be holy and without blame before Him in love, HAVING PREDESTINED US TO ADOPTION AS SONS by Jesus Christ to Himself, according to the good pleasure of His will." (see Ephesians 1:4-5). And so we believers are also begotten sons of God only because we are in Christ and are **one with Him** in Spirit and Body. (see 1 Corinthians 6:15,17; Ephesians 5:30). In the epistles, therefore, Christ is called the first begotten of the Father, and the firstborn among many brethren. (see Romans 8:29). We (believers) are the many brethren, and Christ is not ashamed to call us brethren, because we and Him are of one Father. (see Hebrews 2:11).

Thus, God did not create Adam because He was lonely, as some wrongly believe. Adam was created as a part of a bigger plan which was ultimately intended for God's pleasure. (see Revelation 4:11 KJV). Because Adam was created to live in the earth or natural realm, everything that happened to and with Adam and the entire Old Creation happened in the physical or natural realm. God interacted with Adam through the Sense realm. For instance, God put Adam or man in a special (physical) garden — a garden planted eastward of Eden — where He could visit and interact with him. (see Genesis 2:8, 15). By so doing, God made it easy for Adam to approach Him and to be in His presence. God also appeared to man as a Voice (or audible sound) in the garden to interact with man. (see Genesis 3:8-10). And in this manner also God walked in the Garden. Consequently, when man sinned, all God had to do to drive man out of His presence was to drive him out of the Garden of Eden and put measures in place to prevent him from coming back into the Garden. (see Genesis 3:22-24). Satan, likewise, had to interact with man through the physical senses. For instance, Satan had to enter and speak audibly through a physical creature — the serpent — in order to interact with and deceive Eve. (see Genesis 3:1-7). Thus, the Bible says that the spiritual Man — Jesus Christ — (who brought the spiritual life) was not first; the natural man — Adam — (who brought the natural life) was first, and afterward, the spiritual. (see 1 Corinthians 15:46). Jesus Christ is the Second and Last Adam — the Representative of man who brought eternal life and ushered in a new species of man (a spiritual man) called the New Creation. It was Jesus Christ who brought the SPIRITUAL life. The Bible states: "And so it is written, "The first man Adam became a **living being**." The last Adam (Jesus Christ) became a **life-giving spirit**. However, **THE SPIRITUAL (Jesus Christ) IS NOT FIRST**, but THE NATURAL (Adam), and AFTERWARD THE SPIRITUAL (Jesus Christ). The **FIRST MAN** (Adam) WAS OF THE EARTH, made of dust; **THE SECOND Man** (Jesus Christ) is the Lord FROM HEAVEN. As was the man of dust (Adam), SO ALSO are those who are made of dust (the Old Creation men); and AS IS THE HEAVENLY Man (Jesus Christ), SO ALSO are those who are heavenly (the New Creation men, or the saints). And AS WE (the Old Creation men) HAVE BORNE THE IMAGE of the man of dust (Adam), WE (the New Creation men) SHALL ALSO BEAR THE IMAGE of the heavenly Man (Jesus Christ)." (I Corinthians 15:45-49). From these verses it is clear that the spiritual Man — Jesus Christ — (who brought the spiritual life) was not first; the natural man — Adam — (who brought the natural life) was first, and afterward, the spiritual. (see 1 Corinthians 15:46). Hence, **the first or Old Creation man (Adam) was not a spiritual man** and could, therefore, neither live nor walk in the Spirit. Living and walking in the Spirit, then, is a reality that was brought by Jesus Christ and is thus exclusive to the New Creation man, because only the New Creation man has the nature and the capability to live and walk in the Spirit. The New Creation man (when he is fully mature) is a spiritual man (see 1 Corinthians 3:1), because he bears the image of Jesus Christ the heavenly and spiritual Man. (see 1 Corinthians 15:49; 1 John 4:17; Romans 8:29-30).

People need to stop guessing God's intentions and imposing (or forcing) explanations on God's words. God doesn't need any man to guess or make assumptions about what He was thinking before creation, or what He is thinking at any given time; nor does He need any man to guess what He is trying to say when He speaks. **God always says what He thinks and He speaks very clearly**; that is what the Bible is all about — it contains the clear thoughts and opinions of God — for all Scripture is God-breathed. (see 2 Timothy 3:16 NIV). Therefore if we want to know what God was thinking before He created Adam, we just have to look in the Bible and allow ourselves to be aided by the Holy Spirit to understand it. (see 1 John 2:27). The Bible says, "Then God said, "Let Us make man in Our IMAGE, according to Our LIKENESS; LET THEM HAVE DOMINION over the fish of the sea, over the birds of the air, and over the cattle, OVER ALL THE EARTH and over every creeping thing that creeps on the earth." (Genesis 1:26). Here, we see that God's original plan was to create MAN in His image, according to His likeness, and for Man **TO HAVE DOMINION, OR RULE OVER HIS CREATION**. The Bible also adds, "The Lord God PLANTED A GARDEN eastward in EDEN, and there He put the man whom He had formed. Then the Lord God TOOK THE MAN AND PUT HIM IN THE GARDEN of Eden **TO TEND AND KEEP IT.**" (Genesis 2:8, 15). Here also, we see that God intended for man to be a CARETAKER or KEEPER of the garden He planted eastward in Eden.

Was Adam Created in God's Nature?

Now, what does it mean that God created man in His image, according to His likeness? It is important to understand what this means, because many people confuse "the IMAGE and LIKENESS of God," with "the NATURE of God." And thus, many people have forced explanations on this verse that were never spoken nor intended by God. Many people think "the image and likeness of God" is the same as "the nature of God." But the truth is that the word "nature" does not appear even once in the whole of the Old Testament section of the Bible. And so one wonders how that interpretation even became a part of the conversation. The two words IMAGE (OR LIKENESS) and NATURE are not the same. The Hebrew word that was translated IMAGE is the word **"tselem"** which is from a root word that means "to shade" as in shadow. STRONG'S DEFINITIONS: "צֶלֶם *tselem, tseh'-lem; from an unused root meaning to shade; a phantom, i.e. (figuratively) illusion, resemblance; hence, a representative figure, especially an idol:—**image**, vain shew."* As you can see, IMAGE is a fitting translation of this Hebrew word. The Hebrew word that was also translated LIKENESS is the word **"dĕmuwth."** STRONG'S DEFINITIONS: *"תּוּמָד dᵉmûwth, dem-ooth'; from H1819; resemblance; concretely, model, shape; adverbially, like:—fashion, **like** (-ness, as), manner, similitude."* Obviously, this Hebrew word is also rightly translated as LIKENESS. **These two words (Image and Likeness), therefore, don't have the same meaning as "NATURE."** They are not even similar; they are as different as a man is different from a woman. In fact, if you were looking for a Hebrew word for NATURE in the Bible, you wouldn't find one.

And so here is the truth: **Man (the Old Creation) was created in the IMAGE and LIKENESS of God (see Genesis 1:26); this is what the Bible teaches. Man (the Old Creation) was NOT created in the NATURE of God**; the Bible never teaches that he was. In fact, whenever the truth of man (or the Son of Man) being in the IMAGE and LIKENESS of God is quoted in the New Testament (as in First Corinthians 11:7, Second Corinthians 4:4 and Colossians 3:10), the Greek word that is translated IMAGE is always the word **"eikōn."** STRONG'S DEFINITIONS: *"εἰκών eikṓn, i-kone'; from G1503; a **likeness**, i.e. (literally) statue, profile, or (figuratively) representation, resemblance:—**image**."* The meaning of this word is obviously very different from the Greek word **"phýsis"** which is translated NATURE (as used in 2 Peter 1:4; Galatians 2:15; Galatians 4:8; Ephesians 2:3). STRONG'S DEFINITIONS: *"φύσις phýsis, foo'-sis; from G5453; growth (by germination or expansion), i.e. (by implication) **natural production** (lineal descent); by extension, a genus or sort; figuratively, native disposition, constitution or usage:—(man-)kind, **nature**(-al)."* In fact, if man (the Old Creation) had been created in the NATURE of God, then, as this definition points out, **he would've been produced naturally out of God (as by birth), having the same innate constitution as God**, and thus would never have sinned or failed, because God cannot sin or fail. (see 1 John 3:9; James 1:13; 1 John 1:5).

Thus, even though IMAGE and LIKENESS are often used as synonyms, they are **never** used as synonyms with NATURE — never in the Hebrew language, never in the Greek language, and never in the English language are these words used as exact replacements for each other. In fact, if you look in the dictionary right now for the definition of IMAGE, you will find something like this: *"a REPRESENTATION of the **EXTERNAL FORM** of a person or thing in art,"* or *"a reproduction or imitation of the FORM of a person or thing"* (Merriam-Webster's dictionary). LIKENESS is also defined by Merriam-Webster's dictionary as *"the quality or state of being ALIKE or SIMILAR especially in*

APPEARANCE." Now, contrast this with NATURE, which is defined by Merriam-Webster's dictionary as: *"the INHERENT character or basic CONSTITUTION of a person or thing"* or *"the genetically controlled qualities of an organism."* **Evidently, IMAGE and LIKENESS of God are descriptive of His EXTERNAL QUALITIES or APPEARANCE, and not His nature or innate character.** Thus, man (the Old Creation) was not created in the same NATURE or inherent character and constitution as God. Man was only created to resemble God in external physical characteristics or form. As we know, God is Spirit (see John 4:24), but He is not without form. (see Numbers 12:8). The Bible teaches that God has the image or external appearance of a man, and thus man was created or formed in the image and likeness of God. (see Genesis 1:26; Genesis 2:7). Man was formed to look like God in appearance. Therefore, if you need a mental picture or image of God, just look at man.

To understand this further, we have to find out completely what God's external appearance or form is. And what better place to get this information than the Bible. As stated earlier, the Bible says that **God is Spirit.** (see John 4:24). The Spirit of God is spoken of repeatedly in the Bible. (see Genesis 1:2; 6:3; Exodus 31:3; Numbers 27:18; Isaiah 61:1; Ezekiel 36:27; Joel 2:28-29; Job 33:4; Romans 8:14, etc). Therefore the first point where man bears the image and likeness of God is that man is a spirit-being; man has a spirit (see 1 Thessalonians 5:23). Moreover, the Bible speaks of God as eternal. (see Genesis 21:33; Deuteronomy 33:27; Isaiah 57:15; Psalm 90:1-4; 1 Timothy 1:17; Revelation 1:8). Thus, God is an eternal Spirit. This is another external characteristic of God that is borne by man. The Bible teaches that, just like God, man is an eternal spirit; man's spirit is eternal.

(see Daniel 12:2-3; Ecclesiastes 12:7; Matthew 25:46; 1 Corinthians 15:12-19; Psalm 22:26; Ecclesiastes 3:11). When man dies, his body (which was made from the dust of the earth) returns to the earth, and his spirit — which is the breath of God (see Job 33:4) — returns to God who gave it (see Ecclesiastes 12:7) to spend eternity either in eternal life or eternal punishment. (see Daniel 12:2-3; Matthew 25:46).

The Bible also makes mention of the different body parts of God, which affirms that **God has a body** (a celestial body, of course — see 1 Corinthians 15:40) that is in the form, appearance or likeness of the body of man. For instance, God has a face (see Genesis 3:14; Genesis 32:30; Exodus 33:19-20; Psalm 34:16; Ezekiel 39:29; Numbers 6:25; Isaiah 59:1-2). God has eyes that see (see 2 Chronicles 14:2; 2 Chronicles 16:9). God has ears that hear (see Psalm 34:15; Isaiah 59.1; 1 Peter 3:12; Psalm 18:6). God has a nose with which He smells (see Genesis 8:21; Psalm 18:8). God has a voice and can speak (see Genesis 3:8; John 5:37; Exodus 33:19-20). God has a heart. (see 1 Samuel 2:35; 1 Samuel 13:14; Genesis 8:21). God has hands (see Luke 23:46; Ezra 7:28; Exodus 33:22-23; Psalm 16:11; Ecclesiastes 9:1; Acts 7:55). God has feet (see Exodus 24:9-11; Isaiah 66:1), and God walks or moves (see Micah 6:8; Deuteronomy 23:4; Genesis 3:8). God has a back (see Exodus 33:23). The full picture of God (and for that matter, Jesus Christ) having the appearance of a Man in Heaven is painted for us in Revelation 1:13-18. Since God made man in His own image, He gave man a body also (a terrestrial or earthly body) that is like God's own body in appearance or form. The Bible says that after God created man — the spirit being — (see Genesis 1:26), He put man in a body formed from the dust of the earth. (see Genesis 2:7). Man's body then is just an earthen vessel (see 2 Corinthians 4:7 KJV) in which his spirit lives. Thus, another point where man was made in the image and likeness of God is that man has a body (see 1 Thessalonians 5:23).

Again, the Bible speaks of God's soul (see Psalm 11:5; Isaiah 42:1), which means that **God has a soul**. And so, God gave man a soul (see 1 Thessalonians 5:23; Psalm 62:1; Psalm 42:11). The soul, as we know, consists of the mind (or intellect), will, and emotions. Man has all these three elements of the soul, just like God. God has a mind (see 1 Samuel 2:35) with which He chooses to remember or forget, as He pleases. (see Jeremiah 31:34; Genesis 8:1). And thus, God has thoughts (see Isaiah 55:8-9). God also has (free) will and so He gave man free will. The will is free to make and execute decisions (or plans) based on inputs from the mind, emotions, and the spirit. God's will is spoken of extensively in the Bible (see Psalm 40:8; John 1:12-13; James 1:18; John 6:40; Ephesians 1:1; Ephesians 1:5-12; 1 Thessalonians 5:18; 1 Thessalonians 4:3; 1 Peter 2:15; Matthew 6:10; Hebrews 13:21; Jeremiah 29:11). In fact, the entire Bible reveals God's will. God also has emotions. The Bible speaks of a wide range of the emotions of God. For instance, God LOVES and shows mercy and COMPASSION (see Hosea 11:1; Psalm 103:11; John 3:16; Romans 5:8; 1 John 4:8:11; 1 John 4:16; Psalm 145:9). God HATES sin, wickedness, the wicked and the one who loves violence; He hates all workers of iniquity (see Deuteronomy 12:31; Deuteronomy 16:22; Psalm 5:4-6; Psalm 11:5; Proverbs 6:16-19). God has wrath and gets ANGRY with the wicked (see Romans 1:18; Romans 5:9; John 3:36; Ezekiel 25:17; Numbers 1:2-6; Psalm 7:11; Psalm 30:5; 1 Kings 11:9-10). God LAUGHS at the wicked (see Psalm 37:13). God has JOY (see Nehemiah 8:10).

God is JEALOUS (see Exodus 20:4-6; Isaiah 42:8; Exodus 34:14). God can be GRIEVED. (see Genesis 6:5-7; Psalm 78:40; Ephesians 4:30). God can be SADDENED and SORROWFUL (see Jeremiah 8:18-9:3). Thus, another point in which man was made in the image and likeness of God is that man has a soul. (see 1 Thessalonians 5:23). All that we have discussed here is what it means when the Bible says that God made Man in His image and likeness.

Is the Holy Spirit the Same as the Breath of God/the Breath of Life ?

Many people have also been erroneously taught that the Old Creation man — Adam — had the Holy Spirit dwelling in him. But the Bible never says anything like that. The Bible calls the Holy Spirit the Spirit of God or the Spirit of Christ. (see Romans 8:9). Nowhere in the Bible is the Holy Spirit called the breath of God or the breath of life. **People often confuse the breath of life mentioned in Genesis 2:7 with the Holy Spirit; but they are not the same.** The Bible reports concerning the great flood in Noah's day, that God had said, "And behold, I Myself am bringing floodwaters on the earth, to destroy from under heaven ALL FLESH **in which is THE BREATH OF LIFE**; everything that is on the earth shall die." (Genesis 6:17). Consequently, when the floodwaters came, indeed "all flesh died that moved on the earth: birds and cattle and beasts and every creeping thing that creeps on the earth, and every man. ALL IN WHOSE NOSTRILS WAS THE BREATH OF **the Spirit of Life**, all that was on the dry land, died" (Genesis 7:21-22). Of course, the Spirit of life is God, the Holy Spirit (see Romans 8:2). And so, clearly, the breath of the Spirit of life is a reference to **the breath of God** or the breath of the Holy Spirit. His breath is the breath of life, and His breath is in every living creature. **The Holy Spirit Himself is obviously NOT in every living creature.** What these Scriptural verses are saying then is that all creatures that had life as we know it, perished in the flood in Noah's Day. Life as we know it proceeded from the breath of the Holy Spirit (the Spirit of Life). Every man alive today has the breath of the Almighty (see Job 33:4; Job 27:3) or the breath of the Spirit of life (see Genesis 7:22) or simply, the breath of life (see Genesis 2:7; Genesis 6:17; Genesis 7:15) in him; that is what is keeping us alive. That is what keeps every living creature alive. For man, it is called the human spirit, or the spirit of man; it is not the Spirit of God or the Holy Spirit.

The Two Kinds of Death

Now, the Bible talks about two kinds of death: **physical death** and **spiritual death**. We die PHYSICALLY when our spirit leaves our body. (see Luke 23:46; Matthew 27:50; Acts 7:59; Ecclesiastes 12:7; Genesis 25:8; James 2:26). We also die SPIRITUALLY when we are separated from God or alienated from the life of God, which can either happen now with its effects continuing after we have died physically from this life (see Matthew 25:41, 46; Matthew 10:28; Daniel 12:2-3; Genesis 2:17 with 1 Corinthians 15:22), or happen for a limited time while we are still physically alive in this life until we come to Christ and receive life (see 1 Timothy 5:6, Ephesians 2:1; Ephesians 4:18; Isaiah 59:1-2; with 1 John 5:11-13). Adam surely DIED (SPIRITUALLY) **on the same day** he ate of the tree of the knowledge of good and evil, just as God said he would (see Genesis 2:17). It was Adam's spiritual death which gave birth or led to his PHYSICAL DEATH. (see Genesis 5:5). On that very day Adam sinned, he was literally separated from God, driven out and banished from the presence of God, from the garden of Eden. (see Genesis 3:22-24). Adam's physical death followed later — as a natural consequence of his spiritual death — when he was 930 years old. (see Genesis 5:5). Thus, **spiritual death gave birth to physical death.** Spiritual death is the mother of all deaths.

Adam Did Not Have The Holy Spirit Dwelling in Him

Adam did not have the Holy Spirit dwelling in him, as explained earlier. In fact, anybody who has the Holy Spirit or the Spirit of God dwelling in him CANNOT die spiritually, because the Holy Spirit is joined as one with the spirit of that individual. This explains why the New Creation man or the true believer in Christ has **eternal life.** The believer is joined as one spirit with the Lord. (see 1 Corinthians 6:17). "He who is joined to the Lord is **one spirit** with Him." (I Corinthians 6:17). Hebrews 6:4 also affirms that those who believe in Jesus Christ have been made partakers (sharers or partners) of the Holy Spirit. If you are a believer, you and God are one Spirit. Peter also adds that the exceedingly great and precious promises of God have been given to us so that through them (or by laying hold on them) we may be partakers of the divine (or God) nature, having escaped the corruption that is in the world through lust. (see 2 Peter 1:4). Every sincere believer (who has laid hold on eternal life and is walking in the Spirit) is a partaker of the divine (or God) nature. And so, for such a true believer to die spiritually, God has to die spiritually, which is just impossible. This is also the reason why Jesus said whoever believes in Him has passed from (spiritual) death into (eternal) life. (see John 5:24). Whoever believes in Jesus Christ has the Spirit of God (which is also called the Spirit of Christ) in him (see Romans 8:9), and is joined as one with the Spirit of God (see 1 Corinthians 6:17). Thus, the Bible says anyone who does not have the Spirit of Christ does not belong to Christ. (see Romans 8:9). Adam did not have the Spirit of Christ.

Again, it is impossible for anyone in whom the Spirit of God permanently dwells to suffer spiritual death. It is impossible for the New Creation man to die spiritually. This is why Jesus also said, "whoever lives and believes in Me **shall NEVER die**." (John 11:26). Jesus knew this statement would come as a shock to many people, and so He asked, "Do you believe this?" (see John 11:26). Jesus wasn't talking about physical death here, because obviously **all His disciples died physically**, even though they lived on in the Spirit. Thus, Jesus was talking about spiritual death. You cannot die spiritually when you have the Holy Spirit living on the inside of you. This is true, and so you better believe it!

If Adam had the Holy Spirit living inside him, he would never have sinned and died spiritually (or fallen) as he did. In fact, if God made the New Creation man to be like what the Old Creation man (Adam) was before his fall in the garden of Eden, as many erroneously believe is the case, then the New Creation man, just like Adam, would be susceptible to failing or suffering spiritual death. Therefore, that kind of thinking or teaching is inimical to the truth of the Bible and the divine purpose of God. My friend, God is too smart to make a New Creation man that is subject to the same weaknesses as the Old Creation man. This is why God made the New Creation man a spiritual (or heavenly) man like Jesus Christ, and not a natural (or earthy) man like Adam. (see 1 Corinthians 15:45-49). God our Savior alone is wise (see Jude 1:25), and His thoughts are higher than your thoughts. (see Isaiah 55:9). In fact, God gave Adam the **choice** to receive **eternal life or the**

life and nature of God and become the son of God simply by eating of the tree of life which was also in the midst of the garden of Eden (see Genesis 2:9), instead of eating of the (forbidden) tree of the knowledge of good and evil (or more bluntly the tree of death). But as we all know, **Adam rejected eternal life and chose (eternal) death instead.** Adam rejected God or Jesus Christ who is the Eternal Life (see 1 John 5:20; John 14:6), who brings righteousness and life, and chose to obey Satan who brings sin and death. If Adam had believed God and thus chosen to eat of the tree of life, then he would've received the Spirit of God (or the Holy Spirit), just as all believers have. Thus, Adam's sin was rooted in **UNBELIEF**. He didn't believe God's Word and thus rebelled against it. He rather believed Satan's word and thus acted on it. Adam knowingly **chose** Satan over God. The Bible says that **Adam was not deceived.** (see 1 Timothy 2:14). Adam knew what he was doing. Hence, Adam was not a believer, which is why throughout the Bible Adam is **contrasted** with the Lord Jesus Christ (see 1 Corinthians 15:22; 1 Corinthians 15:47-49; Romans 5:15-19), whereas the believer is spoken of as being **one** with the Lord Jesus Christ, and as **conformed to the image** of the Lord Jesus Christ. (see 1 John 4:17; Colossians 1:18; Ephesians 5:30; Romans 8:29-30; Hebrews 2:11; 1 Corinthians 15:48-49; 1 Corinthians 12:12, 27; Romans 12:5; John 15:1-5; 1 Corinthians 6:15, 17). In fact, whereas Adam was created **in the image and likeness** of God, we believers, just as the Lord Jesus Christ is, are the very image or **the express image of God and the brightness of His glory**; believers are **conformed** to the image of Jesus Christ (see Romans 8:29-30), and Jesus Christ is the express image of God and the brightness of His glory. (see Colossians 1:15; Hebrews 1:3; 2 Corinthians 4:4).

I guess I was jumping ahead of myself here; but we will talk more about this when we get to (Chapter 14) the part of this book bordering on the New Creation realities. I just can't wait!

Now, back to our discussion of the Old Creation, let me reemphasize that the breath of life spoken of in Genesis 2:7 is not the Holy Spirit. Someone may say, "Well, Jesus also breathed on His disciples and said, "receive the Holy Spirit" (see John 20:22). Yes He did, but look at the exact wording in that verse; it doesn't say Jesus breathed the Holy Spirit on His disciples. You cannot breathe the Holy Spirit on anyone. The Holy Spirit is a Person; He is God. And so after Jesus had breathed on His disciples, the Bible says he spoke to impart the Holy Spirit to the disciples; He spoke the Holy Spirit into them, if you may. He said, "Receive the Holy Spirit." (see John 20:22). The Holy Spirit was the Word that was spoken, just as Jesus is the Word and God is the Word. (see John 1:1, 14; Revelation 19:13). Thus the Bible affirms that the words of Jesus are **Spirit** and they are life. (see John 6:63).

Needless to say, if the breath of life were the Holy Spirit, then every living creature, including all animals, and every man alive today (the regenerate and the unregenerate alike) has the Holy Spirit or the Spirit of God in them, which is just not the case. The only mention of the Spirit of God in the whole account of creation — that is, from Genesis chapter 1 to chapter 3 — is in Genesis 1:2 which says, "The earth was without form, and void; and darkness was on the face of the deep. And **the Spirit of God** was hovering over the face of the waters." (Genesis 1:2). Note that the Hebrew word translated "Spirit" here is the word **"ruwach."** This word is used throughout the Old Testament of the Bible for "spirit," whether it is talking about the Spirit of God (as in Genesis 1:2; Job 33:4), the spirit of man (as in Ecclesiastes

12:7); or an evil spirit (as in Judges 9:23). The only way you can know what specific spirit it is referring to is when it is qualified, as in "the Spirit of God" (ruwach elohiym) or "an evil spirit" (ra`ruwach). So, according to the account of the creation of man that is given to us in Genesis, "And the Lord God formed man of the dust of the ground, and breathed into his nostrils THE BREATH OF LIFE; and man became a living being." (Genesis 2:7). Believe it or not, this is what makes people believe that Adam had the Holy Spirit. And yet, there is obviously no mention of the Holy Spirit or the Spirit of God here. The only thing mentioned here is "the breath of life" which in Hebrew is "něshamah chay." And so, the Lord God (Yěhovah) breathed into his nostrils the breath of life (něshamah chay). This is all we're told. The breath of life is obviously not the Spirit of God, as we can see in the Hebrew as well as the explanation that was given earlier in this book. God is the source of life (see John 1:4; John 5:26); His breath is the breath of life. Hence, "the breath of life" is used interchangeably with "the breath of the Almighty." Job said, "The Spirit of God has made me, and the breath of the Almighty gives me life." (Job 33:4). The Spirit of God which was mentioned in Genesis 1:2 is the One who created or made man. In Genesis 1:26-27, the "God, who gives life to the dead and calls those things which do not exist as though they did (see Romans 4:17), called or spoke the spirit of man into being; then in Genesis 2:7, He created a body (for the man) from the dust of the earth, and put the spirit of man (which He had already spoken into existence) into the body He had created, by breathing into his nostrils **the breath of life**. The Bible says, and man became a living soul or a living being. (see Genesis 2:7).

Now, before we continue with our discussion on Adam and the Old Creation he heads, I wish to emphasize the truth of God's Word, because as I mentioned earlier, Adam rebelled against God's WORD and chose to be on the side of Satan's word (or the lie), instead of God's Word (or the Truth).

Would You Choose to Be on the Side of the Truth?

The Lord Jesus Christ, in praying for His disciples before His crucifixion said, "Sanctify them by Your truth. **Your WORD IS TRUTH.**" (John 17:17).

Evidently there are two kinds of knowledge or information in this world: Facts, and Truth. Facts are primarily based on man's scientific research and investigation, whereas truth is directly from God (and is revealed in the Word of God or the inspired Books of the Bible).

When philosophers try to distinguish between facts and truth, they tend to put facts above truth in reliability and superiority, claiming that truth is variable or dependent on the perspective and experience of individuals whereas facts are based on empirical evidence and are thus concrete and verifiable. This clearly shows that **the natural man, just like Pontius Pilate, does not know or understand what truth is**. Pilate asked Jesus, "What is truth?" (see John 18:38). This is the question that the natural man has still not been able to answer correctly and continues to struggle with. Jesus came into the world to bear witness to the truth, and He rightly said that anyone who is of the truth hears Him or pays heed to His words. (see John 18:37). What philosophers don't seem to realize is that Truth is a Person, Truth is Jesus Christ (see John 14:6), Truth is God, Truth is the Spirit of God (see 1 John 5:6), Truth is the Word of God. (see John 17:17). Satan "the god of this age has blinded the minds of unbelievers (or natural men), so that they cannot see the light (or the truth) of the gospel that displays the glory of Christ, who is the image of God." (2 Corinthians 4:4 NIV). And **this blindness of the mind is only removed when one turns to Christ or accepts Jesus Christ as one's Lord and Savior.** (see 2 Corinthians 3:14, 16). Then and only then is man able to know and to walk in the truth. And I can assure you that nothing gives God greater joy than to see men walk in the truth. The Spirit, speaking through the apostle John, says, "I have no greater joy than to hear that my children walk in truth." (3 John 1:4). Yet, Satan works hard to prevent men from knowing the truth and walking in it, because Satan knows that the moment a man comes to know the truth and to walk in it, that man becomes free from bondage to Satan and his deception. "To the Jews who had believed in Him, Jesus said, "If you HOLD TO MY TEACHING, you are really my disciples. Then you will KNOW THE TRUTH, and THE TRUTH WILL MAKE YOU FREE." (John 8:31-32). Indeed, knowledge of the truth makes a man free; and knowledge of the truth only comes when one holds to, or continues in the teachings of Jesus Christ who proclaims light (or truth) to the whole world — both Jews and Gentiles. (see John 8:31-32, with Acts 26:23)

My dear friend, don't let Satan fool you. In a sense, all truth are facts; but not all facts are truth. For instance, it was once accepted as a fact that the earth was flat, but that fact wasn't truth. That fact later changed to conform to the truth of God's Word that the earth is round or circular. (see Isaiah 40:22). There are many similar examples where the Bible or God's Word has remained true and man's so-called scientific facts that challenged the truth of God's Word have been proven to be false. For years, medical science believed that bleeding a sick person would help the sick to recover. Consequently, when George Washington, the first president of the United States was sick, the doctors bled him, then they bled him again till he lost so much blood and died. I don't blame the doctors for doing what they did; they were only following the scientific FACTS of the day. But imagine what would've happened if they had read the Bible and discovered the TRUTH that "the life of a creature is in the blood." (see Leviticus 17:11). Medical science would later learn this truth and CHANGE their FACTS to conform with the TRUTH of the Bible. And so today, when someone is sick, doctors don't bleed him; they rather give him blood (blood transfusion), because the life of a creature is indeed in the blood.

Again, in the 14th century the Bubonic plague killed about a third of Europe's population because medical science knew nothing about putting people with infectious diseases in quarantine. Meanwhile the Bible had instructed years earlier that we are to put an infected person in quarantine for seven days. (see Leviticus 13:4). Medical science learned this truth later (in a very hard and costly way). Indeed, the Bible is always ahead of Science in stating truths.

In fact, many of the things Science convinced all of mankind to believe in the past as "scientific truths" have been proven over the years to be false, whether it is the shape of the earth, the axis of the earth, the bleeding of the sick, the age of the earth, the number of planets in the solar system, the single cell protoplasm, etc. And yet we know that truth is never supposed to change. In the Louvre Library today, there's a huge section that contains obsolete science books. Once-held scientific "truths" have been, and are always being revised or replaced by new "truths" as scientists make new discoveries. And so the science textbooks in our schools keep being revised. It is just puzzling and astonishing how fast scientific facts do change. But the Bible (in its original text and language) has not undergone a single revision. In fact, the Bible has survived all the attacks launched against it by scientists and historians over the years, as they struggled to align themselves with some of the Bible's truths after years of studies and discoveries. This only goes to affirm the Bible as the eternal and flawless Word of God. Jesus said, "Heaven and earth will pass away, but My words will by no means pass away." (Matthew 24:35). The Bible remains the same and endures forever. Indeed, the truths of the Bible remain truths regardless of what Science claims, because, well, what does Science know about truth anyway, given its shifting stance on almost every issue?

The Theory of Evolution is Just Another of Satan's Lies

Today, scientists claim that the theory of evolution is a fact; that man evolved from apes. But any honest scientist will admit that Evolution (though they call it a fact) is not truth; it is just another of Satan's many lies. The Evolution Theory is just as fictional as Dan Brown's "The Da Vinci Code." It is not backed by any empirical evidence; nor is it independently verifiable through the scientific method of investigation. It is purely the wisdom of men. Men by their craftiness have concocted this theory and reviewed it among themselves, endorsing one another's lies in what is called "peer review." There is not a single concrete evidence in the long period since this theory was concocted, of any ape becoming a man. Thus The Theory of Evolution does not even pass scientists' own standard of what constitutes a scientific fact.

Just as on many other subjects, only the Bible has the truth regarding the origin of man. And the truth is that **God created man**. Not just that, God created man in His image, according to His likeness. (see Genesis 1:26-27). Thank God I am on the side of truth. Thank God I know the truth; thank God I walk in the truth; thank God that I am a worker for the truth. (see 3 John 1:8). My life and my hope is built on the truth of God's Word, because God's Word is unshakable; it doesn't change (see Numbers 23:19), and it endures forever (see Isaiah 40:8; 1 Peter 1:25). I encourage you also to choose to be on the side of truth and be a fellow worker for the truth. Don't be fooled by facts that are not truth. Don't be fooled by the philosophies of men. The Bible says, "BEWARE lest anyone CHEAT YOU through PHILOSOPHY and empty deceit, according to THE TRADITION OF MEN, according to the BASIC PRINCIPLES OF THE WORLD, and not according to Christ." (Colossians 2:8). The choice to be deceived or not to be deceived is ultimately yours. Be enlightened by choosing to believe the Word of God, by choosing to believe in Jesus Christ who is the Light of the world, and who is The Way, The Truth and The Life. (see John 9:5, with John 14:6). Jesus Christ is not just one of many ways to God, He is The Way, The only Way to God. Jesus Christ is not just one of many truths in the world, He is The Truth, The only Truth in the world. Jesus Christ is not just one of many ways or forms of life; He is The Life, The Eternal Life. Jesus Christ is not just one of many saviors, He is the only Savior of mankind. (see Acts 4:12; 1 Timothy 2:5). Whoever follows Jesus will not walk in darkness but will have the light of life. (see John 8:12).

Indeed Satan is the invisible being behind every lie in this world. He is the one who keeps people in darkness (or in ignorance of the truth).

Jesus pointed out during His earth ministry that Satan is a liar and the father of it, and that Satan does not stand in the truth, because there is no truth in him. (see John 8:44). **Satan's goal is and has always been to deceive mankind by opposing or disputing the truth of God's Word.** Moreover, because Satan is the god of this world (see 2 Corinthians 4:4) and the whole world is under his control (see 1 John 5:19), he propagates his lies everywhere through the world's educational, political, religious, economic, cultural and social systems. In fact, Satan's most potent weapon against man is and has always been his ability to deceive subtly. **If Satan ever loses the power of deception, he will cease to be relevant.** Thus Satan works very hard to stay relevant. And the Bible says that he deceives the whole world. (see Revelation 12:9). In the garden of Eden he deceived Eve by his craftiness. (see 2 Corinthians 11:3). **He was able to trick Eve into believing his lies over the truth of God's Word** (see Genesis 3:1-6); and that is what he continues to do today, not only through secular literature, but also through the doctrine of false apostles who have infiltrated Christian churches. No wonder Jesus told us (His true disciples) to be on our guard against the yeast (or doctrine/teachings) of the Pharisees and Sadducees. (see Matthew 16:6, 11-12). No wonder Jesus said, "Beware of false prophets, who come to you in sheep's clothing, but inwardly they are ravenous wolves." (Matthew 7:15). Beloved, don't allow anyone to teach you doctrines that are not Scriptural, for Jesus said, "**Scripture cannot be set aside**." (see John 10:35 NIV). All of man's opinions and traditions will pass away, but the Word of God will never pass away. Therefore, stick with the Word, and never be ashamed of it. God said, "My covenant I will **not** break, **nor alter the word that has gone out of My lips.**" (Psalm 89:34).

Indeed God loves the world so much (see John 3:16), and yet Satan, through the power of deception has been able to turn the world against God, making many men rebellious against God and against the Word of God. How sad!

God Has Given Us the Same Choice He Gave Adam in the Garden of Eden

The Bible reveals, as we noted earlier, that after God created man in His own image and likeness, He made man His under-ruler. God gave man dominion over all the works of His hands. (see Genesis 1:28; Psalm 8:3, 6). Man thus became ruler over all creation on earth, subject to no one but God. God made Man so intelligent that he was able to name the many different species of animals God created, and whatever he called each living creature, that was its name. (see Genesis 2:19-20). Man indeed had God's authority to rule over His creation on earth. He was the master or lord of the earth; he was the god of this world, only answerable to the Almighty God and Creator. God loved man so much, and so He told man the truth about LIFE and DEATH and commanded man to choose life and avoid death. Thus, after God had planted a garden eastward in Eden and had made every tree grow out of the ground that was pleasant to the sight and good for food, including THE TREE OF LIFE which was also in the midst of the garden, as well as THE TREE OF THE KNOWLEDGE OF GOOD AND EVIL (see Genesis 2:9), "the Lord God COMMANDED the man, saying, "Of EVERY TREE of the garden YOU MAY FREELY EAT; **but** OF THE TREE OF THE KNOWLEDGE OF GOOD AND EVIL YOU SHALL NOT EAT, for IN THE DAY that you EAT of it YOU SHALL SURELY DIE." (Genesis 2:16-17). Thus,

God set before Adam **LIFE** and **DEATH**, blessing and cursing, and told him to CHOOSE life. My dear friend, the way of the truth is the way of LIFE.

Since the creation of the first man (Adam), God has always told man the same truth, that there is a CHOICE that has to be made between LIFE and DEATH, and God will not violate man's free will or man's freedom to choose. In fact, God has always gone the extra mile by recommending to us that we CHOOSE LIFE, because obviously life is a better choice over death. To the children of Israel, Moses said, "I call heaven and earth as witnesses today against you, that I HAVE SET BEFORE YOU **LIFE** AND **DEATH**, blessing and cursing; THEREFORE **CHOOSE LIFE**, that both you and your descendants may live." (Deuteronomy 30:19). God basically said the same thing to Adam. God's command to Adam was very simple. God's command to man is always very simple. And yes, the truth is always very simple. So today God commands us to BELIEVE in the Lord Jesus Christ and be saved (see John 3:16; Acts 16:31; Romans 10:9-10; Romans 10:13) — a truth so simple it's scary! And thus the apostle Paul says, "But **I fear**, lest somehow, as the serpent deceived Eve by his craftiness, so your minds may be corrupted from **the SIMPLICITY that is in Christ**." (II Corinthians 11:3). Even after God has told us to CHOOSE LIFE by believing in Jesus Christ, many people today are still choosing death over life. Many people today criticize Adam for his choice in the garden of Eden; they criticize Eve for allowing Satan (the serpent) to deceive her. And yet they themselves are like Adam and Eve; they are also following the deception of Satan as he sways them away from the truth of God's Word; and they are making the same stupid choice Adam made, choosing death over life by rejecting

Jesus Christ who is the Life. The Bible says, "And this is the testimony: that God has given us eternal LIFE, and THIS LIFE IS IN HIS SON. **He who HAS the Son HAS LIFE**; he who DOES NOT HAVE the Son of God DOES NOT HAVE LIFE." (1 John 5:11-12).

My dear friend, God has set before you life and death. This is the truth, and it has always been the same since the beginning of the world. If you haven't already, I encourage you to CHOOSE LIFE by choosing the Son Jesus Christ. Jesus Himself said, "Most assuredly, I say to you, **he who believes in Me has everlasting life**." (John 6:47). If you accept Jesus Christ today as your Lord and Savior, you will have LIFE. So be wise and eat of the tree of life. "For God so loved the world that He gave His only begotten Son, that WHOEVER BELIEVES in Him SHOULD NOT PERISH but HAVE everlasting LIFE. He WHO BELIEVES in Him IS NOT CONDEMNED; but he WHO DOES NOT BELIEVE is CONDEMNED ALREADY, because he has not believed in the name of the only begotten Son of God." (John 3:16, 18).

Given the time-tested and proven truth of God's Word, every man must be able to make the right choice today. God is trusting each one of us to make an informed choice. Evidently, God trusted Adam to make an informed choice, and so He held Adam accountable for his choice. Adam could've done the wise thing by eating of the TREE OF LIFE, which would've united him with God or given him eternal life and immortality for his body. But instead, and sadly, Adam failed to obey God's command (see Genesis 3), and chose to obey Satan instead. Adam chose to eat of the (forbidden) TREE OF THE KNOWLEDGE OF GOOD AND EVIL (or more bluntly, the tree of death), and thus suffered its consequence of spiritual death and mortality for his body. Adam, by his disobedience, set into motion **the law of sin and death**. (see Romans 5:12, with Romans 8:2). The Bible says, "death reigned from Adam to Moses, even over those who had not sinned according to the likeness of the transgression of Adam, who is a type of Him who was to come." (see Romans 5:14). "Through one man's offense judgment came to all men, resulting in condemnation" (see Romans 5:18). And so "by one man's (or Adam's) disobedience many were made sinners" (see Romans 5:19). But the good news today is that "as by one man's disobedience many were made sinners, so also by one Man's obedience many will be made righteous." (Romans 5:19). And this one Man whose obedience has made and will make many righteous is the Lord Jesus Christ. For God "made Him who knew no sin to be sin for us, that we might become the righteousness of God in Him." (2 Corinthians 5:21). If you're in Christ you are the righteousness of God; you have come out of the first Adam, and you are in Christ the Second and Last Adam, and so you are no longer a sinner but a righteous man. "Therefore, if anyone is in Christ, he is a new creation; old things have passed away; behold, all things have become new." (II Corinthians 5:17).

Adam's Treason Affected All His Descendants

Man (represented by Adam, for Adam's name means **mankind**) committed high treason by choosing to obey Satan over God, by choosing to be a servant or slave of Satan rather than a servant or slave of God (see Romans 6:16), by choosing to eat of the (forbidden) tree of the knowledge of good and evil. (see Genesis 3:6). And by so doing, man turned over the legal rulership or dominion over the earth into the hands of God's enemy, Satan (the Devil). As noted earlier, Adam was culpable in that he knew exactly what he was doing when he transgressed against God's Word. The Bible says Eve was deceived, and fell into transgression, but **Adam was not deceived**. (see 1 Timothy 2:13-14). Adam knew exactly what he was doing. Adam knew the consequences of his transgression, and still went ahead with it. Thus, the natural result of Adam's treason or sin was DEATH — first, **spiritual death** (or separation from God), which ultimately resulted in **physical death**. When Adam sinned and died, all of his descendants (the entire humanity, or mankind) also sinned and died with him, not only because he was our representative, but also because we were all still in his loins when he sinned and died. Therefore, "through one man (Adam) sin entered the world, and death through sin, and thus death spread to all men, **because ALL sinned**" (see Romans 5:12). Thus Adam sold himself (and thus mankind) into slavery to Satan and into bondage to sin (wickedness or lawlessness) and death, which explains why our great God and Savior Jesus Christ had to redeem, buy or purchase us back with his own precious blood. (see 1 Corinthians 6:20; Acts 20:28; 1 Peter 1:18-19; Titus 2:13-14).

Man, as a result of his sin, became dead in trespasses and sins (see Ephesians 2:1); he became alienated from the life of God (see Ephesians 4:18, with 1 John 1:3). Prior to this sin, man's physical body had been neither mortal nor immortal; and so man's destiny was in his own hands. Man, therefore, could've eaten of **the tree of life,** which was also in the midst of the garden, and lived forever (see Genesis 3:22-24), but instead, he chose to eat of the (forbidden) tree of the knowledge of good and evil, and died. Man became mortal. What a tragedy this was! Adam's choice brought death to all His descendants, to all mankind. The Bible says that **"in Adam all die."** (see 1

Corinthians 15:22). Therefore, for all to be made alive, all have to be redeemed, delivered, rescued or taken out of Adam, and translated or brought into Christ, For **"in Christ all shall be made alive."** (see 1 Corinthians 15:22). This also means that for all to be made alive all have to be created anew, created in Christ, born again. Thus, the only reason God embarked on the New Creation project is because **the first or Old Creation died.**

Adam Made Satan the god of this World and Ruler Over Man

By obeying, yielding, surrendering, or submitting to Satan, Adam gave Satan dominion over all of God's creation on earth, including mankind. This thus put Adam and his descendants in **bondage (captivity** or **slavery)** to Satan and to sin, and so man became Satan's slave or servant. Man became **a slave of sin** (see John 8:34); man was **taken captive** by Satan **to do his will.** (see 2 Timothy 2:26). And thus, today Satan is called the god (or ruler) of this world. (see 2 Corinthians 4:4). Evil as Satan is, he exploits this position by demanding worship from man through the lure of worldly possessions. During Satan's temptation of Jesus Christ in the wilderness, for instance, the Bible says, "Then the devil, taking Him up on a high mountain, showed Him ALL THE KINGDOMS OF THE WORLD in a moment of time. And the devil said to Him, "ALL THIS AUTHORITY **I will give You, and their glory**; FOR THIS HAS BEEN DELIVERED TO ME, and I give it to whomever I wish. Therefore, **if You will WORSHIP BEFORE ME, all will be Yours."** And Jesus answered and said to him, "Get behind Me, Satan! For it is written, 'You shall worship the Lord your God, and **Him only** you shall serve.'" (Luke 4:5-8). Obviously, Jesus did not deny or challenge it when Satan said all the authority over all the kingdoms of the world had been delivered to him (Satan) together with their glory, and that he (Satan) could give it to whomever he wished. Jesus did not challenge Satan's claim because it was true. The authority and dominion over all the kingdoms of the world was originally given to man by God (see Genesis 1:26), and man had delivered that authority to Satan, just as Satan claimed. How tragic! How great a fall man had fallen! Man had fallen **from master to slave**. He had fallen into the captivity of Satan to do his will. (see 2 Timothy 2:26; 2 Peter 2:19). The fall of man did not only put man in bondage or slavery to Satan and sin, it also brought blighting curses upon Eve, the serpent, and for the sake of the man, the ground and its vegetation. (see Genesis 3:17). But did Adam really have the legal right to transfer man's dominion and authority over all of God's creation on earth into the hands of Satan? And how did the descendants of Adam end up being redeemed or rescued from Adam and from slavery to Satan and sin? We will explore these questions and more in Chapter 2 of this book. We will discuss how God made and executed a redemption plan for mankind that ultimately led to the New Creation man.

Chapter 2
Adam's Fall and How God Came To The Rescue of Mankind

The Hopeless State of Man Under Satan's Rule, and How God Came to the Rescue

W<small>E</small> <small>ENDED</small> C<small>HAPTER</small> One by discussing the failure or fall of the Old Creation man (Adam) — how he disobeyed God by eating of the (forbidden) TREE OF THE KNOWLEDGE OF GOOD AND EVIL and suffered its consequence of spiritual death, and mortality for his body. We noted that Eve was deceived by the serpent — Satan — and fell into transgression, but Adam was not deceived. (see 1 Timothy 2:13-14). Adam knew exactly what he was doing; he was fully aware of the choice he had to make between LIFE and DEATH, and **he chose death.** Adam knew the consequences of his transgression and still went ahead with it. In this regard, we also noted that Adam, by his disobedience, set into motion the law of sin and death. (see Romans 5:12, with Romans 8:2). The Bible says that "**death reigned** from Adam to Moses, even over those who had not sinned according to the likeness of the transgression of Adam, who is a type of Him who was to come." (see Romans 5:14). "Through one man's offense **judgment** came **to all men**, resulting in **condemnation**" (see Romans 5:18).

"By one man's disobedience many were made sinners" (see Romans 5:19). Therefore, Adam's sin was not against only God, but against all of us who were to be born as his descendants. Adam sold himself (and thus mankind) into slavery to Satan and into bondage to sin (wickedness or lawlessness) and death, which explains why our great God and Savior Jesus Christ had to redeem, buy or purchase us back with his own precious blood. (see 1 Corinthians 6:20; Acts 20:28; 1 Peter 1:18-19; Titus 2:13-14).

Indeed Adam committed high treason against both God and posterity by choosing to obey Satan over God, by choosing to be a servant of Satan rather than a servant of God, by choosing death over life, by choosing to eat of the (forbidden) tree of the knowledge of good and evil, instead of the tree of life. (see Genesis 3:6). Thus by choosing to obey Satan, Adam handed over the legal rulership or dominion over the earth to the adversary — Satan, the Devil. (see Romans 6:16; with 1 Peter 5:8). Also, by submitting to Satan and giving Satan dominion over all of God's creation on earth — including man himself — man put himself in bondage (or slavery) to Satan and thus to sin, and man became Satan's slave or captive. Man became a slave of sin (see John 8:34); he was taken captive by Satan to do his will. (see 2 Timothy 2:26). And thus, today Satan is called the god (or ruler) of this world (see 2 Corinthians 4:4), a title that used to belong to man. The apostle John said, "The whole world is under the control of the evil one" (see 1 John 5:19 NIV), and that Satan "deceives the whole world" (see Revelation 12:9). It is a very sad reality! When Jesus was talking to His disciples, He referred to Satan as **the ruler or prince of this world** (see John 14:30). But in the same breath Jesus also declared confidently that Satan has no hold over Him. And so if you're in Christ today, you're as Jesus is in this world (see 1 John 4:17), and Satan has no hold over you. (see 1 John 4:4; Romans 8:37; Revelation 12:11). Jesus also told us, His disciples, on the night of his betrayal that He was going to the Father and would send the Holy Spirit to, among other things, prove the world to be in the wrong about judgment, because the prince of this world (Satan) **now stands condemned**. (see John 16:7-11). Praise God!

Now, in this Second Chapter, we are going to explore whether Adam had the legal right to transfer or hand over his dominion over all of God's creation on earth to Satan (the Devil). We will also discuss the result of Satan's dominion over the earth and over man, as well as how God initiated the process of redeeming/rescuing us out of Adam, and thus redeeming us from slavery/captivity to Satan and sin and creating us anew in Christ. Also, we will examine what kind of man God sought to create in Christ, and eventually did create, when He embarked on the New Creation project.

Did Adam Have the Legal Right to Transfer His Dominion Over All of God's Creation on Earth to Satan?

Adam evidently had the legal right to transfer his dominion and authority over all of God's creation on earth into the hands of Satan the adversary, because that authority belonged to him; it had been given to him legally by God Himself (see Genesis 1:26-28); Adam had been created for this very purpose; He was created to be a ruler over God's creation on earth, so the dominion and authority he had over all of God's creation on earth was **his legal birthright**. (see Genesis 1:26-28). And because the authority the Old Creation man (Adam) had was legally given to him by God and recognized by the Supreme Justice of the Universe, he had the legal right to transfer that authority to whomever he pleased. The Bible clearly tells us how one becomes a slave of another. It says, "Do you not know that to whom you present yourselves slaves to obey, YOU ARE THAT ONE'S SLAVES WHOM YOU OBEY, whether of sin leading to death, or of obedience leading to righteousness?" (Romans 6:16). Adam had the choice of obeying God and becoming God's slave (which would lead to righteousness, and of course life), or obeying Satan (the author of sin — see 1 John 3:8), and becoming Satan's slave, which would lead to sin and death. The choice was clear: God or Satan? Righteousness or sin? Life or Death? Adam chose Satan and thus sin and death. Consequently, **Adam died**; the Old Creation **died**. Hence, **the need** for the New Creation.

As we learned in the previous Chapter, **everything that happened to the Old Creation man (Adam) happened in the flesh or Sense realm, because he was a natural man (see 1 Corinthians 15:46-48) who could only respond to the world through his five traditionally recognized senses of sight, hearing, taste, smell, and touch.** So Satan (being a spirit who lives in the heavenly realms — see Ezekiel 28:14; Ephesians 2:2; Ephesians 6:12; Isaiah 14:13,14) couldn't interact with man in the spiritual or heavenly realm, which is why he devised and executed a plan to enter into the flesh or Sense realm through a physical creature on earth, THE SERPENT, to interact with and deceive Eve and cause man to disobey God. (see the story in Genesis 3:1-7). Thus from that point onward, **the serpent became associated with Satan**, and today one of the many names by which Satan is called in the Bible is "the serpent" (see 2 Corinthians 11:3), "the gliding serpent" (see Job

26:13; Isaiah 27:1), "the coiling serpent" (see Isaiah 27:1), or "that ancient serpent." (see Revelation 12:9). Note that the serpent who caused man to disobey God was a physical creature on earth, so the serpent was actually under the dominion of man, since God had put all things on earth under the dominion of man (see Genesis 1:26-28). Thus **by obeying the serpent, the Old Creation man (Adam) was basically obeying his subject or a creature that was under his authority.** That was just plain stupid! And yet, many believers still do that today. Satan (the serpent) is our subject; he has been defeated by Jesus Christ and put under the authority of the believer as a subject or a slave (see Colossians 2:15; Hebrews 2:14; Luke 10:20; Mark 16:17; Matthew 28:18-20; Ephesians 2:4-6; 1 John 4:4; Matthew 10:1; with Philippians 2:9-10; Acts 16:16-18; 2 Corinthians 10:3-6; Ephesians 4:27; James 4:7); so the New Creation man (or the believer) is a master over Satan, and yet many believers submit to Satan — they obey Satan when he tells them to sin — to doubt, hate, or fear. How stupid! Beloved, you have authority in the name of Jesus to trample upon serpents and scorpions, and over all the power of the devil (see Luke 10:19), so give no place to the devil. Resist the devil, and he will flee from you.

By submitting to the serpent or obeying the serpent, the Old Creation man (Adam) deposed or demoted himself from the position of a master over the serpent, to that of a slave of the serpent (and for that matter, a slave of Satan and sin). Man (Adam) thus **transferred his birthright** of dominion and rulership over all of God's creation on earth to Satan the serpent in an act of stupidity which was repeated later in human history by "Esau, who for one morsel of meat sold his birthright." (see Hebrews 12:16, with Genesis 25:29-34). Adam sold his birthright to Satan for a morsel of food (by **EATING** of the tree of the knowledge of good and evil**).**

As stated earlier, man (Adam) had the legal right to transfer his dominion over the earth to Satan. Therefore, God, because of His **perfect justice** (see Isaiah 30:18; Job 34:12; Deuteronomy 32:4; Psalm 99:4; Acts 10:34-35; Proverbs 11:1; Romans 2:11), has been obliged throughout the long period of human history, to recognize Satan's legal standing and legal right and authority to exercise dominion and rule over all of God's creation on earth. This explains **the legal side** of God's plan for the redemption of mankind. Indeed God is Sovereign and Almighty, but because He is also a God of justice, He has never taken advantage of Satan. Adam had legally transferred to Satan the authority which God had invested in him to rule the earth. And God respected that. It was enough that **Adam surely died** when he committed that sin. Had God not been absolutely Just, He would've immediately stripped Satan of the authority Adam had given away, and punished the descendants of Adam for Adam's sin or treason. But instead, God's GRACE and LOVE made provision for Adam's descendants to be redeemed or rescued out of the fallen Adam and out of the dominion of Satan and sin, based upon perfect justice. Oh, what a loving God we serve! God wanted the descendants of Adam to have the same privilege Adam had — to be able to make a choice for themselves between LIFE and DEATH. It saddens me that many people today are still choosing death over life by rejecting Jesus Christ who is the Life. It saddens me that many people today take God's grace for granted, and prefer to work for their own salvation, instead of just accepting the **gift** of Salvation God offers through Jesus Christ. How foolish! (see Romans 6:23, with Galatians 3:1-4).

The Devastating Result of Satan's Dominion or Rule Over the Earth and Over man

Beloved, never crave to be under Satan's dominion again. Nothing comes out of Satan, except sin and death. Satan will lure you with worldly possessions, but his ultimate intent is to steal, and to kill, and to destroy. (see John 10:10; John 8:44; 1 Peter 5:8). Indeed Satan is a liar, a thief, and a murderer. The day Satan took dominion over the earth was the real doomsday of human history. Today, we are still seeing remnants of what it looks like to be under the dominion and rule of Satan. We all know what happened the moment Satan took authority over man and the whole earth. The first thing that happened was that, God backed off from man (Adam). God drove Adam out of His presence; He drove man out of the garden of Eden and put measures in place to ensure that man could not return to the garden, to His presence. (see Genesis 3). God didn't banish man from His presence because He hated man. No! A thousand times No! A million times No! God loved man, and His love endures forever. The Bible says God so loved the world. (see John 3:16). Of course, this is referring mainly to the world of men. So God loved man. You need to understand what was going on here. God could allow man in His presence only because man was pure, man was very good; God had created a very good man when He created Adam. After God created man, the Bible says He saw everything He had created (including man), and indeed it was **VERY GOOD** (see Genesis 1:31), so God could fellowship with man. But when sin entered into man, Satan himself entered into man, because you see, sin is the spirit or person of Satan; sin is the very nature of Satan. The Bible says Satan is the author of sin: "HE WHO SINS IS OF THE DEVIL, for the devil has sinned from the beginning. For this purpose the Son of God was manifested, that He might destroy the works of the devil." (I John 3:8). And so man (Adam), having sinned, was now **of the Devil**. When sin entered man, it didn't just enter his body. The body is just the earthly tent in which man (the spirit-being) lives (see 2 Corinthians 5:1, 4). So **sin entered the spirit of man**, such that man became a different person from the person God originally created. **Man was corrupted**. Iniquity was found in man. Remember, Satan was also pure or perfect in his ways from the day that he was created until iniquity was found in him. (see Ezekiel 28:15). Thus, because of his sin, man was now of the Devil. Satan was in man, and so God could not fellowship with Satan; God cannot fellowship with evil; God (who is Light) cannot fellowship with darkness. (see 1 John 1:6; Isaiah 59:1-3; Habakkuk 1:13; 2 Corinthians 6:14). He just can't. And yet, out of His abundant grace and mercy, God **clothed** the fallen Adam and Eve, the wicked or evil Adam and Eve, who now found themselves naked, ashamed and afraid before God; God clothed them with tunics of skin. (see Genesis 3:10, 21). What a merciful and gracious God we serve! Jesus said, "He makes His sun rise **on the evil** and on the good, and sends rain on the just and **on the unjus**t." (see Matthew 5:45).

Indeed, when sin (Satan) entered man, man became evil, **man became darkness** (see Ephesians 5:8), and God wouldn't fellowship with man. After all, "What do Righteousness and wickedness have in common? Or **what fellowship can light have with darkness**?" (see 2 Corinthians 6:14 NIV). Nothing! Absolutely nothing! Wickedness had taken over the spirit of man (see Ephesians 2:2-3); darkness had fallen upon man and the whole earth; man had become a slave of sin (see John 8:34); sin had entered man and the world (see Romans 5:12); death had entered the world (see Romans 5:12). Man had become a child of disobedience, and a child of hell; the spirit of the prince of the power of the air had entered man to make him do his will and fulfill the lusts of the flesh, to fulfill the desires of the flesh, to fulfill the desires of the mind; man had by nature become the child of wrath; man was now going to be walking in the futility of his mind, having his understanding darkened, being alienated from the life of God, because of the ignorance that is in him, because of the blindness of his heart; man was going to go past feeling, to give himself over to lewdness, to work all uncleanness with greediness. (see Ephesians 2:2-3; Ephesians 4:18-19). That was what Satan had in stock for man, and he executed his plan accordingly. Man was now in the snare of Satan, having been taken captive by him to do his will. (see 2 Timothy 2:26). Man had become a slave of corruption; he was now in bondage, for by whom a person is overcome, by him also he is brought into bondage. (see 2 Peter 2:19). Man was poisoned by bitterness and bound by iniquity. (see Acts 8:23). Under the influence of Satan, man "changed the glory of the incorruptible God into an image made like corruptible man — and birds and four-footed animals and creeping things." (see Romans 1:23). Therefore God also **gave man up** to uncleanness, in the lusts of his heart, to dishonor his body, since **man had exchanged the truth of God for the lie, and worshipped and served the creature rather than the Creator, who is blessed forever**. (see Romans 1:24-25). God's wrath was coming upon the head of the wicked (see Jeremiah 30:23), and who are the wicked but Satan and his sons of disobedience? Jesus said to the natural man, "you are the children of **your father the devil**" (see John 8:44). Thus the wrath of God was coming upon man, who was now the son of the devil, the son of disobedience. (see Colossians 3:6). For God has said, "I will discipline you but only with justice; I will not let you go entirely unpunished." (see Jeremiah 30:11). Thus, God's perfect justice demanded a punishment. And the Bible says, "It is a fearful thing to fall into the hands of the living God." (Hebrews 10:31). The Bible says that God has prepared eternal fire for the devil and his angels on Judgment Day. (see Matthew 25:41; Jude 1:6). Adam was now destined to go into that eternal fire with the devil. **It was a choice Adam had consciously made out of his own free will**. And all of Adam's descendants were going to go into that eternal fire with Adam and the devil — **through no choice of ours**. And so if the descendants of Adam were to avoid the coming wrath of God, then they needed a Savior who would deliver them out of Adam, because "in Adam, all die." (see 1 Corinthians 15:22). And yet, man (the descendant of Adam) didn't even know he needed a Savior. And even if he did, how was he going to find a Savior? No Savior could come from amongst men, because all men have sinned and fall short of the glory of God. (see Romans 3:23). Man was in a hopeless situation; he was destined to perish with his father and new master Satan on the day of wrath that God has set aside, when His righteous judgment will be revealed. (see Romans 2:5). Therefore, having no hope and without God in the world (see Ephesians 2:12), man was fearfully waiting for the day of wrath. He was fearfully waiting for the Day of Judgment. Man had no hope "but only a fearful expectation of judgment and of raging fire that will consume the enemies of God." (see Hebrews 10:27).

God Offered Man a Savior

Beloved, as depressing and hopeless as the plight of man (the descendant of Adam) was at this point, and as badly as man had broken the heart of God, the Bible says, "For God so loved the world that **He gave His one and only Son**, that **whoever believes in Him shall not perish but have eternal life.**" (John 3:16 NIV). God offered man a Savior, and that Savior was God's only begotten Son Jesus Christ. He was the delight of God's heart, God's only comfort and the apple of His eye; Jesus was God's everything. And yet, God did not spare Him. He gave His only begotten Son to save you and I, not because He loved Jesus any less, but because He so loved us, and didn't want us to perish in His coming wrath; He wanted us to be able to **choose** to have eternal life, to spend eternity with Him in Heaven, where He will wipe every tear from our eyes, where there will be no more death or mourning or crying or pain. (see Revelation 21:4). Therefore God punished His own innocent (or sinless) Son Jesus Christ, and satisfied the demands of justice so that you and I will have **the choice** to walk out of Adam and death and come into Christ and be made alive (see 1 Corinthians 15:22) simply by putting our **faith** in Jesus Christ as our Lord and Savior; so that you and I will walk away as free men, as innocent men, as sinless men, as righteous men. (see Romans 3:23-24, 26; 2 Corinthians 5:21). Hallelujah! Instead of us suffering for our sins, Jesus, who knew no sin (see 2 Corinthians 5:21) stepped in as our Substitute, as our Representative to bear the punishment we deserved, so that by simply denouncing sin and Satan as our lord (in what is called repentance), and accepting Jesus as our (new) Lord and Savior (by our confession of faith), we would be acquitted of all charges and declared innocent or righteous. This was an act of grace born out of the loving heart of God our Father. God gave His only begotten Son Jesus Christ as a Substitute to suffer the full brunt of His wrath against sin, which man was supposed to suffer, and to die the shameful and humiliating death, which man was supposed to die, so that whoever believes in Him will live and not die.

The Bible says of Jesus Christ that: *"He was despised and rejected by mankind, a Man of suffering, and familiar with pain. Like one from whom people hide their faces He was despised, and we held Him in low esteem. Surely He took up our pain and bore our suffering, yet we considered Him punished by God, stricken by Him, and afflicted. But He was pierced for our transgressions, He was crushed for our iniquities; the punishment that brought us peace was on Him, and by His wounds we are healed. We all, like sheep, have gone astray, each of us has turned to our own way; and the Lord has laid on Him the iniquity of us all. He was oppressed and afflicted, yet He did not open His mouth; He was led like a lamb to the slaughter, and as a sheep before its shearers is silent, so He did not open His mouth. By oppression and judgment He was taken away. Yet who of His generation protested? For He was cut off from the land of the living; for the transgression of my people He was punished. He was assigned a grave with the wicked, and with the rich in His death, though He had done no violence, nor was any deceit in his mouth. Yet it was the Lord's will to crush Him and cause Him to suffer, and though the Lord makes His life an offering for sin, He will see His offspring and prolong His days, and the will of the Lord will prosper in His hand. After He has suffered, He will see the light of life and be satisfied; by His knowledge My righteous Servant will justify many, and He will bear their iniquities. Therefore I will give Him a portion among the great, and He will divide the spoils with the strong, because He poured out His life unto death, and was numbered with the transgressors. For He bore the sin of many, and made intercession for the transgressors."* (Isaiah 53:3-12 NIV).

What a beautiful picture of the amazing grace that has saved us! And Paul tells us that "He has saved us and called us to a holy life—NOT BECAUSE OF ANYTHING WE HAVE DONE but because of HIS OWN PURPOSE and GRACE. This **GRACE** was GIVEN US IN CHRIST JESUS **BEFORE THE BEGINNING OF TIME**, but it has **now been REVEALED** through the APPEARING of our Savior, Christ Jesus, who has DESTROYED DEATH and has BROUGHT LIFE AND IMMORTALITY to light through the gospel." (2 Timothy 1:9-10 NIV).

Beloved, God foresaw that the Old Creation man (Adam) would commit high treason and put himself and his descendants into bondage to Satan and sin. And God loved man too much to allow Satan to have us entirely forever. So before the beginning of the world, God gave man GRACE in Christ Jesus to save those who believe from perishing (see 2 Timothy 1:9-10) and to give us eternal life or a way of knowing Him, the only true God and Jesus Christ whom He has sent. (see John 17:3). And so today the Bible says that "the grace of God that brings salvation has **appeared** to ALL men" (see Titus 2:11). And yet only those men who accept this grace through faith will be saved. (see Ephesians 2:8-9). **Grace** is what has given us Jesus Christ in whom is life. **Grace** was what put the tree of life in the midst of the garden of Eden, because grace was given to us in Christ Jesus **before the beginning of time**. But **Adam rejected this grace** (which was given us in Christ Jesus before the beginning of time) **through unbelief**, and chose death over life. Every man today also has to make a choice to accept the grace of God which is in Christ Jesus (by faith) or reject it (through unbelief); we all have to choose between LIFE and DEATH — we have the same privilege Adam had. Indeed God's great love for mankind preceded or pre-dated creation; it existed long before the foundation of the world was laid, and it has never changed. *"Give thanks to the Lord, for He is good. HIS LOVE ENDURES FOREVER. Give thanks to the God of gods. His love endures forever. Give thanks to the Lord of Lords: His love endures forever."* (Psalm 136:1-3 NIV). Hallelujah!

Thus right in the garden of Eden, immediately after man sinned, God uttered a prophecy of **a war between Himself** (which He referred to as the Seed of the woman. Obviously a woman has no seed; only man has a seed, so this was referring to the virgin birth or the manifestation of God in the flesh as Jesus Christ — see Isaiah 7:14; Matthew 1:18-23; Galatians 4:4; 1 Timothy 3:16) **and the serpent (Satan)**, in which the serpent (Satan) appears to win a crucial battle (a strike at Jesus' heel — the crucifixion) only to lose the war (or have his head crushed — in the resurrection of Jesus Christ). In this prophecy, God says to the serpent, "I will put enmity between you and the woman, and between your seed and **her Seed**; He shall bruise your head, and you shall bruise His heel." (Genesis 3:15). The universal significance of this statement is understood in the light of the manifestation of God as Jesus Christ of Nazareth who was born of the virgin Mary (see John 1:1, 14; 1 Timothy 3:16). We see in the Gospels how Satan attempts to destroy Jesus in one way or another from the day of His birth until His death by crucifixion. While Satan eventually succeeds in having his human proxies crucify Jesus, Satan (the serpent) loses the war when Jesus destroys Satan's works through his death and resurrection (see Colossians 2:15; Hebrews 2:14; 1 John 3:8; 2 Timothy 1:10; Revelation 1:18), as God gives birth to multitudes of children through the resurrection of Jesus, by the Word of truth (see 1 Peter

1:3; James 1:18; 1 Peter 1:23) — children who are just as Jesus is, in this world. (see 1 John 4:17). Thus, man (the descendant of Adam) was to be saved by God Himself paying the penalty for man's sin or purchasing man with His own blood (see Acts 20:28; 1 Corinthians 6:20), giving birth to man out of His own will (see James 1:18; John 1:12-13) and giving man His own (righteous and holy) nature (see Ephesians 4:24; 2 Peter 1:4), so that man could come boldly to God's throne of grace (see Hebrews 4:16), stand in God's presence without guilt or fear (see Romans 8:1; Hebrews 10:1-3; 1 John 4:18), and fellowship with Him. (see 1 Corinthians 1:9; 1 John 1:3). God is Righteous in doing this. (see Romans 3:23-26). Hence, those who think today that they can save themselves through their own good works or their own righteous deeds are just kidding themselves. You have to be born again (born from above, or born of God) to be able to see or enter the Kingdom of God. (see John 3:3). And this only happens when you believe in Jesus Christ as your Lord and Savior. "I tell you, now is the time of God's favor, now is the day of salvation." (2 Corinthians 6:2b NIV). Only Jesus saves. "Salvation is found in no one else, for there is no other name under heaven given to mankind by which we must be saved." (Acts 4:12 NIV). And so, today "if you CONFESS with your mouth THE LORD JESUS and BELIEVE in your heart that God has raised Him from the dead, YOU WILL BE SAVED. For with the heart one believes unto righteousness, and with the mouth confession is made unto salvation." (Romans 10:9-10).

Beloved, the story of the New Creation is a beautiful love story. **The Old Creation had surely died,** having eaten of the (forbidden) tree of the knowledge of good and evil. Satan had completely asserted his rule over man's spirit, body and soul, with the goal of stealing, killing and destroying man. (see John 10:10; John 8:44; 1 Peter 5:8). Man had consequently become one with Satan. The spirit of Satan was at work in man (see Ephesians 2:2) changing the very nature of man into that of Satan himself. (see John 8:44-45). Man had become a sinner by nature, because of the spirit of Satan that was at work in him. (see Ephesians 2:2-3; Psalm 143:2; Isaiah 48:8; Psalm 51:5). Man had become a murderer and a liar, a complete enemy of the truth. (see John 8:44-45). Thus, man's whole being had become the temple of Satan, and man's deeds had become evil and unrighteous. (see Psalm 14:2-3, 10; Romans 3:10). There was not a single righteous man on earth, none who does good and does not sin. (see Ecclesiastes 7:20; Ecclesiastes 9:3; Psalm 143:2; Proverbs 20:9; Psalm 14:2-3). **All of mankind had become like an unclean thing, and all our righteous acts were like filthy rags**; we were all shriveling up like a leaf, and like the wind our sins swept us away. And yet no one called on the name of the Lord nor strove to lay hold of Him, for He had hidden His face from us and had given us over to our sins. (see Isaiah 64:6-7). Still today, man's "carnal mind is enmity against God; for it is not subject to the law of God, nor can it be. So those who are in the flesh (or sense realm) cannot please God." (see Romans 8:7). Satan, the god of this world, has blinded the eyes of the natural man to the will of God. (see 2 Corinthians 4:4). Paul sums up the natural man's condition in Ephesians 2:12 — **without covenant claims on God, having no hope and without God in the world.** How tragic! Just imagine how dire man's condition was — living in a world with the authority (or the keys) of death and hell in Satan's hands, and having no legal approach to God, no legal rights to prayer. Man was a doomed criminal, condemned by his own sin. Therefore, **for God to be able to fellowship with man, man had to become sinless, man**

had to become righteous; and the only way for this to happen was for God to create man anew. The Old Creation man had to be **born again** or **born of God**. And God chose to give birth to man out of His own will. (see John 1:12-13; James 1:18). Praise God!

What Manner of Man Did God Seek to Create When He Embarked on the New Creation Project?

"The men marveled, saying, WHAT MANNER OF MAN IS THIS, that even the winds and the sea obey Him!" (Matthew 8:27 KJV).

When the First or Old Creation **surely died**, God embarked on the process of revealing or manifesting the New Creation project — a project to redeem man and to create man anew. This was a project that had been **hidden from the foundation of the world** but was now about to be **revealed** or manifested. (see Ephesians 1:4-5; Romans 8:29; Revelation 13:8; 1 Peter 1:20). This time, God was going to create not a natural man (or earthy man) like the first Adam, but **a heavenly or spiritual man** and **a life-giving spirit** (see 1 Corinthians 15:45-49) who from the onset would have not just the image and likeness of God, but **the very nature of God** (see 2 Peter 1:4, with Ephesians 4:24; 1 John 5:1, 4) and **the very life of God in him** (see 1 John 5:11-13; John 3:35-36; John 5:26-27; John 6:47), who would be an **incorruptible spirit-being** (see 1 Peter 1:23, with Hebrews 12:23) with **complete authority and dominion over both the natural world and the spirit world.** (see Matthew 28:18-20; Mark 16:17-18; Luke 10:20; Mark 9:23; Philippians 4:13; 1 John 4:4). This new man would be a true super man to whom all things are possible. (see Mark 9:23; Philippians 4:13). God was, out of His own will, going to **give**

birth to this new man (see James 1:18; John 1:12-13), so that he will be a truly begotten son of God (see 1 John 3:1; James 1:18) and **a truly spiritual or heavenly man** (see 1 Corinthians 15:46-48; 1 Corinthians 3:1) whose **citizenship is in Heaven** (see Philippians 3:20), who has the incorruptible seed of God in him (see 1 Peter 1:23) and **is thus incapable of sinning** or committing the treason of the Old Creation man Adam (see 1 John 3:9). And that is not all, God was going to also put **His seal** (that is, the Holy Spirit) on this man and in this man's heart as a guarantee that he belongs to Him forever (see Ephesians 1:13; 2 Corinthians 5:5; 2 Corinthians 1:21-22), and that Satan cannot steal him, kill him or destroy him. (see John 5:24; John 11:25-26; 1 John 3:14; 2 Timothy 1:10).

This New Creation man would be **God's own son**, born of Him to overcome the world (see 1 John 5:4; 1 John 3:9; 1 John 5:1). God Himself would live in him and abide in him, and he would also live in God and abide in God (see 1 Corinthians 3:16; 1 Corinthians 6:19; 1 John 4:15-16; 1 John 4:4; Ephesians 4:6, with Colossians 3:3). Therefore, **he and God would be one**; he would be joined as **one spirit** with God (see 1 Corinthians 6:17), and he would be a member of Christ's own Body, of His bone and of His flesh. (see Ephesians 5:30). He would be a god-man (see Psalm 82:6; John 10:33-36), a partaker (or sharer) of the Holy Spirit and a partaker of the divine (or God) nature. (see 2 Peter 1:4; Hebrews 6:4). This new Creation man would be a true champion and **a spiritual giant, just as Jesus Christ is**. (see 1 John 4:17). He would be more than a conqueror. (see Romans 8:37). And he would **live simultaneously in Heaven and on Earth**, as his life is hidden with Christ in God (see Colossians 3:3), as he sits on the right hand of God on His throne with Christ and in

Christ (see Ephesians 2:4-6), and lives in this world without being of this world. (see John 17:16; John 15:19; 1 John 3:1). Moreover, unlike the Old Creation man, this New Creation man would be **in the Spirit**, (see Romans 8:9), **live in the Spirit**, and **walk in the Spirit** (see Galatians 5:25 KJV), and NOT in the flesh or Sense realm. (see Romans 8:9; Romans 8:13). This new Creation man would also have **a new body** (see 1 Corinthians 15:50-54; Philippians 3:21), but he would not receive this new body until his days on earth are over and the Lord Jesus Christ returns. (see 2 Corinthians 5:1-8; Philippians 3:20-21; 1 Thessalonians 4:15-18). So, **for now, he would still live in this old body of corruption** (see 1 Corinthians 15:42, 50; 2 Corinthians 5:1), having this **treasure in earthen vessel**, so that **the excellence of the power** (he has) **may be of God and not of him**. (see 2 Corinthians 4:7).

Beloved, the old man (or the old creation man) had died; he had become darkness (see 2 Corinthians 6:14; Ephesians 5:8), but God was going to create the new man as the light of the world. (see Matthew 5:14, with 2 Corinthians 6:14; Ephesians 5:8). Thus, God in creating this new man was going to **call light out of darkness** the way He did in the beginning when He created the heavens and the earth (see Genesis 1:1-3); God was going to call this new man out of darkness **into His marvelous light** (see 1 Peter 2:9; Colossians 1:13); He was going to call (or make) this new man out of the dead old man; He was going to **give life to the dead.** (see Ephesians 2:1; Colossians 2:13). God was going to prove that He is indeed "God, who **gives life to the dead** and calls those things which do not exist as though they did." (see Romans 4:17). Therefore, as a necessary first step in manifesting or revealing this new creation project, God needed the consent and cooperation of man (the old man). And since man (humanity in general) had lost his way to God, God had to initiate contact with man out of His pure and amazing grace, and make a covenant with man. This is where or how Abram (or Abraham) came into the picture.

Just as He did in delivering the children of Israel (or the descendants of Abraham) from slavery in Egypt and bringing them to the promised land, God redeemed or delivered man (or the descendants of Adam) from slavery to sin/Satan in this mighty way, and manifested the new creation to the world at the appointed time, so "that all the peoples of the earth may **know** the hand of the Lord, that it is mighty, **that you may fear the Lord your God forever**." (Joshua 4:24).

In the next Chapter, we will discuss how God initiated and executed a redemption plan for mankind that ultimately led to the New (Creation) man.

Chapter 3

Grace Was Given To Us in Christ Jesus Before Time Began

How God Revealed The Redemption Plan for Mankind that Ultimately Led to the Manifestation of Our Lord Jesus Christ

THE BIBLE SAYS that God chose us (that is, man — believers); He chose us IN CHRIST JESUS "**BEFORE THE FOUNDATION OF THE WORLD**, that we should be holy and without blame before Him in love, HAVING PREDESTINED US TO ADOPTION AS SONS by Jesus Christ to Himself, according to the good pleasure of His will" (see Ephesians 1:4-5). This means that God foresaw that the Old Creation man Adam would commit high treason and put himself, his descendants and this whole world into bondage to Satan and sin. But God loved the world so much and wouldn't allow Satan to have us entirely forever. So before the beginning of the world, God gave man GRACE in Christ Jesus to save us (believers) from perishing (see 2 Timothy 1:9-10) and to adopt us (believers) as His son(s) by Jesus Christ to Himself (see Ephesians 1:4-5); God made the same **grace** that put the tree of life in the midst of the garden of Eden available to all mankind; He gave us grace so that we (who would believe in

Him or accept this grace) would have eternal life (see John 3:16) or a way of knowing Him, the only true God, and Jesus Christ whom He has sent. (see John 17:3). Thus GRACE "was given to us **in Christ Jesus** before time began" (see 2 Timothy 1:9). God gave man GRACE even before He created the world, and **this grace was in His Son Jesus Christ**. Indeed grace was always around; it wasn't given when Jesus Christ our Savior appeared; it was only REVEALED by His appearing. (see 2 Timothy 1:10). Grace was right there in the garden of Eden. The Bible calls the Word of God the Word of HIS GRACE. (see Acts 20:32). Adam rejected grace when he rejected the Word of God that was spoken to him in the garden of Eden; he rejected grace when he rejected the tree of life that God, by His great grace, had put in the midst of the garden of Eden. Adam rejected Life and chose Death when he chose the (forbidden) tree of the knowledge of good and evil over the tree of life; and that Life which Adam rejected was Jesus Christ (see John 14:6) who is also the Word of God (see John 1:1, 14; Revelation 19:13), and in whom also is grace. (see 2 Timothy 1:9; 2 Peter 1:2). In spite of this, God extended grace to us also — the descendants of Adam. Therefore the Bible says that, "the grace of God that brings salvation has **appeared to ALL men**" (see Titus 2:11). But unfortunately, just like Adam, many men today are rejecting the grace of God by rejecting Jesus Christ in whom is grace, by rejecting Jesus Christ who is the Word of God, by rejecting Jesus Christ who is the Life. And so many are condemned, just like Adam; many have surely died or perished just like Adam, whereas those of us who have accepted the Lord Jesus Christ are saved, we have eternal life. "For as in Adam all die, even so in Christ all shall be made alive." (1 Corinthians 15:22).

Beloved, God's great love and grace for mankind preceded or pre-dated creation; it existed long before the foundation of the world was laid, and it has never changed. God's love and grace is still available today to all who would accept it.

Thank God For Grace

Not too long after the Old Creation man (Adam) disobeyed God, suffered spiritual death (or separation from God) and fell under the dominion of Satan, physical death and devastation also became a hideous reality to him. Adam and Eve had a first son named Cain, and a second named Abel. (see Genesis 4:1-2). Suffering under Satan's yoke, the first family of the human race had already started yearning for the presence of God. And of course it is in God's nature to respond to those who diligently search for Him with all their heart, as He said to the Israelites that "you will seek Me and find Me, when you search for Me with all your heart." (see Jeremiah 29:13). The Book of Hebrews also says that without faith it is impossible to please God; that God is pleased with men who believe that He exists and that He is **a rewarder of those who diligently seek Him**. (see Hebrews 11:6). Thus "in the process of time it came to pass that Cain brought an offering of the fruit of the ground to the Lord. Abel also brought of the FIRSTBORN of his flock and of their FAT. And the Lord respected Abel and his offering, but He did not respect Cain and his offering. And Cain was very angry, and his countenance fell." (Genesis 4:3-5). Evidently God accepted Abel's offering because Abel offered it **by faith** (see Hebrews 11:4), Abel believed God and did what was acceptable and pleasing to God; he followed god's instruction (or God's Word) by offering the FIRSTBORN of his flock and the FAT PORTIONS. (see Genesis 4:4-7 AMP). Hence the Bible says that **Abel's deeds were righteous**. (see 1 John 3:12). "**By FAITH** Abel offered a more excellent sacrifice than Cain, through which he obtained witness that **he was righteous**, God testifying of his gifts…" (see Hebrews 11:4). Cain, on the contrary, did not offer his offering by faith, he did not believe God but ignored God's instruction (or God's Word) and failed to do what was acceptable and pleasing to God, and so God had no respect for Cain and his offering. (see Genesis 4:5-7 AMP). Consequently, Adam's firstborn son Cain got very angry, and **he murdered his brother Abel** (see Genesis 4:5, 8). Sin had taken hold of Cain and was ruling over him. (see Genesis 4:7). So Adam painfully saw and felt firsthand the devastating effect of his sin; Adam had not only sinned against God but also against posterity, against his children one of whom had now manifested the murderous nature of Satan his father. (see John 8:44; 1 John 3:12). The Bible says that **Cain was of the devil**, and **his deeds were evil**. (see 1 John 3:10-15). Hatred, the very nature of Satan, had entered the world and was snarling at Adam and his family; sin had taken root. The voice of Abel's righteous blood cried out to God for vengeance, for justice (see Genesis 4:10 AMP) and thus brought **judgment** and **a curse** upon Cain. God pronounced a curse on Cain, such that Cain became afraid that someone may also kill him. But God showed **grace** to Cain and pronounced that "whoever kills Cain, vengeance shall be taken on him sevenfold." And the Lord set a mark on Cain, lest anyone finding him should kill him." (Genesis 4:15). It's amazing what God's grace does: here, it protected a murderer, an evil man, a man who was of the devil, just as it clothed Adam and Eve with tunics of skin after they had sinned. As we noted earlier, the Bible says that God "makes His sun rise on the evil and on the good, and sends rain on the just and on the unjust." (see Matthew 5:45). That is grace — unmerited, unearned, undeserved favor of God!

Beloved, the voice of Abel's righteous blood cried out to God for vengeance, for justice (see Genesis 4:10 AMP) and thus brought judgment and a curse upon Cain. Hence the Bible says that the blood of sprinkling (or the blood of Jesus) speaks better things than that of Abel. (see Hebrews 12:24). Whereas Abel's blood cried out for justice or vengeance and brought judgment and a curse to Cain, Jesus' blood cried out for mercy and brought forgiveness and blessings to us all who believe. Hallelujah! At the cross Jesus, with His dying breath, pleaded for His murderers: "Father, forgive them, for they do not know what they do." (see Luke 23:34).

Now, Cain the murderer had a son and named him Enoch. (see Genesis 4:17). One of Enoch's great grandchildren whose name was Lamech was the first man to practice what is known today as polygamy. (see Genesis 4:18-19). Not only that, Lamech also followed after his grandfather Cain's footsteps and murdered a young man (see Genesis 4:23), and then he remorselessly pronounced upon himself that "If Cain shall be avenged sevenfold, then Lamech seventy-sevenfold" (Genesis 4:24), thus alluding to the grace God showed Cain, in his attempt to justify himself. Paul asks, "What shall we say then? Shall we continue in sin that grace may abound? Certainly not!" (see Romans 6:1-2). Shame on Lamech!

The Bible says that Adam and Eve also bore another son and named him Seth. "And as for Seth, to him also a son was born; and he named him Ē′nosh. THEN MEN BEGAN TO CALL ON THE NAME OF THE LORD." (Genesis 4:26). Here, we are told that it was when

Ē'nosh was born that men began to CALL ON THE NAME OF THE LORD. Burdened by the yoke of slavery to Satan, men began to yearn for God and to call on Him. The Bible also reports that five generations after the birth of Ē'nosh, a man named ENOCH who was of the seventh generation in Adam's genealogy (see Jude 1:14) was born to Jared (see Genesis 5:18); it was this Enoch who begat Methuselah, the man who lived the longest in the entire history of the human race — he died at the age of 969. We are told that "After he begot Methuselah, **ENOCH** WALKED WITH GOD THREE HUNDRED YEARS, and had sons and daughters." (Genesis 5:22). That was certainly a long walk with God. Thus the Bible also records an amazing thing that happened to this Enoch: he did not taste physical death; **God took him**. The Bible says, "And Enoch WALKED WITH GOD; and he was not, for **God took him**." (Genesis 5:24). The Book of Hebrews also explains that, "BY FAITH Enoch was taken away so that **he DID NOT SEE DEATH**, "and was not found, because **God had taken him**"; for before he was taken he had this testimony, that HE PLEASED GOD. But WITHOUT FAITH IT IS IMPOSSIBLE TO PLEASE Him, for he who comes to God must believe that He is, and that He is a rewarder of those who diligently seek Him." (Hebrews 11:5-6). Here also, we are introduced to an important truth about God: that He is pleased with men who come to Him believing that He exists, and that He is a rewarder of those who diligently seek Him; but **without faith it is IMPOSSIBLE to please God.**

Grace is Accessed by Faith

Obviously, the testimony (or citation) Enoch had from God before he was taken to Heaven did not cite his good works; it did not say anything about him doing some extraordinary humanitarian work in the poorest part of the ancient world, or perhaps living a sinless life, even though all such things are good. No, it only cited his FAITH. It stated that "**he pleased God. But without faith it is impossible to please Him**." Hallelujah! Sincere (or genuine) faith (in Jesus Christ) is all you need if you want to please God, if you want to be saved, if you want to enter the Kingdom of God, if you want to be with God, because **the grace which God has given to man is IN Christ Jesus** (see 2 Timothy 1:9) and **can only be accessed by faith** (see Romans 5:2); salvation is found IN no other, "for there is no other Name under heaven given among men by which we must be saved." (see Acts 4:12). The Kingdom of Heaven is indeed an exclusive domain; admission is granted solely to those who have FAITH in JESUS the King. Hence the Bible says to the New Creation man: "For BY **GRACE** YOU HAVE BEEN SAVED **through FAITH**, and that not of yourselves; IT IS THE GIFT OF GOD, NOT OF WORKS, lest anyone should boast." (Ephesians 2:8-9). **Faith** is all you need to access grace and be saved; nothing else will do. And to those who think telling people this truth will make them sin, all I can say to you is that you don't know anything about faith, because **genuine faith will make you please God in every way imaginable**; it will not make you live in sin. Genuine faith will give you access to more and more grace; and the Bible says that sin shall not have dominion over you when you're under grace. (see Romans 6:14). Moreover, faith always produces corresponding works; faith cannot even be separated from works. This is why James uses faith and works interchangeably in his famous exposition on faith and works (see James 2:21, with James 2:23). James also says in his epistle that "faith without works is dead." (see James 2:26). Faith without works is useless, and cannot save. Period.

Beloved, we are still building our discussion toward the complete genealogy of Abram (or Abraham) the father of all who believe, but for now let us note that Enoch begat Methuselah; Methuselah begat Lamech; and Lamech begat **Noah**. (see Genesis 5:21-29). Now, let us have a brief discussion about Lamech's son **Noah**, because he would give us a very important picture of what has been from the beginning and still is God's only requirement for salvation.

Salvation Has Always Been By Grace Through Faith

We will be talking in detail about Noah soon, about how God saved him and his family in the great flood, thereby proving to us that no matter how much sin is in your genealogy or in your own past, God can still use you for His will and purpose, God can still save you. In fact, no man born of Adam has ever qualified to be saved or to work for God based on his own merit; it is always **the GRACE of God** that qualifies man. You just have to be willing to be used by God; you just have to make yourself available for use by surrendering or offering your body as a living sacrifice, holy, acceptable to God (see Romans 12:1), and surrendering your members (or body parts) as instruments of righteousness to God (see Romans 6:13), so that you will be a vessel for honor, sanctified and useful for the Master, prepared for every good work (see 2 Timothy 2:20-21). God will use you mightily if you would cooperate with Him and with His grace. For it is the grace of God that teaches us to deny ungodliness and worldly lusts, and to live soberly, righteously, and godly in this present age. (see Titus 2:11-12). Throughout the Bible we see God, by His great grace, calling and using all kinds of otherwise sinful men for great works. God called and used Abraham (who prior to his calling was worshipping other gods with his father Terah — see Joshua 24:2-4) to bless all the nations of the earth. (see Genesis 12:1-3; Genesis 22:18). God also called and used Moses (a murderer — see Exodus 2:11-12) to deliver the Israelites from slavery in Egypt. (see Exodus 14). God called and used King David (who was also covetous, an adulterer and a murderer — see 2 Samuel 11&12)) to do mighty works to the glory of God; and the Bible says that the Messiah (Jesus Christ) was a descendant of David, so that Jesus was even called the Son of David. (see Mark 12:35-37; Luke 1:32). Thus David even exclaimed, "Who am I, O Lord? And what is my house, that You have brought me this far?" (see 2 Samuel 7:18). God also put Rahab (the prostitute — see Hebrews 11:31; James 2:24-26) in the direct lineage of our Lord Jesus Christ. (see Matthew 1:5). God used the apostle Paul — who murdered, harassed and persecuted Christians — to bring salvation to the Gentiles (see Acts 9:4-5; Galatians 2:8; 1 Timothy 1:12-13; Ephesians 3:2-12, with Acts 26:17-18) and to write two-thirds of the New Testament epistles. Paul even made a famous statement that he was the chief or worst of sinners (see 1 Timothy 1:15). Praise be to God, for it is only **the grace of God** that makes such things possible! Thus Paul said, "I am the least of the apostles, who am not worthy to be called an apostle, because I persecuted the church of God. **But by the grace of God** I am what I am, and **His grace** toward me was not in vain; but I labored more abundantly than they all, yet not I, but **the grace of God which was with me.**" (see I Corinthians 15:9-10).

And so by the grace of God, Noah was also used mightily to teach us about God's way of salvation. The Bible says, "And Noah was five hundred years old, and Noah begot Shem, Ham, and Japheth." (Genesis 5:32). During Noah's day is when man's wickedness under

Satan's reign became great and evil was being committed continually. It is unveiled to us in more detail here: *"Now it came to pass, when men began to multiply on the face of the earth, and daughters were born to them, that THE SONS OF GOD SAW THE DAUGHTERS OF MEN, that they were beautiful; AND THEY TOOK WIVES FOR THEMSELVES OF ALL WHOM THEY CHOSE. And the Lord said, "My Spirit shall not STRIVE with MAN forever, FOR HE IS INDEED FLESH; yet* **HIS DAYS SHALL BE ONE HUNDRED AND TWENTY YEARS.***"* *There were GIANTS on the earth in those days, and also AFTERWARD, when* **the sons of God came in to the daughters of men and THEY BORE CHILDREN TO THEM.** *Those were the mighty men who were of old, MEN OF RENOWN. Then the Lord saw that* **THE WICKEDNESS OF MAN WAS GREAT IN THE EARTH,** *and that* **EVERY INTENT OF THE THOUGHTS OF HIS HEART WAS ONLY EVIL CONTINUALLY.** *And THE LORD WAS SORRY THAT HE HAD MADE MAN ON THE EARTH, and He was* **GRIEVED** *in His heart. So the Lord said,* **"I WILL DESTROY MAN** *whom I have created FROM THE FACE OF THE EARTH, BOTH MAN AND BEAST, creeping thing and birds of the air,* **FOR I AM SORRY THAT I HAVE MADE THEM.***"* (Genesis 6:1-7).

Clearly this is a very sad picture of the state of affairs on earth in Noah's day as man labored in his slavery to Satan and sin, producing all manner of works of the flesh. Wickedness had reached such a stupendous height that God decided to reduce man's lifespan on earth to 120 years. God was grieved in His heart; He was sorry that He had made man on the earth, and thus decided to destroy man from the face of the earth. In talking about the wickedness of man during Noah's day, mention is also made of the sons of God marrying the daughters of men and having children with them. But who are "the sons of God" mentioned here as marrying and having children with the daughters of men?

Who Were these "Sons of God" Who Married the Daughters of Men in Noah's Day?

The term "sons of God" in the Old Testament is also used elsewhere but only of angels, never of men. In Job 1:6, for instance, the "sons of God" were presenting themselves to God and Satan also came with them; these were angels. And so these are fallen angels here in Genesis 6 that actually began to intermingle and intermarry with the daughters of men, and had children with them, who grew up to become giants (not quite unexpected, with Satan being the ruler or god of this world).

Someone may say, but wait a minute, Jesus said the angels in heaven neither marry nor are given in marriage. (see Matthew 22:30; Mark 12:25). That is true. But note that Jesus said, "the ANGELS IN HEAVEN" don't marry; He didn't include the fallen angels that are on earth. And the fact that these were rebellious or fallen angels meant that they could break all the laws of God or do whatever they wanted. After all, Jesus did not say that angels were sexless; He just said there was no marriage among angels in heaven. And it is interesting that, always, angels are referred to in the masculine gender. Also note that angels are not limited to the spirit realm either; they can manifest in the flesh as humans (strangers — see Hebrews 13:2), as they did when they visited Lot and saved Lot from God's wrath upon Sodom and Gomorrah. Even those wicked men in Sodom wanted to have sex with these angels. (see Genesis 19:1-5). Angels have the ability to do this. And the Bible teaches that those angels who fell (Satan and his angels) didn't lose their wisdom or power, it was just corrupted (see James 3:15; Ezekiel 28:12-17; Ephesians 6:12), so they indulge in all kinds of wicked acts, inventing creative ways to sin. Satan and his angels can manifest in any form they choose to; we are even told that Satan can transform himself into an angel of light and masquerade as an angel of light. (see 2 Corinthians 11:14). But you will know him by his fruits (see Matthew 7:16, 20); his speech will even give him away, because he is a liar, there is no truth in him, and he does not stand in the truth. (see John 8:44).

The Salvation of Noah in the Great Flood

Now, the Bible says that sin had increased tremendously on earth in Noah's day. God saw that THE WICKEDNESS OF MAN WAS GREAT IN THE EARTH, and that EVERY INTENT OF THE THOUGHTS OF HIS HEART WAS ONLY EVIL CONTINUALLY. So God regretted creating man on the earth; God was grieved, and decided to destroy man together with beast, creeping thing and birds of the air from the face of the earth. Essentially, all of God's creation on earth were doomed to destruction. No man or animal DESERVED to be saved. The Bible says, "God looked upon the earth, and indeed it was corrupt; for **ALL flesh** HAD CORRUPTED THEIR WAY on the earth." (Genesis 6:12). **ALL flesh** (including Noah) "had corrupted their way" or sinned on the earth. All means all. The apostle Paul echoes this in his letter to the Romans when he writes that "All have sinned and fall short of the glory of God." (see Romans 3:23). And, of course, the wages of sin is death. (see Romans

6:23). Therefore all were destined to die, to perish in the impending wrath of God. The Almighty God Himself was bringing floodwaters on the earth, "to DESTROY from under heaven ALL FLESH IN WHICH IS **THE BREATH OF LIFE**; everything that is on the earth SHALL DIE." (see Genesis 6:17). But then, there is a glimmer of hope in the midst of this gloom, as we are told of an interesting thing that happened to one man — Noah. The Bible says, "But Noah **found GRACE** in the eyes of the Lord." (Genesis 6:8). Hallelujah! Noah accessed grace by faith; Noah found or received his share of the grace that was given to us in Christ Jesus before the beginning of the world (see 2 Timothy 1:9-10). Noah had younger brothers and sisters (see Genesis 5:30), and yet Noah was the only one among his siblings who found GRACE in the eyes of the Lord, and he was saved in the flood together with his wife, his 3 sons and their wives — 8 in all. (see 1 Peter 3:20; Hebrews 11:7; Genesis 6:18; Genesis 7:7). Noah and his household were saved by God's GRACE (unmerited, unearned, undeserved favor) through faith.

Indeed GRACE saves through faith! Grace was what saved Noah, through faith, not his good works. The Bible says that Noah (just like Enoch) walked with God. (see Genesis 6:9). The story of Noah's salvation is concrete proof that since the beginning of human history salvation has always been by GRACE through FAITH. Grace freely justified Noah, through faith. Hence the Bible says, "Noah was A JUST MAN, PERFECT in his generations. Noah WALKED WITH GOD." (see Genesis 6:9). The Book of Hebrews gives us more details: "**BY FAITH** Noah, being divinely warned of THINGS NOT YET SEEN, MOVED WITH GODLY FEAR, PREPARED AN ARK FOR THE SAVING OF HIS HOUSEHOLD, by which HE CONDEMNED

THE WORLD and BECAME HEIR OF THE RIGHTEOUSNESS which is ACCORDING TO **FAITH**." (Hebrews 11:7). Beloved, does this picture look familiar? Noah was justified freely and saved by grace through faith, just like believers today. And he became heir of **the righteousness which is according to FAITH**. Thus, Paul says that even though all have sinned and fall short of the glory of God, ALL are "JUSTIFIED FREELY **by His GRACE** through the REDEMPTION that is in CHRIST JESUS, whom God set forth as a propitiation by His blood, **THROUGH FAITH**, to demonstrate His righteousness, because in His forbearance GOD HAD PASSED OVER THE SINS THAT WERE PREVIOUSLY COMMITTED, to DEMONSTRATE AT THE PRESENT TIME His RIGHTEOUSNESS, THAT He MIGHT BE JUST and the **JUSTIFIER** OF **THE ONE WHO HAS FAITH in JESUS**." (see Romans 3:24-26).

Beloved, righteousness has always been by FAITH. Salvation has always been by grace through faith. (see Ephesians 2:8-9). Noah believed in an impending flood he hadn't seen, and he prepared himself for it by doing according to all that God commanded him. The Bible states that **Noah did according to all that God commanded him**. (see Genesis 6:22). That is FAITH! Today we also believe in an impending Day of Wrath, or a Judgment Day we haven't seen. (see Romans 2:5). And we are preparing ourselves for it by doing according to all that God has commanded us. The only evidence Noah had of the impending flood was God's Word (which is also the only evidence we have today). And yet Noah, moved with godly fear, prepared an ark for the saving of his household, just as God had commanded him. We are also commanded to hold fast our faith in Jesus Christ till He comes (see Revelation 3:11; Revelation 2:25; Revelation 3:21; Hebrews 4:14; with 1 John 5:4-5),

"For we have become partakers of Christ **if we hold the beginning of our confidence steadfast to the end**" (Hebrews 3:14).

Faith Has Corresponding Works or Actions; Faith is Work

As noted earlier, Noah did according to all that God commanded him. (see Genesis 6:22). Because Noah believed God's Word, he acted on it by building the ark God commanded. Faith always moves us into action. Faith works. Faith is produced when we act on the Word of God, when we trust God's Word enough to act on it, trusting and expecting that God will do what He has promised to do. Today all men need to act on God's Word which commands us to confess with our mouth the Lord Jesus and believe in our heart that God has raised Him from the dead, and we will be saved. (see Romans 10:9-10). All Christians also need to believe and act on God's Word which says that we are saved, that we have eternal life because of our sincere faith in Jesus Christ as our Lord and Savior. (see 1 John 5:13; John 3:35-36; John 6:47). Today if you claim to be a Christian and yet deny that you have eternal life, or are not sure that you have everlasting life, then obviously you're not truly a Christian, you don't believe in the Lord Jesus Christ, because Jesus said, "Most assuredly, I say to you, **he who believes in Me has everlasting life.**" (John 6:47).

Faith is the Victory that Overcomes the World

The Bible says that Noah condemned (or overcame) the world and became heir of the righteousness which is according to FAITH. (see Hebrews 11:7). In other words, Noah's name was written in the Book of Life as a recipient or beneficiary of the "faith righteousness" or "righteousness by faith" which was in Christ Jesus and was to be revealed or manifested to us through the crucifixion, death and RESURRECTION of our Lord and Savior Jesus Christ. The Bible says, "For in the gospel the righteousness of God is **REVEALED** —a righteousness that is **BY FAITH FROM FIRST TO LAST**, just as it is written: "The righteous will live BY FAITH." (Romans 1:17 NIV). "For WITH THE HEART ONE BELIEVES UNTO RIGHTEOUSNESS" (see Romans 10:10). What all of this means for us today is that righteousness is attained only by FAITH. And this "faith righteousness" has now been REVEALED to us in the gospel and is being enjoyed today by all who believe in Jesus Christ. We believers, just like Noah, are righteous not because of what we do, but because of what Jesus has done. For God made Jesus who knew no sin to be sin for us, **"that we might become the righteousness of God in Him."** (see II Corinthians 5:21). Thus Paul says, "But NOW the righteousness of God apart from the law is **REVEALED**, being witnessed by the Law and the Prophets, even THE RIGHTEOUSNESS OF GOD, **THROUGH FAITH IN JESUS CHRIST**, TO ALL AND ON ALL **WHO BELIEVE**..." (Romans 3:21-22). So **by faith** Noah condemned or overcame the world. The apostle John also tells us in his First epistle that "this is the victory that has overcome the world—**OUR FAITH**. Who is he who overcomes the world, but he who BELIEVES that Jesus is the Son of God?" (see I John 5:4-5). All of us who believe in Jesus have condemned or overcome the world, just as Noah did. And in the same way as our Lord Jesus Christ said of Himself, we can say that the devil has no claim on us and no power over us (see John 14:30), for we overcame the devil by the blood of the Lamb (Jesus Christ) and by the word of our testimony (or our confession of the

Word of God), not loving our lives even unto the death. (see Revelation 12:11). Glory to God!

God's Covenant with Noah

As we continue to eavesdrop on God's conversation with Noah in Genesis 6, we will also hear the very first mention in the Bible of the word "COVENANT." God said as part of His plan to save Noah and his household, that "I will establish My COVENANT with you; and you shall go into the ark—you, your sons, your wife, and your sons' wives with you." (Genesis 6:18). Noah's part in the Covenant was to trust God or have FAITH in God — faith which was sincere enough to act on God's word or God's command regarding the building of an ark into which Noah, his wife, his sons, his sons' wives, and a male and female of each kind of living creature on earth will enter to be saved from the coming floodwaters. Through this Covenant, Noah's entire family was to be saved together with him in the impending flood. This makes me believe in family salvation, and I pray that my entire family or household will accept Jesus and be saved. In Acts 16:31 Paul and Silas said to the jailer, "Believe on the Lord Jesus Christ, and you will be saved, YOU AND YOUR HOUSEHOLD." (Acts 16:31). So try to get you and your household to believe in the Lord Jesus Christ, and be saved.

God Keeps His Covenant

The story of Noah's salvation proves that God keeps His covenant. The Bible says, "Therefore know that the Lord your God, He is God, the faithful God WHO KEEPS COVENANT and mercy for a thousand generations with those who love Him and keep His commandments" (Deuteronomy 7:9). Indeed God is a covenant-keeping God, and He will keep His covenant to us, which is **Jesus Christ** of whom He said, "I, the Lord, have called You in righteousness, and will hold Your hand; I will keep You and **GIVE You AS A COVENANT** TO THE PEOPLE, as a light to the Gentiles, to open blind eyes, to bring out prisoners from the prison, those who sit in darkness from the prison house." (Isaiah 42:6-7). Indeed God has given Jesus Christ to us as **A COVENANT** — the New Covenant is in Jesus' blood (see Luke 22:20) — and our part in this Covenant is simply to believe in the Lord Jesus Christ for our salvation. (see Acts 16:31; John 3:16). God Himself has said, "My covenant I WILL NOT BREAK, nor alter the word that has gone out of my lips." (Psalms 89:34). Indeed God will fulfill His covenant to us in the same way as He fulfilled His covenant with Noah. The Bible says that when the ark Noah was to build was ready, just as God's Covenant with Noah had established, "they went into the ark to Noah, two by two, of all flesh in which is **the breath of life**. So those that entered, male and female of all flesh, went in as God had commanded him; and THE LORD SHUT HIM IN." (Genesis 7:15-16).

Beloved, when you come into Jesus Christ the New Covenant, when you come into Jesus Christ the Way, the Truth and the Life (see John 14:6), when you come into Jesus Christ the ARK OF SALVATION, you don't need to worry about falling out or stumbling, because the Lord Himself SHUTS YOU IN, as we're told He did for Noah. It wasn't Noah who closed the door of the ark; it wasn't Noah who was responsible for security in the ark. The Bible says God Himself shut him in. Once you enter God's ark (which is Jesus Christ), God shuts you in; He shuts the door. Shutting you in is a picture of the security of the believer. God secures salvation for the believer. Thus Jude says, "Now to Him who is ABLE TO KEEP YOU FROM STUMBLING, and to present you faultless before the presence of His glory with exceeding joy, to God our Savior, who alone is wise, be glory and majesty, dominion and power, both now and forever. Amen." (Jude 1:24-25). Paul also says, I am "confident of this very thing, that He who has begun a good work in you **will complete** it until the day of Jesus Christ" (see Philippians 1:6). Paul adds: "Now He **who establishes us** with you in Christ and has anointed us is God, who also **has sealed us** and given us the Spirit in our hearts **as a guarantee.**" (2 Corinthians 1:21-22). God has established us (believers) in Christ and has SEALED US or SHUT US IN; the seal He used is the HOLY SPIRIT who lives with us and in us forever. (see 2 Corinthians 1:21-22; Ephesians 1:13-14; 2 Corinthians 5:5; with John 14:16). And so we cannot be "un-sealed." Hallelujah! We have been sealed for good; we have been shut in! Our salvation is guaranteed by the seal of the Holy Spirit. We are in Christ, and we are members or parts of His body, of His flesh, and of His bones. (see Ephesians 5:30). Nothing can separate us from Him.

It gives me hope to learn that Noah and his family and all the living creatures IN THE ARK were saved from the floodwaters, whereas everyone and everything else OUTSIDE THE ARK perished. Noah rose above the destructive floodwaters and ascended higher and higher in the ark into safety, whereas all who were outside the ark descended into destruction and sunk lower and lower into the destructive floodwaters. I can just imagine the praises in the mouth of Noah at this point when he came out of the ark after the flood and stepped on dry land, and saw brand new vegetation. I can just imagine the smile on his face. I can imagine his heart filled with thanksgiving. He must've been singing with his family the same song believers are singing today, that: "AT ONE TIME we too were foolish, disobedient, deceived and enslaved by all kinds of passions and pleasures. We lived in malice and envy, being hated and hating one another. BUT when the kindness and love of GOD OUR SAVIOR appeared, **HE SAVED US**, NOT BECAUSE OF RIGHTEOUS THINGS WE HAD DONE, but because of HIS MERCY. He saved us through the washing of rebirth and renewal by the Holy Spirit" (Titus 3:3-5 NIV).

Noah's Sacrifice of Praise

Noah was obviously beaming with gratitude to God. The Bible says, "Then Noah BUILT AN ALTAR TO THE LORD, and took of every clean animal and of every clean bird, and OFFERED BURNT OFFERINGS on the altar. AND THE LORD SMELLED A SOOTHING AROMA. Then the Lord said in His heart, "I WILL NEVER AGAIN CURSE THE GROUND FOR MAN'S SAKE, although the imagination of man's heart is EVIL FROM HIS YOUTH; nor will I again destroy every living thing as I have done." (Genesis 8:20-21). How pleasing Noah's sacrifice must've been to God for Him to say these wonderful words in His heart. He said that NEVER AGAIN would He curse the ground for man's sake, nor would He again destroy every living thing in the manner He had done. And God has kept His covenant up to this day.

Today, **Jesus Christ is our burnt offering** (see Hebrews 10:8-10), and just like Noah, we who are saved today through the blood of our Lord and Savior Jesus Christ, should **by Him** "**continually offer** THE SACRIFICE OF PRAISE to God, that is, THE FRUIT OF OUR LIPS, GIVING THANKS to His name." (see Hebrews 13:15). God indeed loves it when we continually offer Him praises and thanksgiving in the name of the Lord Jesus Christ, as a sacrifice. And so the Bible says that God the Holy One is enthroned in the praises of Israel. (see Psalm 22:3). In other words, He has made His home in our praises and reigns therein. No wonder God's presence becomes so tangible and His glory manifests whenever we spend time with Him in worship, continually offering Him praises and thanksgiving in the name of Jesus. Oh, we are so pleasing to God, and He delights in us and in our praises! (see Zephaniah 3:17; Psalm 147:11). "For WE ARE TO GOD THE PLEASING AROMA OF CHRIST among those who are being saved and those who are perishing." (2 Corinthians 2:15 NIV). Let us, therefore, "be imitators of God as dear children. And walk in love, as Christ also has loved us and given Himself for us, AN OFFERING AND A SACRIFICE TO GOD FOR A SWEET-SMELLING AROMA." (Ephesians 5:1-2).

God Established His Covenant With Noah and All Living Creatures

The Bible also says that after the flood, God blessed Noah and his family, and told them to "be fruitful and multiply; bring forth abundantly in the earth and multiply in it." (Genesis 9:7). And thus through Noah and his family, new generations of humans populated the whole earth. (see Genesis 9:18-19). The Bible says, *"Then God spoke **to Noah and to his sons with him**, saying: "And as for Me, behold, **I establish My covenant with you and with your descendants after you, and*** *with every living creature that is with you: the birds, the cattle, and every beast of the earth with you, of all that go out of the ark, every beast of the earth. Thus I establish My covenant with you:* **Never again shall all flesh be cut off by the waters of the flood; never again shall there be a flood to destroy the earth."** *And God said: "This is the SIGN of the covenant which I make between Me and you, and every living creature that is with you, for perpetual generations: I set My RAINBOW in the cloud, and it shall be for* **the SIGN of the covenant** *between Me and the earth. It shall be, when I bring a cloud over the earth, that the rainbow shall be seen in the cloud; and I will remember My covenant which is between Me and you and every living creature of all flesh; the waters shall never again become a flood to destroy* **all** *flesh. The rainbow shall be in the cloud, and I will look on it to remember the EVERLASTING COVENANT between God and every living creature of all flesh that is on the earth." And God said to Noah, "This is THE SIGN OF THE COVENANT which I have established between Me and all flesh that is on the earth."* (Genesis 9:8-17).

From these verses we notice that the first covenant God made with man was **an everlasting covenant**, and it came with **a sign** (the sign of the Covenant), and so all future Covenants God would make with man were also to be EVERLASTING and to have a SIGN. Here, the sign was the RAINBOW.

I hope you're still following the discourse in this Third Chapter, because we are about to get to the main point we are building toward, which is the Blood Covenant God made with Abraham, whom the Bible calls "the father of all of us" who believe. (see Romans 4:16). It is the Blood Covenant God made with Abraham that culminated in the manifestation of our Lord Jesus Christ as the New Covenant (see Isaiah 42:6-7). The Abrahamic Covenant is thus the basis for the New (Blood) Covenant God gave us through Jesus Christ (see Luke 22:20), which gave birth to all of us (believers). Therefore, a proper understanding of the Abrahamic Covenant is key to understanding God's purpose for Israel and the Nations, or God's redemption plan for humankind (in general).

As you would remember, Noah went into the ark with three sons namely **Shem, Ham, and Japheth** (see Genesis 7:13). So, after the flood, when they came out of the ark, they lived together. The Bible says, "Noah began to be a farmer and he planted a vineyard. Then he drank wine and WAS DRUNK and became UNCOVERED (or naked) in his tent. And HAM, the father of Canaan, SAW THE NAKEDNESS of his father, and told his two brothers outside. But SHEM and JAPHETH took a garment, laid it on both their shoulders, and went backward and covered the nakedness of their father. Their faces were turned away, and THEY DID NOT SEE THEIR FATHER'S NAKEDNESS." (see Genesis 9:22-23). As the story relates, Noah woke up, and realizing what had happened, he CURSED Canaan, Ham's son, to be a servant of servants to his brethren. Then Noah BLESSED **Shem** and Japheth and pronounced that Canaan will be their servant. (see Genesis 9:24-28). Now, this leads us to the genealogy of Abram, whose name was later changed to Abraham, the father of all who believe.

Abram (or Abraham)

Abram descended from Noah along the direct lineage of **Shem**, whom Noah blessed. (see Genesis 11:10-27). The Bible says that Noah died at the age of 950. So Abram is our man of interest now. Abram was **the son of Terah**. Terah (the father of Abraham) lived beyond the Euphrates River and **worshipped other gods**. (see Joshua 24:2-4). Abram had two brothers, Nahor and Haran. Haran begat a son whose name was **Lot**, and Haran died before his father Terah died. So Terah (Abram's father) took Abram, Lot (who was Abram's nephew) and Sarai (who was Abram's wife), and they went from Ur of the Chaldeans to go to the land of Canaan, and settled in Haran, where Terah died at the age of 205. So from this point forward we have Lot (the nephew of Abram) under the care of Abram and his wife Sarai, and all of them were still living in the land called **Haran**. But before they dwelt in Haran, the Lord had appeared to Abram in **Mesopotamia** (see Acts 7:2), and this was where **God made a Covenant with Abram**, a Covenant that would expand and take shape over the passage of time.

God's Covenant With Abram (or Abraham)

The Bible says, "Now the Lord had said to Abram: "GET OUT OF YOUR COUNTRY, from YOUR FAMILY and from YOUR FATHER'S HOUSE, to A LAND THAT I WILL SHOW YOU. I will MAKE YOU A GREAT NATION; I will BLESS YOU and MAKE YOUR NAME GREAT; and YOU SHALL BE A BLESSING. I will bless those who bless you, And I WILL CURSE HIM WHO CURSES YOU; and **IN YOU ALL THE FAMILIES OF THE EARTH SHALL BE BLESSED**." (Genesis 12:1-3). Here once again we see God initiating contact with man out of His amazing grace, and seeking to reconcile man to Himself or bring man back into fellowship with Himself. Thus God seeks one man's cooperation through which He seeks to bless **ALL the families of the earth**, these families of sinful men who are still under the dominion and rule of Satan (as a result of Adam's treason). Oh, the grace and mercy of our God! God is indeed the Father of mercies. (see 2 Corinthians 1:3). He is indeed the God of love and peace. (see 2 Corinthians 13:11).

Now, this offer or promise God made to Abram formed the basis of what is today called the Abrahamic Covenant through which Jesus the Messiah was revealed or manifested. In this Covenant, God commanded Abram to LEAVE his country, LEAVE his family, LEAVE his father's house. Are you getting the picture here? **Abram was to LEAVE his comfort zone, to CUT TIES with his past, to CUT TIES with his present world, to LEAVE his present and past life behind and LAY HOLD on a NEW LIFE God was offering him**. Hallelujah! God was telling Abram to leave a land he could see and thought to be safe, and embark on a journey to **a land he hadn't seen**. Have we also been made a similar offer today by God? Yes. We have been asked to seek first the Kingdom of God and His righteousness (see Matthew 6:33), to set our minds on things above and not on things on earth. (see Colossians 3:2). We haven't seen the things above, but we can see the things on earth. So are you going to obey God? Are you going to seek first the Kingdom of God and His righteousness? Are you going to set your mind on things above and not on things on earth? You will notice that God did not require much from Abram. **He only required trust and obedience, or what we now know to be FAITH. (see Romans 4:16; Hebrews 11:8-10).** God made all manner of promises to Abram; God was giving up so much in this covenant; in fact, He was giving His all; He was making this one man Abram heir of the world (see Romans 4:13) — a blessing this man would share with all his descendants. God promised Abram a NEW LAND (He was going to show him). He promised Abram a great new and bigger family or A GREAT NATION. God promised Abram A BLESSING and A GREAT NAME. God promised Abram that He would make him THE EMBODIMENT of this very thing called BLESSING. God promised to BLESS THOSE WHO BLESS Abram, and CURSE him who curses Abram. God promised Abram that in him ALL THE FAMILIES OF THE EARTH SHALL BE BLESSED. In other words, any family on earth that has ties with Abram would be blessed. This promise makes me glad, because the Bible says, "**ONLY** THOSE WHO ARE **OF FAITH** are SONS OF ABRAHAM" (see Galatians 3:7). "And if you are Christ's, then you are **Abraham's seed**, and **heirs according to the promise.**" (Galatians 3:29). Since I am of faith, since I am Christ's and therefore the seed of Abraham or the son of Abraham, I am entitled to every blessing God has given to Abraham. So by now you may be asking, "Did Abraham (or Abram) accept God's offer?" But before I answer your question, let me ask you: have you accepted God's offer? The Bible says, "For God so loved the world that He gave His only begotten Son, that whoever believes in Him should not perish but have everlasting life." (John 3:16). God is offering you salvation through **faith** in His Son Jesus Christ. Will you accept His offer? Will you believe in Jesus Christ? Because if you believe or accept Jesus Christ right now as your Lord and Savior, you are Abraham's seed and heirs according to the promise. (see Galatians 3:29). And the promise is that you would be heir of the world. (see Romans 4:13). Everything in the world would be yours, including things in this present world, and in the world which is to come. (see 1 Corinthians 3:21-23). That was what God was offering Abram in Genesis 12:1-3. And I am thankful that **Abram accepted God's offer and thus entered into a covenant with God.**

I am thankful that God had found a man through whom He could establish a covenant and reveal or manifest His plan for the redemption of mankind and the creation of "the New man."

Stephen tells us by the Spirit in the Acts of the Apostles that Abram obeyed God; "he came out of the land of the Chaldeans and dwelt in Haran. And from there, when his father was dead, He (God) moved him (Abram)…" (see Acts 7:4). And thus the Book of Hebrews tells us that "**BY FAITH** Abraham **OBEYED** when he was called to go out to the place which he would receive as an inheritance. And he went out, **not knowing** where he was going. **By FAITH** he dwelt in the land of promise as in a foreign country, dwelling in tents with Isaac and Jacob, the heirs with him of the same promise; for he waited for the city which has foundations, whose builder and maker is God. **By FAITH** Sarah herself also received strength to conceive seed, and she bore a child when she was past the age, because she judged Him faithful who had promised. Therefore FROM ONE MAN, and him as good as dead, WERE BORN AS MANY AS THE STARS OF THE SKY IN MULTITUDE —innumerable as the sand which is by the seashore." (Hebrews 11:8-12). Oh, I'm glad that I am one of these multitudes of children born to Abraham, the father of all who believe! And you can become one of us also simply by believing in the Lord Jesus Christ. "And if you are Christ's, then you are Abraham's seed and heirs according to the promise." (see Galatians 3:29). What are you waiting for? Lay hold on the new life God is offering you in Christ, and be blessed. Jesus Himself said, "Most assuredly, I say to you, he who believes in Me has everlasting life." (John 6:47). So believe in the Lord Jesus Christ and receive this new life, so that you can join me in telling the whole world all about this new life. (see Acts 5:20 NIV).

In the next chapter we will discuss how God's Covenant with Abram evolved or expanded into a Blood Covenant that eventually gave us the Ten Commandments, the ceremonial laws and its Priesthood; the Sabbath and New Moon celebrations, and much more, that were just a shadow of the good things that were to come in Christ Jesus. Paul tells us in his letter to the Colossians: "So let no one judge you in food or in drink, or regarding a festival or a new moon or sabbaths, WHICH ARE A SHADOW OF THINGS TO COME, but THE SUBSTANCE IS OF CHRIST." (Colossians 2:16-17). The Book of Hebrews also says, "For the law, HAVING A SHADOW OF THE GOOD THINGS TO COME, and **not** the very image of the things, **can never** with these same sacrifices, which they offer continually year by year, make those who approach perfect." (Hebrews 10:1). Paul again adds that "the law was our TUTOR to bring us to Christ, that we might be **justified BY FAITH**. But after faith has come, we are NO LONGER UNDER A TUTOR." (Galatians 3:24-25). And so we will continue in Chapter 4 as we discover how the walk with God was for the Old Covenant believer, and how different the walk with God is for you, the New Covenant believer who is the beneficiary of the glories that were to follow the sufferings of Christ (see 1 Peter 1:9-12 NIV). By the time we are through with this book, I believe you will understand and appreciate the necessity of living and walking in the Spirit as a new creation, and why you can't afford to walk in the flesh. "For if you live according to the flesh you will die; but if by the Spirit you put to death the deeds of the body, you will live." (Romans 8:13).

Chapter 4

The Evolution of God's Everlasting Covenant With Abraham and His Descendants

How God's Covenant with Abram Evolved or Expanded into an Everlasting Blood Covenant that Eventually Led to the Manifestation of Our Lord Jesus Christ

THE BIBLE SAYS that Abram was 75 years old when he departed from Haran in response to God's command. (see Genesis 12:4). We are also told that "Abram took with him Sarai his wife and Lot his brother's son, AND ALL THEIR POSSESSIONS THAT THEY HAD GATHERED and the people whom they had acquired in Haran, and they departed to go to the land of Canaan." (see Genesis 12:5). You see, contrary to what many believe, God does not require everyone who wants to follow Him to sell all their belongings/possessions and become poor first; He certainly didn't require that of Abram, and He hadn't required it from Noah or any of the previous generations. God does not frown upon wealth. Rather, **He gives the power to gain wealth.** (see Deuteronomy 8:18). **"The blessing of the Lord makes one rich**, and He adds no sorrow with it." (Proverbs 10:22). There was only one person in the Bible that we are told Jesus asked to sell all his possessions and give to the poor, and then come and follow Him (see Matthew 19:21; Mark 10:21; Luke 18:22). And it was mainly because Jesus knew what was in the heart of man (see John 2:24-25), and He knew that in this man's heart he had made a god out of his wealth or possessions. Therefore Jesus was bringing him to the realization that no one can serve two masters — he couldn't serve God and mammon. (see Matthew 6:24; Luke 16:13). The Bible does not call money (or wealth) the root of all evil as many wrongly believe. It is "**the LOVE of money**" that is the root of all evil. (see 1 Timothy 6:10). We can't love money and desire money more than we love and desire God and then claim to serve God. God knows we need money in this world in order to be able to promote the gospel and send it to every corner of the world. And so the Bible says that our Lord Jesus Christ, though He was rich, became poor for our sakes, in order that **we through His poverty might become RICH.** (see 2 Corinthians 8:9). So if you believe in Jesus Christ, expect to become rich, because you are rich. The apostle John prayed for believers that we may **prosper** and be in health, just us our soul prospers. (see 3 John 1:2). This was a prayer inspired by the Holy Spirit. It is God's will for believers to prosper, and so He causes us to prosper. Thus Abram departed Haran **with ALL HIS POSSESSIONS and servants or followers.** And when he passed through the land of Canaan to the place of Shechem, as far as the terebinth tree of Moreh, God "appeared to Abram and said, "To your descendants I will give this land." (see Genesis 12:7). Here, we see God putting details into His promise to Abram regarding the land He was going to give him and his descendants, as Abram continued his walk with the Lord, building altars and calling on the name of the Lord as he journeyed along. (see Genesis 12:7-9).

God Protects His People and Provides for Them

At this point the Bible gives us an interesting insight regarding a FAMINE IN THE LAND where Abram was living, a famine which was so severe that it made Abram GO DOWN to Egypt to dwell there. (see Genesis 12:10). The man who had the promise of God's blessing and provision was going through a famine, so he went DOWN to Egypt. Several years later, Abram's descendant (or grandson) Jacob (whose name God changed to Israel) also went through a famine and went DOWN to Egypt. (see Acts 7:11, 15). Can you relate to this, beloved? Are you going through a famine or a DOWN period? Do you think, based on your current circumstances, that God has forsaken you or forgotten about you? No, He hasn't. Our God is a faithful God. (see 1 Corinthians 1:9; 2 Timothy 2:13; Hebrews 10:23). And He will never leave us nor forsake us. (see Hebrews 13:5). God never promises anyone who seeks Him that he wouldn't go through trouble or adverse circumstances. On the contrary, He promises that we will go through trouble, but then He also promises protection, and He urges us both in the New and Old Testament to not fear or be afraid. He says: "FEAR NOT, for I HAVE REDEEMED YOU; I have called you by your name; **you are Mine**. WHEN (note: He didn't say IF. He says WHEN) YOU PASS THROUGH THE WATERS, I WILL BE WITH YOU; and through the rivers, THEY SHALL NOT OVERFLOW YOU. When you WALK THROUGH THE FIRE, YOU SHALL NOT BE BURNED, NOR SHALL THE FLAME SCORCH YOU. For I am the Lord your God, The Holy One of Israel, YOUR SAVIOR…" (see Isaiah 43:1-3). Hallelujah! In the New Testament also, Jesus says, "These things I have spoken to you, that in Me YOU MAY HAVE PEACE. In the world you WILL (note again:

He doesn't say you MAY. He says you WILL) HAVE TRIBULATION; but BE OF GOOD CHEER, (why? Because) I HAVE OVERCOME THE WORLD." (see John 16:33). Therefore, as believers we don't have to fear when we go through afflictions or trials and tribulations. We should rather be of good cheer, knowing that the Lord our Savior is with us and we have overcome the world with Him. (see Matthew 28:20 with 1 John 5:4-5). The apostle Paul writes: "WHO SHALL SEPARATE US FROM THE LOVE OF CHRIST? Shall tribulation, or distress, or persecution, or famine, or nakedness, or peril, or sword? As it is written: "For Your sake we are killed all day long; We are accounted as sheep for the slaughter." Yet IN ALL THESE THINGS **WE ARE MORE THAN CONQUERORS** through Him WHO LOVED US. For I am persuaded that neither death nor life, nor angels nor principalities nor powers, nor things present nor things to come, nor height nor depth, nor any other created thing, shall be able to separate us from THE LOVE OF GOD WHICH IS IN CHRIST JESUS OUR LORD." (Romans 8:35-39).

Thus God was with Abram through this severe famine as he journeyed to Egypt; and the Bible says of Abram when he came out of Egypt, that he "WAS **VERY RICH** IN LIVESTOCK, IN SILVER, AND IN GOLD." (see Genesis 13:2). Hallelujah! Abram and his nephew Lot were both **very rich** when they came out of Egypt. The Bible says "Now the land was not able to support them, that they might dwell together, for **THEIR POSSESSIONS were SO GREAT that they could not dwell together.**" (Genesis 13:6). As we recall and reflect on the promises God made to Abram from the beginning when He made a covenant with him in Genesis 12:1-3, we realize that Abraham became rich because God was keeping His covenant to bless him and make him a blessing. God will also keep His covenant to all the descendants of Abraham, including you, if you believe in Jesus Christ. (see Galatians 3:29). "For no matter how many promises God has made, **they are "Yes"** in Christ. And so through Him the "Amen" is spoken by us to the glory of God." (2 Corinthians 1:20, NIV). Abram and Lot separated, because they needed more space for their GREAT POSSESSIONS. The Bible says Lot chose to move to the plain of Jordan, dwelt in the cities of the plain and pitched his tent even as far as **Sodom** (which was inhabited by men who were exceedingly wicked and sinful against the Lord), whereas Abram dwelt in **the land of Canaan**. (see Genesis 13:10-13).

God Made Abram and His Descendants the Heir of the World

The Bible also says that after Lot had separated from Abram, the Lord said to Abram: **"LIFT YOUR EYES NOW AND LOOK from the place where you are**—NORTHWARD, SOUTHWARD, EASTWARD, and WESTWARD; for **ALL the land which you see** I give to you and your descendants **forever**. And I WILL MAKE YOUR DESCENDANTS AS THE DUST OF THE EARTH; so that if a man could number the dust of the earth, then your descendants also could be numbered. ARISE, WALK IN THE LAND through its length and its width, FOR I GIVE IT TO YOU." (Genesis 13:14-17). Praise God! As you would remember, God had said to Abram in His covenant with him in Genesis 12:1-3, "GET OUT OF YOUR COUNTRY, from YOUR FAMILY and from YOUR FATHER'S HOUSE, to **A LAND THAT I WILL SHOW YOU**." Now God was showing Abram the land, just as He promised He would. And the land had no limit; it stretched **as far as Abram**

could SEE. Its limit depended on how far Abram could see. Here, God was training Abram to see with the eyes of his mind. He told Abram to look FROM THE PLACE WHERE HE WAS (standing), and to look Northward, Southward, Eastward, and Westward. (see Genesis 13:14). Now think about it, how far can you see when you stand at one spot? Not far when you look with the eyes of your body (or your physical eyes), but when you look with the eyes of your mind (or your imagination), there is no limit to how far you can see. And so Abram looked with the eyes of his mind and saw the whole world, and thus God gave the whole world to Abram as his inheritance, just as He had promised. (see Romans 4:13, with Genesis 13:15, 17). The Bible says that the land (or the whole world) was given not only to Abram, but to Abram's descendants also, and it is theirs **forever**. (see Genesis 13:15, with Romans 4:13). Beloved, you are a descendant of Abram, if you believe in Jesus Christ. The Bible says that if you belong to Christ, you are Abraham's seed, and heir according to the promise (see Galatians 3:29); you are heir of the world (see Romans 4:13); the land belongs to you; the whole world belongs to you; but how much of it you will actually possess (or lay hold on) depends on how far you can see. Don't limit yourself, because as a believer, all things are yours, the whole world is yours — Heaven (things to come) and Earth (things present) are yours. (see 1 Corinthians 3:21-23). So lay hold on it through faith.

Indeed, God's blessing to Abram and his descendants entailed EVERY blessing that can be conceived. It was an all-inclusive or all-encompassing blessing that entailed the blessing of wealth, health, protection, safety, security, peace of mind, joy, and much more, which is why believers today are blessed with EVERY spiritual blessing in the heavenly realms in Christ. (see Ephesians 1:3). Hallelujah!

God Delivered Abram's Enemies into His Hand

Now the Bible says Abram's nephew Lot got in trouble when war or conflict broke out in Sodom and Gomorrah and its vicinities and the people of Sodom and Gomorrah were defeated and spoiled of all their provisions or possessions. (see Genesis 14:1-11). The victors in this war or conflict "also took Lot, Abram's brother's son who dwelt in Sodom, and his goods, and departed." (see Genesis 14:12). Thus, Lot had lost all his possessions and was now a captive. As the story relates, one of Lot's people escaped and reported the incident to Abram the Hebrew. (see Genesis 14:13). "Now when Abram heard that his brother (or nephew) was taken captive, he armed his three hundred and eighteen trained servants who were born in his own house, and went in pursuit as far as Dan. He divided his forces against them by night, and HE AND HIS SERVANTS ATTACKED them and PURSUED them as far as Hobah, which is north of Damascus. So HE BROUGHT BACK ALL THE GOODS, AND ALSO BROUGHT BACK HIS BROTHER (or nephew) LOT AND HIS GOODS, AS WELL AS THE WOMEN AND THE PEOPLE." (Genesis 14:14-16). This was total victory for Abram and his forces, and there is no doubt that God was responsible for this victory (see Genesis 14:20), because Abram was under God's blessing and protection. Beloved, you also have victory over your enemies; God has delivered your enemies into your hands, because you are a descendant of Abraham. As a believer, you are a partaker of the victory Jesus won over Satan through His death and resurrection. The Bible says that you are more than a conqueror through Christ who loved you. Jesus said, "Behold, I give you the AUTHORITY to trample on serpents and scorpions, and OVER ALL THE POWER OF THE ENEMY, and nothing shall by any means hurt you." (Luke 10:19). All your enemies such as diseases, poverty, lack, addictions, depression, doubts, fear, worry, and so forth, are defeated in Jesus' name. Claim this victory now, because it belongs to you through the redemption we have in Christ Jesus. You have authority over ALL the power of the enemy, so exercise your authority.

Abram Voluntarily Paid a Tithe to Melchizedek

Now, an interesting thing happened when Abram returned following his victory in the war. The Bible says, "Then Melchizedek KING OF SALEM brought out BREAD AND WINE; he was THE PRIEST of God Most High. And HE BLESSED him (Abram) and said: "Blessed be ABRAM **OF GOD Most High**, possessor of heaven and earth; and blessed be God Most High, WHO HAS DELIVERED YOUR ENEMIES INTO YOUR HAND." And he (Abram) gave him (Melchizedek) a **TITHE** of all." (Genesis 14:18-20). Melchizedek, the Priest of God Most High brought bread and wine, which we now know symbolizes the body and blood of our Lord Jesus Christ (see Matthew 26:26-27; Mark 14:22-24; 1 Corinthians 11:23-26). In the breaking of Jesus' body and the shedding of His blood, we have our victory today — we have our healing (see Isaiah 53:5; 1 Peter 2:24) and the forgiveness of our sins (see Hebrews 9:22; 1 Peter 2:24); we have our blessing (see Ephesians 1:3). Praise God! Thus Melchizedek brought bread and wine, and he blessed Abram, and blessed God. And Abram, in return, gave Melchizedek a TITHE OF ALL (the spoils he brought from the war). Of course, we know that Abram was not under any obligation to give a tithe, because he was not under any law; he was under grace. So he **voluntarily** gave a tithe. The Bible says Melchizedek was a type of our High Priest Jesus Christ, who remains a Priest forever (see Psalm 110:4; Hebrews 7:1-10, with Hebrews 3:1 and Hebrews 4:14). So today we believers who are also under grace (see Romans 6:14) are encouraged to VOLUNTARILY give a tithe, since we have victory (see 1 Corinthians 15:57; 2 Corinthians 2:14) and have been so blessed by the Most High God. (see Ephesians 1:3). We shouldn't be forced to pay a tithe, but we are ENCOURAGED to pay a tithe to our Lord Jesus Christ who is a High Priest forever, and whose Priesthood is in the order of Melchizedek. (see Hebrews 7:1-22). We give to Jesus our High Priest when we give a tithe to the ministers of the new covenant, so that they may continually have the needed resources to bring the gospel of Christ to the whole world, as Jesus commanded us to do. (see Mark 16:15; Matthew 24:14). And as you give cheerfully, Jesus promises that "it will be given to you: good measure, pressed down, shaken together, and running over will be put into your bosom. For with the same measure that you use, it will be measured back to you." (see Luke 6:38).

God Gave Abram His Word

"After these things THE **WORD** of the Lord CAME to Abram in a **vision**, saying, "DO NOT BE AFRAID, Abram. I am YOUR SHIELD, YOUR EXCEEDINGLY GREAT REWARD." But Abram said, "Lord God, WHAT WILL You GIVE ME, SEEING I GO CHILDLESS, and the heir of my house is Eliezer of Damascus?" Then Abram said, "Look, You HAVE GIVEN ME NO OFFSPRING; indeed ONE BORN IN MY HOUSE IS MY HEIR!" And behold,

THE **WORD** of the Lord came to him, saying, "This one shall not be your heir, BUT ONE WHO WILL COME FROM YOUR OWN BODY SHALL BE YOUR HEIR." Then He brought him outside and said, "**Look** now toward heaven, and COUNT THE STARS if you are able to number them." And He said to him, "SO SHALL YOUR DESCENDANTS BE." And **he BELIEVED in the Lord**, and **He ACCOUNTED IT TO HIM FOR RIGHTEOUSNESS.** Then He said to him, "I am the Lord, who brought you out of Ur of the Chaldeans, TO GIVE YOU THIS LAND TO INHERIT IT." And he said, "Lord God, HOW SHALL I KNOW THAT I WILL INHERIT IT?" (Genesis 15:1-8).

Here again we see God expounding His Covenant with Abram. And we see God giving Abram HIS **WORD** in a vision. He tells Abram not to be afraid, because He (God) is his shield, his exceedingly great reward. Then when Abram asks God for a child, God trains Abram again to lay hold on the promise God made in Genesis 12:2 that He would make him a great nation; in this regard, God told him to **look** toward heaven, and count the stars if he is able to number them (and thus use the eyes of his mind to see his children as numerous as the stars of the sky). And so Abram looked toward heaven, and with the eyes of his mind, he saw each star as representing his children, bearing the beautiful images of his children, whom he couldn't count. **And Abram believed in the Lord**. Beloved, what you look at makes all the difference. What you are conscious of affects your peace of mind. For example, you can either look at (or be conscious of) the sickness that the doctor says is in your body, or you can look at the healing that the Bible says is yours; you can look at the Word of God, or the word of the enemy. The choice is ultimately yours. The Word of God says that by the stripes of Jesus, you were healed (see 1 Peter 2:22), so behold your healing; be conscious of your healing. If you are a believer and you need a child right now, the Bible also promises that "**No one** shall suffer **miscarriage** or be **barren** in your land" (see Exodus 23:26); it says, "You shall be blessed above all peoples; **there shall not be a male or female barren among you** or among your livestock." (Deuteronomy 7:14). Again, if you're a man, the Bible promises that "Your wife shall be like **a fruitful vine** in the very heart of your house; your children like olive plants all around your table." (Psalm 128:3). Lay hold on these promises of God, and give glory to Him. Consider not the limitations of your physical body, but focus on the promises of God, and be FULLY PERSUADED that what God has promised, He is also able to perform; be convinced that He who has promised is faithful, who also will do it. The Bible says of Abraham that he "**against hope believed in hope**, that he might become the father of many nations; according to that which was spoken, so shall thy seed be. And **being not weak in faith, he CONSIDERED NOT his own body now dead**, when he was about an hundred years old, **neither yet the deadness of Sara's womb**: he STAGGERED NOT at **the promise of God** through **unbelief;** but was STRONG IN FAITH, giving glory to God; and being FULLY PERSUADED that, **what He had promised, He was also able to perform.**" (Romans 4:18-21 KJV). Beloved, whatever God has promised in His Word is yours to claim today, thanks to our Lord Jesus Christ. All you have to do is LOOK in the Bible for the word or promise of God concerning your situation. And once you find a promise, believe it, act on it, claim it, picture it as yours and say Amen to it, giving glory to God. (see 2 Corinthians 1:20). If you can picture the fulfillment of the promise, or see it with the eye of your mind, if you can capture it in your imagination, then you can believe for it, and it will manifest or materialize to the glory of God. If you need children, look, and see your children like olive plants (or anointed children) all around your table, and believe God, just as Abraham looked at the stars and saw his descendants as innumerable as the stars of the heaven, and believed God, giving glory to Him. If you are burdened by guilt and condemnation, you can also look and see the forgiveness of all your sins in Christ Jesus. (see Psalm 103:3). If you feel sick, look and see your healing. If you are struggling in your business or with your finances, look and see your prosperity. If you have legal troubles, look and see your deliverance. Believe God's promises, and you will see their fulfillment in your life. David said, "I would have lost heart, **unless I had believed** that I would see the goodness of the Lord in the land of the living." (Psalm 27:13).

God Used Abram as Another Example to Teach Us that Righteousness is by Faith

When the Word of the Lord came to Abram, **he believed it**. Hence, the Bible says that Abraham believed God (see James 2:23), thus equating the Word with God. Indeed the Word of God is God (see John 1:1), and the Word of God has come to each of us; God has given His Word to us in the Person of Jesus Christ (see John 1:1, 14); and as believers, we are told in First John 2:14 that the Word of God abides in us. Let us therefore sing with the Psalmist that "The LORD is my strength and my shield; my heart trusts in Him, and He helps me. My heart leaps for joy, and with my song I praise Him." (Psalm 28:7). We must indeed be thankful for the Word of God because when God gives His Word, He has given Himself. God is His Word. (see John 1:1). God and His Word are one. Obviously Abram didn't have this revelation; yet the Bible says that when God gave him His Word, when God told him that he will have his own biological child and that his descendants will be as numerous as the stars of the sky, Abram was able to grasp it, **Abram BELIEVED God**, and God accounted it to him for RIGHTEOUSNESS. And so here we see God again declaring a man (this time, Abram) RIGHTEOUS because of His BELIEF (or FAITH) in God or in the Word of God (see Genesis 15:6), just like He did with Noah (see Hebrews 11:7) — yet another proof that RIGHTEOUSNESS HAS ALWAYS BEEN BY FAITH, and not by the works of the Law. (see Romans 3:20). The apostle Paul thus writes: "For what does the Scripture say? **Abraham BELIEVED God, and it was ACCOUNTED TO HIM FOR RIGHTEOUSNESS.**" Now to him who works, the wages are not counted as grace but as debt. But to HIM WHO DOES NOT WORK but BELIEVES on Him who justifies the ungodly, HIS **FAITH** IS ACCOUNTED FOR **RIGHTEOUSNESS**" (Romans 4:3-5). James also writes: "And the Scripture was fulfilled which says, "**Abraham BELIEVED God, and IT WAS ACCOUNTED TO HIM FOR RIGHTEOUSNESS.**" And he was called the friend of God." (James 2:23). Again, Paul reproving the churches of Galatia for walking in the flesh and seeking to be made righteous through the keeping of the Law of Moses, instead of walking in the Spirit and accepting righteousness by faith, writes: "O foolish Galatians! Who has bewitched you that you should not obey the truth, before whose eyes Jesus Christ was clearly portrayed among you as crucified? This only I want to learn from you: DID YOU RECEIVE **the Spirit** BY THE WORKS OF THE LAW, or by the hearing of FAITH? Are you so foolish? Having **begun in the Spirit**, ARE YOU NOW BEING MADE PERFECT BY THE FLESH? Have you suffered so many things in vain—if indeed it was in vain? Therefore He who supplies the Spirit to you and works miracles among you, does He do it by THE WORKS OF THE LAW, or **BY the hearing of FAITH**?— just as Abraham "BELIEVED God, and IT WAS ACCOUNTED TO HIM FOR RIGHTEOUSNESS." Therefore know that **ONLY** THOSE WHO ARE OF **FAITH** are SONS OF ABRAHAM. And the Scripture, foreseeing that God would JUSTIFY THE GENTILES BY FAITH, **preached the gospel to Abraham beforehand**, saying, "In you ALL THE NATIONS shall be blessed." So then THOSE WHO ARE **OF FAITH** ARE BLESSED WITH BELIEVING ABRAHAM." (Galatians 3:1-9). Therefore, I say with Paul that, "I DO NOT set aside the GRACE of God; for IF RIGHTEOUSNESS COMES THROUGH THE LAW, then CHRIST DIED IN VAIN." (Galatians 2:21).

God Solemnized His Covenant with Abram

Now, let us pay particular attention to these next few verses from Genesis 15, as God gives Abram a gracious visitation because of his faith, and thus solemnizes His covenant with Abram or gives him a token or a symbol of his having been brought into covenant relationship with God. Let us also pay particular attention to the prophecy God gives Abram in these verses, of the things that will happen to Abram's promised seed or descendants in the future. "And he (Abram) said, "Lord God, HOW SHALL I KNOW THAT I WILL INHERIT IT (the Promised Land)?" So He said to him, "BRING Me A THREE-YEAR-OLD HEIFER, a three-year-old female goat, a three-year-old ram, a turtledove, and a young pigeon." Then he BROUGHT ALL THESE to Him and cut them in two, down the middle, and placed each piece opposite the other; but he did not cut the birds in two.

And when the VULTURES came down on the carcasses, ABRAM DROVE THEM AWAY. Now WHEN THE SUN WAS going down, a deep sleep fell upon Abram; and behold, horror and great darkness fell upon him. Then He said to Abram: "KNOW CERTAINLY THAT **YOUR DESCENDANTS** WILL BE STRANGERS IN A LAND THAT IS NOT THEIRS, AND **WILL SERVE THEM**, and **they will AFFLICT THEM FOUR HUNDRED YEARS**. And also the nation whom they serve I will judge; afterward THEY SHALL COME OUT WITH GREAT POSSESSIONS. Now as for you, you shall go to your fathers in peace; YOU SHALL BE BURIED AT A GOOD OLD AGE. But in the FOURTH GENERATION THEY SHALL RETURN HERE, for the iniquity of the Amorites is not yet complete." And it came to pass, WHEN THE SUN WENT DOWN AND IT WAS DARK, that behold, THERE APPEARED A SMOKING OVEN AND A BURNING TORCH that passed between those pieces. **ON THE SAME DAY the Lord MADE A COVENANT WITH ABRAM, saying: "TO YOUR DESCENDANTS I HAVE GIVEN THIS LAND**, from the river of Egypt to the great river, the River Euphrates— the Hittites, the Perizzites, the Rephaim, the Amorites, the Canaanites, the Girgashites, and the Jebusites." (Genesis 15:8-18, 20-21).

Indeed God is good. Here, God solemnizes His covenant with Abram through a sacrifice determined by God Himself. Then He confirms that He has given the promised land to the descendants of Abram. Then God gives Abram a prophecy regarding things that will happen to his descendants before they finally inherit the promised land.

God Sealed His Covenant With Abraham With the Sign of Circumcision

The Covenant God made with Abram made Abram and his descendants God's Covenant People, and God, Israel's Covenant God. (see Genesis 17:7; Jeremiah 32:38; Ezekiel 37:27). No wonder Abraham was recognized as **"a mighty prince"** among strangers (see Genesis 23:6). And no wonder God changed Abraham's wife's name from Sarai, to Sarah, which in Hebrew means **"a princess."** Thus, through this Covenant, God had lifted Abraham (and his descendants) into the Royal Family of the universe.

Moreover, as we learned from Chapter 3 in our study of God's Covenant with Noah and all living creatures on earth, God seals His Covenant with a sign. In the case of Noah after the flood, the sign was a **rainbow**. (see Genesis 9:13,17). But in the case of Abraham, God gave **the sign of CIRCUMCISION.** (see Genesis 17:8-12). The Bible gives us further details that, "When Abram was ninety-nine years old, **the Lord appeared to Abram** and said to him, "I am Almighty God; WALK BEFORE Me AND BE BLAMELESS. And I will make My COVENANT between Me and you, and WILL MULTIPLY YOU EXCEEDINGLY." Then Abram fell on his face, and God talked with him, saying: "As for Me, behold, **MY COVENANT IS WITH YOU**, and YOU SHALL BE A FATHER OF MANY NATIONS. No longer shall your name be called ABRAM, but **YOUR NAME SHALL BE ABRAHAM**; for I HAVE MADE YOU A FATHER OF MANY NATIONS. I will make you **EXCEEDINGLY FRUITFUL**; and I WILL MAKE NATIONS OF YOU, and KINGS SHALL COME FROM YOU. And I WILL ESTABLISH My COVENANT BETWEEN Me AND YOU AND YOUR DESCENDANTS after you in their generations, for **AN EVERLASTING COVENANT**, to be GOD TO YOU AND YOUR DESCENDANTS after you. **Also I GIVE TO YOU AND YOUR DESCENDANTS after you THE LAND IN WHICH YOU ARE A STRANGER, all the land of Canaan, as AN EVERLASTING POSSESSION**; and **I WILL BE THEIR GOD**." And God said to Abraham: "As for you, YOU SHALL KEEP My COVENANT, YOU AND YOUR DESCENDANTS after you throughout their generations. THIS IS MY COVENANT which you shall keep, between Me and you and your descendants after you: EVERY MALE CHILD AMONG YOU SHALL BE **CIRCUMCISED**; and you shall be CIRCUMCISED IN THE FLESH OF YOUR FORESKINS, and it shall be **a SIGN OF THE COVENANT** between Me and you. He who is EIGHT DAYS OLD among you SHALL BE **CIRCUMCISED**, every male child in your generations, he who is born in your house or bought with money from any foreigner who is not your descendant. He who is born in your house and he who is bought with your money **must be circumcised**, and My COVENANT SHALL BE **IN YOUR FLESH** for an EVERLASTING COVENANT. And THE UNCIRCUMCISED MALE child, who is not circumcised **in the flesh** of his foreskin, that person SHALL BE CUT OFF FROM HIS PEOPLE; he has BROKEN My covenant." Then God said to Abraham, "As for Sarai your wife, YOU SHALL NOT CALL HER NAME SARAI, but SARAH shall be her name. And I WILL BLESS HER and also give you A SON by her; then I will bless her, and she shall be A MOTHER OF NATIONS; KINGS OF PEOPLES SHALL BE FROM HER." Then Abraham fell on his face and laughed, and said in his heart, "Shall a child be born to A MAN WHO IS ONE HUNDRED YEARS OLD? And shall Sarah, who is NINETY YEARS OLD, bear a child?" And Abraham said to God, "Oh, that Ishmael might live before You!" Then God said: "No, Sarah your wife shall bear you A SON, and you shall call his name **ISAAC**; I will establish My COVENANT with him for an EVERLASTING COVENANT, and with his descendants after him. And as for Ishmael, I have heard you. Behold, I have blessed him, and will make him fruitful, and will multiply him exceedingly. He shall beget twelve princes, and I will make him a great nation. BUT My COVENANT I WILL ESTABLISH WITH ISAAC, whom Sarah shall bear to you at this set time next year." Then He finished talking with him, and God went up from Abraham." (Genesis 17:1-22).

We are told from the preceding paragraph that after the Covenant was solemnized and confirmed, God changed Abram's name to **Abraham** (which means a father of many nations) and changed Sarai's name to Sarah. Thus, with his new name, every time Abraham introduced himself to a stranger, he was basically confessing that he is the father of many nations, even though he as yet had no child with Sarah. In this manner also, God was teaching Abraham to confess what he believed, to confess the promises of God, to confess the Word of God and hold fast his confession.

The Bible also says that God sealed the Covenant with the sign of Circumcision and declared the Covenant to be an EVERLASTING COVENANT. In other words, the Covenant could only be amended or expanded over time, but it couldn't be annulled or obliterated. Circumcision became how one entered into the Abrahamic Covenant. And as a result of this Covenant, God was bound to Abraham and his descendants by indissoluble ties, and God had to sustain and protect Abraham and his descendants forever. (see Genesis 22:16-17). Later, God would test Abraham's faith a few years after the birth of his promised son Isaac by asking Abraham to sacrifice his son Isaac as **a burnt offering** to God, which Abraham obeyed. But as the story relates (see Genesis 22:1-14), God did not allow Abraham to kill Isaac, but instead, God Himself provided a ram to Abraham to be offered as a burnt offering in the stead of Isaac, thus pointing to Jesus Christ, God's only begotten Son whom God was to send to be sacrificed as our burnt offering to save mankind. Because Abraham was obedient to God, God again confirmed His Covenant with Abraham and said: "By Myself I HAVE SWORN, says the Lord, because you have done this thing, and HAVE NOT WITHHELD YOUR SON, YOUR ONLY SON — blessing I will bless you, and multiplying I will multiply your descendants as the stars of the heaven and as the sand which is on the seashore; and YOUR DESCENDANTS SHALL POSSESS THE GATE OF THEIR ENEMIES. In **YOUR SEED** all the nations of the earth SHALL BE BLESSED, because YOU HAVE OBEYED My VOICE." (see Genesis 22:16-18). Indeed there is great reward in obeying God's Voice. Let us always obey God's Voice (or God's Word).

Concerning the oath sworn by God to bless Abraham, the Book of Hebrews says, "For when God made a promise to Abraham, BECAUSE He COULD SWEAR BY NO ONE GREATER, **He swore by Himself**, saying, "Surely blessing I will bless you, and multiplying I will multiply you." And so, after he (Abraham) had patiently endured, **HE OBTAINED THE PROMISE**. For men indeed swear by the greater, and an oath for confirmation is for them an end of all dispute. Thus God, determining to show more abundantly TO THE HEIRS OF PROMISE the IMMUTABILITY of His counsel, CONFIRMED IT BY AN OATH, that by **two immutable things**, in which IT IS IMPOSSIBLE FOR GOD TO LIE, we might have strong consolation, who have fled for refuge to lay hold of the hope set before us." (Hebrews 6:13-18).

In God's covenant with Abraham, not only had God committed eternally to being the God — the Provider and Deliverer — for Abraham and his descendants, but Abraham also had made an unqualified committal of himself and his descendants to God, which meant that all that he and his descendants were and would ever be belonged to God; Abraham and his descendants now must worship only the one true God (Jehovah) forever. Therefore Abraham gave himself to God in utter abandonment of self. Stated differently, Abraham denied himself, picked up his cross daily, and followed God Almighty. Today the Lord Jesus Christ also commands: "If anyone desires to come after Me, LET HIM DENY HIMSELF, AND TAKE UP HIS CROSS DAILY, and FOLLOW Me. For whoever desires to save his life will lose it, but WHOEVER LOSES HIS LIFE FOR My SAKE WILL SAVE IT. For what profit is it to a man if he gains the whole world, and is himself destroyed or lost? For whoever is ashamed of Me and My words, of him the Son of Man will be ashamed when He comes in His own glory, and in His Father's, and of the holy angels." (see Luke 9:23-26). Following the Lord Jesus Christ requires a total committal of one's self, or an utter abandonment of one's own selfish interests, ambitions and desires. Jesus requires total commitment, or nothing at all. He says, "He who loves father or mother more than Me is not worthy of Me. And he who loves son or daughter more than Me is not worthy of Me. And he who does not take his cross and follow after Me is not worthy of Me." (Matthew 10:37-38). It is not enough to just add Jesus to your life and call Him Lord, Lord; you have to totally submit your life to His loving Lordship. Jesus is either your Lord in deed, or He is not your Lord at all. (see Matthew 7:21-23). Also, Jesus requires us to hold on to our faith in Him till He comes. (see Revelation 2:25, with Hebrews 3:14). He says, "No one, having put his hand to the plow, and looking back, is fit for the kingdom of God." (see Luke 9:62).

Stephen's Recap of the History of Israel

Now, as we bring this Fourth Chapter to a close, let us allow Spirit-filled Stephen to give us a recap of the history of Israel, as we listen to his address to the Council in Acts Chapter 7: "But God spoke in this way: that his (that is, Abraham's) descendants would dwell in a foreign land, and that they would bring them into bondage and oppress them four hundred years. 'And the nation to whom they will be in bondage I will judge,' said God, 'and after that they shall come out and serve Me in this place.' Then He gave him THE COVENANT OF CIRCUMCISION; and so Abraham begot Isaac and circumcised him on the eighth day; and Isaac begot Jacob, and Jacob begot the twelve patriarchs. "And the patriarchs, becoming envious, sold Joseph into Egypt. But God was with him and delivered him out of all his troubles, and gave him FAVOR and WISDOM in the presence of Pharaoh, king of Egypt; and he made him governor over Egypt and all his house. Now a famine and great trouble came over all the land of Egypt and Canaan, and our fathers found no sustenance. But when Jacob heard that there was grain in Egypt, he sent out our fathers first. And the second time Joseph was made known to his brothers, and Joseph's family became known to the Pharaoh. Then Joseph sent and called his father Jacob and all his relatives to him, seventy-five people.

So Jacob went down to Egypt; and he died, he and our fathers. And they were carried back to Shechem and laid in the tomb that Abraham bought for a sum of money from the sons of Hamor, the father of Shechem. "But WHEN THE TIME OF THE PROMISE DREW NEAR which God had sworn to Abraham, the people grew and multiplied in Egypt till another king arose who did not know Joseph. This man dealt treacherously with our people, and oppressed our forefathers, making them expose their babies, so that they might not live. At this time MOSES WAS BORN, and WAS WELL PLEASING TO GOD; and he was brought up in his father's house for three months. But when he was set out, Pharaoh's daughter took him away and brought him up as her own son. And MOSES WAS LEARNED IN ALL THE WISDOM OF THE EGYPTIANS, and was MIGHTY IN WORDS AND DEEDS. "Now when he was FORTY YEARS OLD, it came into his heart to visit HIS BRETHREN, THE CHILDREN OF ISRAEL. And seeing one of them suffer wrong, he DEFENDED AND AVENGED HIM WHO WAS OPPRESSED, AND STRUCK DOWN THE EGYPTIAN. For he SUPPOSED that his brethren WOULD HAVE UNDERSTOOD that GOD WOULD DELIVER THEM BY his HAND, but they DID NOT understand. And the next day he appeared to two of them as they were fighting, and tried to reconcile them, saying, 'Men, YOU ARE BRETHREN; why do you wrong one another?' But he who did his neighbor wrong pushed him away, saying, 'WHO MADE YOU A RULER AND A JUDGE OVER US? Do you want to kill me as you did the Egyptian yesterday?' Then, at this saying, MOSES FLED AND BECAME A DWELLER IN THE LAND OF MIDIAN, where HE HAD TWO SONS. "And WHEN FORTY YEARS HAD PASSED, an Angel of the Lord appeared to him IN A FLAME OF

FIRE IN A BUSH, IN THE WILDERNESS OF MOUNT SINAI. When Moses saw it, he MARVELED at the sight; and as he drew near to observe, THE VOICE OF THE LORD CAME TO HIM, saying, 'I am the God of your fathers—the God of ABRAHAM, the God of ISAAC, and the God of JACOB.' And Moses TREMBLED and DARED NOT LOOK. 'Then the Lord said to him, "TAKE YOUR SANDALS OFF YOUR FEET, FOR THE PLACE WHERE YOU STAND IS HOLY GROUND. I have surely **SEEN** the OPPRESSION of My PEOPLE WHO ARE IN EGYPT; I have **HEARD** their GROANING and **HAVE COME DOWN** TO DELIVER THEM. And now come, I will send you to Egypt.'" "This Moses WHOM THEY REJECTED, saying, 'Who made you a ruler and a judge?' IS THE ONE GOD SENT TO BE A RULER AND A DELIVERER BY THE HAND OF THE ANGEL WHO APPEARED TO HIM IN THE BUSH. He brought them out, after he had shown **wonders** and **signs** in the land of Egypt, and in the Red Sea, and IN THE WILDERNESS FORTY YEARS. "This is that Moses who said to the children of Israel, 'The Lord your God WILL RAISE UP FOR YOU **a Prophet LIKE me** from your brethren. **HIM YOU SHALL HEAR.**' (see Acts 7:6-37). What a beautiful recap of Israel's long history! God indeed kept His Covenant with Israel His people, and He was their God and still is our God, and is still keeping His covenant with us — the Church of God (see Deuteronomy 7:9, with Acts 20:28), and "the Israel of God." (see Galatians 6:16). Hallelujah!

In the next chapter of this book, we will discuss how God continued to work with Israel and expanded His covenant with Israel by giving them the Ten Commandments through Moses, the ceremonial laws or laws governing the sacrifices, the atonement, and the Priesthood;

the Sabbath and New Moon celebrations, and much more, that were just a shadow of the good things that were to come in Christ Jesus. Paul tells us in his letter to the Colossians: "So let no one judge you in food or in drink, or regarding a festival or a new moon or sabbaths, WHICH ARE **A SHADOW** OF THINGS TO COME, but THE SUBSTANCE IS OF CHRIST." (Colossians 2:16-17). The Book of Hebrews also says, "For the law, HAVING **A SHADOW** OF THE GOOD THINGS TO COME, and not the very image of the things, can never with these same sacrifices, which they offer continually year by year, make those who approach perfect." (Hebrews 10:1). Paul again adds that "the law was our TUTOR to bring us to Christ, that we might be justified BY FAITH. But after faith has come, we are NO LONGER UNDER A TUTOR." (Galatians 3:24-25). And so we will continue in Chapter 5 as we discover how the walk with God was for the Old Covenant believer, and how different the walk with God is for you, the New Covenant believer who is the beneficiary of the glories that were to follow the sufferings of Christ (see 1 Peter 1:9-12 NIV). By the time we are through with this book, I believe you will understand and appreciate the necessity of living and walking in the Spirit as a new creation, and why you can't afford to live according to the flesh. "For if you live according to the flesh you will die; but if by the Spirit you put to death the deeds of the body, you will live." (Romans 8:13).

Chapter 5

The Law Was Given Through Moses

How God's Covenant with Abraham Evolved or Expanded to Give Israel the Ten Commandments, the Ceremonial Laws, the Sacrifices and Priesthood, Which Foreshadowed the Manifestation of Our Lord Jesus Christ

IN THE PREVIOUS Chapter we learned that God's Covenant with Abraham was an everlasting Covenant that would expand and take shape over the passage of time to culminate in the coming of our Lord Jesus Christ, who fulfilled the Old Covenant, and established the New Covenant, and who also is Himself the New Covenant. We additionally learned that God sealed the Covenant with the sign of Circumcision. Thus the Covenant was also known as "the Covenant of Circumcision." (see Acts 7:8). Any male descendant of Abraham who refused circumcision was declaring himself to be outside of God's covenant, which explains why God was angry with Moses when Moses failed to circumcise his son. (see Exodus 4:24–26). As a result of the Covenant of Circumcision, God was bound to Abraham and his descendants by indissoluble ties, and God had to sustain and protect Abraham and his descendants forever. (see Genesis 22:16-17). Hence, not only had God committed eternally to being the God — the Provider and Deliverer — for Abraham and his descendants, but Abraham also had made an unqualified committal of himself and his descendants to God, which meant that all that he and his descendants were and would ever be belonged to God. Abraham and his descendants now must worship only the one true God (Jehovah) forever.

God was faithful to His Covenant with Abraham, so that even after Abraham died, God confirmed His Covenant with Abraham's son Isaac (see Genesis 26:2-5), and then with Isaac's son Jacob, whose name was later changed to Israel (see Genesis 28:13-22; Genesis 35:9-15), and then with subsequent generations of the descendants of Abraham (who became known as the children of Israel). God protected Abraham's descendants and delivered them from a great famine through Joseph — the son of Jacob — whom God sent ahead to be governor in Egypt (see Acts 7:9-14; Psalm 105:17, 21). God, through Joseph, delivered the children of Israel and preserved them from being wiped out by the famine (see Genesis 45:7). And so through Joseph, all the children of Israel migrated and settled in Egypt (see Genesis 46:1-7; Genesis 47:11; Acts 7:11-15), in a sojourn that lasted 430 years. (see Exodus 12:40-41).

The Children of Israel Became Slaves and Were in Bondage in Egypt

God protected the children of Israel throughout this period because of His Covenant with Abraham and his descendants. Thus the Psalmist says of God that "**He remembers His covenant forever**, the word which He commanded, for a thousand generations, the covenant which He made with Abraham, and His oath to Isaac, and confirmed it to Jacob for a statute, to Israel as an everlasting covenant, saying, "To you I will give the land of Canaan as the allotment of your inheritance" (Psalms 105:8-11).

The children of Israel — God's Covenant People — multiplied in number in Egypt, became very prosperous, and thus became the envy of the Egyptians. The Bible says: "**the children of Israel were fruitful and increased abundantly, multiplied and grew exceedingly mighty**; and the land was **filled** with them." (Exodus 1:7). The Egyptians felt threatened by the growth and prosperity of the children of Israel. Therefore, after the death of Joseph as well as Pharaoh (the King who appointed Joseph as Governor), the Egyptians oppressed the children of Israel, and put them into captivity. The Bible says, "Now there arose A NEW KING over Egypt, WHO DID NOT KNOW JOSEPH. And he said to his people, "Look, THE PEOPLE OF THE CHILDREN OF ISRAEL ARE **MORE** and **MIGHTIER** THAN WE; come, let us deal SHREWDLY with them, LEST they multiply, and it happen, in the event of war, that they also join our enemies and fight against us, and so go up out of the land." Therefore they SET TASKMASTERS OVER THEM to **AFFLICT THEM** with their BURDENS. And they built for Pharaoh supply cities, Pithom and Raamses. But THE MORE THEY AFFLICTED THEM, THE MORE THEY MULTIPLIED AND GREW. And they were IN DREAD OF THE CHILDREN OF ISRAEL. So the Egyptians made the children of Israel SERVE WITH RIGOR. And they MADE THEIR LIVES BITTER with HARD BONDAGE — in mortar, in brick, and in all manner of service in the field. All their service in which they made them serve was with RIGOR. Then the king of Egypt spoke to the Hebrew midwives, of whom the name of one was Shiphrah and the name of the other Puah; and he said, "When you do the duties of a midwife for the Hebrew women, and see them on the birthstools, IF IT IS A SON, THEN YOU SHALL KILL HIM; but if it is a daughter, then she shall live." But the midwives FEARED GOD, and DID NOT DO AS THE KING OF EGYPT COMMANDED them, but saved the male children alive. So the king of Egypt called for the midwives and said to them, "Why have you done this thing, and saved the male children alive?" And the midwives said to Pharaoh, "Because the Hebrew women are not like the Egyptian women; for they are lively and give birth before the midwives come to them." Therefore God dealt well with the midwives, and THE PEOPLE MULTIPLIED AND GREW VERY MIGHTY. And so it was, **because the midwives feared God**, that He provided households for them. So PHARAOH COMMANDED all his people, saying, "EVERY SON WHO IS BORN you shall CAST INTO THE RIVER, and every daughter you shall save alive." (Exodus 1:8-22). Thus the oppression of the children of Israel continued, as they served as slaves to the Egyptians, as they suffered in that iron-smelting furnace. (see Deuteronomy 4:20; Jeremiah 11:4).

God Offered Redemption to the Children of Israel

But God was with the children of Israel, and hearing their groaning and their cry, He "remembered **His Covenant** with Abraham, with Isaac, and with Jacob. And God looked upon the children of Israel, and God acknowledged them." (see Exodus 2:24-25). God appeared to Moses and "sent Moses His servant, and Aaron whom He had chosen" (see Psalm 105:26), to go and lead the children of Israel, as

God delivered them from the land of Egypt and from the hands of Pharaoh through mighty signs and wonders that were heard throughout the earth. (see Exodus 3 — 17; Psalm 105:26-45). The Bible says that God did not just deliver the Israelites from slavery in Egypt in order to give them the land that He had promised to Abraham and his descendants (see Exodus 3:7-8), but that God delivered the children of Israel for another important reason: **for them to serve Him** (see Exodus 3:12; Exodus 4:22-23; Exodus 8:1, 20; Exodus 9:1, 13) and **"that they might observe His statutes and keep His laws."** (see Psalm 105:45). As you would remember, God's Covenant with Abraham and his descendants had a provision that God would be Israel's God (see Genesis 17:7; Exodus 6:7). But God had as yet not demanded worship from the children of Israel. God had been fulfilling His part of the Covenant as the God of Israel (see Exodus 3:6-8) by protecting them, providing for them, and eventually delivering them from captivity in Egypt, but He had never demanded that Israel fulfill their part by worshipping only Jehovah as their God. Until now, God had basically been dealt the short end of the stick as far as the keeping of His Covenant with Abraham and his descendants (the Israelites) was concerned. Therefore, in sending Moses to deliver the children of Israel from bondage in Egypt, God said, **"I will certainly be with you.** And this shall be a sign to you that I have sent you: When you have brought the people out of Egypt, **YOU SHALL SERVE GOD on this mountain."** (Exodus 3:12). God was now going to enforce the terms of the Covenant by demanding that the children of Israel serve or worship only Him. (see Exodus 20:2-6). But how was Israel going to worship or serve God? They had never done it in Egypt, and they didn't know how God wanted to be served or worshipped, or with what they must serve the Lord, as Moses admitted to Pharaoh in Exodus 10:26. And so God started giving the children of Israel guidelines or instructions for serving Him. He started giving them laws or commandments, statutes, and ordinances, as He renewed and expanded His Covenant with Israel through Moses (see Exodus 34:10-28). Thus the Ten Commandments were also called "**the words of the covenant**" (see Exodus 34:28).

God continued to work with the children of Israel in manifesting His plan of redemption for humanity, by expanding His covenant with Israel and giving them ordinances, statutes, and laws through His servant Moses — ordinances that instituted **the Passover feast or the Feast of Unleavened bread** and its regulations, **the Sabbaths**, the consecration of the firstborn or the law of the firstborn, the Ten Commandments, the ceremonial laws or laws governing the sacrifices, the atonement, and the Priesthood, the Sabbaths and New Moon celebrations, and much more, that were just a shadow of the good things that were to come in Christ Jesus. (see Colossians 2:16-17). Thus John writes: "the LAW WAS **GIVEN** THROUGH MOSES, but grace and truth came through Jesus Christ." (see John 1:17).

Israel Was Delivered By The Blood of a Lamb Without Blemish

When God announced to Moses the tenth and last plague — the death of all the firstborn of animals and humans in the land of Egypt (see Exodus 11:4) — that would compel Pharaoh to free the children of Israel and let them go out of Egypt, God also announced and instituted **the Lord's Passover Feast** as a memorial to be kept throughout the generations. (see Exodus 12:14-28). Israel was to be delivered by the BLOOD of A LAMB WITHOUT BLEMISH (see Exodus 12:5), which every household was to apply or put on their two doorposts and on the lintel of the houses where they would eat the lamb (see Exodus 12:7). The blood was to be a sign for the children of Israel on their houses, so that when God saw THE BLOOD, He would PASS OVER them, and not allow the plague to be on them to destroy the (firstborn) children of Israel when He struck the land of Egypt. (see Exodus 12:13, 22-23). Thus God instituted **the PASSOVER ordinance**, and gave regulations to govern it. (see Exodus 12:43-51). Then it came to pass that **by THE BLOOD of a Lamb without blemish, God delivered Israel from the land of Egypt**. (see Exodus 12:28-42). Clearly, it wasn't the good or righteous works of the children of Israel that saved them from being killed by the "destroyer," and caused them to be delivered from bondage in Egypt; it was **the blood of the Lamb without blemish** alone that saved them. Israel's good works didn't play any part in it. Whoever didn't have the blood of a Lamb without blemish on their doorposts and on the lintel of their houses had their firstborn children killed, regardless of their good works or righteous deeds. But whoever had the blood of a Lamb without blemish on their doorposts and on the lintel of their houses were passed over, and saved.

Likewise, it wasn't because of Israel's good works or righteous deeds that God brought them into the promised land. Moses himself acknowledged this when he said to the children of Israel: "**Do not think in your heart**, after the Lord your God has cast them out before you, saying, 'Because of **my righteousness** the Lord has brought me in to possess this land'; but it is because of the wickedness of these nations that the Lord is driving them out from before you. **It is not because of your righteousness or the uprightness of your heart** that you go in to possess their land, **but because of the wickedness of these nations** that the Lord your God drives them out from before you, and **that He may fulfill the word which the Lord swore to your fathers, to Abraham, Isaac, and Jacob.** Therefore understand that the Lord your God is **not** giving you this good land to possess **because of your righteousness**, for **you are a stiff-necked people**." (Deuteronomy 9:4-6). Indeed, God keeps His covenant; God keeps His promises. The Bible says that, **"Not one of all the Lord's good promises to Israel failed; every one was fulfilled."** (Joshua 21:45 NIV).

Beloved, Israel's deliverance or redemption from the hands of Pharaoh in Egypt was a deliverance from slavery and an empty way of life. And just as Israel was delivered by the blood of a Lamb without blemish, the Bible says we believers today have also been delivered from slavery to Satan and sin by the blood of Jesus Christ, **a Lamb without blemish or defect**. And thus Peter writes: "For you know that it was not with perishable things such as silver or gold that **you were redeemed** from the empty way of life handed down to you from your ancestors, BUT WITH THE PRECIOUS BLOOD OF CHRIST, a LAMB WITHOUT BLEMISH OR DEFECT." (1 Peter 1:18-19 NIV). God, in delivering the children of Israel through the blood of the lamb, was giving these Old Covenant believers a foretaste or a shadow of the good things that were to come, whose substance is of Christ.

In starting to give the children of Israel guidelines and instructions for serving Him, God not only ordained the Passover Feast and sacrifice, but He also gave a law requiring the CONSECRATION to God of ALL the FIRSTBORN children of Israel, both of man and beast. (see

Exodus 13:1-2; Exodus 13:11-16). The same day of the Passover was also ordained by the Lord as **the Feast of Unleavened Bread** (see Exodus 13:3-9). Then God led the children of Israel out of Egypt, going before them by day in a pillar of cloud to lead the way, and by night in a pillar of fire to give them light, so as to go by day and night. (see Exodus 13:21). God also saved the Israelites in the wilderness by parting the Red Sea and allowing them to go through it like dry ground to escape the pursuit of Pharaoh and his army. (see Exodus 14). "Thus, Israel **saw** the great work which the Lord had done in Egypt; **so** the people FEARED THE LORD, and BELIEVED THE LORD and His servant Moses." (Exodus 14:31). The people believed God and believed His servant Moses also. Likewise, Jesus Christ the Holy Servant of God (see Acts 4:30) said, "you believe in God, BELIEVE ALSO IN ME." (see John 14:1). God wants those who believe Him to believe His servants also.

The People Under the Old Covenant (of Law) Could Not Boldly Enter the Presence of God

One thing is noteworthy here in how God saw the children of Israel: God considered them as unrighteous people, as transgressors and sinners (see 1 Timothy 1:9; Galatians 3:19). God considered them as unholy people who needed to be holy (see Leviticus 11:44-45; Leviticus 19:2; Leviticus 20:26; Deuteronomy 23:14). And so God gave them the Law and restricted them from coming into His holy presence. (see Exodus 19:10-13). God would only communicate with them through His own appointed ways — through God's own chosen prophets whom He often spoke to through Angels, and often by means of visions, dreams, and many different ways. (see Hebrews

1:1). For example, the Bible says of Moses before he was sent to Egypt to deliver the children of Israel out of slavery, that "And when forty years had passed, an ANGEL OF THE LORD appeared to him in a flame of fire in a bush, in the wilderness of Mount Sinai. When Moses saw it, he marveled at the sight; and as he DREW NEAR to observe, the voice of the Lord came to him, saying, 'I am the God of your fathers—the God of Abraham, the God of Isaac, and the God of Jacob.' And Moses TREMBLED and DARED NOT LOOK. 'Then the Lord said to him, "TAKE YOUR SANDALS OFF YOUR FEET, FOR THE PLACE WHERE YOU STAND IS HOLY GROUND." (Acts 7:30-33). God wouldn't allow Moses to come close to the Holy presence of His Angel. The Bible says the voice of God came to Moses from the midst of the burning bush saying, "**DO NOT DRAW NEAR THIS PLACE**. Take your sandals off your feet, for the place where you stand is holy ground." (see Exodus 3:5). Moses, during this time, couldn't come near God's Holy presence, and Moses was also afraid and wouldn't dare look. (see Exodus 3:6). Yet, once the Spirit of God came upon Moses as God's anointed servant to deliver the children of Israel from slavery in Egypt (and because Moses himself was a faithful servant before God), Moses could speak with God face to face. (see Exodus 33:11; Numbers 12:8).

For the most part, the children of Israel under the Old Covenant could not come into the presence of God without a bleeding sacrifice (see Leviticus 4; Numbers 6), and amidst much fear. As you would remember, the spirit of fear entered the world with Adam's fall. Adam was unable to stand in the presence of God after his sin; he hid himself from God because he was afraid. (see Genesis 3:9-10, 22-24). When the spirit of Satan entered and started working in man as a result of man's disobedience (see Ephesians 2:2), the spirit of bondage to fear had entered into man. But as a new creation in Christ, the Bible says, **"you DID NOT receive the spirit of bondage again to fear**, but you received the Spirit of adoption by whom we cry out, "Abba, Father." (see Romans 8:15). Because all believers today (under the New Covenant) are righteous by faith in Christ Jesus (see 2 Corinthians 5:21; Romans 5:17), we are bold as a lion. (see Proverbs 28:1). God's perfect love has cast out fear from the New Covenant believer (see 1 John 4:18), so that we can boldly enter God's presence at any time. (see Hebrews 4:16). The Bible says that, in Christ Jesus our Lord, "**we have boldness** and access **with confidence** through **faith** in Him." (see Ephesians 3:12). We have "**boldness to enter the Holiest** by the blood of Jesus, by **a NEW and LIVING WAY** which He consecrated for us, through the veil, that is, His flesh." (see Hebrews 10:19-20). The Old Covenant people did not have such glories. (see 1 Peter 1:10-12). In fact, there are many examples of terrible things that happened to the Old Covenant people whenever they, being sinful men, tried to force themselves into the presence of our Holy Father and God, without being invited; they were suddenly smitten with death. Some of these incidents are recorded in Leviticus 10:1-3, and First Samuel 6:19, both of which, I believe, occurred in order to cause the Old Covenant (man) to know his spiritual condition before God.

Israel Was Delivered to Worship and Serve the Living God

As mentioned earlier, one of the main reasons God delivered the children of Israel from Egypt was for them to serve Him. (see Exodus 3:12; Exodus 4:22-23; Exodus 8:1, 20; Exodus 9:1, 13). God desired to have a special people through whom all the nations or families of the earth would be blessed. God desired to have a people who, BY OBEYING His VOICE AND KEEPING His COVENANT, would be a special treasure to Him above all people, and also be a KINGDOM OF PRIESTS and a HOLY NATION. (see Exodus 19:4-6). And so at Mount Sinai, on what became known as **the Day of Pentecost**, God proposed **the Law of the covenant** to Israel. "So Moses came and called for the elders of the people, and laid before them all these words which the Lord commanded him. Then all the people answered together and said, **"All that the Lord has spoken we will do."** Hence, Moses brought back the words of the people to the Lord." (Exodus 19:7-8). Thus Israel accepted the terms of God's covenant and signed up for it. And so God, seeking to make Israel a special treasure to Himself above all people, seeking to make Israel an example and a witness or a testimony to the rest of the world regarding the right way to live, gave the children of Israel the Ten Commandments (see Exodus 20:1-17), as well as the ceremonial laws or statutes (see Leviticus 19), to form **a composite Law** which was holy, just, and good. (see Romans 7:12). **If** Israel kept the Law **perfectly**, God was prepared to **bless** Israel abundantly (see Deuteronomy 28:1-14) and set Israel apart, set Israel high above all the nations of the earth. However, **if** Israel **failed** to keep the Law **perfectly**, Israel would come under blighting **curses**. (see Deuteronomy 28:15-68). These were the terms of the Law of the Covenant.

After reading both the blessings and the curses associated with the Law God gave to Israel, let me say honestly that I love the blessings, but I loathe the curses. Therefore if I were one of the elders of Israel at the time the Law was given, and if I knew, as they did, that this perfect Law was to be kept perfectly, or else curses were to be incurred, I would have asked God for GRACE instead of the Law, because clearly, it is impossible for any man born of (sinful) Adam to keep God's perfect Law perfectly. Hence, Paul, who knew the Law and lived under the Law before he came to Christ, says dejectedly that, "NO ONE WILL BE DECLARED RIGHTEOUS **in GOD'S SIGHT** by the WORKS of the LAW; rather, through the law we become **CONSCIOUS of our SIN.**" (Romans 3:20 NIV). And James, who also knew the Law and lived under the Law before he came to Christ, tells us by the inspiration of the Holy Spirit, that "whoever shall KEEP THE WHOLE Law, and yet STUMBLE in ONE POINT (or offend in one single instance), he is GUILTY of (breaking) ALL (of the Law)." (James 2:10). And so whoever offends in one single instance of the Law comes under the curses of the Law. "For AS MANY as are of the WORKS OF THE LAW are UNDER THE CURSE; for it is written, "**CURSED is EVERYONE who does not continue in ALL the things which are written in the book of the LAW, to DO them.**" (Galatians 3:10). Thus the whole of Israel was under the curse of the Law, because they couldn't keep the Law. (see Jeremiah 11:7-8). Indeed I am thankful, that "Christ has redeemed us from the curse of the law, having become a curse for us (for it is written, "Cursed is everyone who hangs on a tree"), that the blessing of Abraham might come upon the Gentiles in Christ Jesus, that we might receive the promise of the Spirit through faith." (Galatians 3:13-14). Hallelujah! My prayer is for God to have mercy on those who still want to be under the Law and its curses! But I know it is a prayer that cannot and will not be answered, because the Law cannot be tampered (or mixed) with mercy and grace, or else, it will cease to be the Law. The Spirit, speaking through Paul, said that it is impossible to be under the Law and be under Grace at the same time; you cannot mix Grace (or unmerited, unearned, undeserved favor) with the Law. (see Galatians 5:4; Romans 11:6). Therefore people have a choice between the two. You can either choose to be under Law, or you can choose to be under Grace, "for the grace of God that brings salvation has appeared to all men." (see Titus 2:11). And thus, James says that, for those who are under Law, judgment is without mercy, because by breaking the Law, the lawbreakers themselves have not shown mercy; they have not loved their neighbor as themselves. So judgment is without mercy. (see James 2:13). I choose not to be under Law, because the Bible says, "sin shall not have dominion over you, for **you are NOT under LAW** but under GRACE." (see Romans 6:14). Sin cannot have dominion over me, because I'm not under law but under grace. In fact, I rather have dominion over sin. (see 1 John 3:9). Thank God for His grace!

The Real Purpose of the Law Was to Convict All Men of Sin

Obviously, it was not fun for Israel to be under the Law. The apostle Paul tells us in his epistles that before faith came, Israel was kept under guard by the law, kept for **the faith** which would afterward be **revealed**. (see Galatians 3:23). "Therefore, the law was our TUTOR to bring us to Christ, that we might be **justified** BY FAITH. But after faith has come, we are NO LONGER UNDER A TUTOR." (Galatians 3:24-25). Israel was given the Law because of transgressions, **till** Christ (the Seed) should come. (see Galatians 3:19). The children of Israel were transgressors, they were sinners, and they didn't even know they were sinners. (see 1 John 1:10). The Bible says where there is no law, there is no transgression. (see Romans 4:15). So the Law was given to point out their sin or transgression to them, to make all men realize that they were guilty before God. Thus Paul writes:

"Obviously, **the law applies to those to whom it was given**, for **ITS PURPOSE** IS TO KEEP PEOPLE FROM HAVING EXCUSES, and **to show that** THE ENTIRE WORLD IS **GUILTY** BEFORE GOD." (Romans 3:19 NLT). The law, then, is the strength (or power) of sin (see 1 Corinthians 15:56). So by being under the law, Israel was under the dominion of sin. (see Romans 6:14). Thus, the Bible says that "**the law is not made for a righteous man**, but for the lawless and disobedient, for the ungodly and **for sinners…**" (see 1 Timothy 1:9). This also means that the law is not made for the believer in Christ who, according to the Bible, has been made righteous and holy by the precious blood of Jesus Christ. (see 2 Corinthians 5:21; 1 Corinthians 1:30; Ephesians 4:24; 1 Corinthians 3:16-17). Hence, Paul writes: "Knowing that a man is NOT JUSTIFIED by the WORKS OF THE LAW, but by the FAITH of Jesus Christ, even **we have believed in Jesus Christ, that we might be justified by the faith of Christ**, and not by the works of the law: for BY THE WORKS OF THE LAW SHALL **NO FLESH** BE JUSTIFIED." (Galatians 2:16 KJV).

The Law Was Given to Only the Children of Israel or the Jews, But They Failed to Keep It and Broke Their Covenant With God

The Law of Moses was given to only the people who were under the Covenant of Circumcision. It was given to only the children of Israel, who were the only Covenant people of God on earth at the time, and who were the only people God delivered out of the land of Egypt and gave a physical land that was promised to Abraham and his descendants (see Exodus 20:2; Exodus 20:12; Exodus 31:13,17; Ezekiel 20:12-13; Ezekiel 20:20; Deuteronomy 5:15; Deuteronomy 5:1-5).

And for these people who were under the Law, the Law had dominion over them as long as they lived. (see Romans 7:1).

Beloved, the Law of Moses was not given to the Gentiles (or non-Jews). Before Jesus Christ came to fulfill the Old Covenant, and established the New Covenant, the Gentiles were not in a Covenant with God. And so Paul writes: "Therefore, remember that **at one time you were Gentiles (heathens) in the flesh**, called Uncircumcision by those who called themselves Circumcision, [itself a mere mark] in the flesh made by human hands. [Remember] that **you were at that time separated (living apart) from Christ** [excluded from all part in Him], **utterly estranged and outlawed from the rights of Israel as a nation**, and **strangers with no share in the sacred compacts of the [Messianic] promise** [with **no knowledge of or right in God's agreements, His covenants**]. And you had no hope (no promise); you were in the world without God. **But now** in Christ Jesus, you who once were [so] far away, through (by, in) the blood of Christ have been brought near." (Ephesians 2:11-13 AMP). Peter also adds (of all believers): "Once you were not a people [at all], but now you are God's people; once you were unpitied, but now you are pitied and have received mercy." [Hos. 2:23.] (1 Peter 2:10 AMP). Obviously, the Gentiles only became the seed of Abraham, and thus beneficiaries of the Covenant, through faith in Christ, and not through the Law or the Covenant of Circumcision. (see Romans 4:16-17, with Galatians 3:29, and Galatians 5:1-3). Even **Israel who received the Law did not keep the Law** (see Acts 7:53), because they couldn't keep it. The Bible says, "the people of Israel, who tried so hard to get right with God by keeping the law, **never succeeded.**" (see Romans 9:31 NLT). The Law being spiritual (see Romans 7:14), could not be kept by the natural or carnal man; it takes a spiritual man to keep the Law. Jesus (the Spiritual Man) came and fulfilled the Law (see Matthew 5:17), and has made us spiritual men through faith in Him (see 1 Corinthians 15:45-49; 1 Corinthians 3:1), so "that the righteous requirement of the law might be fulfilled in us who do not walk according to the flesh but according to the Spirit." (see Romans 8:4). Thus the Bible says, "Christ is the end of the Law [the limit at which it ceases to be, for the Law leads up to Him who is the fulfillment of its types, and in Him the purpose which it was designed to accomplish is fulfilled. That is, the purpose of the Law is fulfilled in Him] as the means of righteousness (right relationship to God) for everyone who trusts in and adheres to and relies on Him." (Romans 10:4 AMP). Praise God!

On a certain occasion during His earthly ministry, Jesus asked the Jews, "Did not Moses give you the law, yet **none of you keeps the law**? Why do you seek to kill Me?" (see John 7:19). Obviously, Israel who received the law failed to keep the Law and the Covenant of the Lord. The Psalmist says, "They **did not** keep the covenant of God; they **refused** to walk in His law, and **forgot** His works and His wonders that He had shown them." (Psalms 78:10-11). How tragic! Second kings 17:7-16 speaks of the sins of the children of Israel: *"For so it was that the children of Israel had **sinned against the Lord their God**, who had brought them up out of the land of Egypt, from under the hand of Pharaoh king of Egypt; and **they had feared other gods**, and had **walked in the statutes of the nations whom the Lord had cast out** from before the children of Israel, **and of the kings of Israel**, which they had made. Also the children of Israel secretly did against the Lord their God things that were not right, and they **built for themselves high places** in all their cities, from watchtower to fortified city. They **set up*** *for themselves sacred pillars and wooden images* on every high hill and under every green tree. *There they burned incense on all the high places*, like the nations whom the Lord had carried away before them; and *they did wicked things to provoke the Lord to anger, for they served idols*, of which the Lord had said to them, "You shall not do this thing." Yet the Lord testified against Israel and against Judah, by all of His prophets, every seer, saying, "Turn from your evil ways, and keep My commandments and My statutes, according to all the law which I commanded your fathers, and which I sent to you by My servants the prophets." Nevertheless they would not hear, but **stiffened their necks**, like the necks of their fathers, who did not believe in the Lord their God. And **they rejected His statutes and His covenant that He had made with their fathers**, and His testimonies which He had testified against them; **they followed idols, became idolaters**, and went after the nations who were all around them, concerning whom the Lord had charged them that they should not do like them. So **they left all the commandments of the Lord their God**, made for themselves a molded image and two calves, made a wooden image and worshiped all the host of heaven, **and served Baal.**" (II Kings 17:7-16). How tragic!

God Proposed a New Covenant

Israel failed miserably because her heart was not right; Israel had a heart of stone (see Ezekiel 11:19; Ezekiel 36:26-27). Thus the problem of sin and rebellion had to do with the Old Creation man's heart, mind and spirit, which Satan had taken over (see Ephesians 2:2, with 2 Corinthians 4:4). The Bible says, "the carnal mind is enmity against God; for it is not subject to the law of God, nor indeed can be. So then, those who are in the flesh cannot please God." (Romans

8:7-8). I love how the New Living Translation renders the 7th verse: "For **the sinful nature** is always hostile to God. It never did obey God's laws, and it never will." (Romans 8:7 NLT). Indeed it never will. Therefore God decided that man needed **a new heart**, and **a new spirit**; man needed **a new nature and a new mind**. God decided that the Old Creation man needed to be **born again** or **created anew**. That was the only solution to the sin problem. That was the only solution to the Old Creation man's rebellion against God. That was the only solution that would prevent man from perishing in hell with his master Satan on the Day of Judgment. So God spoke through the prophet Ezekiel to the Children of Israel, saying: "**I will give you** a NEW HEART and put a NEW SPIRIT within you; I will take the heart of stone out of your flesh and give you a heart of flesh. **I will put My Spirit within you** and **cause you** to walk in My statutes, and you will keep My judgments and do them." (Ezekiel 36:26-27). The prophet Jeremiah also prophesied: "Behold, the days are coming, says the Lord, when I will make a **NEW COVENANT** with the house of Israel and with the house of Judah—NOT according to the covenant that I made with their fathers in the day that I took them by the hand to lead them out of the land of Egypt, My COVENANT WHICH THEY BROKE, though I was a husband to them, says the Lord. But this is the covenant that I will make with the house of Israel after those days, says the Lord: I will put My law IN THEIR **MINDS**, and WRITE IT ON THEIR **HEARTS**; and I will be their God, and they shall be My people. No more shall every man teach his neighbor, and every man his brother, saying, 'Know the Lord,' for they all shall know Me, from the least of them to the greatest of them, says the Lord. For I WILL FORGIVE THEIR INIQUITY, and THEIR SIN I WILL REMEMBER NO MORE." (Jeremiah 31:31-34). This New

Covenant God spoke about is the Covenant Jesus came to establish for us. Thus, the Book of Hebrews quotes this prophecy of Jeremiah and emphasizes its fulfillment in Christ. (see Hebrews 8:6-13). The Book of Hebrews also calls the New Covenant **a better covenant established on better promises**; the New Covenant has Jesus Christ as its Mediator (see Hebrews 8:6) and its guarantor or surety (see Hebrews 7:22). In fact, the New Covenant is Jesus Christ Himself (see Isaiah 42:6-7); the New Covenant is in Jesus' blood (see Luke 22:20). Moreover, by establishing the New Covenant, God has made the first or Old Covenant (with its law and rituals) **obsolete**, and what is obsolete and growing old is ready to vanish away. (see Hebrews 8:13). Praise God!

All the Scriptures Testify of Jesus Christ

During Jesus' earth ministry, before His crucifixion and resurrection, He said to the Jews: "You search THE SCRIPTURES, **for in them you think you have eternal life**; and THESE ARE THEY WHICH TESTIFY OF Me. But you are not willing to come to Me **that you may have life.**" (John 5:39-40). Here, Jesus claimed that the Old Testament Scriptures (which were, of course, the only Scriptures they had at the time) are all about Him — they testify or bear witness of Him. Also, after Jesus' resurrection from the dead, the Bible says He appeared (initially incognito) to two of His disciples who were saddened by His death and were on their way to Emmaus, and had a conversation with them. "Then He (Jesus) said to them, "O foolish ones, and slow of heart to believe in all that the prophets have spoken! Ought not the Christ to have suffered these things and to enter into His glory?" And beginning at MOSES and all THE PROPHETS, He

(Jesus) expounded to them IN **ALL** THE SCRIPTURES **the things concerning Himself.**" (Luke 24:25-27). Thus Jesus affirmed, both before and after His death and resurrection, that the Old Testament Scriptures (including the law and the sacrifices) testify of Him or bear witness of Him; He even taught the two disciples from the Old Testament Scriptures (the books of Moses & the prophetic books) the things concerning Himself. Then later when He appeared again to His eleven disciples and those who were together with them in Jerusalem, Jesus again reminded them of the words which He had spoken to them before His death and resurrection, "that all things must be fulfilled *which were written in **the Law of Moses** and **the Prophets** and **the Psalms** concerning **Me**.*" (see Luke 24:44). "And He opened their understanding, that they might comprehend the Scriptures." (see Luke 24:45). The apostle Paul also writes by the Spirit in his epistle to the Romans that, **the gospel of God** was "**promised before through His prophets in the Holy Scriptures, concerning His Son Jesus Christ our Lord.**" (see Romans 1:1-2). So the Old Testament Scriptures are indeed all about Jesus Christ our Lord.

Christ is the Substance of the Old Testament Types and Shadows

Now, as we can learn from the Book of Exodus, in instructing the children of Israel on how to serve or worship Him, God commanded them to build a tabernacle, and instructed them on how to build it. (see Exodus 35 to 40). God also appointed priests (see Exodus 40:13-15) and instructed the children of Israel on how and when to offer burnt sacrifices and offerings, including the sin offering. (see Exodus 20:24-26, with Leviticus 4). Thus, under the Old Covenant of Law, there was a physical tabernacle; they had the priesthood that offered the sacrifices at the tabernacle. Israel also had to observe the festivals and feasts that were mentioned earlier. But today, under the New Covenant, the Bible says Jesus Christ is our burnt offering (see Ephesians 5:2; Hebrews 9:26; Hebrews 10:12-14; 1 Corinthians 15:3-4); He is our Passover. (see 1 Corinthians 5:7). Therefore, as stated earlier, you are not to let anyone "judge you in food or in drink, or regarding a festival or a new moon or sabbaths, WHICH ARE A SHADOW OF THINGS TO COME, but THE SUBSTANCE IS OF CHRIST." (Colossians 2:16-17).

Quite unfortunately, in some Christian denominations today emphasis is still placed on observing the laws, Sabbaths, feasts and rituals of the Old Covenant, even though the Bible clearly teaches that these laws, rituals and feasts were not an end in themselves, but a shadow of the good things that were to come (see Hebrews 10:1), and that the substance is of Christ. (see Colossians 2:17). In and of themselves there is no value in these rituals, as the book of Hebrews explains. (see Hebrews 10:11-14). All the rituals under the Old Covenant served only to point us to the real thing, which is Christ. As an illustration, a photo of your baby taken while the baby is still in the womb is of value inasmuch as it points you to the child you're going to have; it gives you an image or a shadow of the real thing that is to come, and for that purpose it is worth cherishing or adoring. But once your child comes out of the womb and is present and alive, it would be foolish to be content with the photo, and to continue to kiss the photo when the substance (the real child) is laying right there to be kissed and adored. Common sense tells you that when you see your baby, you don't kiss or embrace the photo instead of your baby. But that is what we do when we focus on the rituals, laws, and feasts of the Old Covenant instead of the real truth and substance that is of Christ. For example, the Priesthood God instituted under the Old Covenant was only a shadow of the Priesthood of Christ and the holy and royal priesthood of all believers. It is sheer folly today to have priests in some of our churches offering sacrifices daily for the sins of believers. How can one even offer sacrifices without blood? How can you serve God the Old Covenant way without using blood to sanctify everything in the tabernacle? Besides, the Bible says without the shedding of blood, there is no forgiveness of sins. (see Hebrews 9:22). What blood exists today that is superior to the blood of Jesus and can forgive sins better than the blood of Jesus has already done? In fact, in the New Covenant, all believers are priests, and we are all implored to offer only spiritual (not physical) sacrifices that are acceptable to God through Jesus Christ. (see 1 Peter 2:5). "Therefore by Him let us continually offer the SACRIFICE OF PRAISE to God, that is, the fruit of our lips, GIVING THANKS to His name." (Hebrews 13:15). "For we are to God the fragrance of Christ among those who are being saved and among those who are perishing." (II Corinthians 2:15).

The Book of Hebrews thus explains that "not even the first covenant was dedicated without blood. For when Moses had spoken every precept to all the people according to the law, he took THE BLOOD OF CALVES AND GOATS, with water, scarlet wool, and hyssop, and SPRINKLED BOTH THE BOOK ITSELF and ALL THE PEOPLE, saying, **"THIS IS THE BLOOD OF THE COVENANT** which God has commanded you." Then likewise he SPRINKLED WITH BLOOD BOTH THE TABERNACLE AND ALL THE VESSELS OF THE MINISTRY. And according to the law ALMOST

ALL THINGS ARE PURIFIED WITH BLOOD, and **WITHOUT SHEDDING OF BLOOD THERE IS NO REMISSION**. Therefore it was necessary that the COPIES of the things in the heavens should be purified with these, but THE HEAVENLY THINGS THEMSELVES with **BETTER SACRIFICES** THAN THESE. For Christ has NOT entered the holy places MADE WITH HANDS, WHICH ARE COPIES OF THE TRUE, but **INTO HEAVEN ITSELF**, now to APPEAR IN THE PRESENCE OF GOD FOR US; NOT THAT He should OFFER Himself OFTEN, as the high priest enters the Most Holy Place every year with blood of another—He then WOULD HAVE HAD TO SUFFER OFTEN SINCE THE FOUNDATION OF THE WORLD; but now, **ONCE** at the end of the ages, He has APPEARED TO PUT AWAY SIN BY THE SACRIFICE OF Himself. And as it is appointed for men to die once, but after this the judgment, so Christ WAS OFFERED **ONCE** TO BEAR THE SINS OF MANY. To those WHO EAGERLY WAIT for Him He will APPEAR A SECOND TIME, APART from sin, FOR SALVATION. (Hebrews 9:18-28). Hallelujah! This is the good news that reveals the superiority of the New Covenant to the First or Old Covenant. This is the good news that needs to be preached and emphasized every day in our churches. Any so-called priest that wants to continue to offer physical sacrifices as was done under the old covenant has to sacrifice blood that is equal to the blood of Jesus, because that is the only sacrifice (and the only blood) God accepts and has accepted today. Besides, God does not even desire physical sacrifices, nor does He have pleasure in burnt offerings and sacrifices for sin. (see Hebrews 10:5-6).

Under the Old Covenant, the high priest had to offer animal sacrifices, first for his own sins and then for the people's. He had to be covered by the blood sacrifice before he could intercede on behalf of the people, for he himself was imperfect; he was a sinner. Year after year, on the Day of Atonement, the high priest had to offer up sacrifices. These sacrifices were only good for COVERING the sins of the nation FOR A YEAR. It was a temporary solution, "For IT IS NOT POSSIBLE that the blood of bulls and goats could TAKE AWAY SINS." (Hebrews 10:4). The blood of bulls and goats could not TAKE AWAY SINS; it could only temporarily cover the sins of the people, so the people were always **living under sin-consciousness** knowing that every year they had to offer sacrifices again and again through their high priest to atone for their sins. God knows how many goats and bulls had to die for this purpose! These animal sacrifices that were offered during Israel's 1,500 years under the law only served one purpose: they foreshadowed or pointed to the true Lamb of God — Jesus Christ — who was to come and sacrifice Himself to take away the sins of the world. So when John the Baptist introduced Jesus as the Lamb of God who takes away the sins of the world (see John 1:29, 36), the Jews (or Hebrews) got an instant picture of it, even though they didn't fully understand it until the finished work of Christ was revealed in the New Testament epistles. And so Israel was living under sin-consciousness because of the daily and annual sacrifices that had to be made for sin. The Book of Hebrews says: "For the law, having a SHADOW of the good things to come, and not the very image of the things, can NEVER with these same SACRIFICES, which they OFFER CONTINUALLY YEAR BY YEAR, make those who approach PERFECT. For then WOULD THEY NOT HAVE CEASED TO BE OFFERED? For the worshipers, ONCE PURIFIED, **WOULD**

HAVE HAD NO MORE CONSCIOUSNESS OF SINS. But in those sacrifices there is a REMINDER OF SINS EVERY YEAR. For it is **NOT POSSIBLE** that the BLOOD OF BULLS AND GOATS could take away sins. Therefore, when He (Jesus Christ) came into the world, He said: "Sacrifice and offering You DID NOT DESIRE, but a body You have prepared for Me. In BURNT OFFERINGS and SACRIFICES for SIN You had NO pleasure. Then I said, 'Behold, I have come— In the volume of the book it is written of Me— To do Your will, O God.'" Previously saying, "Sacrifice and offering, burnt offerings, and offerings for sin You did not desire, nor had pleasure in them" (which are offered according to the law), then He said, "Behold, **I have come to do Your will**, O God." He TAKES AWAY THE FIRST that He may ESTABLISH THE SECOND. **By that will** WE HAVE BEEN **SANCTIFIED** through THE OFFERING of the BODY of Jesus Christ **ONCE FOR ALL**. And every priest stands MINISTERING DAILY and OFFERING REPEATEDLY THE SAME SACRIFICES, which can NEVER TAKE AWAY SINS. But this Man (Jesus Christ), after He had OFFERED ONE SACRIFICE FOR SINS FOREVER, **SAT DOWN** at the right hand of God, from that time waiting till His enemies are made His footstool. For BY ONE OFFERING He has PERFECTED FOREVER **those who are being sanctified**." (Hebrews 10:1-14). The point that is being made in Hebrews 10:1-3 is that when Jesus Christ came into the world and made one sacrifice for sins forever, and perfected us forever, we were to have **NO MORE consciousness of sin**. And thus Romans 8:1 says that there is now no condemnation to those who are in Christ Jesus.

The Imperfect Sacrifices of the Old Covenant Have Been Made Obsolete by the One Perfect Sacrifice of Jesus Christ

Under the law, we had an imperfect high priest who offered imperfect sacrifices. But under the New Covenant, we have the perfect High Priest (Jesus Christ) who offered up Himself as the perfect sacrifice, and thus has perfected all believers once for all. We no longer need priests to offer sacrifices for our sins, because the one time sacrifice of Jesus is perfect and eternally efficacious. The Book of Hebrews tells us of Jesus Christ that: "if He were on earth, He would not be a priest, since there are priests who offer the gifts according to the law; who serve the COPY AND SHADOW OF THE HEAVENLY THINGS, as Moses was divinely instructed when he was about to make the tabernacle. For He said, "See that you make all things according to the pattern shown you on the mountain." (see Hebrews 10:11-14). Thus because the shadow pointed to the true heavenly sanctuary, Moses was instructed to make all things according to the pattern shown. It had to reflect the real thing. The value is in the real thing, not the shadow. And so the real substance of all the rituals under the law is the Person of Jesus Christ. Therefore it doesn't make sense today to focus on and argue over rituals and festivals, feasts, Sabbaths, and sacrifices, which are a SHADOW, instead of focusing on the revelation of Jesus Christ who is the SUBSTANCE.

Indeed, the story of God's redemption of mankind (the descendants of Adam) from the dominion of Satan and sin is an amazing love story as well as an amazing revelation of the merciful, loving and gracious heart of God our Father. God has always loved man, and He has always been a Father to us. (see Acts 17:28; Isaiah 64:8). But He is a righteous Father. Righteousness and justice is the foundation of His throne (see Psalm 89:14). So His children ought to be as righteous and perfect as Himself. (see Matthew 5:48). Israel did not realize that they were an unrighteous people in covenant with a righteous God. In fact, they were transgressors who boasted that whatever God commanded them to do, they will do it. (see Exodus 19:8). So God gave them the law through Moses at Mt. Sinai. God showed Himself as a Lawgiver and Judge (see Isaiah 33:22). The Law of Moses demanded perfect righteousness from man. But man could not attain to the righteousness of the law. (see Romans 9:31). Israel broke the Covenant with God and sinned against Him. (see Jeremiah 31:32). The Law showed the people that they were sinners (see Romans 3:20). When the Law passed its verdict, all of mankind was found guilty. "For all have sinned and fall short of the glory of God." (see Romans 3:23). None was found righteous. (see Romans 3:10; Ecclesiastes 7:20; Psalm 14:1-3). Our sins separated us from God and hid His face from us so that He will not hear us. (see Isaiah 59:2). God is a just God, so His justice demanded for the death of the sinner. The Law stipulated that the soul who sins shall die (see Ezekiel 18:20). The wages of sin is death (see Romans 6:23). So sinful man was destined to die or perish with his master Satan on the Day of Judgment. And naturally, man became afraid of God and hid himself from the presence of God just as Adam did in the garden of Eden (see Genesis 3:8-10). But God did not want to see us die. God is love, and He does not delight in the death of the wicked (see Ezekiel 33:11). So He made provision for blood sacrifices to cover our sins and deliver us from death. This was a temporary provision that had to be repeated every year to keep the sins of the people covered, because, as we noted earlier, it is impossible for the blood of bulls and goats to take away sins (see Hebrews 10:4). Moreover, God did not desire sacrifice and offering; God had no pleasure in burnt offerings and sacrifices for sin. (see Hebrews 10:5-6). So these sacrifices were just a shadow of the good things that were to come. (see Hebrews 10:1-2). And the reality (or substance) is found in Christ. (see Colossians 2:17). "For God so loved the world that He gave His only begotten Son, that whoever believes in Him should not perish but have everlasting life." (John 3:16).

Jesus fulfilled the Law (see Matthew 5:17); He died in our place (as our Substitute and Representative), so that we will be declared righteous in Him, and live. (see 2 Corinthians 5:21; Romans 3:23-24). Jesus thus satisfied and exhausted the judgment and the full punishment for our sins on the cross. "He was pierced for our transgressions, He was crushed for our iniquities; the punishment that brought us peace was on Him…" (see Isaiah 53:5 NIV). He satisfied the full justice of God through the one perfect sacrifice of Himself. And today, because we are in Christ, we are new creations (see 2 Corinthians 5:17); we are the children of God (see John 1:12) who are accepted in the Beloved. (see Ephesians 1:6). God is our Father. Jesus has made us perfect, holy and righteous as our Father is. "For by one offering He has perfected forever those who are being sanctified." (Hebrews 10:14). God laid on Jesus the sins of all mankind (see Isaiah 53:6; 1 John 2:2), and gave the righteousness of Jesus to us as a gift to be received **by faith**. (see Romans 5:17, 2 Corinthians 5:21, Romans 1:17). We are no longer separated from God by our sins. God has reconciled us to Himself through Jesus Christ and does not count or impute our sins to us anymore once we accept His offer of reconciliation (see 2 Corinthians 5:18-19, Jeremiah 31:31-34; 1 Corinthians 13:5). So it is up to us to accept God's offer of reconciliation by believing (or putting our faith in) what Jesus has done for us. Today, we can enjoy a new and intimate relationship or fellowship with God through our Lord Jesus Christ. (see Ephesians 2:18; 1 John 1:3; 1 Corinthians 1:9). We no longer have to fear God's judgment or keep a distance. The judgment for our sins has been exhausted on Jesus, and there is none left for the believer. As a child of God, you should never harbor a fear of judgment which involves torment. First John 4:17-18 says, "Love has been perfected among us in this: that we may have boldness in the day of judgment; because **as He is, so are we in this world.** There is no fear in love; but PERFECT LOVE CASTS OUT FEAR, because fear involves torment. But he who fears has not been made perfect in love." For the believer, God's perfect love has removed all fear.

Today, he who fears has not been made perfect in love. He who has been made perfect in love has **no fear.** We no longer have to fear the wrath and judgment of God. We no longer have to feel uncomfortable in God's presence. We have peace with God through our Lord Jesus Christ. (see Romans 5:1). Christ Himself is our peace (see Ephesians 2:14); the punishment that brought us peace was upon Him. (see Isaiah 53:5). In fact, God has come so close to us that we are joined as one with God in spirit (see 1 Corinthians 6:17). It cost God dearly for us to freely obtain this kind of relationship with Him. It cost God His dearest and only begotten Son for us to also become God's children (begotten of Him). If God loved us any less, He would not have sent Jesus Christ to die for us. God could have left us to perish without hope. But see what manner of love He has loved us! "By this, we KNOW LOVE, because He LAID DOWN HIS LIFE for us." (1 John 3:16). The Bible says that there is no greater demonstration of love than to lay down your life for another (see John 15:13). God's love is so great that nothing can ever separate us from the love of God which is in Christ Jesus. Even death cannot separate us from His love (see Romans 8:38-39). So be convinced that neither your sins nor failings nor mistakes can separate you from the love of God in Christ. You should be eternally grateful to Jesus Christ, and live your life for Him, just as He died for you. (see 2 Corinthians 5:15). As a child of God, you should live a life that brings honor and glory to God your Father. Declare with the apostle Paul that "I am crucified with Christ: nevertheless I live; yet not I, but Christ liveth in me: and the life which I now live in the flesh I live by the faith of the Son of God, who loved me, and gave himself for me." (Galatians 2:20 KJV).

In the subsequent Chapters of this book we will continue our discussion by exploring how God established the New Covenant through which we became new creations, and what our true identity is as new creations in Christ. We will also explore what it means to walk in the Spirit, and how we can accomplish that every moment of our life. By the end of this book, I am confident that you will understand and appreciate the necessity of living and walking in the Spirit as a new creation, and why you can't afford to walk in the flesh. "For if you live according to the flesh you will die; but if by the Spirit you put to death the deeds of the body, you will live." (Romans 8:13).

Chapter 6

Jesus the Spiritual Man Brought and Established the Spiritual Life

The Birth of Jesus Christ Was a Prophecy Fulfilled

GOD, THROUGH DIFFERENT prophets, affirmed and reaffirmed His commitment to manifesting in the flesh as Jesus Christ the Lamb slain from the foundation of the world (see 1 Timothy 3:16, with Revelation 13:8) — to fulfill the Old Covenant and establish the New Covenant. Not only was the coming of Jesus Christ in fulfillment of God's everlasting Covenant promise to Abraham, that in his "**Seed** ALL THE NATIONS OF THE EARTH SHALL BE BLESSED" (see Genesis 22:18; Galatians 3:29 with Romans 4:16-17), it was also in fulfillment of God's promise to David (who was also a descendant of Abraham) saying: "WHEN YOUR DAYS ARE FULFILLED and you rest with your fathers, I will set up **your SEED** after you, WHO WILL COME FROM YOUR BODY, and I will ESTABLISH HIS KINGDOM. He shall build a house for My name, and **I WILL ESTABLISH THE THRONE OF HIS KINGDOM FOREVER**. I will be HIS Father, and HE SHALL be My SON. If he commits iniquity, I will chasten him with the rod of men and with the blows of the sons of men. But My MERCY SHALL NOT DEPART FROM HIM, as I took it from

Saul, whom I removed from before you. And YOUR HOUSE and YOUR KINGDOM SHALL BE ESTABLISHED FOREVER before you. YOUR THRONE SHALL BE ESTABLISHED FOREVER." (2 Samuel 7:12-16). Of course, part of this promise to David was fulfilled in his son Solomon, but the part that had to deal with establishing the throne of David's kingdom forever was to be fulfilled in Jesus Christ (see Luke 1:31-33), who is also the Seed or Son of David according to the flesh. (see Romans 1:3, with Luke 18:38).

Additionally, the manifestation of Jesus Christ in the flesh was in fulfillment of God's prophecy in the garden of Eden, where He said to the serpent: "And I will put enmity between you and the woman, and between your seed and **her Seed**; He shall bruise your head, and you shall bruise His heel." (Genesis 3:15). In Chapter Two of this book we cited this verse and explained that this prophecy was uttered by God Himself immediately after man sinned, and that in this prophecy God was speaking of a war between Himself (which he referred to as the **Seed** of the woman. Obviously a woman has no seed; only man has a seed, and so this was referring to **the virgin birth** or the manifestation of God in the flesh as Jesus Christ) and Satan the serpent, in which the serpent (or Satan) appears to win a crucial battle (a strike at Jesus' heel — the crucifixion), only to lose the war (or have his head crushed — in the resurrection of Jesus Christ). And thus the prophet Isaiah prophesied, saying: "Therefore the Lord Himself will give you a sign: Behold, **THE VIRGIN SHALL CONCEIVE and bear a Son**, and shall call His name Immanuel." (Isaiah 7:14). The prophet Micah also added a remarkable prophetic utterance that this Son that the virgin was to bear would be born in Bethlehem, and would be "the One to be Ruler in Israel, **whose goings forth are from of old, from everlasting**."

(see Micah 5:2). This prophecy obviously speaks of the pre-existence of Jesus Christ, the Ruler (or Lord) that was to be born through the virgin. The identity of this Child (Jesus Christ) becomes even clearer as God gives more details through the prophet Isaiah, saying: "For unto us a Child is born, unto us a Son is given; And the government will be upon His shoulder. And His name will be called Wonderful, Counselor, **MIGHTY GOD**, **Everlasting FATHER**, Prince of Peace." (Isaiah 9:6). And so here we have an astounding confirmation that the Son the virgin was going to bear would be no ordinary Man — He would be God Himself, as His name **Mighty God** and **Everlasting Father** clearly indicates. Deity was to become united with humanity in this Child. God was to send His own Son into the world "in the likeness of sinful flesh" (see Romans 8:3), the Son having offered Himself without spot to God through the eternal Spirit. (see Hebrews 9:14). God was to visit man incognito. God Himself was to break into the Sense (or flesh) realm and take an identity as the Son of Man (see 1 Timothy 3:16), and offer Himself as a Savior, as a Substitute to bear sins, to pay the penalty of man's transgressions with His own blood (see Acts 20:28), to die for the sins of the Old Creation man, so as to deliver or redeem us (the descendants of Adam) from the dominion of Satan and sin, and give us eternal life (in a supernatural rebirth or regeneration called the New Creation).

Jesus Christ Was Born in the Fullness of The Time

Thus, "when the fullness of the time had come, God sent forth His Son, born of a woman, born under the law, to REDEEM those who were under the law, THAT WE MIGHT RECEIVE THE ADOPTION AS SONS." (see Galatians 4:4-5). The Gospel according to Luke gives us a detailed account of **the virgin birth** of our Lord Jesus Christ: "Now in the sixth month the angel Gabriel was sent by God to a city of Galilee named **Nazareth**, to a VIRGIN betrothed to a man whose name was **Joseph**, OF THE HOUSE OF DAVID. The virgin's name was **MARY**. And having come in, the angel said to her, "Rejoice, HIGHLY FAVORED ONE, the Lord is with you; blessed are you among women!" But when she saw him, she was troubled at his saying, and considered what manner of greeting this was. Then the angel said to her, "Do not be afraid, Mary, for YOU HAVE FOUND FAVOR WITH GOD. And behold, YOU WILL CONCEIVE in your womb **and bring forth a Son**, and shall **call His name JESUS**. He will be **great**, and **will be called the Son of the Highest**; and the Lord God WILL GIVE Him THE THRONE OF His father DAVID. And He will **reign** over the house of Jacob FOREVER, and OF His KINGDOM THERE WILL BE NO END." Then Mary said to the angel, "How can this be, SINCE I DO NOT KNOW A MAN?" And the angel answered and said to her, "**The Holy Spirit** will come upon you, and **the power of the Highest** will overshadow you; therefore, also, that **Holy One** who is to be born will be called **the Son of God**." (Luke 1:26-35).

Mary BELIEVED the Word of God that was spoken to her by the Angel. The Bible says, "Then Mary said, "Behold the maidservant of the Lord! LET IT BE TO ME ACCORDING TO YOUR WORD." (see Luke 1:38). Here, Mary gives us a perfect lesson on how we are to respond to, or receive the promises of God that are in the Bible. When the Bible says, for instance, that by His stripes you're healed, say, "Lord, LET IT BE TO ME ACCORDING TO YOUR WORD." This is the Amen that we are to speak, according to Second Corinthians 1:20.

By believing the Word of God, Mary possessed what the Word had promised. Thus when Mary went to visit her relative Elizabeth, Spirit-filled Elizabeth spoke saying, "BLESSED IS **SHE WHO BELIEVED**, for THERE WILL BE A FULFILLMENT **of those things which were told her from the Lord.**" (Luke 1:45). Beloved, you are blessed if you BELIEVE the Word of God, if you believe the promises of God, for there will be a fulfillment of whatever the Word promises you. Indeed Mary conceived and brought forth the Son Jesus Christ, as promised by the Word. And thus with the coming of Jesus Christ, "Grace and Truth came." (see John 1:17).

The First Man Adam Was a Natural Man, But the Second and Last Adam Jesus Christ is a Spiritual Man

The Bible states: "And so it is written, "The first man Adam became a living being." The last Adam (Jesus Christ) became **a life-giving spirit**. However, THE SPIRITUAL (Jesus Christ) IS NOT FIRST, but **THE NATURAL** (Adam), and AFTERWARD **THE SPIRITUAL** (Jesus Christ). The FIRST MAN (Adam) WAS OF THE EARTH, made of dust; THE SECOND Man (Jesus Christ) is the Lord FROM HEAVEN. As was the man of dust (Adam), SO ALSO are those who are made of dust (the Old Creation man); and AS IS THE HEAVENLY Man (Jesus Christ), SO ALSO are those who are heavenly (the New Creation man). And AS WE (the Old Creation men) HAVE BORNE THE IMAGE of the man of dust (Adam), WE (the New Creation men) SHALL ALSO BEAR THE IMAGE of the heavenly Man (Jesus Christ)." (I Corinthians 15:45-49). In Chapter One of this book we explained that the spiritual Man — Jesus Christ — (who brought and established the spiritual life) was not first; the natural man —

Adam — (who brought the natural life) was first, and afterward, the spiritual. (see 1 Corinthians 15:46). And so, clearly, the first or Old Creation man **Adam was not a spiritual man** and could, therefore, neither live nor walk in the Spirit. Living and walking in the Spirit, then, is a reality that was brought by Jesus Christ, and is thus exclusive to the New Creation man, because only the New Creation man has the nature and the capability to live and walk in the Spirit. The New Creation man (when he is fully mature) is a spiritual man, because he bears the image of Jesus Christ, the heavenly and spiritual Man. (see 1 Corinthians 15:46; Romans 8:29; 1 John 4:17, with 1 Corinthians 3:1)

The Birth of Jesus Christ Was Proclaimed as Good News that Will Cause Great Joy For All the People

After the birth of Jesus **in Bethlehem** as prophesied, an angel of the Lord appeared to some shepherds who were keeping watch over their flock by night (see Luke 2:8-9). "**The angel** said to them, "Do not be afraid. I bring you **GOOD NEWS** THAT WILL CAUSE GREAT JOY FOR ALL THE PEOPLE. Today in the town of David **A SAVIOR** HAS BEEN BORN TO YOU; He is **the Messiah**, the **Lord**." (Luke 2:10-11 NIV). "And suddenly there was with the angel a MULTITUDE of the heavenly host PRAISING GOD AND SAYING: "Glory to God in the highest, and on earth PEACE, GOODWILL TOWARD MEN!" (Luke 2:13-14). Here, we learn a few things about this Child Jesus from the angel, and from the multitude of the heavenly host that appeared with him. First, the birth of this Child Jesus is **good news** that will cause great joy for all the people. Why? Because this Child Jesus is the MESSIAH, the LORD; He is a SAVIOR that has been born to man. "For unto us (men) a Child is born, unto us a Son is given…" (see Isaiah 9:6). "For God so loved the world (of men) that He GAVE us (men) His only begotten Son, that whoever believes in Him should not perish but have everlasting life." (John 3:16). And so this was good news that will cause great joy for **all the people.**

The Birth of Jesus Christ Brought Glory to God in the Highest, and On Earth Peace, Goodwill Toward Men

The second thing we learn from the angel and the multitude of the heavenly host that appeared with him is that, this Child Jesus is to bring "**glory to God** in the highest, and on earth, **peace, goodwill toward men.**" (see Luke 2:14). Jesus Himself also confirmed during His earth ministry that He came to bring glory to God the Father — the One who sent Him. To those who questioned His teaching authority in the Temple, "Jesus answered, "My teaching is NOT MY OWN. IT COMES FROM **THE ONE WHO SENT ME.** Anyone who chooses to do the will of God will find out whether **my teaching comes from God** or whether I speak on my own. WHOEVER SPEAKS ON THEIR OWN DOES SO TO GAIN PERSONAL GLORY, but HE WHO **SEEKS THE GLORY OF THE ONE WHO SENT HIM** is a man of truth; there is nothing false about him." (John 7:16-18 NIV). And so Jesus, by His own admission, came to earth **seeking the glory of the One who sent Him**, and thus Jesus was a Man of truth; there was nothing false about Him. In John 17:4, Jesus, as He prayed to God the Father at the conclusion of His earth ministry, said, "**I HAVE BROUGHT YOU GLORY ON EARTH** by finishing the work you gave me to do." (John 17:4 NIV). Therefore, the glory Jesus was to bring the Father explains the angels' proclamation that "Glory to God in the highest."

Beloved, just as Jesus was sent by God the Father to bring glory to the Father, Jesus has also sent us (believers — His disciples) to bring glory to Jesus and to God the Father through the ministry of reconciliation. After His resurrection and before His ascension to Heaven, "Jesus said to His disciples (which includes all of us who believe in Him): "As the Father has sent Me, **I also send you**." (see John 20:21). Then He added, "All authority has been given to Me in heaven and on earth. Go therefore and **make disciples** of all the nations, baptizing them in the name of the Father and of the Son and of the Holy Spirit, teaching them to observe all things that I have commanded you; and lo, I am with you always, even to the end of the age." Amen." (Matthew 28:18-20). And so we have been sent to proclaim the gospel of Christ and make disciples for Christ, we who were once alienated from God and enemies in our mind by wicked works (see Colossians 1:21), we who were once not a people. Thus Peter says, "But you are a chosen generation, a royal priesthood, a holy nation, **His own special people**, that YOU MAY PROCLAIM THE PRAISES of Him who called you out of darkness into His marvelous light; WHO ONCE WERE NOT A PEOPLE but **are NOW the PEOPLE OF GOD**, who had not obtained mercy but NOW have obtained mercy." (1 Peter 2:9-10). Clearly, Jesus died to make each believer somebody, to make each believer God's own special person, to make each believer a special treasure. (see 2 Corinthians 4:7). Before, you were nobody, I was nobody. (see 1 Peter 2:10). But now you and I have obtained mercy; we are the people of God. And not just that, Jesus died to make you and I the sons or children (born) of the Living God. (see

John 1:12; 1 John 5:1; Galatians 3:26; 1 John 3:1-2). Today I am God's special and beloved son with whom He is well pleased. Jesus washed me in His own blood, and has made me a king and a priest unto His God and Father. (see Revelation 1:5-6). I am a royal. I am an heir of God and joint-heirs with Christ. I am holy. Jesus died for my glory (see Colossians 1:27; John 17:22). And so I live for His glory. (see 1 Corinthians 6:20; 2 Corinthians 5:15). I proclaim His praises. Praise God! And thus the apostle Paul reminds us: "For you see your calling, brethren, that **NOT** many wise ACCORDING TO THE FLESH, **NOT** many mighty, **NOT** many noble, ARE CALLED. But GOD HAS CHOSEN THE FOOLISH THINGS of the world to put to shame the wise, and GOD HAS CHOSEN THE WEAK THINGS of the world to put to shame the things which are mighty; and THE BASE THINGS of the world and THE THINGS WHICH ARE DESPISED God has chosen, and THE THINGS WHICH ARE NOT, to bring to nothing the things that are, that NO FLESH SHOULD GLORY IN His PRESENCE." (1 Corinthians 1:26-29). Hallelujah! I cannot glory in God's presence, because everything I am, I owe it to Him. "As it is written, "He who glories, let him glory in the Lord." (see 1 Corinthians 1:31). God alone deserves all the glory. And God has given us the Holy Spirit to help us bring glory to Jesus, as His witnesses. (see John 16:14, with Acts 1:4-5, 8).

The multitude of the heavenly host who appeared with the angel that announced the birth of Jesus Christ to the shepherds also proclaimed PEACE and GOODWILL TOWARD MEN ON EARTH. (see Luke 2:14). Indeed the birth of Jesus was not just to bring glory to God in the highest, but also to bring peace and goodwill toward men on earth, because "God was in Christ reconciling the world (including all men) to Himself, not imputing their trespasses to them, and has committed to us the word of reconciliation." (see 2 Corinthians 5:19). Jesus Christ was going to die for sins as man's Representative and Substitute, and be raised from the dead for man's justification. (see Romans 4:25). God was going to forgive all our sins and justify (or declare as righteous) all men who would put their faith in Jesus and His substitutionary sacrifice on the cross. Paul says, "Therefore, having been **justified by faith**, WE HAVE **PEACE** WITH GOD **through** our Lord Jesus Christ" (Romans 5:1). Christ Himself is our peace (see Ephesians 2:14); the punishment that brought us peace was upon Him (see Isaiah 53:5). Thus, men who were once alienated from God, and were enemies of God in our own minds because of our evil behavior (see Colossians 1:21), now have peace with God, having been reconciled to God through our Lord Jesus Christ. The gospel of Christ is, therefore, also called **the gospel of peace**. (see Ephesians 6:15). In Acts 10:36, Peter said that God sent the Word to the children of Israel, **PREACHING PEACE** through our Lord Jesus Christ. How fitting it is then that the angels would proclaim peace and goodwill toward men because of the birth of Jesus Christ. How fitting that the angel of God would proclaim the birth of Christ as GOOD NEWS THAT WILL CAUSE GREAT JOY FOR ALL THE PEOPLE.

You see, the peace that the angels were proclaiming was not the peace that the United Nations and the war-torn countries around the world are craving today. It is not the peace all nations seek to establish through their legal justice system. Jesus did not come so that wars or violence in the earth would cease. If that were the peace that was being proclaimed by the angels, then obviously Jesus failed to make it a reality, because He Himself suffered a violent death, and there is still no such peace in the world today. Gun violence, terrorism and wars are still prevalent and rampant today. Jesus Himself said, "**Do not think that I came to bring peace on earth.** I did not come to bring peace but a sword. For I have come to 'set a man against his father, a daughter against her mother, and a daughter-in-law against her mother-in-law'; and 'a man's enemies will be those of his own household.' He who loves father or mother more than Me is not worthy of Me. And he who loves son or daughter more than Me is not worthy of Me. And he who does not take his cross and follow after Me is not worthy of Me. He who finds his life will lose it, and he who loses his life for My sake will find it." (Matthew 10:34-39). What this means is that following Jesus Christ comes at a cost. Accepting Jesus as one's Lord requires a complete surrender to Him, a total denial of oneself, and quite often, an abandonment of one's family, if they're not believers and are not supportive of such a decision; it requires an unqualified committal of one's life to Christ. This explains why many people are not willing to accept Jesus Christ as their Lord. For many people, the cost is just too high. Many people prefer to just add Jesus to their life, rather than submit their life to Jesus. Many people like to have Jesus as their Savior, but they are not willing to submit to Him as Lord over their life. But that is exactly what Jesus has to be and wants to be in your life —Lord. Jesus can't be your Savior if He is not also your Lord. Jesus wants to rule your life and have a say in everything you do — in the kind of words you use in communicating with others, how you treat yourself and others, the kind of lifestyle you lead, even the sort of movies you watch, the kind of songs you listen to, the way you make and spend your money, how you spend your time, etc. Jesus wants to be the Lord of your life, and so you can choose to say "Yes" or "No" to Him. Unfortunately, many people choose to say "No", because they want to be their own boss; they want to be their own god, not realizing what a difficult yoke or a heavy burden that is, not realizing that only Jesus' yoke is easy and His burden light (see Matthew 11:30). And so, to such people Jesus maintains, "he who does not take his cross and follow after Me is not worthy of Me. He who finds his life will lose it, and he who loses his life for My sake will find it." (Matthew 10:38-39). Many believers have lost their lives for Jesus' sake, yet in losing their lives, they found eternal life — the God-kind of life, the highest form of life. The apostle Paul said, "I affirm, by the boasting in you which I have in Christ Jesus our Lord, I DIE DAILY." (I Corinthians 15:31). We all have to crucify or put to death the deeds of the flesh (by the Spirit), we have to die daily so that Christ may live in us and reveal or manifest His life in our mortal bodies.

Today tribulations and persecutions follow believers everywhere. Many believers have been rejected by their families because of their faith in Jesus Christ. Many non-Christian families consider it a shame and a disgrace to the family when their relatives accept Jesus Christ as their Lord and Savior. And so they often reject such relatives, and sometimes persecute them continually. Many countries today also specifically target Christians for persecution. The blood of martyrs cry from every corner of the earth. And yet, the believer (who is walking in the Spirit) can have peace in the midst of trials and tribulations, and be of good cheer, because Jesus has overcome the world (see John 16:33), and the believer has overcome the world with Him (see 1 John 5:4-5). Thus, the peace Jesus brought is not the peace the world gives; it is **inner peace**, assurance and quietness that cannot be disturbed by any trial, persecution, affliction, tribulation, or trouble. The peace Jesus brought is the kind of peace that comes from knowing that we have right standing with God; the kind of peace that comes from being "persuaded that neither death nor life, nor angels nor principalities nor powers, nor things present nor things to come, nor height nor depth, nor any other created thing, shall be able to separate us from the love of God which is in Christ Jesus our Lord." (Romans 8:38-39). It is the peace of God, which surpasses all understanding, which guards or garrisons our hearts and minds through Christ Jesus. (see Philippians 4:7). This is the kind of peace Jesus was speaking of when He said, "Peace I leave with you, My peace I give to you; **not as the world gives** do I give to you. Let not your heart be troubled, neither let it be afraid." (John 14:27). This is the kind of peace the angels were proclaiming toward men on earth. And indeed, knowing what we know today about Jesus and His finished work at the cross, we should all be able to join the angels and the multitude of the heavenly host in proclaiming: "Glory to God in the highest, and on earth PEACE, GOODWILL TOWARD MEN!" Hallelujah! The Birth of Jesus Christ is worth celebrating every single day of the year. Glory to God!

From an early age, Jesus kept His focus on the goal of bringing glory to God the Father. The Bible says of Jesus that "the Child grew and became STRONG IN SPIRIT, filled with wisdom; and the grace of God was upon Him." (Luke 2:40). Jesus understood that He had to always do His Father's business (see Luke 2:49), because He and His Father are one. (see John 10:30). And so at the young age of 12, Jesus, while He was in Jerusalem with His parents for the Passover feast, chose not the playground nor the company of His friends and family; He chose to linger around in Jerusalem and to stay in the Temple of God even when it was time to go back home to Nazareth with His parents. At age twelve, the Boy Jesus was "in the temple, sitting in the midst of the teachers, both **listening to them and asking them questions**. And **all who heard Him were astonished at His understanding and answers**." (see Luke 2:46-47). And when His parents were worried upon discovering after a day's journey back towards Nazareth, that the Boy Jesus was not with them, they searched for Him, and when they found Him after three days of searching, and told Jesus that they had searched for Him anxiously, "He said to them, "Why did you seek Me? DID YOU NOT KNOW THAT I **MUST** be about **My Father's business**?" (Luke 2:49). To Jesus, doing God the Father's work or business and bringing glory to the Father was **a MUST**. And He knew this even at the young age of 12. Beloved, you are also God's child today, just as Jesus is, and so I ask, "What is your attitude towards doing the Father's business?" Do you consider it a MUST to be about the Father's business? You must! The full story of the Boy Jesus' visit to Jerusalem for the Passover feast with His parents can be found in Luke 2:41-52. I encourage you to read it because it is the only story we have in the Bible that gives us a glimpse into Jesus' childhood.

The Bible says, "And Jesus INCREASED in WISDOM and STATURE, and in FAVOR with God and men." (Luke 2:52). May we also increase in wisdom, because Jesus Christ Himself is our wisdom (see 1 Corinthians 1:30). May we also increase in stature "till we all come to the unity of the faith and of the knowledge of the Son of God, to a perfect (or complete) man, **to THE MEASURE OF THE STATURE OF THE FULNESS OF CHRIST**; that we should NO LONGER BE CHILDREN, tossed to and fro and carried about with EVERY WIND OF DOCTRINE, by THE TRICKERY OF MEN, in the CUNNING CRAFTINESS OF DECEITFUL PLOTTING, but, speaking THE TRUTH in LOVE, may GROW UP IN ALL THINGS INTO Him who is the head—Christ— from whom the whole body, joined and knit together by what every joint supplies, according to the EFFECTIVE WORKING by which EVERY PART does its share, CAUSES GROWTH OF THE BODY for the EDIFYING of itself in LOVE" (Ephesians 4:13-16). May we also grow in favor with God and men, as God surrounds us with His favor as with a shield (see Psalm 5:12). Indeed, God has given each one of us grace or favor (see Ephesians 4:7). This grace came through Jesus Christ (see John 1:17). May you receive abundance of grace (together with the gift of righteousness) to reign in life. (see Romans 5:17). Amen.

How Jesus the Spiritual Man Lived and Walked in the Spirit, And What We Can Learn From Him

As noted earlier, Jesus is a spiritual Man, and so are all (mature) believers today. (see 1 Corinthians 15:45-49, with 1 Corinthians 3:1). One mark or characteristic of a spiritual man, as we can learn from Jesus, is that **he is a man of PRAYER**. Jesus, during the days of His life on earth, was a Man of prayer. The first time Jesus is introduced to us as an adult in the Bible is when, at about age 30 (see Luke 3:23), He comes from Nazareth (which is in the province of Galilee) to John the Baptist to be baptized in the Jordan, in what is known as the baptism of repentance. (see Luke 3:21-22; Matthew 3:13-17; Mark 1:9-11, with Acts 19:4). The Bible says Jesus **PRAYED** during or immediately after His baptism in the Jordan, and that "**while He PRAYED**, the heaven was opened. And the Holy Spirit descended in bodily form like a dove upon Him." (see Luke 3:21-22). "And suddenly a voice came from heaven, saying, "This is My beloved Son, in whom I am well pleased." (Matthew 3:17). The Bible also records that John the Baptist saw the Spirit descending upon Jesus in bodily form like a dove, and that this was the evidence to John that Jesus was the Messiah, the Lamb of God who takes away the sins of the world, the One who baptizes with the Holy Spirit. (see John 1:29-36). And thus John testified that Jesus Christ is the Son of God.

Now, this Scripture about the Holy Spirit descending upon Jesus in bodily form like a dove (see Matthew 3:16; Mark 1:10; Luke 3:22; John 1:32-33) is often misunderstood and misinterpreted to mean that the Holy Spirit looks like a dove in appearance or form. A close reading of these verses, however, (with the help of the Holy Spirit), will reveal that the Holy Spirit is NOT being likened to a dove in form or appearance at all. The image or symbolism of the dove is used in these verses ONLY to describe the WAY or MANNER in which the Holy Spirit DESCENDED upon Jesus Christ. His descent was like that of a dove. Imagine how a dove in flight descends to the earth. That is the imagery these verses of Scripture are giving us about how the Holy Spirit came down in bodily form upon Jesus. Now, if you were to describe me as jumping like a cat from the floor onto the bed, I bet nobody would think for a minute that you meant to say that I look like a cat in form or appearance. And yet Satan has caused many people to think (based on the verses above) that the Holy Spirit looks like a dove. May you be guided by the Spirit in studying the Scriptures.

Why Jesus Was Baptized

I have always wondered why Jesus needed to be baptized, since He had no need of repentance. And John the Baptist felt that way too as can be seen from his attempt to prevent Jesus from being baptized, saying, "I need to be baptized by You, and are You coming to me?" But Jesus answered and said to him, "Permit it to be so now, for thus it is fitting for us to fulfill all righteousness." Then he allowed Him." (see Matthew 3:14-15). Now, what did Jesus mean by saying "it is fitting for us to fulfill all righteousness"? You see, Jesus did not come into this world for His own sake, but for our sake — to save us, to make us righteous, to establish us in righteousness. Jesus was very content in Heaven being equal with God (see Philippians 2:5-8), and so He didn't need anything from earth; He only came **for our sake**; He came to stand in our place, as **our Representative, as our Substitute** to bring us into **right standing** with God. As Our Substitute, Jesus underwent the baptism of repentance **in our stead**, in our place, so that today we don't have to receive John's baptism again. Today, we receive a different kind of baptism, which is baptism into the Body of Christ. We are baptized into the Body of Jesus Our Substitute the moment we believe in Him, so that we become ONE with Him. This is why John says that as Jesus is, so are we in this world (see 1 John 4:17); it is also why Paul says that "we are members of His body, of His flesh and of His bones." (see Ephesians 5:30). Paul says of all believers that "BY **one Spirit** we were all BAPTIZED INTO ONE BODY — whether Jews or Greeks, whether slaves or free—and have all been MADE TO **DRINK** into **one Spirit.**" (see I Corinthians 12:13). What this means is that our baptism into the Body of Christ is BY that one Spirit (the Holy Spirit); it is the work of the Holy Spirit, (and NOT the work of any man), and so this is not referring to water baptism (which is the work of man). The Holy Spirit has baptized each one of us into the Body of Christ, and having baptized each one of us into that One Body of Christ, the Holy Spirit has also come into each one of us; we have all been made to **drink** into **one Spirit**. This is a fulfillment of Jesus' promise that whoever drinks of the water (that is, the Holy Spirit) that Jesus gives him will never thirst, but that the water will become in him a fountain of water **springing up into everlasting life**. (see John 4:14; with John 7:37-39). Thus the apostle Paul emphasizes in his letter to the Ephesians that when we believed in Jesus Christ, we "were **sealed with the Holy Spirit of promise**" (see Ephesians 1:13); and again to the Corinthians, Paul said of those of us who have believed in Jesus, that God "has **sealed us** and **given us the Spirit in our hearts** as a guarantee." (see 2 Corinthians 1:21-22). And so the baptism spoken of in First Corinthians 12:13 is the only baptism that saves, and it is the baptism that has saved all of us who believe in Jesus Christ. This was also the baptism Jesus was speaking of when He said that whoever believes (the gospel) and **is baptized** will be saved. (see Mark 16:15-16). Water baptism does not save anyone, which is also why Paul (even after he had baptized a few believers) could boldly say that, "Christ did not send me to baptize, but to preach the gospel…" (see 1 Corinthians 1:17). We only get baptized in water because it is symbolic of the actual baptism that was performed on us by the Holy Spirit when we believed in Jesus. Moreover, Jesus commanded the early disciples to baptize believers in His name, and so we do it in obedience to our Lord. The thief on the cross who professed faith in Jesus and was promised salvation did not need to come off the cross to be baptized in water first, because water baptism doesn't save anyone; water baptism only gives us a picture or an outward (physical) sign of what has already happened (spiritually) to those of us who have believed in Jesus Christ — it shows us that when we believed we were baptized into (or became partakers of) Jesus' death, we were buried with Jesus, and were raised with Him, that just as Jesus "was raised from the dead by the glory of the Father, even so we also should walk in newness of life." (see Romans 6:3-4, with Ephesians 2:6). Water baptism also shows us that when we believed in Jesus Christ, we were baptized into Christ or became united with Christ as one body, we put on Christ, or we clothed ourselves with Christ. (see Galatians 3:27). And so, again, the baptism that is spoken of in First Corinthians 12:13 is not water baptism. It actually refers to **the new birth** which occurs when we believe in Jesus Christ. The Bible says that "He saved us through **the washing of rebirth and renewal by the Holy Spirit**." (see Titus 3:5 NIV). Thus through the washing of regeneration and renewing of the Holy Spirit, we become members of the Body of Christ, with Christ as the Head (see Colossians 1:18); we become "members of His **body**, of His **flesh**, and of His **bones**" (see Ephesians 5:30); we become partakers of the Holy Spirit (see Hebrews 6:4); we become partakers of the divine (or God) nature. (see 2 Peter 1:4). And all of this happens when we believe in our heart the Lord Jesus and confess with our mouth that God has raised Him from the dead. (see Romans 10:9-10, with 1 Corinthians 12:13). Hallelujah!

Now, one may ask, "Doesn't the Bible say that there is one Lord, one faith, **one baptism**?" Yes, the Bible says this, but many people take it out of context because they don't understand it. And by the way, this is not talking about water baptism either, but rather the baptism explained earlier, which saved us. Now, let's fully quote the verses this statement appears in. "There is **ONE BODY** and **ONE Spirit**, just as you were called in ONE HOPE OF YOUR CALLING; ONE Lord, ONE faith, **ONE baptism**; ONE God and Father of all, who is above all, and through all, and in you all." (Ephesians 4:4-6). Indeed there is one Body — this is referring to the Body of Jesus Christ (also called the Church) into which we were all baptized when we believed. There is one Spirit — this is also referring to the Holy Spirit who baptized us into the Body of Christ, and of whom we have all been made to drink, as we explained earlier. And so we were called in one hope of receiving salvation through one (or the same) faith (which we profess) in one Lord (Jesus Christ); and thus when we profess this same (or one) faith in Jesus Christ, (at that very instant) we are baptized into the one Body of Christ (by the one Holy Spirit) in one (and the same) baptism (or new birth) that gives us eternal life. As a result of this new birth, we all become sons or children of one God, who is the Father of us all (see John 1:12, 1 John 3:1; 1 John 5:4), who is above all, and through all, and **is in us all** (or dwells in all of His children). This is what this **"one baptism"** means in Ephesians 4:4-6. It is not in any way limiting believers to experiencing only one baptism throughout our Christian walk; otherwise what can we make of the other baptisms that we all know about, including **water baptism, and the Holy Spirit baptism?** What can we make of the use of the phrase "**the doctrine of BAPTISMS**" (plural) in Hebrews 6:2? Would we then say that the Bible contradicts itself because it says in Ephesians 4:4-6 that there is "one baptism"? No. The Bible never contradicts itself. It is the people who don't know how to rightly divide the Word of truth, who make it seem contradictory. Hence Paul's advice to the young preacher Timothy was this: "STUDY to shew thyself APPROVED unto God, a workman that needeth not to be ashamed, RIGHTLY DIVIDING THE WORD OF TRUTH." (2 Timothy 2:15 KJV). Study the Word of God to become approved of God, and don't be ashamed of the gospel, but rightly divide the Word of truth, because God wants His Word to be rightly divided, so that it will be rightly understood and interpreted to reveal truths that have no contradictions whatsoever. This is also why God gave us the Holy Spirit as our teacher. (see 1 John 2:27). Every believer needs to submit to the teaching authority of the Holy Spirit. This is the only way out of false doctrines and teachings.

What We can Learn From The Prayer Life of Our Lord Jesus Christ

We are still on the subject of what we can learn from the earth walk of Jesus Christ the Spiritual Man, and we have noted that He was a Man of prayer, and that He prayed during or immediately after His baptism by John in the Jordan. Our Lord Jesus Christ **began His earth ministry with prayer**. Hence, during His earth walk, He (Jesus) spoke a parable to His disciples in which He made the astounding statement, "that **MEN ALWAYS OUGHT TO PRAY AND NOT LOSE HEART**" (Luke 18:1). For Jesus, prayer was a way of life. He lived praying and died praying. Throughout His earth walk He prayed at every opportunity. He understood the power of prayer, and He emphasized the importance of prayer. Even though He was often followed by the multitudes, Jesus "often withdrew into the wilderness and prayed." (Luke 5:16). Sometimes He would also pray publicly, right in the presence of the crowd as in when He blessed the five loaves of bread and two fish to feed 5000 people (see John 6:11, 23), and when He raised Lazarus from the dead. (see John 11:41-44). He prayed at all times of the day. He would sometimes withdraw **to a solitary place** in the **morning — having risen a long while**

before daylight — to pray (see Mark 1:35), and in the **night** also. The Bible reports that Jesus **prayed all night** to God on the night before He chose His twelve apostles. (see Luke 6:12). "And when it was day, He called His disciples to Himself; and from them He chose twelve whom He also named apostles" (Luke 6:13). Jesus also prayed during or immediately after His baptism in the river Jordan, as we noted earlier, and the Bible says that the heaven was opened and the Holy Spirit descended in bodily form like a dove upon Him. (see Luke 3:21-22). **The transfiguration** of Jesus also occurred **while He prayed**. The Bible says, "**As He prayed**, the appearance of His face was altered, and His robe became white and glistening." (Luke 9:29). Jesus' miracle of walking on water also happened **after He had spent time praying** on the mountain. (see Mark 6:46-51). In the Garden of Gethsemane, it was through prayer that Jesus received strength to face the agony of the cross in His substitutionary death for mankind. (see Luke 22:41-44). Hebrews 5:7 tells us that, "In the days of His flesh, Jesus offered up prayers and supplications, with loud cries and tears, to Him who was able to save Him from death, and **He was heard because of His reverence**." Jesus was heard when He prayed, because of His reverence (for God). This means that reverence gets us the attention of the Father. Jesus got the Father to hear His prayer, because of His reverence for the Father. And He also got the answer to His prayer. God sent an angel to strengthen Him in the Garden of Gethsemane to face the agony of the cross for you and I. And there in the Garden, Jesus also commanded us, His disciples, to WATCH AND PRAY that we do not fall into temptation. (see Matthew 26:41). Even today Jesus is still praying for us in Heaven as our High Priest. The Book of Hebrews says, "He always lives **to make intercession** for those who draw near to God" (see Hebrews 7:25). Romans 8:34 also says that He is "at the right hand of God, **interceding for us**."

Indeed Jesus knew something about prayer that He wants us, as spiritual men, to also know and act on. He says "**men always ought to pray and not lose heart.**" (Luke 18:1). In other words, we should pray continually and never give up on prayer. Prayer is like oxygen to the believer; we need it to survive in this world. And without it, we will fall into various temptations. Paul emphasizes the importance of prayer by telling us in First Thessalonians 5:16-18 that God's will for us is that we rejoice always, **PRAY WITHOUT CEASING**, and **give thanks in everything** (or in all circumstances). Indeed, that both the Holy Spirit baptism of Jesus and the transfiguration of Jesus occurred **while He prayed** is a testament to the power and sanctity of prayer. We can never underestimate the role of prayer in our Spirit walk.

Today I want to encourage you to **make prayer a habit, and always pray fervently and earnestly**. Become addicted to prayer. Withdraw from the busyness of life each day and at every opportunity to pray to God. If Jesus could not, or would not conduct His earthly ministry without prayer, neither can you, and neither should you. Prayer changes things. Jesus has promised us that whatever we ask the Father in the name of Jesus, He would give us. (see John 16:23-24). We have Jesus' authority to use His name in prayer. And we have His promise that our prayers in His name will be heard and answered by God. When we pray in the name of Jesus, it is as though Jesus Himself were praying. And the Bible tells us that God always hears Jesus (see John 11:41-42), which means that God always hears us when we pray in the name of Jesus. His ears are open to the prayers of the righteous. (see 1 Peter 3:12). Moreover, Jesus has assured us that the Father

Himself loves us as much as He loves Jesus (see John 16:27; John 17:20, 23), so nothing should prevent us from going to the Father in prayer. The Bible urges us to "come boldly to the throne of grace, that we may **obtain mercy** and **find grace** to **help in time of need.**" (see Hebrews 4:16). What are you waiting for? Get into the habit of prayer. The early apostles understood the significance and power of prayer. They made it their goal to devote themselves continually to **prayer** and to the ministry of the Word. (see Acts 6:4). In one instance, the Bible says, "And **when they had prayed**, the place where they were assembled together was shaken; and they were all filled with the Holy Spirit, and they spoke the word of God with boldness." (see Acts 4:31). In another instance, when Paul and Silas were thrown into prison, the Bible says, "at midnight Paul and Silas **were praying** and singing hymns to God, and the prisoners were listening to them. Suddenly there was a great earthquake, so that the foundations of the prison were shaken; and immediately all the doors were opened and everyone's chains were loosed." (Acts 16:25-26). May you never underestimate the significance and power of prayer in your Christian walk.

We will continue to explore the life of Jesus further in the next few chapters of this book, as we examine and learn from His faith, which was evident in His confessions, His love and His works. We will also discuss all the other ways in which Jesus lived in the Spirit and walked in the Spirit, and not according to the flesh. Additionally, we will examine how Jesus fulfilled the Old Covenant, and established the New Covenant.

Chapter 7

Jesus' Walk of Faith

How Jesus Walked in the Spirit (by Faith, and Not by Sight), and What We Can Learn From Him

IT IS EVIDENT that Jesus Christ was not just a Man of Prayer, but also **a Man of Faith**. In fact, it was faith working through love (see Galatians 5:6) that brought Jesus to earth to die for the sins of man. Jesus believed or had faith that if He came down to earth to die or lay down His life in the greatest display of love to pay the full penalty for the sins of man, man would put his faith in Him, accept His Substitutionary sacrifice, and thus be saved from the dominion of Satan and sin and from God's impending wrath on the Day of Judgment. Jesus had faith that man would accept Him as Savior and Lord, that man would respond to His great love and accept His offer of eternal redemption. That was the faith that brought Jesus to earth. And so, even before He came to be born on earth as a Man to be our Representative, our Substitute and our Savior, Jesus' faith was evident.

The Bible teaches that Jesus Christ existed in Heaven in the form of God and was equal with God. (see Philippians 2:5-8). The Bible also adds that ALL things were made through Jesus Christ and by Jesus Christ (see John 1:1-3, 14; Hebrews 1:2; Colossians 1:16), and without Him nothing was made that was made. (see John 1:3). Jesus Christ is the image of the invisible God, and **BY HIM all things were created** that are in heaven and that are on earth, visible and invisible, whether thrones or dominions or principalities or powers; all things were created through Him and for Him, and He is before all things, and in Him all things are held together. (see Colossians 1:15-17). The Bible further teaches that all things were created by the **faith** of the Creator — God (see Romans 4:17), and that this faith was exercised through or by the Word of God (Hebrews 11:3). Thus, the Bible says that Jesus Christ who is over all, the eternally blessed God (see Romans 9:5; 1 Timothy 3:16; Acts 20:28), "gives life to the dead and CALLS THOSE THINGS WHICH DO NOT EXIST AS THOUGH THEY DID" (see Romans 4:17).

This means that Jesus Christ, who is Himself God, is a faith God. After all, what defines faith better than calling "those things which do not exist as though they did?" Clearly, Jesus when He walked here on earth as a Man, was a faith Man. No wonder the Bible calls Jesus the author (or source) and finisher (or perfecter) of our faith. (see Hebrews 12:2). No wonder the Bible also calls God's Family or Household "the Household of Faith" (see Galatians 6:10). This means that one unique or distinguishing characteristic of the people who belong to the Household of God or "the household of faith" is that we all have faith — starting from our Father God (see Romans 4:17) and our Brother Jesus (see Hebrews 12:2), to the least of our brethren. (see Romans 12:3; 2 Peter 1:1). We all have faith; this is the only reason we are called the family or household of faith. Thus the Bible says of believers (the children of the household of faith) that God has given each one of us "THE MEASURE OF FAITH" (see Romans 12:3);

we have obtained the same (or like) precious faith (see 2 Peter 1:1). In other words, we have all obtained faith which is of equal value and honor. This faith came when we heard the Word (or Gospel) of Christ. (see Romans 10:17). Therefore, if you're a believer and you don't think you have faith, then perhaps you don't know who you are, or perhaps you're not a believer; perhaps you don't belong to "the household of faith," because everybody in "the household of faith" has faith. Otherwise we wouldn't be called "the household of faith," we wouldn't be called "believers." Believers need to stop struggling to find faith, and just act on the Word of God, which says that we have already been given the measure of faith. (see Romans 12:3; 2 Peter 1:1). When we act on the Word of God, God considers it as evidence that we believe the Word, and so He counts us as "believers," He counts us as His children, and He counts our faith to us as righteousness. Believing (which is a verb) is acting on the Word of God; and faith (which is a noun) is what results when we act on the Word of God. God and His Word are one. (see John 1:1). When Abraham believed God's Word, it was the same as believing God, and so God counted it to him as righteousness. (see Genesis 15:6; Romans 4:3). Also, when Abraham believed God's Word, he acted on the Word, for example, by waiting on God for the promised son, and also bringing his son Isaac to the mountain and laying him on the altar to be sacrificed to God, as commanded by God's Word. God credits righteousness to people who believe Him, who believe His Word and act on His Word. (see Romans 4:5). He did it not only for Abraham but previously for Noah, when Noah acted on God's Word by building the ark through which God saved him and his family from the great flood. (see Hebrews 11:7). Moses also acted on God's Word to lead the children of Israel out of bondage in Egypt, and through the red sea. (see Hebrews 11:23-29). Today when we also believe God's Word and act on Romans 10:9-10, God sees it as faith in Jesus, and so He declares us righteous, because we have believed God. Hebrews 11:6 tells us that "without faith it is impossible to please God." Aren't you glad (as a Christian) that God has given you the measure of faith (see Romans 12:3) so that you can please Him? Habakkuk 2:4 also says my righteous one will **walk** by faith. And Hebrews 10:38 says, "Now the just shall **live** by faith; but if anyone draws back, My soul has no pleasure in him." Then, Verse 39 adds, "But WE ARE NOT of those who draw back to perdition, BUT OF THOSE WHO BELIEVE TO THE SAVING OF THE SOUL." Hallelujah!

The Old Creation Man Was Always Implored to Have Faith

In the old Testament and in the Four Gospels, the natural man had to continually struggle to find faith to walk with God. In the Old Testament, God had even said of the children of Israel: "I will hide My face from them, I will see what their end will be, For THEY ARE a perverse generation, CHILDREN IN WHOM is **NO FAITH**." (Deuteronomy 32:20). Again, when Jesus arrived on the scene (here on earth), He echoed the same theme or truth, telling the natural or Old creation man (even His disciples before they were born again) in the Gospels that "IF YOU HAVE FAITH **as a mustard seed**, you can say to this mulberry tree, 'Be pulled up by the roots and be planted in the sea,' and it would obey you." (see Luke 17:6). Also, Jesus would often say to the Old Creation man, "O you of little faith." (see Matthew 6:30; Matthew 8:26; Matthew 14:31; Matthew 16:8; Luke 12:28). One time Jesus also MARVELED and spoke to the crowd that followed Him about a Roman centurion's faith — a Gentile's faith — in these words: "I say to you, I have not found such **great faith**, not even in Israel!" (see Luke 7:9; Matthew 8:10). Evidently, the natural man scarcely had faith, such that when one was found who had faith, it was a marvel even to Jesus. (see Luke 7:9). On another occasion Jesus spoke of the great faith of another Gentile — this time a Syrophoenician woman whose daughter was severely demon-possessed and thus needed healing; Jesus said to her in an exchange, "O woman, **great is your faith**! Let it be to you as you desire." And her daughter was healed from that very hour." (see Matthew 15:28). It is quite obvious that these two people Jesus commended had faith because they were Gentiles — they were not under the Jewish law or the Law of Moses. Faith was very scarce among the Old Creation men, especially the Jews, because they were under the Law. The Bible says that the Law is not of faith. (see Galatians 3:12). The Law is not based on faith, and so doing the works of the law is the opposite of walking by faith. The law was intended to bring us to the realization that we need a Savior, and for the Savior to justify us by faith.

The Bible says that Jesus Christ is the author and finisher of our faith. (see Hebrews 12:2). In other words, Jesus is the source of our faith as well as the One who brings our faith to completion or perfection. Today those who still choose to be under the Law and seek the righteousness that comes through the Law, are those who have **no faith** in the finished work of Jesus Christ. "For they being ignorant of God's righteousness, and seeking to establish their own righteousness, have not submitted to the righteousness of God. For Christ is the end of the law for righteousness **to everyone who believes**. For Moses writes about the righteousness which is of the law, "The man who does those things shall live by them." But the righteousness of faith speaks in this way, "Do not say in your heart, 'Who will ascend into heaven?'" (that is, to bring Christ down from above) or, "'Who will descend into the abyss?' " (that is, to bring Christ up from the dead). But what does it say? "The word is near you, in your mouth and in your heart" (that is, the word of faith which we preach): that if you confess with your mouth the Lord Jesus and believe in your heart that God has raised Him from the dead, you will be saved. For **with the heart one believes unto righteousness**, and **with the mouth confession is made unto salvation**. For the Scripture says, "Whoever believes on Him will not be put to shame." For there is no distinction between Jew and Greek, for the same Lord over all is rich to all who call upon Him. For "whoever calls on the name of the Lord shall be saved." (Romans 10:3-13). Thank God that I am not under law but under grace. (see Romans 6:14). Thank God that I have been justified by faith. (see Romans 5:1).

When Jesus' disciples (who were then natural men, and under the law) asked Jesus to increase their faith (see Luke 17:5), Jesus immediately pointed out to them that they didn't need their faith to be increased; they just needed faith, period. I mean, how can you increase something you don't have? And so Jesus said, "IF YOU HAVE FAITH as a mustard seed, you can say to this mulberry tree, 'Be pulled up by the roots and be planted in the sea,' and it would obey you." (Luke 17:6). Before they were born again, Jesus' disciples were always struggling for faith. On another occasion, when the disciples couldn't cast out a demon and they asked Jesus why they couldn't cast it out (see Matthew 17:19), "Jesus said to them, "Because of YOUR UNBELIEF (or lack of faith); for assuredly, I say to you, if you have faith as a mustard seed, you will say to this mountain, 'Move from here to there,' and it will move; and nothing will be impossible for you." (Matthew 17:20). In this same story, Jesus called the disciples a FAITHLESS and perverse generation. (see Matthew 17:17).

The New Creation Man Already Has Faith

The Old Creation man was always implored to have faith, but in the epistles, which are mainly letters to and about the New Creation man in the light of the finished work of Christ, you will never find the New Creation man being implored to have faith. This is because, as a product of faith, the New Creation man is already a faith-man; the new creation man was born by grace **through faith** (see Ephesians 2:8-9, with 2 Corinthians 5:17), and so he has faith. Having been born through faith, the New Creation man walks by faith (see 2 Corinthians 5:7), just like the Lord Jesus Christ. Under the New Covenant (of Grace), when we accept Jesus as our Lord and Savior, or when we believe in Jesus Christ, we are no longer natural men; we are born again (see 1 Peter 1:23); we are new creations (see 2 Corinthians 5:17), and so we are given the measure of faith (see Romans 12:3), we obtain the same (or like) precious faith. (see 2 Peter 1:1). Therefore the believer DOES NOT pray for faith or struggle for faith to walk with God. To pray for faith is to confess your own unbelief. Indeed, as a believer, to walk in the Spirit is to walk in the knowledge and consciousness of the truth that you ALREADY have faith, and then walk by that faith. In the epistles, we are told that we have "the same Spirit of faith" (see 2 Corinthians 4:13). And so whenever the believer is implored regarding faith, in the epistles, he is only implored to **continue steadfastly in the faith**. (see Acts 14:22; Colossians 1:23; Colossians 2:5; 1 Corinthians 16:13; 2 Corinthians 1:24). If Jesus were to reproach the

New Creation man (or the believer) for his faith today, all He can say and would say is: "Use the faith you've got!" Jesus would never tell the believer or New Creation man to have faith, because that would be contrary to His own Word (especially, the Pauline revelation) which says that we already have the measure of faith. (see Romans 12:3). God has given to each believer (the required) measure of faith. This faith came when we heard the Word of Christ or the Gospel of Christ (see Romans 10:17). And so we all begin our Christian walk with the same measure of faith. The degree to which we use or exercise this faith and grow or increase it is what differs from one believer to another, because it completely depends on our free will; it is also what determines the magnitude of the works of each believer's faith.

Beloved, the only reason you are called a believer (see Acts 5:14; 1 Timothy 4:12) is because you believe — you have faith, so don't let anybody tell you otherwise. The believer always believes. There is not a single sincere or genuine believer who stops believing. Hence, you're either a believer or you're not. The believer already has the measure of faith, so all he has to do is use or exercise the faith he has. We can also grow, increase or strengthen the faith we already have by CONTINUALLY HEARING and DOING the Word of Christ. (see Romans 10:17, with James 1:22). You can as well desire and receive the gift of faith, which is a special gift of highly developed faith that is given by the Holy Spirit to some believers for the profit of all believers. (see 1 Corinthians 12:9). As you continually hear and act on the Word of Christ, I am confident that your faith will grow exceedingly, just like the faith of the church of the Thessalonians during the apostle Paul's day. (see 2 Thessalonians 1:3).

Jesus Christ Did Not Walk or Judge by Sight

Now back to our discussion of the faith of Jesus, the prophet Isaiah prophesied about Jesus even before His birth, that, "His delight is in the fear of the Lord, and He SHALL NOT JUDGE BY THE SIGHT OF HIS EYES, nor decide by the HEARING of His ears;…He shall strike the earth with the rod of His mouth." (see Isaiah 11:3-4). Indeed when Jesus walked on this earth, **He never walked by the sight of His eyes, nor by the hearing of His ears**; He walked by **FAITH**. Jesus struck, even shook the earth with the rod of His mouth (that is, His words, His CONFESSION, or the Word of His Testimony). Whenever Jesus spoke, things happened, circumstances changed for the better: demons left their victims, diseases and sicknesses disappeared, the dead came back to life, the rowdy and turbulent winds and the waves of the sea became still. Thus, the evidence that Jesus walked by FAITH throughout His earth walk can be found in His confession, His love, and His miraculous works (which were also the result of His confession). The Bible teaches that when we truly believe something in our heart, we must speak that which we claim to believe (see 2 Corinthians 4:13); in this is the full expression of faith. Genuine or "living" faith (see James 2:26) always culminates in a confession. Therefore our faith cannot be separated from our confession, and/or our works (or deeds). Thus, Jesus' entire walk on earth was a walk of confession, resulting in great works of faith. His life is a true example of what it means to walk by faith and not by sight; it is a true example of what the New Creation man can do with the faith that we have; it is a true example of what it means to live and walk in the Spirit and not in the flesh (or sense realm).

Every Believer Has the Spirit (or Anointing) Without Measure

As the Son of God, Jesus was led by the Spirit of God. "For as many as are led by the Spirit of God, these are sons of God." (Romans 8:14). After Jesus' baptism in the Jordan, when He had prayed and the Spirit had descended upon Him in bodily form like a dove, the Bible says, "Then Jesus, being **filled with the Holy Spirit**, returned from the Jordan and WAS LED BY THE SPIRIT into the wilderness" (Luke 4:1). Jesus was LED by the Spirit, and He also walked "in the power of the Spirit" (see Luke 4:14), just like all believers today are required to do. The Bible says that "God anointed Jesus of Nazareth with the Holy Spirit and with power," and Jesus "went around doing good and healing all who were under the power of the devil, because God was with Him." (see Acts 10:38). "For He **whom God has sent** speaks the words of God, for GOD **DOES NOT** GIVE the Spirit BY MEASURE." (John 3:34). Thus Jesus had the Spirit without measure.

Today every believer has the Spirit or Anointing without measure, because God DOES NOT give the Spirit by measure. (see 1 John 2:20, 27; 2 Corinthians 1:21-22, with John 3:34). We believers, just like Jesus, have also been sent by God, and so we speak the words of God. (see John 17:18, 20; John 20:21; Matthew 28:18-20; Mark 16:15-18; with 2 Peter 1:15-21; 1 Corinthians 2:1-8; Colossians 3:17; 1 Peter 4:11). Therefore, after we have accepted Jesus and have received the Holy Spirit baptism, we don't need to pray again for the Anointing (or the Holy Spirit), because we already have Him without measure; we don't need to ask for "a double portion" of the Anointing (the Holy Spirit) as some ignorantly do. We are responsible for being filled (or remaining filled with the Spirit). Paul said, "And do not be drunk with wine, in which is dissipation; but **BE FILLED** with the Spirit, speaking to one another in psalms and hymns and spiritual songs, singing and making melody in your heart to the Lord, giving thanks always for all things to God the Father in the name of our Lord Jesus Christ, submitting to one another in the fear of God." (Ephesians 5:18-21). This is obviously instructive. We have the responsibility to **be filled with the Spirit**. A man whose life is filled with prayer, praise, thanksgiving, love, the study of the Word, meditation on the Word and confession of the Word, will be a man filled with the Spirit.

You see, many believers make the mistake of supposedly trying to imitate Elisha by asking God for a double portion of the Anointing (the Holy Spirit and His power); what they fail to realize is that Elisha NEVER ASKED GOD for a double portion of the Anointing (the Holy Spirit). Neither did Elisha ask ELIJAH for a double portion of the Anointing (the Holy Spirit). I will tell you what Elisha asked for. Now open your Bible to Second Kings 2:9, and I quote: "And so it was, when they had crossed over, that ELIJAH said to ELISHA, "Ask! What may I do for you, before I am taken away from you?" Elisha said, "Please LET A DOUBLE PORTION OF **your spirit** BE UPON ME." (II Kings 2:9). Many people don't understand this verse, and yet it is in plain language. Elisha asked for a double portion of the spirit of Elijah, not the Spirit of God. How can you even confuse the spirit of Elijah in this context with the Spirit of God? The spirit of Elijah is not the same as the Spirit of God. Besides, the Bible says God does not give the Spirit by measure (see John 3:34), so Elisha could not possibly be talking about getting a double portion of the Spirit of God; Elisha knew better. You need to remember that Elisha was also a prophet whom God had previously asked Elijah to anoint to replace or succeed him (see 1 Kings 19:16); he was the prophet Elijah's protégé and servant (see 1 Kings 19:21), and so he already had the Spirit of God and the power of God upon him; he already had the Anointing, and he already was the prophet God had appointed (without contention) to succeed Elijah. Thus Elijah was Elisha's master until he was translated into Heaven, and then Elisha took over the office of the prophet. Therefore the major difference between the two of them at this stage was that Elisha was not as courageous, strong, powerful and bold as Elijah regarding the things of God, or the prophetic ministry. Elijah had a strong spirit; he had courage and boldness of faith. He could do things that the ordinary prophet couldn't even imagine let alone try. Elijah was so courageous and powerful that he could remove his mantle, roll it, and strike the Jordan River to divide it for his own traveling (or crossing) convenience. (see 2 Kings 2:8). Such was the courage Elisha admired in Elijah and wanted a double portion of. And so when Elisha asked for a double portion of Elijah's spirit, he was basically asking for a double portion of Elijah's courage and boldness of faith, and he got it. (see 2 Kings 2:10-12). The Bible says, on Elisha's return trip from the Jordan, "He also took up the mantle of Elijah that had fallen from him, and went back and stood by the bank of the Jordan. Then he took the mantle of Elijah that had fallen from him, and struck the water, and said, "Where is the Lord God of Elijah?" And when he also had struck the water, it was divided this way and that; and Elisha crossed over. Now when the sons of the prophets who were from Jericho saw him, they said, "**The spirit of Elijah** (Note: not the Spirit of God, but the spirit of Elijah) rests on Elisha." And they came to meet him, and bowed to the ground before him." (2 Kings 2:13-15). Now, having received a double portion of the spirit of Elijah, Elisha went on to perform great miracles such as the healing of Jericho's waters (see 2 Kings 2:21), the raising from the dead of the

Shunammite's son (see 2 Kings 4:18-37), and the healing of Naaman's leprosy (see 2 Kings 5). Indeed, some of Elisha's miracles, including the multiplication of 20 barley loaves to feed 100 men, foreshadowed some of the miracles of our Lord Jesus Christ (see 2 Kings 4:42-44, with Matthew 16:9-10).

Again, Elisha was not asking for a double portion of the Spirit of God, as 2 Kings 2:9 clearly shows. You cannot ask for a double portion of the Holy Spirit (the Anointing or the Spirit of God). The Spirit of God (or the Anointing) is one. You either have the Spirit fully in you or upon you, or you don't have the Spirit at all, because again, "God does not give the Spirit by measure." (see John 3:34). You would remember that when the angel of God appeared to Zechariah to tell him about the son (John the Baptist) that he and his wife Elizabeth were going to have, the angel said that this son (John the Baptist) will go before Jesus Christ "IN the **spirit** and POWER OF ELIJAH." (see Luke 1:17). This meant that John the baptist was to possess the qualities of Elijah — his courage, power, and boldness of faith. And so Jesus testified of John the Baptist, that "If you are willing to accept it, he is the Elijah who was to come." (see Matthew 11:14 NIV). John the Baptist thus came in the spirit and power of Elijah; he possessed the qualities Elisha wanted double of when he asked for a double portion of Elijah's spirit. And according to Jesus, John the Baptist was the greatest of all men born of women (which includes all the prophets); yet, Jesus said of John the Baptist that, even though he is the greatest among those born of women (i.e natural or old creation men), whoever is least in the Kingdom of Heaven (i.e. the least new creation man) is greater than he. (see Matthew 11:11). Every believer today is greater than John the Baptist, because we come in the Spirit and power of the Lord Jesus Christ Himself. As Jesus is, so are we in this world. (see 1 John 4:17). Indeed it thrills my heart to be able to proclaim, just like Jesus did, that "The one who looks at me is seeing the One who sent me." (John 12:45 NIV). Therefore, today it is an act of ignorance and self-demotion for any believer to ask for the spirit of Elijah, even if you're asking for a triple or quadruple portion of it.

There are also those who try to defend this false doctrine of asking for a "double portion anointing" by referring to the story of Moses and the 70 elders of Israel where "the Lord came down in a cloud, and spake unto him (Moses), and took of **the Spirit THAT WAS UPON him** (Moses), and gave it unto the seventy elders: and it came to pass, that, when the Spirit RESTED UPON THEM, they prophesied, and did not cease." (Numbers 11:25 KJV). Many people read this and they say, "You see, God gave the spirit of Moses to the seventy elders too, and they prophesied." But obviously, that is not what the Bible is saying here. Sometimes I just wonder how some people read the Scriptures. The Bible doesn't say that it was of Moses' spirit God took and gave to the 70 elders. Rather God took OF **the Spirit (of God) that was UPON Moses** and gave it to the seventy elders. And when the Spirit RESTED UPON them, they prophesied and did not cease. (Read Numbers 11:25 again). This is a completely different scenario from the case of Elisha and Elijah. In the case of Moses and the 70 elders, even Moses himself acknowledged in verse 29 that it wasn't his own spirit that was given to the elders but **the Spirit of the Lord**. The Bible says that when the Spirit rested upon Eldad and Medad also (who had been listed among the 70 elders but had remained in the camp and did not go out to the tent) and they prophesied IN THE CAMP, Joshua upon hearing report of it told Moses to stop them from prophesying. But what did Moses say in response to Joshua? "Moses said unto him, Enviest thou for my sake? would God that all the Lord's people were prophets, and that **the Lord** would put **HIS SPIRIT** upon them!" (Numbers 11:29 KJV). In other words, Moses was happy that God had put His Spirit upon Eldad and Medad also, and even wished that all the children of Israel were prophets and that **God** would put **His Spirit** (note: not Moses' spirit, but God's Spirit) upon all His people. And so the point here is that the Spirit of God is one; you either have it (or more accurately, Him) in you or upon you in full measure or you don't have Him at all. The Bible says that the Spirit is one and the same in every anointed individual, but the work of the Spirit in (and through) the individual can vary from one individual to another. (see 1 Corinthians 12:4-11). Moreover, because the Spirit that is upon every anointed man is the Spirit of God Himself, God can, for instance, take of the Spirit that is upon me and give it to another person if necessary, just like He did with Moses and the 70 elders. Alternatively, God has ordained that I (or any apostle for that matter) can lay hand on any believer who has not yet received the Holy Spirit baptism, and the Spirit of God will come upon that believer. (see Acts 8:17-19; Acts 19:6).

As a New Creation saint, praying for a double portion of the Anointing or the Holy Spirit is just a mark of ignorance or a sign of unbelief, because you already have the Anointing (or the Holy Spirit) fully, without measure. The Bible says, "YOU HAVE AN ANOINTING from the Holy One, and you know all things. But the ANOINTING WHICH YOU HAVE RECEIVED from Him ABIDES IN YOU, and you do not need that anyone teach you; but as the same Anointing teaches you concerning all things, and is true, and is not a lie, and just as it has taught you, you will abide in Him." (see 1 John 2:20, 27). And so believers have the Anointing (or the Holy Spirit), and the Bible says that, to the one whom God has sent, God does not give the Spirit (or the Anointing) by measure. In the Old Testament, not every child of Israel had the Anointing or the Holy Spirit, because not every child of Israel was sent by God. God only anointed a select few with the Holy Spirit for His work and for His various purposes. But under the New Covenant, every believer has been sent by God; every believer has the Anointing; every believer is an anointed one. We all who were baptized into Christ have clothed ourselves with Christ or the Anointed One. (see Galatians 3:27). Christ means "the Anointed One". And so we have become members or parts of Christ's or the Anointed One's Body — of His flesh and of His bones (see Ephesians 5:30), which is why God has anointed us in the same way He anointed Jesus. We are permanently in the Anointing. Praise God! Hence, Paul writes: "Now He who establishes us WITH YOU in Christ and **HAS ANOINTED US** is God, who also HAS SEALED US and GIVEN US the Spirit in our hearts as a guarantee." (see 2 Corinthians 1:21-22). It doesn't get any clearer than this. Every believer is anointed. But the Anointing manifests only to the extent that you believe it and have a personal, deeply private encounter with the Holy Spirit, surrendering yourself completely to Him as a vessel for honor, sanctified and useful for the Master, prepared for every good work. (see 1 Timothy 4:14-15, with 2 Timothy 2:20-21). The manifestation of the Anointing continues and grows with a deep fellowship and communion with the Holy Spirit that only you can establish. And so today instead of praying for a double portion of the Anointing, after you have received the baptism in the Holy Spirit all you need to do is stir up (kindle afresh or fan into flame) the Spirit or the Anointing that is already in you (see 2 Timothy 1:6-7), surrendering your body to God as a living sacrifice and as a vessel for honor, walking by faith, praying, singing or worshipping in hymns, Psalms and spiritual songs, and speaking in tongues continually. (see Ephesians 5:17-19, with 2 Peter 1:5-8). In Acts 4:31, the early apostles (who had experienced the infilling of the Holy Spirit at Pentecost a few chapters earlier) prayed to the Lord and the place was shaken: "And THEY WERE FILLED with the Holy Spirit and spoke the word of God boldly." A study of their prayer will reveal that they didn't ask specifically to be filled with the Spirit. (see Acts 4:23-30). Nevertheless, prayer opens us up to be filled with the Spirit to accomplish the work God has called us to do. This is why we need to pray without ceasing. (see 1 Thessalonians 5:17). Ephesians 5:18-19 contrasts being filled with the Holy Spirit with being drunk with wine in the natural. It is an intoxicating spiritual experience indeed to be filled with the new wine of the Holy Spirit. May you be filled with the Spirit.

How Jesus Exercised His Faith

Now, back to our discussion on the faith of Jesus and how He exercised it throughout His earth walk, it is evident that Jesus exercised His faith by **confessing what He believed**. As we noted earlier, when the prophet Isaiah prophesied about Jesus before His coming, he said of Him that, "His delight is in the fear of the Lord, and He SHALL NOT JUDGE BY THE SIGHT OF HIS EYES, nor decide by the HEARING of His ears;…He shall strike the earth with the rod of His mouth." (see Isaiah 11:3-4). Indeed when Jesus walked on this earth, He never walked by the sight of His eyes, nor by the hearing of His ears; He walked by faith. And He struck, even shook the earth with the rod of His mouth — **His words**, His CONFESSION. Whenever Jesus spoke, things happened, circumstances changed for the better: demons left their victims, diseases and sicknesses disappeared, the dead came back to life, the rowdy and turbulent winds and the waves of the sea became still. Not only that, Jesus was always making one confession or another in agreement with or in line with what the Father had spoken about Him. (see John 12:49). For example, at the young age of twelve, Jesus knew and believed that God was His Father, and that it was a must for Him to be about His Father's business, and so He CONFESSED that belief to His earthly parents Mary and Joseph. (see Luke 2:49). Also, when Jesus was tempted by Satan in the wilderness, He CONFESSED **His faith in the Word of God**, and CONFESSED **His dependence on the Word of God** by declaring to Satan that "**It is written,** 'Man shall not live by bread alone, but BY EVERY WORD OF GOD.'" (see Luke 4:4). And so **Jesus lived by every Word of God**. Again, when Satan baited Jesus with worldly possessions in an attempt to lure Him into bowing and worshipping Satan, Jesus CONFESSED His **allegiance and faithfulness to God and His Word** by saying to him, "Away with you, Satan! For IT IS WRITTEN, 'You shall worship the Lord your God, and HIM ONLY you shall serve.'" (see Matthew 4:10). Jesus thus resisted Satan's temptation by faith in the Word of God, by CONFESSING the Word of God. Beloved, FAITH (in God and in His Word) is our shield against the temptations or attacks of the enemy. (see Ephesians 6:16). The Word of God is also our sword in our spiritual warfare against Satan our adversary (see Ephesians 6:17). Therefore, the shield of FAITH, and the sword of the Spirit, which is THE WORD OF GOD, are two important pieces of the armor of God which we are to put on to withstand the evil day and to stand against the wiles of the devil. (see

Ephesians 6). Jesus believed the Word of God and CONFESSED it, so He was able to withstand the evil day and stand against the wiles and temptations of the devil. And thus the Bible says that Jesus "was **in all points tempted** as we are, **yet without sin**." (see Hebrews 4:15). We must also resist the devil by confessing the Word of God, if we claim to believe it. The Spirit said through Paul that we should give no place to the devil. (see Ephesians 4:27). We must all learn to say, "It is written," and then confess the Word of God always.

Faith is "Work"

When His disciples asked Him, "What must we do to do the **works** God requires?" Jesus answered, "The **work** of God is this: to **believe** in the One He has sent." (John 6:28-29). Thus Jesus calls believing in Him the only work that God requires of us; He calls faith "work." No wonder the Book of Hebrews implores us to LABOR to enter into His rest (see Hebrews 4:11), and then adds that we who have BELIEVED do enter that rest. (see Hebrews 4:3). Our only work or labor is to believe in Jesus Christ, and believe in the Word of Christ. This is why we are called "believers." Believing is what we do. We are doers of God's Word. (see James 1:22). This means we believe and act on God's Word; we don't act on human wisdom or opinions. (see 1 Corinthians 2:5). Our only work is faith in the finished work of Christ, faith in the power of God. Indeed, FAITH is work. The early apostles understood this. Hence, James uses "work" and "faith" interchangeably in his epistle. (see James 2:21, with James 2:23). This means that when we believe and act on God's Word, God counts it as work; He sees it as faith, but He counts it as work. When we believe, we are agreeing with God. (see Amos 3:3). True faith always moves us to agree with God and speak the words of God (2 Corinthians 4:13), even in the face of contradictory sense evidence. Therefore there is no true or genuine faith that does not culminate in a confession. And since the believer's daily walk is a walk of faith (see 2 Corinthians 5:7), our daily walk, in essence, must be a walk of CONFESSION. We have to believe the Word of God with our heart, and then use our mouth to confess the Word daily unto salvation (see Romans 10:10, with Hebrews 4:14) — salvation from diseases, poverty, and every power of darkness or every negative circumstance. That is how we work out our salvation, as the apostle Paul urges us to do with fear and trembling. (see Philippians 2:12-13). Therefore working OUT our salvation does not mean we should work FOR our salvation, since we already have salvation (see 1 John 5:13; John 5:24; John 6:47). It simply means fighting the good fight of faith and laying hold on the salvation or eternal life that is already ours. (see 1 Timothy 6:12).

Jesus has truly given us a great example to emulate as we fight the good fight of faith, as we walk by faith or walk in the Spirit. Jesus was **always making confessions of the Word of God**. He Himself stated that the words He spoke were not His own words but the words of God the Father. (see John 7:16; John 8:28; John 14:10; John 12:49; John 17:8). And thus Jesus was always confessing the Word of God, **holding fast His confession**. No wonder the Bible calls Jesus the Apostle and High Priest of our CONFESSION (see Hebrews 3:1 ESV). Today Jesus is the Lord we all confess to be saved. (see Romans 10:9-10). We confess the Word of God, which is Jesus Christ. (see John 1:1, 14; Revelation 19:13). And we are urged to hold fast our confession of Jesus Christ and of the Word of God. (see Hebrews 4:14). This means we are to commit to continually making a confession of what God's Word says about who we are in Christ, what we have in Christ, and what we can do in Christ. We are to commit to continually confessing everything that God has said (in the Bible), every declaration and every promise which we claim to believe. That is the obedience of faith or obedience to the faith that the apostle Paul talks about. (see Romans 1:5; Romans 16:26, with 2 Corinthians 4:13). The Christian walk is truly a walk of faith (see 2 Corinthians 5:7); and CONFESSION is the proof of faith (see 2 Corinthians 4:13). Jesus said that out of the abundance of the heart the mouth speaks. (see Luke 6:45). When our hearts are full of Christ, we will always confess Christ; when our hearts are full of the Word of God, we will always confess the Word. Confession, then, is at the heart of our Christian walk. Hence, Christianity is also known in some circles as "The Great Confession." There is simply no salvation without a confession, "for with the mouth CONFESSION is MADE UNTO SALVATION." (see Romans 10:10). Jesus was a great confessor, and we have to imitate Him. The Bible says that we ought to walk **just as** Jesus walked. (see 1 John 2:6).

Study to Know the Word of God and Confess it Continually

Jesus knew the Word of God and He confessed it all the time. The first step to a life of faith is to hear and to know the Word of God (or the Word of Christ). The Bible says, "faith comes from hearing, and hearing through the Word of Christ." (see Romans 10:17 ESV). When you hear what the Word of God says, then are you able to believe it, for you cannot believe what you haven't heard. And so the hearing of the Word of God brings faith. And confession is the proof of faith. Jesus knew what the Word said about Him; He knew who He was and He confessed it all the time. Let us look at a few of Jesus' confessions. Jesus said (sometimes by inference) that, "**My Father loves Me**, because I lay down My life that I may take it again (see John 10:17); I am the Son of the living God (see Matthew 16:15-17; Luke 22:70); I and My Father are one (see John 10:30); he who has seen Me has seen the Father (see John 14:9); I came from the Father; again, I am going to the Father (see John 16:28); Before Abraham was, I Am (see John 8:58); I am the Way, the Truth and the Life: no one comes to the Father except through Me (see John 14:6); I am the Light of the world (see John 8:12); I am the true Vine (see John 15:1-5); I am the good Shepherd (see John 10:11); I am the Door of the sheep (see John 10:7); I am the Bread of life (see John 6:35); If anyone thirsts, let him come to Me and drink. He who believes in Me, as the Scripture has said, out of his heart will flow rivers of living water (see John 7:37-38); I am the Resurrection and the life (see John 11:25); I am the Messiah (see John 4:26; Matthew 26:63-64; Mark 14:61-62); I am the Lord of the Sabbath (see Matthew 12:8);" and so forth.

Jesus also used words or His confession to perform practically all His miracles, whether it was saying to the leper, "I am willing; be cleansed" (see Luke 5:13), or crying out to dead Lazarus, "Lazarus, come forth!" (see John 11:43). The Word of God on Jesus' lips healed all who were oppressed by the devil. (see Acts 10:38). The Word of God on your lips will do the same thing, if you trust in the Word. Jesus trusted in the Word of God. Only those who trust in God's word are able to sincerely confess it or act on it (which is also how we walk by faith). When you sincerely trust in God's Word and confess it, it will produce miraculous results, just as Jesus' confessions produced extraordinary miracles. Indeed, Jesus knew who He was and He confessed it continually. That is what the Christian walk should be for us also. We are to follow the example of Jesus Christ the Apostle and High Priest of our CONFESSION, and commit to continually confessing or saying the same things in agreement with what God our Father has said about us. And to be able to do this effectively, we have to study to know the Word of God, especially what the Father has said concerning us.

The Word of God is The Glory of the Lord and a Mirror for the Believer

The Word of God is **the glory of the Lord** and it is also **a mirror** that reflects back to you the true image God has of you. If you want to know who you truly are and how God sees you in Christ, you have to look in the Mirror of God, which is the Word of God. In fact, if you're not already abiding in the Word or walking by meditation on the Word, confession of the Word, and doing of the Word, begin immediately. Get into the Word, find out what it says about who you are and what you have and can do in Christ, then believe it, confess it continually, and act upon it. As believers, the Word of God is our mirror indeed, and it is important that whenever we look in it and walk away, we don't forget what we looked like. The Spirit, speaking through the apostle Paul, says that "we all, with unveiled face, BEHOLDING AS IN A MIRROR **the glory of the Lord**, are being transformed into the same image from glory to glory, just as by the Spirit of the Lord." (2 Corinthians 3:18). In other words, as we continually look in the Mirror (or Word) of God, which is also the GLORY OF GOD and meditate on the Word, beholding it and not departing from its teachings, we are being transformed by the Spirit of God into the image we see, and that image is the glory of the Lord; and so, we are being transformed from one level of glory to another. This also means that we believers are the glory of God; hence we see our own reflection as we look in the Mirror (or the Word) of God, and thus are being transformed into the substance of that image by the Spirit of God from glory to glory. In this regard, James also adds that we are not just to look in the Mirror (or the Word), but **do the Word** also. He says, "But **be doers of the word**, and not hearers only, deceiving yourselves. For if anyone is a hearer of the word and not a doer, he is like a man observing his natural face IN A MIRROR; for he observes himself, goes away, and immediately forgets what kind of man he was. But he who looks into the perfect law of liberty (that is, the Word of God) AND CONTINUES IN IT, and IS NOT A FORGETFUL HEARER but A DOER of the work, this one WILL BE BLESSED IN WHAT HE DOES." (James 1:22-25). Simply put, looking in the Word of God or hearing the Word without acting on the Word or believing it and doing (confessing, and claiming, and laying hold on) what it says about you, is a useless exercise that benefits no one. You need to act on the Word of God. You need to believe the Word of God enough to be moved to confess what it says, do what it says and claim or lay hold on what it says. When you READ the Word and you BELIEVE the Word, you will CONFESS or SPEAK the Word (see 2 Corinthians 4:13); you will act on the Word. Of course we all speak and do what we believe, and we believe what we do. And so those who believe right will act right, and those who believe wrong will act wrong. Right actions (or right living) will be born out of your right believing, and vice versa.

Beloved, it is important that you believe and speak the truth of God's Word and not the words of this world or your own (idle) words. It is important that you don't go about saying or confessing what you feel, see or hear in the natural realm (particularly if it's contrary to what the Word of God says). Don't confess the ugly picture your current circumstance may be presenting to you; instead, continually say or confess what God's Word says about you, even in the face of contradictory sense evidence. Agree with the opinion of God by speaking and doing God's Word, rather than agreeing with and communicating what your senses tell you. Be a doer of God's Word. God's Word expresses God's opinions, plans and thoughts. God's Word has integrity. The Bible is truly a revelation from God to us; it is God Himself speaking to us; "it is God-breathed" (see 2 Timothy 3:16 NIV). Therefore, as a believer, the Word of God is your creative material. It will definitely give you what it promises, if you go for it. Trust in God's faithfulness to keep His promises, and then claim those promises through your confession and actions. In your day-to-day conversations and confessions, don't use your own words or the words of this world but the Father's words. We noted earlier that when Jesus walked here on earth, He CONFESSED His faith in the Word of God, and CONFESSED His dependence on the Word of God by declaring to Satan that "It is written, 'Man shall not live by bread alone, but BY EVERY WORD OF GOD.'" (see Luke 4:4). In whose word have you also put your faith today? Whose word are you living by. On whose word are you depending? I hope it is God's Word. Make a decision that you will not believe anything that is contrary to God's Word — it doesn't matter if it is the pastor's word, the doctor's word, the banker's word, the lawyer's word, your teacher's word, your friend's word, your boss' word, your siblings' word or your parents' word. Don't let their titles fool you; ONLY God's Word is life. (see John 6:63; Prov. 4:22). Anything contrary to God's Word is death. Moreover, you cannot walk with God unless you agree with Him, unless you agree with His Word. (see Amos 3:3).

Indeed when you choose to believe the Word of God and to depend on the Word of God, when you choose to live by the Word of God, when you choose to fully agree with the Word of God and to act on the Word of God, it will put you not only in opposition with your own senses (or feelings) sometimes, but also in disagreement with many men. It will even bring much persecution upon you. But that's OK. Don't apologize for it. And let not your heart be troubled, because the Lord Jesus who has overcome the world is with you, and you have overcome the world with Him. (see Matthew 20:28; John 16:33, with 1 John 5:4). The Bible says, "And they (believers) overcame him (the adversary) by the blood of the Lamb and by the word of their testimony (or confession of the Word of God), and they did not love their lives to the death." (Revelation 12:11).

I don't know what trials or afflictions you're going through today. Perhaps you're experiencing some challenges with your health, or the doctor has diagnosed you with a deadly sickness or disease, and you're troubled and wondering what to do about your condition. But I want you to cheer up and realize that though the doctor's report may be a medical fact, in the eyes of God, such a report isn't true, because it's not in line with God's image of you or God's provisions for you in Christ Jesus, that are revealed in His Word. The prophet Isaiah said, "Who has believed our report?" (see Isaiah 53:1). God's Word is our report, and God's Word is truth (see John 17:17); it is the only true report, and it is in our own interest to believe it. God's Report is that Jesus Himself took up our infirmities and bore our diseases, and by His stripes we were healed and are healed. (see 1 Peter 2:24, with Isaiah 53:5; Matthew 8:17). Therefore, whatever report the doctor has given you is contrary to God's report, so you have to decide which of the two reports you will believe; and I suggest you believe God's report. Look in God's Mirror and see yourself healed. Whatever condition you have been diagnosed with is not consistent with God's report about you or God's image of you, so refuse to think or meditate on it with your heart and mind. Reject that condition in Jesus' Name. Don't think on it, and don't say or utter it. Jesus said, "Therefore TAKE NO THOUGHT, SAYING,…" (Matthew 6:31 KJV). Saying something out or voicing it is basically how you take (hold of) a thought. Hence, Jesus is saying that you shouldn't take (hold of) an evil or negative thought by saying it. Again Jesus said, "Take heed what you hear" (see Mark 4:24), and not just what you hear, but also "how you hear" (see Luke 8:18). We have to be careful what we hear, and how we hear it. When we hear something that is contrary to the truth revealed by the Spirit of God, we must shut the doors of our hearts against it, so that it will not come out of our hearts (through our confession) to defile us. Jesus said that it is not what goes into the mouth that defiles a man, but what comes out of the mouth (from the heart) that defiles a man. (see Matthew 15:11, 17-20). When you focus on, process and (from your heart) say a negative or evil thought that you heard, you give birth to that thought; you endorse it and give it substance; YOU GIVE IT POWER TO EXIST IN A TANGIBLE FORM AND TO RULE OVER YOU, because you are a king and where your word is, there is power. (see Revelation 1:6, with Ecclesiastes 8:4). Remember also that "Death and life are in the power of the tongue, and those who love it will eat its fruit." (Proverbs 18:21). Thus the apostle Paul, in his letter to the Philippians said, "Finally, brethren, whatever things are TRUE, whatever things are NOBLE, whatever things are JUST, whatever things are PURE, whatever things are LOVELY, whatever things are OF GOOD REPORT, if there is any VIRTUE and if there is anything PRAISEWORTHY—MEDITATE ON THESE THINGS." (Philippians 4:8). In other Words, we are to MEDITATE on God's Word, since God's Word is the only thing that is true, noble, just, pure, lovely, of good report, excellent and praiseworthy. You have to train yourself to only think or meditate on things that are consistent with the truth of God's Word. For as a man thinks in his heart, so is he. (see Proverbs 23:7).

Beloved, you cannot stop Satan from suggesting negative or evil thoughts to you (because that is his job), but you can stop yourself from accepting those thoughts, focusing on them, processing them and saying them from your heart. You cannot stop others from saying, for instance, that you are sick, or you are going to die, but you can stop yourself from saying, "I am sick." You can stop yourself from saying "I'm going to die," and say instead with the Psalmist that, "I shall not die, but live, and declare the works of the Lord." (Psalm 118:17). As believers, we don't walk by feelings nor by sight; we walk by faith. When you voice a negative thought or condition by saying, "I am …(whatever negative condition it is)" or "I have …(whatever negative condition it is)," you endorse that condition as your own, as your new image or identity. In other words, you accept or choose Satan's opinion or image of you (which is the lie that you're sick) over God's opinion or image of you (which is the truth that you're healed). And in that instant, that negative condition gains the right of mastery over you. (see Romans 6:16). This is also why the Bible says, "And no inhabitant [of Zion] will say, "I AM SICK"; the people who dwell there will be forgiven their iniquity and guilt." (Isaiah 33:24 AMP). Every believer is an inhabitant of Zion. (see Hebrews 12:22). And so you should never say, "I am sick," regardless of how you feel. Never confess sickness and other negative or deadly conditions. Your confession must always be a confession of life and godliness. Your confession must always be consistent with God's opinion of you that is revealed in His Word. Our Lord Jesus Christ said that we must be careful with our confession or the words we speak, because on the day of judgment we will answer for every careless or idle word we have spoken. (see Matthew 12:36). Jesus knows the power of words; He knows that every word we speak is a seed we are sowing, which will take flesh and bear fruit, whether good or evil. (see Matthew 13:24-26; Mark 4:26-29). And so our confession is important to Jesus, who is the Apostle and High Priest of our confession. (see Hebrews 3:1).

Therefore, as a believer, always make sure to confess your true image or identity in Christ; always make sure that whatever you think or say after the words "I AM…" is true, pure, just, lovely, of good report, virtuous and praiseworthy. Reject every thought that is contrary to the mind and will of God for your life. The Bible says, "If any man be in Christ, he is a new creature: old things are passed away; behold, all things are become new" (2 Corinthians 5:17 KJV). This means that even if you were born with a sickness or a curse, now that you're in Christ, you don't have it anymore; it has passed away. Every old image or condition that you used to claim as your own has now passed away (or is dead; it's gone). You are now a new creature — a perfect being that didn't exist before. And you have been given ALL THINGS that pertain to LIFE and GODLINESS. (see 2 Peter 1:3). You now live in divine health. The Holy Spirit is in you giving life to your mortal body. (see Romans 8:11). So sickness or disease no longer has a place in you. If you see any sickness in your body, it has no right to exist there, so you can command it to leave in the Name of Jesus, and expect it to leave. Sin also no longer has a place in you. Poverty, defeat and failure no longer have a place in you, so give them no place. Satan no longer has authority over you, praise God! You now have authority over Satan and his angels. The Bible says you have overcome them. Now, note that it doesn't say you are trying to overcome them, or you are about to overcome them, or you are going to overcome them; it says you HAVE OVERCOME them, because He who is in you is greater than he who is in the world. (see 1 John 4:4). The victory that overcomes them is our faith. (see 1 John 5:4). So believe that you have divine health. Believe that you are a world-overcomer, that you are more than a conqueror through Christ who loved you. (see Romans 8:37). This is the image and the consciousness that God wants you to have of yourself; this is how He wants you to think about yourself. So this must be your daily confession. You have overcome that sickness in your body, so don't try to overcome it; just walk right out of it; speak to that sickness and say, "Get out of my body in Jesus' name because I have overcome you!" Glory be to God! Give no place to the devil. Allow the life of Jesus to be manifested in your mortal body.

Someone will say, "But didn't James ask if there is any sick among you?" Yes he did. He said, "IS ANYONE AMONG YOU SICK? Let him call for the elders of the church, and let them pray over him, anointing him with oil in the name of the Lord." (James 5:14). Clearly, James said "Is anyone among you sick?" (see James 5:14). He didn't say "Is there anyone among you who is not sick?" Sickness is an anomaly in the church; it is not the norm; it is not supposed to be there. The norm is divine health. But you can only live at the level of your revelation or knowledge. As we mentioned earlier, the Bible says, "And no inhabitant [of Zion] will say, I am sick; the people who dwell there will be forgiven their iniquity and guilt." (Isaiah 33:24 AMP). As a believer, you are an inhabitant of Zion. (see Hebrews 12:22). But Mount Zion, like any other mountain, has levels — there is the top or the peak, but there is also the bottom or the base and the sides, so you have to decide which part of Mount Zion you want to dwell. You can dwell in the heights, at the peak with God, where you will never say "I am sick." Or you can choose to dwell at the base, on the slopes or go up and down the slopes. In other words, you can choose to be a baby or carnal Christian and dwell at the base, or you can desire the sincere milk of the Word and grow and come to maturity and be a mature son of God, a spiritual man who dwells at the peak of Mount Zion with God and imitates God, walking in love, in divine health, and in every blessing that belongs to the inhabitants of Mount Zion. The Spirit says through the apostle Paul that, the heir, as long as he is a child (or underage), does not differ at all from a slave, although he owns the whole estate. (see Galatians 4:1). This means that **for as long as** you remain a child or underage in Mount Zion, for as long as you remain a baby Christian, you will live like a slave, being ruled by sicknesses, sin, depression, fear, and every power of darkness, although you are a master over all these things. So I decided long ago that I would not remain a child; no, not when I have full access to a Bible. I choose to study the Word and grow; I choose to wait on the Lord. For the Bible says, "But those who wait on the Lord Shall renew *their* strength; They shall mount up with wings like eagles, They shall run and not be weary, They shall walk and not faint." (Isaiah 40:31). Like the eagle, I choose to dwell at the peak of the mountain, at the top of Mount Zion; I choose to dwell in the secret place of the Most High, where no plague shall come near my dwelling. But for those who choose to dwell at the base or go up and down the slopes of Mount Zion and so do not live consistently in divine health, God has still made provision for your healing whenever you get sick: He says call for the elders of the church (those who are dwelling at the peak of Mount Zion), and let them pray over you, anointing you with oil in the name of the Lord; and the prayer of faith will save you, and the Lord will raise you up. (see James 5:14-15).

As a believer, whether sickness will have dominion over you or not depends on what you believe about sickness. If you want to live in divine health, you must renew your mind with the Word of God until you not only believe, but KNOW in your spirit, body and soul that you are THE HEALED of God (see Isaiah 53:5; 1 Peter 2:24; Psalm 103:3; Psalm 107:20), and that the Spirit of life is in you giving life to your mortal body. (see Romans 8:11). In fact, if you have been diagnosed with any sickness, you can walk right out of that sickness right now in the NAME OF JESUS. Believe that it is God's will for you to prosper and BE IN HEALTH even as your soul prospers. (see 3 John 1:2). Believe that NO PLAGUE shall come near your dwelling. (see Psalm 91:10). And believe that it is Jesus who has made healing an eternal provision and reality for you through the redemption that came through His blood. He is the precious chief cornerstone laid in Zion, and anyone who believes in Him will by no means be put to shame (see 1 Peter 2:6). You will by no means be put to shame for believing in Jesus and believing that He Himself bore all your sins and all your diseases and sickness in His own body on the cross, so that you wouldn't have to bear them again. (see Isaiah 53:5; 1 Peter 2:24; Matthew 8:17). Nothing shall by any means harm you, because the Lord Jesus is with you always, even to the end of time.

Beloved, God wants you to have a glorious image or picture of yourself and maintain a victory mindset, because you are glorious and victorious in Christ. The Bible says, "But thanks be to God, who in Christ always leads us in **triumphal** procession, and through us spreads the fragrance of the knowledge of Him everywhere." (2 Corinthians 2:14 ESV). There is such a thing as the mindset of the righteous; it is a victory mindset, and God wants you to have this mindset because you are righteous in Christ. This is why He has given you His Word (His Mirror) to meditate on and renew your mind with, so that you will be transformed not just in your quality of life, but foremost, in your pattern of thinking, not conforming to the ways of the world. (see Romans 12:2, with Joshua 1:8). May this be a reality for you.

Be Consistent in Your Confession – Hold Fast Your Confession

To emphasize further the importance of consistent positive confession, the Bible says, "Death and life are in **the power of the tongue**, and those who love it will eat its fruit." (Proverbs 18:21). Ask yourself what kind of fruit you want your tongue to bear: Life or Death? Always choose life; always speak life, for your tongue indeed controls your life, just as a rudder controls a ship. (see James 3:1-5). Jesus knew this, and so He consistently spoke life during His earth walk. He declared that the words He spoke were Spirit and LIFE. (see John 6:63). When you abide in Jesus and allow His words to abide in you, you will speak the way He spoke, you will speak the words He spoke, and your words, just like His, will be no ordinary words but SPIRIT and LIFE. (see John 6:63, with Colossians 3:16-17). Ordinary words don't create miracles; words that are spirit and life do. Thus Peter said, "If anyone speaks, they should do so as one who speaks THE VERY

WORDS OF GOD." (see 1 Peter 4:11). The very words of God are Spirit and life. Jesus performed practically all His miracles with the very words of God. (see John 12:49; John 14:10). And we can also, by speaking the very words of God perform many miracles. Everything in the Word of God that ever was possible to Jesus Christ the Son of Man is likewise possible to the believer. We can do all things through Christ who strengthens us. (see Philippians 4:13). Praise God!

Beloved, be careful what you believe in your heart and say with your mouth, because Jesus said in Mark 11:23-24 that whatever you believe in your heart and say with your mouth will come to pass. Believe and confess positive things only. As believers we should never confess failure or defeat. Victory is ours in Jesus' name. Success is ours in Jesus' name. Therefore, no matter how you feel, don't say, "I'm sick," but rather say, "I'm healed," because that is what the Word of God says about you. (see Isaiah 53:5; 1 Peter 2:24). Don't confess your (negative) feelings, confess the Word of God. Never say, for example, that "I'm catching a cold" or "I have cancer." That is a bad confession; in fact, you're agreeing with the enemy and thus empowering the enemy by making such a confession. Rather, say something like this: "Satan, Jesus bore all my sins and diseases on the cross, and by His stripes I was healed and I am healed, and so you have no right to attack me with a cold (or cancer). Therefore, in the name of Jesus I reject the cold (or cancer) and cling to my healing. I am healed in the mighty name of Jesus." This is the right confession, because it agrees with the Word of God. After you have made such a confession, begin to act like you're truly healed, begin to do what you couldn't do before, and you will see yourself made whole; indeed there will be a manifestation of your healing when you truly believe and confess the Word of God regarding your healing in Christ. The Word of God never fails. When you stick with the Word, you will by no means be put to shame; God will make His Word good, for He watches over His Word to perform it (see Jeremiah 1:12), and He has also said that His Word shall not return to Him void, but it shall accomplish the thing for which it was sent (see Isaiah 55:11). So don't be afraid to believe and to speak and claim God's promises, for He who has promised is faithful, who also will do it. Proverbs 18:7 says, "A fool's mouth is his destruction, and his lips are the snare of his soul." Don't speak anything that will bring destruction upon you, because whenever you speak death or confess destructive things like disease or poverty, you are ensnaring or trapping yourself by your own words (see Proverbs 6:2). Beloved, you are not a fool, so don't speak like one. You are wise; Christ is your wisdom. (see 1 Corinthians 1:30). You have the mind of Christ. (see 1 Corinthians 2:16). You are also righteous in Christ. (see 2 Corinthians 5:21). And the Bible says, "The mouth of the righteous is a well of life" (see Proverbs 10:11). So always speak life. Speak positive thoughts.

It is highly important to be consistent in your confession (or the things you speak in agreement with the Word of God). Don't be a double-minded person. Don't make a positive confession now, and then confess the opposite later because of your feelings or your fluctuating circumstances, because the second will nullify the first. For instance, don't say "I'm healed" now, and the next moment you see another symptom of the sickness, turn around to say, "I'm sick." Don't walk by sight (or sensory perception), walk by faith (or by the Word of God). For your confession to be effective or for it to work for your good, you must not stagger (or base your confession on observable changing circumstances and sensory perceptions); you have to be fully persuaded about the Word or promise of God, and base your confession on it, giving glory to God, just like our father Abraham did (see Romans 4:19-21). You have to believe the Word before you speak or confess it (see 2 Corinthians 4:13), so that you will continually make the same confession without doubting it or contradicting yourself, regardless of what you feel, see, or hear. The Bible says you are to hold fast your confession. (see Hebrews 4:14). People who make contradictory confessions do so because they walk or judge by the sight of their eyes, and decide by the hearing of their ears; they harbor doubts in their heart; they waver between two opinions because they don't completely believe or trust God's Word (God's opinion). James says, "he who doubts is like a wave of the sea driven and tossed by the wind. For **let not that man suppose that he will receive anything from the Lord**; he is a double-minded man, unstable in all his ways." (see James 1:6-8). Don't be a double-minded man, or else, you won't receive anything from God.

God's Word has integrity; God's Word has power. Therefore you can trust God's Word. The Bible says, "No word from God will ever fail" (see Luke 1:37 NIV). When you stand on God's Word, you are standing on a word that will never fail, you are standing on steady ground. When you build your hope on God's Word, you are building on an immovable Rock. The Bible says, as we noted earlier, that the words Jesus spoke during His earth walk were the words of the Father (see John 12:49), and so Jesus performed practically all His works or miracles with the words of the Father. (see John 14:10, 24). Just as God's words in Jesus' mouth never failed, they won't fail in your mouth. They didn't fail in Peter's mouth when he commanded the lame man at the gate of the temple which is called Beautiful to rise up and walk in the name of Jesus. (see Acts 3:1-9). We must all submit to the Word of God; we must all bring ourselves to believe and to speak the words of the Father, just as our Lord Jesus Christ did. It is in our own interest to do so. God's Words are creative words; they're healing words; they're demon-dominating words; they are words filled with God and His faith. Indeed, God's Word is powerful. The Bible says that the worlds were framed by the Word of God. (see Hebrews 11:3). So, go for the Word! Begin to frame your world with the Word of God: meditate on the Word, trust the Word, act on the Word, and God will make good His promises. Indeed God watches over His Word to perform it (see Jeremiah 1:12). Therefore, be an imitator of God as a dear child (see Ephesians 5:1) and begin to speak or confess the Word of God; begin to claim all the exceedingly great and precious promises that have been given to us by God; begin to call those things which do not exist as though they did (see Romans 4:17), and they will become. That is the God-kind of faith; that is how you partake of the divine (or God) nature. (see 2 Peter 1:4). God is watching over His Word to perform it, as you believe and speak it.

Today, if you will just look into the Mirror (or Word) of God, it will show you who you truly are. And once you look and see your true reflection from the Mirror of God, grasp that image, lay hold on it, never forget it, and never stop speaking or confessing it. As a start, here are a few truths about your image or identity, and your rights and privileges in Christ that you can begin to confess right now. Commit to continually saying or confessing these truths, and your life will never be the same: "Jesus Christ is my Lord and Savior, and I believe God has raised Him from the dead. (see Romans 10:9-10). He is alive forevermore! (see Revelation 1:18). I have the Son of God, and so I have the life of God in me; I have eternal life; I have "zoe" in me. (see 1 John 5:11-13). I no longer bear the image of the first Adam, for I bear the image of Jesus Christ the Son of God, I am conformed to His image. (see Romans 8:29; 1 Corinthians 15:49). I am the righteous and glorified son of God. (see Romans 8:29-30). I have the Living God as my Father; I am the begotten child of God (see James 1:18; John 1:12). I have God's incorruptible seed in me. (see 1 Peter 1:23; 1 John 3:9). I have the nature of God. (see Ephesians 4:24). I am a partaker of the divine (or God) nature (see 2 Peter 1:4). I am the brother of Jesus, and Jesus is not ashamed to call me His brother. (see Hebrews 2:11). As Jesus is, so am I in this world. (see 1 John 4:17). I have the mind of Christ. (see 1 Corinthians 2:16). I have the Spirit of the Son of God in me. (see Galatians 4:6). I am one with Christ not just in Spirit but also in body. (see 1 Corinthians 6:15, 17). As a member (or part) of the Body of Christ, of His flesh and of His bones, I am one with the Lord of the Universe (see Ephesians 5:30), and His matchless, mighty power is mine. I have the resurrection life in me; I have the Spirit of life in me; I have the same Spirit that raised Jesus from the dead in me. (see Romans 8:11). I have the same power that raised Jesus from the dead in me. (see Ephesians 1:19-20). I am a conscious possessor of the Spirit of God, and the power of God. The authority and power I have is that of Jesus Christ Himself, and it cannot fail. Oh yes, I am a success; I am an overcomer! (see 1 John 4:4; 1 John 5:4). I am complete in Christ. (see Colossians 2:9-10). I am the anointed of God. (see 1 John 2:20, 27; 2 Corinthians 1:21). I am the sanctified child of God. (see Hebrews 10:10). I have been perfected by Christ. (see Hebrews 10:14). I am holy. (see 1 Corinthians 3:16-17; 1 Peter 2:5, 9). I cannot fail; I cannot be defeated; I am a victor. (see 2 Corinthians 2:14; 1 Corinthians 15:57). I live the

Spirit Life

abundant life. (see John 10:10). I live a life of victory. (see 2 Corinthians 2:14). I live a life of favor. (see Ephesians 1:6; Psalm 5:12). I permanently stand in grace (unmerited favor), and I have access to grace by faith. (see Romans 5:2). God surrounds me with favor as with a shield. (see Psalm 5:12). I have peace with God. (see Romans 5:1). Christ Himself is my peace. (see Ephesians 2:14). I permanently have fellowship with God through His Son Jesus Christ. (see 1 Corinthians 1:9; 1 John 1:3-4). I permanently have fellowship with the Holy Spirit. (see 2 Corinthians 13:14). I am led by the Holy Spirit as a son of God (see Romans 8:14). I am born into God's Family as a son (see James 1:18; Romans 8:16), and so the Father's home is my home. I come from above; I am a citizen of Heaven. (see Philippians 3:20). Whatever I ask the Father in the name of Jesus, He will give me. (see John 16:23). Whatever I ask (or demand) in the name of Jesus will be done. (see John 14:13-14). I will not and do not live in lack; I lack nothing. (see Psalm 23:1). I am more than a conqueror through Christ who loved me. (see Romans 8:37). I am God's elect. (see Romans 8:33). I have found the light of life. (see John 8:12). I am no longer walking in the darkness of sense knowledge; I walk by faith and not by sight. (see 2 Corinthians 5:7). All things are possible to me because I believe. (see Mark 9:23). I am blessed (together) with Abraham the believer. (see Galatians 3:9). I am blessed with every spiritual blessing in the heavenly places in Christ. (see Ephesians 1:3). I have been freely given all things. (see Romans 8:32). I am an heir of the world. (see Romans 4:13, with Galatians 3:29). I am an heir of God and joint-heirs with Christ. (see Romans 8:17). I am an heir of all things; all things are mine; the whole world is mine. (see 1 Corinthians 3:21-22). I am rich. (see 2 Corinthians 8:9). Yes, the Almighty is my gold and my precious silver. (see Job 22:25). I eat the good of the land. (see

Isaiah 1:19). I have the peace of God. (see Philippians 4:7; John 14:27). I have the joy of God; the joy of the Lord is my strength. (see John 15:11; Nehemiah 8:10, Galatians 5:22). Jesus Himself bore all my sins and diseases, and by His stripes I was, and I am healed. (see Isaiah 53:5; 2 Peter 2:24; Matthew 8:17). I have divine health, because the Spirit of life is in me giving life to my mortal body. (see Romans 8:11). No plague shall come near my dwelling. (see Psalm 91:10). I am a new creation in Christ, a new species of being. (see 2 Corinthians 5:17). There is now no condemnation for me because I am in Christ Jesus. (see Romans 8:1). I have no more consciousness of sin. (see Hebrews 10:1-3). I am a kind of firstfruit of God's creation, I'm God's absolute best. (see James 1:18). I'm God's workmanship. (see Ephesians 2:10). I am fearfully and wonderfully made. (see Psalm 139:14). I am created according to God in true holiness and righteousness. (see Ephesians 4:24). I am the righteousness of God in Christ Jesus. (see 2 Corinthians 5:21). God has established me in righteousness. (see Isaiah 54:14). I am created to do good. (see Ephesians 2:10). I know who I am. I am no ordinary being; I am not a mere man. (see 1 Corinthians 3:3). I am a god-man. (see Psalm 82:6; John 10:34-36). I am the beloved and special child of the Most High God. (see John 1:12; James 1:18; Psalm 82:6; 1 Peter 2:9). I am the Father's will; I am born of His will (see James 1:18), so I am able to do His will. God is working in me both to do and to will for His good pleasure. (see Philippians 2:13). My sufficiency (or ability to meet all needs) is from God. (see 2 Corinthians 3:5). God's power is at work within me. (see Ephesians 3:20). Christ's working works in me mightily. (see Colossians 1:29). I can do all things through Christ who strengthens me. (see Philippians 4:13). I fear nothing; I am bold as a lion. (see Proverbs 28:1). No weapon formed against me shall prosper, and every tongue that rises against me in judgment I shall condemn, for this is my inheritance, and my righteousness is of God. (see Isaiah 54:17). Just as the mountains surround Jerusalem, so the Lord surrounds me, both now and forever. (see Psalm 125:2). God's divine power has given to me all things that pertain to life and godliness. (see 2 Peter 1:3). I have authority in the Name of Jesus over demons, over the laws of nature, and over all circumstances. (see Matthew 28:18-20; Mark 16:17-18). I was bought at a price. (see 1 Corinthians 6:20). My Father loves me. (see John 16:27). I am the head and not the tail; I am above only and not beneath. (see Deuteronomy 28:13). I am born to win. I am seated in the heavenly realms with Christ and in Christ. (see Ephesians 2:4-6). My life is hidden with Christ in God. (see Colossians 3:3). I am in God (see Colossians 3:3), and God is in me. (see 1 John 4:4; 1 Corinthians 3:16; Ephesians 4:6). I am one Spirit with the Lord; I and the Lord are one. (see 1 Corinthians 6:17). I am a branch of the true Vine. (see John 15:5). I am a member of the Body of Christ. (see Romans 12:5; 1 Corinthians 12:12). Christ Himself is my life. (see Colossians 3:4). My life is hidden with Christ in God. (see Colossians 3:3). I am seated above all principalities and powers, and all things are in subjection under my feet. (see Ephesians 2:4-6, with Ephesians 1:20-23). The spirits are subject to me in the name of Jesus. (see Luke 10:17-20). I am the light of the world. (see Matthew 5:14-16). I am the salt of the earth. (see Matthew 5:13-16). I am an ambassador for Christ. (see 2 Corinthians 5:20). I am a king and a priest to my God and Father. (see Revelation 1:6). I reign in life; I reign above every circumstance and situation. (see Romans 5:17). And I proclaim the praises of Him who called me out of darkness into His marvelous light. (see 1 Peter 2:9; Hebrews 13:15)." "To God our

Savior, who alone is wise, be glory and majesty, dominion and power, both now and forever. Amen." (Jude 1:25).

We believers are truly blessed, and we should never stop confessing our blessings. We have been given exceedingly great and precious promises in Christ. And the Bible says that all the promises of God in Christ are Yes, and in Him Amen, to the glory of God through us. (see 2 Corinthians 1:20). It is through laying hold of these precious promises of God that we become partakers of the divine (or God) nature. (see 2 Peter 1:4). May this be a reality for you.

Use Your Words to Get Things Done

There is a story in the Bible about a Roman centurion who came to Jesus to seek healing for his servant who was lying at home "paralyzed, dreadfully tormented." The Bible says that when Jesus offered to go home with the centurion and heal his servant, "The centurion answered and said, "Lord, I am not worthy that You should come under my roof. But ONLY SPEAK A WORD, and my servant will be healed. For I also am a man under AUTHORITY, HAVING soldiers UNDER ME. And I SAY to this one, 'GO,' and HE GOES; and to another, 'COME,' and HE COMES; and to MY SERVANT, 'Do this,' and he does it." (Matthew 8:8-9).

Beloved, the Centurion in these verses above spoke a very profound truth, and Jesus even marveled at that. (see verse 10). Indeed, people in positions of authority ONLY SPEAK A WORD, and things get done. They only speak words and their subjects carry out those words. For example, when I worked as a manager/supervisor at a certain job, I would say, "I want this table moved from point A to point B." And those workers under me would carry out those WORDS and the table was moved from point A to point B. You would notice in this example that MY WORDS MOVED THE TABLE without me moving even a finger. Jesus said that WORDS spoken in faith (faith here signifies authority) can MOVE a mountain. (see Matthew 17:20). You have no authority in the spirit realm until you believe and exercise the authority God has given to you as a disciple of Christ. The Bible assures us as disciples of Christ that the spirits are subject to us in the name of Jesus (see Luke 10:17-20). And so all we have to do is speak a word, and they will obey it, they will do our word.

Now, here's another example in the natural realm. When you ask anybody, "Which President of the United States killed Osama Bin Laden?" Everybody would immediately say that it was President Barack Obama. But ask yourself this, "How did President Obama kill Osama?" He killed him with A WORD. He just authorized or ordered Osama killed. He only SPOKE A WORD that Osama should be killed at such and such a time. And his generals (working through the Navy Seals) carried out his WORD.

It is the same principle at work in the spirit realm. The Bible says, "Bless the Lord, you His angels, who excel in strength, WHO DO His **word**, heeding the voice of **His word**." (Psalms 103:20). It is the angels who DO or execute the Word of God. As a believer you are authorized, IN THE NAME OF JESUS, to heal the sick, cast out demons, take up serpents, etc. (see Mark 16:17-18; Matthew 10:8; Mark 3:14-15). Therefore you are in a position of authority, and your authority was given to you by the Lord Jesus Christ Himself. It is an authority that answers to no one but God. You have Satan and all his angels under your authority (see Colossians 2:15; Hebrews 2:14; 1

John 4:4; Mark 16:17-18; Matthew 28:18-20; James 4:7; Ephesians 4:27; Ephesians 2:4-6, with Ephesians 1:20-23); they submit to you in the Name of Jesus. (see Luke 10:17, 20). You also have all of God's angels under your authority; they also minister FOR you or serve you. (see Hebrews 1:14). Today all you have to do to assert or exercise your authority is to SPEAK A WORD. The Bible says, "And whatever you do IN WORD or DEED, do all in the name of the Lord Jesus, giving thanks to God the Father through Him." (Colossians 3:17). This means you are an authorized representative or ambassador for the Lord Jesus, and so when you SPEAK or DO anything in His name, it is as though the Lord Jesus were speaking or doing it Himself. You have Jesus' authority to function in His name. And that authority can never fail; it can never be subverted.

I will never forget what the Lord Jesus told me when He called me into ministry; He said, "Know your authority, for it is My authority." Indeed, you can never be intimidated when you know that your authority is that of God Himself. God has conferred on every believer His own authority. We are all heirs of God and joint-heirs with Christ. (see Romans 8:17). And we are all called to be partakers of the divine (or God) nature. (see 2 Peter 1:4). We have the angels of God ministering FOR us (see Hebrews 1:14), just as they minister for God our Father. And the Bible says their number is INNUMERABLE; we have an innumerable company of angels. (see Hebrews 12:22). Praise God! Therefore, all we have to do is SPEAK a word, and the Lord Jesus will make sure that the angels execute our WORD; they will bring it to pass.

Indeed, as believers we speak in the name of the Lord Jesus, and so our words are the words of Jesus, they are the very words of God (see

1 Peter 4:11), and "NO WORD from God will ever fail." (see Luke 1:37 NIV). The Bible also says that we are kings (see Revelation 1:6; Luke 22:29), and where the WORD of a king is, there is power (see Ecclesiastes 8:4). Whatever decrees we make will be established for us. (see Job 22:28). When, for instance, you decree or say to a sick person, "Be healed," and you do not doubt it in your heart, it will be so — the angels will move into action right away to bring that WORD to pass — to get that sick person healed. Thus the Bible says that God watches over His Word to perform it. (see Jeremiah 1:12). All things are possible to the believer. (see Mark 9:23). We can have what we say. (see Mark 11:23). We just need to believe, and then speak what we want. Paul said, "And since we have the same Spirit of faith, according to what is written, "I believed and therefore I spoke," WE ALSO BELIEVE AND THEREFORE SPEAK " (II Corinthians 4:13). Now, what do you desire today? Is it healing? Is it money? Is it a job? Is it a promotion? Is it a house? Is it a car? Is it a baby? Is it a husband, or wife? If you can BELIEVE in your heart and SPEAK it with your mouth, you will have it. These are the words of Jesus, not mine (see Mark 11:23-24). O, how I love these words! I am meditating on this all my life, and I am laying hold of it. I can have whatever I say if I believe what I say. Awesome! Just awesome! Why say what I don't want, when I can say what I want? Why say I am sick, when I can believe and say I am healed? Why say I'm broke, when what I really desire is to be rich? Believers need to watch our confession, really! You will have what you say and believe! May you never stop BELIEVING and SPEAKING what you truly desire. You are in a position of authority, so use your words to get things done. Hold fast your confession as you claim the exceedingly great and precious promises of God and partake of the divine (or God) nature, having

escaped the corruption that is in the world through lust. (see 2 Peter 1:4).

In the next Chapter, we will continue our discussion of how Jesus lived and walked in the Spirit, by examining His love for mankind, because His faith which we just discussed, was expressed through love. The Bible says that faith works through love (see Galatians 5:6), and so we cannot talk about Jesus' faith without talking about how that faith worked through love.

Chapter 8
Jesus' Faith Worked Through Love

What We Can Learn From How Jesus Loved the World or Walked in Love

TODAY MANY PEOPLE are looking for love, acceptance, and security. The world is yearning for love. Yet, love (in its purest form) has eluded the world, because there is no true love (or agape) outside of God. The world (of sinners) cannot love. And when they try, they only end up with a fake (conditional and selfish) kind of love. Indeed Satan (who is the god of this world — see 2 Corinthians 4:4) cannot love, and neither can his children (see 1 John 3:10). Satan has no capacity for love, and people who are in his kingdom have no capacity for love either. This is why there are so many dysfunctional relationships in the world today. It is also the reason for the increase in crime and wars. God is the only source of true love. The Bible says "LOVE IS OF GOD; and **everyone who loves is born of God and knows God**. He who does not love does not know God, for GOD IS LOVE." (see 1 John 4:7-8). Jesus is born of God. Jesus is God's only begotten Son, and so Jesus has the love nature of God, and He manifested this love nature throughout His earth walk. The Bible says that Jesus loved His own to the last and highest degree. (see John 13:1 AMP). As we noted in the previous Chapter of this book, it was faith working through love (see Galatians

5:6) that brought Jesus into this world to die for our sins. Jesus said, "For God **SO LOVED** THE WORLD, that **HE GAVE** His **only begotten Son**, that whosoever believes in Him should not perish, but have everlasting life." (John 3:16 KJV). There is only one reason Jesus Christ was born unto us. And the reason (according to John 3:16) is LOVE. God loved us with His great love (see Ephesians 2:4), and He loved us while we were still sinners. (see Romans 5:8). Because God loved us so greatly, He DEMONSTRATED His own love toward us by GIVING His only begotten Son Jesus Christ to die for us while we were still sinners. Indeed, Love GIVES. Love DEMONSTRATES itself. Love is ACTION-ORIENTED; Love is ACTIVE. Love is not just expressed in word or tongue, but in DEED and in TRUTH. (see 1 John 3:18). The Bible says, "In this the love of God was MANIFESTED toward us, that God has sent His **only begotten Son** into the world, **that we might live through Him**." (1 John 4:9). God loved us and **manifested** His love through the GIVING of Jesus Christ, **His only begotten Son,** to die for us, so that we might live through Him. In this same love act of God we also see the love of Jesus or how Jesus also loved us. Jesus allowed Himself to be given to the world by God the Father; He yielded to the Father's will every step of the way (see John 4:34; John 6:38; Luke 22:42; Hebrews 10:7-10; Philippians 2:5-8). The Bible says that Christ, through the eternal Spirit, **OFFERED Himself** without spot to God. (see Hebrews 9:14). This evidently points us to the love Jesus Himself also has for us. The Book of Revelation says of believers that, JESUS "**LOVED US** and washed us from our sins in His own blood, and has made us kings and priests to His God and Father." (see Revelation 1:5-6). Jesus indeed was God (that is, Love) manifested in the flesh. (see 1 Timothy 3:16, with 1 John 4:8). The apostle Paul writes that JESUS CHRIST "**HAS**

LOVED US and **GIVEN Himself for us**, an offering and a sacrifice to God for a sweet-smelling aroma." (see Ephesians 5:2). Jesus' love for mankind is summed up in the sacred act of GIVING Himself or laying down His life for us. Jesus Himself said, "Greater love has no one than this: to lay down one's life for one's friends." (John 15:13 NIV). After saying this, Jesus went ahead to lay down His life for us to demonstrate and teach us this greater love. Thus, John also writes, "BY THIS WE KNOW LOVE, because He laid down His life for us. And WE ALSO OUGHT TO LAY DOWN OUR LIVES FOR THE BRETHREN." (1 John 3:16).

Have You Accepted God's Great Love?

Indeed, God is LOVE (see 1 John 4:8); there isn't a more accurate description of God than this. LOVE is the single most accurate word that characterizes God. Don't let anybody deceive you into thinking any differently of God. God is not out to get you (or harm you), as some will have you wrongly believe; He is for you, He loves you, and He wants to fellowship with you if you're willing to have Him. "For I know the thoughts that I think toward you, says the LORD, **thoughts of peace and not of evil**, to GIVE YOU **a future** and **a hope**. Then you will **call upon Me** and go and **PRAY to Me**, and I WILL LISTEN TO YOU. And you will SEEK Me and FIND Me, **when** you **search for Me with all your heart.**" (Jeremiah 29:11:13). Indeed, God has extended an open invitation to everyone. (see John 3:16; 1 John 1:3; Matthew 11:28; Revelation 3:19-20). God loves you greatly; but, you see, He will never violate your free will by forcing you to accept His love, which is in Christ Jesus. When Jesus walked on this earth as the exact representation of God (see Hebrews 1:3; 1 Timothy 3:16), He wouldn't violate anybody's free will. In fact, it is deeply touching to observe a vivid expression of the Father's love as Jesus laments, "O Jerusalem, Jerusalem, the one who kills the prophets and stones those who are sent to her! HOW OFTEN I WANTED TO GATHER YOUR CHILDREN TOGETHER, AS A HEN GATHERS HER CHICKS under her wings, BUT YOU WERE NOT WILLING!" (Matthew 23:37). THEY WERE **NOT** WILLING! How tragic! And Jesus wouldn't violate their will. That is God!

My dear friend, whether or not you will accept God's love is your decision to make, and God respects that. But know this: Love is God's very nature, and He loves you unconditionally (all the time), and I mean, ALL THE TIME, regardless of what you have done or failed to do. God knows your every failure, every weakness, every sin; He knows every hidden secret of your heart, and still loves you anyway. In fact, nobody ever merited or earned God's love, and nobody ever will. The Bible says, "But God demonstrates His own love toward us, in that **while we were still sinners**, Christ died for us." (Romans 5:8). God's love is ours simply by grace (unmerited, undeserved favor). And His love and goodness leads us to repentance and salvation. (see Romans 2:4; Titus 3:4-5). God "desires ALL MEN to be SAVED and to come to the knowledge of the truth." (1 Timothy 2:4). He "is longsuffering toward us, not willing that ANY should perish but that ALL should come to repentance." (see 2 Peter 3:9). That "ALL, " my dear friend, includes YOU. "For there is no partiality with God." (Romans 2:11).

Truly, the ultimate expression of God's great love for us is in the giving of His only begotten Son Jesus Christ as a propitiation for the sins of mankind. (see John 3:16, with Hebrews 2:17; 1 John 3:16; 1 John 2:2). "IN THIS THE LOVE OF GOD WAS MANIFESTED TOWARD

US, that GOD HAS SENT His ONLY BEGOTTEN SON INTO THE WORLD, **THAT WE MIGHT LIVE THROUGH HIM.**" (1 John 4:9). And so ask yourself today whether you're living through Christ. If you're not, then you haven't yet accepted the great love of God, and I encourage you to do so.

It behooves every man and woman today (out of our own free will) to accept God's love which is in Christ Jesus. I testify that I know and have experienced God's great love; yes, I am loved, and I feel loved every second of the day, because I have chosen to accept God's great love which is in Christ Jesus. I recommend that you do the same right now, so that you can say with me: "Behold what manner of love the Father has bestowed on us, that we should be called children of God! Therefore the world does not know us, because it did not know Him." (1 John 3:1).

Know How Jesus Has Loved You, And Love The Same Way

Indeed Jesus Christ has left us a great example of the highest degree of love. Jesus' faith and love were working together when He gave Himself and died on the cross for us. Jesus believed that, by giving us the example of His love, believers would be bearers and sharers of His love — this selfless and unconditional kind of love — all around the world. And so He gave us a commandment to love one another AS He HAS LOVED US. He said, "This is My Commandment, that you LOVE ONE ANOTHER AS I HAVE LOVED YOU." (John 15:12). Beloved, you can only love as Jesus has loved you, when you know and understand how Jesus has loved you. Jesus laid down His life for you and I. He took our death, and gave us His life — eternal life. That is how Jesus has loved each one of us. Each one of us has to know how Jesus has loved him or her. You have to know how Jesus has loved you. I know how Jesus has loved me, and so I say with Paul that, Jesus "LOVED me and GAVE HIMSELF FOR me." (see Galatians 2:20). Today the greatest way we can also express our love for the brethren is to give ourselves or LAY DOWN OUR LIVES for them. (see 1 John 3:16). We walk in the Spirit when we walk in love; and we walk in love by GIVING ourselves for others or for the brethren. Paul says, "For the love of Christ compels us, because we judge thus: that if One died for all, then all died; and He died for all, that **those who live should live no longer for themselves**, but for Him who died for them and rose again." (2 Corinthians 5:14-15). We no longer live for ourselves but for Christ. And the way to live for Christ is to live and walk in love (agape). We walk in love by giving ourselves, as Christ did. Love is giving. Hence the Bible says, "it is more blessed to give than to receive." (see Acts 20:35). In other words, it is more blessed to love than to be loved. Paul said in his letter to the Corinthians that the more abundantly he loved them, the less he was loved. (see 2 Corinthians 12:15). Such is the walk of love. And so we are to learn to be imitators of Paul, and more so "imitators of God," as beloved children, walking in love even as Christ has loved us. (see 1 Corinthians 4:15-16, with Ephesians 5:1-2). Walking in love means giving ourselves to the brethren. And one major way to do this is to be bold and fearless in preaching the gospel everywhere, regardless of the threat of imprisonment, stoning, or death, just as Jesus did for us, just as the early apostles did for us.

The gospel is a Person; the gospel is Jesus Christ. To preach the gospel is to preach Christ. Those who preach the true gospel preach Christ, not commandments and laws or philosophical moral lessons which can neither change anyone nor save anyone. Philip preached Jesus to the Ethiopian Eunuch. (see Acts 8:35). Paul also preached Jesus (see Acts 17:18), he preached Christ. (see 2 Corinthians 1:19; 1 Corinthians 15:12). All the apostles preached Jesus Christ. Indeed Jesus Christ is the gospel of the Kingdom. Christ is the wisdom of God and the power of God. (see 1 Corinthians 1:24). Christ (the gospel) is the power of God unto salvation to all who believe. Christ is God's only saving power for the world, for all who believe. God has no alternative way to save anyone. We have to make this information known to the whole world. Peter said, "Nor is there salvation in any other, for there is no other name under heaven given among men by which we must be saved." (Acts 4:12). Paul also said, "Therefore let it be known to you, brethren, that through this Man (Jesus Christ) is preached to you the forgiveness of sins; and by Him everyone who believes is justified from all things from which you could not be justified by the law of Moses." (Acts 13:38-39). Then writing to the Corinthian Church, Paul again said, "For the Son of God, JESUS CHRIST, **WHO WAS PREACHED among you by us**—by me, Silvanus, and Timothy—was not Yes and No, but in Him was Yes. For all the promises of God in Him are Yes, and in Him Amen, to the glory of God through us." (II Corinthians 1:19-20).

Indeed, the preaching of the gospel is the only means by which we may bring eternal life to every creature. Therefore let us preach the gospel, let us preach Christ! In Him is salvation, in Him is victory. The Bible says that Jesus came into the world to seek and to save that which was lost. (Luke 19:10). He sought us, saved us, and left us in this world for a while, so that we can proclaim the good news of salvation to those who are ignorant of it, to those who don't know that Jesus has completed the work of salvation for the whole world and that all we need to do to receive this salvation and enter into the victory is to accept or believe in Jesus Christ the Savior. Thus, we win souls for the Kingdom of God by simply preaching Jesus Christ who is Salvation, who is the gospel. The Bible says, "…and he who wins souls is wise" (Proverbs 11:30). There is nothing wiser for a Christian to do than to preach Christ, and by so doing win souls for the Kingdom. This is why Jesus, who became our wisdom from God (see 1 Corinthians 1:30) commands us to "go into all the world and preach the gospel to every creature" (see Mark 16:15), and thus demonstrate wisdom by winning souls. Will you respond to the voice of Wisdom? Clearly, the preaching of the gospel is not optional; it is a command given to each disciple of Christ; it is our mission in this world. To each of us Jesus says, "As the Father has sent Me, I also send you." (see John 20:21). Let us therefore go into all the world and preach the gospel, for our time in this world is limited, and we cannot relent, for the Lord Jesus Christ is coming soon. Glory to God! Paul said, "For if I preach the gospel, I have nothing to boast of, for NECESSITY is laid upon me; yes, **woe is me if I do not preach the gospel!**" (1 Corinthians 9:16). No matter where you find yourself today, preach Christ to somebody. For in this is our love demonstrated. Indeed, the highest and greatest expression of love is to give or lay down one's life for the brethren.

Jesus walked in love from His birth to His death. His whole life was the definition of love. Every step Jesus took was a step rooted and grounded in love. From the time He was 12 years old, Jesus knew He was on this earth to carry out His Father's (love) business. (see Luke 2:49). Jesus came into the world as a product or a demonstration of the Father's love (see John 3:16; Romans 5:8; 1 John 4:9), and so the business of the Father that He had in mind all along was to reveal the Father's love to the world by first teaching the Word of God to the poor, healing the brokenhearted and all those who were oppressed by the devil, and then going to the cross to pay the penalty of man's disobedience (with His own life), so as to set us (the captives of Satan) free, open the eyes of the blind, and proclaim the acceptable year of the Lord. (see Luke 4:18-19). Beloved, Jesus was a Man on a mission, and the mission was Love. Jesus came to reveal God the Father as Love, "For God is Love." (see 1 John 4:8). Love is the nature of God. Therefore today all of us who have been born of God have been born of Love. And so we have the love nature of God; we have the capacity to love just like our Father God and just like our Brother Jesus. We are partakers of the divine (God or Love) nature (see 2 Peter 1:4), and so we are to imitate God our Father. (see Ephesians 5:1-2). "Behold what manner of love the Father has bestowed on us, that we should be called children of God!" (see I John 3:1). Today we are children of God because of the manner of love the Father has bestowed on us, and since God is Love, we can also say that we are children of Love. "We love Him because He first loved us." (1 John 4:19). Thus the Bible commands us that "if God so loved us, WE ALSO OUGHT TO LOVE one another." (see I John 4:11). We are to walk in love, as Christ loved us and gave Himself for us. (see Ephesians 5:2). Walking in love is the proof that we are walking in the Spirit; it is the proof that we are spiritual men, and not mere men. (see 1 Corinthians 3:1-3). It is the proof that we are born of God. (see 1 John 4:7-8).

Jesus' walk of love began and continued with humility, and ended with exaltation by God (see Philippians 2:5-11, with John 13:3-17).

And so Jesus tells us also that whoever humbles himself as a little child is the greatest in the Kingdom of Heaven. (see Matthew 18:4). Jesus who, being in the form of God was equal with God, gave up the prestige, majesty, glory, and honor of being God, and made Himself of no reputation, taking the form of a bondservant, and coming (to earth) in the likeness of men. And being found in appearance as a Man, He humbled Himself and became obedient to the point of death, (and not just any ordinary death), even the death of the cross. (see Philippians 2:5-8). Jesus the Holy One (see Luke 1:35) first humbled Himself to be baptized by a man (John the Baptist) in the baptism of repentance (even though He had nothing to repent of), so as to fulfill all righteousness (see Matthew 3:13-15) for the sake of sinful man whom He had come to Substitute/Represent and die for. Jesus, because of His great love, also allowed Himself to be led by the Spirit into the wilderness to be tempted by Satan. (see Matthew 4; Luke 4). The God of the whole Universe, because of His great love for mankind, was now a Man identifying with the weaknesses of men in the temptations of Satan, which He overcame and lived a sinless life. (see Hebrews 4:15).

Evidently, Jesus' entire earth ministry was the definition of love. The Bible says that from the time following His temptation by Satan in the wilderness, Jesus **began to preach** and to say, "Repent, for the kingdom of heaven is at hand." (see Matthew 4:17). The Bible also says, "And Jesus went about all Galilee **teaching** in their synagogues, **preaching the gospel** of the Kingdom, and **healing** all kinds of sickness and all kinds of disease among the people." (Matthew 4:23). "And they were astonished at His teaching, for His word was with authority." (Luke 4:32). The Bible also adds that Jesus "went through

EVERY CITY AND VILLAGE, preaching and bringing the glad tidings of the kingdom of God. And the twelve (apostles) were with Him" (see Luke 8:1). Jesus loved mankind so much and desired for all to be saved and to come to the knowledge of the truth, such that, even when His mother and brothers (who thought He was out of His mind — see Mark 3:21, 31) came to Him while He was teaching, and could not approach Him because of the crowd, and thus sent for Him saying, "Your mother and Your brothers are standing outside, desiring to see You," Jesus answered and said to them, "My mother and My brothers are these who hear the word of God and do it." (Luke 8:19-21). Oh, see what manner of love makes a Man put the work of God and the salvation of mankind above His own personal interests! Such was, and is the love of Jesus Christ.

Having come into the world as a demonstration of the Father's love, Jesus did everything He did because of love. **Jesus never sought His own interest; He never lived for Himself. He did not please Himself.** (see Romans 15:1-3). He preached the gospel everywhere because of His love for mankind. For Him, it was a must to preach the Kingdom of God; for this very purpose He was sent. (see Luke 4:43). Being always in harmony with the will of the Father, Jesus desired (above all things) and still desires for all men to be saved and to come to the knowledge of the truth. (see 1 Timothy 2:4; 2 Peter 3:9). And so Jesus preached the gospel declaring Himself as **the way, the truth and the life** without whom no one can come to the Father (see John 14:6). He is the only Mediator between God and man. (see 1 Timothy 2:5). Indeed, salvation is found in no other but Jesus Christ, "for there is no other name under Heaven given among men by which we must be saved." (see Acts 4:12). And so today if we claim to love our neighbors as ourselves, if we claim to love others as Christ has loved us, we have to preach the gospel of Christ to them and make them understand that "whoever calls on the name of the Lord (Jesus Christ) shall be saved." (see Romans 10:13). Paul asks, "How then shall they call on Him in whom they have not believed? And how shall they believe in Him of whom they have not heard? And how shall they hear without a preacher? And how shall they preach unless they are sent? As it is written: "How beautiful are the feet of those who preach the gospel of peace, who bring glad tidings of good things!" (Romans 10:14-15).

Jesus preached the gospel because of His love for mankind, and we who walk in love today must also preach the gospel out of love, because we have been sent for this very purpose. (see Mark 16:15-16). It is only when people hear the gospel that they can believe, call on the Name of the Lord, and be saved. "So then faith comes by hearing, and hearing by the Word of God." (Romans 10:17).

Jesus' Miraculous Works Were the Fruits of Love

Besides preaching the gospel everywhere, Jesus also performed many wonderful love deeds. Indeed all His miraculous works were the fruits of love. Jesus' faith worked through love to produce many works of faith or fruits of love, as He went about **doing good** and **healing all** who were oppressed by the devil. (see Acts 10:38). The very first miracle Jesus performed, for instance, reveals how His faith worked through love. The Bible says Jesus and His disciples were invited to a wedding in Cana of Galilee, and Mary the mother of Jesus was also at the wedding. "And when they ran out of wine, the mother of Jesus said to Him, "They have no wine." Jesus said to her, "Woman, what does your concern have to do with Me? My hour has not yet come." His mother said to the servants, "Whatever He says to you, do it." (John 2:3-5). And so, here we are informed about a shortage of wine at the wedding, which (as those of us who have been in a wedding before would acknowledge) was a potentially disastrous and embarrassing situation for the hosts of this wedding. And so when Mary the mother of Jesus noticed and informed Jesus about the situation, even though Jesus indicated that the timing was quite premature, that His hour had not yet come, His love nature constrained or compelled Him to act against time to save the day and protect the honor of the bridegroom. Paul tells us that the love of Christ has a compelling or constraining effect. (see 2 Corinthians 5:14). And thus, Jesus, out of His great love, performed the great miracle of changing water into the finest wine (see John 2:6-10) at this wedding feast (which in itself was a celebration of love). Oh, what an amazing miracle of love at such an august celebration of love! How fitting that Jesus' first miracle in a series of miracles in which His faith worked through love, was performed at a love celebration or wedding! How fitting that Jesus' first miracle changed water into wine for mankind, which was a SIGN **manifesting His glory** (see John 2:11) and pointing to His blood which He was to pour out for the salvation of mankind. (see Mark 14:24; Matthew 26:28).

In Capernaum, a city of Galilee, we continue to see the faith of Jesus working through love, as He casts out an unclean spirit from a demon-possessed man (see Luke 4:33-37), heals Peter's mother-in-law from a high fever (see Luke 4:38-39; Matthew 8:14-15), and heals all those brought to Him who were sick or demon-possessed (see Luke 4:40-41; Matthew 8:16-17). We also see how by the Lake of Gennesaret, Jesus, having used Simon's fishing boat as a podium to teach the Word of God to the multitudes, lovingly rewards Simon mightily by giving him an astonishing net-breaking catch of fish — a miracle which caused Peter to confess that he is a sinful man and to confess Jesus as Lord — which caused Peter and all who were with him to forsake all and follow Jesus. (see Luke 5:1-11). In another instance, we see Jesus cleansing a leper and declaring His ever enduring willingness to heal, when the leper implores Him saying, "Lord if You are willing, You can make me clean." (see Luke 5:12-14). Here, Jesus showed that He is as willing to heal the sick as He is to save the sinner. Jesus' love deeds continue throughout the gospels as He forgives the sins of a paralytic and heals him (see Luke 5:17-26), calls Levi (or Matthew), a tax collector to follow Him, and accepts the invitation to attend a great feast (or dinner) held in His honor in the house of Levi — a dinner which had Him eating with a bunch of tax collectors considered sinners by the scribes and the Pharisees. At this feast, we also see Jesus responding to the complaints of the scribes and the pharisees against His association with sinners, not by distancing Himself from "sinners," but rather, by lovingly identifying Himself with sinners (whom He had come to Substitute and die for), and declaring the calling to repentance of sinners (and not the righteous) as the reason for His coming to earth. (see Luke 5:27-32).

Again, we see His love revealed, as Jesus the Lord of the Sabbath (see Matthew 12:8; Mark 2:28) puts doing good and saving men's lives above the ceremonial keeping of the Sabbath Day. (see Luke 6:6-11; Matthew 12:11-12). At the tomb of Lazarus we also see the love of Jesus in full manifestation as He weeps with those who were weeping. (see John 11:35, with Romans 12:15). Jesus also displayed His love for Martha, Mary and Lazarus (see John 11:5) and comforted them, as He silenced all doubts, all fears, and all sorrows, and turned all grief into gladness, turned all tears of sorrow into tears of joy by crying out to dead Lazarus "with a loud voice, "Lazarus, come forth!" And he who had died came out bound hand and foot with graveclothes, and his face was wrapped with a cloth. Jesus said to them, "Loose him, and let him go." Then many of the Jews who had come to Mary, and had seen the things Jesus did, believed in Him." (John 11:43-45). Hallelujah! What a testimony of Jesus' love Lazarus, Mary and Martha now had! Jesus also proved by raising Lazarus from the dead, that He is indeed the resurrection and the life. (see John 11:25).

There are many other miracles Jesus performed that we need to examine more closely to further understand how the faith of Jesus worked through love. The Bible says that on a certain occasion Jesus "went into a city called Nain; and many of His disciples went with Him, and a large crowd. And when He came near the gate of the city, behold, a dead man was being carried out, the ONLY SON of his mother; and she was a WIDOW. And a large crowd from the city was with her. When the Lord saw her, HE HAD **COMPASSION** ON HER and said to her, "Do not weep." Then He came and touched the open coffin, and those who carried him stood still. And He said, "Young man, I say to you, arise." So HE WHO WAS DEAD SAT UP AND BEGAN TO SPEAK. And He PRESENTED him TO HIS MOTHER. Then fear came upon all, and they glorified God, saying, "A great prophet has risen up among us"; and, "God has visited His people." And this report about Him went throughout all Judea and all the surrounding region." (see Luke 7:11-17). In this story, the great love and unbridled compassion of our Lord Jesus Christ is palpable.

Indeed, Jesus had, and still has compassion for mankind. The Bible tells us of many other instances where Jesus was moved with compassion for people. In one of these instances, He saw the multitudes, and "was moved with **COMPASSION** for them, because they were weary and scattered, like sheep having no shepherd." (see Matthew 9:36). "Then He said to His disciples, "The harvest truly is plentiful, but the laborers are few. Therefore pray the Lord of the harvest to send out laborers into His harvest." (Matthew 9:37-38). Jesus' compassion was also what made Him feed 4000 men with 7 loaves of bread and a few little fish. The Bible says, "Now Jesus called His disciples to Himself and said, "**I have COMPASSION on the multitude**, because they have now continued with Me three days and HAVE NOTHING TO EAT. And I DO NOT want to send them away HUNGRY, lest they FAINT on the way." Then His disciples said to Him, "Where could we get enough bread in the wilderness to fill such a great multitude? Jesus said to them, "How many loaves do you have?" And they said, "Seven, and a few little fish." So He commanded the multitude to sit down on the ground. And He took the seven loaves and the fish and gave thanks, broke them and gave them to His disciples; and the disciples gave to the multitude. So they all ate and were filled, and they took up seven large baskets full of the fragments that were left. Now those who ate were four thousand men, besides women and children." (Matthew 15:32-38). Jesus also had compassion on everyone who came to Him for healing. There is this particular story in the Bible about a time when Jesus entered Capernaum and a centurion came to Him, pleading with Him, saying, "Lord, my servant is lying at home paralyzed, dreadfully tormented." And Jesus said to him, "**I will come and heal him.**" (see Matthew 8:5-7). Such was the compassion of Jesus; He never turned anyone away who had faith in Him for healing, and He won't turn you away today when you need Him, and believe in Him for your healing or whatever you need.

The disciples of Jesus saw firsthand the love and faith of Jesus in action, and they did not hesitate to record them for us. On a certain occasion, Jesus was in a boat with His disciples crossing over to the other side. "But as they sailed He FELL ASLEEP. And a windstorm came down on the lake, and they were filling with water, and were in jeopardy. And they came to Him and AWOKE HIM, saying, "Master, Master, we are perishing!" Then HE AROSE and rebuked the wind and the raging of the water. And they ceased, and there was a calm. But He said to them, "WHERE IS YOUR FAITH?" And they were afraid, and marveled, saying to one another, "Who can this be? For He commands even the winds and water, and they obey Him!" (Luke 8:23-25). Beloved, as we all know, unbelief displeases Jesus (see Hebrews 11:6), and it is a sign of unbelief for us to be afraid, to worry or to panic over any situation when Jesus is present with us, and of course, we know He is always present with us, for He has said He will never leave nor forsake us (see Hebrews 13:5), and that He is with us always, even till the end of time. (see Matthew 28:20). Thus, the disciples, by panicking or entertaining fear in the presence of Jesus in that boat had displeased Jesus, and yet Jesus' love for them was so selfless that He allowed His sleep to be disrupted, and He arose to rebuke the wind, and calmed the raging sea to assuage their fears. Today I can see Jesus rebuking every wind and calming every sea of trouble that is raging against you, as you call on Him; I can hear Jesus lovingly reassuring all of us and saying, "Fear not, for I am with you; Be not dismayed, for I am your God. I will strengthen you, Yes, I will help you, I will uphold you with My righteous right hand." (Isaiah 41:10). Hallelujah!

Jesus Loves You More Than You Can Ever Imagine

Jesus loves you more than you can ever imagine. His love for you is an everlasting love, and His kindness towards you is an unfailing kindness. (see Jeremiah 31:3). If Jesus loved you and died for you while you were still a sinner, be convinced that He loves you even more so, because you are righteous in Him. (see 2 Corinthians 5:21, with Romans 5:8-11). During His earth walk, Jesus truly demonstrated His love for the poor, the sinful, the sick, and the downtrodden. Jesus never condemned sinners nor shunned their company. He never judged sinners nor made them feel guiltier than they already felt. Look at the stories of the tax collectors, the prostitutes, the fishermen, the blind, the lame and the sick that Jesus encountered, some of which we have already discussed. All He did was love them in a way that brought them to repentance and forgiveness, healing and transformation. The Bible says that God's kindness is intended to lead us to repentance. (see Romans 2:4). No wonder Jesus was so kind to sinners! He never made any sinner feel more guilty or ashamed than he already felt. Indeed Jesus was a friend of sinners. **On a certain occasion Jesus went out of His way just to meet with a Samaritan woman — a sinner (see John 4:1-42).** The Samaritan woman's name was not mentioned in the story because she represents every sinner; she represents who I was and who you were before we came to Christ. What motivated Jesus to meet with the Samaritan woman was love, and love is what motivated Him to meet with us in our own personal encounters with Christ that has given us eternal life today. And so today love should be the force that motivates or compels us to also share the gospel of Christ with others. The Bible says that Jesus considered it a must or a need to go through Samaria, as He left Judea and departed again to Galilee (see John 4:3-4). And the obvious reason was that He had an imperative divine appointment with this Samaritan woman — an appointment that would bring her the good news of the Kingdom of God and change her life forever from a rotten, shameful, lonely and empty sinner, to a delightful, joy-filled, unashamed, and effective evangelist heralding the sighting of the Messiah to the men of her city and leading them to saving faith. What an amazing transformation the love of Christ brings! And what an amazing expression of love from Jesus our Lord to this Samaritan woman!

It is important to note also that this woman in the story wasn't just a sinner, she was a Samaritan. And the Jews, during this period in history, considered the Samaritans as enemies — as dogs, as demons with whom they had no dealings (see John 8:48; Matthew 15:26; John 4:9). And so, for Jesus to visit this Samaritan woman, Jesus needed not only to break the gender barrier that was very prevalent also during this period in history, but the racial, religious, social, as well as political barriers between the Jews and the Samaritans. And He did! By meeting and interacting with the Samaritan woman at the well, Jesus gave her a firsthand experience of His love — the kind of love that knows no bounds. Jesus gave her not just a taste, but a full serving of what it means to be wanted, to be cared for, and to be loved selflessly. Jesus showed this Samaritan woman His great love, and gave her grace. He knew every sin she had ever committed, and still reached out to her and loved her anyway. This Samaritan woman had a thirst for true love that no man had been able to satisfy until now.

She had been abused and used by many men in her village as she was married and divorced by five men, one after another, and the man she had now was not even her husband. (see John 4:17-18). Jesus knew about this Samaritan woman's thirst for everlasting life and for true love — the God-kind of love — and He satisfied that thirst, just as He has satisfied your thirst and my thirst, and will satisfy the thirst of all who are willing to embrace Him. As Jesus Himself told the Samaritan woman, whoever drinks of the water Jesus gives will NEVER thirst. But the water that He shall give him will become in him a fountain of water springing up into everlasting life. (see John 4:14).

Indeed, Jesus is the ultimate lover; He is Love. Today I recommend Jesus to you if you haven't accepted Him yet as your Lord and Savior. He is the cure for your lonely heart. He knows everything about you and loves you anyway. If you thirst for everlasting life, if you thirst for true love, come to Jesus, because He alone can satisfy your thirst; He alone can fill the void or the emptiness within. If you rely on man for love, or if you drink from human relationships alone, you will thirst again; only Jesus can satisfy the thirst of your soul for true love and eternal life. And Jesus is reaching out to you today just as He reached out to the Samaritan woman, just as He reached out to me. He says "Come to Me, all you who are weary and burdened, and I will give you rest." (see Matthew 11:28 NIV). Then He adds for the benefit of those who still find it difficult to come; He says, "Here I am! I stand at the door and knock. If anyone hears my voice and opens the door, I will come in and eat with that person, and they with me." (Revelation 3:20 NIV). What an amazing invitation to a love feast, to a love relationship and fellowship with Jesus! What an amazing love Jesus has for us! He loves you, and He wants to fellowship with you if you're willing to have Him. He has extended an open invitation to everyone. He loves you greatly. But, you see, He will never violate your free will by forcing you to accept His love. Jesus' love extends to people of all race, age, gender, or creed. His love and warmth always attracted all manner of people to Him during His earth walk. It made faithful disciples out of the worst sinners. It attracted parents to bring their little children to Him for blessing. And wow, how Jesus loved these little children! On a certain occasion when His disciples rebuked and tried to prevent the little children from coming to Jesus, the Bible says that "When Jesus saw this, he was **indignant**. He said to them, "Let the little children come to me, and do not hinder them, for the kingdom of God belongs to such as these." (see Mark 10:13-14). In fact, this was one of the few times Jesus was angry, indignant. Jesus loves it when we, His little children, come to Him, because He loves us greatly. And so He gets angry with anything or anyone who tries to prevent us from coming to Him. May you come to Him today to drink from His fountain of love, so that you will never thirst. May you come to Him today to drink from His fountain of life, so that you will live forever. Amen.

Jesus' Great Love Was Also Evident in His Teachings

Jesus' great love was not only evident in His actions, but also in His teachings. In other words, not only did Jesus walk in love, He also taught us how to walk in love. For example, Jesus taught, saying, "You have heard that it was said, 'An eye for an eye and a tooth for a tooth.' But I tell you not to resist an evil person. But whoever slaps you on your right cheek, turn the other to him also. If anyone wants to sue you and take away your tunic, let him have your cloak also.

And whoever compels you to go one mile, go with him two. Give to him who asks you, and from him who wants to borrow from you do not turn away. You have heard that it was said, 'You shall love your neighbor and hate your enemy.' But I say to you, love your enemies, bless those who curse you, do good to those who hate you, and pray for those who spitefully use you and persecute you, that you may be sons of your Father in heaven; for He makes His sun rise on the evil and on the good, and sends rain on the just and on the unjust. For if you love those who love you, what reward have you? Do not even the tax collectors do the same? And if you greet your brethren only, what do you do more than others? Do not even the tax collectors do so?" (Matthew 5:38-47).

Thus Jesus commanded us not only to love those who love us or do good to those who have something to give us in return, but more so to love those who hate us and seek to harm us, and do good to those who have nothing to give us in return. Moreover, Jesus lived what He taught. We read in the gospels about how Jesus said a prayer asking forgiveness for the sinful men (His wicked enemies) who condemned Him to death, who mocked, flogged and crucified Him. (see Luke 23:34). Jesus also knew all along that Judas Iscariot would betray Him (see John 13:21, 26); He even said that Judas Iscariot was a devil (see John 6:70-71), and yet He loved him to the end, to the last and highest degree (see John 13:1). Jesus even washed the feet of all the disciples, including Judas Iscariot at the Last Supper (see John 13:5), and thus taught us through His example that we are to wash one another's feet — submit to one another or serve one another out of reverence for Christ. (see John 13:12-17; Ephesians 5:21).

Jesus Gave Us A New Commandment To Love One Another

Jesus, as noted earlier, wanted us to share His love or carry the example of His great love around the world, so that all will know that we are His disciples indeed. And so He gave us a new commandment at the Last Supper. He said, "**A new commandment** I give to you, that you **love one another**; AS I HAVE LOVED YOU, that you also love one another. **By this all will know that you are My disciples**, if you have love for one another." (John 13:34-35). Additionally, Jesus said, "He who has My commandments and keeps them, it is he who loves Me. And he who loves Me will be loved by My Father, and I will love him and **manifest** Myself to him…If anyone loves Me, he will keep My word; and My Father will love him, and We will come to him and make Our home with him." (John 14:21, 23). Today we have the example of Jesus' love to follow. We are not to love with our own strength. God is our strength, and God is at work in us with His mighty power or ability (see Philippians 2:13). Jesus is in us (see Colossians 1:27), living and loving through us. (see Galatians 2:20). Our sufficiency (or ability to meet all needs) is from God (see 2 Corinthians 3:5), and so all we have to do to walk in love is to yield to the leading of the Holy Spirit; we are to yield to the power or ability of God that is at work in us. The Bible says that "the love of God has been poured out in our hearts by the Holy Spirit who was given to us." (see Romans 5:5). So we can walk in love, as Christ has loved us, by simply letting His love loose in us or in our lives. The Bible tells us that love is the fulfillment of the law (see Romans 13:10, Galatians 5:14). When we walk worthy of our calling to love, the Law is fulfilled in us. And thus Paul writes: "Be ye therefore followers of God, as dear children; And **walk in love**, AS CHRIST ALSO HATH LOVED US, and hath given himself for us an offering and a sacrifice to God for a sweetsmelling savour. But fornication, and all uncleanness, or covetousness, let it not be once named among you, as becometh saints; Neither filthiness, nor foolish talking, nor jesting, which are not convenient: but rather giving of thanks." (Ephesians 5:1-4 KJV). Many (legalistic) Christians often read these verses and start demanding, "You see, you're to love; you're not to fornicate; you're not to covet; you're to obey these commandments" etc. And whereas all these are true, these legalistic Christians miss the whole point and the revelation which is the basis of these instructions. The truth is that we cannot love through our self-efforts under the law. No one under the Old Covenant could keep the law of Moses that required them to love their neighbor as themselves. Under the Old Covenant, God demanded love from sinful man. And until Jesus came to fulfill the law, no man could love the way God had commanded them to. But thanks be to God, under the New Covenant, Jesus supplies us with love first, and then commands us to share it with others. We ought to first have a revelation of the love of God for us, which is demonstrated through Jesus Christ. We ought to have the revelation in Ephesians 5:2, which actually says to "walk in love, AS CHRIST HAS ALSO LOVED US." Thus we have to first know how Christ has loved us. Hence, Paul prayed earlier in Ephesians 3:14-19 that you may know the width, length, depth and height of the love of Christ towards you. This is the opposite of the Law of Moses which focuses on man's love for God (or the lack thereof). First John 4:19 says, "We love Him because He first loved us." You have to be seated in the revelation of Christ's love for you, before you can walk in that love. When you have the revelation of Christ's love for you, you are seated well. Then walking becomes easy. You are simply to walk by letting the love of God, which has been poured out into your heart (see Romans 5:5), flow through you, instead of "trying" to love. When we allow the love of Christ to flow through us, when we let loose the love of Christ in us, the requirements of the law will be fulfilled without us "trying" to fulfill them. This is why the other verses in Ephesians 5:1-4 tell us against fornication, uncleanness, covetousness, filthiness, foolishness, coarse jesting, etc. When one walks in the love of Christ, one does not harm others or himself by committing any of those sins. It is when we leave the realm of love that we fall into the realm of selfishness and sin. But when we allow the Holy Spirit to guide us in love, our hearts will always be flooded with love, and we will not seek our own interests but the interest of others, for love does not seek its own. (see 1 Corinthians 13:4). The Bible says, "Do nothing out of selfish ambition or vain conceit. Rather, in humility value others above yourselves." (Philippians 2:3 NIV). It is the divine plan of God that as we are filled with the Spirit of His Son and allow His Spirit to lead us, we will have the same attitude of mind toward each other that Christ had (see Romans 15:5-6), we will walk just as Jesus walked (see 1 John 2:6) — we would walk in love, loving righteousness and hating iniquity, just like our Lord Jesus Christ. (see Hebrews 1:9, with Psalm 45:7). May this be a reality for you.

The Realm of Love is Where Prayers are Answered

The realm of love is where prayers are answered and God is glorified. The apostle John writes, "My little children, **let us not love in word or in tongue, but in deed and in truth. And by this** we know that we are of the truth, and **shall assure our hearts before Him.** For if our heart condemns us, God is greater than our heart, and knows all things. Beloved, if our heart does not condemn us, **we have confi-**

dence toward God. AND WHATEVER WE ASK WE RECEIVE FROM HIM, BECAUSE WE KEEP HIS COMMANDMENTS and do those things that are pleasing in His sight. AND THIS IS His COMMANDMENT: that we should BELIEVE on the name of His Son Jesus Christ AND LOVE ONE ANOTHER, as He gave us commandment." (I John 3:18-23). What this means is that regardless of how many promises of God you plead, if, besides believing on the name of Jesus, you are not also walking in love as commanded by Jesus, your prayers will not be effective, because your heart will condemn you for you to not have confidence toward God. Also, no matter how much you pray, your prayers will not be effective until you know God's will and ask everything according to His will. (see 1 John 5:14-15; James 4:3). Asking according to His will in this context simply means asking with the right motive (see James 4:3), and in the manner in which Jesus taught us to ask. Jesus said we should ASK THE FATHER in the NAME of Jesus. (see John 16:23-24). He said that we shouldn't ask Him (Jesus) to pray to the Father for us, because He wouldn't pray to the Father for us, but we should pray directly to the Father in the Name of Jesus, because the Father Himself loves us. (see John 16:26-27). Yes, we can worship Jesus (see Luke 24:52), talk to Him and fellowship with Him (see 1 John 1:3; 1 Corinthians 1:9), and we can also command circumstances to change, or ask anything in the Name of Jesus, and He will do it (see John 14:13-14, Acts 3:1-9). But we are NOT to pray to Jesus when we need something; we are to pray to the Father in the NAME of Jesus. (see John 16:23-24). And once we have prayed with the right motive, and in the manner Jesus asked us to pray, we are to believe and know that whatever we have asked for, we have received. Beloved, if you walk in love, you will never pray with the wrong motive or with an evil conscience, you will have the right motives for asking from God, and so you will have confidence toward God, and whatever you ask the Father in the name of Jesus, you will receive, and your life will be a pleasing aroma of thanksgiving to God.

Indeed, we can only walk in love when we give up on our self-efforts under the law to love, and then submit or yield to the will and purpose of the Holy Spirit who is in us, for those who are led by the Spirit are not under the law. (see Galatians 5:18). May you be led by the Spirit to walk worthy of your calling in Christ.

In the next Chapter, we will continue our discussion by exploring how faith worked through love to move Jesus to lay down His life on the cross as an offering and a sacrifice to God through the eternal Spirit for the sins of mankind — a sacrifice through which we became new creations and beloved children of God who are born of God, born in the Spirit, live in the Spirit, and are to walk in the Spirit. Thus, we will discuss the crucifixion of Jesus and how Jesus' love for mankind is manifested in this story — the greatest story ever told. We will also expound on the truth that Jesus' death on the cross was just a means to the greater end of fulfilling the Old Covenant or the things written in the Law of Moses, the Prophets and the Psalms (see Luke 24:44-48), and establishing the New Covenant (see Hebrews 8:6-13) which led to the creating anew of mankind into what is today known as the New Creation (see 2 Corinthians 5:17), the New Humanity or the New Man (see Ephesians 2:15).

Chapter 9

Jesus Our Sacrificial Lamb and Substitute

How Jesus, Out of Love, Suffered Pain and Agony, and Died to Redeem Us Eternally From the Dominion of Satan and Sin, and Made Us a New Creation

"Greater love has no one than this: to lay down one's life for one's friends." (John 15:13 NIV). "By this we know love, because He laid down His life for us…" (I John 3:16).

The Bible says that Jesus Christ died of His own volition. No man could take His life from Him. This was Jesus' own claim: "Therefore My Father loves Me, because **I lay down My life** that I may take it again. NO ONE TAKES IT FROM ME, but I lay it down of Myself. **I have power to lay it down, and I have power to take it again**. This command I have received from My Father." (John 10:17-18). So Jesus had the authority and the power to lay down His life and take it again, and He did. Thus the Bible says, "[NOW] BEFORE the Passover Feast began, JESUS KNEW (was fully aware) THAT THE TIME HAD COME for Him to LEAVE THIS WORLD and return to the Father. And as He had LOVED those who were His own in the world, He LOVED THEM TO THE LAST AND TO THE HIGHEST

DEGREE." (John 13:1 AMP). How did Jesus love His own to the last and to the highest degree? By laying down His life for them, for us. (see 1 John 3:16). Jesus knowing fully about the pain and agony He was to suffer (see Luke 22:15) as He prepared to leave this world and return to the Father, did not rescind His decision to lay down His life for you and I. He loved us too much to give up on His mission. Love was the reason He had come into the world. And so He loved us to the end, to the last and to the highest degree. He gave us the greatest definition and example of love. Indeed, Jesus held nothing back; He stripped Himself of everything but love. He laid down His life for us because it was NECESSARY; it was the ONLY WAY man could be saved from the dominion of Satan and sin, and from perishing with his master Satan on the Day of Judgment. Through His death and resurrection, Jesus was to fulfill the Old Covenant and establish the New Covenant. (see Luke 24:44-48, with Luke 22:20 and Hebrews 8:6-13).

The Lord's Supper is The One Thing Jesus Wants Us To Do in Remembrance of Him

Therefore at the Last Supper, the Bible says, "And as they were eating, Jesus took BREAD, blessed and broke it, and gave it to the disciples and said, "Take, eat; this is My body." Then He took the cup, and gave thanks, and gave it to them, saying, "Drink from it, all of you. For this is My BLOOD OF THE NEW COVENANT, which is shed for many FOR THE REMISSION OF SINS." (Matthew 26:26-28). In the gospel according to Luke, we are also told that Jesus commanded us (His disciples) to do this in remembrance of Him. (see Luke 22:19). How interesting that Jesus did not ask us to remember anything other than His body and blood which He gave for the remission of our sins. How interesting that He did not ask us to remember our sins, but to remember Him instead, and the sacrifice He made of His body and blood for our sins. How sad then, that many in the Church today have missed this truth and are focusing on sin and remembering sin, instead of focusing on Jesus and remembering Jesus, instead of "looking unto Jesus, the author and finisher of our faith, who for the joy that was set before Him endured the cross, despising the shame, and has sat down at the right hand of the throne of God" (see Hebrews 12:2), instead of remembering how, as the Lamb of God, Jesus condemned sin in the flesh and took away the sins of the world, took away our sins. Oh, how such people have strayed and deviated from the will of Jesus! Evidently, Jesus, by going to the cross to die to take away our sins, was also to take away our consciousness of sin (see Hebrews 10:1-3). Jesus didn't want us to remember our sins anymore. He wanted us to only remember Him. Jesus wanted our memory to always be flooded with thoughts about Him, about His sacrifice for us, about His amazing example of love that was symbolized in the breaking and eating of bread (His Body) and the drinking of the fruit of the vine (His blood).

Jesus Wants Us to Feed on His Flesh, Which is the Word

We noted earlier that Jesus Christ is the New Covenant. (see Isaiah 42:6). According to the gospel of Luke, Jesus also stated that the New Covenant is IN His blood which is shed for us. (see Luke 22:20). The Prophet Isaiah tells us that Jesus' body was broken for our healing. (see Isaiah 53:5). Hence, Jesus said we are to feed on His body and drink His blood in order to have eternal life. He said, "Most assuredly, I say to you, UNLESS YOU **EAT THE FLESH** of the Son of Man AND

DRINK HIS BLOOD, you have NO LIFE IN YOU. Whoever EATS My FLESH and DRINKS My BLOOD **has ETERNAL LIFE**, and I will raise him up at the last day. For My FLESH IS FOOD INDEED, and My BLOOD IS DRINK INDEED. He who EATS My FLESH and DRINKS My BLOOD abides in Me, and I in him. As the living Father sent Me, and I live because of the Father, so he who FEEDS on Me WILL LIVE BECAUSE OF Me. This is the bread which came down from heaven—not as your fathers ate the manna, and are dead. He who eats this bread will live forever." (John 6:53-58). Hallelujah!

Feeding on Jesus' flesh, in this context, simply means believing in Jesus and feeding on the Word of God. (see John 6:47, with Luke 4:4, Matthew 4:4, and John 15:7). The Bible says, "And the Word BECAME **FLESH** and dwelt among us, and we beheld His glory, the glory as of THE ONLY BEGOTTEN (Son) OF THE FATHER, full of grace and truth." (John 1:14). Jesus is the Word made flesh. And so feeding on His flesh is feeding on the Word. It is in feeding on the Word of God or hearing the Word of Christ that we receive faith to be saved or to have eternal life. (see Romans 10:17, with Ephesians 2:8-9). It is in abiding or continuing in Jesus's words that we become His disciples indeed. (see John 8:31). Hence Jesus said unless you eat His flesh and drink His blood, you do not have life in you. (see John 6:53). Then He said the same thing in different words when He said, "I am the vine, you are the branches. He who ABIDES in Me, and I in him, bears much fruit; for WITHOUT Me YOU CAN DO NOTHING. If anyone DOES NOT ABIDE in Me, he is CAST OUT as a branch AND IS WITHERED; and they gather them and throw them into the fire, and they are burned. If you ABIDE in Me, and My WORDS ABIDE IN YOU, you will ask what you desire, and it shall be done for you." (John 15:5-7). My dear friend, unless you hear the Word of Christ and act on it to receive saving faith in Jesus Christ, and then continually feed on the Word of Christ and hold on to your faith till He comes, you do not have life in you. Jesus wants you to believe in Him — to abide or remain in Him (in His Word) and for His Word to abide or remain in you. First John 2:14 says of those of us who are believers — who already believe in Jesus Christ — that the Word of God (already) abides in us (in our spirit). This is because we believe the Word, and have been born of the Word, and so the Word (which is the seed of God) remains or abides in us — in our spirit. (see James 1:18; 1 Peter 1:23; 1 John 3:9). But we have to also get the Word to abide in the mind of our body, by renewing our mind (with the Word) so that the mind of our body will conform to the mind of our spirit, which is the mind of Christ. (see Romans 12:2, with 1 Corinthians 2:16). Thus, to the believer the Bible says, "Therefore let that abide in you which you heard from the beginning (that is, the Word of Christ). If what you heard from the beginning (that is, the Word of Christ) ABIDES IN YOU, you ALSO WILL ABIDE in the Son and in the Father. And this is THE PROMISE that He has promised us—**ETERNAL LIFE.**" (I John 2:24-25). The apostle Paul stated the same truth when he said "Now, brothers and sisters, I want to remind you of the gospel I preached to you, which you received and on which you have taken your stand. **By this gospel you are saved**, IF YOU HOLD FIRMLY TO THE WORD I PREACHED TO YOU. **Otherwise, you have believed in vain**." (1 Corinthians 15:1-2 NIV). Our responsibility today, as believers, is to continue to ABIDE (live or remain) in the Word as we allow the Word to continue to abide in us. We abide in the Word by making a habit of reading and meditating on the Word (see Proverbs 4:20-22; Joshua 1:8; 2 Corinthians 3:18), and doing the Word. (see James 1:22-25). We have to let the Word of Christ dwell in us richly in all wisdom. (see Colossians 3:16). We have to let our mind stay on the Word of God, which is Jesus Christ. (see Hebrews 12:2; Isaiah 26:3, with John 1:1,14; Revelation 19:13). We have to make our home in the Word of God. The Bible says God will keep in perfect peace the person whose mind is stayed on Him, because such a person trusts in Him. (see Isaiah 26:3). Hallelujah! You can be this person. The Psalmist says, "Great peace have those who love Your law (or Your Word), and nothing causes them to stumble.' (Psalm 119:165).

The New Covenant is in the Blood of Jesus

Drinking Jesus' blood has a similar meaning as eating His flesh — it simply means feeding on the Gospel of Christ in the light of His finished work at the cross. Today His blood is the New Covenant message or ministry, because the New Covenant is in His blood. As noted earlier, the Bible records that on the night before His crucifixion, Jesus offered the cup to His disciples and said, "This cup is THE NEW COVENANT IN MY BLOOD, which is poured out for you" (Luke 22:20). Here, we can note that THE NEW COVENANT is IN Jesus' blood. Therefore when we drink (that is, hear and believe, or take in) the New Covenant message or the Gospel of Christ, we are drinking the blood of Christ. You cannot separate the New Covenant (message or gospel) from the blood of Jesus, because the blood contains the New Covenant. The New Covenant is in His blood. The blood of Jesus and the New Covenant are one. Having the New Covenant is having the blood of Jesus, because Jesus' blood is the blood of the New Covenant. Drinking the blood of Jesus, then, is drinking the blood of the New Covenant or hearing and believing the New Covenant gospel, which is the gospel of Christ in the light of New Covenant realities. The Bible says that God has "also made us sufficient as MINISTERS OF THE NEW COVENANT, not of the letter (or the Law) but of the Spirit; for the letter (or the Law) kills, but the Spirit gives life." (2 Corinthians 3:6). We are not to be ashamed of the New Covenant ministry. We are not to be ashamed that we are ministers of the Spirit and not of the Law. In fact, as ministers of the New Covenant, we have a superior and a more excellent ministry, because we are ministers of a better covenant (the New Covenant) which was established on better promises — (see Hebrews 8:6). Therefore we should continually be the ministers of reconciliation that the Lord Jesus Christ has called us to be (see 2 Corinthians 5:18-20), and not ministers of condemnation and death, not ministers of the Old Covenant or the Law. (see 2 Corinthians 3:5-6). The apostle Paul in his first letter to the young pastor Timothy, rebuked those who had strayed from the ministry of reconciliation, "desiring to be teachers of the law, understanding neither what they say nor the things which they affirm." (see 1 Timothy 1:7). Then in his second letter he urged Timothy to "**Study** to shew thyself approved unto God, a workman that needeth **NOT TO BE ASHAMED**, rightly dividing the word of truth." (2 Timothy 2:15 KJV). Again, speaking in the light of the New Covenant ministry, the apostle Paul says, "For I am **not ashamed** of the gospel of Christ, for it is THE POWER OF GOD to SALVATION for EVERYONE WHO BELIEVES, for the Jew first and also for the Greek. For in it the RIGHTEOUSNESS OF GOD is **revealed** from FAITH to FAITH; as it is written, "The just shall live by faith." (Romans 1:16-17). The Gospel of Christ is not something to be ashamed of. The Gospel of Christ is the POWER OF GOD to salvation for everyone who believes. The New Covenant ministry unveils to us (by the Holy Spirit) the things which have been freely given to us by God, which are all summed up in one gift — THE GIFT OF RIGHTEOUSNESS, THE RIGHTEOUSNESS OF GOD. The righteousness of God is a gift to the believer in Christ (see Romans 5:17), and it is given and received through faith (see Romans 3:22) as it is revealed in the Gospel of Christ (from faith to faith) by the Spirit of God which is in us. (see 1 Corinthians 2:12, with 1 John 2:27).

The Lord's Supper is a Memorial of the New Covenant

Jesus instituted the Lord's Supper on the night before His crucifixion as a memorial of the New Covenant, and we are to continue to honor the Lord's Supper and to do so in remembrance of our Lord Jesus Christ. Just as it was necessary for Jesus to die and to rise again, today it is necessary for us to also continually remember Him in the Lord's Supper (or the Love Feast, as it is called in Jude 1:12) in the same manner as the early disciples did. (see Acts 2:46–47; 1 Corinthians 11:17–34).

It Was Necessary for Jesus to Die and to Rise Again

Indeed, it was necessary for Jesus' body to be broken and for His blood to be shed for us. It was necessary for Him to die (for our transgressions) and to rise again (for our justification) — (see Romans 4:25). In fact, Jesus affirmed the NECESSITY of His death and resurrection when He reminded His disciples after His resurrection by saying to them, "These are the words which I spoke to you while I was still with you, THAT ALL THINGS **MUST** BE FULFILLED WHICH WERE WRITTEN in **THE LAW OF MOSES** and **the PROPHETS** and **the PSALMS** concerning Me." And He OPENED THEIR UNDERSTANDING, that they might COMPREHEND THE SCRIPTURES. Then He said to them, "Thus it is written, and thus **IT WAS NECESSARY** for THE CHRIST TO SUFFER and to RISE FROM THE DEAD the third day, and that **REPENTANCE and REMISSION OF SINS should be PREACHED in His NAME to ALL NATIONS**, beginning at Jerusalem." (see Luke 24:44-47). Jesus' death was NECESSARY not only to FULFILL the things written in the Law of Moses, the writings of the Prophets, and the things written in the Psalms concerning Him, but also to offer REMISSION OF SINS to all mankind, and eternal life to all who believe. And thus Jesus, after His resurrection, invoked the Disciples as **witnesses** to the things that had been fulfilled in Him from the Law of Moses, the Prophets, and the Psalms. (see Luke 24:48, with Luke 24:44).

Thank God They Did Not Know!

It is indeed amazing that Jesus knew He was going to be crucified, and imperatively so. He predicted or prophesied His own death and resurrection on several occasions. On one of these occasions He gave the details of His suffering. The Bible says, "Now Jesus, going up to Jerusalem, took the twelve disciples aside on the road and said to them, "Behold, we are going up to Jerusalem, and the Son of Man will be BETRAYED to the chief priests and to the scribes; and they will CONDEMN Him to DEATH, and deliver Him to the Gentiles to MOCK and to SCOURGE and to CRUCIFY. And the THIRD day

He will RISE AGAIN." (Matthew 20:17-19). How detailed! How vivid! And how amazing that everything Jesus predicted happened with divine precision. It is also worth noting that although Jesus had a foreknowledge of His impending death and resurrection, the chief priests, the scribes, and the elders of the people who plotted to kill Him and eventually delivered Him up for crucifixion, had no idea that they were fulfilling a prophecy and a foreordained plan of God. Paul said, "NONE OF THE RULERS OF THIS AGE KNEW; for had they known, they WOULD NOT have crucified the Lord of glory." (see I Corinthians 2:8). They did not know that Jesus was to be delivered up for crucifixion by the determined purpose and foreknowledge of God for the salvation of mankind. Yes, Caiaphas, who was the high priest in the year the Lord was crucified, prophesied that Jesus would die for the Jewish nation, and not only for that nation but also for the scattered children of God, to bring them together and make them one. (see John 11:47-53). But the Bible says that Caiaphas **did not say this on his own** (see John 11:51), but as high priest that year, he spoke by the Spirit of God, and so he did not know what he himself was prophesying. Even Satan the god of this age (see 2 Corinthians 4:4) didn't know that Jesus' death was to fulfill a prophecy, and that the ultimate purpose of Jesus' death (and resurrection) was to redeem man from his dominion and make man his master; for had Satan known, he wouldn't have powered it, he wouldn't have fueled the strong hatred and fury of the people who crucified Christ. Satan and his human proxies did not know that, through them, God was going to punish His own innocent (or sinless) Son Jesus Christ and satisfy the demands of justice, so that you and I will walk away as free men, as innocent men, as sinless men, as righteous men. (see Romans 3:23-24, 26; 2 Corinthians 5:21). They did not know that instead of every man suffering for his own sins, Jesus, who knew no sin (see 2 Corinthians 5:21) had stepped in as every man's Substitute and Representative to bear the punishment we deserved, so that we (who believe in Jesus) would be acquitted of all charges and declared innocent and righteous. Satan and his cohorts did not know that the death of Jesus was a foreordained plan of God for the redemption of mankind; that it had happened from the foundation of the world but was to be **manifested** in the flesh for all to see (see Revelation 13:8); that it was an act of grace born out of the loving heart of God the Father. They did not know that God had given His only begotten Son Jesus Christ as a Substitute to suffer the full brunt of His wrath against sin, which man was supposed to suffer as a result of his disobedience. They did not know that Jesus was to die the shameful and humiliating death, which man was supposed to die. Indeed, Satan and his human proxies had no clue that through the crucifixion, death and resurrection of Jesus Christ, the Old Creation man (the descendant of Adam) was to be born again or created anew. And unfortunately, many people in the world today still don't know.

Thus, Paul writes that the unsearchable riches of Christ is **a "MYSTERY, which from the BEGINNING of the ages HAS BEEN HIDDEN IN GOD** who created all things through Jesus Christ; TO THE INTENT THAT **NOW** the manifold wisdom of God might be **MADE KNOWN BY THE CHURCH** to the PRINCIPALITIES and POWERS IN THE HEAVENLY PLACES, according to the eternal purpose which He (God) accomplished in Christ Jesus our Lord, in whom we have boldness and access with confidence through faith in Him." (see Ephesians 3:9-12). We (the Church) are the ones that have to make these truths known to Satan and his cohorts, and even to the heavenly angels, through **our confession,** which includes our preaching. We have to confess what Jesus has done, and then hold fast our confession. (see Hebrews 4:14). Truly, none of the rulers of this age who crucified Jesus knew what they were doing. No wonder Jesus prayed for them on the cross and said, "Father, forgive them, for THEY DO NOT KNOW WHAT THEY DO." (see Luke 23:34). They certainly did not know what they were doing. They only started to realize what they had done when the disciples started confessing or testifying about the manifold wisdom of God, beginning with Peter who stood up on the Day of Pentecost to speak after the outpouring of the Holy Spirit, and said, "Men of Israel, hear these words: Jesus of Nazareth, a Man attested by God to you by miracles, wonders, and signs which God did through Him in your midst, as you yourselves also know— Him, BEING DELIVERED BY THE DETERMINED PURPOSE AND FOREKNOWLEDGE OF GOD, you have taken by lawless hands, **have crucified**, and put to death; **whom God raised up**, having loosed the pains of death, because it was not possible that He should be held by it." (Acts 2:22-24). Then he added, "This Jesus God has raised up, of which **we are all witnesses.**" (Acts 2:32).

Beloved, aren't you glad that the rulers of this age didn't know what they were doing when they crucified Jesus Christ? Because if they had known, they wouldn't have crucified Him (see 1 Corinthians 2:8), and you and I couldn't have been saved. Therefore, not knowing that they were about to fulfill a prophecy from God and facilitate the performance of the greatest miracle man has ever experienced or witnessed — the miracle of the new creation — and not knowing that **glories were to follow** the sufferings of Christ (see 1 Peter 1:11), "the chief priests, the scribes, and the elders of the people assembled at the palace of the high priest, who was called Caiaphas, and **plotted to take Jesus by trickery and kill Him**." (see Matthew 26:3-4; — see also Mark 14:1-2). They plotted to take Jesus by TRICKERY and KILL Him. Doesn't this sound familiar? Beloved, you would remember from the earlier parts of this book, particularly the parts where we discussed the life of the Old Creation man in the garden of Eden, that **trickery** (or deception) and **murder** are the primary devices or weapons of Satan that he uses against man. (see Genesis 3:1-7; Genesis 4:3-8; 1 John 3:8-12; 2 Corinthians 11:3). The Bible says we are not ignorant of Satan's devices. (see 2 Corinthians 2:11). And by the way, these human proxies of Satan who were plotting to trick (lie) and kill (murder) Jesus, were **the religious leaders of the day**. How familiar this also sounds when one thinks of the Inquisition and the Reformation, when one thinks of the torture and heinous crimes against true believers that the Roman Catholic Church and its religious leaders committed during what has now gained notoriety in church history as the Dark Ages? It is baffling that today SOME PEOPLE still see the Roman Catholic Church and its religious leaders as harmless, as a part of the true Body of Christ, instead of seeing them as the tares among the wheat that they truly are. (see Matthew 13:24-30). How deceived SUCH PEOPLE are, given the obvious idolatry and blasphemies of the Roman Catholic Church. Thus those religious leaders — the chief priests, the scribes, and the elders of the people — were only taking from their father the devil's own resources or his playbook. No wonder Jesus had previously said to them, "You are of your father THE DEVIL, and the desires of your father you want to do. He was a MURDERER from the beginning, and does not stand in the truth, because there is no truth in him. When he speaks a LIE, he SPEAKS FROM his OWN RESOURCES, for he is a LIAR and

THE FATHER OF IT." (John 8:44). Evidently these religious leaders were plotting to do the works of their father the devil.

"Then one of the twelve, called JUDAS ISCARIOT (the son of perdition — see John 17:12), went to the chief priests and said, "What are you willing to give me if I deliver Him (Jesus) to you?" And they counted out to him THIRTY PIECES OF SILVER. So from that time he sought opportunity to BETRAY Him." (Matthew 26:14-16). Meanwhile, Jesus had already predicted or prophesied at the Last Supper that one of the disciples (specifically Judas Iscariot) would betray Him. (see Matthew 26:20,25; Mark 14:17-21). It is amazing that Jesus knew Judas Iscariot was a devil (see John 6:70) and would betray Him, and yet He loved him to the end. (see John 13:1).

Indeed, Jesus knew everything about His impending arrest, sufferings and death, to the exact hour of His betrayal by Judas Iscariot (see Matthew 26:45-46; Mark 14:41-42); not that having such foreknowledge of His betrayal and crucifixion made it any less painful. That Jesus was to suffer and be killed for our sins, was written of Him in the Law, the Prophets, and the Psalms, and had to be fulfilled (see Matthew 26:24; Mark 14:21); it could not be avoided or thwarted. Therefore Jesus repeatedly predicted His death and assured the disciples that He would be RAISED FROM THE DEAD on the THIRD DAY (see Matthew 16:21; Matthew 20:17-19; Matthew 26:32; Mark 8:31-32 Mark 9:31-32; Mark 10:33-34; Mark 14:28), but the disciples paid no heed to these assurances. They didn't even remember that Jesus had said He will rise again (see John 20:9), nor did they understand or even believe it when they were informed about His resurrection (see Mark 9:32, with Luke 24:8,11; Mark 16:11-14; Luke 24:41; Mark 16:14), until long afterward when Jesus OPENED THEIR

UNDERSTANDING, that they might COMPREHEND THE SCRIPTURES. (see Luke 24:44-47).

Jesus Prayed and Yielded to the Will of the Father

It is also important to note that Jesus, in the face of death and agony, did not forget to pray. He did not deny or forsake His God and Father. The Bible says, "Jesus came with them (His eleven disciples) to a place called GETHSEMANE, and said to the disciples, "Sit here **WHILE I GO AND PRAY over there**." And He took with Him Peter and the two sons of Zebedee (that is, John and James), and He BEGAN TO BE SORROWFUL AND **DEEPLY DISTRESSED**. Then He said to them, "**My soul is EXCEEDINGLY SORROWFUL, EVEN TO DEATH**. Stay here and watch with Me." He went a little farther and fell on His face, and PRAYED, saying, "O My Father, **IF IT IS POSSIBLE**, let this cup PASS from Me; NEVERTHELESS, NOT AS I WILL, BUT AS You WILL." (see Matthew 26:36-39).

The Bible also records that in Gethsemane Jesus prayed the same prayer **three times**. (see Matthew 26:36-46). Now, why three times? Because He was "deeply distressed" and His soul was "EXCEEDINGLY SORROWFUL, EVEN TO DEATH." (see Matthew 26:37-38). Besides, Jesus' prayer here was not a prayer of faith, which must be prayed once, without doubting; it was a prayer of petition, which can be prayed repetitively and with perseverance and reverence until the answer comes. Yes, Jesus shared in the weaknesses of man; He was "deeply distressed" and "exceedingly sorrowful" in the face of danger. And so the Bible says that Jesus our High Priest understands and can relate to our weaknesses; He sympathizes with our weaknesses (see

Hebrews 4:15), and He always lives to make intercession for us. (see Hebrews 7:25; Romans 8:34). "Likewise the Spirit also helps in our weaknesses. For we do not know what we should pray for as we ought, but the Spirit Himself makes intercession for us with groanings which cannot be uttered." (Romans 8:26). Sometimes sorrow and anxiety or distress can indeed make us pray the same prayer repetitively. And yet, even in such situations, our beloved and eternally faithful Father still hears us and answers us, because of our reverence for Him.

An Amazing Picture of Love

Jesus, in each of the three consecutive times He prayed in the garden of Gethsemane, asked or petitioned God to let the cup pass from Him "IF IT IS POSSIBLE." If what is possible? If remission/forgiveness of sins is possible without Jesus dying on the cross; if man could be saved in any other way; if God had any alternative means by which man could be saved. Beloved, if man could be saved by simply being moral, sincere, kind or religious, then Jesus was asking God the Father to let the cup — that shameful and agonizing death on the cross, that cup of God's wrath — pass from Him. But the Bible says that "without shedding of blood there is no remission." (see Hebrews 9:22). Oh, how this speaks against the blasphemy of men who think their own so-called "good works" — which God sees as filthy rags (see Isaiah 64:6) — can save them or make them accepted by God. How this speaks against those who think that they can offer to God their own "good works" in order that they might receive the remission of their sins. How this speaks against every one of man's efforts to bypass Jesus and be accepted by God. Indeed, how this speaks against the world-religions, how this speaks against Purgatory and Indulgences, Penance, and prayers to Mary and the "Saints" that the Roman Catholic Church falsely teaches and practices. Jesus was basically saying to the Father, "If there is some other way by which sins might be remitted, let this cup pass from me." He was inquiring into the possibility of an alternative plan of salvation, an alternative means by which the sins of mankind could be forgiven or remitted. And yet, knowing the will of God, and having come to the world to do the will of God (see Hebrews 10:5-9; John 6:38; John 8:29), Jesus understood that it was not possible for man to be saved in any other way, and so He humbly declared in submission: "nevertheless, NOT AS I WILL, but AS You WILL." (see Matthew 26:39). Hallelujah! Jesus knew the will of the Father and submitted to the Father's will. (see also Mark 14:36). Inasmuch as Jesus had offered up prayers and supplications, with vehement cries and tears to God the Father who was able to save Him from death (see Hebrews 5:7), inasmuch as Jesus wanted the cup to pass from Him if it were possible, He also knew it wasn't possible.

Jesus' prayers were thus heard and answered by the Father. (see Hebrews 5:7, with Luke 22:43). The answer came in the form of the strengthening of Jesus by an angel from heaven, and a confirmation from the Father that it was not possible for man to be saved in any other way or by any other means. Therefore Jesus had to drink the cup (of God's wrath and judgment against sin), He had to carry His cross, He had to die that painful and shameful but necessary death for you and I, because He loved us too much to give up on us. The Gospel according to Luke tells us that "an ANGEL appeared to Him (Jesus) from heaven, STRENGTHENING Him. And BEING IN AGONY, He PRAYED MORE EARNESTLY. Then His SWEAT BECAME

LIKE GREAT DROPS OF BLOOD falling down to the ground." (see Luke 22:43-44). Now, come with me to join Jesus in Gethsemane as we picture this scene together: Jesus, having fallen on His face in prayer, praying more earnestly for the possibility that there might be an alternative means by which man could be saved so that the cup would pass from Him, so that He wouldn't have to become sin and become a curse (see 2 Corinthians 5:21, with Galatians 3:13), so that He wouldn't have to suffer spiritual death or separation from God and be forsaken by God (see Matthew 27:46), so that He wouldn't have to go to hell for three days or descend into the abyss, into the lower parts of the earth (see Ephesians 4:8-9), into the center of the earth where the imprisoned spirits were (see 1 Peter 3:19-20, with Matthew 12:40). Let's continue to picture Jesus, still on His knees in a more earnest prayer, groaning in His Spirit, agonizing, sweating till His sweat becomes like great drops of blood falling down to the ground, falling like raindrops, falling like hailstones, falling down to the ground — sweat like great drops of blood. And despite all His agony, despite all His earnest prayers, despite all His sweating and His sweat which has now become like great drops of blood, nothing changes. Yes, angels come from Heaven to strengthen Him, but the cup still stands, and Jesus must still drink the cup, because God cannot find an alternative means by which man could be saved. The only alternative is for man to suffer for his own sins, for man to suffer eternal death and perish with his master Satan in the terrible, fierce, unforgiving, unquenchable and everlasting fires of hell, where there will be wailing and gnashing of teeth.

Jesus had seen the fires of hell. As the Creator of all things He knew the condition in hell; and He didn't desire any man to perish in hell.

Hell was not made for man but for Satan and his cohorts. Peter writes that "The Lord is not slack concerning His promise, as some count slackness, but is longsuffering toward us, not willing that any should perish but that all should come to repentance." (2 Peter 3:9). The Lord Jesus Christ didn't and still doesn't desire that any man should perish or go to hell. He even warned that no man should desire to go to hell. He taught and cautioned that, "If your right eye causes you to sin, pluck it out and cast it from you; for it is more profitable for you that one of your members perish, than for your whole body to be cast into hell. And if your right hand causes you to sin, cut it off and cast it from you; for it is more profitable for you that one of your members perish, than for your whole body to be cast into hell." (Matthew 5:29-30). In fact, it was so important to Jesus that man would at all cost avoid going to hell, so much so that Jesus emphasized and cautioned us a second time saying, "If your hand or foot causes you to sin, cut it off and cast it from you. It is better for you to enter into life lame or maimed, rather than having two hands or two feet, to be cast into the everlasting fire. And if your eye causes you to sin, pluck it out and cast it from you. It is better for you to enter into life with one eye, rather than having two eyes, to be cast into hell fire." (Matthew 18:8-9). Therefore, knowing that the only alternative to Him drinking the cup was for man to perish in hell, Jesus offered to die and go to hell for man as man's Representative and Substitute, so that man by accepting His Substitutionary death (by Faith) will have eternal life, instead of the eternal death he deserves. Oh, what an amazing picture of love! What an amazing picture of grace (unmerited, undeserved favor)! This is the amazing grace we so often sing about. Jesus truly loved us to the end, to the highest and greatest degree. And thus, right there in Gethsemane, He yielded Himself or submitted to the will of God the Father, and allowed Himself to be arrested by evil men, and to be mocked, scourged, and ultimately crucified.

In the next Chapter, we will continue to stay with Jesus in the garden of Gethsemane in this story of God's amazing love for mankind. We will insert ourselves into the scene and walk closely with Jesus throughout His arrest and trial. Yes, we would even claim to be the few of Jesus' disciples who stood by Him and followed Him closely throughout to the end. And our reward will be the golden nuggets of truth and fresh revelations we will gather and pick up along the way.

Chapter 10

Love Still Won

How Jesus Was Oppressed and Afflicted and Led as a Lamb to the Slaughter, Yet Opened Not His Mouth

THE BIBLE SAYS that, in the garden of Gethsemane, when Jesus had finished praying, "He came to His disciples and said to them, "Are you still sleeping and resting? Behold, the hour is at hand, and the Son of Man is being betrayed into the hands of sinners. Rise, let us be going. See, My betrayer is at hand." And while He was still speaking, behold, **Judas,** one of the twelve, WITH A GREAT MULTITUDE WITH SWORDS AND CLUBS, came FROM THE CHIEF PRIESTS AND ELDERS of the people. Now His betrayer had given them a sign, saying, "**WHOEVER I KISS**, He is the One; **seize Him**." Immediately he went up to Jesus and said, "Greetings, Rabbi!" and KISSED Him." (Matthew 26:45-49). Here, you have just witnessed the greatest treason in human history next to Adam's treason; and ironically, it was committed with a kiss. Judas Iscariot betrayed Jesus with a kiss. As is always the case with Satan and his minions, Judas chose a symbol of love (i.e. the kiss), and corrupted it to glorify evil; Judas chose a symbol of love (the kiss) and turned it into a symbol of hate and betrayal. How evil, how dishonorable, how tragic! Satan always seeks to corrupt the good, to turn the good into evil. Indeed, we are not ignorant of his devices. (see 2 Corinthians 2:11). And unfortunately, Satan often succeeds (even if temporarily). He succeeded with Eve in the garden of Eden. (see Genesis 3:1-7; 2 Corinthians 11:3). And here in the garden of Gethsemane, he did it again through Judas Iscariot in betraying Jesus. In the early stages of the New Covenant Church, Satan also sought to corrupt the great love that the believers shared, by making Ananias and Sapphira lie and keep back part of the proceeds from their property which they had sold to share with the other believers in that communal living that the early believers practiced. Satan influenced Ananias and Sapphira to turn that symbol of love into an opportunity to defraud and cheat their fellow believers, thereby revealing their own hypocrisy and paying the penalty for it. (see Acts 5:1-11). Ananias and Sapphira died (physically) because they were living or walking according to the flesh and not according to the Spirit, just as Romans 8:13 warns will happen to those who live as such. (We will discuss the case of Ananias and Sapphira further in Chapter 17).

Again, in the Corinthian Church, Satan sought to corrupt the Lord's Supper by making some believers turn what was instituted as a memorial and symbol of love and a proclamation of the death of our Lord Jesus Christ, into an opportunity or an occasion for greed and selfishness. (see 1 Corinthians 11:17-34). Later, Satan also sought to corrupt the entire Church of God by working through the Roman Catholic Church to introduce idolatry and teachings that are blasphemous and contrary to the finished work of Christ — false practices and teachings that are still prevalent in the church today. Indeed, the Roman Catholic Church has rebelled against God and betrayed Jesus by corrupting and turning the innocent image of Mary the mother of

Jesus into an idol or a goddess that the multitudes are being deceived to pray to and worship against the will of the one true God (see Deuteronomy 5:8; Isaiah 44:17; 1 John 5:21; Colossians 2:18, Revelation 9:20). They are like the rebellious Israelites who "secretly did things against the Lord their God that were not right. From watchtower to fortified city they built themselves **high places** in all their towns. They set up **sacred stones** and **Asherah poles** on every high hill and under every spreading tree. At every high place they **burned incense**, as the nations whom the Lord had driven out before them had done. They did wicked things that aroused the Lord's anger. They **worshiped idols**, though the Lord had said, "You shall not do this." (2 Kings 17:9-12 NIV). And the Lord said, "They **set up their vile images in the house that bears my Name and defiled it**." (Jeremiah 32:34 NIV). The Roman Catholic Church is doing all of this against Jesus' insistence that we worship the Lord our God, and serve Him only (see Matthew 4:10; Luke 4:8), against Jesus' command that we only pray to God the Father in the name of Jesus our Lord (see John 16:23), against Jesus' command that we worship God in spirit and in truth (see John 4:24). "They profess to know God, but in works they deny Him, being abominable, disobedient, and disqualified for every good work." (Titus 1:16). What a betrayal of Jesus! And so God says, "And they will know that I am the Lord, when their people lie slain among their idols around their altars, on every high hill and on all the mountaintops, under every spreading tree and every leafy oak—places where they offered fragrant incense to all their idols." (Ezekiel 6:13 NIV). Beloved, don't participate in the blasphemies of the Roman Catholic Church. God says, "Come out of her, My people, that ye be not partakers of her sins, and that ye receive not of her plagues." (Revelation 18:4 KJV). "Come out of her, My people! Run for your lives!

Run from the fierce anger of the Lord." (Jeremiah 51:45 NIV). Here in Gethsemane, such betrayal of Jesus began, as Judas Iscariot, the son of perdition, betrayed Jesus with a kiss, giving Him up to the multitudes (the detachment of troops, and officers from the chief priests and Pharisees — see John 18:3) who had come with lanterns, torches, swords, and clubs to arrest Jesus. But even in this moment when Jesus was being arrested — in this moment when He was seemingly helpless and defenseless — our Lord Jesus Christ was still in control of the situation. He was still the Lord, and could not be arrested until He allowed Himself to be arrested.

Describing the divine power Jesus wielded and exercised during His arrest, the Bible says, "Jesus therefore, KNOWING ALL THINGS that would come upon Him, WENT FORWARD and said to them, "Whom are you seeking?" They answered Him, "Jesus of Nazareth." Jesus said to them, "I AM He." And Judas, who betrayed Him, also stood with them. Now when He said to them, "I am He," THEY **DREW BACK** AND **FELL** TO THE GROUND. Then He asked them again, "Whom are you seeking?" And they said, "Jesus of Nazareth." Jesus answered, "I have told you that I am He. Therefore, if you seek Me, LET THESE GO THEIR WAY," that the saying might be fulfilled which He spoke, "Of those whom You gave Me I have lost none." (John 18:4-9). It is obvious here that Jesus did not cower at the sight of the MULTITUDES that had come with SWORDS and CLUBS to arrest Him. Instead, Jesus STEPPED FORWARD, and didn't even wait for the multitudes to question Him; He rather questioned them with authority. And when He SPOKE, they DREW BACK and FELL DOWN, without anyone touching them. Then Jesus commanded them to let His disciples go, and they obeyed and allowed the disciples, including Peter to go, in spite of Peter's aggression in cutting the right ear of Malchus, the servant of the high priest. (see Mark 14:47; Matthew 26:51). And so all the disciples deserted Jesus and fled. (see Matthew 26:56).

Indeed, the Word of God which was on the lips of Jesus (see John 12:49; John 14:10) had power, and it still has power today on the lips of the believer. The Bible says, "For no word from God will ever fail." (Luke 1:37 NIV). Jesus commanded the situation surrounding His arrest, just as He commanded the storms and the raging seas of Galilee. (see Mark 4:39). Jesus yielded Himself into the hands of those evil men. He allowed Himself to be arrested. Indeed, Jesus laid down His life for us of His own volition, and no one could take His life from Him. (see John 10:17-18). The Bible says that when Peter drew his sword and cut the right ear of Malchus, the servant of the high priest, in trying to defend Jesus his Master, Jesus told Peter to put his sword away because the Scriptures had to be fulfilled. (see Matthew 26:51-54; with John 18:10-11). Jesus said to Peter, "Do you think I cannot call on my Father, and he will at once put at my disposal more than twelve legions of angels? But how then would the Scriptures be fulfilled that say it must happen in this way?" (Matthew 26:53-54 NIV). The Scriptures also tell us that after Peter cut Malchus' right ear, Jesus touched his ear and healed him (see Luke 22:51) — yet another amazing example from Jesus of how we are to love our enemies, as He commanded (see Matthew 5:44). Jesus also called Judas Iscariot "friend" after he betrayed Him. (see Matthew 26:49-50). What an amazing love Jesus exemplified!

Now, in regard to Peter drawing his sword to strike Malchus' ear in defense of Jesus, Peter was clearly working outside the will of God.

Peter was clearly ignorant of, and out of step with the will of God, and thus tried to thwart the foreordained plan of God, just as he had done previously when Jesus taught openly for the first time that "the Son of Man must suffer many things, and be rejected by the elders and chief priests and scribes, and be killed, and after three days rise again." (Mark 8:31; see also Mark 8:32-33). Oh, how many things we do in the church today thinking we are helping the Kingdom of God or doing the will of God, and not knowing we are hurting the Kingdom! For example, how many times we preach the Law and preach condemnation thinking we are preventing sin, and not knowing we are strengthening sin rather. (see 1 Corinthians 15:56, with Romans 6:14). Indeed, we should learn from the mistakes poor Peter made, that it is very important for us to know and to act in accordance with all the will of God (see Colossians 1:9-12). We need to have a perfect knowledge of the will of God. And we can only attain this by praying continually, reading and meditating on the Word of God (see Joshua 1:8; Proverbs 4:20-27; Proverbs 3:1-6), being attentive to the teachings of the Holy Spirit (see 1 John 2:27), and learning to rightly divide the Word of truth (see 2 Timothy 2:15).

Now, back to our story, Jesus Christ had come into the world to manifest the love of God by dying for the sins of man, as man's Representative and Substitute, and He wasn't going to back off from that or allow anything to prevent Him from fulfilling that mission. Therefore Jesus allowed Himself to be ARRESTED and BOUND by those evil men (see John 18:12). "And they led Him away to ANNAS first, for he was the father-in-law of CAIAPHAS who was HIGH PRIEST that year. Now it was Caiaphas who advised the Jews that it was EXPEDIENT that ONE MAN SHOULD DIE FOR THE

PEOPLE." (John 18:13-14). As we noted earlier, as the high priest that year, Caiaphas spoke (not on his own) but by the Spirit, that "one man should die for the people." Therefore, now that they had this "one Man" in custody who could perhaps be the fulfillment of that prophecy by Caiaphas, they couldn't wait to get Him over to him. Therefore after Annas the high priest's father-in-law had questioned Jesus about His disciples and doctrines (see John 18:19-23), "Then Annas sent Him bound to Caiaphas the high priest." (John 18:24).

Important Lessons From Peter's Denial of Jesus

Before we discuss what happened to Jesus from this moment forward, let us look at a sad but interesting thing that happened to Peter as he followed Jesus AT A DISTANCE right into the high priest's courtyard and sat with the servants of the high priest **to warm himself at their fire**. (see Mark 14:54). As you would remember, Jesus had told His disciples after the Last Supper and over at the Mount of Olives that they would all be made to stumble tonight because of Him (see Matthew 26:30-31). But Peter had insisted that even if all the other disciples would deny or forsake Jesus, and even if he (Peter) would have to die with Jesus, he would never deny Jesus (see Matthew 26:32-33), to which Jesus had responded that, "Assuredly, I say to you that this night, before the rooster crows, you will deny Me three times." (Matthew 26:34). And so this prophecy of Jesus' was awaiting its fulfillment in Peter. "Now Peter sat outside in the courtyard. And a servant girl came to him, saying, "You also were with Jesus of Galilee." But he DENIED it before them all, saying, "I DO NOT KNOW WHAT YOU ARE SAYING." And when he had gone out to the gateway, another girl saw him and said to those who were there, "This fellow also was with

Jesus of Nazareth." But again he DENIED WITH AN OATH, "I do not know the Man!" And a little later those who stood by came up and said to Peter, "Surely you also are one of them, for your speech betrays you." Then he BEGAN TO CURSE AND SWEAR, saying, "I DO NOT KNOW THE Man!" Immediately a rooster crowed. And PETER REMEMBERED THE WORD OF JESUS who had said to him, "Before the rooster crows, you will deny Me three times." SO HE WENT OUT AND WEPT BITTERLY." (Matthew 26:69-75). Luke's gospel adds another important detail, that after Peter denied Jesus the third time, "THE LORD TURNED AND LOOKED AT PETER. Then Peter remembered the word of the Lord, how He had said to him, "Before the rooster crows, you will deny Me three times." So Peter went out and wept bitterly." (see Luke 22:61-62).

Beloved, Peter made a lot of mistakes in this story, that led to his fall — mistakes that are worth noting and learning from. The first lesson we can learn from Peter's fall is that there is grave danger in putting our confidence in our own faithfulness to the Lord. You see, the New Covenant is all about God's faithfulness displayed through Jesus Christ. It is not so much about our faithfulness. God doesn't want us to put our confidence in ourselves. He wants us to put our confidence in His Son Jesus Christ and in His faithfulness. In fact, the Bible says that "If we are faithless, He remains faithful; He cannot deny Himself." (2 Timothy 2:13-14). Can you believe that? Well, you should! Even when we are faithless (or unfaithful), God remains faithful. And so today, if you are blessed, it's not because you have been faithful to God; it's because God has been faithful to you. God's blessing is a free gift that comes through faith in Jesus Christ, so that no one can boast. (see Ephesians 2:8-9, with Ephesians 1:3). Our

Christian walk changes for the better when we start to look upon His faithfulness rather than our own faithfulness, when we start to put our confidence in His faithfulness. God is always faithful to us, because faithfulness is His very nature and character. He cannot deny Himself by being unfaithful. So those who think or say that God is faithful only to those who are faithful to Him are basically saying that God can deny Himself, which is just not true. Now, before anybody misconstrues what I have said thus far, let me intimate that I am not saying we don't have to be faithful to God. Certainly not! After all, faithfulness is a fruit of the Spirit (see Galatians 5:22), and so we will be faithful as long as we walk in the Spirit and not according to the flesh. Thus, I'm only emphasizing that, as believers, we don't live on the basis of our faithfulness; we live on the basis of His faithfulness. The Bible says we are to "TRUST IN THE LORD, and do good; dwell in the land, and FEED ON HIS FAITHFULNESS." (Psalms 37:3). This is what the Bible teaches. We are to feed on the faithfulness of God, not on our own faithfulness. When Peter focused or fed on his own faithfulness to Jesus, he spoke vehemently saying to Jesus, "If I have to die with You, I will not deny You!" (see Mark 14:31). And yet, just as Jesus had prophesied, Peter denied Him three times before the cock crowed (see Mark 14:66-72). Still, Jesus was faithful to Peter, and hired Him for His work following His resurrection. (see John 21:15-17). Now, tell me the truth: Would you hire somebody who betrayed you three times, and then put him in charge of your flock? You certainly wouldn't, unless faithfulness was your nature and you couldn't deny yourself. That is Jesus! That is God!

The second lesson we can learn from Peter's fall has to do with the fact that He did not follow our Lord Jesus Christ closely enough.

The Bible says Peter followed Jesus AT A DISTANCE (see Mark 14:54; Luke 22:54). Beloved, it is very dangerous to follow Jesus at a distance. There are many people today who admire or LIKE Jesus. They have heard great stories about how good of a Man Jesus was during His earth walk, how great a Teacher He was and How great a Miracle Worker He was. And so they like Him and mentally assent to His teachings. They can even quote some of His teachings and claim that somehow they believe in Him. But unfortunately such people don't want to stay close enough to Him. They don't want to submit their lives to Him and make Jesus their Lord and Savior. There are also some who claim to have made Jesus their Lord and Savior, who claim to believe in Jesus, and yet they can't or don't approach Jesus directly, even though the Lord has told us to "come boldly to the throne of grace that we may obtain mercy and find grace to help in time of need." (see Hebrews 4:16). Such so-called believers don't stay close to Jesus or approach Him directly, but instead, they prefer to follow Jesus at a distance, and thus approach Him through "Saints" and through "Mary" as well as so-called priests. Following Jesus at a distance is dangerous, as we can see from the story of Peter's fall. The believer cannot follow Jesus at a distance; the believer cannot approach Jesus any other way except directly. (see Hebrews 4:16; 1 Corinthians 1:9; John 15:5-7; John 16:23; 1 Timothy 2:5). Temptations will abound when we follow Jesus at a distance, as we may end up denying Jesus, just like Peter did. Indeed many people today "profess to know God, but in works they deny Him, being abominable, disobedient, and disqualified for every good work." (see Titus 1:16). The secret to following Jesus closely is to know the Word of Christ, to abide in His Word as His Word abides in you. (see John 15:7). The Psalmist says, "Your word I have hidden in my heart, that I might not sin against

You." (Psalms 119:11). You have to "Let the word of Christ dwell in you richly in all wisdom, teaching and admonishing one another in psalms and hymns and spiritual songs, singing with grace in your hearts to the Lord. And whatever you do in word or deed, do all in the name of the Lord Jesus, giving thanks to God the Father through Him." (Colossians 3:16-17).

We also have a lot to learn from Peter's tragic mistake of seeking warmth at the enemy's fire. (see Mark 14:54; Luke 22:55). The Bible says, "Now when **they had kindled a fire in the midst of the courtyard and sat down together**, PETER SAT AMONG THEM." (Luke 22:55). How many times I have heard stories about so-called believers who go to sorcerers, mediums and necromancers to seek comfort or seek answers and solutions to their problems. This is not only dangerous but stupid and outrageous, because as believers we have the same power that raised Jesus from the dead living inside of us (see Ephesians 1:19-20); we have God Himself working in us with His mighty power or ability. (see Philippians 2:13; Colossians 1:29). And so we don't need the enemy's fire (or power) for warmth or comfort. It is dangerous for us to sit in the company of the ungodly, as Peter did. The Bible says, "Blessed is the man who walks not in the counsel of the ungodly, nor stands in the path of sinners, NOR SITS IN THE SEAT OF THE SCORNFUL" (Psalms 1:1). Peter was in violation of this admonition when he sat among those sinners, when he sat in the seat of the scornful. Hence he made himself vulnerable to the temptations that derailed his faith and made him deny the Lord. And so Paul admonishes us in his Second letter to the Corinthians that "Do not be unequally yoked together with unbelievers. For what fellowship has righteousness with lawlessness? And what communion has light with darkness? And what accord has Christ with Belial? Or what part has a believer with an unbeliever?" (2 Corinthians 6:14-15). Let us, therefore, heed Paul's admonition. Let us learn from the fall of Peter, so that we will not make the mistake of fellowshipping with unbelievers, feeding on our own faithfulness, and following Jesus at a distance, because we will make ourselves vulnerable to temptations/failure when we do so.

Jesus Was Falsely Accused of Blasphemy

Now, let us continue our walk with the Lord Jesus Christ as He is brought bound to Caiaphas the high priest and put before the Sanhedrin — the assembly of the high priest, the scribes, the chief priests and elders of the people (see Matthew 26:57; Mark 14:53). The Bible says that these lawless men **sought false testimony against Jesus** to put Him to death, but **found none.** (see Mark 14:55; Matthew 26:59-61). Many came forward to bear false witness against Jesus, but their testimonies did not agree. (see Mark 14:56). But at last two false witnesses came forward "and said, "This fellow said, 'I am able to destroy the temple of God and to build it in three days.'" And the high priest arose and said to Him, "Do You answer nothing? What is it these men testify against You?" BUT JESUS KEPT SILENT. And the high priest answered and said to Him, "I PUT You UNDER OATH BY THE LIVING GOD: Tell us if You are THE CHRIST, the Son of God!" Jesus said to him, "IT IS AS YOU SAID. Nevertheless, I say to you, hereafter you will see the Son of Man sitting at the right hand of the Power, and coming on the clouds of heaven." Then the high priest tore his clothes, saying, "**He has spoken BLASPHEMY**! What further need do we have of witnesses? Look, now you have heard His

BLASPHEMY! What do you think?" They answered and said, "He is DESERVING OF DEATH." (Matthew 26:61-66). Thus, desperate for the blood of Jesus and struggling to no avail to find an offense based on which to sentence Him to death, these evil men became more frustrated by Jesus' silence and decided to put Him under oath by the living God to testify if He was the Christ (the Messiah), the Son of God. It was only when Jesus was put under oath by the living God to testify, that He spoke and affirmed that He was indeed the Christ, the Son of God. Then He went on to declare that His Kingdom is not of this world; He also declared His glory in the Kingdom that was to come. And so Jesus' truthful confession of who He was, had Him falsely convicted of blasphemy. It was Jesus' confession that infuriated the enemy and got Him killed, because the enemy couldn't stand it!

Today Satan still can't stand to hear us confess who we are as new creations in Christ. He can't stand to hear us confess that we are the beloved sons of God who are blessed with every spiritual blessing in the heavenly realms in Christ Jesus. (see John 1:12; 1 John 3:2, with Ephesians 1:3). Satan can't stand to hear us confess that we are the righteousness of God in Christ Jesus (see 2 Corinthians 5:21), and that there is therefore now no condemnation for us because we are in Christ Jesus. (see Romans 8:1; Romans 8:33-39). Satan can't stand to hear us confess that sin shall not have dominion over us because we are not under Law but under Grace. (see Romans 6:14). This is why the Bible tells us to hold fast our confession. (see Hebrews 4:14). We have to continually confess who we are in Christ. Indeed, we overcome the enemy by the blood of the Lamb, and by the WORD (logos) OF OUR TESTIMONY, **not loving our lives unto death**. (see Revelation 12:11). Jesus wasn't afraid to confess who He was even if it meant death, and neither should we be afraid to confess who we are in Christ, even if it means death, because that is how we overcome the enemy. Jesus' death was to bring a crushing defeat to Satan the enemy, and an astounding victory to all of us who believe in Jesus Christ. And it did. Praise God!

Jesus was falsely convicted of blasphemy by the Sanhedrin and declared to be deserving of death, all because of His truthful confession that He was the Christ, the Son of God. And so here He was in the hands of His own people — now His enemies — as they numbered Him with the transgressors (see Luke 22:37; Matthew 15:28). Israel's covenant God, the God who made a covenant with Abraham, the God who saved the family of Jacob from being wiped out by a famine in Canaan, the Lord who delivered Israel out of bondage in Egypt with a mighty hand and performed great miracles for Israel in the wilderness, the Immanuel who was God with them, the Messiah who was prophesied to be sent to them (see Isaiah 9:6), had finally come in the fullness of time, having been born of a woman, born under the Law to redeem those who were under the Law that they might receive the adoption as sons (see Galatians 4:4-5); but Israel couldn't recognize or receive Him. "He was in the world, and the world was made through Him, and the world did not know Him. **He came to His own, and His own did not receive Him.**" (John 1:10-11). Rather, they rejected Him and condemned their God and their Savior as deserving of death. What a tragedy!

Thus Jesus, having been condemned to death, was blindfolded (see Mark 14:65). Then they spat in His face, and beat Him; and others struck Him with the palms of their hands, saying, "Prophesy to us, Christ! Who is the one who struck You?" (see Matthew 26:67-68).

"And many other things they blasphemously spoke against Him." (Luke 22:65). And this (I suppose) was done throughout the night until morning. Obviously these lawless Jews desired so much to kill Jesus, but it was not lawful (under Roman law) for them to put anyone to death (see John 18:31). This explains their earlier efforts to find false witnesses and false testimonies to present against Jesus before the Roman Authorities.

The Bible says that "Immediately, in the morning, the chief priests held a consultation with the elders and scribes and the whole council; and they bound Jesus, led Him away, and delivered Him to Pilate. Then Pilate asked Him, "Are You **the King of the Jews**?" He answered and said to him, "**It is as you say**." (Mark 15:1-2). Thus, the Bible says that Jesus Christ witnessed the **good confession** before Pontius Pilate. (see 1 Timothy 6:13). Before Pilate, Jesus did not deny who He was; neither should we deny who we are in Christ before Satan and his minions. And so the Jews had delivered their own God and King to a pagan governor for trial, and demanded His crucifixion. They took Jesus to Pilate in the Praetorium. According to John's gospel, the Jews themselves didn't enter the Praetorium with Jesus because they didn't want to defile themselves by going into a Gentile's court, so that they would (be ceremonially clean to) be able to eat the Passover. (See John 18:28). Hypocrites indeed! "Pilate then went out to them and said, "What accusation do you bring against this Man?" They answered and said to him, "If He were not an EVILDOER, we would not have delivered Him up to you." (John 18:29-30). But Pilate knew better after questioning Jesus. He knew that Jesus was no evildoer. Pilate declared Jesus as a just Man (see Matthew 27:24; Mark 15:13); he said, "I find no fault in Him at all." (see John 18:38).

As you can glean from Pilate's line of questioning, he was obviously more interested in securing his seat as governor (or king, if you may) over the people. Pilate was more concerned about the perceived threat Jesus might pose to his position if He indeed were the King of the Jews — the insurrection He might incite against his government. And so Pilate first asked Jesus, "Are you the King of the Jews?" And then Jesus got his attention when He responded that it was so, and that it was for the reason or cause of being a King and bearing witness to the truth that He was born. (see John 18:37). Jesus also perhaps put Pilate at ease when He explained that His Kingdom is not of this world. (see John 18:36). Meanwhile the chief priests and elders also continued to falsely accuse Jesus before Pilate. And the Bible says that, "while He (Jesus) was being accused by the chief priests and elders, He ANSWERED NOTHING. Then Pilate said to Him, "Do You not hear how many things they testify against You?" But He ANSWERED him NOT ONE WORD, so that the governor MARVELED GREATLY." (see Matthew 27:12-14). Here, it is obvious that Jesus' silence fulfilled the Prophecy of Isaiah that "He was **oppressed** and He was **afflicted, yet He opened not His mouth**; He was led as a lamb to the slaughter, and as a sheep before its shearers is silent, so **He opened not His mouth.**" (Isaiah 53:7). And thus Pilate marveled greatly that Jesus wouldn't defend Himself against His accusers. (see Matthew 27:14; Mark 3:5). Pilate marveled all the more because he knew that the chief priests and elders had handed Jesus over because of ENVY. (see Mark 15:10; Matthew 27:18). Pilate himself found no fault in Jesus Christ; he said, **"I find no fault in Him at all."** (see John 18:38). And so Pilate sought a way to release Jesus, to set Jesus free. (see John 19:12). "But they (the Jews) were the more fierce, saying, "He stirs up the people, teaching throughout all Judea, beginning from Galilee to this place." When Pilate heard of Galilee, he asked if the Man were a Galilean. And as soon as he knew that He belonged to Herod's jurisdiction, he sent Him to Herod, who was also in Jerusalem at that time. Now when Herod **saw** Jesus, HE WAS EXCEEDINGLY GLAD; for he had DESIRED FOR A LONG TIME TO SEE Him, BECAUSE he had heard many things about Him, and **he HOPED TO SEE SOME MIRACLE DONE BY Him.** Then he questioned Him with MANY WORDS, but He ANSWERED HIM NOTHING. And the chief priests and scribes stood and vehemently accused Him. Then Herod, with his men of war, treated Him WITH CONTEMPT and MOCKED Him, arrayed Him in a gorgeous robe, and sent Him back to Pilate. THAT VERY DAY PILATE AND HEROD BECAME FRIENDS with each other, for PREVIOUSLY THEY HAD BEEN AT ENMITY with each other." (Luke 23:5-12).

What is Your Reason for Seeking Jesus?

It is interesting that King Herod was exceedingly glad to see Jesus. Obviously Jesus didn't feel the same way about seeing Herod. This Herod was the same king who ordered John the Baptist to be beheaded as a present for Herodias' daughter (see Mark 6:16-29), and so Jesus had also heard some unflattering things about him. (see Matthew 14:12-13). Jesus had even called Herod a fox. When some Pharisees came to tell Jesus to leave Galilee and go somewhere else because Herod wanted to kill Him, "He replied, "Go tell THAT FOX, 'I will keep on driving out demons and healing people today and tomorrow, and on the third day I will reach my goal.'" (Luke 13:32 NIV). Herod, however, was obviously impressed by the things he had heard about Jesus and the great miracles He was performing; Herod had even thought it was John the Baptist who had risen from the dead. The Bible says, "Now King Herod heard of Him (Jesus), for His NAME HAD BECOME WELL KNOWN. And he (Herod) said, "John the Baptist is RISEN FROM THE DEAD, and therefore these powers are at work in him." (Mark 6:14). And so Herod desired to meet Jesus.

Of course, we are told the reason Herod was exceedingly glad to see Jesus — he had heard many great things about Jesus and had desired for a long time to see Him **in the hope that** He MIGHT PERFORM SOME MIRACLE **FOR HIM TO SEE**. What a lousy reason undergirded Herod's long-held desire to see Jesus! What a phony Herod really was! It is sad that even today, there are some people who seek Jesus for the same lame reason Herod had. They're not seeking Him so that they would make Him their Lord and Savior and receive eternal life. No, they only want to satisfy the lusts of their eyes — they only want to see miracles done by Jesus. It would be shocking to know just how many people go to evangelistic meetings just for this purpose. My friend, if you're one such person, know that Jesus has no desire to meet you at all; He is not glad at all to see you at these gatherings, regardless of how exceedingly glad you may be to see Him. However, if you desire to meet Jesus for the right reasons, if you desire to meet Jesus for salvation, which also brings healing and wholeness, then know that Jesus desires to meet you also, and He will be exceedingly glad to see you. In fact He is calling you right now. He says, "Come to Me, all you who labor and are heavy laden, and I will give you rest." (Matthew 11:28). And to those who still find it hard to come, He says, "Behold, I stand at the door and knock. If anyone hears My voice and opens the door, I will come in to him and dine with him, and he with Me." (Revelation 3:20). Hallelujah! Jesus seeks to fellowship with those who come to Him with a humble spirit, and a broken and contrite heart — a heart broken over sin and repentant of sin. David writes, "The sacrifices of God are a broken spirit, a broken and a contrite heart — these, O God, You will NOT DESPISE." (Psalm 51:17). King Herod had no such spirit nor heart. No wonder we are told that Jesus gave King Herod silent treatment. And after Jesus gave Herod silent treatment (and obviously refused to perform any miracle for him to see), "Herod, with his men of war, treated Him with contempt and mocked Him, arrayed Him in a gorgeous robe, and sent Him back to Pilate. That very day Pilate and Herod became friends with each other, for previously they had been at enmity with each other." (see Luke 23:11-12). Indeed, it is baffling how people so often unite around evil deeds — Herod and Pilate present a classic example.

What is Your Judgment Concerning Jesus Christ?

Now, the Bible says that at the feast of the Passover, the governor (Pilate) was accustomed to releasing to the multitude one prisoner whom they wished. (see Matthew 27:15). Perhaps he did this only as a goodwill gesture to please the people and garner the support of the masses, because we are told in John's gospel that this custom of releasing one prisoner to them during the Passover was actually a custom of the Jews. (see John 18:39). Perhaps it was a custom they had fought hard for. And thus, since at that time they had a notorious prisoner called Barabbas (see Matthew 27:16), Pilate (seeking to release Jesus or set Him free — see John 19:12) said to the people, "But YOU HAVE A CUSTOM that I SHOULD release someone to you at the Passover. Do you therefore want me to release to you the King of the Jews?" Then they all cried again, saying, "NOT THIS Man, but Barabbas!" Now Barabbas was a ROBBER." (John 18:39-40). Why would the Jews choose to request the release of a notorious murderer and robber over Jesus the innocent and just Man, you ask? The Bible says that the chief priests and elders of the people persuaded or stirred up the multitudes to ask for the release of Barabbas and destroy Jesus. (see Matthew 27:20; Mark 15:11). And so they did. And "Pilate said to them, "WHAT THEN SHALL I DO WITH JESUS WHO IS CALLED CHRIST?" They all said to him, "Let Him be crucified!" (Matthew 27:22).

Pilate asked a very interesting and important question when he asked, "What then shall I do with Jesus who is called Christ?" You see, everyone of us has to make a decision concerning Jesus Christ. We have to decide what we want to do with Jesus who is called Christ. We have to be the judges who decide whether we're going to receive Him or deny Him, whether we're going to accept Him or reject Him, whether we are going to believe in Him or not believe in Him. We cannot be excluded in this matter. Pilate recognized that burden. He recognized that being the judge concerning Jesus was not an exclusive burden. And thus he asked for the involvement of the people in making the judgment. It was a very unusual move from such a prominent judge, and yet it was a significant move, because the fact of the matter is that we are all judges when it comes to Jesus. Everybody has to make a personal judgment concerning Jesus. It is a personal judgment that cannot be made for you by Pilate. You have to make a decision for yourself, and you are responsible then for that decision that you make. What are you going to do with Jesus who is called the Messiah? You can't escape this decision. You can't escape this judgment. Jesus will not allow you to sit on the fence. He said, "he that is not for Me is against Me" (see Matthew 12:30). Therefore you must decide in your heart whether you are for Him or against Him. Failing to accept Him today is the same as rejecting Him. There is no neutrality. And the interesting thing about your decision or judgment concerning Jesus is that it does not determine the destiny of Jesus; it only determines your own destiny. Jesus is the Son of God, and Jesus is God (see Philippians 2:6; 1 Timothy 3:16; Acts 20:28; Romans 9:5), whether you accept it or not. Jesus is who He is regardless of what you believe or think, regardless of the judgment you make concerning Him. "The Jewish leaders insisted, "We have a law, and according to that law He (Jesus) must die, because **He claimed to be the Son of God.**" (John 19:7 NIV). "**For this reason** they tried all the more to kill him; not only was he breaking the Sabbath, but **he was even calling God his own Father, making himself equal with God.**" (John 5:18 NIV).

You see, Godliness is a mystery. The Jewish leaders didn't know that. The Bible says, "And without controversy great is the mystery of godliness: God was **manifested in the flesh**, Justified in the Spirit, Seen by angels, Preached among the Gentiles, Believed on in the world, Received up in glory." (1 Timothy 3:16). This is obviously referring to Jesus. So Jesus is the eternally blessed God; He is God over all (see also Romans 9:5), whether you believe it or not. The Jewish leaders chose not to believe in Him. So they called for His crucifixion. But by crucifying Him, they only gave Him the opportunity to affirm His divinity by raising Himself from the dead. Today, your refusal to accept or believe in Jesus will not determine the destiny of Jesus, but it will determine your own eternal destiny. Your refusal to submit yourself to Jesus and accept Him as your Lord and Savior will not affect Jesus' Lordship; it will only affect your own eternal destiny. The Bible says, "He who believes in Him **is not condemned**; but he who does not believe **is condemned already**, because he has not believed in the name of the only begotten Son of God." (John 3:18).

Therefore Pilate's decision really didn't determine the destiny of Jesus, because **Jesus was slain from the foundation of the world** (see Revelation 13:8); rather, it determined Pilate's own destiny. You are in the same position today as judge concerning Jesus. You have to judge in your own heart whether Jesus was a liar and a fraud, or whether He is indeed the Son of God, whether He is indeed "the way, the truth and the life" that He claimed to be (see John 14:6). And in making this judgment, you are ultimately judging yourself and determining your own destiny by choosing to accept or reject Jesus. And thus, no one can blame God for their destiny, because God has given to each man the capacity of choice. The choice you make today concerning Jesus determines your eternal destiny. "For as many as received Him, to them gave He the power to become the sons of God, even **to those who believed upon His name**" (see John 1:12). "For God so loved the world, that He gave His only begotten Son, that **whosoever believes in Him, should not perish, but have everlasting life.**" (see John 3:16). But if you don't believe in Him, then you will perish. "He who does not believe will be condemned." (see Mark 16:16). And this is where you're sitting in the judgement seat: you are determining your own destiny, as you choose to believe or not to believe in Jesus Christ, as you choose to be saved or to be condemned.

May you make the right decision as you sit in judgment concerning what you would do with Jesus who is called Christ. May you carefully examine all the evidence concerning Jesus and make the right decision, because ignorance is no excuse for the wrong decision. It doesn't help to make a decision about Jesus based on the testimony of people who don't know Him. It doesn't help to make a decision concerning Jesus based on pressure from the crowd or from your science books at school. Search the Bible yourself, and you will arrive at the truth that no one can get to God without going through Jesus Christ. Jesus is the only Way to God, because He Himself is God. He Himself has reached out to man and reconciled us to Himself through His sacrifice on the cross. (see 2 Corinthians 5:18-19). Those who try to point you to God through any other way are themselves lost; either they're ignorant, or they're thieves and robbers. Jesus said, "Most assuredly, I say to you, he who does not enter the sheepfold by **the door**, but climbs up some other way, the same is **a thief and a robber**. Then Jesus said to them again, "Most assuredly, I say to you, **I am the door of the sheep**. All who ever came before Me are thieves and robbers, but the sheep did not hear them. **I am the door. If anyone enters by Me, he will be saved, and will go in and out and find pasture.**" (John 10:1, 7-9).

Indeed, ignorance is no excuse for making the wrong decision concerning Jesus; ignorance is no excuse for rejecting Jesus. The Bible warns that "God **overlooked** people's ignorance about these things **in earlier times**, but **now** He commands everyone everywhere to **repent** of their sins **and turn to Him**. For He has set a day for judging the world with justice by the Man He has appointed, and **He proved to everyone who this is by raising Him from the dead**." (Acts 17:30-31 NLT). There are many people today who have weighed all the evidence concerning Jesus and have arrived at the inevitable conclusion that He is innocent, He is without sin; He is indeed the Son of God, the King of kings and the Lord of Lords; He is indeed who He claimed to be. And yet, just like Pilate, they have yielded to pressure from people (be it professors, religious leaders, friends or family), and have rejected Jesus. But I feel sorry for such people. Woe to the one who has rejected Jesus Christ. You'd be much better off if you were never born than to live without Jesus Christ, because to live without Jesus Christ is to live without hope, to live in fearful expectation of death, in a certain fearful expectation of judgment. And in the end, those who don't have Jesus will have to face that certain fiery wrath of God which will devour His adversaries. "Anyone who has rejected Moses' law dies without mercy on the testimony of two or three witnesses. OF HOW MUCH WORSE PUNISHMENT, do you suppose, will he be thought worthy who has trampled the Son of God underfoot, counted the blood of the covenant by which he was sanctified a common thing, and insulted the Spirit of grace? For we know Him who said, "Vengeance is Mine, I will repay," says the Lord. And again, "The Lord will judge His people." It is a fearful thing to fall into the hands of the living God." (Hebrews 10:28-31). Better that you'd never been born than to incur God's wrath.

God loves man too much to see anyone suffer His wrath. This is why He sent Jesus Christ into the world. The Bible says, "But God demonstrates His own love toward us, in that while we were still sinners, Christ died for us. Much more then, having now been justified by His blood, **we shall be saved from wrath through Him.**" (Romans 5:8-9). If you receive Jesus Christ as your Lord and Savior, you will be justified by His blood, you will receive eternal life, and you will be saved from God's wrath and live in joyful expectation of the appearing of our Lord Jesus Christ.

Jesus – the Substitute for the Sinner

And now, back to our story, the multitudes asked for Barabbas to be released, and for Jesus to be crucified, notwithstanding the fact that Barabbas was a robber and a murderer, and Jesus was innocent, just and sinless. Pilate the governor was even dismayed by this decision and declaration of the multitudes. And so the Bible says, "Then the governor said, "Why, what evil has He done?" But they cried out all the more, saying, "Let Him be crucified!" When Pilate saw that he could not prevail at all, but rather that a tumult was rising, he took water and washed his hands before the multitude, saying, "I am innocent of the blood of this just Person. You see to it." And all the people answered and said, "His blood be on us and on our children." Then he released Barabbas to them; and when he had scourged Jesus, **he delivered Him to be crucified.**" (Matthew 27:23-26).

It is interesting that the Jews asked for the release of the unjust man or the sinner Barabbas, and the death of the just Man Jesus Christ. Jesus therefore became the Substitute for the sinner and died the death the sinner was supposed to die. Thus the Bible says, "For Christ also hath once suffered for sins, **the just for the unjust**, that he might bring us to God, being put to death in the flesh, but quickened by the Spirit" (1 Peter 3:18 KJV). It is also interesting that the Jews asked for the blood of Jesus Christ to be on them and on their children. In other words, they were unabashedly accepting responsibility and blame for the lawless and wicked act of killing a just and innocent Man. How tragic! These Jews were indeed murderers like their father the devil, just as Jesus had spoken of them. (see John 8:44). And of course, the blood of Jesus will forever be on them and their children. You would remember that when Peter stood up on the Day of Pentecost, after the outpouring of the Holy Spirit to speak, he said, "Men of Israel, hear these words: Jesus of Nazareth, a Man attested by God TO YOU by miracles, wonders, and signs which God did through Him in your midst, as you yourselves also know— Him, being delivered by the determined purpose and foreknowledge of God, **YOU HAVE TAKEN BY LAWLESS HANDS, HAVE CRUCIFIED, AND PUT TO DEATH."** (Acts 2:22-23). Thus Peter put the blood of Jesus squarely on the Jews. Peter put the blame on them just as they had wished at the trial of Jesus. But Peter also knew that Jesus had forgiven them (see Luke 23:34), and so he implored them to repent and be baptized in the name of Jesus Christ for the remission of their sins, so that they will also receive the gift of the Holy Spirit. (see Acts 2:38).

Back to the trial of Jesus, the Bible says, "So Pilate, WANTING TO GRATIFY THE CROWD, released Barabbas to them; and he DELIVERED JESUS, after he had SCOURGED Him, **TO BE CRUCIFIED.** Then the SOLDIERS led Him away into the hall called Praetorium, and they called together THE WHOLE GARRISON. And they clothed Him with PURPLE; and they TWISTED A CROWN OF THORNS, put it on His HEAD, and began to salute Him, "Hail, King of the Jews!" Then they STRUCK Him ON THE HEAD with a REED and SPAT on Him; and bowing the knee, they worshiped Him. And when they had MOCKED Him, THEY TOOK THE PURPLE OFF Him, put His own clothes on Him, and led Him out TO CRUCIFY Him." (Mark 15:15-20). A few things are noteworthy here. First, Pilate delivered Jesus to be crucified NOT because He was GUILTY, but because Pilate wanted to GRATIFY or PLEASE the crowd. (see Mark 15:15). Woe to the people-pleasers! Paul said, "Am I now trying to win the approval of human beings, or of God?

Or am I trying to please people? If I were still trying to please people, I would not be a servant of Christ." (Galatians 1:10 NIV). Pilate was more interested in pleasing people than pleasing God. Second, the soldiers took Jesus into the Praetorium and gathered the WHOLE GARRISON (or troops) around Him. And they STRIPPED Him (naked) and put a scarlet (or purple) robe on Him. (see Matthew 27:27-28; Mark 15:16-17). Third, they twisted a CROWN OF THORNS and PUT IT ON HIS HEAD, and put in His right hand a REED (a weak grass, perhaps symbolizing in mockery that Jesus was a weak King). Then they bowed the knee before Him and mocked Him, saying, "Hail King of the Jews!" (see Matthew 27:29; Mark 15:17-19). Fourth, they SPAT on Jesus, and took the REED and struck Him on the head. (see Mark 15:19). When they had mocked Him (and were satisfied), they TOOK the robe OFF Him (that is, stripped Him naked again), put His own clothes on Him, and led Him away to be crucified. (see Matthew 27:31; Mark 15:20).

The gospel according to John says, "Now it was the Preparation Day of the Passover, and **about the sixth hour**. And he (Pilate) said to the Jews, "BEHOLD YOUR KING!" But they cried out, "AWAY WITH HIM, away with Him! CRUCIFY HIM!" Pilate said to them, "Shall I crucify your King?" The chief priests answered, "We have no king but Caesar!" Then he DELIVERED Him TO THEM **TO BE CRUCIFIED.** So they TOOK JESUS AND LED HIM AWAY." (John 19:14-16).

In the next Chapter, we will follow Jesus on His trip to Golgotha and witness as He is nailed to the cross and dies to take away the sins of the world. Indeed, we will die with Him, be buried with Him, and rise with Him into newness of life. And having had our minds illuminated by the Savior after His resurrection, we will begin to reveal, to unravel who we truly are as new creations in Christ. It is my hope and prayer that you will read this book to the end. For I am confident that by the end of the book, you will understand and appreciate the necessity of living and walking in the Spirit as a new creation, and why you can't afford to live or walk according to the flesh. "For if you live according to the flesh you will die; but if by the Spirit you put to death the deeds of the body, you will live." (Romans 8:13).

Chapter 11

Jesus Our Ransom

Jesus Died on the Cross for Our Sins

LET US BEGIN this Chapter with a recap (from the gospel according to Luke) of the final moments of Jesus' trial and the sentence that was issued thereof. *"Then Pilate, when he had called together the CHIEF PRIESTS, THE RULERS, and THE PEOPLE, said to them, "You have brought this Man to me, as ONE WHO MISLEADS THE PEOPLE. And indeed, having EXAMINED Him in your presence,* **I HAVE FOUND NO FAULT in this Man** *concerning those things of which you accuse Him; no, NEITHER DID HEROD, for I sent you back to him; and indeed NOTHING DESERVING OF DEATH HAS BEEN DONE BY Him. I will therefore CHASTISE Him and RELEASE Him"* (*for it was NECESSARY for him to RELEASE ONE TO THEM AT THE FEAST). And they all cried out at once, saying, "AWAY WITH THIS Man, and RELEASE TO US BARABBAS"— who had been thrown into prison for a certain REBELLION made in the city, and FOR MURDER. Pilate, therefore, WISHING TO RELEASE JESUS, again called out to them. But* **they SHOUTED, saying, "CRUCIFY Him, CRUCIFY Him!"** *Then he said to them the THIRD TIME, "Why, what evil has He done? I HAVE FOUND NO REASON FOR DEATH in Him. I will therefore chastise Him and let Him go." But they were*

*INSISTENT, DEMANDING WITH LOUD VOICES that He be CRUCIFIED. And **the VOICES of these men and of the chief priests PREVAILED.** So PILATE GAVE SENTENCE THAT IT SHOULD BE AS THEY REQUESTED. And he RELEASED to them THE ONE THEY REQUESTED, who for REBELLION and MURDER had been thrown into prison; but he DELIVERED JESUS TO THEIR WILL."* (Luke 23:13-25).

Here in Luke's Gospel, we see Jesus in whom no fault was found, taking the place of Barabbas (the murderer and rebellious one) to die in his place, to die as his Substitute, to die the death Barabbas was supposed to die. In the previous chapter, we noted that Jesus was the Substitute for the sinner. Indeed, there is no gainsaying the fact that Barabbas represents each and every one of us. Each of us is Barabbas. We are the guilty ones that deserved to die. Like Barabbas, we are the rebellious ones and the murderers, having rebelled against God's law at every stage in human history, beginning in the garden of Eden. There in the Garden also, we became murderers (represented by Cain), having been enslaved by Satan after Adam had voluntarily given over the dominion over the earth to him. Thus, Jesus said of the "Old Creation man," "You are of YOUR FATHER THE DEVIL, and the desires of your father you want to do. He was a MURDERER from the beginning, and does not stand in the truth, because THERE IS NO TRUTH IN HIM. When he speaks a lie, he speaks from his own resources, for he is A LIAR and the father of it." (John 8:44). The whole human race after the fall of Adam is considered collectively as the offspring (or seed) of Satan. First John 5:19 says that the whole world is under the sway of Satan. This is why we needed to be created anew and redeemed from the dominion of Satan (the devil). Moreover, explaining who a murderer is, John wrote that anyone who hates his brother or sister is a murderer (see 1 John 3:15); Jesus said anyone who is angry with a brother or sister is subject to judgment in the same way as a murderer is subject to judgment. (see Matthew 5:21-22). You see, many people find it difficult to embrace the Good News (of grace) because they don't understand the bad news that we are all guilty before God and deserve to die. In Romans 1:22-32, the apostle Paul lists over 23 different kinds of sin including idolatry, murder, envy, gossip, disobedience to parents, lack of understanding, pride, and deceit, and then declares that "all who do such things DESERVE DEATH." In Romans 14:23, Paul expands the list of sins to include anything that is not of faith (which will include our doubts or worries). James also expands the list of sins further to include anything we know is good but fail to do. (see James 4:17). Such all-encompassing definition of sin makes Paul's pronouncement in Romans 3:23 that "ALL HAVE SINNED and fall short of the glory of God" all the more compelling. It also makes the declaration in Romans 6:23 that "the wages of sin is death" all the more scary.

Like Barabbas, we were all sinners or lawbreakers destined to die, destined to perish with our father the devil on the Day of Judgment. We were all in the same condition and position as Barabbas, waiting hopelessly for the Day we will be thrown into the eternal fires of hell to perish. And yet, while we were still sinners, while we were still hopelessly waiting to die, Jesus Christ the sinless Man was delivered up to be killed for our sins, to die in our place so that we would be released and live, so that we would be saved from the wrath of God (see Romans 5:8), just as Barabbas was saved from the wrath of Pilate. How amazing the grace that saved us! How deep the love that ransomed us, that took our place on that rugged cross! Oh, how can we ever pay our debt of gratitude! Today, all we have to do to be declared innocent and walk away justified in the eyes of God is to believe in the Lord Jesus Christ and thus accept the payment He made for our sins. (see John 3:16; Romans 3:23-26). If you're not already saved, you will be saved today if you will simply accept the substitutionary death Jesus died for you on the cross, by confessing Jesus as your Lord and believing in your heart that God has raised Him from the dead. (see Romans 10:9). And once you have done this, you will join the many sons of God who continually offer Him our sacrifices of Praise. You will also join us in offering our bodies as a living sacrifice to God, so that we can all say with the apostle Paul: "I am crucified with Christ: nevertheless I live; yet not I, but Christ liveth in me: and the life which I now live in the flesh I live by the faith of the Son of God, who loved me, and gave himself for me." (Galatians 2:20 KJV). Praise God!

We Are All Commanded to Bear Our Cross Daily After Jesus

The Bible says that after Jesus was unfairly and unjustly sentenced to death for no offense at all — for no sin at all — He was delivered up for crucifixion and led away bearing His own cross to a place called the Place of the Skull, which in Hebrew is called **Golgotha**. (see John 19:17). The Gospel according to Luke also tells us that, "Now as they led Him away, THEY LAID HOLD of a certain man, SIMON a Cyrenian, who was coming from the country, and ON him THEY LAID THE CROSS that he might BEAR IT AFTER JESUS. And a GREAT MULTITUDE of the people FOLLOWED Him, and WOMEN WHO ALSO MOURNED and LAMENTED

Him. But Jesus, turning to them, said, "Daughters of Jerusalem, DO NOT WEEP FOR Me, but WEEP FOR YOURSELVES AND FOR YOUR CHILDREN. For indeed the days are coming in which they will say, 'Blessed are the barren, wombs that never bore, and breasts which never nursed!' Then they will begin 'to say to the mountains, "Fall on us!" and to the hills, "Cover us!"' For if they do these things in THE GREEN WOOD, what will be done in the DRY?" (Luke 23:26-31).

Simon of Cyrene was made (or compelled) to bear the cross after Jesus. (see Matthew 27:32; Mark 15:21). In the same way as Simon was compelled by the soldiers to bear the cross after Jesus, the love of Jesus compels us today to bear our cross daily after Jesus; Jesus is asking all of us (who desire to be His disciples) **to take up our cross daily and follow Him**. We are to share in His suffering, so that we will also share in His glory. He said, "If anyone desires to come after Me, let him deny himself, and TAKE UP HIS CROSS, AND FOLLOW Me." (Matthew 16:24). Thus, Paul says of those of us (the apostles) who preach the gospel, that, "We are hard-pressed on every side, yet not crushed; we are perplexed, but not in despair; persecuted, but not forsaken; struck down, but not destroyed — **always carrying about in the body the dying of the Lord Jesus**, THAT **THE LIFE OF JESUS** ALSO MAY BE **MANIFESTED IN OUR BODY**. For we who live are ALWAYS DELIVERED TO DEATH FOR JESUS' SAKE, that THE LIFE OF JESUS ALSO MAY BE MANIFESTED IN OUR MORTAL FLESH. So then death is working in us, but life in you." (2 Corinthians 4:8-12). Indeed we are all commanded to crucify the flesh (by the Spirit) or die daily, so that Christ might live (and manifest) in us. We are commanded to deny ourselves (of all selfish or worldly desires, ambitions and interests), take up our cross DAILY, and follow the Lord Jesus Christ. (see Luke 9:23). Yet, although, like Simon of Cyrene we must take up our cross and follow Jesus, ultimately Jesus' death alone saves us, for He died to save us. We cannot die to save ourselves, but even if we should lose our life bearing our cross after Jesus, we will find our life back — we will be saved. And thus Jesus added: "For whoever desires to save his life will lose it, but whoever loses his life for My sake will find it." (Matthew 16:25). In the light of this truth, Paul also said (of those of us who take our cross daily to follow Jesus) that if we are children of God, then we are heirs of God and joint-heirs with Christ, if indeed we SUFFER WITH HIM, that we may also be GLORIFIED TOGETHER. (see Romans 8:17). Then he added: "For I consider that the SUFFERINGS of this present time ARE NOT WORTHY TO BE COMPARED with THE GLORY which shall be revealed in us." (Romans 8:18). Hallelujah! Peter also emphasized the same truth when he wrote: "Beloved, do not think it strange concerning the FIERY TRIAL which is to try you, as though some strange thing happened to you; but REJOICE to the extent that YOU PARTAKE OF CHRIST'S SUFFERINGS, that when His GLORY is revealed, you may also be GLAD with EXCEEDING JOY. If you are REPROACHED FOR THE NAME OF CHRIST, **BLESSED ARE YOU**, for the Spirit of glory and of God rests upon you. On their part He is blasphemed, but on your part He is glorified. But let none of you SUFFER as a murderer, a thief, an evildoer, or as a busybody in other people's matters. Yet **IF ANYONE SUFFERS AS A CHRISTIAN, LET HIM NOT BE ASHAMED, but LET him GLORIFY GOD IN THIS MATTER."** (I Peter 4:12-16). As believers, we suffer with the Lord Jesus Christ, as we bear our cross daily after Him — we share in His suffering — so that we will also share in His glory. For no disciple is greater than his teacher, nor a servant greater than his master. (see Matthew 10:24). Jesus said, "If the world hates you, you know that it hated Me before it hated you. If you were of the world, the world would love its own. Yet because you are not of the world, but I chose you out of the world, therefore the world hates you. Remember the word that I said to you, 'A SERVANT IS NOT GREATER THAN HIS MASTER.' IF THEY PERSECUTED Me, THEY WILL ALSO PERSECUTE YOU. If they kept My word, they will keep yours also. But all these things they will do to you for My name's sake, because they do not know Him who sent Me." (John 15:18-21).

Just as Jesus Christ our Teacher and Master was persecuted despite being faultless, even so we also will be persecuted for the simple reason of bearing the name of Christ and testifying of Him. Thus, the Bible says, "Yes, and all who desire to live godly in Christ Jesus WILL SUFFER PERSECUTION." (2 Timothy 3:12). Again, "we must through many tribulations enter the Kingdom of God." (see Acts 14:22). Paul writes in his letter to the Thessalonians, "For you, brethren, BECAME IMITATORS OF THE CHURCHES of God which are IN JUDEA in Christ Jesus. For YOU ALSO SUFFERED the same things FROM YOUR OWN COUNTRYMEN, just as they did from the Judeans, WHO KILLED BOTH THE Lord Jesus AND THEIR OWN PROPHETS, AND HAVE PERSECUTED US; and THEY DO NOT PLEASE GOD AND ARE CONTRARY TO ALL MEN, forbidding us to speak to the Gentiles THAT THEY MAY BE SAVED, so as always to FILL UP THE MEASURE OF THEIR SINS; but WRATH HAS COME UPON THEM to the uttermost." (1 Thessalonians 2:14-16). Then he encouraged them, saying, "that no one should be shaken by these AFFLICTIONS; for you yourselves know that WE ARE APPOINTED TO THIS. For, in fact, we told you before when we were with you THAT WE WOULD SUFFER TRIBULATION, just as it happened, and you know." (1 Thessalonians 3:3-4).

Indeed we are NOT above Him or greater than our Lord Jesus Christ, and so we will suffer just as He suffered; we will be persecuted just as He was persecuted. And those of us who are willing to endure such suffering, who are willing to be perfectly trained as disciples (or students) will, when we are perfectly trained, BE LIKE OUR TEACHER AND OUR LORD JESUS CHRIST, having the power He had and doing the works He did. Jesus Himself said, "A disciple is not above his teacher, but everyone who is perfectly trained WILL BE LIKE HIS TEACHER." (Luke 6:40).

The Road to Golgotha

Back to our story, Simon the Cyrenian carried Jesus' cross after Him to a place called the Place of the Skull, which is called in Hebrew, Golgotha. Luke's Gospel tells us that this place — Golgotha — where Jesus was crucified, is also called Calvary. (see Luke 23:33). Moreover, we are told that a great multitude of the people followed Jesus as He was led away, even though, as we can glean from their behavior at the scene of the crucifixion, not all of the multitude of the people followed Jesus for the right reasons. Some only followed Him to mock Him (see Mark 15:29; Matthew 27:39-40) — they didn't follow Him because they believed in Him. Others followed just to look on. (Luke 23:35). Similarly, there are many people today that only follow Jesus to mock

Him; many false believers and false prophets are following Jesus — mocking Him. Others are following Him just out of curiosity, looking on. And yet, there are many true followers too who genuinely love the Lord. And so we are told that among the multitude that followed Jesus were WOMEN WHO ALSO MOURNED and LAMENTED Him. But Jesus told them not to weep for Him, but to weep for themselves and their children. (see Luke 23:28). Indeed, we (mankind in general) cannot read or listen to the account of Jesus' crucifixion and weep for Him. No, we should rather weep for ourselves and for our children, because we are the ones that are pitiful, not Him. We are the ones that have sinned and are bound for hell. We are the dry wood — alienated from the life of God. (see Ephesians 4:18). Jesus is the Green Wood — sinless and full of life (see John 5:26; 1 John 5:11) — who stepped in on His own volition to save us. (see John 10:18). He laid down His life out of His own free will — out of His great love, having come into the world for this very purpose; so there is no weeping for Him. But we should weep for ourselves and for our children, especially those who hear the good news of Christ and the eternal life He offers, and yet refuse to accept Him as their Lord and Savior. Jesus asked, "for if they do these things in the green wood, what will be done in the dry?" (see Luke 23:31). In other words, if they treated Jesus the Green Wood this way; if they subjected the sinless one in whom is life to such cruel punishment and suffering, imagine what would be done to the dry wood — the sinners who have no life in them. Indeed, such sinners would cry and beg for the rocks and mountains to fall on them and hide them, than for them to face the fiery wrath of God that would be revealed in the last day. In the Book of Revelation, we are told that when the sixth seal was opened, "the kings of the earth, the great men, the rich men, the commanders, the mighty men, every slave and every free man, hid themselves in the caves and in the rocks of the mountains, and said to the mountains and rocks, "Fall on us and hide us from the face of Him who sits on the throne and from the wrath of the Lamb! For the great day of His wrath has come, and who is able to stand?" (Revelation 6:15-17).

Jesus Was Numbered With the Transgressors; God Made Him Who Knew No Sin to be Sin for Us, That We (You and I) Might Become the Righteousness of God in Him

Now, the Bible says that when they got to Golgotha, they gave Jesus sour wine mingled with gall and myrrh to drink. But when He had tasted it, He would not drink. (see Mark 15:21-23; Matthew 27:33-34). This fulfilled the prophecy in the Messianic Psalm 69 which says, "Reproach has broken My heart, and I am full of heaviness; I looked for someone to take pity, but there was none; and for comforters, but I found none. They also GAVE ME GALL FOR MY FOOD, And FOR MY THIRST they gave me VINEGAR TO DRINK." (Psalm 69:20-21).

After this, they crucified Jesus, and two robbers (criminals, transgressors) with Him, one on either side, and Jesus in the center. (see John 19:18; Matthew 27:38; Luke 23:33). This also fulfilled the Scripture which says, "And He was numbered with the transgressors." (see Mark 15:27-28). There on the cross, Jesus identified with sinners — He identified with you and I in sin, so that we might also identify with Him in righteousness. God "made Him who knew no sin to be sin **for us**, that we might become the righteousness of God in Him." (see 2 Corinthians 5:21).

"Now Pilate wrote a title and put it on the cross. And the writing was: JESUS OF NAZARETH, THE KING OF THE JEWS." (John 19:19). This inscription was also the official accusation against Jesus, and it was put up over His head on the cross. (see Matthew 27:37). And thus, the King was nailed to the cross, as the people looked on, stared at Him and mocked Him. "Then Jesus said, "FATHER, FORGIVE THEM, FOR THEY DO NOT KNOW WHAT THEY DO." (see Luke 23:34). Oh, the merciful heart of Jesus! The forgiving heart of Jesus! How I wish that all mankind would imitate Him! And yet I know that no man can imitate Jesus unless he is born again, unless he is born of God to be as Jesus is, unless he is helped by the power (or ability) of the Holy Spirit, unless Jesus lives in him and he yields to Jesus and follows His leading. Jesus forgave His enemies and prayed for them. The Bible says, "And they divided His garments and cast lots." (see Luke 23:34). The Roman soldiers divided Jesus' garments, casting lots, that it might be fulfilled which was spoken by the prophet: "They divided My garments among them, and for My clothing they cast lots." (see Matthew 27:35; Mark 15:24).

The Bible also records that it was **the third hour** when they crucified Jesus. (see Mark 15:25). Then, sitting down, they kept watch over Him there. (see Matthew 27:36). "And those who passed by blasphemed Him, wagging their heads and saying, "Aha! You who destroy the temple and build it in three days, save Yourself, and come down from the cross!" (Mark 15:29-30). "And the people stood looking on. But even the rulers with them sneered, saying, "He saved others; let Him save Himself if He is the Christ, the chosen of God." The soldiers also mocked Him, coming and offering Him sour wine, and saying, "If You are the King of the Jews, save Yourself." (Luke 23:35-37).

"Likewise the chief priests also, mocking among themselves with the scribes, said, "HE SAVED OTHERS; HIMSELF HE CANNOT SAVE. Let the Christ, the King of Israel, descend now from the cross, that we may see and believe." EVEN THOSE WHO WERE CRUCIFIED WITH Him REVILED Him." (Mark 15:31-32).

It is interesting that while Jesus was still up on that cross the people mocked Him and ridiculed Him, perplexed and astonished by the fact that He couldn't or wouldn't save Himself. "Likewise the chief priests also, mocking with the scribes and elders, said, "He saved others; Himself He cannot save. If He is the King of Israel, let Him now come down from the cross, and we will believe Him. He trusted in God; let Him deliver Him now if He will have Him; for He said, 'I am the Son of God.'" (see Matthew 27:41-43). This was a mockery, and yet how true a testimony that He saved others and He believed in God! In fact it was the chief priests, mocking with the scribes and elders, that said these two things about Jesus. They said it in mockery, yet what a testimony concerning Jesus! He saved others and He trusted in God. Weren't the chief priests ashamed of themselves that they had connived against a Man who saved others and trusted in God? Weren't they really condemning themselves by their own testimony? So-called chief priests shamelessly condemning an innocent Man who saved others and trusted in God! How tragic! What an astonishing display of Hypocrisy! And yet that's what vain religion does to people. That is what religious zeal without knowledge does to people.

Beloved, "He saved others; Himself He cannot save." How true this is, because if He saved Himself, He could not save others; He could not save you and I. It was only by not saving Himself on that cross that He was able to save us. He did it all out of love, because without the shedding of blood, there is no forgiveness of sins. (see Hebrews 9:22). It wasn't the nails of the Roman Soldiers that held Jesus to that rugged cross; it was love that held Him there to lay down His life for us. Jesus loved us too much to save Himself from the death on the cross and watch us perish in our sins. If there was any other way we could be saved, if it were possible for mankind to be saved through the keeping of the Law of Moses, if it were possible for mankind to be saved without Jesus dying on the cross, then He wouldn't have died. Dying was the only option. Sacrificing Himself was the only means. And Jesus wouldn't allow anything to stop Him from saving mankind: not even the shame and agony of dying on the cross and becoming sin and a curse; not even the mockery of the very people He was dying to save. He loved us too much to worry about any of that. He had to be lifted up on the cross to save mankind. He said, "And as Moses lifted up the serpent in the wilderness, even so MUST the Son of Man be lifted up, that whoever believes in Him should not perish but have eternal life." (John 3:14-15). Hence, when Peter pulled the sword and began to flail it back there in the garden of Gethsemane where Jesus was arrested, Jesus essentially said, "Put it away Peter. They that take up the sword will die by the sword. Don't you realize, Peter, that I am in control here? At this moment I could call for twelve legions of angels to deliver me out of their hands, but then how could the scriptures be fulfilled? How could I save man? How could I redeem mankind, if I would deliver myself from this?" (a paraphrase of Matthew 26:51-54; John 18:10-11).

Indeed, we should all be thankful and happy that Jesus did not save Himself on that cross. He bore the full punishment for our sins, and today, all we have to do to be saved is repent and BELIEVE in Him, believe in His Substitutionary death for our sins. This is the Good News Paul and all the other apostles preached. Paul affirms this good news when he declares: "Be it known unto you therefore, men and brethren, that through this Man is preached unto you the forgiveness of sins: And by Him ALL THAT BELIEVE are JUSTIFIED from ALL things, from which ye could not be justified by the LAW OF MOSES." (Acts 13:38-39 KJV). Paul additionally "preached that they should repent and turn to God and **DEMONSTRATE their REPENTANCE BY their DEEDS.**" (see Acts 26:20 NIV). John also declares that Jesus Christ "Himself is the propitiation for our sins, and not for ours only but also for the whole world." (1 John 2:2). Moreover, Jesus Himself said He was to die for the believer, the One for many, His life a ransom for many. (see Mark 10:45). And He declared, "this is My blood of the new covenant, which is shed for many for **the remission of sins**" (see Matthew 26:28). Thus, Jesus has paid the penalty for everyone's sins. This is called grace (unmerited, undeserved favor). But you have to accept the payment Jesus has made, you have to put faith in what Jesus has already accomplished in order to be saved (see Ephesians 2:8-9). Jesus bore the full extent of God's wrath against sin, as He who knew no sin was made sin (see 2 Corinthians 5:21) and was forsaken by God (see Matthew 27:46), so that you and I will be reconciled to God (see 2 Corinthians 5:19) and become the righteousness of God in Him. (see 2 Corinthians 5:21). "In Him (Jesus) we have redemption through his blood, THE FORGIVENESS OF SINS, IN ACCORDANCE WITH THE RICHES OF GOD'S GRACE." (see Ephesians 1:7). Peter also proclaimed the same message when he said: "For Christ also hath ONCE SUFFERED FOR SINS, the just for the unjust, that He might bring us to God…" (see 1 Peter 3:18 KJV). Today, all who believe in Jesus Christ have eternal life, and have become members of the family of God (see 1 John 5:13, with John 1:12-13). We must all thank Jesus for His unfathomable love.

Beloved, none of us deserved to be saved. That Jesus died to save us is an act of God's grace, and so we are all beneficiaries of unmerited, unearned, undeserved favor from God. "Surely He has borne our griefs and carried our sorrows; Yet we esteemed Him stricken, smitten by God, and afflicted. But He was wounded for our transgressions, He was bruised for our iniquities; The chastisement for our peace was upon Him, And by His stripes we are healed. All we like sheep have gone astray; We have turned, every one, to his own way; And the Lord has laid on Him the iniquity of us all." (Isaiah 53:4-6). As the last verse indicates, **the Lord laid the iniquity of us all on Jesus**, including the iniquity of those people who crucified Him. Jesus died even for the sins of those criminals that were crucified with Him; and yet they reviled Jesus with the same thing as the chief priests, scribes, and elders (see Mark 15:32; Matthew 27:44), until one of them eventually repented and woke up to the reality that Jesus indeed was innocent, that He was the Messiah. The Bible says, "Then one of the criminals who were hanged blasphemed Him, saying, "If You are the Christ, save Yourself and us." But the other, answering, rebuked him, saying, "Do you not even fear God, seeing you are under the same condemnation? And we indeed justly, for we receive the due reward of our deeds; but this Man has done nothing wrong." Then he said to Jesus, "Lord, remember me when You come into Your kingdom." And Jesus said to him, "Assuredly, I say to you today, you will be with Me in Paradise." (Luke 23:39-43). As you can see, I have moved the punctuation in verse 43 to where it is supposed to be. Jesus did not go to Paradise the same day He died; He went to hell as our Substitute, having died as sin. (We will expound on this truth when we get to our discussion on what happened within those three days and three nights leading to the resurrection). And so what Jesus said here was not to be translated as the criminal going to paradise with Him that same day. Yes, the criminal went in Christ to paradise — to Abraham's bosom — that day, as promised, but not with Christ; Jesus joined Him later after He defeated Satan in hell and freed the captives. (see 1 Peter 3:19-20; Ephesians 4:8-10; Acts 2:27,31; Matthew 12:40; and Psalm 88; with Colossians 2:15 and Hebrews 2:14). It must be noted that the original Greek manuscript of the New Testament Bible does not use punctuations consistently, so it was the translators who mostly inserted the punctuations, and thus, here, they inserted it wrongly. Yes, the Bible is without errors, but only in the original manuscript, not in the translations, so we must fix any errors that we notice in the translations we have today, especially if the error alters the intended meaning as revealed by the Holy Spirit. Thus, Jesus said to the criminal who expressed faith in Him: "Assuredly, I say to you today, you will be with Me in Paradise." And I believe Jesus kept His promise, thereby proving to us once again that salvation is only by GRACE through FAITH, and not by works of the law, so that no one should boast. (see Ephesians 2:8-9).

The Bible records that, having been crucified in the third hour, Jesus was still on the cross by the ninth hour. And as He hanged on the cross, His figure was so marred from the scourging and sufferings that He had "no form or comeliness; and when we see Him, there is no beauty that we should desire Him." (see Isaiah 53:2). Jesus was unrecognizable as a human being on that cross, as He hanged there for six solid hours — from the 3rd hour to the 9th hour. The Bible says that from the sixth hour until the ninth hour, **there was darkness over all the land** (see Matthew 27:45; Mark 15:33), as Jesus Christ the Light of the world was taken away and the power of darkness reigned, as Jesus was made sin with our sins and God the Father turned His face away from Him, forsaking His only begotten Son for our sakes, so that we would be accepted in Him. Jesus had said to the chief priests, captains of the temple, and the elders who had come to Him to arrest Him that, "this is your hour—when darkness reigns." (see Luke 22:53 NIV). And so even now darkness was reigning — literally.

The Bible says, "And about **the ninth hour** Jesus cried out with a loud voice, saying, "Eli, Eli, lama sabachthani?" that is, "My God, My God, WHY HAVE YOU FORSAKEN Me?" (Matthew 27:46). In fact, the statement Jesus uttered here is the first line of the Messianic Psalm 22. Perhaps Jesus was too weak at this point to cry out the entire Psalm, but I believe that in His spirit He said it all; and it is really sad when you ponder over the entirety of what Jesus was going through on the cross as revealed in the 22nd Psalm quoted below:

*"**My GOD, My GOD, WHY HAVE You FORSAKEN Me?** Why are You so far from helping Me, And from the words of My GROANING? O My God, I CRY IN THE DAYTIME, but You DO NOT HEAR; And IN THE NIGHT SEASON, and am not silent. But You are holy, Enthroned in the praises of Israel. Our fathers trusted in You; They trusted, and You delivered them. They cried to You, and were delivered; They trusted in You, and were not ashamed. But I AM A WORM, AND NO MAN; A REPROACH OF MEN, and DESPISED BY THE PEOPLE. All those who see Me RIDICULE Me; They shoot out the lip, THEY SHAKE THE HEAD, saying, "**HE TRUSTED IN THE LORD, LET Him RESCUE Him; Let Him DELIVER Him, since He delights in***

Him!" *But You are He who took Me out of the womb; You MADE Me TRUST WHILE ON My MOTHER'S BREASTS. I was CAST UPON You FROM BIRTH. From My mother's womb You HAVE BEEN My GOD. Be NOT far from Me, For TROUBLE IS NEAR; For THERE IS NONE TO HELP. Many BULLS HAVE SURROUNDED Me; Strong bulls of Bashan have ENCIRCLED Me. They GAPE AT Me WITH THEIR MOUTHS, Like a raging and roaring lion. I am POURED OUT LIKE WATER, And ALL My BONES ARE OUT OF JOINT; My heart is like WAX; It has MELTED WITHIN Me. My STRENGTH IS DRIED UP like a potsherd, And My TONGUE CLINGS TO My JAWS; You have brought Me to the DUST OF DEATH. For DOGS HAVE SURROUNDED Me; The CONGREGATION OF THE WICKED HAS ENCLOSED Me. They PIERCED My HANDS AND My FEET; I CAN COUNT ALL My BONES. They LOOK AND STARE at Me.* **They DIVIDE My GARMENTS AMONG THEM, And for My clothing THEY CAST LOTS.** *But You, O Lord, DO NOT BE FAR FROM Me; O My Strength, hasten to help Me! Deliver Me from the sword, My precious life from the power of the dog. SAVE Me FROM THE LION'S MOUTH And from the horns of the wild oxen!* **YOU HAVE ANSWERED Me.** *I will declare Your name to My brethren; In the midst of the assembly I will praise You. You who fear the Lord, praise Him! All you descendants of Jacob, glorify Him, And fear Him, all you offspring of Israel! For He has not despised nor abhorred the affliction of the afflicted; Nor has He hidden His face from Him; But when He cried to Him, He heard. My praise shall be of You in the great assembly; I will pay My vows before those who fear Him. The poor shall eat and be satisfied; Those who seek Him will praise the Lord. Let your heart live forever! All the ends of the world Shall remember and turn to the Lord, And all the families of the nations Shall worship before You. For the kingdom is the Lord's,*

And He rules over the nations. All the prosperous of the earth Shall eat and worship; All those who go down to the dust SHALL BOW BEFORE Him, Even he who cannot keep himself alive. A posterity shall SERVE Him. It will be recounted of the Lord to the next generation, They will come and DECLARE His RIGHTEOUSNESS TO A PEOPLE WHO WILL BE BORN, That He has done this." (Psalm 22:1-31). And so Jesus, in so much agony and suffering on the cross, was saying these things in prayer, ending it all with praise to God for answering Him. The answer was to come in His resurrection. And so Jesus received it here by faith.

On the cross, God the Father had forsaken Jesus. Jesus was suffering spiritual death or separation from God, having borne our sins in His own body (see 1 Peter 2:24), and having been made sin (see 2 Corinthians 5:21) and a curse (see Galatians 3:13). The Prophet Isaiah said that it pleased the Lord to bruise Jesus; God put His only begotten Son Jesus Christ to grief and made **His soul** an offering for sin (see Isaiah 53:10), so that you and I could be saved. Jesus being made sin is the only plausible reason for God to forsake Him, and yet it was also the only way Jesus could die as the sinner's Substitute. Thus, God took our sin (and our spiritual death) and laid it all on the soul of Jesus, making His soul an offering for sin, so that Jesus became the very embodiment or persona of sin and of a curse, as He hanged on the cross. Then God looked at the travail of Jesus' soul, and **was satisfied**. (see Isaiah 53:11). Justice was served; God's wrath against sin was exhausted on Jesus, as Jesus hanged on the cross as sin. If you looked at Jesus' soul in that very moment on the cross, you were looking at sin (see 2 Corinthians 5:21), you were looking at a curse (see Galatians 3:13). And because Jesus had become that ugly thing called sin, which is the very nature of Satan, because our sin had made Jesus a subject of Satan on the cross, God the Father had forsaken Him. The Father could not fellowship with Jesus at this point on the cross, just as He couldn't fellowship with Adam after he sinned in the garden of Eden. For the first time in His life, Jesus was separated from the Father, alienated from the life of God the Father, and forsaken by the Father, because the Father was holy, and Jesus was not — Jesus was sin (see 2 Corinthians 5:21), Jesus was a worm. (see Psalm 22:6). Such was the anguish and agony in which Jesus was, as He hanged on that cross and cried out to God, bearing the full wrath and indignation of God against sin (for you and I).

Thus, on the cross, Jesus Christ the second and last Adam died two deaths — **spiritual death** first, followed by **physical death** — just like the first Adam. Until Jesus died spiritually (through being made sin — see 2 Corinthians 5:21), He couldn't die physically, because He was without sin (see 1 Peter 2:22; 1 John 3:5) and was thus immortal. Jesus' blood was not tainted by Adam's original sin because He was not born of Adam but of God, having been conceived by the power of the Holy Spirit and born of the blessed virgin Mary. (see Luke 1:34-35). The Bible says that death entered the world through sin — Adam's sin. (see Romans 5:12). Therefore, in order to take away death from the world and bring life and immortality to light, sin had to be taken away first. This explains why Jesus the Lamb of God came on a mission to take away the sins of the world. (see John 1:29). It was through taking away the sins of the world that Jesus could abolish or destroy death and bring life and immortality to light through the gospel. (see 2 Timothy 1:10). Being made sin therefore was a necessary first step for Jesus to be able to take away the sins of the world.

Jesus, the Lamb of God, Took Away the Sins of the World

Now, let's explain this in more detail. The Bible says that Jesus was without sin. (see Hebrews 4:15; 1 John 3:5; 1 Peter 2:22). Being without sin, Jesus was not subject to death, and could therefore not die in that sinless state; He was not mortal or death-doomed. Jesus was not a subject of Satan, and thus death could not lay hold of Him, until He was made sin on the cross and became a subject of Satan and death. It was necessary for Jesus to be made sin so that He could die for us. Jesus was made sin with the sins of the world, so that, as the Lamb of God, He would take away the sins of the world (see John 1:29, 36) to make it possible for man to pass from death to life, for man to have eternal life, to live forever in perpetual fellowship with the only true God and Jesus Christ whom He has sent. (see John 3:16; John 5:24; with John 17:3; 2 Timothy 1:10). As you would remember from our discussion in the first three chapters of this book, sin was also what made Adam a subject of Satan and death, but in the case of Adam, it was his own sin, his own disobedience. Adam was neither mortal nor immortal, until he sinned and became mortal; Jesus the second and last Adam was not mortal until He was made sin on the cross (with our sin). This is why Jesus said during His earth walk that no one could take His life from Him, and that He had the authority to lay down His life and take it again. (see John 10:18). Jesus had a Body which God prepared for Him to sacrifice (see Hebrews 10:5, 10) — a Body that was in the likeness of sinful flesh. (see Romans 8:3). And so Jesus was immortal. And yet, our sin made Him mortal on that cross. Oh, how He loved us! He Himself bore our sins in His own Body on the cross. (see 1 Peter 2:24). Jesus sacrificed or offered His Body for our sanctification once-for-all. (see Hebrews 10:10). Praise God!

It is also worth noting that both sin and death, and of course hell, were the paramount enemies of man, and they were formidable enemies prior to Jesus' sacrifice on the cross. Hence, Jesus came to deal with the sin problem, which was the parent problem — sin gave birth to death. (see Romans 5:12). Thus, the Bible says that Jesus, through His death and resurrection, was to destroy, and did destroy Satan (the author of sin and the one) who had the power of death (see Hebrews 2:14). Jesus took the keys (or power) of death and of Hell from Satan, so Jesus now has the keys of death and of Hell. (see Revelation 1:18). The Bible says that Jesus has destroyed death and brought life and immortality to light through the gospel. (see 2 Timothy 1:10). However, whereas **spiritual death** has been utterly destroyed, **physical death** still remains a formidable (but not scary) enemy — in this life — and it will remain so for as long as we remain in these mortal bodies. The Bible says that (physical) death is the last enemy that will be destroyed. (see 1 Corinthians 15:26). Spiritual death has already been destroyed, which is why everyone who believes in Jesus today has eternal life and will never die. (see 1 John 5:13, with John 5:24, and John 11:26). Physical death, on the other hand, will be destroyed when Jesus comes back for the Church and we are transformed into our glorious immortal bodies. (see 1 Corinthians 15:51-54). "And God will wipe away every tear from (our) eyes; there shall be NO MORE DEATH, nor sorrow, nor crying. There shall be no more pain, for the former things have passed away." (Revelation 21:4).

Indeed Jesus was made sin on the cross — all our sins were laid on Him — so that He would bear our sins away as our sin offering. The Bible says, as noted earlier, that He Himself bore our sins in His own **body** on the cross. (see 1 Peter 2:24). Therefore, when Jesus was taken away from the cross and buried, sin was taken away from the world and buried, never to be resurrected again; Jesus condemned sin in the flesh or body. (see Romans 8:3). Hebrews 9:26 says that Christ appeared ONCE to PUT AWAY SIN by the sacrifice of Himself. Therefore, sin has been put away; sin has lost its power or dominion over the believer, because the believer is not under Law but under Grace. (see Romans 6:14). Sin has lost its power to put the believer (the New Creation man) under condemnation and guilt (see Romans 8:1; Romans 8:33-39; Hebrews 10:1-3); it has lost its power to put the believer to spiritual death or separation from God. This is why Jesus said, "I am the resurrection and the life. He who believes in Me, though he may die, he shall live. And WHOEVER lives and BELIEVES IN Me SHALL NEVER DIE. Do you believe this?" (see John 11:25-26). Obviously Jesus wasn't speaking of physical death because all His twelve apostles died (physically). And so Jesus was primarily talking about spiritual death in this context. But we also know that ultimately, upon His second coming, physical death will also be swallowed up by life, and will be no more. (see Revelation 21:4).

Clearly, the real Substitutionary death of Jesus Christ for mankind was a composite and holistic death — it was both spiritual and physical death. Jesus was our Substitute in His spiritual death (or separation/alienation from the life of God), as well as His physical death (or separation of the spirit from the body). This explains why we (believers) have the benefit of being alive to God in Christ Jesus now in this present life, and forever (see Romans 6:11); it explains why we have permanent fellowship with God the Father and with His Son Jesus Christ, as well as with the Holy Spirit (see 1 Corinthians 1:9; 1 John

1:3; 2 Corinthians 13:14). It also explains why, although we will die physically (or fall asleep in Christ), we have the promise from the Lord that we will receive a new and immortal physical body in the resurrection of the dead which is to come. (see 2 Corinthians 5:1-8; 1 Corinthians 15:51-54; 1 Thessalonians 4:13-18). Hence, the Bible says, "Inasmuch then as the children have partaken of flesh and blood, He Himself likewise shared in the same, that through death He might destroy him who had the power of death, that is, the devil" (Hebrews 2:14). Jesus, who was equal with God (see Philippians 2:6-8), had to become a Man (flesh and blood) and die in our place (as our Representative) in order that He might destroy the devil who had the power of death. Man gave the devil that power of death through our disobedience (or our sin), and so Man had to take back that power. And to accomplish this, the Man Jesus Christ (who was sinless and righteous) was delivered up for our sins (see Romans 4:25); He stood in as our Representative and our Substitute, was made sin in the spirit, and thus died in the spirit (see 2 Corinthians 5:21) as well as in the body, went to hell in the spirit (see 1 Peter 3:19-20; Ephesians 4:8-10; Acts 2:27,31; Matthew 12:40; Psalm 88), was justified in the Spirit (see 1 Timothy 3:16), born again in the Spirit (see Acts 13:33; Romans 1:4), defeated Satan in the spirit (see Colossians 2:15; Hebrews 2:14), and was raised to life for our justification (see Romans 4:25). All of this must be spiritually discerned. (see 1 Corinthians 2:14). The natural mind cannot grasp it. Paul summarized this truth for us when He said, "Therefore, as through one man's offense JUDGMENT came to all men, resulting in CONDEMNATION, even so through one Man's righteous act **the FREE GIFT** came to all men, resulting in JUSTIFICATION of LIFE. For as by ONE MAN'S DISOBEDIENCE many were made **SINNERS**, so also by ONE Man's OBEDIENCE many will be made **RIGHTEOUS**." (Romans 5:18-19). Thus, after His death, Jesus, having been carried away for burial as sin, was going to be raised from the dead not as the sin that was taken away from the world, but as a justified (or righteous) Man (see 1 Timothy 3:16) who will Himself be the righteousness of all who believe in Him (see 1 Corinthians 1:30). Jesus was going to be raised from the dead as the First begotten Son of God, begotten through the resurrection (see Acts 13:33; Romans 1:4), the Firstborn among many brethren (see Romans 8:29), the Firstborn from the dead (see Colossians 1:18), the Firstborn of the New Creation (see Acts 13:33), and the Firstfruits of those who have fallen asleep. (see 1 Corinthians 15:20, 23).

Beloved, the GOOD NEWS today is that, because Jesus paid the penalty for every man's sins and suffered both spiritual death and physical death on our behalf when He died as our Representative and Substitute on the cross, every human being gets to have eternal life as a free gift simply by BELIEVING IN JESUS CHRIST, by believing in His substitutionary death for our sins, and His resurrection from the dead. (see John 3:16, with Romans 10:9-10). And so we should praise Jesus and boast in the Lord. (see 1 Corinthians 1:31). And when praising Him and showing our gratitude to the Lord, we must also remember that the sufferings of Jesus for the sins of mankind went beyond His physical sufferings and death on the cross. There was also a spiritual suffering and death. Jesus died for each of us spiritually before He even died for us physically. He tasted death for every man. (see Hebrews 2:9). Indeed it was His spiritual death that even made His physical death possible. He died spiritually first, and because of that spiritual death or separation from the life of God, Jesus went to hell for each one of us, so that we (believers) never have to die spiritually again nor go to hell ever. Never ever can or will a believer go to hell! Whoever believes in Jesus Christ will never perish, but have eternal life. (see John 3:16; 1 John 5:13). Similarly, never ever can any man go to heaven without accepting (by faith) the payment Jesus made on the cross for the sins of mankind. Never will anyone go to heaven without accepting Jesus as their Substitute, as their Lord and Savior. In fact, if God ever sends one "unbeliever" to heaven, that would make God unjust, and He would have to apologize to Jesus for His sufferings and deaths on the cross. Sending even one person who doesn't believe in Jesus to heaven, will only go to show that God could've, and should've saved all of mankind the same way without the need for Jesus to die on the cross, which would thus make God unjust. In the same vein, if God ever sends one sincere believer to hell, He would be unjust, and He would need to apologize to Jesus for His deaths and sacrifice on the cross. But God can never be unjust. And thus, the Bible says that God demonstrates His righteousness at the present time, "**that He might be JUST** and the justifier of the one who has **faith in Jesus**." (see Romans 3:26). And so you can bank on the truth that God will send those who believe in Jesus Christ to heaven, and those who don't believe in Him to hell. May you be among the former.

It is urgent, indeed imperative for everyone to accept Jesus Christ as their Lord and Savior. And those who do so, those who believe in Jesus have eternal life (see 1 John 5:13; John 6:47), and will not come into judgment, but have passed from death into life. (see John 5:24). Hallelujah! This is why we should praise God and worship Him alone. This is why we should love Jesus and live for Him. He died for us; He really did — not just physically, but spiritually too. He took our death, and gave us His life — eternal life. Hence, the Bible says that "**everlasting destruction** from the presence of the Lord and from the glory of His power" is the punishment that will be meted out to sinners who still refuse to accept the remission of sins that is preached through Jesus Christ. (see 2 Thessalonians 1:9). But, for those of us who believe in Jesus, He already bore the punishment for our sins when He became sin on the cross (and died spiritually and physically or bodily) — to reconcile us to God and make us the righteousness of God in Him. (see 2 Corinthians 5:21). And so I repeat: there is not a single sincere believer today who will suffer spiritual death or separation from God ever again. Praise God!

Thus far, we have proven that Jesus' spiritual death was necessary for His physical death to be possible; and His physical death was necessary because His blood was needed for the remission of our sins. "And according to the law almost all things are purified with blood, and WITHOUT SHEDDING OF BLOOD THERE IS NO REMISSION." (Hebrews 9:22). Let us, therefore, appreciate Jesus' death for us in its totality, and let us continually praise and thank Jesus for His precious blood that was shed for us. "In Him we have redemption THROUGH His BLOOD, the FORGIVENESS OF SINS, according to the riches of His GRACE" (Ephesians 1:7). And the redemption we have through the blood of Jesus is AN ETERNAL REDEMPTION. (see Hebrews 9:12). Hallelujah!

Jesus Dismissed His Spirit and Died a Majestic Death

Now, back to the scene of the crucifixion, Jesus our blessed Savior when He cried out to God on the cross, asking why God had forsaken Him, was mocked that He was calling for Elijah. (see Mark 15:35).

"After this, Jesus, knowing that all things were now accomplished, that the Scripture might be fulfilled, said, "I thirst!" (John 19:28). "Then someone ran and filled a sponge full of sour wine, put it on a reed, and offered it to Him to drink, saying, "Let Him alone; let us see if Elijah will come to take Him down." (Mark 15:36). So when Jesus had received the sour wine, He cried out again with a loud voice, and said "It is finished!" (see John 19:30). And bowing His head, He yielded His Spirit up, saying, "Father, into Your hands I commit My spirit.'" (see Luke 23:46). Having said this, He breathed His last. (see Matthew 27:50; Mark 15:37; Luke 23:46).

Beloved, by dying in such majestic way — crying out with a loud voice on the cross saying "it is finished" and then delivering up His spirit into the hands of His Father (see Matthew 27:49-50; Luke 23:46), Jesus gave us the most convincing evidence that indeed He laid down His life, and no one could take His life from Him. Jesus, obviously unconquered by death, dismissed His spirit, and until He did that, He wouldn't die; they couldn't kill Him. No one else in history had ever died in this manner, but Jesus made it possible for the believer to die this way also, as exemplified by Stephen (see Acts 7:59). Jesus had the power to say to His spirit, "All right, you may leave the body now," after He had made that loud cry of victory, "It is finished" (see John 19:30), indicating that the Abrahamic Covenant was fulfilled, and the redemption of man was complete, never to be repeated again. "For by one sacrifice he has made perfect forever those who are being made holy." (Hebrews 10:14 NIV). In "laying down" His life this way, Jesus' death was distinguished from all other deaths.

In the next Chapter, we will revisit this final scene of Jesus' death on the cross and reveal the truths hidden in the report that when Jesus finally cried out and gave up His Spirit, the veil of the temple was torn in two from top to bottom; and the earth quaked, and the rocks were split, and the graves were opened; and many bodies of the saints who had fallen asleep were raised; and coming out of the graves after the resurrection of Jesus, they went into the holy city and appeared to many. (see Matthew 27:51-53). We will also reveal the truths hidden in the reactions and proclamations of the centurion and those with him who were guarding Jesus, when they saw the earthquake and the things that happened. In Chapter 12, we will also explore the truth of Jesus' resurrection, and discuss what happened within those three days and three nights leading to the resurrection of Jesus Christ, as well as how we were born again as new creations through the resurrection. Please turn the page and read this book to the end. For I am confident that by the end of the book, you will understand and appreciate the necessity of living and walking in the Spirit as a new creation, and why you can't afford to live or walk according to the flesh. "For if you live according to the flesh you will die; but if by the Spirit you put to death the deeds of the body, you will live." (Romans 8:13).

Chapter 12

The Death, Burial and Resurrection of Jesus Christ and How it Changed the Destiny of Man Forever

The Final Scene at the Crucifixion of Jesus and Its Significance

THE BIBLE SAYS, "And Jesus cried out again with a loud voice, and yielded up His spirit. Then, behold, THE VEIL OF THE TEMPLE was TORN in two FROM TOP TO BOTTOM; and the EARTH QUAKED, and THE ROCKS WERE SPLIT, and THE GRAVES WERE OPENED; and MANY BODIES OF THE SAINTS who had fallen asleep WERE RAISED; and COMING OUT OF the graves **AFTER His RESURRECTION**, they WENT INTO THE HOLY CITY and APPEARED TO MANY. So when the CENTURION and THOSE WITH HIM, WHO WERE GUARDING Jesus, SAW the EARTHQUAKE and the THINGS THAT HAD HAPPENED, they FEARED GREATLY, saying, "TRULY this was the Son of God!" (Matthew 27:50-54).

The Significance of the Tearing of the Veil in the Temple in Two From Top to Bottom

To better understand the significance of the tearing of the veil of the temple in two from top to bottom following the death of Jesus Christ, we need to first understand the purpose the veil served in the temple, as well as how the sacrifice of Jesus Christ on the cross fulfilled the Law of Moses, and thus eliminated the need for the veil. Under the Old Covenant (of law), there is a physical tabernacle, which God asked Moses to erect according to the pattern of the true tabernacle in heaven that was shown to him on the mountain; Moses was to build the tabernacle as a shadow or a copy of the true tabernacle in heaven which God Himself erected, and not man. (see Hebrews 8:1-5; Exodus 25:8-9, 40). So there is this physical tabernacle erected by Moses under the Old Covenant. Then there is the priesthood that offered the sacrifices at the tabernacle. The children of Israel were also required to keep the Sabbaths and to observe other rituals, new moon celebrations and feasts, including the Day of Atonement, and the Passover. Today, some so-called Christians, out of ignorance or sheer unbelief, still focus a lot on these rituals, Sabbaths and laws of the Old Covenant, but the Bible tells us that these laws and rituals are not an end in themselves, but are shadows that point to Jesus Christ the Substance. (see Colossians 2:16-17). In other words, all the laws and rituals of the Old Covenant find their fulfillment in Jesus Christ, just as Jesus Himself affirmed after His resurrection. (see Luke 24:44-48). Today under the New Covenant (of grace), there is no value in physically observing all those Old Covenant laws, Sabbaths, feasts and rituals again, since they have taken on a spiritual meaning in Christ.

Thus, when Jesus started His earth ministry, He told the Jews that He had not come to abolish the Law or the Prophets, but to fulfill. (see Matthew 5:17). And so the Bible tells us that, "The law and the prophets were until John. Since that time the kingdom of God has been preached, and everyone is pressing into it." (Luke 16:16). The New International Version puts it this way: "The Law and the Prophets were proclaimed until John. Since that time, the good news of the kingdom of God is being preached, and everyone is forcing their way into it." (Luke 16:16 NIV). What this simply means is that the preachers among the children of Israel prior to John the Baptist preached or proclaimed the law and the prophetic writings, urging people to fear God and keep His laws (the ten commandments and the ceremonial laws), as they waited for the Messiah and His Kingdom to be revealed. But all that preaching of the law and the writings of the prophets changed when John the Baptist came along; John started preaching that people should repent (or change their mind) because the kingdom which all the prophets prophesied about is now here. (see Matthew 3:1-2). And so John preached the gospel of the kingdom — that Jesus the King is now here and everyone should change their mind from sin and turn to Him in faith. Jesus Himself also preached the gospel of the kingdom (see Matthew 4:17, 23; Mathew 9:35; Acts 1:3) calling on all people to have faith in Him because He is the way, the truth and the life, and no one comes to the Father except through Him. (see John 14:6). Today we His disciples are also preaching the gospel of the kingdom (see Acts 20:25; Acts 28:31), urging people to repent and believe in the Lord Jesus Christ for salvation. Thus since the time of John the Baptist, we are no longer preaching the Law and the Prophets as the way to life; we are preaching the Lord Jesus Christ as the Life. "Therefore **the law was our tutor** to bring us to Christ, that we might be justified by faith. But **after faith has come, we are no longer under a tutor.**" (Galatians 3:24-25). Indeed the Law was fully fulfilled in Christ through His death, burial and resurrection. This is why after Jesus' resurrection, He opened the understanding of His disciples for them to comprehend the Scriptures and bear witness to the truth that He had indeed fulfilled the things which were written in the Law of Moses, the Prophets, and the Psalms concerning Him. (see Luke 24:44-48).

As mentioned earlier, the Jews served a copy or shadow of the true tabernacle which is in heaven, and this true tabernacle — the substance — is Christ Jesus who dwells (or tabernacles) with and in believers today. (see Colossians 1:27; Matthew 28:20, with 2 Corinthians 6:16). The Bible says that the Lord God almighty and the Lamb (Jesus Christ) are the Temple (and for that matter, the True Tabernacle) of the heavenly Jerusalem. (see Revelation 21:22). The Bible also says that Jesus is "a Minister of the sanctuary and of THE TRUE TABERNACLE WHICH THE LORD ERECTED, and NOT MAN." (Hebrews 8:2). Thus, the Tabernacle Moses constructed in the wilderness contained many prophetic images that explain how the Old Covenant believer's approach to God differs from the New Covenant believer's approach. (see Hebrews 8:1-5; Hebrews 4:14-16). The tabernacle had three distinct sections: the Outer Court, the Inner Court (or Holy Place), and the Holy of Holies (or the Most Holy Place). The Temple in Jerusalem was also set up in a similar fashion as the Tabernacle, and served the same purpose, except the Temple was more magnificent and grand. There was only one way or gate into the Outer Court of the tabernacle (see Exodus 27:16-17; Exodus 38:18-20), and only one door into the Holy Place (see Exodus 26:36-37; Exodus

36:37-38), just as Jesus Christ is the only Door, the only Way to the heavenly Father. (see John 10:9, with John 14:6). There was also a veil separating the Holy of Holies from the other parts of the Tabernacle, and the Temple. (see Exodus 26:31-35; Exodus 36:35-38). The high priest had to go through this veil to enter the Holy of Holies. This was also the veil that was torn in two from top to bottom when Jesus died on the cross.

In the outer court of the Temple and the Tabernacle was the Brazen Altar. It is at this altar that animals were sacrificed as sin offering to make way into the presence of God. Therefore, the way into the presence of God began at the Brazen Altar. No sinner could come empty handed into the tabernacle; they had to come with a sacrificial animal, and the animal had to be without blemish. (see Leviticus 4:1-5:13; 6:24-30). Similarly, the only way to the presence of the Father today is through the cross of Jesus Christ. To come to the Father, we must all believe the crucifixion, burial and resurrection of the Lord Jesus Christ; we must put our faith in Jesus the Lamb of God who took away the sins of the world, and confess Him as Lord. Under the Old Covenant, when an Israelite brought an animal without blemish as his sin offering, he laid his hand on it first, and then killed it (see Leviticus 4:1-4). By laying his hand on the sin offering first, his sins were transferred (or imputed) to the innocent animal. Then the animal would die with/for his sins, and he would go free. The anointed priest would then take some of the blood of the sacrificial animal and bring it to the tabernacle of meeting for the cleansing rituals. (see Leviticus 4:5-10). Thus, only by the shedding of innocent blood, in accordance with the instructions of God, could one's sins be atoned for and forgiven. In this regard, God said, "For the life of the flesh is in the blood, and I have given it to you upon the altar to make atonement for your souls; for it is the blood that makes atonement for the soul." (Leviticus 17:11).

In the same manner as the sinner had to lay hands on his sin offering and kill it as the atonement for his sins, even so did the high priest, chief priests and elders of the people (representing the Jewish nation), together with the Roman governors and soldiers (representing the Gentiles or non-Jews) lay hand on Jesus our Passover Lamb (see 1 Corinthians 5:7) and killed Him on the brazen altar of the cross, as the propitiation for the sins of the whole world. (see 1 John 2:2). The Book of Hebrews also explains: "And according to the law almost all things are purified with blood, and **without shedding of blood there is no remission.**" (Hebrews 9:22). The Brazen (or Bronze) Altar in the outer court of the tabernacle is a picture of the cross of Jesus. Bronze speaks of judgment, and the sacrificial animal without blemish points to Jesus the Lamb of God without blemish and without spot (see 1 Peter 1:19). Jesus our sacrificial Lamb bore our sins in His own body (1 Peter 2:24) and tasted death for every man (see Hebrews 2:9), offering a better and once-for-all sacrifice that did not just cover sin, but removed it (or put it away) altogether (see Hebrews 9:8-14, 26) and perfected believers forever. (see Hebrews 10:14). On the cross, Jesus bore our sins and took our judgment. (see 1 Peter 2:24; Isaiah 53). As our sin offering, His blood was shed for the remission of our sins (see Matthew 26:28), and as our burnt offering, He was burnt by the fire of God's judgment for a sweet-smelling aroma to God. (see Isaiah 53:11; Hebrews 10:10-14; Ephesians 5:2).

Clearly, every furniture in the tabernacle or Temple points to the inner working of Jesus Christ within the believer today. We have already pointed out that the Brazen Altar points to Jesus the Lamb of God who took away our sins. The Brazen Laver (see Exodus 38:8), which is also located in the outer court of the tabernacle, points to Jesus our sanctification (see Ephesians 5:25-27; 1 Corinthians 1:30). The Golden Lampstand (see Exodus 25:31-40) located in the Holy place of the tabernacle points to Jesus our baptizer in the Holy Spirit and the Head of the Church. The Table of Showbread (see Exodus 25:23-30), which is located inside the Holy Place of the tabernacle also points to Jesus our Bread of Life. The Altar of Incense which is also located in the Holy Place (see Exodus 40:26) points to Jesus our High Priest. The Mercy Seat, located in the Holy of Holies on top of the Ark of the Covenant (see Exodus 25:17-22), points to Jesus our merciful Savior and the Lamb upon the Throne. Everything in the tabernacle points to the revelation of Jesus Christ. They point to the ministry of Jesus Christ in the believer who today is the temple of God and the temple of the Holy Spirit. (see 1 Corinthians 3:16-17; 1 Corinthians 6:19). Indeed it is amazing that the believer's body is today God's temple on earth, and his heart is today God's Holy of Holies on earth.

Under the Old Covenant the Holy of Holies was God's special dwelling place or throne in the tabernacle and in the Temple (see Leviticus 16:2); it was a perfect cube or square measuring 20 cubits or 30 feet on each side (see 2 Chronicles 3:8; 1 Kings 6:16; Ezekiel 41:4), and inside it was the Ark of the Covenant, also called the Ark of the Testimony (see Exodus 26:33; Exodus 40:3, 21; 1 Kings 8:6-9), which represented the presence of God. Indeed the Holy of Holies was a shadow or representation of Heaven — the true throne of God (see Isaiah 66:1) — as we are told in John's vision of heaven that the new Jerusalem is also a perfect cube or square. (see Revelation 21:16).

The Bible says that a thick curtain divided or separated the Holy of Holies (God's dwelling place) from the Holy Place (see Exodus 26:33) and the tabernacle of meeting which Aaron and his sons and all succeeding priests tended from evening until morning before the Lord. (see Exodus 27:21). This thick curtain, known as the "veil," was woven of blue, purple, and scarlet thread, and fine woven linen; it was woven with an artistic design of cherubim. (see Exodus 26:31). The veil of the temple thus existed to always show the people the separation between God and sinful man and the difficulty for the Old Creation man to approach God. It showed the people that God's eyes are too pure to look on evil and He can tolerate no sin (see Habakkuk 1:13). Indeed, God considered the people as transgressors and sinners (see 1 Timothy 1:9; Galatians 3:19); God considered them as unholy people who needed to be holy (see Leviticus 11:44-45; Leviticus 19:2; Leviticus 20:26; Deuteronomy 23:14). And so God restricted them from coming into His presence, by installing the veil (see Exodus 26:33), just as He restricted them from coming into His presence at Mount Sinai by setting bounds. (see Exodus 19:10-13).

Moreover, because whoever entered the Holy of Holies entered into the very presence of God, the Law permitted only the high priest to enter the Holy of Holies, and even he couldn't go in whenever he pleased, but could enter only once a year (on the Day of Atonement), and not without blood sacrifices to atone for his own sins and the sins of the people that were committed in ignorance. (see Leviticus 16; Hebrews 9:6-7). The high priest also had to make some meticulous preparations before entering the Holy of Holies on the Day of Atonement — he had to wash himself, put on special clothing, bring burning incense for the smoke to cover his eyes from a direct view of

God (represented by the mercy seat), or else he would die; then also he had to bring blood with him to make atonement for his own sins and for the sins of the people. (see Leviticus 16). In fact, if anyone else apart from the high priest entered the Holy of Holies at any time, that person would die. In Chapter 5 of this book we noted many examples of terrible things that happened to the children of Israel whenever they, being sinful men, tried to force themselves into the presence of our Holy Father and God without being invited; they were immediately smitten with death. Some of these incidents are recorded in Leviticus 10:1-3, and 1 Samuel 6:19, both of which, I believe, occurred in order to cause Israel to know her spiritual condition before God. What astounds me the most is the fact that even Aaron the high priest was warned not to come into the Holy of Holies just any time he wanted, lest he die. (see Leviticus 16:1-2). This thus makes the tearing of the veil of the temple following Jesus' death very significant. For the first time in Israel's history, the Holy of Holies was exposed deliberately by God Himself, offering unlimited access to all men. God's presence was no longer in that man-made Holy of Holies; His presence had vacated the Temple. The Bible says, "God, who made the world and everything in it, since He is Lord of heaven and earth, does not dwell in temples made with hands." (Acts 17:24). Jesus had prophesied to the Samaritan woman that the hour was coming when they would neither worship the Father on Mount Gerizim in Samaria, nor (in the Temple) in Jerusalem. (see John 4:21). This hour had now come with the tearing of the veil. The Father could now only be worshipped in spirit and in truth, and He seeks true worshippers to do such. (see John 4:23-24). Remember that Jesus had also said in Matthew 23:38, "See! Your house is left to you desolate." Here, Jesus had uttered a prediction of the most confounding event that would ever happen to the Israelites. The presence of God was to depart the Temple's Holy of Holies. And it did happen when the veil of the temple was torn in two from top to bottom. The "house" had indeed been left desolate. Again, in Matthew 26:61, we learn that two witnesses had testified against Jesus before the Sanhedrin that He had said, "I am able to destroy the temple of God and build it in three days." Little did they know that, even though the temple Jesus was referring to was His own body (see John 2:21) which was to be raised from the dead in three days, the physical temple in Jerusalem was also to be destroyed upon the death of Jesus, as God's presence vacated the Holy of Holies and left the house desolate with the tearing of the veil of the temple. And in three days, a new temple was to be erected through the resurrection of Jesus — all men who believe in Jesus were to become that new temple in whom God would dwell. Consequently, Jesus breathed on His disciples on the same night of His resurrection (on that third day) and said to them, "Receive the Holy Spirit,' thereby making those men the new temple of God on earth. (see John 20:19-22, with 1 Corinthians 3:16-17; 1 Corinthians 6:19; Ephesians 2:22).

Indeed, the temple was destroyed as the place where God dwelt, and Jesus built it in three days through His resurrection. The temple was destroyed the moment Jesus said "It is finished" and gave up His spirit. The temple was finished — God no longer dwelt there; the Holy of Holies in the temple was finished; the Old Covenant that had given Israel its home, national life and culture was finished: it was fulfilled, and its law (the Law of Moses) was annulled and set aside. (see Hebrews 7:18). The Priesthood was finished; the Sacrifices were finished — the Law was finished! Thus, not only was the Old Covenant made obsolete, everything connected with the Old Covenant had also come to an end and become obsolete, including the Old Covenant Law — the Ten Commandments. (see Hebrews 8:13, with Colossians 2:13-14 and Galatians 3:24-25). A New Covenant was inaugurated — the New Covenant in Jesus' blood. (Luke 22:20; Matthew 26:28). And this New Covenant was to bring into being one new humanity and a special people of God, a holy nation and a royal priesthood made up of Jews and Gentiles; this new humanity was to be called the Body of Christ or the Church of God (see Ephesians 2:15-22; 1 Corinthians 10:32; 1 Corinthians 12:13; Colossians 1:18, with 1 Peter 2:5,9-10); it was to be called the New Creation — children of God, born of God, created or born in Christ Jesus through His resurrection and by the Word of truth. (see 2 Corinthians 5:17, with 1 Peter 1:3, 1 Peter 1:23, and James 1:18). Indeed, the New Covenant was to bring into existence a new temple (see 1 Corinthians 3:16; 1 Corinthians 6:19; Ephesians 2:19-22), a new law (see John 13:34-35), a new High Priest (see Hebrews 4:14-16), and a new priesthood (see 1 Peter 2:5, 9-10; Revelation 1:6) offering new (spiritual) sacrifices acceptable to God through Jesus Christ. (see Romans 12:1; 1 Peter 2:5; Hebrews 13:15-16; Philippians 4:18).

The children of Israel, however, were obviously not happy about the change. When Jesus said, "It is finished," the whole of Heaven heard it and acknowledged it, but many people in Israel who had ears would not hear it nor accept it. Israel was shaken to its very core by this declaration. No wonder there was an earthquake. The children of Israel had worshipped the Law of Moses, even though they didn't and couldn't keep it. They had revered the Ten Commandments and worshipped it more than they had revered and worshipped God. And yet, it was a law of death, a law of sin, and a law that begat fear in the hearts of men. The Bible calls it "the law of sin and death" (see Romans 8:2) and "the ministry of condemnation." (see 2 Corinthians 3:9). And even though the law itself is spiritual (see Romans 7:14) and can only be kept through the Spirit or by walking in the Spirit, it is made for the natural man and not for the spiritual or righteous man (see 1 Timothy 1:9), and so the natural man loved it, and didn't want to part with it and embrace the spiritual life that had come through Jesus Christ. (see 1 Corinthians 15:45-49). Ironically, the natural man did not want to part with the law, even though he didn't and couldn't keep the law. Even today, there are many people (including Gentiles) who still can't let go of the Law of the Old Covenant, who still cling to the law and other shadows from the Old Covenant, instead of embracing the substance which is of Christ. How sad, and how tragic!

Beloved, the tearing of the veil in the temple says it all: the Old Covenant is finished; a New Covenant is born. The Old Covenant has been fulfilled and set aside. (see Luke 8:44-48, with Hebrews 8:13 and Hebrews 7:18). The old way of approaching God has been annulled and is no longer valid. A new and better way to the Holy of Holies — to heaven, to God — is now open, and this new Way is Jesus Christ. (see John 14:6; Acts 4:12; 1 Timothy 2:5). Jesus presents a better way and "a better hope through which we draw near to God." (see Hebrews 7:19). The presence of God is no longer shielded from man behind a thick veil. Sin, the obstacle that stood between man and God for generations, has been put away forever through Jesus' sacrifice of Himself on the cross. (see Hebrews 9:26). The Law of Moses which was a veil that blinded their minds and hearts and separated unrighteous men from a righteous God, has been removed and nailed to the cross of Jesus. (see 2 Corinthians 3:14-16, with Colossians 2:14-15).

When Jesus died, the veil of the Jerusalem temple was torn in half, from the top to the bottom. Only God could have carried out such an incredible act because the veil was too high for human hands to have reached from the top, and too thick to have torn it. Only God could've torn it from top to bottom the way it happened. And when God acts, who can reverse it? (see Isaiah 43:13). Thus, the Way to God is open to all mankind: this is what the tearing of the veil of the temple was heralding. We can now boldly enter God's Presence behind the veil "where the forerunner has entered for us, even Jesus, having become High Priest forever according to the order of Melchizedek." (see Hebrews 6:19-20). Praise God! "Let us therefore come boldly unto the throne of grace, that we may obtain mercy, and find grace to help in time of need." (Hebrews 4:16 KJV).

The High Priesthood of Jesus Christ and Its Significance

The Bible also makes it clear that Jesus' High Priesthood is not according to the order of the Levitical priesthood, but according to the order of Melchizedek. It is important, therefore, to know the differences between Jesus' perfect High Priesthood and the "imperfect" Levitical priesthood. Under the Old Covenant, priests came from the tribe of Levi, and the first high priest in that order of priests was Aaron, whom God Himself appointed. (see Exodus 28:1-3). These high priests were sinful men who had to offer animal sacrifices, first for their own sins and then for the people's. They themselves had to be covered by the blood sacrifices before they could intercede on behalf of the people, for they were imperfect. Besides the daily sacrifices offered by the priests, year after year, on the Day of Atonement, the high priest had to offer sacrifices. These sacrifices were only good for covering the sins of the nation for a year. It was a temporal solution, for it is not possible for the blood of bulls and goats to take away sins. (see Hebrews 10:4). These Levitical high priests were not just imperfect with regards to their own sinful nature and the imperfect sacrifices they offered, but also by the fact that they were prevented by death from continuing in office. (see Hebrews 7:23). Their sacrifices also couldn't make anyone perfect. (see Hebrews 7:11). And so, to fix this problem, God Himself became a Man in the Person of Jesus Christ (see John 1:1-5, 14; 1 Timothy 3:16) to become our great High Priest forever (see Hebrews 4:14) and to offer Himself as the sacrifice for our sins, to put away sin once for all. (see Acts 20:28, with Hebrews 9:12, 26). He had to be made "**fully human in every way**, in order that He might become a merciful and faithful high priest in service to God, and that he might make propitiation for the sins of the people." (see Hebrews 2:17). He had to become a Man also because "every high priest is selected from among the people." (see Hebrews 5:1). However, Jesus' High Priesthood is after the order of Melchizedek (see Hebrews 5:1-10), which is a perfect and eternal priesthood. It is not after the order of Aaron (or the Levitical priesthood), which was temporary and imperfect.

Levitical priests inherited their office by law and only held the position temporarily until death, but God swore to make Jesus our **High Priest forever**. (see Hebrews 5:5-6). Since Jesus wasn't a Levi, His Priesthood required a change in the law. (see Hebrews 7:18-22). Jesus became a priest by oath sworn by God Himself declaring Him a Priest forever after the order of Melchizedek. And because of this oath, Jesus has become the guarantor of a New and better Covenant (see Hebrews 7:22). Since the Old Covenant (of law) was tied to the sacrifices made by the Levitical high priest, the people's fate was linked to the acceptability or right standing of the high priest before God. Hence the high priest had to secure good standing before God through sacrifices for his own sins before he could offer sacrifices for the people to also be in good standing before God. And since the high priest's standing before God was never stable because of his sinful nature, the people's standing before God was never stable either. So God changed the priesthood of the Old Covenant and replaced it with the perfect and better priesthood of Jesus Christ, confirming with an oath to make His priesthood permanent and everlasting, so that our right standing before God will also be permanent and everlasting. Today we can be at ease because our High Priest is God's own sinless Son, in whom He is well pleased (see Matthew 17:5). We can be certain of God's acceptance and blessings in our life. No wonder Paul says in Ephesians 1:6 that we are accepted in the Beloved. We cannot lose our right standing before God, because Jesus is our eternal High Priest. Jesus' priesthood is after the order of Melchizedek, which is a priesthood of righteousness and peace. Hence, Jesus came to make peace between God and man and to establish us in righteousness through faith (see Romans 5:1, with 2 Corinthians 5:21; Romans 3:22; Isaiah 54:14; Isaiah 53:11). For those of us who believe in Him, Jesus is our righteousness forever (see 1 Corinthians 1:30, with Daniel 9:24)); and He Himself is our peace. (see Ephesians 2:14). Thus blessings are perpetually on our head, because the Bible says that blessings are on the head of the righteous (see Proverbs 10:6). We are blessed with every spiritual blessing in the heavenly realms in Christ Jesus (see Ephesians 1:3). Hallelujah!

Jesus has a permanent priesthood, and is able to save completely those who come to God through Him, because He always lives to intercede for them (see Hebrews 7:23-25). Also, since Jesus our High Priest is sinless and perfect in every way (see Hebrews 7:26-28), He offered **His own blood** once for all for our **eternal redemption**. He did not need to sacrifice the blood of goats and bulls, which cannot take away sins. Jesus is the One John the Baptist introduced twice as the Lamb of God who takes away the sins of the world (see John 1:29; John 1:36). He Himself became our perfect sacrifice, entering the Most Holy Place once for all with His own blood; and God has accepted His sacrifice as sufficient in itself for our ETERNAL redemption (see Hebrews 9:11-12). This means that we were not redeemed for just a year or until our next sin; we were redeemed for eternity. The Bible says that Jesus, having been perfected (through suffering), became "the author of **ETERNAL salvation** to all who obey Him." (see Hebrews 5:9). He is the Captain of our salvation. (see Hebrews 2:10). Indeed Jesus Christ is the Shepherd and Overseer of the believer's soul. (see 1 Peter 2:25). Our soul is in good hands. So we can be secure in His salvation, for our salvation is eternal. The Bible says we have been made holy forever through Jesus' sacrifice (see Hebrews 10:10). We have been made perfect. (see Hebrews 10:14). Jesus our High Priest has done what the Levitical priests couldn't do. The Levitical priests could never make anyone perfect (see Hebrews 7:19; Hebrews 10:1); they could never sit down because their work was never done, and their sacrifices could never take away sins (see Hebrews 10:11). But when Jesus our great High Priest "had offered for all time one sacrifice for sins, He SAT DOWN at the right hand of God." (see Hebrews 10:12). To me, this is by far the most distinguishing characteristic affirming the superiority of our great High Priest Jesus Christ's priesthood to that of the Levitical priesthood: He is sitting down. Just reflect on that picture for a minute. And be reminded that the Levitical priests never sat down because their work was never finished. They just kept offering more and more sacrifices because the sacrifices they offered were only good for the time until they committed the next sin. So they kept at it, going on and on, never sitting down. There wasn't even a single chair in the Tabernacle for them to sit down, because it would be unnecessary since their job was never done. The only seat there was the Mercy Seat of God in the Holy of Holies, which no one dared sit on. No priest ever sat down. But Jesus offered one perfect sacrifice, **and sat down**, because the work was finished. Did I hear you say, "Amen!?" Jesus accomplished what the entire Levitical system could never accomplish: He sat down. "For by one sacrifice He has made perfect forever those who are being made holy." (Hebrews 10:14 NIV). And this one sacrifice was the sacrifice of Himself. Jesus did it all. As far as our salvation is concerned, the work is finished, and Jesus has sat down; He is resting. Hallelujah! You have to believe it so that you can also enter that rest, so that you can also sit down with Him and rest in Him and with Him. The Bible says that "we who have believed do enter that rest." (see Hebrews 4:3). There is nothing to add to the salvation Jesus has purchased for us. "For he who has entered His rest has himself also ceased from his works as God did from His." (Hebrews 4:10). All of us who claim to believe in Jesus as our Savior must also cease from our own works; we must cease from working FOR our salvation. Salvation has been given to us by grace, and we must accept (or receive) it by faith. (see Ephesians 2:8-9; Romans 10:9-10). Through Jesus' one perfect sacrifice, God has reconciled us to Himself and made peace with us forever (see Colossians 1:19-20; 2 Corinthians 5:18-19; Romans 5:1), so that now we can come boldly and with confidence to the throne of grace (which is the throne of God) whenever we like, without fear or trepidation (see

Ephesians 3:12; Hebrews 4:16). ALL our sins — past, present and future — are forgiven. (see Colossians 2:13). "All" means ALL. Jesus' one time sacrifice took ALL of our sins away. All our sins are forgiven or remitted once we accept Jesus Christ as our Lord and Savior. "And where these (sins) have been forgiven, **sacrifice for sin is no longer necessary.**" (Hebrews 10:18 NIV). Thanks to our great High Priest Jesus Christ, today we no longer need an endless line of priests who aren't perfect, offering sacrifices that aren't sufficient, in a sanctuary that isn't permanent. "For Christ did not enter a sanctuary made with human hands that was only a copy of the true one; **He entered heaven itself, now to appear for us in God's presence**. Nor did He enter heaven to offer Himself again and again, the way the high priest enters the Most Holy Place every year with blood that is not his own. Otherwise Christ would have had to suffer many times since the creation of the world. But He has appeared ONCE FOR ALL at the culmination of the ages to do away with sin by the sacrifice of Himself. Just as people are destined to die once, and after that to face judgment, so Christ was sacrificed ONCE TO TAKE AWAY THE SINS OF MANY; and He will appear a second time, not to bear sin, but TO BRING SALVATION to those who are waiting for Him." (Hebrews 9:24-28 NIV). Hallelujah! This is the good news we are all commanded to preach to the world.

Today God doesn't want us to approach Him through anyone else but Jesus our great High Priest. "For there is one God and one Mediator between God and mankind, the Man Christ Jesus." (1 Timothy 2:5 NIV). When we believe in Him and depend on Jesus Christ as our High Priest and our Mediator, He brings us to the Father. Jesus Himself said, "My Father's will is that everyone who looks to the Son and BELIEVES in Him shall HAVE eternal life, and I will raise them up at the last day." (see John 6:40 NIV). This is our hope in the New Covenant. "Therefore, holy brethren, partakers of a heavenly calling, **consider Jesus, the Apostle and High Priest of our confession.**" (Hebrews 3:1 NASB). "Let us hold fast the confession of our hope without wavering, for He who promised is faithful." (Hebrews 10:23 NASB). "Let us therefore come boldly to the throne of grace, that we may obtain mercy and find grace to help in time of need." (Hebrews 4:16). The throne of grace is the new Holy of Holies. For the Old Covenant men, it was a throne of judgment which they approached in fear. But for us the New Covenant men, it is a throne of grace which we approach boldly in faith and with confidence. Jesus said that as we come boldly to the throne of grace with our needs, the Father will give us whatever we ask in His name. (see John 16:23-24). "Therefore, brethren, having **boldness to ENTER** the Holiest BY THE BLOOD OF JESUS, **by a NEW AND LIVING WAY which He consecrated for us, THROUGH THE VEIL, that is, His FLESH**, and having a High Priest over the house of God, LET US DRAW NEAR with a true heart in full assurance of FAITH, having our hearts sprinkled from an evil conscience and our bodies washed with pure water." (Hebrews 10:19-22). Amen!

The Significance of the Statement or Testimony of the Centurion and Those With Him at the Crucifixion of Jesus Christ

Now back to the scene of the crucifixion, the tearing of the veil of the temple, the quaking of the earth, and other events associated with the death of Jesus Christ were obviously astounding and frightening to many, if not all those who witnessed it. The Bible says that, "when the CENTURION and THOSE WITH HIM, WHO WERE GUARDING Jesus, SAW the EARTHQUAKE and the THINGS THAT HAD HAPPENED, they FEARED GREATLY, saying, **"TRULY this was the Son of God!"** (Matthew 27:54). Today, there are many who question why the three Gospel writers — Matthew, Mark, and Luke — who recorded these events that occurred upon the death of Jesus, reported different variations of the CENTURION'S words or statement. Here, Matthew records the centurion as saying, "Truly this was the Son of God," while Mark says substantially the same thing, adding only the word "Man," and rendering it, "Truly this Man was the Son of God!" (see Mark 15:39). Luke records the words of the centurion as follows: "Certainly this was a righteous Man!" (see Luke 23:47). So what did the Centurion really say? Well, Matthew gives us an explanation for the variations here in Chapter 27 verse 54, by noting that it was "the Centurion AND THOSE WITH HIM who were guarding Jesus" WHO SAID THESE THINGS. So it wasn't just one person's words, which thus explains why we have different variations of it. Each writer recorded whatever they heard and could grasp from the centurion and those soldiers that were standing guard with him in great fear and saying these things. Each Gospel writer recorded what best served their purpose. Therefore there is no reason to doubt that all those words were spoken of Jesus, as the centurion and those with him struggled to comprehend all that had happened. Now, come to think of it — the things that happened astounded, shocked, terrified and overwhelmed everyone. Besides the tearing in two FROM TOP TO BOTTOM of the multi-layered, thick VEIL OF THE TEMPLE, Jesus' last words and last breath were accompanied by other supernatural events: "the EARTH QUAKED, and THE

ROCKS WERE SPLIT, and THE GRAVES WERE OPENED; and MANY BODIES OF THE SAINTS who had fallen asleep WERE RAISED; and COMING OUT OF the graves **AFTER His RESURRECTION**, they WENT INTO THE HOLY CITY and APPEARED TO MANY" (see Matthew 27:51-53). And so the centurion's words need not be limited to one phrase or sentence, because the centurion's recorded words were not the words of a single individual, but many; and thus "they" could have said each of the things the centurion was quoted as saying. In accordance with his own emphasis on Christ as the perfect Man, Luke may have chosen to use the phrase, "Certainly this was a righteous Man!" rather than the ones used by Matthew and Mark. In fact, Mark tells us at the beginning of his gospel that he was writing "the gospel about Jesus Christ the Son of God" (see Mark 1:1), even as he proceeded to present Jesus to us as the suffering "Servant." And so, for Mark, after all that Jesus had suffered as a "Servant," the declaration by the centurion that, "Truly this Man was the Son of God!" (see Mark 15:39), was the most telling, the most memorable and the most fitting for His purpose in writing the gospel. Amongst men, what greater testimony of Jesus' innocence, righteousness, perfection and divinity than from the lips of His executioners!

The Significance of the Day on Which Jesus Was Crucified, Died, and Was Buried

The Bible also records that as Jesus gave up His spirit or breathed His last and all those supernatural things were happening, many women who ministered to Jesus or served Him were also looking on from afar, including Mary Magdalene, Mary the mother of James the Less and of Joses, and Salome the mother of the sons of Zebedee. (see Matthew

27:55-56; Mark 15:40-41; Luke 23:49). Now, the Gospel according to John also adds: "Therefore, because it was **the PREPARATION DAY**, that the bodies should not remain on the cross on the Sabbath (for that Sabbath was **A HIGH day**), THE JEWS asked PILATE that their LEGS MIGHT BE BROKEN, and THAT THEY MIGHT BE TAKEN AWAY. Then the SOLDIERS came and BROKE THE LEGS of THE FIRST and of THE OTHER WHO WAS CRUCIFIED with Him. BUT WHEN THEY CAME TO JESUS and **SAW** that **He WAS ALREADY DEAD**, they DID NOT BREAK His legs. But one of the soldiers PIERCED His SIDE with a SPEAR, and immediately BLOOD AND WATER CAME OUT. And he who has seen has testified, and his testimony is true; and he knows that he is telling the truth, so that you may believe. For these things were done that the Scripture should be fulfilled, "Not one of His bones shall be broken." And again another Scripture says, "They shall look on Him whom they pierced." (John 19:31-37).

Thus, we can learn from these verses that the day Jesus was crucified, died, and was buried was the **Preparation Day** (or the Day before the Sabbath); and this Sabbath in question was **a high day**. (see John 19:31; Mark 15:42). What this means is that this particular Sabbath on whose eve Jesus died was **not** a regular Sabbath day — it was not a Saturday, but a high (Sabbath) day. Now, during the Passover feast, the first and the last day of the Passover feast were called high days or holy convocation (see Exodus 12:16; Leviticus 23:4-8); they were extra Sabbath days. So, this particular Sabbath day, since it was a high (Sabbath) day and not the regular (Saturday) Sabbath, was most likely a Friday, which would thus put the Preparation Day, the Day Jesus died, on a **Thursday**. Obviously the Preparation Day couldn't be pushed back beyond Thursday, because according to the biblical records, Jesus was raised from the dead on the morning of the THIRD DAY after His burial, and this third day was also **the first day of the week,** which obviously is Sunday. (see Matthew 27:64; Matthew 28:1-6; Mark 16:1-6; Luke 24:1-3; John 20:1-10). And so for those people who are confused about how Jesus could possibly have been three days and three nights in the heart of the earth if He were crucified on Friday, this information should perhaps solve the puzzle for you, because Jesus obviously wasn't crucified on Friday as is popularly believed and celebrated, but on Thursday. Clearly, the high (Sabbath) day on this occasion was the Friday after Jesus' crucifixion and burial, thereby giving the Israelites a double Sabbath day — the Friday (high Sabbath day) and the Saturday (regular Sabbath day). The fact that the previous two days were Sabbath days also explains why the women who discovered the empty tomb couldn't bring the spices to the tomb of Jesus any sooner than they did — on the resurrection morning, the first day of the week. (see Luke 24:1). Jesus was evidently crucified during the day on Thursday, and was buried in the evening of that same day. And then early in the morning of the first day of the week, which was Sunday, they came and found the tomb empty. Therefore, Jesus was actually three days and three nights in the heart of the earth just as He had prophesied. (see Matthew 12:40). Indeed, Jesus our Savior fulfilled all the prophecies concerning Him.

Was Jesus Truly Dead When He Was Taken From the Cross For Burial?

If anybody still has any doubts that Jesus was dead when He was taken off the cross for burial (as I have learned many Muslims do), John (the disciple of Jesus) being an eyewitness himself and testifying of the truth of Jesus' death, also calls the soldiers to the witness stand as eyewitnesses who also SAW that Jesus was dead (see John 19:33). Then, of course, there is the blood and water that came out of Jesus' side when He was pierced by the spear of the soldiers. Moreover, the Bible records that when, in the evening of Jesus' crucifixion, Joseph of Arimathea — the courageous rich man, prominent council member, and a good and just man who had also become a disciple of Jesus — went to Pilate and asked for the body of Jesus, Pilate marveled that Jesus was already dead, and only granted Jesus' body to Joseph after VERIFYING WITH THE CENTURION that Jesus was indeed DEAD and had been DEAD FOR SOME TIME. (see Mark 15-43-45; Matthew 27:57-58; Luke 23:50-52). After Joseph came and took the body of Jesus, the Bible also says that, "Nicodemus, who at first came to Jesus by night, came, bringing a MIXTURE OF MYRRH AND ALOES, about a HUNDRED POUNDS. Then they TOOK THE BODY OF JESUS, AND BOUND IT IN STRIPS OF LINEN WITH THE SPICES, as the custom of the Jews is to bury." (John 19:39-40). At this point, even if Jesus had not died on the cross, the embalming performed by Nicodemus and Joseph with the mixture of myrrh and spices would have killed Him. And so there is no question that Jesus was dead when He was buried in that new tomb belonging to Joseph, which had been hewn out of the rock (see Matthew 27:59-60; Mark 15:46); there is no doubt that He was dead when Joseph rolled that heavy stone against the door of the tomb with the help of Nicodemus, and departed (see John 19:38-41, with Matthew 27:60). Indeed, there is no doubt that the women who had come with Jesus from Galilee and had followed after Joseph and Nicodemus and observed the tomb and how Jesus' body was laid, knew that Jesus was dead when they returned and prepared spices and fragrant oils. (see Luke 23:55-56). Again, there is no doubt that the chief priests and Pharisees who gathered together the next day to Pilate (breaking the high Sabbath day in their hypocrisy), knew that Jesus was dead when they asked for a guard to be set at His tomb until the third day. (see Matthew 27:62-64). There is absolutely no doubt that Pilate knew Jesus was dead when he gave the chief priests and Pharisees permission to put a guard at the tomb and they responded accordingly, making the tomb secure, sealing the stone and setting the guard. (see Matthew 27:65-66). And so Jesus Christ was very very dead when He was laid in the tomb. And everybody knew it! But thank God that is not where the story ends; Jesus was also raised from the dead on the third day. Glory to God!

The Significance of the Events of the Resurrection Morning

The Bible says that after the Sabbath, as the first day of the week began to dawn, Mary Magdalene, and Mary the mother of James the Less and Joses, and Salome came to see the tomb of Jesus; they had bought spices and prepared it, so they brought it that they might come and anoint Him. (see Matthew 28:1; Mark 16:1-2; Luke 24:1). They got to the tomb when the sun had risen, only to realize that the sun wasn't the only light-giving body that had risen, but that the Son had also risen, the Sun of Righteousness had risen with healing in its rays. (see Malachi 4:2). Hallelujah! The Bible says, "they found the stone rolled away from the tomb. Then they went in and did not find the body of the Lord Jesus. And it happened, as they were greatly perplexed about this, that behold, two men stood by them in shining garments. Then, as they were afraid and bowed their faces to the earth, they said to them,

"WHY DO YOU SEEK THE LIVING AMONG THE DEAD? He IS NOT HERE, BUT IS RISEN! Remember how He spoke to you when He was still in Galilee, saying, 'The Son of Man must be delivered into the hands of sinful men, and be crucified, and the THIRD DAY rise again.'" And they remembered His words. Then they returned from the tomb and told all these things to the eleven and to all the rest." (Luke 24:2-9). What joyous news the resurrection of the Lord must've been to these women, who prior to arriving at the tomb had been contemplating who was going to roll away that very large stone from the door of the tomb for them; and what a surprise and shock it must've been to them when they first looked up and saw that the stone had been rolled away. (see Mark 16-3-4; Luke 24:2). But how was the stone rolled away? The Bible says there was a great earthquake; for an angel of the Lord descended from heaven, and came and rolled back the stone from the door, and sat on it. (see Matthew 28:2; Mark 16:4). I love this angel, for he has good sense of humor: he rolled the stone and sat on it! The angel's countenance was like lightning, and his clothing as white as snow. (see Matthew 28:3). Matthew tells us in an earlier report that following the death of Jesus, there was also an earthquake in which "THE ROCKS WERE SPLIT, and THE GRAVES WERE OPENED; and MANY BODIES OF THE SAINTS who had fallen asleep WERE RAISED; and COMING OUT OF the graves **AFTER His RESURRECTION**, they WENT INTO THE HOLY CITY and APPEARED TO MANY" (see Matthew 27:51-53). What this is saying is that after Jesus was raised from the dead, many bodies of the saints who had fallen asleep WERE RAISED also, and they came out of their graves, went into the Holy city and appeared to many. What an amazing day this must've been! What a great day to be alive! There is no doubt that these saints were raised by the same

Power that raised Jesus from the dead — the power of the Holy Spirit. (see Romans 8:11, with Ephesians 1:19-20).

In a few moments we would discuss what happened to these raised bodies of the saints. But for now, aren't you at this point wondering what happened to the guards at the tomb? Well, promise you won't laugh. The Bible says that they shook for FEAR of the angel and became like DEAD MEN. (see Matthew 28:4). My heart leaps for joy as I ponder over the good news the angel carried to the women at the tomb: "He is not here; for He is risen, as He said. Come, see the place where the Lord lay." (Matthew 28:6). How amazing! Jesus had died as sin and a curse, as a subject of Satan; yet He was raised as the LORD — the Lord over life and death, the Lord over Satan and his cohorts, the Lord over all principalities and powers, the Lord of Heaven and Earth, THE LORD OF LORDS! Hallelujah! The resurrection of Jesus Christ is indeed the greatest event that ever happened on earth both in the spirit realm and the physical (or sense) realm. Satan was defeated, and will stay defeated forever.

What Happened to Those Saints Who Were Raised Bodily With Jesus Christ on Resurrection Morning?

As you probably know, Matthew 27:52-53 is the only passage in the entire Bible that reports the event of some saints being raised bodily with the Lord and coming into the Holy City and appearing to many. Clearly, this passage alone does not give us complete information about what happened to these resurrected saints afterwards. Nevertheless, we can point out a few truths based on the information we are provided in Matthew's gospel, in addition to other scriptural references from the New Testament epistles:

First, those who were raised from the dead were saints (believers; righteous people).

Second, they were raised bodily (their bodies were raised). Here the word "glorified" is not used to describe their risen bodies, but that is immaterial to any conclusion we draw on this, because when Jesus' body was raised, the word "glorified" was not used in Matthew's gospel to describe His risen body in reporting the actual account of His resurrection either. (see Matthew 28:1-10). And yet we know, based on other scriptural references, that it was a glorified body. Paul tells us of the believer's body, that it is sown (or buried) in corruption, but it is raised incorruptible; that it is sown (or buried) in dishonor, but raised in glory. (see 1 Corinthians 15:42-43). And since this account in Matthew's gospel is the first account of believers being raised (bodily) together with the Lord Jesus Christ in His resurrection, we can conclude that they were raised in glory or in a glorified body, just like the Lord Jesus Christ.

Third, those saints who were raised (only) APPEARED to many (people). The Bible doesn't say that they afterward lived with the people whom they appeared to. The word "appeared" seems to suggest a temporary presence. Whenever Jesus visited His disciples after His resurrection, the same word "appeared" as well as the phrases "was seen" or "presented Himself to" and other similar phrases were also used to describe His visits, thus denoting a temporary physical presence with the disciples, which the Bible tells us lasted over a period of 40 days. (see Acts 1:3; 1 Corinthians 15:3-8; Luke 24:34-36). Moreover, the

Bible says of Jesus, that "When He ASCENDED on high, HE TOOK MANY CAPTIVES (with Him) and gave gifts to His people." (see Ephesians 4:8 NIV). And so we are told here that JESUS DIDN'T ASCEND ALONE but took many captives with Him, which seems to suggest that those saints who were raised with Christ also ascended with Him to Heaven. Now, the use of the word "captives" is understood in the sense that every man born of Adam (after the fall, of course) is a captive of Satan, and does the will of Satan, until he accepts Jesus Christ as his Lord and Savior in all sincerity. (see 2 Timothy 2:26; John 8:44). And so believers were also once captives of Satan until we believed in Jesus, who redeemed us. Thus, when Jesus began His ministry on earth after being anointed with the Holy Spirit and with power, He said, "The Spirit of the Lord is upon Me, because He has anointed Me to preach the gospel to the poor; He HAS SENT Me to heal the brokenhearted, **TO PROCLAIM LIBERTY TO THE CAPTIVES**…" (see Luke 4:18). We all are the captives Jesus proclaimed liberty to and has freed. And so He took all believers with Him when He ascended to Heaven. We were all in Christ when He was raised, having died with Him and been buried with Him (see Romans 6:4-11); we were all raised together with Him (together with those saints who were raised bodily on resurrection morning); then we all ascended with Him and God seated us together with Him in the heavenly places in Christ Jesus. (see Ephesians 2:4-6). Now, this is referring to our spirit. But for those saints who were raised bodily with Christ on Resurrection Morning, it also includes their glorified body.

Regarding the bodily resurrection of the rest of us who may die before the Lord returns, the apostle Paul said, we know "that He who raised up the Lord Jesus WILL ALSO RAISE US UP WITH JESUS, and

WILL PRESENT US WITH YOU. For all things are for your sakes, that grace, having spread through the many, may cause thanksgiving to abound to the glory of God." (see 2 Corinthians 4:14-15). He also said, "Now if Christ is preached that He has been raised from the dead, how do some among you say that there is no resurrection of the dead? But if there is no resurrection of the dead, then Christ is not risen. And if Christ is not risen, then our preaching is empty and your faith is also empty. Yes, and we are found false witnesses of God, because we have testified of God that He raised up Christ, whom He did not raise up—if in fact the dead do not rise. For if the dead do not rise, then Christ is not risen. And if Christ is not risen, your faith is futile; you are still in your sins! Then also those who have fallen asleep in Christ have perished. If in this life only we have hope in Christ, we are of all men the most pitiable." (1 Corinthians 15:12-19). Those saints who were raised together with Christ on His resurrection morning, present us with an additional evidence for our hope as we await the return of our Lord Jesus Christ, and the resurrection of the dead. And, of course, we know, as Paul tells us, that "the Lord Himself will descend from heaven with a shout, with the voice of an archangel, and with the trumpet of God. AND THE DEAD IN CHRIST WILL RISE FIRST. Then we who are alive and remain shall be caught up together with them in the clouds to meet the Lord in the air. And thus we shall always be with the Lord." (1 Thessalonians 4:16-17). Amen.

What Makes Jesus Christ Different From All The Great Philosophers and Founders of the World's Religions?

Now, as we bring this chapter to a close, I wish to comment briefly on what makes the Lord Jesus Christ different from all the great philosophers and founders of the world's religions. All the great philosophers of old, and the founders of the world's religions obviously had great ideas, perhaps they had good intentions too; but they couldn't give life to anybody. They themselves died and found themselves helpless in the hands of death, utterly defeated and swallowed up by the grave. And those who follow after them will no doubt suffer the same fate, because the disciple cannot be greater than his master. But Jesus Christ came into the world not just with great ideas, not just with good intentions, but with WORDS OF LIFE. In fact, He was the only Man to ever claim to be THE RESURRECTION and THE LIFE (see John 11:25, with John 14:6), and then prove it by His death and resurrection. All the great philosophers of the world spoke mere human words, words of the flesh which could not give life to anyone. But when Jesus came, He said, "It is the Spirit who gives life; the flesh profits nothing. THE WORDS THAT I SPEAK TO YOU ARE SPIRIT, and THEY ARE LIFE." (John 6:63). And so Jesus spoke words that were spirit, and that **gave life to men**. He spoke the words of God the Father (see John 12:49-50), the words of life. The apostle John says of Jesus, that, "In Him was life, and the life was the light of men." (John 1:4). Yes, Jesus also died; yes, He was also buried; but what sets Him apart is that He was raised from the dead on the third day, thereby proving His deity — proving that He is over all the eternally blessed God. Amen. (see Romans 9:5; 1 Timothy 3:16; Acts 20:28). Before His death, Jesus had said, "My Father loves Me, because **I lay down My life that I may take it again.** NO ONE TAKES IT FROM Me, but I LAY IT DOWN of Myself. I have **POWER to lay it down**, and I have POWER TO TAKE IT AGAIN. This command I have received from My Father." (see John 10:17-18). And Jesus was right. He did just that — He laid down His life, and He took it again. Truly, He is risen!

He is alive forevermore! The Bible says that Jesus presented Himself ALIVE to His disciples after His suffering "BY MANY INFALLIBLE PROOFS, being seen by them during forty days and speaking of the things pertaining to the kingdom of God." (see Acts 1:3).

Thus, the resurrection of Jesus Christ is truth which cannot be denied, for it is supported by many infallible proofs; it is a divine truth, and it is a historical fact. Jesus, finding Himself in the hands of death, and coming face-to-face with the devil who had the power of death, tied the devil up, stripped him of all his power, and destroyed him. (see Hebrews 2:14, with Colossians 2:15). Then He walked out of the grave with the keys of hell and of death. When He appeared to John in a vision, He laid His right hand on him, saying to him, "Do not be afraid; I am the First and the Last. I am He who lives, and was dead, and behold, I AM ALIVE FOREVERMORE. Amen. And I HAVE THE KEYS OF HADES AND OF DEATH." (Revelation 1:17-18). What a glorious declaration of victory!

Indeed, our Savior Jesus Christ "has ABOLISHED DEATH and BROUGHT LIFE and IMMORTALITY to light through the gospel," (see II Timothy 1:10). Today all you have to do to receive this life and IMMORTALITY Jesus brought is to **believe the gospel**. "Believe on the Lord Jesus Christ, and you will be saved, you and your household." (Acts 16:31). Jesus Himself said, "I am the resurrection and THE LIFE. He who believes in Me, THOUGH HE MAY DIE, he SHALL LIVE. And whoever lives and believes in Me SHALL NEVER DIE. Do you believe this?" (John 11:25-26). Truly, those who believe in the Lord Jesus Christ do not die; we only fall asleep, and when we are absent from this earthly body, we are still alive, present with the Lord Jesus Christ in Heaven. (see 2 Corinthians 5:8). Glory to God! Soon, when the Lord Jesus Christ comes back in glory, and we are already asleep in Christ, our bodies will be raised incorruptible, and we shall be changed. "For this corruptible must put on incorruption, and this mortal must put on immortality. So when this corruptible has put on incorruption, and this mortal has put on immortality, then shall be brought to pass the saying that is written: "Death is swallowed up in victory." (I Corinthians 15:53-54). Hallelujah!

Accept Jesus Christ as your Lord and Savior today, and you will have eternal life. The Bible says, "And this is the testimony: that God has given us eternal life, and this life is in His Son. He who has the Son has life; he who does not have the Son of God does not have life." (I John 5:11-12). "Nor is there salvation in any other, for there is no other name under heaven given among men by which we must be saved." (Acts 4:12). If you are ready to sincerely give Jesus your heart, to make HIM your Lord and Savior and thus receive eternal life, pray this prayer from your heart:

"Almighty God, Your Word says that if I confess my sins, You are faithful and just to forgive me my sins and to cleanse me from ALL unrighteousness. Today I acknowledge and confess that I am a sinner in need of salvation, and I thank you for sending your beloved Son, Jesus Christ to die for me and to bear the judgment for my sins. I believe that Jesus Christ was crucified for my sins and was raised from the dead for my justification. I accept Jesus today as my Lord and Savior. And I thank You that I have received eternal life in the name of Jesus. Amen."

In the next Chapter, we will expound on the truth and power of the resurrection of Jesus Christ. We will also discuss what happened within those three days and three nights Jesus spent in the heart of the earth before His bodily resurrection. Indeed we will also unveil how the resurrection of Jesus Christ gave birth to the New Creation man, and what makes the new creation man such a super man — unique and superior to the First or Old Creation man.

Chapter 13

He is Risen: The Power of the Resurrection of Jesus Christ

What Happened Within Those Three Days and Three Nights Jesus Spent in the Heart of the Earth

THE BIBLE SAYS that Jesus Christ was made sin on the cross (see 2 Corinthians 5:21); all the iniquity of humanity was laid on Him (see Isaiah 53:6). Therefore Jesus died as sin and as a subject of Satan. He died as man's Representative and Substitute bearing the punishment man deserved for his sins. And since man was destined for hell, Jesus our sin-bearer, having suffered on the cross and died as sin, was cast into hell as man's Substitute. And so He spent three days and three nights in hell, in the heart of the earth (see Matthew 12:40); He descended into the lower parts of the earth (see Ephesians 4:8-10); He went (to prison) and preached to the spirits in prison (see 1 Peter 3:19); He was counted with those who go down the pit, and was laid in the lowest pit, in darkness, in the depths (see Psalm 88:4, 6). But His soul was not left in hell (see Psalm 16:10; Acts 2:27). Jesus was in hell for three days and three nights bearing the full punishment for our sins. And once the demands of Justice had been met, once He had suffered enough to pay the full penalty for man's disobedience, He was justified (or made righteous) in the Spirit (see 1 Timothy 3:16). Jesus was born again (or created anew) in the Spirit, as God declared: "Thou art my Son, this day have I begotten thee." (see Acts 13:33; Psalm 2:7; Romans 1:4). This means that Jesus was born out of **both** spiritual and physical death (the realm of Satan and sin) into life (the realm of God and righteousness). He is the firstborn from the dead — that is, the composite death (or spiritual and physical death combined) — (see Colossians 1:18), the firstborn over all creation (see Colossians 1:15), and the Head of the Body — the Church, the New Creation, the New Humanity (see Colossians 1:18). The Bible says that once Jesus was made alive by the Spirit (see 1 Peter 3:18) in that awful darkness of hell, He met Satan the strong man head-on, and tied him in his own house, and plundered his house, just as He had alluded to during His earth walk. (see Mark 3:27; Matthew 12:29). Paul describes it colorfully for us, that Jesus disarmed principalities and powers (that is, Satan and his angels) and made a public spectacle of them (that is, put them to public shame), triumphing over them in it. (see Colossians 2:15). Hebrews 2:14 also adds that in this battle, Jesus — who Himself became a Man and died for this very purpose — destroyed the devil who had the power of death; Jesus stripped the devil of his power and brought him to nought (or left him paralyzed), defeating him right in his own camp before his own army, and releasing those who through fear of death were all their lifetime subject to bondage. (see Hebrews 2:15). Jesus the New Creation Man or the Spiritual Man took back (for the entire new humanity) the dominion over the earth, which Adam the First or Old Creation man or the natural man handed over to Satan by his disobedience in the garden of Eden.

Indeed, Jesus possessed "the gate of His enemies" (see Genesis 22:17); He took "the keys of death and of hell" (see Revelation 1:18) from the devil. Then He preached also **to those that are dead,** so that they may be judged according to (that is, on the same grounds or in the same manner as) men in the flesh (see 1 Peter 4:6) — the dead heard the words of Jesus, just as men in the flesh have, and they had the choice to either accept the words of Jesus and be saved, or reject them and be condemned. Peter also clarifies for us that **the dead Jesus preached to in this context were the dead from the flood in the time of Noah**, these were those disobedient people who died in the wrath of God or the destruction that came upon the earth (long before God's covenant with Abraham), **they were the spirits (of men who formerly were disobedient in the days of Noah) that were imprisoned there in hell** (see 1 Peter 3:19-20); Jesus preached to them the gospel of grace — repentance and remission of sins in His name (see Luke 24:47). And those prisoners or captives who believed were freed. (see Ephesians 4:8; Isaiah 42:7; Luke 4:18). And once this was accomplished, Jesus ascended out of hell with the freed captives (see Ephesians 4:7-10), and was raised bodily from the dead in a transformed and glorified body (see Philippians 3:20-21; 1 Corinthians 15:3-5). The Bible says that God did not leave the soul of Jesus in hell, just as He had promised in His divine contract or covenant with Him (see Psalm 16:10); neither did God allow Jesus' Body to suffer corruption or decay (see Acts 2:27). Therefore, having been delivered up to death for our sins (or our offenses), Jesus was raised when we were justified (or declared righteous); He was raised for our justification. (see Romans 4:25). Hallelujah!

Just as the first Adam sinned (as man's representative to make all of us sinners), Jesus the second and last Adam was crucified and died as man's Representative and Substitute to make all of us (who believe in Him) righteous. (see Romans 5:18-19). That Jesus was our Representative and Substitute means that in the eyes of Justice, we (believers) were all crucified with Him and died with Him when He was crucified and died (see Galatians 2:20; Romans 6:4-6); we were all buried with Him when He was buried (see Romans 6:4-6; Colossians 2:12); and we were all raised with Him when He was raised (see Romans 6:4-8; Ephesians 2:4-6; Colossians 2:12-13). Then we were all made to sit together with Him in the heavenly places in Christ Jesus (see Ephesians 2:4-6) at God's right hand, far above all principality and power and might and dominion, and every name that is named, not only in this age but also in that which is to come. (see Ephesians 1:20-21). The Bible thus explains that when Jesus was born again or created anew in the Spirit as the Son of God (see Acts 13:33), we (believers) were created IN Him (see Ephesians 2:10). Jesus became our new world or habitation — for we were created in Him to live or abide in Him (see John 15:5-7) and walk in Him (see Colossians 2:6) — so that whatever we do in word or deed, we are to do all in the name of the Lord Jesus, giving thanks to God the Father, through Him. (see Colossians 3:17).

We (Believers) Were Born Again Through the Resurrection

Thus, we (believers) were begotten by God or born again to a living hope through the RESURRECTION of Jesus Christ from the dead. (see 1 Peter 1:3, with John 3:3; 1 John 5:1). Having been created in Christ (see Ephesians 2:10), we were born out of God's own will, through the resurrection of Jesus Christ and by the incorruptible seed or Word of God which lives and abides forever. (see 1 Peter 1:23; James 1:18; John 1:12). Therefore we are children of God, children of the Word, children of the Spirit, children of the resurrection. Also, because we have been born again (see John 3:3, with 1 Peter:1:23) or born of God and are therefore the sons of God, the Bible says that the seed (sperma) of God remains in us, and we cannot sin. (see 1 John 3:9). As a believer, you are a new creation (see 2 Corinthians 5:17); you are a re-created man, a new spirit (see John 3:6, with Ezekiel 11:19-20) who can also be called the new man (see 2 Corinthians 5:17, with Ephesians 4:24). In Chapter One of this book we learned that man is a spirit who lives in a body; therefore the real you is your spirit. Your spirit is also the part of you that has been created anew; you have a new spirit in you. (see Ezekiel 11:19-20; Ezekiel 36:26). This is why the Bible calls your spirit "the new man" (see Ephesians 4:24), "the inner man" or "inward man" (see Ephesians 3:16), "the new self" or "the hidden man of the heart" (see 1 Peter 3:4). You are born to be a heavenly or spiritual man, and a life-giving spirit, just as Jesus is. (see 1 Corinthians 2:14-15; 1 Corinthians 3:1; 1 Corinthians 15:45-49). You are born of God, and God's seed (or sperma) remains in you. Therefore, (in your spirit or new self), you cannot sin, for you were created according to God (or in the nature of God) in true righteousness and holiness. (see Ephesians 4:24). Your spirit is united or joined as one with the Spirit of God (see 1 Corinthians 6:17). As a believer, your spirit and God's Spirit are no longer two, but one spirit. You are united with God in spirit. And not just that, you're also united with Christ in Body. (see 1 Corinthians 6:15, with Ephesians 5:30). You and God have become one. You and Jesus Christ have become one in spirit and body, for there is one Body and one

Spirit. (see Ephesians 4:4). Jesus is the vine and you are the branch (see John 15:5); Jesus is the Head and you are the body (see Colossians 1:18). This is why the Bible says that the body is for the Lord, and the Lord is for the body. (see 1 Corinthians 6:13). This is also why the Bible says that as Jesus is, so are you in this world. (see 1 John 4:17). You are the visible image of the invisible Christ; you are conformed to His image; you have clothed yourself with Christ. (see Romans 8:29, with 1 Corinthians 15:49; Galatians 3:27). It is no longer you who live, but Christ lives in you. (see Galatians 2:20). The fullness of God dwells in you. (see John 1:16; 1 Corinthians 3:16-17; Ephesians 3:19; John 1:16; 2 Corinthians 6:16). Indeed, the Believer is in Christ (see 2 Corinthians 5:17), and Christ is in the believer. (see Colossians 1:27). The believer is in the Spirit, and the Spirit is in the believer. (see Romans 8:9, 11). The believer is in God (see Colossians 3:3), and God is in the believer. (1 Corinthians 3:16; Philippians 2:13; 1 John 4:4). Therefore, the fullness of the Godhead dwells in the believer, just as in Christ; and the believer is complete in Christ. (see Colossians 2:9-10, with Ephesians 3:19). The Bible says, "And of His fulness we have all received, and grace for grace." (John 1:16). Truly, the believer is united as one with God by a divine act of God. Therefore, what God has joined together, let no man put asunder. (see Mark 10:9). Amen!

There is no doubt that believers who have not caught the revelation that they are joined or united as one with God in spirit, often get confused about the Bible's interchangeable use of spirit and Spirit when talking about the believer and God. But, beloved, don't try to separate the spirit of a believer from the Spirit of God, because the two are one — they are joined inseparably as one. (see 1 Corinthians 6:17). Thus, whether you write to a believer to "walk in the Spirit" or "walk in the spirit," you're saying the same thing — don't let the capitalization or the lack thereof confuse you. The Bible calls the believer a partaker (or sharer) of the Holy Spirit (see Hebrews 6:4), and a partaker of the divine (or God) nature. (see 2 Peter 1:4). This is a very important revelation, because once you catch this revelation (that you're a member of the God-Family), you will never see yourself as a "mere man" again (see 1 Corinthians 3:3); you will begin to see yourself rightly as a true son or child of God, just as Jesus Christ is; and thus you will see yourself as a god-man (see Psalm 82:6; John 10:34-36) who has full access to the power of God (see Ephesians 1:19-20), and who can, and must always imitate God, walking in love (see Ephesians 5:1), in faith, in wisdom and in power. Truly, once you catch this revelation, you will be able to say confidently with Jesus: "I and my Father are one." (see John 10:30). And you will also be able to say with Jesus: "Do you not believe that I am in the Father, and the Father in Me? The words that I speak to you I do not speak on my own authority; but the Father who dwells in me does the works." (John 14:10). Such is the glory of the believer: the believer is as Jesus is in this world, and the spirit of the believer cannot be separated from the Spirit of God and the Spirit of Christ. As a believer, you and Jesus your Brother (see Hebrews 2:11) and God your Father are one in spirit. Hallelujah! This is the truth that makes the apostle John declare: "Behold what manner of love the Father has bestowed on us, that we should be called children of God! Therefore the world does not know us, because it did not know Him." (John 3:1). Indeed, the world does not know you, but you must know who you are. Throughout the New Testament and throughout this book, you will notice that the only reason the spirit of the believer and the Spirit of God are mentioned or treated separately is for discussion and teaching purposes only. But in reality the two are joined as one spirit (see 1 Corinthians 6:17); the two have become one. The body of the believer has also become a member or part of Christ Himself. (see 1 Corinthians 6:15). Glory to God!

Indeed, as a believer, the life of God is in you; the power of God is in you; the righteousness of God is in you; the mind of Christ is in you; the wisdom of God is in you; the love of God is in you; the faith of God is in you; the Spirit of God is in you. You are set for the glorious life! Praise God!

The Truth About Hell and Heaven

Now, there seems to be some confusion surrounding the meaning of Hell and who goes there. This confusion stems mainly from the way the Hebrew word "Sheol" has been translated in the King James Version of the Bible. And since this confusion has led some into an erroneous understanding of what the Bible really teaches about the intermediate state and the final state of the dead, it is imperative that we address this subject to unveil the truth before we continue expounding on the power of Jesus' resurrection. It is my prayer that you will let go of the lies that have been told to us over the years, and have an open mind for this true and faithful revelation that is coming from the Word of God (by the Spirit of God). In this regard we will explain a few details about Heaven and Hell and bring to light the true meaning of words (and phrases) such as Paradise, Abraham's bosom, Hades, Gehenna, Sheol, grave, etc. Needless to say, there is a major difference between Hell and the Grave, between Hell and Heaven, and between "Hades" and "Gehenna." But all of them are real places; they are not just metaphors as some erroneously believe to their own ruin. The Hebrew word for Hell is "Sheol" and the Greek equivalent is "Hades." "Tartarus" is another Greek Word for Hell used only once in the Bible (see 2 Peter 2:4), and it seems (from the context) to be synonymous with "Hades." Then there is the Greek word "Gehenna" (see Luke 12:5), which is often translated as Hell but is actually the ultimate hell or lake of fire into which Death and Hades will be cast on the Judgment Day. (see Revelation 20:14). "Gehenna" is thus often referred to in Scripture as the place of "outer darkness" (see Matthew 8:12; 25:30), and also described as a "furnace of fire" (see Matthew 13:42), "everlasting punishment" (see Matthew 25:46), "the mist of darkness" (see 2 Peter 2:17), "the second death" (see Revelation 2:11, 20:6,14; 21:8), and "a lake of fire burning with brimstone" (see Revelation 19:20; 20:10; 21:8).

Some Bible translators, notably the (old) King James Bible translators, erroneously translated the Hebrew word "Sheol" sometimes as the grave, and other times as hell, thereby giving it a dual meaning and unfortunately treating "the grave" and "hell" as though they were synonymous. But the real Hebrew word in the Bible for the grave or sepulcher is "Queber," and thus the correct translation of "Sheol" is Hell. Therefore in the old King James Version of the Bible, the Hebrew word "Sheol" has been erroneously translated about thirty-five times as "Grave." Obviously, when they first translated it, the translators did not have the knowledge and understanding of the Hebrew language that we have gained over the last several years or centuries. Neither did they have the revelation of the message of the Bible the way we do today. And so such translation errors in the King James Version of the Bible have necessitated new or revised translations, and I think, as far as the translation of the word "Sheol" particularly is concerned, the American Standard Revision does well by simply transferring this Hebrew word into the English language untranslated.

It is interesting to note that in the Old Testament, the word "Sheol" is used in about seventy-six places, and "Queber" is also used in several places. Therefore, when the usage of these two Hebrew words "Sheol" and "Queber" in the Old Testament are compared, their true meanings become apparent, and the fact that they are not synonymous and cannot be used interchangeably also becomes incontrovertible. Now, the following differences in usage are noteworthy:

The word "Sheol" is never used in the plural, whereas the word "Queber" is used in the plural several times.

"Sheol" is never located on the surface of the earth, whereas "Queber" is spoken of as being located on the surface of the earth thirty-two times.

Bodies are never put into "Sheol" by man, whereas bodies are put into "Queber" thirty-seven times.

No individual has a "Sheol" of his own, whereas individuals are said to have "Quebers" forty-four times.

Man never puts another man into "Sheol," but man puts man into his Grave or "Queber" thirty-three times.

Man never digs a "Sheol," but man digs a "Queber" six times.

Man never touches "Sheol," but the Bible speaks of man touching "Queber" six times.

(These 7 points of comparison are adapted from "The Father and His Family" by E.W. Kenyon, Kenyon's Bible Publishing Society, 1998, p.77).

Thus, by their usage, it is clear that "Sheol" and "Queber" are not the same, and that "Sheol" cannot be translated grave; "Queber" is the correct Hebrew word for Grave (and, of course, we all know what a grave is). This is why the translators who gave us the American Standard Revision, also known as the American Standard Version (ASV), rather than cause confusion, simply left "Sheol" in the English language untranslated. In fact, the correct translation of "Sheol" is Hell in the English language. And clearly, "Grave" and "Hell" cannot, and are not synonymously used in the Bible; nor are they synonymously used even in the English language, because they are not and cannot be the same. Therefore, "Sheol" in the Old Testament (see Psalm 16:10) must be rightly translated as Hell, since its Greek equivalent in the New Testament — "Hades" — also means Hell. (see Acts 2:27). With this understanding, let us proceed to explain what Hell, Heaven, Paradise and Abraham's bosom refer to in the Bible, so that we can better understand what our Lord Jesus Christ accomplished in His death, burial and resurrection.

Hell (Hades) is the prison (see 1 Peter 3:19) where the wicked dead are locked up to await trial before the Judgment seat (or white throne) of Christ, and to receive their eternal punishment of spending eternity in the lake of fire (or the "Gehenna" of the New Testament). Hell (Hades), therefore, is eternal in one sense, but also temporary in another sense. Hell (Hades) is eternal in the sense that it will exist forever, even though in the end it will be cast into the lake of fire together with death. (see Revelation 20:13-15). But in another sense, hell (Hades) is a temporary holding place for those destined for the lake of fire burning with brimstone, the lake of fire or "Gehenna" being the final place of punishment for the damned souls and for everything and everyone that is evil (see Revelation 20:7, 10, 13-15). The Bible says Hell (in every sense of the word) was never made for man; it was made for the devil and his angels. (see Matthew 25:41). But God is compelled to send men who don't believe in Jesus Christ, or who reject Jesus Christ, to hell. (see John 3:18; Mark 16:16; Hebrews 10:26:31; Matthew 25:41, 46). Such men go to hell because they have deliberately chosen to go there; they have shown by their life choices that they want to serve Satan as their god, that they prefer to be with Satan than to be with the God and Father of our Lord Jesus Christ. And this is what makes it very sad and unfortunate, because it is appointed for men to die once, but after this the judgment. (see Hebrews 9:27). It is unfortunate and sad that many die who have not accepted Jesus Christ as their Lord and Savior, and thus get thrown into hell. It is indeed unfortunate because it is very easy to escape hell. Today, everyone can easily predict where they will spend eternity, by simply answering for themselves whether they sincerely believe in Jesus Christ as their Lord and Savior or not. (see John 3:16-18). It is that simple. The Bible says that on the Judgment Day, Jesus will divide men into two broad categories: the sinners (or goats), and the righteous (or sheep) — (see Matthew 25:31-46). The sinners are those who have rejected Jesus Christ (see John 8:24; John 16:9), and the righteous are those who believe in Jesus Christ or have accepted Him as our Lord and Savior. (see 2 Corinthians 5:21; Romans 3:22: Ephesians 4:24; 1 Corinthians 1:30; 1 John 3:9; 1 John 5:13). And so the sinners "will go away into everlasting punishment, but the righteous into eternal life." (see Matthew 25:46). Until the Judgment Day, however, when a sinner dies, his disembodied spirit/soul goes to hell (Hades) to remain there until the second resurrection when his body will be raised full of corruption to be judged before the great white throne of Jesus Christ and be cast into Gehenna or the eternal lake of fire with the devil, the false prophet, and the fallen angels. (see Revelation 20:10-15). Thus, even though there are people in Hades (Hell) today, no one has as yet been put into "Gehenna" the lake of fire burning with brimstone, but I can promise you that it is not going to be fun for those who will be cast in there.

Again, the Hebrew word for Hell in the Old Testament is **"Sheol"** and the Greek equivalent in the New Testament is **Hades.** Isaiah 14:3-11 gives us a vivid picture of Sheol (hell) as it describes the descent into hell (Sheol) of Nebuchadnezzar, the great king of Babylon. Verses 9 to 11 are especially noteworthy as it says of Nebuchadnezzar: "Hell from beneath is excited about you, to meet you at your coming; it stirs up the dead for you, all the chief ones of the earth; it has raised up from their thrones all the kings of the nations. They all shall speak and say to you: 'Have you also become as weak as we? Have you become like us? Your pomp is brought down to Sheol, and the sound of your stringed instruments; the maggot is spread under you, and worms cover you.'" (Isaiah 14:9-11). Here, we see all the inhabitants of hell, some who were kings and rulers on earth sitting on their mock thrones, mocking King Nebuchadnezzar, the greatest ruler of our dispensation, as he is brought down writhing in agony into hell, looking as helpless and wretched as everyone else in hell. And so we must note here that **even though the grave is for every man who dies, hell is not for every man who dies; hell is for the evildoers** — Satan, his angels, and his children. The Bible tells us in Jude 1:6 that God has reserved or kept the fallen angels (Satan and his cohorts) in everlasting chains under darkness for the Judgment Day. Psalm 9:7 also says, "The wicked shall be turned into hell (Sheol), and all the nations that forget God." Therefore all evildoers — the fearful and unbelieving and abominable, or all whose names are not found written in the Book of Life — are cast into hell upon their death, to await being cast into the lake of fire burning with brimstone (see Revelation 21:8; Revelation 20:15); and the righteous also go to Heaven or Abraham's bosom upon their death. Thus, during Jesus' public ministry on earth, He told a story about an incident that happened to certain (two) men after their death, to teach us about the reality of Hell (Hades) and Heaven. (see Luke 16:19-31). One of these men in the story was a certain beggar named **Lazarus**, a righteous man, and the other one was **a certain rich man** and a sinner whose name was not mentioned. Now, mind you, this story was not a parable, because Jesus told it as an incident that actually happened, and even mentioned one of the names. In this story, Jesus said: *"There was A CERTAIN RICH MAN who was clothed in purple and fine linen and fared sumptuously every day. But there was A CERTAIN BEGGAR **named** LAZARUS, full of sores, who was laid at his gate, desiring to be fed with the crumbs which fell from the rich man's table. Moreover the dogs came and licked his sores. So it was that THE BEGGAR DIED, and WAS CARRIED BY THE ANGELS to **ABRAHAM'S BOSOM**. The RICH MAN ALSO DIED and was BURIED. And being in TORMENTS in **HADES**, he **LIFTED UP his EYES** and SAW Abraham **AFAR OFF**, and LAZARUS in HIS BOSOM. "Then he cried and said, 'Father Abraham, have MERCY on me, and send Lazarus that he may dip the tip of his finger in water and COOL MY TONGUE; for I am TORMENTED in this FLAME.' But Abraham said, 'Son, REMEMBER that in your* *lifetime you received your good things, and likewise Lazarus evil things; but now HE IS COMFORTED and YOU ARE TORMENTED. And besides all this, BETWEEN US AND YOU there is **A GREAT GULF FIXED**, so that those who want to pass from here to you CANNOT, nor can those from there pass to us.' "Then he said, 'I beg you therefore, father, that you would send him to my father's house, for I have five brothers, that he may testify to them, lest they also come to **this place of torment.**' Abraham said to him, 'They have Moses and the prophets; let them hear them.' And he said, 'No, father Abraham; but if one goes to them from the dead, they will repent.' But he said to him, 'If they do not hear Moses and the prophets, neither will they be persuaded though one rise from the dead.'"* (Luke 16:19-31).

In this story quoted above, a few things are noteworthy for our discussion here. First, there are two real places waiting for man after death, and each man or woman will go to one of these two places — Hades (Hell) and Abraham's bosom (which we will soon learn is just another expression for Heaven or Paradise). And so man is destined to go to one of these two real places immediately after death. The righteous Lazarus, after his death, was taken or carried immediately by the angels to Abraham's bosom, whereas the (sinful) rich man was buried, and went to Hades (or Hell). Of course, we know Lazarus was righteous and the rich man was a sinner, because the Scriptures teach that sinners go to Hades and the righteous to Heaven. (see Psalm 9:17; 2 Peter 2:4-9; Psalm 31:17; Psalm 49:14-15; Isaiah 5:14; Matthew 25:46).

Now, here is where I need you to pay particular attention, because many people have twisted God's Word here to their own ruin. We are not told here that Lazarus went to Hades (Hell) or a compartment of Hades (Hell), as some erroneously teach. The only thing we are told here is that Lazarus (the righteous man) went to **Abraham's bosom**. We are not told that Abraham's bosom was a compartment of Hades (Hell). What we are rather told is that there is a GREAT GULF (a deep ravine, chasm, or abyss) FIXED between Abraham's bosom and Hades (Hell), which no man can cross to the other side. And so the emphasis here is not on "commonality" of the two places Hades (Hell) and Abraham's bosom, as it is obvious that the two places share no common wall — they have nothing in common. The emphasis is rather on the deep or great divide or separation between the two places. Jesus even emphasized this in the story when He said that the rich man "**lifted his eyes**" or "**looked up**" (as the NIV translation of Luke 16:23 puts it) and saw Abraham **AFAR OFF** (far away). You will notice that the rich man was **down** in hell, in the heart of the earth, in the abyss, and so to see Abraham, he lifted his eyes or **LOOKED UP**, up toward Heaven (if you may), **up** toward Abraham, and saw Abraham **AFAR OFF** (far away, far **up** there), and Lazarus in his bosom. The rich man didn't look down (below) or straight ahead on the same plane; the rich man looked **up** (above). Obviously, Abraham's bosom was up (above) when one looked from hell where the rich man was. Thus, the rich man's location and Abraham's location were not on the same plane. Indeed no one should even remotely suggest that Abraham the father of all who believe (see Romans 4:16), Abraham the friend of God (see James 2:23), Abraham the righteous man (whom God Himself justified because of his faith, just as we believers are justified today by faith) went to a compartment of Hades (or Hell) when he died, because this insults the very foundation of the Christian faith. Beloved, when God justifies, who is it that condemns? (see Romans 8:33).

Now, we will prove in a moment (from Scriptures) that all the Old Testament saints went to be with God (in Heaven, also known as Abraham's bosom or Paradise) immediately when they died. But before then, let us continue to point out the core points in the story of the rich man and Lazarus. We can learn from the story that there is a **flame** in Hades (Hell) that torments those who go there, and that Hades (Hell) is a place of torment. We can also learn that in Hades (Hell), all of man's senses (sense of hearing, sight, feeling or touch, smell, and taste) still function. Thus, the rich man lifted his EYES, and SAW Abraham afar off. The rich man FELT the torment and the anguish in Hades (Hell). The rich man FELT the burning of his tongue and needed water (to cool off his tongue). The rich man could SPEAK and HEAR in Hades (Hell), and he could REMEMBER; his memory still functioned — Abraham asked him to remember. The rich man also pleaded for mercy, which we learned none could be given in Hades (Hell). There is no mercy in Hades (Hell). Then when the rich man realized the hopeless situation in hell, he begged for Abraham to send somebody to warn his family (his brothers) to do all they can to avoid joining him in Hades (Hell). You see, Hades (Hell) is such an awfully hideous place of torment that even the evil men who go there don't wish for anybody to come there. It is that bad! But Abraham told the rich man that his family — his brothers — have Moses and the Prophets; they have the Bible. If they won't believe what is written by Moses and the Prophets, they wouldn't believe anyone who comes from the dead to tell them about the torment in hell. And how true this is! Jesus went to hell, and came back to tell us about hell, even in this story, but how many people believe it? Now, for the righteous, we can also learn in this story one important lesson about Heaven or Abraham's bosom: it is a place of COMFORT, where the righteous go to be comforted by the God of all comfort. There, we are made to forget all the troubles, tribulations and persecutions, and sufferings we go through in this life. We are comforted in Abraham's bosom! Hallelujah!

Abraham's bosom is just another descriptive phrase for Heaven or the presence of the Lord. This phrase is descriptive of the fact that since Abraham is the father of all who believe, we all go to rest in his bosom — in the bosom of our father — when we die. In fact, the Bible is replete with evidence to support this truth. The Bible is replete with evidence that all the Old Testament saints looked forward to dwelling in Heaven, the house of the Lord (see Isaiah 66:1; Acts 7:49) forever, as the Psalmist says in Psalm 23:6. In Psalm 73:24-25, the Psalmist expressed his belief that after the Lord had guided him with His counsel here in this life, the Lord would receive him to glory. Then as he looked forward to this heavenly encounter with the Lord, he said, "Whom have I in Heaven but Thee? And there is none upon earth that I desire beside Thee." (Psalm 73:25 KJV). Hebrews 11:10 also tells us that our father Abraham looked forward to going to heaven after death — he looked for the city which has foundations, whose builder and maker is God. Then in Hebrews 11:13-16, we are also told that all the Old Testament saints died in faith looking forward to their (heavenly) homeland, their heavenly country, which God has prepared for them. And so it is safe to believe that all these men went to be at home with the Lord in Heaven when they died, just as the Bible promises all believers. (see 2 Corinthians 5:8; Philippians 1:23). Of course, the part where the Book of Hebrews says (of all the saints both from the Old Testament and the new Testament), that, "And all these, having obtained a good testimony through faith, DID

NOT RECEIVE THE PROMISE, God having provided something better for us, **that they should not be made perfect apart from us**" (Hebrews 11:39-40) is to be understood in the sense that they did not receive the promise of a new Heaven and a new earth yet. Even after Jesus' physical death and resurrection, we today are still waiting with all the saints who have died, for the promise of a new Heaven and a new earth. (see Revelation 21; Hebrews 13:14; 2 Peter 3:13-14). Also, we are still waiting (with the majority of the saints who have died and are already in Heaven) for the Lord Jesus Christ to return to earth before we will receive our transformed and glorified bodies. (see 1 Corinthians 15:51-55; 1 Thessalonians 4:13-18). And yet when we die, we still go to heaven to be with the Lord and wait there for that glorified body, which we will receive at the resurrection of the dead. The Old Testament saints are also waiting for the same promise. Meanwhile, talking about us (believers today), Hebrews 12:22-23 says that, not only have we come to Heaven (or the heavenly Jerusalem) the city of the living God, and to Jesus, but that we have also come to (be with) the spirits of just men made perfect. These "spirits" in this context are all the saints (both from the Old Testament and the New Testament). We (together with the Old Testament saints) are all inhabitants of the heavenly Jerusalem, and members of the General Assembly and Church of the Firstborn. Hallelujah!

Unfortunately, there are many sincere Christians and ministers of the gospel today who believe that no one could go to Heaven until Jesus physically came to earth and died for our sins. They claim that Jesus had to come to earth to die first and perfect all men before any man could enter Heaven. But this is just NOT true. You see, what many people don't seem to realize is that God does not live within the confines of time, as we (men) do here on earth. God lives outside time — there is no night in Heaven, and no lamp or sun is needed, as all light in Heaven is given by the Lord God (see Revelation 22:5). Therefore, as far as God is concerned, Jesus Christ the Lamb was slain from the foundation (or creation) of the earth (see Revelation 13:8); the Bible says that "His works have been finished since the creation of the world" (see Hebrews 4:3 NIV), and so Jesus only came to reveal or manifest the finished works to us, so that those of us who believe will enter His rest (see Hebrews 4:3). This is also why the Bible says that God **"chose us (believers) in Him** (Jesus) BEFORE THE FOUNDATION OF THE WORLD, that we should be holy and without blame before Him in love, having predestined us to adoption as sons by Jesus Christ to Himself, according to the good pleasure of His will" (see Ephesians 1:4-5). Thus, God didn't need Jesus' physical suffering and death on earth as evidence (or to prove anything to Himself) before justifying any man who believed in Him; God already knew Jesus had been slain from the foundation (or creation) of the earth; it was men who needed physical evidence of this truth, and so God gave the evidence to us by sending Jesus Christ physically into the world (at the culmination or the end of the ages — see Hebrews 9:26) to be slain for us to see. God gave us the physical evidence or PROOF that we needed, because we were natural men just like Adam (see 1 Corinthians 15:44-49) and, therefore, would otherwise not receive these spiritual truths or things of the Spirit of God as they are being preached today; neither could we know them because they are spiritually discerned. (see 1 Corinthians 2:14). Thus everything had to be manifested in the flesh (in the physical or sense realm) for man to see; it had to be done FOR OUR SAKE. To affirm this truth, Peter tells us that Jesus Christ "was FOREKNOWN indeed BEFORE the foundation of the world, but WAS **MANIFESTED** at the end of the times **FOR YOUR SAKE**" (1 Peter 1:20 ASV). Paul also adds: "Therefore since we are God's offspring, we should not think that the divine being is like gold or silver or stone—an image made by human design and skill. In the past God overlooked such ignorance, but now He commands all people everywhere to repent. For He has set a day when He will judge the world with justice by the Man He has appointed. He HAS GIVEN **PROOF** OF THIS TO EVERYONE BY RAISING HIM FROM THE DEAD." (Acts 17:29-31 NIV). Thus, God wanted to give us **proof** that He has appointed Jesus Christ as the Man by whom He will judge the world with justice; He wanted us to see Jesus crucified and raised from the dead by the power of God, "so that we might KNOW that the Lord is God; besides Him there is no other." This was also the reason God delivered the children of Israel out of Egypt. The Bible says, "Has any god ever tried to take for himself one nation out of another nation, by testings, by signs and wonders, by war, by a mighty hand and an outstretched arm, or by great and awesome deeds, like all the things the Lord your God did for you in Egypt before your very eyes? You were SHOWN THESE THINGS **SO THAT** you might KNOW that the Lord is God; besides him there is no other." (Deuteronomy 4:34-35 NIV). By sending Jesus to die, be buried, and rise again to redeem or deliver us from the kingdom of darkness, God also **made a name for Himself**, just as He made a name for Himself by delivering the children of Israel out of Egypt with a mighty hand. The Bible says, "And who is like Your people, like Israel, the one nation on the earth whom God went to redeem for Himself as a people, **to MAKE FOR HIMSELF A NAME**—and to do for Yourself great and awesome deeds for Your land—before Your people whom You redeemed for Yourself from

Egypt, the nations, and their gods?" (II Samuel 7:23). The children of Israel were a rebellious people. "Yet He saved them **for His name's sake**, to **make His mighty power known**." (Psalm 106:8 NIV). Thus when Jesus' work of redemption was also finished or fully manifested here on earth, the Bible says that God exalted Him to the highest place and gave Him the NAME that is above every name. (see Philippians 2:9). In other words, God made a Name for Himself. He saved us for His name's sake, to make His mighty power known. God made the exceeding greatness of His power known by the works and miracles Jesus performed while He walked here on earth (see Acts 10:38), and by raising Jesus from the dead (see Ephesians 1:19-20; Acts 17:31) and creating a new humanity in Christ through the resurrection, a new humanity who are children of God and the visible image of the invisible Christ, who are just as Jesus is in this world.

Indeed, if God had not sent Jesus to be slain (or killed) and raised from the dead for us (men) to see physically and for witnesses to write it down for the sake of those of us who weren't around to see it ourselves, if God (without such additional physical evidence) had only told us to believe as a spiritual truth and preach that Jesus was slain (for us) from the foundation of the world for our sins and was raised from the dead for our justification, we would've considered it as foolishness, as many natural men still do even today; I mean how many men would've believed or accepted that Jesus had suffered all the things written about Him in the four gospels and had died for our sins from the foundation of the earth (if there wasn't any physical manifestation of these things)? No (natural) man would've accepted or received it, because "the natural man receiveth not the things of the Spirit of God: for THEY ARE FOOLISHNESS UNTO HIM: neither can he know them, because they are spiritually discerned." (see 1 Corinthians 2:14 KJV). No wonder the death, burial and resurrection of the Lord Jesus Christ was not preached **explicitly** in the Old Testament in the same way as we are preaching it to you today by the Holy Spirit sent from Heaven. The Old Testament believers did not possess the full revelation of the Gospel, neither did they enjoy the glories that were to follow the sufferings of Christ (see 1 Peter 1:10-12); and yet by believing God and obeying His Word — His statutes and precepts — they were believing in Jesus Christ (who is the Word of God, who is God, and who is the Lamb slain from the foundation of the world) and thus were receiving the end result of their faith — the salvation of their soul. In the fullness of time, however, God gave us **the proof** — for us to SEE so that we might KNOW that Jesus had indeed been slain from the foundation of the world — by sending Jesus to come to the earth **in the flesh** to be slain for us to see. (see Galatians 4:4-7, with 1 John 4:2-3; 2 John 1:7; 1 Timothy 3:16). At the beginning of his epistles, therefore, the apostle John who saw Jesus slain, bears witness for all men to believe in Jesus' physical manifestation on earth to bring us eternal life, by stating: "THAT **WHICH WAS FROM THE BEGINNING**, which we have HEARD, which we have SEEN WITH OUR EYES, which we have LOOKED UPON, and OUR HANDS HAVE HANDLED, concerning the Word of life— **THE LIFE WAS MANIFESTED**, and WE HAVE SEEN, and BEAR WITNESS, and DECLARE TO YOU that ETERNAL LIFE which WAS WITH THE FATHER and was **MANIFESTED TO US** — that which WE HAVE SEEN and HEARD we DECLARE TO YOU, **that** YOU ALSO MAY HAVE FELLOWSHIP WITH US; and truly our fellowship is with the Father and with His Son Jesus Christ. And these things we write to you **that your joy may be full**." (1 John

1:1-4). Indeed John, in these verses, convincingly bears witness of the physical manifestation of the Word of Life or the Life that was from the beginning, Jesus Christ the Lamb that was slain from the beginning. As an eye witness to these things and one who was in fellowship with Christ throughout His manifestation in the flesh, John declares these things to us (who were not eye witnesses or in fellowship with Christ), so that we also may have fellowship with all who profess faith in Christ; and truly our fellowship is with the Father and with His Son Jesus Christ. In verse 4, John states that the reason he is telling us all these things (all these details about the manifestation of Christ in the flesh) is just so our joy may be full. How? By having the **evidence** or **the testimony of an eyewitness**, that indeed these glorious things are so — that Jesus (the Life — see John 14:6), who was from the beginning (or who existed from the beginning and was slain from the beginning), was truly manifested (in the flesh) and was seen and heard, and held — and that He indeed brought us eternal life (as John emphasizes in First John 5:13).

The apostle Paul, also bearing witness to the manifestation of God in the flesh as Jesus Christ, writes (by revelation) in his first letter to Timothy that; "And without controversy great is the mystery of godliness: God was **manifested in the flesh**, justified in the Spirit, seen by angels, preached among the Gentiles, BELIEVED ON IN THE WORLD, received up in glory." (1 Timothy 3:16). He again emphasizes this truth in his first letter to the Corinthians, where he writes: "Moreover, brethren, I declare to you **THE GOSPEL** which I preached to you, which also YOU RECEIVED and IN WHICH YOU STAND, **BY WHICH ALSO YOU ARE SAVED**, IF YOU HOLD FAST THAT WORD WHICH I PREACHED TO YOU

—unless you believed in vain. For I delivered to you first of all THAT WHICH **I ALSO RECEIVED**: that CHRIST **DIED** FOR OUR SINS according to the Scriptures, and that HE **WAS BURIED**, and that HE **ROSE AGAIN** the third day according to the Scriptures, and that HE **WAS SEEN** by Cephas, then by the twelve. After that HE WAS SEEN by over five hundred brethren at once, of whom the greater part remain to the present, but some have fallen asleep. After that HE WAS SEEN by James, then by all the apostles. Then last of all HE WAS SEEN BY ME ALSO, as by one born out of due time." (1 Corinthians 15:1-8).

Luke (the writer of the Acts of the Apostles) also confirms that, to the apostles whom He had chosen, Jesus "presented Himself alive after His suffering BY MANY INFALLIBLE PROOFS, being seen by them during forty days and speaking of the things pertaining to the Kingdom of God." (see Acts 1:3)

Today I preach to you that which I also received, and it is the same gospel of Christ which Paul and all the early disciples preached.

The Gospel of Christ is an Everlasting Gospel, and It Saves

John records in the Book of Revelation: "Then I saw another angel flying in the midst of heaven, having **THE EVERLASTING GOSPEL** to preach to those who dwell on the earth— to every nation, tribe, tongue, and people—" (Revelation 14:6). Here, John calls the gospel of Christ **the everlasting gospel**. The gospel of Christ is EVERLASTING indeed. God's revelation of Himself to the world has been progressive, culminating in the manifestation of Jesus Christ in the flesh, and the compilation of the complete Scriptures that we have today. At every stage in history the people of God had a certain amount of revelation, but it was the same gospel — the everlasting gospel of Christ. It is the same gospel that has been revealed progressively and preached throughout the generations, beginning with Adam — the gospel that offers man a choice between LIFE and DEATH, the Kingdom of God (Jesus) and the kingdom of Satan (see Genesis 2:9, 16-17; John 3:16-18), the gospel by which those who believe are saved. (see 1 Corinthians 15:1-2). The gospel is the same yesterday, and today and forever. It has never changed, and it will never change. The same gospel was preached to Abraham (see Galatians 3:8), preached to the children of Israel (see Hebrews 4:2), and is being preached to us today. (see Hebrews 4:2). Indeed, it is an everlasting Gospel, and it is the power of God to salvation for everyone who believes. (see Romans 1:16). All the people in the Old Testament who believed the gospel (including Abel, Enoch, Noah, Abraham, Daniel, Job, Moses, David, Elijah, and Isaiah) were saved, just as we have also believed the gospel today and are saved. The only difference between us and the Old Testament saints is that we have the full revelation of the gospel, or the substance, which is of Christ; we understand the things they did which they themselves didn't even understand. For instance, they didn't know that the Passover Lamb (without spot or blemish) that was slain to redeem the children of Israel from slavery in Egypt was Jesus Christ. (see 1 Corinthians 5:7). They also didn't know that the Rock that gave the children of Israel water in the wilderness was Jesus Christ. (see 1 Corinthians 10:4). They did not know that they were bitten by serpents and destroyed because THEY TEMPTED CHRIST. (see Numbers 21:4-6, with 1 Corinthians 10:9). They didn't know that the Sabbath rest is entered or attained when one believes the gospel of Christ. (see Hebrews 4:3; Matthew 11:28). And so they only had a shadow of the things that were to come — they didn't have the substance, which is of Christ. (See Colossians 2:17). The Bible says that there were Old Testament prophets, including Isaiah, who saw Jesus' glory and spoke about Him. (see 1 Peter 1:10-12, with John 12:41). Today we are the beneficiaries of Jesus' glory (see John 17:22; Colossians 1:27); we have the substance, which is Christ Himself — Christ Himself was manifested in the flesh. Paul, in his letter to the Romans, said that the gospel of God was "promised before through His prophets in the Holy Scriptures, concerning His Son Jesus Christ our Lord, who was born of the seed of David according to the flesh, and declared to be the Son of God with power according to the Spirit of holiness, by the resurrection from the dead." (see Romans 1:1- 4). Thus the promised gospel has been received in full. Today we have the full revelation of the gospel, and we understand the things the Old Testament saints did not understand. And, of course, with more revelation or knowledge and understanding comes more victory in this life, for the Bible says that **through knowledge the righteous will be delivered.**" (see Proverbs 11:9). This is the main difference between us and the Old Testament saints. We have the glories that were to follow the sufferings of Christ. (see 1 Peter 1:11). Hallelujah! Thank God that the Lamb that was slain from the foundation of the world (see Revelation 13:8) was manifested in the flesh to us, or in our dispensation. (see 1 Timothy 3:16; 1 John 1:1-2).

Beloved, the truth that Jesus was slain from the foundation of the world is what allowed the God of Justice to justify (by faith) or declare as righteous such great men of faith as Abel, Enoch, Noah, Abraham, Lot, etc — see Hebrews 11:4-10). And it is also what allowed God to send these men to Heaven, where the souls of all the righteous go immediately after death. (see 2 Corinthians 5:8; Philippians 1:23). Even some of these Old Testament men of faith — specifically, Enoch and Elijah — did not taste death at all, but were taken by God to Heaven; they were taken bodily or translated right into God's Holy presence. (see Genesis 5:24, with Hebrews 11:5; 2 Kings 2:1, 11). So the question is this: if (supposedly) no one could go to Heaven until Jesus physically came to the world to be slain for our sins, then how come Elijah, for instance, was taken alive to Heaven? (see 2 Kings 2:1, 11). This just completely tears apart this false doctrine that no one could go to Heaven until Jesus physically came to the world to die for our sins; it completely debunks the false belief that Abraham, or any Old Testament believer for that matter, was kept in a compartment of Hades (or Hell) until the physical death, burial and resurrection of our Lord Jesus Christ. It refutes and invalidates the doctrine that the Old Testament believers (or saints) were the prisoners or captives that Jesus set free or took with Him when He arose or ascended on high, as reported in Ephesians 4:8. What many people don't seem to realize is that all men were (formerly) the captives of Satan; and all believers were freed by Christ and taken with Christ when He ascended (see Ephesians 2:4-6), and not just the Old Testament saints. We (both the New and Old Testament saints) were all **IN** Christ before the foundation of the world (see Ephesians 1:4-5), having been created **in** Christ (see Ephesians 2:10); we were **IN** Christ when He was crucified, we were in Christ when He died and was buried, we were in Christ when He was justified and raised from the dead, or born again through the resurrection, we were in Christ when He ascended into Heaven, and we are still **IN** Him today. Thus, speaking of all believers, the Bible says: "But God, who is rich in mercy, because of His great love with which He loved us, even when we were dead in trespasses, MADE US

ALIVE TOGETHER with Christ (by grace you have been saved), and RAISED US UP TOGETHER, and MADE US SIT TOGETHER in the HEAVENLY PLACES **IN** Christ Jesus" (Ephesians 2:4-6). Indeed this statement is true and has been true from the foundation of the world for all who believe, because Jesus was slain from the foundation of the world. (see Revelation 13:8).

Many people today are confused and find it contradictory also (especially in the light of the prophet Elijah's ascension to Heaven in a chariot of fire), that the Lord Jesus Christ stated during His earth walk that: "NO ONE has ASCENDED TO HEAVEN but He who came down from heaven, that is, the Son of Man who is in heaven." (John 3:13). But this statement by Jesus is neither confusing nor contradictory at all. In fact, Jesus did not say anything new here as He was only echoing what was written in the Book of Proverbs, where it says: *"I neither learned wisdom Nor have knowledge of the Holy One. WHO HAS ASCENDED INTO HEAVEN, OR DESCENDED? Who has gathered the wind in His fists? Who has bound the waters in a garment? Who has established all the ends of the earth? What is His name, and what is His Son's name, if you know? Every word of God is pure; He is a shield to those who put their trust in Him. Do not add to His words, Lest He rebuke you, and you be found a liar."* (Proverbs 30:3-6). The revelation many people haven't caught yet is that no one can ascend to Heaven unless they go THROUGH or **IN** Jesus Christ the glorious Son of God. Jesus Himself said, "I am the way, the truth, and the life. NO ONE COMES TO THE FATHER except THROUGH Me." (John 14:6). And of course, we know that the Father is in Heaven. (see Matthew 6:9; Isaiah 66:1). So no one ascends or goes to Heaven except through Jesus Christ. You have to be **IN** the Lord Jesus Christ to be able to get to Heaven. And you can't be IN Jesus unless you believe in Him, unless you believe the gospel. All those who believe in Jesus Christ are created **IN** Him (see Ephesians 2:10) and are new creations (see 2 Corinthians 5:17); they are born again, and can therefore enter the Kingdom of Heaven or the Kingdom of God. (see John 3:3). Therefore, all those who ever went to Heaven (including Enoch and Elijah) went **IN** Jesus Christ; they didn't ascend to Heaven on their own or apart from Christ; they were **IN** Christ and went as members or parts of the Body of Christ — of His flesh and of His bones — Jesus Himself being the Head. (see Colossians 1:18, with Ephesians 5:30). Thus in Heaven, Christ is **all** and in all, just as Colossians 3:11 says He is, in the Church. Jesus is and will forever remain the only one who has ascended to Heaven, or descended, and we (believers) are all in Him, being members of His Body — of His flesh and of His bones. Yes, we are all citizens in Heaven (see Philippians 3:20), but we don't ascend to Heaven on our own; we ascend to Heaven **IN** Jesus Christ our Head, our Savior, "He who came down from heaven, that is, the Son of Man who is in heaven." He is the only one who has ascended to Heaven, carrying all of us (the members of His Body) **IN** Him. Thus Speaking of believers, the Book of Hebrews says: "But you have come to Mount Zion and to the city of the living God, THE HEAVENLY JERUSALEM, to an innumerable company of angels, to the general assembly and CHURCH of the firstborn who are registered in heaven, to God the Judge of all, to the spirits of just men made perfect, TO JESUS the Mediator of the new covenant, and to the blood of sprinkling that speaks better things than that of Abel." (Hebrews 12:22-24). When you come to Jesus Christ, you have come to Heaven, you have come to the Heavenly Jerusalem. Indeed, when you are in Christ, you are in Heaven. Hallelujah! All the Old

Testament saints went to Heaven because they were **IN** Christ. Jesus Christ is the only Ladder between Heaven and Earth; He has to carry you to Heaven, and bring you down from Heaven or you can do neither on your own. Jesus Himself said, "without Me you can do nothing." (see John 15:5). Even the angels of God cannot descend from Heaven and ascend to Heaven unless they do so ON or UPON Jesus Christ the Ladder. Genesis 28:12 records a dream Jacob had about this truth. The Bible says, "Then he dreamed, and behold, **A LADDER** was set up on the earth, and its top reached to heaven; and there THE ANGELS OF GOD were ascending and descending on it." (Genesis 28:12). Echoing the truth that He is this Ladder which is referenced in Genesis 28:12, the Lord Jesus Christ also said to Nathanael during His earth ministry: "Most assuredly, I say to you, hereafter you shall see heaven open, and THE ANGELS OF GOD **ascending and descending** UPON **the Son of Man**." (John 1:51). Praise God!

Again, all the old Testament saints (including Abel, Enoch, Noah, Abraham, Elijah, Moses, etc) believed in Christ when they believed and acted on the Word of God, because the Word of God is Jesus Christ. (see John 1:1, 14; Revelation 19:13). This is why God declared them as righteous. Their righteousness was by faith, just like ours. And so they are called saints just like us. The Bible says that "faith comes by hearing, and hearing by **the Word of God**." (see Romans 10:17). Like the Old Testament saints, we believers of today didn't come into Christ by seeing Him on the street somewhere and saying to Him, "Hey Jesus, here you are, I believe in you!" No. We just heard the Word of truth, the gospel of our salvation, and **we believed it**; and by believing **the Word of God**, we were born again, we were saved and were sealed with the Holy Spirit of promise. (see Ephesians 1:13). Thus Peter was fond of the people of his day who hadn't seen Jesus Christ and yet believed in Him; and so in speaking to them, he said: "of Jesus Christ, whom **having not seen** you love. Though **now you do not see Him**, yet believing, you rejoice with joy inexpressible and full of glory, receiving the end of your faith — the salvation of your souls." (1 Peter 1:8-9). Therefore, Beloved, I will be the first to admit that I am not in Christ because I have seen Him with my natural eyes, but that I am in Christ only because I believed the Word of God and acted on it. That Word of God is Jesus Christ. (see John 1:1, 14; Revelation 19:13). The Old Testament saints were also in Christ only because **they believed the Word of God or the gospel** and acted on it. Again, that Word of God is Jesus Christ. And so, just like us today, the Old Testament saints believed in Christ whom they hadn't seen. This is how we are born again: By faith in the Word of God, which is Jesus Christ, and not by sight nor by works of the law. This has always been true since the foundation of the world, and will forever remain true. Paul said, 'For "whoever calls on the name of the Lord shall be saved." How then shall they call on Him in whom they have not believed? And how shall they believe in Him of whom they have not **heard**? And how shall they **hear** without a preacher? And how shall they preach unless they are sent? As it is written: "How beautiful are the feet of those who preach **the gospel of peace**, who bring glad tidings of good things!" (Romans 10:13-15). Salvation has everything to do with **hearing the Word of God or the gospel**, which is the power of God to salvation for everyone who believes. (see Romans 1:16).

The Bible even cites Abraham's faith and obedience as an example for all of us (believers) today, and calls Abraham the father of all believers. (see Hebrews 11:8-10; Romans 4:3-5, 16; Galatians 3:5-9). The Bible also says, as we have noted repeatedly, that the same gospel you and I have believed unto salvation today, was preached to Abraham beforehand, and he believed it. (see Galatians 3:8-9). Abraham heard the gospel of Christ and believed it before you and I heard it. The same gospel was also preached to the children of Israel who rebelled in the wilderness, who did not believe it. (see Hebrews 4:2). And so ask yourself, how could the gospel of Christ have existed in Abraham's day if Jesus wasn't slain from the foundation of the world? And how could Abraham who believed the gospel of Christ go to (a compartment of) hell after his death? Doesn't this even insult the very foundation of Christianity? Sadly, many of us have been falsely taught the Word of God for so long that we have become rebellious against the truth. False teachings abound because there have been and still are too many sense-knowledge men preaching or teaching the Word of God — men who have limited revelation of the heart of God or the theme of the Bible, men who have neither yielded to the teachings of the Holy Spirit nor heeded to Paul's advice to Timothy to "Be DILIGENT to present yourself APPROVED to God, a worker who does not need to be ashamed, RIGHTLY DIVIDING THE WORD OF TRUTH." (2 Timothy 2:15). In fact, I was once a victim of these false teachings myself, and I have often wondered how we all came to believe these false teachings without asking questions. Obviously, those who maintain that no one could go into Heaven until Jesus physically came to the world to die for our sins can't explain why the Bible says Enoch and Elijah went into Heaven, or at least, they can't explain it without twisting God's Word.

I truly thank God for the Holy Spirit, the greatest Teacher on earth today! I commend all believers to the Holy Spirit to be taught directly by Him. Indeed, we can still find more evidence in the Bible to refute the erroneous belief and teaching that Abraham's bosom was a compartment of Hades (Hell) and a prison from which the Old Testament saints were set free when Jesus ascended on high. From what we've learned so far, it is even puzzling and baffling that someone could come up with such a doctrine or teaching that has no Scriptural basis whatsoever — that even contradicts the Scriptures — and still manage to get so many sincere believers to accept it and believe it. I see the fingerprints of Satan the deceiver all over this. Now, you will remember that in the account of **the transfiguration of our Lord Jesus** Christ on the mountain (see Mark 9:1-4; Matthew 17:1-3; Luke 9:28-36), we are told that two Old Testament saints — Moses and Elijah — appeared **IN GLORY** with Jesus and talked with Him about His death which He was to accomplish at Jerusalem. (see Luke 9:31). And so the question is: "If Moses and Elijah were in Abraham's bosom, and if Abraham's bosom were a compartment of hell so that Moses and Elijah were supposedly captives or prisoners who were to be set free by Jesus in His resurrection or ascension on high, then how come they were able to appear **IN GLORY** with Jesus here in His transfiguration? Who freed them from prison or captivity and glorified them to join Jesus in His glory there on the mount (of transfiguration) and to have this glorious conversation with Jesus?" Beloved, that Moses and Elijah appeared **IN GLORY** with Jesus should tell you that they had been living in glory (in Heaven) ever since Elijah was taken away into Heaven in that chariot of fire (see 2 Kings 2:1, 11), and ever since Moses died at the age of 120 in the land of Moab, on Mount Nebo, on top of Pisgah and was buried by God Himself — through His archangel Michael. (see Deuteronomy 34:1, 5-7, with Jude 1:9). We are also told in Jude 1:9 that Michael the archangel had to contend with the devil, when he (the devil) disputed about **the body** of Moses. Please note here that the devil did not contend for the soul or spirit of Moses, just his BODY — his spirit/soul indisputably belonged to God and was with God, because he believed in God and was a faithful servant of God. His body, on the other hand, belonged to God (as a purchased possession) not in its corrupted state but in its transformed and glorified state, which would occur at the resurrection of the dead when our Lord Jesus Christ returns. Thus, Satan had the right to contend for Moses' body (of corruption) although he didn't win custody of it, as the Lord (through His archangel Michael buried Moses). I mention this here because many people misunderstand and misrepresent this verse also.

Thus far, we have proven beyond every doubt that Abraham's bosom is just a descriptive phrase in reference to Heaven where all believers will rest in the bosom of our father Abraham when we fall asleep in Christ or leave this earthly tent (or body). Yet another word which means the same thing as Heaven and Abraham's bosom is **"Paradise."** The first time we see this word used in the Bible is in Luke 23:43 where Jesus promised the thief on the cross who expressed faith in Him that he would be with Him in Paradise. The second time we see the word Paradise used is in the epistles, specifically, Second Corinthians 12:4 where Paul, speaking of his visions, narrates "how he was caught up into **Paradise** and heard inexpressible words, which it is not lawful for a man to utter." (2 Corinthians 12:4). Then in its third and final appearance or usage in the Bible, we are promised in the Book of Revelation, that to him who overcomes, Jesus "will give to eat from the tree of life, which is IN THE MIDST OF THE **PARADISE** OF GOD." (see Revelation 2:7). And so, clearly, Paradise is just another name for Heaven, just like Abraham's bosom. Thus, the three names — Abraham's bosom, Paradise, and Heaven — all refer to the same place, which is the presence of God. The Bible also tells us that Heaven as it is today is a temporary place which will pass away just like the earth as it is today, and that there will be a new Heaven and a New Earth which will be the permanent place of dwelling for the righteous. (see Matthew 24:35; Revelation 3:12; Revelation 21:1-2; Isaiah 65:17-19; Isaiah 66:22-24). Hallelujah! Let God be true, but every man a liar. (Romans 3:4).

Get to Know Jesus and the Power of His Resurrection

From the foregoing discussion, we can truly appreciate the death, burial and resurrection of our Lord Jesus Christ; we can truly appreciate the truth that Our Lord Jesus Christ — the Lamb of God — was slain from the foundation of the world, and was manifested at the end of the world for our sake. Today, we (believers) are citizens of Heaven (see Philippians 3:20) because of the love of our Lord and Savior Jesus Christ, "who was delivered up for our offenses, and was raised again for our justification." (Romans 4:25 KJV). We (believers) are righteous because of the resurrection of our Lord Jesus Christ.

It is my prayer that all of humanity will strive to know Jesus and the power of His resurrection. Knowing Jesus and the power of His resurrection was the apostle Paul's life goal also. In his epistle to the Philippians, he wrote:

"Finally, my brethren, REJOICE IN THE LORD. For me to write the same things to you is not tedious, but for you it is safe. Beware of DOGS, beware of EVIL WORKERS, beware of THE MUTILATION! For **WE ARE THE CIRCUMCISION, who WORSHIP GOD IN THE SPIRIT, rejoice in Christ Jesus, and HAVE NO CONFIDENCE IN THE FLESH**, *though I also might have confidence in the flesh. If anyone else thinks he may have confidence in the flesh, I MORE SO: circumcised the eighth day, of the stock of Israel, of the tribe of Benjamin, a Hebrew of the Hebrews; concerning the law, a Pharisee; concerning zeal, persecuting the church; concerning THE RIGHTEOUSNESS WHICH IS IN THE LAW, blameless. But what things were GAIN to me, these I have counted LOSS for Christ. Yet indeed I also count all things loss FOR THE EXCELLENCE OF THE KNOWLEDGE OF CHRIST JESUS my Lord, for whom I have suffered the loss of all things, and COUNT THEM AS RUBBISH, that I MAY GAIN CHRIST and be found in Him, NOT HAVING MY OWN RIGHTEOUSNESS, which is from the law, BUT THAT WHICH IS THROUGH FAITH IN CHRIST, the righteousness which is from God by faith;* **THAT I MAY KNOW HIM AND THE POWER OF HIS RESURRECTION**, *and the fellowship of His sufferings, being conformed to His death, if, by any means, I may attain to the resurrection from the dead."* (Philippians 3:1-11).

Beloved, the moment you confessed with your mouth that Jesus is your Lord, and believed in your heart that God has raised Him from dead, YOU WERE SAVED. (see Romans 10:9). But that is not all; when you believed in your heart that God has raised Jesus from the dead, the Bible says you were not believing for nothing; you were believing unto RIGHTEOUSNESS. (see Romans 10:10). In other words, you were believing to become righteous. And so you did become righteous the moment you believed in your heart that God has raised Jesus from the dead. At that very moment you ceased being a sinner — your old (sinful) self died with Christ (see Romans 6:6) and you were born again or created according to God in true holiness and RIGHTEOUSNESS (see Ephesians 4:24). At that very moment you became a new creation (see 2 Corinthians 5:17); you became God's workmanship, created in Christ Jesus for good works, which God prepared beforehand that you should walk in them. (see Ephesians 2:10). Thus, RIGHTEOUSNESS is a GIFT (see Romans 5:17). And believing that God has raised Jesus from the dead makes available to the believer the gift of righteousness. This also conforms with the apostle Paul's declaration that Jesus "was delivered over to death for our sins and WAS RAISED TO LIFE FOR OUR JUSTIFICATION (or our righteousness)." (Romans 4:25 NIV). Isn't this just awesome? All believers need to unite in thanking our Lord and Savior Jesus Christ for the gift of righteousness. Indeed, what He has done for us is beyond human comprehension. And He did it all out of love. Today, we (believers) are righteous because of the resurrection of our Lord Jesus Christ. We must all learn, like the apostle Paul, to appreciate the righteousness which is through faith in Christ.

It is truly amazing when one comes to clearly understand the point Paul is making in Philippians 3:1-11, which is quoted above. Paul exhorts us (believers) that we should rejoice in the Lord (Jesus Christ), and beware (or stay clear) of those who seek to put us back in bondage to the Law to strive to attain the righteousness which is in the Law. (see also Galatians 2:4; Romans 7:6; Galatians 4:21-26; Galatians 5:13-18). Paul refers to such people (who seek to put us back in bondage to the Law) as "dogs," "evil workers," "the mutilation," and later in verse 18, "enemies of the cross of Christ." Paul evidently detests the attitude of such people and describes them as "evil workers" primarily because of their pride and insistence on their ability (and faithfulness) to perform the works of the Law and earn their own righteousness, which by God's standard, is just impossible (see Romans 3:20; Galatians 3:11; Galatians 2:16; Galatians 2:21). And thus, in that sense, these people have become evil workers, because they oppose the work of God, and in reality they do not keep the Law (see Acts 7:53; Romans 9:31; Jeremiah 11:10; Hosea 6:7), and are even sinning more, since the Law is the strength of sin. (see 1 Corinthians 15:56). Moreover, these "dogs" and "enemies of the cross" fail to realize that the presumption that one can keep the law to gain merit with God is itself inimical to the gospel; it is diametrically opposed (in the strongest way) to the will and purpose of God in giving the Law, and in sending Jesus Christ to redeem mankind from the curse of the Law. (see Galatians 2:24; Romans 3:20; Galatians 3:10-13). Our focus today should be on knowing Jesus Christ and the power of His resurrection.

In his epistle to the Philippians, which we quoted above, Paul wrote: "That I may know Him (Jesus) and THE POWER OF HIS RESURRECTION…" (see Philippians 3:10). There is power in the resurrection of Jesus Christ indeed, and everyone should have the same hunger or burning desire (as Paul) to know Jesus Christ and the power of His resurrection, and to participate in His sufferings so that we can share in His glory. The power of Jesus' resurrection is such that no one can be saved without believing (in their heart) the resurrection of Jesus Christ. The Bible says, as we noted earlier, that in order for anyone to be saved, not only must he confess with his mouth the Lord Jesus, but **he must also believe in his heart that God has raised Jesus from**

the dead. (see Romans 10:9). It is the power of Jesus' resurrection that gave birth to me and to you, and to all who are in Christ, whom the Bible calls the new creation (see 1 Peter 1:3; Acts 13:33; with 2 Corinthians 5:17). As a believer, the resurrection of Jesus Christ not only gave birth to you, but also gave you "an inheritance incorruptible and undefiled and that does not fade away, reserved in heaven for you, who are kept by the power of God through faith for salvation ready to be revealed in the last time." (I Peter 1:4-5). The power of His resurrection has also made the believer righteous (through faith) by birth (see Ephesians 4:24). It has made the believer a partaker of the Holy Spirit (see Hebrews 6:4) and a partaker of the divine (or God) nature, and thus one with God. (see 2 Peter 1:4; 1 Corinthians 6:17; Romans 8:9; Romans 8:16; John 3:6). Jesus Himself was born or begotten of God by the power of His resurrection. (see Acts 13:33; Romans 1:4). And so today, the Bible calls Jesus the firstborn Son among many brethren. (see Romans 8:29). Jesus is also the Firstborn from the dead (see Colossians 1:18; Revelation 1:5), and has become the firstfruits of those who have fallen asleep. (see 1 Corinthians 15:20). Now, **the firstborn or the first begotten from the dead and the firstfruits of those who have fallen asleep** is talking about the fact that Jesus is the first to come out (or be raised bodily) from **the composite death** (i.e. both physical and spiritual death) **with a glorious body**. Jesus was the first Man (dead both spiritually and physically) to be raised to life both spiritually and physically (or bodily), and to receive the glorious body. Jesus was the first Man to be born through the resurrection in that sense, the first Man to be raised from the dead with a spiritual and glorious body. We have all been raised from spiritual death with Jesus, but we are yet to be raised from physical death and to receive our spiritual and glorious body. If we should all die (physically) before the

Lord returns, we will also be raised (at the resurrection) with that same spiritual and glorious body Jesus now has. If we don't die before Jesus returns, however, our bodies will be transformed into that glorious spiritual body upon Jesus' return, and we will be caught up together in the clouds with the dead in Christ (who will rise first) to meet the Lord in the air. And thus we shall always be with the Lord. (see 1 Corinthians 15:50-55; 1 Thessalonians 4:13-17). Indeed Jesus is the Firstborn Son among many brethren. And we are the many brethren. Both the firstborn Son and the many brethren are born of the same Father (God) by the resurrection (see Acts 13:33; Romans 1:4; with 1 Peter 1:3). And both the firstborn Son and the many brethren are the same in divine life and nature. (see 2 Peter 1:4, with 1 John 5:11-12). Hence, Jesus is not ashamed to call us brothers. (see Hebrews 2:11). Hallelujah!

In fact, prior to His resurrection, the most intimate term Jesus used for His disciples was "friends" (see John 15:14-15). But after His resurrection, He began to call them "brothers" (see John 20:17), because through His resurrection, His disciples (since they believed in Him) had been regenerated or begotten of God (see 1 Peter 1:3). Therefore, the fact that the Lord is not ashamed to call us brothers indicates that we are one with Him in life and share His divine nature indeed. We are truly the sons of God, and we have the full rights of sons. And now because we are God's sons, God has given us the Spirit of His Son. (see Galatians 4:4-7). So today we have the power or the legal right to make the claim that we are sons of God. We have the same rights (as sons) that Jesus has. The Bible says Jesus Christ is the heir of ALL THINGS. (see Hebrews 1:2). And the Bible also says that all believers are heirs of God and joint-heirs with Christ (see Romans 8:17). This means that collectively, believers are heirs of ALL THINGS together with Christ. No wonder Paul told the Corinthian Church that "let no one boast in men. For **ALL THINGS ARE YOURS**: whether Paul or Apollos or Cephas, or THE WORLD or life or death, or things present or things to come—ALL ARE YOURS." (see I Corinthians 3:21-22). Indeed, all things are ours — things present (Heaven and earth), and things to come (the new earth and the new Heaven) are ours — because we are heirs of God and joint-heirs with Christ. All things are yours, beloved. And all things are mine. This is great news. And it has all been made possible by the power of Jesus' resurrection.

Thus, we always have to remember that we are the heirs of God and joint-heirs with Christ only because we are **IN** Christ. In all things Christ has the preeminence, because He is the Head of the Body. (see Colossians 1:18). We are the Body of Christ. We have to abide in Him and let His Word abide in us in order to experience the fullness of our inheritance and power as members of His Body, and as sons of God. God has given all authority in Heaven and on earth to His Son Jesus Christ. And Jesus shares that authority with those of us who believe in Him and thus are members of His Body, and joint-heirs with Him. (see Matthew 28:18-20, with Romans 8:17). He says, in His name we will cast out demons; we will speak with new tongues; we will take up serpents; and if we drink anything deadly, it will by no means hurt us; we will lay hands on the sick, and they will recover. (see Mark 16:17-18). For us to be able to experience all of these, we have to abide in Him and allow His Word to abide in us. This is why Jesus said, "I am the vine, you are the branches. He who abides in Me, and I in him, bears much fruit; for without Me you can do nothing." (John 15:5). The apostle Paul was walking in the consciousness of this truth when he declared that "I can do all things through Christ who strengthens me." (Philippians 4:13).

Beloved, we can do all things through Christ who strengthens us. Let us, therefore, get to know Christ more deeply and intimately through His Word. Let us get to know the power of His resurrection, because the resurrection of Jesus Christ is central to the gospel of Christ. The Book of Acts shows how the early disciples were witnesses of Jesus' resurrection, and how they preached it powerfully to the world. "And with great power the apostles GAVE WITNESS TO THE RESURRECTION OF THE LORD JESUS. And great grace was upon them all" (Acts 4:33; see also 1:21-22; 2:29-32; 4:1-2). Peter witnessed about the resurrection of Jesus Christ in the very first sermon he preached on the Day of Pentecost. (see Acts 2:22-32). He quoted David (in the Psalms) to prove that the resurrection of Jesus Christ was prophesied in the Old Testament, and that it was not possible that death could hold Jesus. (see Acts 2:30-31). Then in 1 Peter 1:3 he says, "Blessed be the God and Father of our Lord Jesus Christ, who according to His abundant mercy has begotten us again to a living hope THROUGH the RESURRECTION of Jesus Christ from the dead." This speaks mightily of the power of Jesus' resurrection. We were begotten through the resurrection of Jesus Christ from the dead. The resurrection of Jesus Christ is the central message of the Church, a message no true church of Christ can deny. Hence the resurrection of Jesus Christ was also at the core of the apostle Paul's teachings. For example, in Athens, Paul spoke forcefully to the philosophers about the resurrection of Christ. "Then certain Epicurean and Stoic philosophers encountered him. And some said, 'What does this babbler want to say?' Others said, 'He seems to be a proclaimer of foreign gods,' because HE PREACHED TO THEM JESUS AND THE RESURRECTION." (Acts 17:18). Paul then told them, "'Truly, these times of ignorance God overlooked, but now commands all men everywhere to repent, because He has appointed a day on which He will judge the world in righteousness by the Man whom He has ordained. He has given assurance of this to all BY RAISING HIM FROM THE DEAD.' And when they heard of the resurrection of the dead, some mocked, while others said, 'We will hear you again on this matter'" (see verses 30-32). Here, Paul made it clear that because of the resurrection of Jesus Christ from the dead ignorance is no longer an excuse for not believing in Jesus Christ.

In his letter to the Corinthian Church, which we quoted earlier, Paul again preached about the resurrection of Jesus Christ. He said, "For I delivered to you first of all that which I also received: that Christ died for our sins according to the Scriptures and that He was buried, and that He rose again the third day according to the Scriptures, and that He was seen by Cephas, then by the twelve. After that He was seen by over five hundred brethren at once, of whom the greater part remain to the present, but some have fallen asleep. After that He was seen by James, then by all the apostles. Then last of all He was seen by me also, as by one born out of due time" (1 Corinthians 15:3-8). Then Paul adds, "Now if Christ is preached that He has been raised from the dead, how do some among you say that there is no resurrection of the dead? But if there is no resurrection of the dead, then Christ is not risen. And if Christ is not risen, then our preaching is empty and your faith is also empty. Yes, and we are found false witnesses of God, because we have testified of God that He raised up Christ, whom He did not raise up—if in fact the dead do not rise. For if the dead do not rise, then Christ is not risen. And if Christ is not risen, your faith is futile; you are still in your sins! Then also those who have fallen asleep in Christ have perished. If in this life only we have hope in Christ, we are of all men the most pitiable. But now Christ is risen from the dead, and has become the firstfruits of those who have fallen asleep. For since by man came death, by Man also came the resurrection of the dead. For as in Adam all die, even so in Christ all shall be made alive." (I Corinthians 15:12-22).

In the Book of Revelation, John also bears witness of the resurrection of Jesus Christ whom he calls "the Faithful Witness, the Firstborn from the dead, and the Ruler over all the kings of the earth." (see Revelation 1:5). Jesus Himself — the Faithful Witness — also bears witness of His own resurrection. He says, "I am HE WHO LIVES, AND WAS DEAD, AND BEHOLD, I AM ALIVE FOREVERMORE. Amen. And I have the keys of Hades and of Death." (Revelation 1:18).

Beloved, just like Peter says, the resurrection of Jesus Christ has indeed given a living hope to mankind; and we have to proclaim to the world the same message Paul preached, that indeed Jesus Christ died for our sins and rose from the dead for our justification. (see Romans 4:25). Let us proclaim this message everywhere. Let us encourage all men to accept Jesus as their Lord and Savior, and to receive the abundance of grace and the gift of righteousness to reign in life. (see Romans 5:17). Amen.

In the next chapter, we will continue to unveil who we are as new creations in Christ, and how, having been born in the Spirit, we are to walk in the Spirit.

Chapter 14
New Creation Realities

The Unveiling of What God Did to Ensure that the New Creation Man (the Believer) Will Not Fail or Fall Like the Old Creation Man Adam

YOU MAY RECALL that in Chapter One of this book we explained that God created the Old Creation man Adam in His own IMAGE and LIKENESS, but not in His own NATURE. In other words, God created Adam to look like Him in external physical appearance or external physical characteristics, but not innate or inherent constitution. Thus, contrary to what many believe, Adam was not a son of God (or born of God) the way Jesus Christ and all of us who believe in Him are. Adam did not have eternal life or the life of God; nor did he have the Holy Spirit indwelling him. But all true children of God have eternal life (see John 5:24, 26; 1 John 5:12-13); and we also have the Holy Spirit (who is also known as the Spirit of God, the Spirit of Christ, or the Spirit of God's Son) in our hearts, the Spirit who cries out, "Abba, Father." (see Romans 8:9, with Galatians 4:6). The Bible further teaches that the sons of God are led by the Spirit of God (see Romans 8:14), and that the sons of God do not and cannot sin because we are born of God and the (incorruptible) seed of God remains in us. (see 1 John 3:9). Also, the sons of God overcome the world, because we are born of God. (see 1 John 5:4-5). Obviously, Adam did not measure up to this standard nor meet any of these requirements. As an earthy (or a natural) man (see 1 Corinthians 15:47-48 KJV), there is no way Adam could've been led by the Spirit of God, because the natural man does not receive the things of the Spirit, and cannot understand them, because they are spiritually discerned. (see 1 Corinthians 2:14). Besides, Adam sinned. Need I say more? I hope you understand the point we're making here. You see, the fact that Adam wasn't born of God or wasn't the (begotten) son of God doesn't mean that God created him as a bad or corrupted person. The Bible says that Adam was created a very good man. After God made Adam, He saw everything he had made (including Adam), and "indeed it was **very good**." (see Genesis 1:31). Therefore, God gave (the very good man) Adam free will and gave him the option to receive eternal life (and thus become the son of God) by simply eating of the tree of life that was in the midst of the garden of Eden. (see Genesis 2:8-17). That tree of life was Jesus Christ (You need to catch this by revelation!). Adam had to make the choice to believe in Jesus Christ and receive eternal life, or reject Jesus Christ and suffer eternal death. In fact, God has today given each one of us the same privileged choice He gave Adam; He has given us the option to eat of Jesus the (tree of) life and become sons of God. (see John 6:53-54; with John 14:6, John 3:16, and John 1:12). But unfortunately, many today reject the opportunity to believe in Jesus Christ and become the sons or children of God (see John 1:11-12), just as Adam did. Adam was the first man who rejected the opportunity to eat of the tree of life and to become the son of God; Adam opted instead to become the son of the devil by obeying the devil (the serpent) and eating of the (forbidden) tree of the knowledge of good and evil (or the tree of death). Adam chose Satan the author of death (see Hebrews 2:14) over Jesus the author of life (see Acts 3:15). By obeying the devil instead of God, Adam became the slave of the devil (see Romans 6:16). By eating of the (forbidden) tree of the knowledge of good and evil, Adam became the son of disobedience (see Ephesians 2:2; Colossians 3:6) or the son of the devil. (see John 8:44). Adam sinned and fell short of the glory of God. Thus, Adam missed a great opportunity to have received eternal life and become the son of God.

Unfortunately and sadly, many of the translators of the New Testament inserted their own word "son" in Luke 3:38 thereby calling Adam "the son of God" and thus confusing many believers. The truth is that the word "son" is not in the original Greek text. The correct translation should've been "Adam of God," which is how the Berean Literal Bible correctly renders it. However, we will not argue about long genealogies (in heeding to Paul's advice to Timothy and Titus — see 2 Timothy 2:23; Titus 3:9); and so it must be pointed out here that calling Adam "son of God" is not wrong when one understands it correctly as meaning that Adam originated directly from God or was the first man God created. As the first man God created, Adam is loosely or figuratively called God's son, not because God literally gave birth to him the way God gave birth to Jesus and to us believers, but because Adam has no biological father or mother in the natural sense, and therefore traces his parentage or lineage directly to God. You would similarly notice that, in Acts 17:27-28, humanity is collectively referred to as the "offspring" of God (in a generic sense), simply because God created us all. (see also Isaiah 64:8). In the strict or legal sense of sonship, however, the Bible says that humanity can be divided into two broad categories: the sons (or children) of God and the sons (or children) of the devil. (see 1 John 3:10).

Moreover, before Jesus' death, burial, and resurrection, the Bible emphasizes that Jesus Christ was God's one and only **begotten** Son (see John 3:16; John 1:14). This exclusive declaration of the Bible refutes any claim that Adam (who did not believe in Christ) was also God's **begotten** son. In fact, for anyone to maintain against the backdrop of this truth, that Adam was also a begotten "son of God" is for that person to claim that John 3:16 and all the other Scriptures that speak of Jesus as the one and only begotten Son of God are lies. But the Bible says, "Let God be true but every man a liar." (see Romans 3:4). I choose to let God be true; I choose to believe the Bible (the power of God), and not the wisdom of man. (see 1 Corinthians 2:5). In Chapter One we explained that if Adam were, in truth, the son of God as many falsely believe, Adam wouldn't and couldn't have sinned (or fallen) the way he did in the garden of Eden, because he would've been born of God and the seed of God would've remained in him, and so he couldn't and wouldn't sin (see 1 John 3:9), just as the Lord Jesus Christ didn't and couldn't sin. (see 2 Corinthians 5:21; 1 Peter 2:22; Hebrews 4:15; 1 John 3:5; 1 John 3:9). We also explained in Chapters 1 and 2 of this book that Adam the Old Creation man lived in the flesh or Sense realm, and not in the Spirit, and that he did not have the indwelling of the Holy Spirit, contrary to what some believe. That Adam did not have the Spirit of God (or the Spirit of Christ) in him means that Adam was not God's. (see Romans 8:9).

The Bible says that Adam was earthy (or fleshly), and so were all those born of him (see 1 Corinthians 15:47-48 KJV), for that which is born of the flesh is flesh. (see John 3:6). Today all those who are **not** in

Christ are still in Adam; they are still earthy; they are still in the flesh; they are still sinners, and they are still dead, because they are born of corruptible seed and have Adam's fallen or sinful nature (see Genesis 3, with Genesis 4:1; Genesis 5:3, and Psalm 51:5; Ephesians 2:3, with 1 Corinthians 15:22). On the contrary, those who are **in Christ** are heavenly, we are spirit because we are born of the Spirit (see John 3:6), and so we live in the Spirit, we have the incorruptible seed of God in us, so we cannot sin (see 1 John 3:9), and we will never die (see John 11:26); we have eternal life, and we are eternally righteous. Glory to God! Thus in Heaven, we will see only one Adam — the Second and Last Adam (Jesus Christ) who lives, and was dead, and is alive forevermore — and we who believe in Him will be in Him and with Him, and will hear Him say, "Here am I and the children whom God has given Me." (see Hebrews 2:13). The first Adam is eternally dead. The Bible says that in Adam, all die or perish; in Christ, all live or are saved. (see 1 Corinthians 15:22). This is a present tense reality. The first Adam brought ETERNAL death; the Second and Last Adam brought ETERNAL Life. The first Adam was not a believer, which is why throughout the Bible Adam is **contrasted** with the Lord Jesus Christ (see 1 Corinthians 15:22; 1 Corinthians 15:47-49; Romans 5:15-19), whereas the believer is spoken of as being ONE with the Lord Jesus Christ, and as CONFORMED to the image of the Lord Jesus Christ (see 1 John 4:17; Colossians 1:18; Ephesians 5:30; Romans 8:29-30; Hebrews 2:11; 1 Corinthians 15:48-49; 1 Corinthians 12:12, 27; Romans 12:5; John 15:1-5; 1 Corinthians 6:15, 17). In fact, the only reason God embarked on the New Creation is because the Old Creation (headed by Adam) died. (see Genesis 2:17, with Genesis 3:6). And so the truth of the New Creation man's legal identity as the SON OF GOD who is one with Christ, and who lives in the Spirit and is to walk in the Spirit, presents the single most significant difference between the New Creation (the believer) and the Old Creation headed by Adam. The New Creation folks (or believers) headed by Jesus Christ (the Second and last Adam) are the children of God (see John 1:12; Galatians 3:26), whereas the Old Creation folks (or unbelievers) headed by the first Adam are the children of wrath (Ephesians 2:3), the children of disobedience (see Ephesians 2:2; Colossians 3:6), the children of the devil. (see John 8:44; 1 John 3:8-10). Therefore, today it is not WHAT people do but WHO they really are (in their spirit) that determines whether they sin or not, and whether they will spend eternity in Heaven with Jesus and God the Father, or in Hell with the devil; it is a question of identity. Your identity today as a goat (sinner — child of the first Adam and child of the devil) or a sheep (righteous — child of the God and Father of Jesus Christ the second and last Adam) is what will determine whether you will go to hell or to heaven if you should die right now. (see Matthew 25:31-46). Hence the Bible says that the Holy Spirit convicts the world of only one sin: the sin of not believing in Jesus Christ. (see John 16:9). This is the truth many people don't seem to get. In Adam, all die; in Christ, all live. (see 1 Corinthians 15:22). Every man today can, and must come out of Adam and death, into Christ and life, by simply believing in Jesus Christ as their Lord and Savior. "For as by one man's (or Adam's) disobedience many were made sinners, so also by one Man's (or Christ's) obedience many will be made righteous." (Romans 5:19). "As in Adam **all die**, even so in Christ **all shall be made alive**." (see 1 Corinthians 15:22).

That the New Creation man (or the believer) is the son of God whom God Himself begat or gave birth to out of His own will (see John

1:12-13; James 1:18; 1 John 5:1) is the greatest and most amazing and glorious thing that ever happened to man. And thus John declares, "Behold what manner of love the Father has bestowed on us, that we should be called children of God! Therefore the world does not know us, because it did not know Him." (1 John 3:1). God, by choosing to give birth to us as His own legal children through the resurrection of Jesus Christ from the dead and by the Word of truth (see James 1:18, with 1 Peter 1:3), has elevated us (from once being hopeless sinners) to being partakers of deity (the God-kind) or the divine (or God) nature. (see 2 Peter 1:4). Therefore, as a believer, you are not a mere man (see 1 Corinthians 3:3), just as Jesus wasn't a mere man when He walked here on this earth; you are a god-man (see Psalm 82:6; John 10:34-36); you belong to the class of God or the God-Family; you are a member of the household of God, and you are a fellow citizen of heaven with all the saints. (see Ephesians 2:19, with Philippians 3:20). And so you can imitate God your Father. (see Ephesians 5:1). Today all believers belong to a whole NEW HUMANITY created in Christ Jesus (see Ephesians 2:10, 15) and born through His resurrection to be called the CHILDREN OF GOD. (see 1 John 3:1). God Himself gave birth to us! And there are multitudes of us that no one can count, from every nation, tribe, people and language. (see Revelation 7:9). God gave birth to all these multitudes of children through the resurrection of Jesus Christ, by the Word of truth (see 1 Peter 1:3; James 1:18; 1 Peter 1:23) — children who are just as Jesus is in this world (see 1 John 4:17), who are eternally righteous (see 2 Corinthians 5:21; Romans 3:22; 1 Corinthians 1:30; Isaiah 61:10; with Daniel 9:24), and who can come boldly to God's throne of grace at any time (see Hebrews 4:16), stand in God's presence without any sense of guilt, sin, or inferiority (see Hebrews 10:1-3), call God "Abba,

Father" (see Galatians 4:6), and fellowship with Him and with His Son Jesus Christ. (see 1 Corinthians 1:9; 1 John 1:3-4). Hallelujah!

As a believer and a child of God, you have a legal right in the Father's presence; you have the same rights in the Father's presence as Jesus Christ (see Romans 8:17). God is legally responsible for taking care of you and supplying all your needs according to His riches in glory by Christ Jesus (see Philippians 4:19; Psalm 23:1; Psalm 34:9-10), because you have been legally born into His Family. The Holy Spirit Himself bears witness with your spirit that you are the child of God. (see Romans 8:16). Therefore, trust God to fulfill all His fatherly responsibilities to you, because He is a good and loving Father.

Beloved, your true legal identity as the son or daughter of God — and all the rights and privileges that come with it — has been made possible solely by the death, burial and resurrection of our Lord and Savior Jesus Christ. Just as it was only when the veil of the temple was torn that access to the Holy of Holies was granted permanently to all (sinful) men, it was only by the tearing of the veil which is Jesus' flesh that a living way or access to God's Holy presence was made permanently available to all of us by the blood of Jesus. (see Hebrews 10:19-20). Today, the believer is a completely new creation or new creature (see 2 Corinthians 5:17) who is able to fellowship permanently with God, because we have become eternally righteous (see 2 Corinthians 5:21), perfect (see Hebrews 10:14), sanctified (see Hebrews 10:10), holy (see 1 Corinthians 3:16-17; 1 Peter 2:5, 9) and sinless (see 1 John 3:9), having been washed and redeemed by the precious blood of Jesus from the empty way of life handed down to us from our ancestors. (see Revelation 1:5-6; 1 Peter 1:18-19). We, as the new creation headed by the Lord Jesus Christ, are superior to the old creation headed by the first Adam, for we are born of God, we have been created in Christ Jesus (see Ephesians 2:10). God did not make imitations (or copies) of the Lord Jesus Christ when He created the new humanity; He made us into the Original, into the Lord Jesus Christ Himself. We were created in Him. There is one Body and one Spirit. (see Ephesians 4:4). We share one Body and one Spirit with the Lord Jesus Christ. We are members of His Body, of His flesh, and of His bone. (see Ephesians 5:30 KJV). And we are joined as one with Him in Spirit. (see 1 Corinthians 6:17). So the believer is one with the Lord Jesus Christ. Of His fullness we have all received. (see John 1:16). We are complete in Him. (see Colossians 2:9-10). As He is, so are we in this world. (see 1 John 4:17). We are blessed with every spiritual blessing in the heavenly realms in Christ. (see Ephesians 1:3). We have been created as world-overcomers (see 1 John 4:4; 1 John 5:4), as more than conquerors through Christ who loved us (see Romans 8:37), and as kings and priests to our God and Father (see Luke 22:29; Revelation 1:6; 1 Peter 2:9). We have been created to reign in life or live a life of victory (see Romans 5:17; 2 Corinthians 2:14; 1 Corinthians 15:57) and a life of favor. (see Ephesians 1:6; Romans 5:2; Psalm 5:12). We have been created to have the power or ability to do all things through Christ who strengthens us. (see Philippians 4:13). Hallelujah! Let us, therefore, say with the Psalmist: "You, God, are awesome in your sanctuary; the God of Israel GIVES POWER and STRENGTH to His people. Praise be to God!" (Psalm 68:35 NIV).

As a new creation, you were created, not as a natural man or earthy man like Adam, but as a spiritual or heavenly man like Jesus Christ (see 1 Corinthians 15:46-48; 1 Corinthians 3:1). You are born of the

Spirit, so you are spirit (see John 3:6); you are a life-giving spirit, just as the Lord Jesus Christ is. You bear the image of Jesus; you are the visible image of the invisible Christ; you are conformed to His image; as He is, so are you in this world. Your citizenship is in Heaven (see Philippians 3:20). Therefore, the mystery surrounding you is that you live SIMULTANEOUSLY in Heaven and on Earth, as you sit in Heaven together with Christ and in Christ on the right hand of God, on the right hand of Power — on God's very throne — (see Ephesians 2:4-6), at the same time as you live in this world without being of this world. (see John 17:16; John 15:19). Just like the Lord Jesus Christ, you can claim that you're from above, even though your birth certificate says you were born somewhere here on earth (see John 8:23; Colossians 3:1-3); you can say that you're in heaven, even while you walk here on earth. (see John 3:13; Ephesians 2:4-6). Indeed, the world will not understand you because it does not know you (see 1 John 3:1), but you must know who you are.

Furthermore, as a new creation man or woman, not only are you conformed to the image of God, but also, you have the very nature of God (see 2 Peter 1:4; Ephesians 4:24); as He is, so are you in this world. (see 1 John 4:17). Hence, the Bible says that you are to imitate God. (see Ephesians 5:1). You have been created according to (the inherent or innate constitution or character of) God — in true holiness and righteousness (see Ephesians 4:24), so it is natural for you to walk in holiness and practice righteousness. Simply put, you are holy and righteous by birth, and there is nothing you can do to change that. (I am talking here to sincere believers who will stand steadfast in the faith till the Lord returns or till you're called home by the Lord). Jesus Himself is your righteousness and your sanctification. (see 1 Corinthians 1:30). Having been born of God, you have the seed (sperma) of God in you, and are therefore incapable of sinning or committing the treason of the Old Creation man Adam (see 1 John 3:9). As God's own son, you also have the Spirit of Christ (see Romans 8:9; Galatians 4:6) and the mind of Christ, and so you have the wisdom of God and you know the mind of the Lord. (see 1 Corinthians 2:16). Jesus Christ Himself is your wisdom (see 1 Corinthians 1:30), just as He is the wisdom of God and the power of God. (see 1 Corinthians 1:24). Also, because Jesus, who is the mystery of God and in whom are hidden all the treasures of wisdom and knowledge (see Colossians 2:3) resides in you (see Colossians 1:27; Galatians 2:20), you have full access to divine knowledge and wisdom; and you will have the exact knowledge of God's will as long as you walk in the Spirit. (see Colossians 1:9-13).

Beloved, as a new creation and the child of God, God has sealed you with the Holy Spirit to guarantee that you belong to Him forever (see Ephesians 1:13; 2 Corinthians 5:5; 2 Corinthians 1:21-22), and that Satan cannot steal you, kill you or destroy you. You have already overcome Satan and his antichrist spirit, because He who is in you is greater than he who is in the world. (see 1 John 4:4). God Himself lives in you, and your life is now hidden with Christ in God (see 1 Corinthians 3:16-17; 1 Corinthians 6:19; 1 John 4:4, with Colossians 3:3). So you and God are one; wherever God goes, you go, and wherever you go, God goes, because you are joined as one spirit with God. (see 1 Corinthians 6:17). God has also promised never to leave you nor forsake you. (see Hebrews 13:5). You are, therefore, a true superman, and a spiritual giant in this world, just as Jesus Christ is. (see 1 John 4:17). You just have to know and walk in the consciousness of this truth.

Moreover, unlike the Old Creation man, you as a New Creation man were created in the Spirit, so you are in the Spirit, (see Romans 8:9). The Bible says that, "they that are in the flesh cannot please God." (see Romans 8:8). This does not apply to you because you are not in the flesh but in the Spirit (see Romans 8:9); so you can please God by walking accordingly. The Spirit of God dwells in you (see Romans 5:5); you live in the Spirit and are to walk in the Spirit (see Galatians 5:25), and NOT according to the flesh. (see Romans 8:13). You as a spiritual man (or new man) cannot survive or live in the flesh (or Sense realm), just as the natural man cannot live in the Spirit. The Bible says that "if you live according to the flesh (or the dictates of your five senses), YOU WILL DIE; but if by the Spirit you put to death the deeds of the body, YOU WILL LIVE." (Romans 8:13). In other words, your natural habitat is the Spirit realm. (see Romans 8:9; Galatians 5:25). The new creation man cannot survive in the flesh or sense realm, just as a fish cannot survive on dry land. Walking in the Spirit thus simply means walking according to who you are in your re-created spirit (as revealed by the Word of God), and not according to your flesh (that is, your senses, the desires and dictates of your body, or who you see yourself to be in the physical realm); it means walking by faith and not by sight. (see 2 Corinthians 5:7). As a believer, all the capabilities and power of God has been imparted to you (in your spirit) through the new birth, so it behooves you to lay hold on it and imitate God (by walking in the Spirit or walking in love).

In fact, as a "new man" or woman, you are such a completely new and different creature from the "Old man" that, you even have a new body (see 1 Corinthians 15:50-54; Philippians 3:21), which you will receive when the Lord Jesus Christ returns. (see 2 Corinthians 5:1-8;

Philippians 3:21). But, for now, you will still live in this old body of corruption (see 1 Corinthians 15:42, 50; 2 Corinthians 5:1), having this treasure in earthen vessel, so that the excellence of the power (you have) may be of God and not of you. (see 2 Corinthians 4:7). Indeed, it is because you still live in this old body of corruption that you are admonished to make a conscious effort to walk in the Spirit (or in harmony with your re-created spirit). It is also because you still live in this old body of corruption that the Bible urges you to (make a conscious decision and effort to) present your body a living sacrifice, holy, acceptable to God, and to not be "conformed to this world, but be transformed by the renewing of your mind, that you may prove what is that good and acceptable and perfect will of God." (Romans 12:1-2). And so this verse, in saying "be transformed," is not talking about transforming your spirit, because your spirit is already transformed and is as perfect as Jesus (see Ephesians 4:24; 2 Corinthians 5:17; Hebrews 10:14; 1 John 4:17); this verse is talking about transforming your bodily conduct, mindset and manner of life so that your thoughts, speech and actions will conform to the righteous and holy nature of your re-created spirit, so that you can enjoy (in the body) the victorious and glorious life that your re-created spirit enjoys.

Be Transformed By the Renewing of Your Mind

The transformation of your bodily conduct, mindset and manner of life is accomplished when you grow in the knowledge of God and are filled with the knowledge of His will in all spiritual wisdom and understanding (see Colossians 1:9), when you are able to prove what is that good and acceptable and perfect will of God (see Romans 12:2), when you are mature, having attained to the whole measure of the fullness of Christ (see Ephesians 4:13), when you are walking worthy of your calling in Christ — walking in love, fully pleasing Him, being fruitful in every good work. (see Colossians 1:10). And the good news is that you can begin that transformation today (if you haven't already) by starting to renew your mind (with the Word of God). Study the Word, meditate on the Word, and do the Word of God. This book is intended to help you in that process.

It must also be noted that the mind that has to be renewed (in the context of Romans 12:2) is the mind of your body (and not the mind of your spirit), because the mind of your re-created spirit is already renewed and is actually the same as the mind of Christ. (see 1 Corinthians 2:16). Thus you have to renew the mind of your body till it is conformed to the mind of your spirit; and thankfully you have the Holy Spirit to help you accomplish this through the study of the Word of God. The Bible says, "Now we have received, not the spirit of the world, but the Spirit who is from God, that we might know the things that have been freely given to us by God." (1 Corinthians 2:12). The renewing of the mind of the body is done through reading and meditating on the Word of God (with the help of the Holy Spirit) to the point where the mind of the body aligns with or conforms to the mind of the Spirit, to the point where we know or are conscious of the things that have been freely given to us by God, to the point where we (through the exceedingly great and precious promises of God) are true partakers of the divine (or God) nature, having escaped the corruption that is in the world through lust. (see 2 Peter 1:4).

When we study and meditate on the Word of God, not only is our mind renewed, but our spirit is stirred as it receives and harmonizes with the information it receives from our mind. Consequently, if we feed our mind with lies or false doctrines and wrong beliefs, especially by fellowshipping with unbelievers, such unwholesome actions and wrong beliefs are received as filth into our spirit, and can keep us from being fully equipped with the power of God to fulfill our calling or to bear fruit in the Kingdom of God. This is why in writing to the Corinthian Church, the apostle Paul said, "Therefore, having these promises, beloved, let us **cleanse ourselves from all FILTHINESS of the flesh and SPIRIT, perfecting holiness in the fear of God." (2 Corinthians 7:1).** Only by walking in the truth of God's Word can we cleanse our flesh and spirit from all filthiness. This is also why Jesus said to His disciples that "You are already clean because of the word which I have spoken to you." (John 15:3). Jesus spoke the truth of God's Word to His disciples, and that was what kept them clean. The truth cleanses and sanctifies. And so while Jesus was praying for His disciples before His crucifixion, He said to the Father, "Sanctify them by Your truth. Your word is truth." (John 17:17). Jesus wants us to stay clean and sanctified by studying, meditating on and walking in the truth of God's Word (as revealed to us by the Holy Spirit). The more our mind is renewed with the truth of God's Word, the more we are cleansed from all filthiness of the flesh and spirit, perfecting holiness in the fear of God.

Indeed the mind of the body has to be renewed to agree or conform to the Word of God. The Bible says, "how can two walk together except they be agreed?" (see Amos 3:3). How can you walk with God while you're still in this body, except the mind of your body agrees with the mind of God (which has been revealed in His Word)? Indeed, you have to renew your mind with the Word until Christ is formed in you — in your soul and body. (see Galatians 4:19). When your mind is renewed, you won't be what James calls "a double-minded man, unstable in all his ways" (see James 1:8); you will not drift away or fall away from the faith but will hold fast your original conviction; you will not doubt God, because you will have one mind with Him. Thus, the transforming of our bodily conduct, mindset and manner of life is fully accomplished when we consistently and continually put the knowledge and wisdom from the renewed mind of the body into practice, or when we become doers of the Word, as James 1:22 commands. The will and desire of your spirit (which according to First Corinthians 6:17 is now joined as one with the Holy Spirit) has to rule or gain the ascendancy over the will and desire of your body, even as your body (or fleshly desire) wars against the Spirit for control and dominance. (see Galatians 5:17). Thus, your part is to subdue your body (by the Spirit) and submit it to the will of God as an instrument of righteousness to God. (see Romans 6:13). You have to crucify the body (or the flesh) by the Spirit (see Romans 8:13), so that you will live, so that you will enjoy the victory which is in Christ. In other words, you have to die daily, so that It is no longer you who live, but Christ lives in you. (see 1 Corinthians 15:31, with Galatians 2:20). Then will you be able to live the victorious and glorious life that is in Christ. Paul said, "I affirm by the boasting in you which I have in Christ Jesus our Lord, I DIE DAILY." (1 Corinthians 15:31). The only people who are truly able to exercise authority over the devil and consistently live the victorious and glorious life that is in Christ are those who choose the way of the cross and dying daily. In this regard, Paul also said, "But I discipline my body and bring it into subjection, lest, when I have preached to others, I myself should become disqualified." (1 Corinthians 9:27). Crucifying the flesh or disciplining your body and bringing it into subjection is not something God does for you, it is something you have to do, and yet you cannot do it by your own strength or effort. Jesus said, "Without Me you can do nothing." (see John 15:5). You cannot crucify the deeds of the body by self-will or willpower. You have to do it BY the (help of the) Holy Spirit, the Spirit of Christ who is in you. (see Romans 8:13).

Beloved, you will not live at your full potential in this life until you consistently discipline your body and submit or surrender your body to the leading and control of the Holy Spirit. You will not bear the fruit of the Spirit (see Galatians 5:22-23) unless you abide in the Spirit and walk in the Spirit. Bearing the fruit of the Spirit — love, joy, peace, long-suffering, kindness, goodness, faithfulness, gentleness, self-control — is the evidence that you are walking in the Spirit, and are thus a spiritual man and not a mere man. (see 1 Corinthians 3:1-3). **Walking in the Spirit, therefore, is an all-encompassing lifestyle** that involves walking in love (see Ephesians 5:2), walking by faith and not by sight (see 2 Corinthians 5:7), walking in the Word of God or in the truth (see 3 John 1:3-4; Matthew 4:4; Ezekiel 36:27), walking in the light (see 1 John 1:7), walking in newness of life (see Romans 6:4), or walking in Christ (see Colossians 2:6). With this understanding, we will continue in the next chapter with a detailed and comprehensive discussion of how to live this all-encompassing lifestyle, beginning with the walk of Faith. And while we are at it, we will be unveiling more truths about who we are as new creations in Christ, what we have, and what we can do. But before we turn the page, here's a short exposition on what Christianity truly is, and how you can be a Christian in DEED and not just in WORD.

What Christianity Truly Is

Christianity is not just another religion, as some wrongly believe. Jesus didn't come from Heaven to die such a painful and horrific death for us, be buried, and rise again on the third day, just to give the world one more empty religion. No! Christianity is the Pure or True Religion. (see James 1:26-27, with Acts 4:12). It is **not** a world-religion; it is God's religion. I know there are many Christians today who believe that Christianity is NOT a religion at all. There are even many great pastors that I personally admire who teach that Christianity is not a religion, and I know they mean well, but that position is unscriptural, and I cannot agree with anything that is unscriptural, even if it is preached by an angel. The Bible says that there is such a thing as **Pure or True and Undefiled Religion** in the sight of our God and Father, and then there is also **Worthless** or **Vain Religion.** (see James 1:26-27). Well, I refuse to accept that any of the world's religions can qualify as the pure and undefiled religion that is mentioned here in Scripture. The world's religions are rather the vain religions. Only Christianity can pass the test of what true and undefiled religion before God and the Father is, because **only Christianity** can equip a man to love with the God-kind of love, visiting orphans and widows in their trouble, and **to keep oneself unspotted (or uncontaminated) from the world.** A man must be born again to be able to meet the standard of what pure and undefiled religion is before God and the Father. And so Christianity is the True religion or the pure and undefiled religion that is mentioned here in the epistle of James. Christianity is THE LIFE OF GOD (the fullness of God, the perfection of God) MADE MANIFEST IN MAN. God lives in and through the believer (or Christian), and reigns in and through us. This is why Paul said, "I have been crucified with Christ; IT IS NO LONGER I WHO LIVE, BUT CHRIST LIVES IN ME; and the life which I now live in the flesh I live by faith in the Son of God, who loved me and gave Himself for me." (Galatians 2:20). It is also the reason John said, "You are of God, little children, and HAVE OVERCOME THEM, because HE WHO IS IN YOU IS GREATER than he who is in the world." (1 John 4:4). Many Christians today may not understand the reality of the fullness of God in the believer because they cannot relate to it. They have been brought up to just attend "church" and perform some routine empty rituals and prayers, and so they think that is Christianity. Beloved, that is not Christianity. There is power in Christianity, and this power is THE POWER OF THE LIVING GOD. Each of us can live and experience this power wherever we are. In fact, Christianity is THE KINGDOM OF GOD CONFERRED OR BESTOWED ON MEN. Jesus said, "And I BESTOW UPON YOU A KINGDOM, just as My Father bestowed one upon Me" (Luke 22:29). And Paul said of this Kingdom, that "the Kingdom of God is NOT A MATTER OF TALK **but OF POWER**." (1 Corinthians 4:20 NIV).

Indeed Christianity was never meant to be another powerless religion having a form of godliness but denying the power thereof. Christ died to make every Christian as Himself: a son of God who has the Spirit and power of God. When you come to understand the mystery of Christ dwelling in the Christian, you will risk everything to be a Christian IN DEED. It is high time the Church realized that we are the visible and tangible Body of Christ, the fullness of His being. We have His power and His authority. Praise God! Jesus (the Head) doesn't seek to operate independently of His Body (the Church). He seeks to operate through us. We are united as one with Him. We have to be conscious possessors of the Spirit of God, and the power/authority of God. We have to walk in the Spirit and power of God. Indeed we can do ALL THINGS through Christ who strengthens us. Glory to God! If you are already a Christian, you can begin to live this life of power and glory that you were called to live, by taking these three (3) simple steps:

1. KNOW and ACKNOWLEDGE every good thing that is in you and is yours in Christ. More importantly, know and acknowledge that Christ is in you (see Colossians 1:27); that God is in you (see 1 Corinthians 3:16-17; 1 John 4:4; Ephesians 4:6); that the Holy Spirit is in you (see 1 Corinthians 3:16; Romans 8:9). Indeed the fullness of God is in you (see John 1:16; Ephesians 3:19); you are complete in Christ. (see Colossians 2:9-10).

Beloved, you cannot acknowledge what you don't know, so you first have to read (or hear), know and understand the Word of God and what it says about you and your life in Christ. Then, once you know who you are and what is in you, according to the Bible, you have to acknowledge (i.e. accept or admit the existence or truth of) every good thing that is in you and is yours in Christ. This was also the apostle Paul's prayer for Philemon when he said, "I pray that the sharing of your faith may become effective and powerful because of YOUR ACCURATE KNOWLEDGE (AND ACKNOWLEDGMENT) OF EVERY GOOD THING WHICH IS OURS IN CHRIST." (PHILEMON 1:6 AMP). Beloved, the life of God is in you (see 1 John 5:11-13; John 6:47); it is yours. The power of God is in you (see Ephesians 1:19-20; Acts 1:8; Ephesians 3:20; Philippians 2:13; 1 Corinthians 1:24); it is yours. The righteousness of God is in you (see

2 Corinthians 5:21; Romans 3:22; Romans 5:17; 1 Corinthians 1:30; Ephesians 4:24); it is yours. The wisdom of God is in you (see 1 Corinthians 1:30; with 1 Corinthians 1:24); it is yours. Not only are you the son or daughter of the Most High God (see John 1:12; Galatians 3:26; 1 John 3:1), God Himself is fully present in you. (see John 1:16; Ephesians 3:19). The Bible says, "I said, "You are gods, and all of you are children of the Most High." (Psalm 82:6). And yet because of your ignorance, "you shall die like men, and fall like one of the princes." (Psalm 82:7). Indeed all the children of the Most High are gods, and yet many Christians today are living in ignorance, and dying like men. They lack knowledge (of the truth of God's Word), and because of that they are living in defeat; they are perishing. (see Hosea 4:6).

Beloved, you are not a mere man, so don't behave like one. (see 1 Corinthians 3:3). You have to lay hold on (eternal) life and live out the life of God (or "zoe") that is in you. Paul said, "Fight the good fight of faith, LAY HOLD ON ETERNAL LIFE, TO WHICH YOU WERE ALSO CALLED and have confessed the good confession in the presence of many witnesses." (1 Timothy 6:12). Truly, you were called to eternal life, so lay hold on it. You have to know every good thing that is in you, and make an acknowledgement of that which you know. You must know who you are in Christ and acknowledge it. That is the first step to living and manifesting the life or fullness of God.

2. Be always CONSCIOUS (or aware) of who you are in Christ, and of every good thing that is in you. You can accomplish this by meditation. Paul said to Timothy, "MEDITATE on these things; GIVE YOURSELF ENTIRELY to them, THAT YOUR PROGRESS MAY BE EVIDENT TO ALL." (1 Timothy 4:15). Beloved, MEDITATION brings CONSCIOUSNESS, and thus PROGRESS. Staying conscious of who you are in Christ, what you have in Christ, and what you can do in Christ (which was also Paul's prayer for the Church of Ephesus — see Ephesians 1:17-19), can be achieved through constant meditation on the Word of God. (see Joshua 1:8-9; Psalm 1:1-6; Proverbs 4:20-22; Acts 20:32). Give yourself entirely to the Word of God. Meditation involves reading the Word of God, pondering over it, and muttering it to yourself. When you meditate on the Word of God and know the truth and are always conscious of the truth, you will neither focus on nor be swayed by the lies of this world that are told through the philosophies of men, and through your own adverse circumstances or afflictions. When you know and are constantly conscious of the truth of God's Word, you will come to understand, like Paul, that every affliction is light and momentary (see 2 Corinthians 4:17), that every affliction comes not to stay, but to pass, and to work for your good. And so you will not look at these temporary afflictions. You will not look at what is seen. You will not walk by sight, but by faith (or by the Word of God). We all as Christians should heed to James' admonition when he says, "My brethren, COUNT IT ALL JOY WHEN YOU FALL INTO VARIOUS TRIALS, knowing that THE TESTING OF YOUR FAITH PRODUCES PATIENCE." (James 1:2-3). Indeed, no trial can overcome the child of God. All trials work to produce patience in us, to perfect us or bring us to maturity in the faith, to a complete man, to the measure of the stature of the fullness of Christ. Therefore, we have to look at all trials through the right lenses. Face all trials with the right attitude. The Bible says, "And WE KNOW that ALL THINGS work together FOR GOOD TO THOSE WHO LOVE GOD, to those who are the called according to His purpose." (Romans 8:28). "And we (believers) KNOW… " Beloved, what do you KNOW? We know that ALL THINGS work together for OUR GOOD. What you know can build you up or break you down. The good things you know must stay in your consciousness.

As believers, the Bible says that even though our outward man (or our body) is perishing, our inward man (or our spirit) is renewed day by day. (see 2 Corinthians 4:16). Therefore we have to set our mind on, and be conscious of the state or condition of our spirit, and not that of our body. Whenever you look at that pain or sickness in your body, you are looking at the wrong thing. Whenever you look at the negative balance in your bank account, you are looking at the wrong thing. Stop looking or focusing on your outward man and your outward circumstances and start focusing on your inward man. Be conscious of the inward man, and see (or focus on) how he is faring, because the inward man is the real you, and he is doing REALLY WELL; he is healthy, rich, and prosperous (see 3 John 1:2; 1 Peter 2:24; 2 Corinthians 8:9), and he is blessed with every spiritual blessing in the heavenly realms in Christ. (see Ephesians 1:3). When you are constantly conscious of who you are on the inside, you will live the life that your inward man lives — a life of victory, a life of prosperity, a life of abundance, a life of joy, a life of peace, a life of good success. Indeed the life of your spirit (which is the life of God) will manifest in your body as you walk in the consciousness of who you are in the spirit.

Beloved, this is so important that I will repeat it: Don't look or focus on your body and your outer circumstances; don't focus on the negative report (or those things which your adverse circumstances tell you), because those things are temporary. You need to focus instead on who you permanently are (in the spirit), as revealed in the Word of God. Focus on the things which are not seen. Paul said, "While we LOOK NOT AT THE THINGS WHICH ARE SEEN, but AT THE THINGS WHICH ARE NOT SEEN: for THE THINGS WHICH ARE SEEN are TEMPORAL; but the things which are NOT SEEN are ETERNAL." (2 Corinthians 4:18). Look at the things which are not seen. Look at who you are in your spirit. Your spirit is prosperous and always flourishing. It is renewed day by day. When you are conscious of this, of the good things God has blessed you with in the spirit, of how your spirit is being renewed day by day, (then in your body also) your youth will be renewed like the eagle's. (see Psalm 103:5). The Psalmist says, "The lines have fallen to me in pleasant places; Yes, I have a good inheritance." (Psalm 16:6). You need to have the same attitude, and say the same thing, because you have a good inheritance. The Bible says that in Christ, "WE HAVE OBTAINED AN INHERITANCE." (see Ephesians 1:11). It is a good inheritance. It includes every spiritual blessing in the heavenly realms in Christ. (see Ephesians 1:3). It includes all things that pertain to life and godliness. (see 2 Peter 1:3). Indeed it is a good inheritance that must be unpacked and possessed. As Paul puts it, this inheritance, this package of salvation must be worked out. (see Philippians 2:12). It must be unpacked and possessed. Just as God gave the children of Israel the (promised) land and told them to go in and possess it (see Deuteronomy 1:8), we are being asked to do the same thing — to possess or lay hold on our inheritance in Christ, lay hold on eternal life. This is where we separate the real or practicing Christians from the lip-service ones (or those who just profess to be Christians, but are not Christians in deed or are not doers of the Word). Beloved, you have to be a doer of the Word. James said that **only the doers of the Word will be blessed in what they do.** (see James 1:25). Now, this brings us to the third and final step to living and manifesting the life or fullness of God.

3. Confess and Do (or Act on) the Word of God, and hold fast your confession (of who you are in Christ, what you have in Christ, and what you can do in Christ). These confessions are also called faith proclamations. And mind you, you don't confess to make the things you're confessing a reality; you confess because they are already the reality, and you believe them. And so you confess out of **conviction**. Also, whenever (by the Spirit) you do the Word or act on the Word, for instance, by healing the sick — praying and laying hands on the sick — casting out demons, preaching and teaching the Word or prophesying, doing various charitable works and other faith-actions or works of faith, you are yielding to God and allowing Him to manifest fully in you.

Thus, the three steps we are discussing here all work together harmoniously and systematically. **First,** you read the Word of God to KNOW and ACKNOWLEDGE who you are, what you have, and what you can do in Christ. **Second**, you meditate on the Word and become conscious of every good thing which is in you and is yours in Christ. **Third**, you speak/confess those things as true and belonging to you in reality, and thus act on them. You confess the Word because you believe it in your heart. (2 Corinthians 4:13). You don't confess in order for you to believe it or have it; you confess because the Bible says you already have it, and you believe from deep within your heart that it is so. Thus when you confess, you say things like: eternal life is mine, prosperity is mine, good success is mine, righteousness is mine, victory is mine, divine health is mine, power is mine, all blessings are mine, the whole world is mine in the name of Jesus. Hallelujah! Jesus said that out of the abundance of the heart, the mouth speaks. (Luke 6:45; Matthew 12:34). The Word of God has to fill your heart and your whole being so abundantly that it would be like a burning fire within you that you can't help but spit out. The prophet Jeremiah said, "Then I said, "I will not make mention of Him, nor speak anymore in His name." But **His word** was in my heart **like a burning fire shut up in my bones**; I was weary of holding it back, AND I COULD NOT." (Jeremiah 20:9). Again, Jesus said, "A good man out of the good treasure of his heart brings forth good; and an evil man out of the evil treasure of his heart brings forth evil. For OUT OF THE ABUNDANCE OF THE HEART HIS MOUTH SPEAKS." (Luke 6:45). If you are a true believer (or Christian), you are a good man; you are the righteousness of God in Christ Jesus. (see 2 Corinthians 5:21). And so your words (which are spoken out of the abundance of your heart) will tell us if you are indeed a true Christian or not. You have to choose to sanctify yourself (or set yourself apart to God) by speaking the truth, which is the Word of God (see John 17:17; Romans 12:1-2), rather than defile yourself with the words of this world. (see Matthew 15:11; Mark 7:15).

Beloved, you have to understand the power of your words, and always speak or confess faith-filled words or words that agree with the Word of God. (see Amos 3:3). The Bible says, "By faith we understand that THE WORLDS WERE FRAMED BY THE WORD of God, so that the things which are seen were not made of things which are visible." (Hebrews 11:3). Indeed, words are the most powerful things in the universe. The whole universe was created with words; God called things that did not exist as though they did. (see Romans 4:17). And they came into existence. In fact, without words, the entire creation wouldn't exist. The Bible says that Jesus holds everything in place by the Word of His power. (see Hebrews 1:3). And so all of creation responds to words. Therefore, the words that proceed from your mouth are important in framing your world or charting the course of your life. Negative or fear-filled words will bring you defeat, and positive or faith-filled words will put you over the top. Many people have habitually spoken Satan's words (or the words of this world which are contrary to the Word of God), and by so doing, they have put themselves in bondage. But God's Word (or promises and declarations) when habitually spoken out in faith from the heart will produce liberty, success and victory in your life. Indeed faith-filled words on your lips will give substance to all of God's promises for you; they will cause God's promises to manifest or materialize in your life. Begin speaking faith-filled words over your life from this moment onwards, and you will see yourself rising higher in life each day.

Moreover, the Bible says that we are to hold fast our confession (see Hebrews 4:14). In other words, we are to continually confess what the Bible says about us, and what we want to see happen in our lives (in the light of the revelation of the Word of God). We are to confess with our mouth unto salvation (see Romans 10:10) — salvation from diseases, poverty, and every power of darkness or negative circumstance. Begin to use your mouth today to chart the course of your life. The Bible says, "Death and life are in the power of the tongue, And those who love it will eat its fruit." (Proverbs 18:21). Every word you speak is a seed you're sowing that will bear fruit unto life or unto death, so always speak words of life, always speak in agreement with the Word of God. In Mark's gospel, Jesus told a parable in which "He said, "The kingdom of God is as if a man should **scatter seed**

on the ground, and should sleep by night and rise by day, **and the seed should sprout and grow**, he himself **does not know how**. For **the earth yields crops by itself**: first **the blade**, then **the head**, after that **the full grain** in the head. But when the grain ripens, immediately he puts in the sickle, because **the harvest has come**." (Mark 4:26-29). The seed in this context is the Word of God, and the ground is your heart. Purpose today to always sow (or study, meditate on, and confess) the Word of God in your heart, and never give up if you don't see the fruit (or the evident progress) just yet; be steadfast and hold fast your confession, for as you sleep by night and rise by day, the Word is definitely working in you — it is sprouting, and growing, even though you don't know how — and it will eventually manifest its power in you for a great harvest of good and miraculous works.

Determine today never to walk or judge by what you see or hear. Don't speak what you see; speak what the Word of God says; speak what you want to see, because the Bible says that you will have whatever you say. (see Mark 11:23). Speak life. Speak God's blessings or promises. Imitate your Father God by calling those things which do not exist as though they did. (see Romans 4:17). Begin to call health where there is sickness or disease, call life where there is death, and call the abundance of provision where there is need. Begin to manifest the life or fullness of God that is in you — preach the gospel, cast out demons, raise the dead, lay hands on the sick and see them recover in the name of Jesus. Paul says preaching has to be in demonstration of the Spirit and of power. The Holy Spirit works with us, bearing witness or confirming the Word of God with signs, wonders and miracles, and with gifts of the Holy Spirit (see Mark 16:20, with Hebrews 2:4); unless these attend our ministry we will have little if any success at all. Paul said, "I will not venture to speak of anything except WHAT CHRIST HAS ACCOMPLISHED THROUGH ME in leading the Gentiles to obey God by what I have SAID and DONE — BY THE POWER OF SIGNS and WONDERS, through THE POWER OF THE SPIRIT OF GOD. So from Jerusalem all the way around to Illyricum, I HAVE FULLY PROCLAIMED THE GOSPEL OF CHRIST." (Romans 15:18-19 NIV).

Beloved, if you take these three steps that have been discussed here, you will never be barren nor unfruitful in your knowledge of Christ. Indeed, if every professed Christian were to follow these steps and become practicing Christians (or Christians in both word and deed), the sharing of our faith (or the preaching of the gospel) would be very effective and powerful, because our normal lives would be supernatural (or spiritual), and all men and women, seeing our works that result from the power we have, would crave to be like us and to be witnesses to Christ with us, to the praise and glory of God the Father.

Chapter 15

The Spirit Walk: A Walk of Faith

THE BIBLE SAYS, "For we walk by faith, not by sight." (2 Corinthians 5:7). "The just shall live by faith." (see Romans 1:17; Hebrews 10:38; Habakkuk 2:4). What this means is that the Christian walk is a walk of faith. Therefore, the walk in the Spirit is a walk by faith, and not by sight. It is obvious that even though we (believers) have all been born of the Spirit as spirits (see John 3:6), no one can see the Spirit; we can only believe in Him or trust Him and His work in us. Jesus said, "The wind blows where it wishes, and you hear the sound of it, but cannot tell where it comes from and where it goes. So is everyone who is born of the Spirit." (John 3:8). Thus, even though we cannot see the Spirit, we can hear Him, and we can see the manifestation of the Spirit and demonstration of His power or the effects of His work in our lives as we believe in Him and yield to Him.

Beloved, we Christians serve a God of faith, and it takes faith to please Him. (see Hebrews 11:6). God could make angels appear to us physically every single day to reassure us of His presence, His love for us, His promises to us and His provisions for us. Indeed, He could make angels appear to us every day to reassure us that we are a new creation, that we are His children, that we are gods, that we are righteous, that we are holy, that we are everything the Bible says we are, that we have the Spirit of God in us and we have everything the Bible says we have, and that we can do everything the Bible says we can do. But that is not faith, and our God doesn't work that way. God wants us to get into His Word and just believe what the Word says. He values it more when we haven't seen and yet believe (in Him and His promises). The Bible says "God is Spirit" so we must worship Him **in spirit and in truth** (see John 4:23-24). Paul said, "God is my witness, WHOM I SERVE **with my spirit** in **the gospel** of His Son…" (Romans 1:9). As mentioned in Chapter One of this book, man is a spirit who lives in a body and has a soul. Natural man, however, is not conscious of his spirit nature in relation to the living God because, besides the fact that he is fleshly or earthly, he is also spiritually dead (or dead to God), and thus his flesh or senses have gained the ascendancy over his spirit. We believers, on the contrary, are alive to God in Christ because our spirits have been born again; we are new creations (see 2 Corinthians 5:17) or re-created **spirits**, born of the Spirit of God. (see John 3:6). Therefore, as believers, we cannot look to our body (our five senses or flesh) for our identity. Paul said, "From now on, **we regard NO ONE according to the FLESH**. Even though we have known Christ according to the flesh, yet now we know Him thus NO LONGER." (see 2 Corinthians 5:16). We are now new creations, we are spirits; our spirits have been created according to God in true holiness and righteousness (see Ephesians 4:24). Therefore, what we presently are in the flesh (or body) no longer accurately represents or captures who we truly are; we are now spiritual men, and life-giving spirits just as Jesus Christ is, for we bear His image, we are conformed to His image. (see 1 Corinthians 15:48-49; 1 John 4:17; Romans 8:29). We are "the spirits of just men made perfect." (see Hebrews 12:23). And thus, the Bible calls our Father (God) the "Father of spirits." (see Hebrews

12:9). It is only when we regard ourselves according to the spirit (our re-created spirit which is joined as one with the Holy Spirit) that we will truly know who we are. We have to develop a keen consciousness or awareness of who we are in the spirit to the point where we are more attuned to our spirit than to our body. Our spirit has to gain the ascendancy over our body to the extent that we will not fulfill the desires of the body, but rather, the desires of the spirit. This is what the Bible means by walking in the Spirit, and bearing the fruit of the Spirit.

Jesus Did Not Walk or Judge By the Sight of His Eyes, and Neither Should We

The Bible says that the Lord Jesus Christ left us an example, that we should follow His steps. (see 1 Peter 2:21). The prophet Isaiah prophesied about Jesus long before His birth, that, "His delight is in the fear of the Lord, and He SHALL NOT JUDGE BY THE SIGHT OF HIS EYES, nor decide by the HEARING of His ears;…He shall strike the earth with the rod of His mouth." (see Isaiah 11:3-4). And indeed when Jesus walked on this earth, He never walked by the sight of His eyes, nor by the hearing of His ears; He walked by **faith**. He struck, even shook the earth with the rod of His mouth — His words, His CONFESSION, the word of His testimony. Whenever Jesus spoke, things happened, circumstances changed for the better: demons left their victims, diseases and every kind of sickness disappeared, the dead came back to life, the rowdy and turbulent winds and the waves of the sea became still. Jesus was a spiritual Man, and He walked in the Spirit, He walked by faith.

Beloved, our Lord Jesus Christ stepped into the word of prophecy that had been spoken of Him long ago by the prophet Isaiah. As believers, we are as Jesus is in this world. (see 1 John 4:17). We also do not judge by the sight of our eyes, nor decide by the hearing of our ears. Just like our Lord Jesus Christ, "we walk by faith, not by sight." (see 2 Corinthians 5:7). Our confession (or what we say) is the rod of our mouth. And we are to use the rod of our mouth — our words, our confession — to change circumstances, like Jesus did with the rod of His mouth, like Moses did with his rod. We are to imitate God by calling the things that do not exist as though they did. (Ephesians 5:1, with Romans 4:17). The Bible says, we are to hold fast our confession (see Hebrews 4:14). We are to continually confess what we want to see happen in our lives, according to what the Word of God has spoken about us. We are to confess with our mouths unto salvation (see Romans 10:10) — salvation from diseases, poverty, and every power of darkness or every negative circumstance. Begin to use your mouth today to chart the course of your life. The Bible says, "Death and life are in the power of the tongue, And those who love it will eat its fruit." (Proverbs 18:21). Determine today never to walk or judge by what you see or hear. Don't speak what you see; speak what you want to see. Speak life. Speak God's blessings or promises. Imitate God your Father — begin to call those things which do not exist as though they did. (see Romans 4:17). Begin to call health where there is sickness or disease, call life where there is death, and call the abundance of provision where there is need.

Unfortunately, there are many believers today who are not even aware that they have the power to change every circumstance. There are many believers who don't know that the same Spirit that raised Jesus from the dead dwells in them with the same power that raised Jesus from the dead. (see Ephesians 1:19-20, with Romans 8:11). Sadly there are many believers who don't know that God Himself is in them, working in them with His mighty ability. (see Philippians 2:13). Indeed God's power is at work in every believer. (see Ephesians 3:20; Colossians 1:29). He that is in us is greater than he that is in the world. (see 1 John 4:4). We are partakers of the divine (or God) nature. (see 2 Peter 1:4). And so we can do all things through Christ who strengthens us. (see Philippians 4:13). The authority (and power) we have as believers, is the authority (and power) of Jesus Christ Himself. (see Matthew 28:18-20; Mark 16:17). Therefore, we cannot fail. We are not some helpless weaklings who have to cry to God in every situation. We have the Helper (the Holy Spirit) already in us, and so we must depend on Him. One time, when Moses forgot about the power God had already given to him, and the frightened children of Israel started crying to God because Pharaoh and his fierce army were pursuing them and furiously drawing near to them, the Bible says, "And the Lord said to Moses, "WHY DO YOU CRY to Me? Tell the children of Israel to GO FORWARD. But LIFT UP **YOUR ROD**, and STRETCH OUT YOUR HAND OVER THE SEA and DIVIDE IT. And the children of Israel shall go on dry ground through the midst of the sea." (Exodus 14:15-16). Oh, how often we cry to God, forgetting the power that is already in our hand! How often we wait for God to move the mountain while God is also waiting for us to command the mountain to move. Beloved, when you are conscious of the power God has already given you, you wouldn't cry to God in every situation; you will exercise the power in the NAME of Jesus. And you will join all the saints in saying, "You, God, are awesome in your sanctuary; the God of Israel

GIVES POWER and STRENGTH to His people. Praise be to God!" (Psalm 68:35 NIV).

Indeed, if you're a believer, you already have God's power working in you mightily (see Ephesians 3:20; Colossians 1:29); use it! You are to honor and praise God instead of crying to Him all the time, for God is already in you; Jesus Christ is already in you, and the Bible says that Jesus Christ is the wisdom of God and the POWER of God. (see 1 Corinthians 1:24). Thus you have the wisdom of God and the power of God living inside you. Begin to speak by faith and change circumstances. (see Matthew 17:20). Begin to command the mountains of diseases, sicknesses, addictions, demon-possession, poverty, and death to be moved, because nothing is impossible to you. All things are possible to the one who believes. (see Mark 9:23). You can do all things through Christ who strengthens you. (see Philippians 4:13). Go, therefore, and change the world, knowing your authority; for it is Jesus' authority, and it cannot fail. Exercise your faith and bring glory to your Father who is in Heaven.

Faith is at the Core of Our Christian Walk

Clearly, spiritual things can only be perceived by our re-created spirit (through faith). Our physical senses can't discern spiritual things. Therefore, faith is at the core of our Christian walk, and we are all commanded to walk by faith, and not by sight. Thus, to the church of God in Corinth, the apostle Paul said, "**Examine yourselves** as to **whether you are in the faith**. Test yourselves. Do you not know yourselves, that Jesus Christ is in you? — unless indeed you are disqualified." (2 Corinthians 13:5). Beloved, if Jesus Christ is truly in you, then you have to walk just as Jesus walked — **by faith**.

Throughout Jesus' ministry on earth before and after His resurrection, His emphasis was always on faith, and not on sight. Even the nature of His birth takes faith to accept: He was conceived of the Holy Spirit, and born of a virgin, and a lowly virgin at that. Although Jesus was the "Mighty God" (see Isaiah 9:6) who had come into the world incognito, He chose not to arrive on earth in some grandiose style. The world He Himself had created even made no room for Him when He arrived in Bethlehem; all the inns were full, so that He was born in a manger. The Lord of the whole universe was born in a manger. Then His birth was announced not to the kings of the world, but to lowly shepherds. When He came of age and started His Ministry on earth, Jesus was referred to as the "carpenter's son" by those who sought to deride Him by his humble background. Thus, when one considered the physical background and circumstances of Jesus, it took faith to recognize that He was God. Those who were looking to accept Him by sight were obviously disappointed. And it was in such manner that Jesus conducted His entire earthly ministry.

Let's consider a few instances where Jesus emphasized Faith as superior to Sight. John the Baptist had introduced Jesus twice as the Lamb of God who takes away the sins of the world (see John 1:29; John 1:36). Yet, when John was imprisoned, he started to harbor doubts about Jesus as the Messiah. So John sent messengers to Jesus to ask Him if He was indeed the Messiah that was to come. (see Matthew 11:1-3). Jesus could have satisfied John's quest for a confirmation by just saying "Yes" to his question. But that was not Jesus' style. He sent back the messengers to John with a message pointing John to the prophecies in the Scriptures about the works of the Messiah (as recorded in Isaiah 35:5-6) and the fulfillment of those prophecies in Him. "Jesus answered and said unto them, Go and shew John again those things which ye do hear and see: The blind receive their sight, and the lame walk, the lepers are cleansed, and the deaf hear, the dead are raised up, and the poor have the gospel preached to them. And blessed is he, whosoever shall not be offended in me." (Matthew 11:4-6 KJV).

Again, from the time Jesus rose from the dead to the time He ascended into Heaven, Jesus never showed Himself to a single person who wasn't already one of His disciples. The Bible says that God showed the risen Christ "openly, not to all the people, but to witnesses chosen before by God." (see Acts 10:40-41). We would think it would've been great for the risen Christ to have walked openly in the streets of Jerusalem and into Pilate's palace so that all the people that had witnessed His crucifixion would see Him in His resurrected body and believe that He was indeed the Christ. But that's not the nature of our God. Hebrews 11:6 says, "But without faith it is impossible to please Him." Even when Jesus appeared to His disciples on the road to Emmaus (on the day of His resurrection), He prevented them from seeing Him as the risen Christ. Instead, He opened their eyes to Scriptures that pointed to His death and resurrection. (See Luke 24:15-16; Mark 16:12). And upon hearing those Scriptural teachings about Christ, their hearts burned within them. (see Luke 24:32). "Is not My Word like a fire?" says the Lord." (see Jeremiah 23:29). No wonder the Bible says that faith comes by hearing, and hearing by the Word of Christ. (see Romans 10:17). Jesus would later appear to all His disciples and declare to Thomas (who had previously doubted the other disciples' account of an earlier visitation by the resurrected Christ) that "blessed are those who have not seen and yet have believed." (see John 20:29). Indeed, in the eyes of God, faith is truly superior to sight.

My dear reader, the Christian walk is truly a walk of faith. The Bible says that through our Lord Jesus Christ **we have access BY FAITH into this grace in which we stand.** (see Romans 5:2). Indeed the Lord loads us daily with benefits. (see Psalm 68:19). And yet every benefit of the finished work of the Lord Jesus Christ is **received by faith**. Thus, we're saved by grace through FAITH in Jesus Christ (see Ephesians 2:8-9). We're made righteous by FAITH in Jesus Christ (see Romans 1:16-17; 2 Corinthians 5:21; Romans 5:17; Romans 3:22). We're healed by FAITH in Jesus Christ. (see Mark 10:52; Isaiah 53:5; 1 Peter 2:24). We inherit the blessings of Abraham by FAITH in Jesus Christ. (see Galatians 3:14-15; Romans 4:13-16). We move the mountains (of our problems) by FAITH in Jesus Christ. (see Matthew 17:20). We overcome the devil by FAITH in the blood of Jesus. (see Revelation 12:11; 1 John 5:4). We fight the good fight of Faith (see 1 Timothy 6:12). Paul admonishes us in Colossians 2:6-7: "**AS** you therefore have received Christ Jesus the Lord, **SO** WALK IN Him, rooted and built up in Him and established in THE FAITH, as you have been taught, abounding in it with thanksgiving." Since we received Christ by GRACE through FAITH, and not by the law or through the works of the law, Paul is basically saying we should walk the Christian walk **in the same way** we got saved and received the Spirit of God — that is, by GRACE through FAITH (see Ephesians 2:8-9). Hence, Paul was angry with the Churches in Galatia when they started moving away from Faith, to the works of the Law. And he said to them, "This only I want to learn from you: Did you receive the Spirit by the WORKS OF THE LAW, or **by the hearing of FAITH?**

Are you so foolish? Having begun in the Spirit, are you now being made perfect by the flesh?" (Galatians 3:2-3). Like the Churches in Galatia, there are many believers today who just can't bring themselves to accept the truth that righteousness is a gift that must be accepted by faith in Christ Jesus. (see 2 Corinthians 5:21; Romans 3:20-22; Romans 5:17; 1 Corinthians 1:30). Many believers insist on being under the Law and working for their own righteousness rather than accepting (by faith) that they are the righteousness of God in Christ Jesus. Unfortunately, it appears that faith is more difficult for many people than works of the law. But Paul said, "I do not set aside the grace of God; for if righteousness comes through the law, then Christ died in vain." (Galatians 2:21). Beloved, we cannot walk the Christian walk by the flesh (or self efforts at keeping the Law of Moses); we are to walk by faith in Jesus our Savior. We are to grow in our dependence on Him — from faith to faith. We are also not to respond to our natural circumstances and situations with human effort, but with faith in the finished work of Christ. God is pleased when we live our lives by faith in Him, in spite of the circumstances in which we may find ourselves. It is only by believing everything the Bible says about who we are in Christ that our lifestyle or conduct will reflect that reality. If we believe right, we will certainly live right. Faith is how we walk in the Spirit.

Understand What Faith Is

"Now faith is **the SUBSTANCE** of things hoped for, **the EVIDENCE** of things not seen." (Hebrews 11:1). A simple glance in any dictionary would reveal that Faith is a noun; it is not a verb. Faith is, therefore, not something you do; it is something you have, and when you have it, you confess it; it moves you into action, because faith is action-oriented. We all respond to faith. Our faith determines our words and actions, and our words and actions reflect our faith. Everything we do as human beings is based on faith, whether we realize it or not. Indeed, in the sense realm we may not call anything "faith." Regardless, it is faith that makes one accept and confess the existence or nonexistence of God. The atheist believes or has "faith" that God does not exist, and so he confesses that "faith" and acts according to that "faith," defending his position with everything he's got. The Christian has faith that God exists, that Jesus is the Son of God who came and died for our sins to redeem humankind and was raised from the dead for our justification, and so the Christian confesses that faith and acts according to that faith, defending his position with everything he's got.

Thus, faith determines our confession and our action. Practically, our faith becomes our confession and the force behind our action; and ultimately our faith becomes our reality. The atheist's "faith" will become his reality when he dies in his sins and is thrown into the outer darkness of hell where God will not exist to him, because God will not be in hell; indeed people will yearn for God in hell but will not find Him, because they are hopelessly dead to God. But for the believer, to be absent from the body is to be present with the Lord (see 2 Corinthians 5:8), and so our faith will become our reality when we also die. Praise God! This is why the Bible says "faith is the substance of things hoped for." It means that faith is tangible; faith is reality. If you look in a dictionary right now for the definition of **"substance,"** you will notice that the definition points to a real physical matter, or something which has a tangible solid presence. **When you have faith**

for something, it is equivalent to having that "thing" physically in your hand right now. Faith calls things that are not as though they were (see Romans 4:17), and they come into manifestation. Whatever it is we need, FAITH considers or imagines it done. In fact, we can only live up to the standard of our faith and our confession. For example, if I have faith for a big church-building for my ministry, it is equivalent to having that church-building right now. And so that faith, which I have, should trigger a corresponding action of confessing that I have a big church-building, celebrating and thanking God for the building, and then moving according to the leading of the Holy Spirit to claim or lay hold on that building. I should also expect that people who are in the flesh or "sense realm" will not understand why I am confessing and celebrating a building they cannot see; they may even think I'm crazy. But if the faith I have is really alive, then I have to hold fast my confession (see Hebrews 4:14) in spite of the sense evidence that points to the contrary. And when people ask for the evidence of the building, all I have to do is point them to my faith, because the Bible says "faith is the EVIDENCE of things not seen." (see Hebrews 11:1). And let's just say that, as I continue to patiently and actively have faith for the building in question, the Holy Spirit leads me to raise a million dollars in donations, and then leads me to construct this church-building with that money. Then, I can rightly say that the building that has been constructed as a result of my faith is no more real or tangible than the faith that brought it into its physical manifestation or existence. And so now, I may not even feel a need or an urge to celebrate the physical building, because I already celebrated when I received the building by faith.

Beloved, all this may seem foolish in the fleshly or sense realm, but guess what, faith doesn't exist in the sense realm. This is why the Bible says, "We walk by faith, not by sight." (see 2 Corinthians 5:7). Sight is in the sense realm (it is one of the five senses); faith is not in the sense realm; **faith is spiritual**. As believers we do not walk according to our flesh or our senses. We walk by faith; we walk in the Spirit.

Now, since Faith is a noun, we can also personify it to bring out more of its distinct characteristics. And, mind you, Faith, as used in this context, DOES NOT refer to a person's religious beliefs or doctrines. If you closely followed the earlier explanation and example that I gave of Faith, or if you yourself are in Faith, you probably already know this: Faith, the God-kind of faith, is self-assured. Faith is narrow-minded. Faith only sees one version of the story — the Bible's version, the positive version. Faith does not reason. Faith doesn't consider contrary opinions or circumstances. Faith is stubbornly certain, unyielding, and does not entertain opposing views. Faith leaves no room for options or alternatives. Faith doesn't know any such thing as "maybe." Faith knows no failure. Faith doesn't know it didn't work. Faith considers it done. Faith knows that it always works. Faith always receives. **Faith doesn't look for proof or evidence that it received whatever it asked for. Faith is the evidence.** Faith doesn't wait for the substance (of whatever is being hoped for) to manifest before the celebration begins. Faith celebrates now, because Faith is the substance. When Faith becomes broad-minded, and begins to consider other versions of the story other than the Bible's version, begins to leave room for options, and starts to consider that "maybe" it is true, "maybe" it isn't, or "maybe" it will work, "maybe" it won't; when Faith starts to waver, and begins to wonder why it didn't receive, or why it didn't work, it immediately ceases to be Faith, because, you see, Faith doesn't know failure; Faith is consistent. Faith doesn't know it didn't work. So far as Faith is concerned, it always works. Faith always wins. Faith doesn't look for evidence of victory; Faith is the evidence. Faith doesn't look for the substance; Faith is the substance. Now, tell me, does this look anything like your faith? It should.

Beloved, genuine faith is what shields the believer in times of trials and tribulations. It is a normal part of the Christian life to be faced sometimes with adverse circumstances (or what the Bible calls trials and tribulations, or afflictions). The Bible says, "**Many** are the **afflictions** of the righteous, but the Lord delivers him out of them all. He guards all his bones; not one of them is broken." (Psalm 34:19-20). The Bible also says in Acts 14:22 that "we MUST **through** MANY TRIBULATIONS enter the Kingdom of God." And so every believer is promised afflictions, trials and tribulations by the Word of God, even though we are additionally promised that God will deliver us out of them all. Indeed it is for good reason that we go through trials. The Bible says we (believers) are grieved by **various trials** for a little while WHEN NEEDED, as a means of TESTING THE GENUINENESS of our (precious) FAITH to see if, when tested, our faith will be found to praise, honor, and glory at the revelation of Jesus Christ, whom we love even though we have not seen. (see 1 Peter 1:6-8). The Bible also says that the testing of our faith is intended to, and does produce PATIENCE or endurance. (see James 1:2-3). James writes, "My brethren, take the prophets, who spoke in the name of the Lord, as **an example of suffering and patience**. Indeed **we count them blessed who endure.** You have heard of **the perseverance of Job** and seen the end intended by the Lord — that the Lord is very compassionate and merciful." (James 5:10-11). Even the Lord Jesus Christ Himself had to learn OBEDIENCE through the things which He suffered (see Hebrews 5:8); and for the joy that was set before Him, Jesus also was patient, He "**endured** the cross, despising the shame, and has sat down at the right hand of the throne of God." (see Hebrews 12:2). And so Jesus forewarned us that in this world we also WILL have tribulations. (see John 16:33). But He added that we should be of good cheer and not let our hearts be troubled, because He has overcome the world. We who believe in Jesus Christ have also overcome the world with Him. (see 1 John 5:4-5; 1 John 4:4). Hence, we need to have an overcomer's attitude whenever we encounter trials or adverse circumstances. It is only by faith in Jesus' finished work that we can keep our hearts from being troubled. Paul, walking in faith, said, "I have learned to be content whatever the circumstances." (see Philippians 4:11). Then he added, "I know what it is to be in need, and I know what it is to have plenty. I have learned **the secret of being content** in any and every situation, whether well fed or hungry, whether living in plenty or in want." (Philippians 4:12 NIV). And **that secret**, my dear believer, **is to set your mind on things above, set your mind on Jesus Christ who is your strength and your life, look unto Jesus who is the author and finisher of our faith, and know that you can do all things through Christ who strengthens you.** (see Philippians 4:13, with Colossians 3:2-4, & Hebrews 12:2). On another occasion Paul again said that "our light affliction, which is but for a moment, is working for us a far more exceeding and eternal weight of glory" (see 2 Corinthians 4:17). Hallelujah!

Faith Overcomes the World

Beloved in Christ, we all need to walk by faith and learn, like Paul, to be content no matter the circumstances we face, and thus praise God through it all, knowing that there is a far more exceeding and eternal weight of glory awaiting us. We need to have a deeper and complete understanding of what happened in the crucifixion of Jesus Christ. Jesus **triumphed** over the devil and his cohorts (see Colossians 2:15) **on our behalf.** He won victory eternally for us; He delivered us from this present evil world (see Galatians 1:4) and seated us with Christ in the heavenly places in Christ Jesus. (see Ephesians 2:4-6). So **every Christian begins the Christian life already seated in victory.** We begin by sitting (or resting) in a position of victory, and then we walk in that victory by accessing (by faith) all the spoils (or benefits) of that victory (some of which are listed in Psalm 103:5-12). As long us we believe the Word of God, we can appropriate all the benefits that are wrought in Jesus' redemptive work. In fact, it is by believing and claiming the promises of God that are in His Word that we become partakers of the divine nature. (see 2 Peter 1:4). This is why Satan's utmost strategy (which he perfected in the garden of Eden) has always been to shift man's focus away from the Word of God. The Bible says that the Word of God is the sword of the spirit (see Ephesians 6:17), so without the Word, the believer basically has no offensive weapon with which to attack Satan the adversary. And that is exactly what Satan desires. **Satan's strategy is to disarm Christians by replacing the Word of God with the philosophies and traditions of men, so that our faith will be in the wisdom of men and not in the power of God.** And so Paul warns believers to "Beware lest anyone cheat you through philosophy and empty deceit, according to the tradition of men, according to the basic principles of the world, and not according to Christ." (Colossians 2:8). And when Paul wrote to the Corinthian Church, he again emphasized the need for our faith to be in the Word of God, and not in the wisdom of men by saying: "And my speech and my preaching were NOT with persuasive words of HUMAN WISDOM, but in demonstration of the Spirit and of power, THAT YOUR FAITH SHOULD NOT BE IN THE WISDOM OF MEN **but in the power of God**." (1 Corinthians 2:4-5).

Many Christians today lack the knowledge of the pure Word of God, and thus have put their faith in the wisdom of men and not in the power of God, because many churches have replaced the pure Word of God with the traditions and philosophies of men and the doctrines of demons. There is no demonstration of the Spirit and of power in many churches today, because they are not preaching by the Holy Spirit; nor are they walking in faith. Indeed many believers don't even know about the victory, the power and blessings they have in Christ, let alone claim them. No wonder the Bible says, "My people are destroyed for lack of knowledge." (see Hosea 4:6). It is disastrous indeed for a believer to lack the knowledge of the Word of God. It is equally disastrous for a believer to doubt the Word of God, because the Bible says that it is through faith that we overcome the world. "And this is the victory that has overcome the world—**our faith**." (see 1 John 5:4). The Bible reminds us that Noah also overcame or condemned the world by his FAITH. (see Hebrews 11:7).

Beloved, the story of Israel entering the promised-land illustrates the utmost necessity and importance of faith, of knowing and believing/trusting the Word of God and walking by it. We can read the story in Numbers 13:17–14:9. Israel had received the Word of God. They had the Word that promised them that the land had been given to them. It was theirs for the taking. All they had to do was to consider it done, to go in and possess or lay hold on the land. But when Moses sent the twelve (12) spies to survey the land, ten of them came back with a bad report that caused Israel to be defeated in faith. They focused on how big the giants that occupied the land were, and how they themselves were like grasshoppers in their own sight. And by so doing, they started to doubt God's Word or God's promise that He had given them the land. They underestimated God by overrating the giants who occupied the land; they failed to magnify God, and magnified the giants instead.

The Bible says that as a man "thinketh in his heart, so is he" (see Proverbs 23:7). What this means is that if the devil can make you feel defeated in the thoughts of your heart, then, for him, the battle is already won. Thus, the key to seeing the blessings of God and the solutions to your problems manifest in your life is to begin changing the way you think in your heart. Begin to align the thoughts of your heart with the Word of God. Begin to anchor your thoughts on the unshakable Word of God and His precious promises to you, so that your thoughts will line up with God's thoughts of peace and not of evil, of hope and a bright future (see Jeremiah 29:11). The Bible says that "whatever is true, whatever is noble, whatever is right, whatever is pure, whatever is lovely, whatever is admirable—if anything is excellent or praiseworthy—think about such things." (see Philippians 4:8 NIV). You need to think about the Word of God; meditate on God's Word. Keep your thoughts on God and begin seeing yourself in possession of all His blessings, just like two of the spies, Joshua and Caleb, who were full of faith. Unlike the other ten spies, **Joshua** and **Caleb** saw by faith how big their God is, and they saw the "giants" that occupied the land as their "bread." And because of their faith, they entered the promised-land, whereas the other ten didn't. The Bible says Joshua and Caleb had a different spirit (see Numbers 14:24). **They had a spirit of faith** and focused on the promises and goodness of God while the others cowered in fear, because they walked by sight, and walked in unbelief. Paul said, "And since **we have the same spirit of faith**, according to what is written, "I believed and therefore I spoke," we also believe and therefore speak." (2 Corinthians 4:13).

Beloved, spiritual warfare basically takes place in the mind (or in our thoughts), as Satan and his demons try to cause us to doubt what the Word of God says about us, and to believe what we see, feel, and hear in the natural realm. (see 2 Corinthians 10:3-6). We fall into the trap of the enemy when we move away from the truth of God's Word. So the good fight of faith spoken of in the Bible (see 1 Timothy 6:12) is the fight to walk according to what God's Word says, regardless of what our circumstances say, or what other people say. It is a fight to walk by faith, and not by sight, a fight to always see through the lens of faith, to always act on the Word of God. Satan truly desires that believers would walk by sight, and not by faith. But the Bible admonishes us to, above all, take "the shield of faith, wherewith ye shall be able to quench all the fiery darts of the wicked." (see Ephesians 6:16 KJV). Satan often throws fiery darts by causing us to look at the physical mountain or storm, and away from the Savior. He did this to Peter when he was walking on the water to meet Jesus. As long as Peter kept his eyes on Jesus, he was able to walk on water (see Matthew 14:29). But the moment he looked away from Jesus to look at the storm, and saw that the wind was boisterous, he was afraid and started to sink (see Matthew 14:30). Satan's strategy is to get you to look away from Jesus, so that you will become afraid. His utmost weapon is to lie and sow thoughts of doubt in your heart. These thoughts can rob you of your faith and ultimately make you respond just like Peter and those ten spies of Israel. But if you hold on to the shield of faith (if you put your faith in Jesus' finished work), if you saturate your mind with thoughts about our beautiful Savior and His goodness, if you look unto Jesus the author and finisher of our faith, none of Satan's fiery darts can touch you. Like Joshua and Caleb, you will reject every negative thought and confess your faith in Jesus. You will not give place to the devil. (see Ephesians 4:27). Indeed you will submit to God, resist the devil and he will flee from you. (see James 4:7). And when you do so, the fiery darts will be quenched and you will stand in victory.

Joshua and Caleb entered the promised-land **by faith**. Jesus said we should come to Him, all of us who labor and are heavy laden, and He will give us rest. (see Matthew 11:28). The only way to enter into the rest offered by Jesus' finished work is **by faith**. Hebrews 4:3 says, "For we who have **believed** do enter that rest." Just like the other ten spies of Israel, it is **unbelief** that will prevent us from entering into the rest offered by Jesus' finished work. Hence the Bible says, "Let us labour therefore to enter into that rest, lest any man fall after the same example of **unbelief**." (see Hebrews 4:11 KJV). Our only labor then is to **believe** that Jesus meant it when He said, "It is finished." (see John 19:30). Thus, to rest is not only to enter into faith; it is also to demonstrate proof of that faith by ceasing from the works of the law. This is why Hebrews 4:10 says, "For he that is entered into His rest, he also hath CEASED FROM HIS OWN WORKS, as God did from His." (KJV). The Bible also says, "The law is not of faith." (see Galatians 3:12). So when we try to keep the law to be righteous, we do not believe in Christ for His righteousness. Walking under the law presumes that we are unrighteous, for "the law is not made for a righteous man." (see 1 Timothy 1:9). Therefore, walking by the law is the opposite of walking by faith; it is the opposite of walking in the Spirit. Under the New Covenant, Jesus has fulfilled the law for us. Our part therefore is simply to believe in Christ, and as we believe that we're righteous in Christ, we will produce the fruits of righteousness, because the fruits of righteousness are by Jesus Christ (see Philippians 1:11) and not by our self-efforts. We don't have to labor under the law anymore. When we believe in the finished work of Jesus, we honor Jesus, and it pleases God the Father.

Indeed we all as believers experience the promises and blessings of God in proportion to our level of faith. The Centurion who needed healing for his servant (see Matthew 8:5-13) and the woman who needed deliverance for her demon-possessed daughter (see Matthew 15:21-28) experienced their miracles because they had great faith. Conversely, Jesus **could not** heal many in His hometown because He was limited by their unbelief (see Matthew 13:58). Jesus said in Matthew 9:29, "According to your faith let it be to you." Faith is always the first step, and the only step. The Bible says, "These signs shall follow **those who believe**…" (see Mark 16:17). Strive or Labor to be among **those who believe**. Mark 11:24 says when we pray, we are to **believe** that we have received; then we shall have it. Yet, many people want to see first before they believe. That certainly isn't faith, and it isn't how we walk in the Spirit.

Faith Comes by Hearing, and Hearing by the Word of God

The Bible says, "So then faith comes by hearing, and hearing by the word of God." (Romans 10:17). Now, this verse is talking about **"living or saving faith,"** which is the God-kind of faith, or faith that is backed by works. It is this kind of faith that comes by hearing, and hearing by the Word of God. We have this kind of faith when we hear the Word of God and **believe** or accept that God will truly do what He has promised that He will do, and then based on this belief **we act on God's Word,** and **receive** (without doubting) **what God has promised,** even though we have not seen it yet. But there is also another kind of faith called **"dead faith**," which cannot save. Thus, James, in the second chapter of his epistle, makes a distinction between "living or saving faith," which is backed by corresponding works of faith, and "dead faith," which has no corresponding works; he writes that "**as the body without the spirit is dead, so faith without works is dead also**." (see James 2:26). James also gives an example of "dead faith" when he says, "You believe that there is one God. You do well. Even the DEMONS BELIEVE — AND TREMBLE!" Even the demons have "faith" that there is one God. And yet the demons are not saved, because their kind of "faith" is not backed by corresponding works, and thus is not saving faith but dead faith, just like the atheist's "faith" mentioned earlier. Indeed, "saving faith" or the God-kind of faith comes by hearing, and hearing by the Word of God. Every Word from God is filled or loaded with FAITH. This faith cannot be invented or manufactured by man. It is a gift (see Ephesians 2:8) that can only come from God through the hearing of His Word. Therefore, one can receive FAITH only as it is imparted to the heart by God Himself through the hearing of His Word. (see Romans 10:17). And the good news is that God is always giving or imparting the gift of faith as we hear His Word preached, and as we read the Bible for ourselves. It is ultimately up to us to receive or accept and lay hold on the faith God gives us through His Word. Right now as you read or hear the message in this book faith is being imparted to you. Thus, it is important what you allow yourself to read or hear on a regular basis. Are you continually hearing the Word of God which will build and grow your faith? Or are you hearing the philosophies of men that will plant doubts in your heart?

Grow and Strengthen Your Faith

Truly, God does many things for us, but He has also given us the **ability** and the **responsibility** to do certain things for ourselves, and exercising, strengthening, and growing our faith is one of them. As a believer, you don't need to struggle to have faith; the Bible says that you already have the measure of faith. (see Romans 12:3). You were saved by grace through FAITH. (see Ephesians 2:8-9). This FAITH was gifted to you when you heard the Word of God. Jesus said, "No one can come to Me unless the Father who sent Me draws him…" (see John 6:44). So God drew you to Jesus by giving you faith through the hearing of the gospel of Christ. God opened your heart to heed the message of the gospel. You couldn't have been saved without faith. Therefore you should know that you have faith. God didn't take the faith away from you after you got saved. No, God's gifts and His calling are irrevocable. (see Romans 11:29). This is why Romans 12:3 says God has given to each believer the measure of faith. We all begin our Christian walk with the (same) measure or amount of faith. And this faith is enough to move a mountain if we would simply exercise it or put it to work. (see Matthew 17:20; Luke 17:6). Jesus said that nothing will be impossible for us if we would just put this faith to use. (see Matthew 17:20). Just as this faith came to us when we heard the Word of God, continually hearing the Word of God is how we can **grow** this faith. Also, exercising our faith or putting our faith into practice is how we **strengthen** our faith. Begin to do everything the Bible says you can do. Begin to lay hands on the sick in the name of Jesus for them to recover. Begin to cast out demons in the name of Jesus. Begin to speak in new tongues in the name of Jesus. Jesus said these signs will follow those who believe. (see Mark 16:17-18). Ask yourself if these signs are following you, and if they're not, are you really one of those who believe? If you are in Christ, you are among those who believe. You don't need to struggle with faith; neither should you focus on your faith; just do what the Bible says you can do; just act on the Word of God. When you study and meditate on the Word of God, the Word will build your faith. (see Romans 10:17). When you act on the Word of God, the Word will strengthen your faith. Take the Word of God for what it is — accept God's Word as true, and act on it. That is faith.

Believers Should Not Pray and Ask for Faith

Beloved, you are what God's Word says you are. You have what God's Word says you have. And you can do what God's Word says you can do. Just believe God's Word and act on it. Faith is simply believing that God's Word is truth, and then acting on God's Word. Be a doer of the Word. Never pray for faith or for God to increase your faith — that is sheer unbelief; and it is unacceptable under the New Covenant. It is just like asking your natural father to help you to believe or trust in his word or help you trust in him. Every father will take this as an insult, and yet many believers do it to God, without seeing anything wrong with it. As believers, we have been born into God's family. Faith should be as normal and natural to us as it is in any beautiful family. We don't have to be faith-conscious; we just have to be love-conscious. We have to know that our dear Father (God) loves us deeply and cares for us greatly. His love should give us confidence in His promises. His love should make us rest and trust that He will provide for us whatever we ask in the name of Jesus. (see John 16:23). We have to become as trusting of God as children are of their natural parents. I don't know of any child who struggles to find faith to receive anything from their father. Children don't even think about faith when asking for something from their father; they just think about their father's love for them. So why should believers struggle for faith when we need something from our Father? Oh, what a difference it would make if we would just think about the Father's love instead of thinking about our faith! What a difference it would make if we were just as convinced as Paul that nothing can separate us from the love of God which is in Christ Jesus our Lord! (see Romans 8:38-39).

Indeed, faith comes by hearing, and hearing by the Word of God. (see Romans 10:17). So, just as you go to the gym to strengthen and grow your muscles, reading the Bible, meditating on it, and being a doer of the Word is how you grow and strengthen your faith. Nothing else will do. You cannot pray to God to give you muscles, because He has already given you muscles. Neither can you pray to God to give you faith, because He has already given you the measure of faith. (see Romans 12:3). You cannot pray to God to increase your muscles, because you can increase it yourself by exercising it. Similarly, no amount of prayer (with your understanding) or fasting can increase your faith. Only the

Word of God can, because "faith comes by hearing, and hearing by the Word of God." (see Romans 10:17). Praying in tongues or praying in the Holy Spirit is also helpful in building yourself up on your most holy faith (see Jude 1:20), and this is mainly because when you pray in tongues you speak mysteries in the spirit to God (see 1 Corinthians 14:2), and these mysteries are the Word or hidden wisdom of God. Paul said, "But we speak the wisdom of God in a MYSTERY, the hidden wisdom which God ordained before the ages for our glory" (1 Corinthians 2:7). The Word of God is God; the Word of God is Jesus Himself (see John 1:1, 14). Revelation 19:13 says, "His name is called The Word of God." And He is the author and finisher of our faith. (see Hebrews 12:2). Get into the Word today and see your faith grow.

In the next chapter we will continue to explore how to walk in the Spirit with emphasis on walking in the Word of God or walking in the truth. I am confident that by the end of this book, you will understand and appreciate the necessity of living and walking in the Spirit as a new creation, and why you can't afford to live or walk according to the flesh (or senses). "For if you live according to the flesh you will die; but if by the Spirit you put to death the deeds of the body, you will live." (Romans 8:13).

Chapter 16

The Spirit Walk: A Walk in the Truth or in the Word of God

WALKING IN THE Truth or walking in (or by) the Word of God is basically the same as walking by Faith. As believers, we are to walk by what God's Word says, and not by what we see, feel, think or hear from people. Thus, discussing "walking by faith" and "walking by the Word of God" as separate topics in this book will lead to unavoidable repetitions, which I hope you don't mind. You may recall that in Chapter One of this book we emphasized how important it is for every man to know the truth and to choose to be on the side of truth. We noted that there are two kinds of knowledge or information in this world: Facts, and Truth. And we explained that Facts are primarily based on scientific research and investigation, whereas Truth is from God (and is revealed in the Word of God or the inspired Books of the Bible). We also mentioned that, in a sense, all truth are facts, but not all facts are truth. Then we explained (with examples) that Truth never changes, but Facts (that are not truth) do change. We will continue that discussion in this chapter by explaining how those who have come to know and to be on the side of truth ought to walk in the truth. Just like the apostle John, I have no greater joy than to hear that believers walk in truth. To walk in truth is to walk in love or in the light of God's Word;

it simply means to walk just as Jesus walked. (see 1 John 2:3-10). Jesus walked according to the truth of God's Word. He said during His earth walk that He came to do the will of the Father (see John 6:38; John 8:29), and that the words that He spoke were not His own, but the Father's words. (see John 12:49-50). So our emphasis in this chapter will be on speaking and doing the Father's words as opposed to speaking the world's words. In other words, we will explain in this chapter how important it is for us to always confess or speak (and act in line with) the truth (which is God's Word) and not the facts (man's wisdom or knowledge) which are opposed to the truth.

When we walk by the Word of God or act on the Word of God, God sees it as evidence that we believe the Word, and so He counts it as faith. Believing (which is a verb) is acting on the Word of God; and faith (which is a noun) is what results when we act on the Word of God. The Bible explicitly teaches that God and His Word are one. (see John 1:1). When Abraham believed God's Word, it was the same as believing God, and so God accounted it to him for righteousness. (see Genesis 15:6; Romans 4:3). God accounts or credits righteousness to people who believe Him, who believe His Word and act on it. (see Romans 4:5). He did it not only for Abraham but previously for Noah (see Hebrews 11:7) and for Abel (see Hebrews 11:4). God also credited righteousness to Phinehas when he acted in zeal to protect the honor of God and of His Word, when he stood up and intervened, and the plague was halted. (see Psalm 106:30-31, with Numbers 25:7-13). Today when we also believe God's Word and act on what God's Word says in Romans 10:9-10, God sees it as believing in Jesus, and so He declares us righteous or credits us with righteousness, because we have believed God. In the preceding chapter, we quoted Habakkuk 2:4, which says that "My righteous one will walk by faith." Hebrews 10:38 also says, "Now the just shall live by faith; but if anyone draws back, My soul has no pleasure in him." Then the 39th verse adds, "But we are not of those who draw back to perdition, but of those who believe to the saving of the soul." Hallelujah!

We also noted in the preceding chapter that when we accept Jesus as our Lord and Savior, we are given the measure of faith (see Romans 12:3). Hence, the believer does not pray for faith or struggle for faith to walk with God, because we already have the measure of faith. The faith the believer has is the reason he is called a believer (or the believing one). Every believer is a new creation (see 2 Corinthians 5:17); every believer is born of God (see I John 5:1); and every believer is a child of God (see John 1:12; 1 John 3:1; Galatians 3:26). Hence, all believers belong to the Family or Household of God, and the Bible calls the Family or Household of God "the household of faith." (see Galatians 6:10 KJV). Thus, one unique or distinguishing characteristic of the people who belong to "the household of faith" is that we all have faith — starting from our Father God (see Romans 4:17) and our Brother Jesus (see Hebrews 12:2; Isaiah 11:3), to the least of our brethren. (see Romans 12:3; 2 Peter 1:1). We all have faith; this is the only reason we are called the family or household of faith. If you think you don't have faith, then you don't belong to this Family. It is as plain and simple as that. Now, since all believers have faith, all we have to do is use the faith we have, and grow or increase it and strengthen it through hearing and acting on the Word of God. (see Romans 10:17, with James 1:22). As you continually hear and act on the Word of God, your faith is developed — increased and strengthened. You can also eagerly desire and receive the gift of faith, which is a special gift of a highly developed faith that is given by the Holy Spirit to some believers for the profit of all believers. (see 1 Corinthians 12:7, 9, with 1 Corinthians 14:1).

Indeed, God has given us grace to help us in our walk with Him. This grace came through Jesus Christ (see John 1:17). And this grace is in the Word of God. Hence, the Word of God is also called "the Word of His Grace." (see Acts 20:32). Thus Peter tells us that grace is increased or multiplied to us through the knowledge of God and Jesus our Lord (see 2 Peter 1:2 KJV), which of course is the same as saying that grace is multiplied to us through the knowledge of the Word of God. Paul also tells us that we have access into this grace by faith (see Romans 5:2). And Peter affirms that all believers, through the righteousness of our God and Savior Jesus Christ, have received THE SAME PRECIOUS FAITH. (see 2 Peter 1:1). Indeed we all have the measure of faith, as Paul tells us in Romans 12:3 and Peter affirms in 2 Peter 1:1.

Believing equals Having

Beloved, believing equals having. If you don't believe you have faith, then you don't have it, and so you're not a believer, you're not one of us; you don't belong to "the household of faith." When you believe the Word of God, you have whatever the word promises. Believing (with patience) is how you inherit or possess the blessings promised by the Word of God. (see Hebrews 6:12). But you have to know or hear what the Word of God says before you can believe it and receive what it promises, which is why the Bible says that faith comes by hearing the Word of God. For instance, John 3:16, John 6:47, and 1 John 5:13

promise that if you believe in Jesus, you have eternal life. So when you hear the Word and act on it by believing in Jesus and confessing Him as your Lord, you should know that you have eternal life. Believing is having. In the same vein, when you hear and believe Ephesians 1:3 that says that God has blessed you with every spiritual blessing in the heavenly realms in christ Jesus, then you should know that you have every spiritual blessing in the heavenly realms in christ Jesus, and that you are truly blessed. Unfortunately many Christians don't rejoice over this verse of Scripture because it says "spiritual blessings" and they don't understand what spiritual blessings are. You see, spiritual things are superior to physical things. Spiritual things gave birth to the physical things. In the beginning there were no physical things around; there was God — who is Spirit — (see Genesis 1:1; with John 4:24); there was the Word — which is also spirit (see John 1:1, with John 6:63). The Bible tells us that the Word was with God and the Word was God (see John 1:1). And so before the physical realm came into being, there was the spiritual realm. Thus the spiritual realm is the mother of the physical realm; it gave birth to the physical realm. Everything that happens here in the physical realm is born out of the spiritual realm. The Bible affirms this when it says, "By faith we understand that THE WORLDS were framed by THE WORD OF GOD, so that **THE THINGS WHICH ARE SEEN WERE NOT MADE OF THINGS WHICH ARE VISIBLE.**" (Hebrews 11:3). That spiritual things are superior to physical things also implies that **spiritual blessings are superior blessings.** Spiritual blessings are the mother of all blessings. Therefore, God has blessed believers with superior blessings (see Ephesians 1:3), so that by believing, we will possess them or see the physical manifestation of our blessings. Faith is how we access and possess our blessings. We cannot access and possess these spiritual blessings any other way. We cannot access and possess them by walking according to sensory perception or what we see and feel. Sense knowledge is limited and unreliable. But the Word of God (which is revelation knowledge) is perfect and infinite; it endures forever. (see Isaiah 40:8; 1 Peter 1:25; Matthew 24:35). Besides, no word from God is void of power. (see Luke 1:37). God says, "I will not violate my covenant or alter what my lips have uttered." (Psalm 89:34 NIV). I encourage you to lay hold on every word God has uttered about you, for He means every word. He says, "I am the Lord: I will speak, and the word that I shall speak shall come to pass." (see Ezekiel 12:25 KJV).

Beloved, **great and strong faith** is the result of hearing and doing the Word of God. (see Romans 10:17, with James 1:22). The Bible says that to **fear God** and **keep His Word** or His commandments is man's duty. (see Ecclesiastes 12:13-14). Therefore it behooves every man and woman to study the Word of God and always keep God's Word or walk according to the Word of God. That is how you walk by faith, and that is how you walk in the Spirit. The Word of God is also called "the Word of Faith" (see Romans 10:8). It gives faith when we read or hear it, and its promises are to be appropriated by faith and patience. All the promises of God in Christ belong to the believer and are to be possessed through faith and patience. (see 2 Corinthians 1:20, with Hebrews 6:12). If you see a promise in the Bible, just claim it — say Amen and in Jesus' name it is yours. Then keep confessing it as yours (see Hebrews 4:14) and possess it; lay hold on it. (see 1 Timothy 6:12). Believing is possessing. When the Angel Gabriel brought the Word of God to the virgin Mary, that she had found favor with God and that she "WILL CONCEIVE" in her womb "and bring forth a Son, and shall call His name Jesus" (see Luke 1:31), Mary believed the Word of God that was spoken to her. The Bible says, "Then Mary said, "Behold the maidservant of the Lord! LET IT BE TO ME ACCORDING TO YOUR WORD." (see Luke 1:38). This is how we are also to receive the promises of God that are in the Bible. When the Bible says, for instance, that by His stripes you're healed, say, "LET IT BE TO ME ACCORDING TO YOUR WORD." This is the "Amen" that we are to speak according to 2 Corinthians 1:20. Thus, by believing the Word of God, Mary possessed what the Word had promised. And when Mary went to visit her relative Elizabeth, the Holy-Spirit-filled Elizabeth spoke saying, "BLESSED IS SHE WHO BELIEVED, for THERE WILL BE A FULFILLMENT of those things which were told her from the Lord." (Luke 1:45). Beloved, **you are blessed if you believe the Word of God**, because there will be a fulfillment of whatever the Word promises you. Indeed Mary conceived and brought forth the Son Jesus Christ, as promised by the Word. John says, "And **the Word became flesh** and dwelt among us, and we beheld His glory, the glory as of the only begotten of the Father, full of grace and truth." (John 1:14).

Another example relates to Simon Peter, who after he had spent all night fishing with his friends and had failed to make a catch, was asked by Jesus in the morning to launch out into the deep and let down his net for a catch. In other words, Jesus was asking Peter to go back to where he had already been and failed, and cast his net again for a catch. Perhaps any other person would've refused for the reason that they had "been there, done that"; they had previously tried that on their own and it didn't work. But not Simon Peter. The Bible says, "Simon answered and said to Him, "Master, **we have toiled all night**

and caught nothing; NEVERTHELESS **AT YOUR WORD** I will let down the net." (see Luke 5:5). Peter **believed the Word** Jesus spoke to him, **and acted on it**. Peter believed the Word of God and acted on it; he was a doer of the Word. Peter launched back into the deep and cast the net again, just as the Word of Christ had commanded. And this time, because he was acting on the Word of Jesus, because He was depending on Jesus and not on his own strength or understanding, because He was standing on the unshakable Word of God, the Bible says he made a large, boat-sinking, net-breaking catch. (see the story in Luke 5:1-11). Hallelujah! Is there anything too hard for the Lord? Beloved, is there anything you have tried on your own and failed? Is it a love relationship or marriage? Is it a business or a job? Is it school or a vocation? Look in the Bible and see what God's Word promises. The Word promises that you can do all things through Christ who strengthens you. (see Philippians 4:13). The Word promises that all things are possible to the believing one or the believer. (see Mark 9:23). The Word promises that everything you do shall prosper. (see Psalm 1:3). The Word says that God is able to do exceedingly abundantly above all that you ask or think, according to His power that works in you. (see Ephesians 3:20). Now based on your faith in these promises of God which are all Yes in Christ, launch out into the deep and try again; try whatever you previously failed at again. And this time, standing on the unshakable Word of God, you are going to have a mind-blowing success. Amen.

All Things Are Possible to the Believer

Now, let me share an amazing revelation with you here. The Bible says that even though some things are impossible with men, "with

God ALL THINGS ARE POSSIBLE." (see Matthew 19:26). Then the Bible adds that "ALL THINGS ARE POSSIBLE to the one who believes." (see Mark 9:23). In other words, all things are possible to the believer, just as all things are possible to God. This simply means that the believer is no ordinary man; the believer is not counted among the class of men spoken of in Matthew 19:26, because the believer is in a different class, a higher class. The believer is the child of the Most High God (see 1 John 3:1; John 1:12; Galatians 3:26), and is thus in the class of God. No wonder Peter said that the believer is a partaker of the divine (or God) nature. (see 2 Peter 1:4). The believer is a partaker of God's righteousness and holiness. (see Ephesians 4:24). The believer is a partaker of the Holy Spirit. (see Hebrews 6:4). Indeed, the believer has full access to God's mighty power. The Bible says that the same exceedingly great power God worked in Christ when He raised Him from the dead has been put inside the believer. (see Ephesians 1:19-20). Therefore, beloved, all things are possible to you if you're truly a believer — if you believe. As a believer in Christ, you partake of God's omnipotence. That's a revelation right there. Never feel weak or ordinary in life, because God Himself is **your glory and strength**. (see Psalm 89:17). The God of Israel gives POWER and STRENGTH to His people. (see Psalm 68:35). Jesus Christ who is the POWER of God and the wisdom of God (see 1 Corinthians 1:24) is in you. (see Colossians 1:27). Never feel like a mere man ever, because you're not a mere man. (see 1 Corinthians 3:3). You have the life of God in you. (see 1 John 5:11-12). God Himself lives in you. (see 1 Corinthians 3:16-17; Ephesians 4:6). He that is in you is greater than he that is in the world. (see 1 John 4:4). God is at work in you with His full power and ability. (see Philippians 2:13; Ephesians 3:20; Colossians 1:29). Of His fullness you have received. (see John 1:16; Ephesians 3:19).

Begin to utilize or exercise the power of God that is in you, and begin to change the seemingly impossible situations you encounter. Be an imitator of God as a beloved child (see Ephesians 5:1), walking in love and bringing glory to your Father's name by demonstrating His power whenever and wherever there is an opportunity to do so. Begin to call life into hopeless situations. Begin to destroy the works of the enemy by making use of the Mighty name of Jesus. The Name of Jesus is your inheritance; it is a strong tower (see Proverbs 18:10); it is Power (see Acts 4:7, 10), and it is yours. All the authority in that Name is yours to exercise. Jesus said, "And these signs will follow those who believe: In My NAME they will cast out demons; they will speak with new tongues; they will take up serpents; and if they drink anything deadly, it will by no means hurt them; they will lay hands on the sick, and they will recover." (Mark 16:17-18). This is describing the authority and power you have as a believer in the Name of Jesus. This is your inheritance as a believer. What else are you waiting for? People who act on the Word of God receive the things promised by the Word. Jeremiah 1:12 shows that God watches over His Word to perform it. It is not praying hard for faith or struggling for faith that brings results or blessings; it is simply by acting on the Word of God that we receive our blessings. May you believe God's Word always. May you act on God's Word always. May you be a doer of God's Word always. And expect to have results as you act on the Word of God.

The Two Main Opinions in the World

Throughout the Bible emphasis is placed on the truth that there are two main opinions in this world: God's opinion and the world's opinion (or Satan's opinion). God's opinion can be found in His Word (the

Bible). And the world's opinion (or Satan's opinion) is every opinion that is contrary to the Word of God. Every single moment, you have a choice between God's opinion (the Truth) and Satan's opinion (the Lie). The Bible makes a clear distinction between these two opinions. On a certain occasion in Israel, the prophet "Elijah came to all the people, and said, "How long will you falter between TWO OPINIONS? If the LORD is God, follow Him; but if BAAL, follow him..." (I Kings 18:21). It is clear from this verse that there is the opinion of God, and the opinion of Baal (or Satan). Either the God of Israel is God, or Baal (Satan) is God; it can't be both. Every man has to make a choice. All men are compelled to consistently choose between the opinions or words of these two beings. God's opinion is in His written Word — the Bible. And the world's opinion or Satan's opinion often includes what is communicated by our own physical circumstances, doctor's reports, news media reports, and the opinions we get from the world through our five senses — hearing, seeing, smelling, feeling or touching, and tasting — and from friends, family and everybody else, which are contrary to the Word of God. God wants us to always choose to believe His opinion (or His Word) and to conduct ourselves or walk according to His opinion. This is called faith. And it is the only way we can truly walk with God, because faith is the only means to access God and to please Him. The Bible says without faith it is impossible to please God. (see Hebrews 11:6). This also means that God is not moved by anything else but faith. God does not want us to falter or waver between two opinions. He wants us to be fully persuaded about His opinion, and to always walk in line with His opinion. Whenever you choose another opinion over God's opinion, you choose a lie over the truth (the reality), you choose Satan's opinion over God's opinion, because, you see, lies are from

Satan. The Bible says Satan is a liar from the beginning; he is the father of lies, and there is no truth in him. (see John 8:44). But God does not lie. (see Titus 1:2). The Bible says, "God is not a man, that He should lie, nor a son of man, that He should repent. Has He said, and will He not do? Or has He spoken, and will He not make it good?" (Numbers 23:19). God's Word is truth. (see John 17:17). His opinion is truth. Hence, the Bible says we are to **walk in the truth**. (see 3 John 1:3-4). **Walking in the Truth is walking in the Word of God, or walking in accordance with the Word of God.** And it is also how we walk in the Spirit.

Beloved, how long will you falter between two opinions? God's opinion is that if you believe in Jesus Christ, you will not perish but have eternal life. (see John 3:16). God's opinion is that whoever calls on the name of the Lord will be saved. (see Romans 10:13; Acts 2:21). God's opinion is that whoever has the Son has life. (see 1 John 5:12). God's opinion is that whoever believes in Jesus Christ has been forgiven of all their sins and declared righteous. (see Colossians 1:14; Romans 3:22, 24; 2 Corinthians 5:21; Romans 5:17; Ephesians 4:24; 1 Corinthians 1:30). God's opinion is that Jesus Himself took our infirmities and bore all our diseases, and by Jesus' stripes we are healed. (see Matthew 8:17; Isaiah 53:5, 1 Peter 2:24). God's opinion is that though the Lord Jesus was rich, He became poor to make you and I rich. (see 2 Corinthians 8:9). Do you believe God's opinion, or do you believe the opinion your present circumstance is giving you? Is your mind fixed on God's opinion, or are you faltering between two opinions? Are you fully persuaded about God's opinion? You need to be, because no one can truly walk with God, unless they are fully persuaded about His opinion. We have to demonstrate the God-kind of faith just like our father Abraham did. The Bible says Abraham **did not waver** at the promise of God through unbelief, but was strengthened in faith, giving glory to God, and being **fully convinced** that what He had promised He was also able to perform." (Romans 4:20-21). Be fully convinced about God's opinion and about God's promises, that what He has promised He is also able to perform. The Bible says two cannot walk together unless they agree. (see Amos 3:3). You have to agree with God's opinion to be able to walk with Him. Besides, God's opinion is the only truth there is. God's opinion is His Word. And God is His Word (see John 1:1). Therefore, anyone who doesn't believe in God's Word (or opinion) doesn't believe in God. Period! The only way to fall in love with God is to fall in love with (and do) His Word. Therefore, study God's Word, and you will know God's will and His ways. Do God's Word, and you will be walking in His will and in His ways.

Indeed, God's Word or opinion is the only truth. Any other opinion is a lie from Satan. So decide whose opinion you would believe today. Every single moment, you have a choice between the two. **In the Garden of Eden, Adam and Eve had a choice between God's opinion and Satan's opinion, and they chose to believe Satan's opinion over God's opinion.** Like the sinners of today, they "exchanged the truth of God for the lie, and worshiped and served the creature rather than the Creator, who is blessed forever…" (see Romans 1:25). They chose to receive the spirit of the world rather than the Spirit of God. And we all know the consequence of that choice. The person whose opinion you choose to believe or obey becomes your master or your god. (see Romans 6:16). This is why the Bible calls Satan the god of this world. (see 2 Corinthians 4:4). Adam made Satan the god of this world by choosing to obey Satan over God. And so all those who are **of the world** today have "the spirit of the world" and thus they love the world and all that is in the world — the lust of the flesh, the lust of the eye, and the pride of life. (see 1 John 2:16). But as believers, we are **not of the world**, we are of God, and the Bible says, "Now we have received, NOT the spirit of the world, but the Spirit who is from God, that we might know the things that have been freely given to us by God." (1 Corinthians 2:12). As believers, Satan is not our god; we are no longer in his kingdom; we are in the Kingdom of God's dear Son (see Colossians 1:13), and in our Kingdom, we only believe in one opinion — the opinion of God. And we have the Spirit of God to teach us the opinion (or Word) of God concerning all things. (see 1 John 2:20, 27).

Unfortunately, there are some "believers" today who doubt the opinion of God; there are some who falter (or waver) between the opinion of God and the opinion of the world. Beloved, how long will you falter between two opinions? If the Lord is God, follow Him; but if Satan (the liar), follow him. The choice is ultimately yours. I choose to believe God's opinion. I choose to obey God's Word. And God's opinion is that I am saved; I am righteous; I am blessed; I am highly favored; I am the beloved child of the Living God; I am healed; I am rich; I have all things that pertain to life and godliness; I am an heir of God and joint-heirs with Christ; the world is my inheritance; I lack no good thing; I eat the good of the land; I am a victor and a success; I am a world overcomer; all because I believe in Jesus Christ. He that is in me is greater than he that is in the world; and I can do all things through Christ who strengthens me. Glory be to God!

Trust the Bible as the Word of God

Here's another important truth: no one can sincerely believe God's opinion in its totality (as presented in the Bible) without first believing and trusting the credibility of the Bible as truly the Word of God and not the word of man. I have met many so-called believers who think that because the Bible was written by men there is no way it could be the literal Word of God. Such people are easily deceived by every wind of doctrine thrown at them by Satan through his human proxies. This is just tragic. If you're one such person I'm not going to try to convince you to accept the Bible as God's Word, because it takes faith to accept the Bible as God's Word. If you can't accept by faith that the Bible is the inspired Word of God, you can't please God, because, you see, God is not pleased by those who seek to follow him by logic or reasoning; He is not impressed by people who seek after scientific evidence to convince them to follow God, because God transcends Science. God is only pleased with those who follow Him by faith.

The Bible, as we know, testifies of itself as the inspired Word of God. "All Scripture is given by inspiration of God, and is profitable for doctrine, for reproof, for correction, for instruction in righteousness, that the man of God may be complete, thoroughly equipped for every good work." (2 Timothy 3:16-17). The NIV translation of verse 16 says that all Scripture is "God-breathed." Thus, the Bible is literally the Word of God written through the hands of men. Therefore the Bible is true and right (see Psalm 33:4); it is pure and flawless. (see Proverbs 30:5). In fact, the Lord Jesus Christ, in His teachings, also confirmed and affirmed the Bible as God's Word, and as truth. (see Matthew 5:18; John 10:35; John 17:17; Luke 11:28; Matthew 22:40; 24:15). For instance, Jesus affirmed the story of the creation of Adam and Eve in the beginning (see Matthew 19:4-6), the story of Noah and the flood (see Luke 17:26), the destruction of Sodom and Gomorrah (see Matthew 10:15), the lifting of the bronze serpent by Moses in the wilderness (see John 3:14), the story of the prophet Jonah who was in the belly of the great fish for three days and three nights (see Matthew 12:39-41), the drought and famine throughout the land in Elijah's time and Elijah's visit to the widow in Zarephath in the region of Sidon whom God directed to supply Elijah with food (see Luke 4:25-26), the healing of Naaman's leprosy by Elisha (see Luke 4:27), and so forth. This is the Bible's own testimony of itself. But if you are someone who believes in scientific evidence, and cannot bring yourself to accept the Bible's own testimony of itself as well as Jesus' confirmation and affirmation of the Bible as truth and as God's Word, you can conduct your own research, and you would discover that the Bible is always way ahead of Science in stating and affirming (scientific) truths. We noted a few examples in Chapter one of this book, but it bears repeating here.

When for so many years scientific evidence insisted that the earth was flat, the Bible maintained that the earth is round, by declaring that "God sits enthroned above the circle of the earth." (see Isaiah 40:22). The Bible never changed its position. It was scientific knowledge that grew until it fell in line with the truth of the Bible that the earth is indeed round or circular. If human wisdom had written the Bible, they would've made the same error Science made. That is just one example.

Another example is in the field of medicine. For years, medical science believed that bleeding a sick person would help the sick to recover. Consequently, when George Washington, the first president of the

United States of America was sick, the doctors bled him, then they bled him again, till he lost so much blood and died. I don't blame the doctors; they were only following the medical principle or wisdom of the day. But imagine what would've happened if they had read the Bible and discovered the Bible's clear declaration that "the life of a creature is in the blood." (see Leviticus 17:11). Medical science would later learn this truth and fall in line with what the Bible had maintained all along. And so today, when someone is sick, doctors don't bleed him; they rather give him blood (blood transfusion), because the life of a creature is indeed in the blood.

Again, in the 14th century the Bubonic plague killed about a third of Europe's population because medical science knew nothing about putting people with infectious diseases in quarantine. Meanwhile the Bible had instructed years earlier that we are to put an infected person in quarantine for seven days. (see Leviticus 13:4). Medical science learned this truth later (in a very hard and costly way). Indeed, the Bible is always ahead of Science in stating truths.

In fact, many of the things Science convinced all of mankind to believe in the past as "scientific truths" have been proven over the years to be false, whether it is the shape of the earth, the axis of the earth, the bleeding of the sick, the age of the earth, the number of planets in the solar system, the single cell protoplasm, etc. And yet we know that truth is never supposed to change. In the Louvre Library today, there's a huge section that contains obsolete science books. Once-held scientific "truths" have been, and are always being revised or replaced by new "truths" as scientists make new discoveries. And so the science textbooks in our schools keep being revised. It is just puzzling and astonishing how fast scientific facts do change. But the Bible (in its original text and language) has not undergone a single revision. In fact, the Bible has survived all the attacks launched against it by scientists and historians over the years, as they struggled to align themselves with some of the Bible's truths after years of studies and discoveries. This only goes to affirm the Bible as the eternal and flawless Word of God. Jesus said, "Heaven and earth will pass away, but My words will by no means pass away." (Matthew 24:35). The Bible remains the same and endures forever. Indeed, the truths of the Bible remain truths regardless of what Science claims, because, well, what does Science know about truth anyway, given its shifting stance on almost every issue? Beloved, I can go on and on with examples, but you see, I don't need to, because I believe that the only way the Bible would have truths that the finest and most popular human wisdom cannot conceive is that it was inspired by God, since only God knows all truth. There are some who may probably still need more evidence to believe the Bible as the Word of God regardless of how much evidence I provide here; this is why I wouldn't argue with such people or even try to convince them, because, you see, it doesn't take logical reasoning to believe the Bible; it only takes faith. I therefore commend the Bible to you as the literal Word of God. And I tell you right now that you don't truly know God nor believe in God until you believe in the Bible, the Word of God.

How Do You Know God?

Now, I have a very simple question for anyone who is still struggling to believe the Bible as the literal Word of God: have you ever seen God? Your obvious answer is "No." So how do you know God? How do you even know He exists? The truth is that everybody knows about

God's existence (even though some self-deceived people deny it). God has made Himself known; He has put an intuitive awareness or knowledge of His existence in every human being that He ever created, and all creation testifies of His invisible qualities, even His eternal power, and His Godhead. (see Romans 1:19-20). Indeed, "the heavens declare the glory of God; the skies proclaim the work of His hands." (see Psalm 19:1). But as a believer, your knowledge of God is not only based on intuition and creation; you know God more intimately through His Word. His Word gives incontrovertible evidence of His existence and of His true nature, His will, His ways and His acts. So the only true and valid concept any believer can have of God must be based on His Word — the Bible. Take the Word away, and you have no true concept of God. Without the Word, you might still perceive some qualities of God, but there will be no way for you to know the complete truth of who He really is, let alone enter into a relationship or fellowship with Him. And you will have no way of allowing God to govern your life.

The Bible says that "No one has ever seen God, but the one and only Son, who is Himself God and is in closest relationship with the Father, has made Him known." (John 1:18 NIV). How has the Son made God known, and how is the Son making the Father known to us today? The answer is simple: through the Word of God — the Bible — and with the help of the Holy Spirit (the Spirit of Christ), who inspired the Bible, and who teaches us and leads us into all truth. (see John 16:13; 1 John 2:27). Jesus is the Word made flesh. (see John 1:1, 14). He is the Living Word. Revelation 19:13 says, "His name is called The Word of God." This is a marvelous revelation! Since Jesus is indeed The Word of God, no one can claim to believe in Jesus and not believe in The Word of God. Jesus and The Word of God are inseparable; they are one and the same. Indeed, Jesus Christ is the closest man has ever gotten to seeing God the Father, because He is God, and He was manifested in the flesh. (see 1 Timothy 3:16; John 1:18; John 14:9; Acts 20:28). Today, the only thing you can physically see that gives a full and vivid revelation or picture of God is The Word of God. God's Word declares Him. If you don't believe in His Word, you don't believe in God.

Emphatically, you can't, and you don't believe in God until you believe in His Word, because God is His Word. (see John 1:1). You can only know God through His Word. Unbelievers don't know God because they don't know or believe His Word. The Bible says the Gospel is veiled to those who are perishing, "whose minds the god of this age has blinded, so that **they do not believe,** lest the light of the gospel of the glory of Christ, who is the image of God, should shine on them." (II Corinthians 4:4). The Word of God is veiled to those who are perishing; they don't understand it, and they don't believe it. They have "**their understanding darkened**, being alienated from the life of God, because of the **ignorance that is in them**, because of the **blindness of their heart**." (see Ephesians 4:18). They are without God and without hope in the world (see Ephesians 2:12). But we, beloved, have had the light of the gospel shine in our heart. We are so blessed. "For it is the God who commanded light to shine out of darkness, who has shone in our hearts to give the light of the knowledge of the glory of God in the face of Jesus Christ." (II Corinthians 4:6). We must be eternally grateful. For there is no other way to truly know God except through the light of His Word. Faith in God only comes through the hearing of God's Word. (see Romans 10:17). And knowledge of God comes through believing and understanding God's Word. As a believer, if you doubt the Word of God, you are doubting God; you're doubting the very Word that saved you, and you're in essence doubting your own salvation. The Bible says God gave birth to us **by** the Word of truth. (see James 1:18, 1 Peter 1:23-25). You can't doubt the Word of truth, the Word that gave birth to you, or you end up doubting your own birth and, thus, your own identity as the child of God. The Bible says that the one who doubts should not expect to receive anything from the Lord. (see James 1:6-8).

The Word of God Endures Forever

God's Word is truth, and it does not change. Jesus said, "Heaven and earth will pass away, but **My words will BY NO MEANS pass away**." (Matthew 24:35). God's Word will never change nor pass away. God does not change. (see Malachi 3:6). Whatever He is, He is permanently. He is the same yesterday, and today and forevermore. (see Hebrews 13:8). So whatever He said yesterday is true today, and tomorrow, and forevermore. In the beginning, He was the Word, and He is still the Word today. He (the Word) became flesh (a Man), and He is still a Man in Heaven today. (see John 1:14; 1 Timothy 3:16, with 1 Timothy 2:5). He is a Spirit, and He is still a Spirit today. (see John 4:24). And He is forever a triune God. Godliness is a mystery. (see 1 Timothy 3:16). God is unchanging. He is His Word. Hence, His Word is unchanging; it endures forever. (see Isaiah 40:8, 1 Peter 1:25). The Psalmist says God has exalted or magnified His Word above His name (see Psalm 138:2), and it's all because He is His Word. God and His Word are one. Believing in His Word (which you can see and read or hear) is how you believe in God (whom you cannot see). This is why you should always believe that you are what God's Word says you are, you have what God's Word says you have, and you can do what God's Word says you can do. Believing the Word and doing the Word is how you walk in the truth; it is how you walk in the Spirit. The Bible says **God's Word is alive and active** (see Hebrews 4:12). This is why we call it the living Word. It is always alive. And whenever we lift a Word from the pages of the Bible and place it in our heart and on our lips, that Word is sharper than any two-edged sword. It cuts through every darkness — every problem, every difficulty, every hopelessness, and it sheds its light abroad. This is why the Bible is also called Good News. When words from the Bible are spoken in faith and with love, news begins to happen — sinners get saved, the sick get healed, the lame leap onto their feet, the dead come to life; and news is made: good news! And this is all because, God watches over His Word to perform it. (see Jeremiah 1:12). The Bible says, "So shall My word be that goes forth from My mouth; It shall not return to Me void, But it shall accomplish what I please, And it shall prosper in the thing for which I sent it." (Isaiah 55:11).

Beloved, trust God's word, because it does exactly what it promises, when mixed with faith. God's word happens when believers act on it in faith; it is always a "Now" Word; it accomplishes whatever it is meant to accomplish, "For no word from God will ever fail." (Luke 1:37 NIV). God's word is always potent; It is always alive, and it always causes the thing for which it is sent to happen. It prospers in the thing for which God sent it. For example, if it is a word for healing, the healing happens once the word is received (believed and acted upon) in faith. Therefore, make the Bible your closest companion and your final authority on all matters: read it, believe it, meditate on it, confess it, act on it. Know the Scriptures, believe what it says, and speak its promises over your life; be a doer of the Word. Let your zeal for the things of God be according to knowledge, so that you will not err. Walk in the truth.

The Bible says that on a certain occasion, Jesus was responding to a question raised by the Sadducees. "And Jesus answering said unto them, **Do ye not therefore err, because ye know not the scriptures, neither the power of God?**" (Mark 12:24 KJV). Jesus spoke these words to the Sadducees — men who felt in their own estimation that they were learned men and gatekeepers of the Law — and yet, how accurately it applies to us today. How accurately it applies especially to many of these man-ordained, self-proclaimed gatekeepers of the doctrines of the Church. And how relevant and timeless it is as a caution to everyone of us against not knowing the Scriptures, nor the power of God. We err or go wrong and wander from the truth when we don't know the Scriptures. And when we don't know the Scriptures, then we also are not able to get a deep revelation and an experiential knowledge of the power of God.

The apostle Paul also made a similar observation of Israel and said, "Brethren, my heart's desire and prayer to God for Israel is that they may be saved. For I bear them witness that THEY HAVE A ZEAL FOR GOD, **BUT NOT ACCORDING TO KNOWLEDGE**. For they being **IGNORANT** OF GOD'S RIGHTEOUSNESS, and SEEKING TO ESTABLISH THEIR OWN RIGHTEOUSNESS, have NOT SUBMITTED to the righteousness of God." (Romans 10:1-3). Clearly, zeal for God without right believing based on knowledge of the truth of God's Word, cannot save anyone. But unfortunately this is also the problem we have among professed Christians today. I bear many professed Christians witness that they have a zeal for God and for the things of God, but not according to knowledge, and so they err. This same doctrine of righteousness by faith that Paul preached about is being rejected by many professed Christians today who seek to establish their own righteousness rather than submitting to or accepting the righteousness of God which is being offered as a gift to all who believe in Christ (see 2 Corinthians 5:21 with Romans 5:17). And this is just one of many areas where otherwise zealous Christians are erring because of a lack of knowledge of the Scriptures and of the power of God. Today there are so many false doctrines and teachings that have been wrapped around a thin layer of truth — I call it the false doctrine burrito — and are being fed to believers who know no better, because they themselves are not reading the Scriptures and verifying things for themselves. These so-called believers are so unlike the Berean Jews in the early Church, whose zeal for God was according to knowledge. These Berean Jews were more fair-minded and would not buy into just any doctrine without going into the Scriptures and verifying things for themselves. The Bible says, "These were more fair-minded than those in Thessalonica, in that they received the word with all readiness, and SEARCHED THE SCRIPTURES DAILY TO FIND OUT WHETHER THESE THINGS WERE SO." (Acts 17:11). You see, the Bible describes people who receive the Word with all readiness and search the Scriptures to verify things for themselves as more fair-minded or noble people. I wonder what the opposite of that is.

Beloved, don't just accept my teaching because it's coming from me. Make sure you verify everything I say by searching the Scriptures for yourself. This is also the reason why I provide a Scriptural reference for everything I say. In fact, I cannot emphasize this enough. Don't just accept any teaching you hear (as truth) without verifying the Scriptures for yourself. And don't allow anybody to convince you that they have their own private interpretation of the Scriptures, and that they are the only people who have the credentials and the right to tell you what the Scriptures mean. Learn from Elihu when he says, "I said, 'Age should speak, and multitude of years should teach wisdom.' But there is a spirit in man, and the breath of the Almighty gives him understanding. Great men are not always wise, nor do the aged always understand justice." (Job 32:7-9). The Scriptures mean one and the same thing even when read by a child. The Bible says, we all should know "this first, that **no prophecy of Scripture is of any private interpretation**, for prophecy never came by the will of man, but holy men of God spoke as they were moved by the Holy Spirit." (II Peter 1:20-21). Read the Scriptures for yourself. It is the Holy Spirit who inspired the writers of the Scriptures, and you also have the Holy Spirit to help you understand the Scriptures. The apostle John, assuring believers that we have the promise of eternal life, said, "These things I have written to you concerning those who try to deceive you. But the anointing (that is, the Holy Spirit) which you have received from Him abides in you, and you do not need that anyone teach you; but as the same anointing teaches you concerning all things, and is true, and is not a lie, and just as it has taught you, you will abide in Him." (I John 2:26-27). Don't allow yourself to be deceived, beloved, and do not be self-deceived either, because you will err if you don't study the Scriptures yourself and come to know the power of God. The blame is squarely on you if you allow anyone to deceive you and lead you to hell with false doctrines and philosophies of men. From my experience, those who clamor for the biggest religious titles are often the ones who have no revelation knowledge of the Scriptures; they are often the ones who try to comprehend the Scriptures by human reasoning, and they often preach or teach sense knowledge, and not revelation knowledge. Nothing is true or makes sense to them (spiritually), unless they can logically explain it. One time Jesus asked a group of such people — who were called the Pharisees — some questions about what the parentage of the Christ is according to the Scriptures, but they couldn't answer Him. (see Matthew 22:41-46). The Bible says, "And no one was able to answer Him a word, nor from that day on did anyone dare question Him anymore." (Matthew 22:46). Ironically these men saw themselves as the learned men and teachers of Israel. Prior to this, they even had the nerve to ask Jesus by what authority He was teaching and conducting His ministry. (see Matthew 21:23). On another occasion Jesus also questioned another Pharisee whose name was Nicodemus; He asked, "Are you the teacher of Israel, and do not know these things?" (see John 3:10). Indeed, it is baffling!

Study the Word to Show Yourself Approved to God

If I could only tell you one thing in conclusion of this chapter, I would echo the inspired words of the apostle Paul, that "Let the word of Christ dwell in you richly in all wisdom…" (Colossians 3:16). And I can promise you that the Word will build your faith (see Romans 10:17), reveal and multiply grace to you (see 2 Peter 1:2), and give you an assurance of salvation (see 1 John 5:13). Indeed, the Word will "build you up and give you an inheritance among all those who are sanctified." (Acts 20:32).

But how can God's Word dwell in you richly in all wisdom? Paul again gives us the answer in his second letter to a young pastor named Timothy. He said, "**STUDY** to shew thyself approved unto God, a workman that needeth not to be ashamed, RIGHTLY DIVIDING THE WORD OF TRUTH." (2 Timothy 2:15 KJV). This is right in line with what God told Joshua in the Old Testament. He said, "This Book of the Law SHALL NOT DEPART FROM **YOUR MOUTH**, but you shall **MEDITATE** IN IT DAY AND NIGHT, that you may OBSERVE TO **DO** ACCORDING TO ALL THAT IS WRITTEN IN IT. For then you will make your way prosperous, and then you will have good success." (Joshua 1:8). In other words, Joshua was being asked to study the Word of God and meditate on it until the Word becomes his consciousness, until everything he **spoke** and **did** was right in line with the Word of God. Joshua was to make his home in the Word of God. God is telling all of us the same thing. In fact, Jesus said to His disciples that we are to abide or make our home in Him (and of course, He is the Word, just as John 1:1, 14 says, and Revelation 19:13 affirms); we are also to allow His words to abide or make their home in us. (see John 15:7). We are all to STUDY the Word of truth or the Word of God to understand it so that we can rightly divide it in a way that is approved by God. We are never to speak anything that is not in agreement with the Word of God, but are to meditate on God's Word day and night, that we may be doers of the Word. (see Joshua 1:8, with James 1:22). And we have the Holy Spirit to help us accomplish this. Thus, if you truly desire to walk in truth, you need to STUDY the Word of God with the help of your Teacher — the Anointing or the Holy Spirit — who abides or remains in you. You have to let the Word of Christ dwell in you richly in all wisdom. Hear God saying, "My Son, give attention to my words, incline your ear to my sayings. Do not let them depart from your eyes; keep them in the midst of your heart; for they are life to those who find them, and health to all their flesh." (Proverbs 4:20-22).

When you give attention to God's Word and the Word of Christ dwells in you richly in all wisdom, it will show in your speech and your actions: you will be a transformed man; you will not speak like the rest of the world do; your speech and actions will not conform to the speech and actions of unbelievers or those who are of the world. (see Romans 12:1-2). You will be unique and distinct from the world, because you will be a man sanctified (or set apart) by the truth, which is the Word of God. (see John 17:17). You will have the mindset of the righteous. You will be as separated from the world as light is separated from darkness. (see 2 Corinthians 6:14-15). Your light will so shine before men, that they will see your good works and glorify your Father who is in Heaven. (see Matthew 5:16). This is the reason Jesus said, "You are the light of the world. A city that is set on a hill cannot be hidden." (Matthew 5:14). You will SHINE in this world and STAND OUT as a city on a hill, when you walk according to the truth of God's Word.

When Jesus walked on this earth, He stood out as Light in this dark world, because not only was He the truth, He also walked in the truth. To the Jews who did not believe in Jesus and sought to kill Him, Jesus said, "You are of your father the devil, and the desires of your father you want to do. He was a murderer from the beginning, and DOES NOT STAND IN THE TRUTH, because there is no truth in him. When he speaks a lie, he speaks from his own resources, for he is a liar and the father of it." (John 8:44). Here, Jesus gave us a very important and profound revelation about Satan (the devil), and the revelation is that the devil **DOES NOT** STAND IN THE TRUTH. This means that when you stand in the truth (of God's Word), Satan will not stand with you. When you walk in the truth (of God's Word), Satan will not walk with you. In other words, Satan is afraid of the truth. This is why every believer must stand and walk in the truth. The only safe ground in this world is the truth, and the Truth is Jesus Christ (see John 14:6); the Truth is the Word of God (see John 17:17). James says, "Therefore submit to God. Resist the devil and he will flee from you." (James 4:7). Submit to the truth. Many people often quote the last part of James 4:7 and ignore the first part. But the point is that you cannot resist the devil without first submitting to God, without first submitting to the Truth. To resist anything, you must first be leaning on something stronger. For instance, in order for you to successfully resist a strong wind, you must be holding on to and allowing yourself to be held by a rock or an object which cannot be moved by the wind. Similarly, God and for that matter, our Lord Jesus Christ, is our Rock (see 1 Peter 2:6-8; Isaiah 26:4), He is the truth (see John 14:6), and we have to submit to and lean on Him in order to successfully resist the devil. Submitting to God and to the Lordship of our Lord Jesus Christ is accomplished by submitting to the Word of God, which is the Truth. We have to submit to or agree with and walk according to what God's Word says about who we are in Christ, what we have in Christ, and what we can do through Christ and with the power and authority that we have in Christ. When we believe God's Word and do (or act on) God's Word, then have we submitted to God, then are we leaning on the immovable Rock, then are we walking in the truth or standing in the truth; and Satan will not stand with us, because he does not stand in the truth. Satan flees when we resist him with the truth of God's Word. When we walk in the truth, we can successfully resist the devil, we can successfully resist every attack and every temptation of the devil. Indeed we know we have truly submitted to God when we have full assurance in our heart that the Bible is in truth the Word of God, and thus renew our minds with what the Bible says, and walk according to what the Bible says. We have to make God's thoughts our thoughts and His opinions our opinions. After all, the Bible says we (i.e in our spirit) have the mind of Christ. (see 1 Corinthians 2:16). We should make this truth manifest in our body, by renewing the mind of our body with the Word of God.

When Jesus walked here on earth, He was able to resist the devil by leaning on the truth of God's Word when the devil tempted Him in the wilderness. (see Luke 4:1-13). Because the devil does not stand in the truth, he fled when Jesus continually confessed and did what the Word of Truth says, as opposed to what Satan wanted Him to do. Confessing and doing the truth (which is God's Word) is how we resist the devil. Satan may also know the written Word of God and may even quote it sometimes, but the truth is that he does not have the revelation and an understanding of the Word, so he cannot rightly divide the Word of truth; nor does he stand in the truth or walk in the truth. This is why the ministers of Satan who have infiltrated Christian churches today are neither able to preach the truth nor do the Word. Yes, they can quote the Scriptures alright, but because they themselves don't understand it and cannot rightly divide it, they deceive their followers with their teachings. On a certain occasion, when the disciples of Jesus asked Him why He spoke the way He did (and in that particular context, why He spoke in parables) to the people, "He answered and said to them, "Because **it has been given to you to know the mysteries of the kingdom of heaven,** BUT TO THEM

IT HAS **NOT** BEEN GIVEN. Therefore I speak to them in parables, because seeing they do not see, and hearing they do not hear, NOR DO THEY UNDERSTAND." (Matthew 13:11, 13). Indeed it has been given to every believer to know the mysteries of the Kingdom of God and to understand the Word of God, and by submitting to it, resist the devil, and he will flee from us.

In the next chapter, we will continue to explore how to walk in the Spirit with emphasis on walking in Love.

Chapter 17

The Spirit Walk: A Walk in Love

Love One Another

THE BIBLE SAYS we are to "LOVE ONE ANOTHER, for LOVE IS OF GOD; and everyone who loves is born of God and knows God. He who does not love does not know God, for GOD IS LOVE." (see 1 John 4:7-8). The commandment to love one another is also accompanied by an endless supply of God's love and ability, because it is a commandment for the new creation. Paul wrote that "the love of God has been poured out in our hearts by the Holy Spirit who was given to us." (see Romans 5:5). Christ Himself is in us, and He is our strength, so we are not to love with our own strength, but by resting in Him, and allowing His love to flow through us to others. You can love effortlessly today and always by resting in Christ and being conscious of His presence and His love.

In Chapter 8 of this book, we discussed how Jesus Christ, having been born of God, walked in love throughout His earth walk and thus left us with an unmistakable example to follow. In fact, much of what we discussed in Chapter 8 bears repeating here. Today it is very easy for us (as believers) to follow Jesus' example of love because, just like Jesus, we have been born of God (see 1 John 5:1), and thus the

Bible says that "as He is, so are we in this world." (see 1 John 4:17). Being born of God also means we have been born of Love, because God is Love. Thus we have the love nature of God. We are partakers of the divine (or God) nature. (see 2 Peter 1:4). We are partakers of the love nature. Love is as natural to the believer as breathing. In fact, any believer who hates his neighbor is not a true believer; he does not have eternal life or the life of God in him; he is not born of God, and he does not know God. This is what the Bible emphasizes in First John 4:7-8, which we quoted above. It is again emphasized when John writes: "He who says he is IN THE LIGHT, and HATES HIS BROTHER, is IN DARKNESS until now. He who LOVES HIS BROTHER abides in the LIGHT, and there is no cause for stumbling in him. But he who HATES HIS BROTHER is IN DARKNESS and walks IN DARKNESS, and does not know where he is going, because the darkness has blinded his eyes." (1 John 2:9-11).

In Chapter One of this book we explained that man is a spirit that lives in a body and has a soul. So the real man is the spirit of a man; the body is just the earthen vessel or tent in which the spirit lives. Therefore when God looks at a man, He looks at the spirit of that man. This is why the Bible says, "The spirit of a man is the lamp of the Lord, searching all the inner depths of his heart." (Proverbs 20:27). Thus, on the Day of Judgment, God will be judging men according to who we are in our spirit, which explains why the believer can have boldness on the Day of Judgment. As a result of God's love demonstrated and perfected in us in the giving of His Son Jesus Christ, the believer's spirit (which is also called the new man) is as perfect as God, having been created according to God in true holiness and righteousness (see Ephesians 4:24); and so, as God is, so is the believer in this world. (see

1 John 4:17). Today anyone who fears the Day of Judgment has not been perfected in love (see 1 John 4:18); such a person is simply not a true believer. The believer is the righteousness of God in Christ Jesus. (see 2 Corinthians 5:21). And God is the righteousness of the believer. (see 1 Corinthians 1:30; Romans 3:26). Hallelujah!

As a believer, your spirit has been created (anew) according to the love nature of God. Your spirit has been created to love. Not only do you have the love nature of God in your spirit, you also have the righteous and holy nature of God. (see Ephesians 4:24). Therefore, you are called to love, to be holy and to practice righteousness. But the challenge is that — as is evident in Ephesians 4:24 — all the amazing transformation (or change) that occurred in you through the new birth occurred in your spirit (the new man) and not in your body. We have explained elsewhere in this book that when we believed in Jesus Christ as our Lord and Savior, it was our spirit (or what Peter calls "the hidden man of the heart") that was born again or created anew; our spirit is the new creation. But our body (together with its mind) remained and still remains the same old corruptible body. In fact, if you had a scar before you were born again, you would notice that you still have that scar; if you had a tattoo, you would still see the tattoo (unless it's been miraculously erased!). The truth here is that it's the same old body you still have. And so, Yes, our body has also been purchased by God (together with our spirit) and belongs to God (see 1 Corinthians 6:19-20), but the purchased body has not been redeemed yet (see Ephesians 1:13-14); it will be redeemed and transformed that it may be conformed to Jesus' glorious body when the Lord Jesus returns (see Philippians 3:21; 1 Corinthians 15:53), but for now it is still in this world, even though it is not of this world. Hence, whereas Satan does not have access to our spirit because it has been redeemed from his kingdom and dominion (see Colossians 1:13-14), he still has access to our body because it is in this world. This explains why the apostle Paul's body could be buffeted by a messenger of Satan; it explains why (to prevent him from being puffed up because of the abundance of revelation) the apostle Paul could be given a thorn in his flesh (body), **a messenger of Satan to buffet him**. (see 2 Corinthians 12:7). It also explains why Paul commanded the Corinthian Church to (in the name of our Lord Jesus Christ, and with the power of our Lord Jesus Christ) hand over or deliver to Satan the body of the believer who was committing sexual immorality with his father's wife, so that Satan will destroy his body, that his spirit may be saved in the day of the Lord. (see 1 Corinthians 5:1-5). It again explains why believers are admonished to not give place to the devil (see Ephesians 4:27), and to resist the devil and he will flee from us. (see James 4:7). Thus, although our body is accessible to Satan, it is more so accessible to us, because we live in this body. What this means is that we are the ones who get to decide what to do with our body even as Satan wrestles against us for the control of our body. Indeed, until the redemption of the purchased possession (or the body of the believer), Satan and his demons and human proxies will always seek to launch attacks on our body; they will seek to even gain control over our body, because our body is still in this world, and Satan is the god of this world. (see 2 Corinthians 4:4). But the Bible says, "You are of God, little children, and HAVE OVERCOME THEM, because He who is in you is GREATER than he who is in the world." (1 John 4:4). Hallelujah!

Satan's favorite part of our body, and his major target for attack is the mind. It is on our mind that Satan often launches his most fatal attacks, as he sets up arguments and pretensions against the knowledge (or Word) of God (see 2 Corinthians 10:5) in seeking to make us conform to (the thinking patterns and conduct of) this world. Thus, since we are in this world but not of this world, our only way to fend off the attacks of Satan and walk in this world as victors, as champions, as overcomers, as the god-men that we truly are in the spirit, is to walk in the Spirit, to walk according to the Word of God, to walk according to the nature and mind of our spirit (the new man). We are to put on the new man. We have to conform our body and its mind to "the new man" which has been delivered from this present evil world (see Galatians 1:4), created in the nature of God (see Ephesians 4:24), joined as one with the Spirit of God (see 1 Corinthians 6:17), and has (or possesses) the mind of Christ. (see 1 Corinthians 2:16). And to accomplish this, the Bible commands us (to make a deliberate decision and take a concerted action) to present our bodies a living sacrifice, holy, acceptable to God (see Romans 12:1). We are also not to offer any parts of our body as instruments of unrighteousness to sin, but are to present all parts of our body as instruments of righteousness to God. (see Romans 6:13). In short, we can accomplish the transformation in the conduct of our body by renewing the mind of our body (with the Word of God), until our mind is conformed to the perfect will of God and to the perfect mind and nature of our new man or our re-created spirit. (see Romans 12:2). And thankfully, we have the Holy Spirit in us to lead us — teach us, help us, guide us, comfort us, counsel us, and give us the ability or power to accomplish all of this transformation — if we will only acknowledge Him and yield or submit to Him.

Beloved, when we love our neighbor as ourselves, we are walking according to the Spirit and not according to the flesh, and the righteous requirement of the law is fulfilled in us. (see Romans 8:4, with Romans 13:10). Therefore, love is the fulfillment of righteousness. We practice and fulfill righteousness by walking in love. The apostle John writes, "If you know that He (God) is righteous, you know that EVERYONE WHO PRACTICES RIGHTEOUSNESS is born of Him." (1 John 2:29). Then he adds for emphasis: "Little children, let no one deceive you. HE WHO PRACTICES RIGHTEOUSNESS IS RIGHTEOUS, just as He (God) is righteous." (1 John 3:7). The apostle Paul also adds, as we mentioned earlier, that we are to present our members (or bodies) as instruments of righteousness to God. (see Romans 6:13). John says we are to practice the truth. (see 1 John 1:6). Practicing righteousness is thus synonymous with practicing the truth; and it is accomplished by simply practicing love or walking in love. Anyone who does not walk in love walks in hate, just like Cain, and is a murderer; and no murderer has eternal life in him. Thus the Bible says, "In this the children of God and the children of the devil are manifest: Whoever DOES NOT PRACTICE RIGHTEOUSNESS is NOT of God, NOR IS he who DOES NOT LOVE his brother. For this is the message that you heard from the beginning, that WE SHOULD LOVE ONE ANOTHER, not as Cain who was OF THE WICKED ONE and murdered his brother. And why did he murder him? Because his works were evil and his brother's righteous. Do not marvel, my brethren, if the world hates you. We know that we have PASSED from death TO LIFE, because WE LOVE the brethren. He who DOES NOT LOVE his brother ABIDES IN DEATH. Whoever HATES his brother IS A MURDERER, and you know that NO MURDERER HAS ETERNAL LIFE abiding in him." (1 John 3:10-15). Indeed it is a blatant lie for anyone to claim to be a believer, to claim to be the righteousness of God in Christ Jesus, and yet fail to walk in love or in righteousness. Walking in love is the proof that you're truly the righteousness of God in Christ Jesus. Walking in love is the very definition of the Christian walk or the Spirit walk; it is the very embodiment of the Christian Way of life. When we walk in love, the righteous requirement of the law is fulfilled in us. Hence the Bible says that "love is the fulfillment of the law." (see Romans 13:10; Galatians 5:14; Romans 8:3-4). Bearing the fruit of the Spirit (which is **love** with its components of joy, peace, longsuffering, kindness, goodness, faithfulness, gentleness, self-control — see Galatians 5:22) is the evidence that you are walking in the Spirit.

Beloved in Christ, you have the very life and nature of God in your spirit, and so long as you walk in the Spirit or allow your (re-created) spirit to rule over your body, you will bear the fruit of the Spirit, which is love (see Galatians 5:22); you will walk in love. Walking in love puts you in the class of God. Any believer who struggles to walk in love is behaving like a mere man; he is carnal or is an infant who has not yet renewed his mind with the Word of God, and is thus unskilled or does not understand the Word of righteousness. (see Hebrews 5:13, with 1 Corinthians 3:1-3). Many believers simply refuse to grow into spiritual people and thus remain babes or carnal for far too long. (see Hebrews 5:11-13). This is the problem Paul was addressing in his first letter to the Corinthians when he said, "And I, brethren, COULD NOT speak to you as to SPIRITUAL PEOPLE but as to CARNAL, as to BABES in Christ. I fed you with milk and not with solid food; for until now you were not able to receive it, and even now you are still not able; for you are STILL CARNAL. For where there are ENVY, STRIFE, and DIVISIONS among you, are you not carnal and BEHAVING LIKE MERE MEN?" (1 Corinthians 3:1-3). You know you're carnal or babes in Christ when you have envy, strife, and divisions among you in your congregation or church. The solution to this carnal behavior is offered by the apostle Peter in his epistles when he writes: "Since you have purified your souls in obeying the truth through the Spirit in sincere love of the brethren, love one another fervently with a pure heart, having been born again, not of corruptible seed but incorruptible, through the word of God which lives and abides forever. Therefore, LAYING ASIDE all malice, all deceit, hypocrisy, envy, and all evil speaking, AS NEWBORN BABES, **DESIRE the pure milk of THE WORD**, that **you may GROW** thereby, if indeed you have tasted that the Lord is gracious." (1 Peter 1:22-23, 2:1-3). Simply put, Peter is making the same recommendation Paul makes in Romans 12:2 that we should renew our minds with, and feed on the pure milk of the Word of God, so that we may grow "till we all come to the unity of the faith and of the knowledge of the Son of God, to a perfect man, to the measure of the stature of the fullness of Christ." (see Ephesians 4:13). Walking in love fervently with a pure heart is the trait of a mature Christian; it is the trait of the complete spiritual man who has attained the measure of the stature of the fullness of Christ.

Our Love Walk Begins With Knowing How Jesus Has Loved Us

As new Covenant believers, we have the example of Jesus to follow in the Way of love; we are to love one another, **as Jesus has loved us**. Jesus said, "As the Father hath loved Me, so have I loved you: continue ye in My love." (John 15:9 KJV). Jesus loved us, as the Father has loved Him. And so He commands us to also love one another, as He (Jesus) has loved us. (see John 13:34-35). Therefore our love walk begins with first knowing how Jesus has loved us. Before we can love others in the same manner as Jesus has loved us, we have to know in what manner Jesus has loved us. We have to know and believe in the love that Jesus has for us. We have to know that Jesus is God (see 1 Timothy 3:16; Acts 20:28; Romans 9:5), and God is love; so Jesus is love, and he who abides in love abides in Jesus, and Jesus in him. (see 1 John 4:16). Thus, the apostle Paul prayed that Jesus (who is love) may dwell in our hearts through faith; that we being rooted and grounded in love, may be able to comprehend with all the saints what is the width and length and depth and height — to know the love of Christ which passes knowledge; that we may be filled with all the fullness of God. (see Ephesians 3:17-19). Like Paul, we need to understand the love of Christ in a personalized way, knowing that Christ loved each one of us individually, and died or gave Himself for each of us (see Galatians 2:20; Hebrews 2:9). Each one of us should be able to say with Paul that, "I have been crucified with Christ; it is no longer I who live, but CHRIST LIVES IN ME; and the life which I now live in the flesh I live by faith in the Son of God, WHO LOVED ME AND **GAVE Himself FOR ME.**" (Galatians 2:20). Indeed Christ lives in every believer, so we are not to love with our own strength or ability by walking in the flesh; instead, we are to love by resting (or believing) in Christ who lives in us, and allowing His love to flow through us to others. The Bible says that "we which have believed do enter into rest." (see Hebrews 4:3). We have ceased from our own works. (see Hebrews 4:10). So it is now God (Love) who is at work in us both to will and to do for His good pleasure (see Philippians 2:13); Christ is in us (see Colossians 1:27) living and loving through us as we rest in Him and walk in the knowledge and consciousness of His presence. (see Galatians 2:20). His working works in us mightily (see

Colossians 1:29). Our sufficiency or ability to meet all (love) needs is from God (see 2 Corinthians 3:5), and so all we have to do to walk in love is to yield to the leading of the Holy Spirit; we are to yield to God (the Holy Spirit) who is at work in us. The Bible says that "the LOVE OF GOD has been POURED OUT in our hearts by the Holy Spirit who was given to us." (see Romans 5:5). Therefore we have an infinite supply of the God-kind of love in us to spread around. We can walk in love (agape), as Christ has loved us, by simply letting His love loose in us or in our lives. When we yield to love and let love loose in our lives, we will effortlessly fulfill the law, because "love is the fulfillment of the law" (see Romans 13:10, Galatians 5:14). Hallelujah!

The Christian Way of Life is the Way of Love

Love, indeed, is the defining nature and inherent characteristic of a true Christian. Love is the evident lifestyle of the believer who is walking in the Spirit. The world has to know us by our love. Love is the fruit by which we are known. As bearers of Christ's name, image, and nature, we are to spread His love or carry the example of His great love around the world, so that all will know that we are truly His disciples. Jesus doesn't want believers to be conformed to this world (see Romans 12:2); He wants us to stand out as the light of the world — to be the holy nation and a peculiar people or His own special people, that He has called us to be. (see 1 Peter 2:9). This is why Jesus gave us a new commandment at the Last Supper. He said, "A new commandment I give to you, that you love one another; **AS I HAVE LOVED YOU**, that YOU ALSO LOVE ONE ANOTHER. **By this** ALL WILL KNOW **THAT YOU ARE My DISCIPLES**, if you have **love for one another.**" (John 13:34-35). As believers, it is our love that sets us apart from the rest of the world; it is our love that makes us the light of the world; it is our unconditional love (agape) for one another that identifies us as the disciples of Jesus Christ. And so we walk as impostors when we claim to be disciples of Jesus and yet fail to walk in love.

The world today is yearning for love; all of creation is yearning for love. Yet, the unbelieving world has no love to give because there is no true love outside of Christ. The world of sinners cannot love; they have no capacity for love. As children of the devil, all they know and have is hate. (see 1 John 3:10, 13). So when they try to love, they only end up with a fake (CONDITIONAL and SELFISH) kind of love. This is why there are so many dysfunctional relationships and marriages in the world today. It is also the reason for the increase in crime and wars. Jesus came to show us a new Way of life — the Way of love (agape). Jesus did not just come to teach us how to love; in fact, it is impossible to teach a sinner to love, because he does not have the capacity for it. This is why sinners had to be born again or re-created in Christ through the death, burial, and resurrection of Jesus Christ, so that, as a new species of human beings, we would have the very nature of God — His love nature. "Therefore, if anyone is in Christ, he is a new creation; old things have passed away; behold, all things have become new." (2 Corinthians 5:17). The new creation — this new humanity (see Ephesians 2:15) — is the very embodiment of love, having been born of Love. This is why Jesus calls us the light of the world (see Matthew 5:14), and the salt of the earth (see Matthew 5:13). We are to shine as light in this world; and as the salt of the world we are also to preserve righteousness (in this world) and heal this wounded world; we accomplish all of this by walking in love. Thus, in Matthew

5:38-47, Jesus commanded us not only to love those who love us or do good to those who have something to give us in return, but more so to love those who hate us and seek to harm us, and do good to those who have nothing to give us in return.

Beloved, love is our nature and character (as believers), because love is the nature of our Father. "For God is Love." (see 1 John 4:8). Therefore, today all of us who have been born of God have been born of Love; we have the love nature of God; we have the capacity to love just like our Father (God) and just like our Brother (Jesus). We are partakers of the divine (God or Love) nature (see 2 Peter 1:4), and so we are to imitate God our Father by walking in love (see Ephesians 5:1-2). "Behold what manner of love the Father has bestowed on us, that we should be called children of God!" (see I John 3:1). Today we are the children of God because of the manner of love the Father has bestowed on us; we are the children of Love. "We love Him because He first loved us." (1 John 4:19). Thus the Bible commands us that "if God so loved us, WE ALSO OUGHT TO LOVE one another." (see I John 4:11). We are to walk in love, as Christ loved us and gave Himself for us. (see Ephesians 5:2). Walking in love then, is the proof that we are walking in the Spirit (see Galatians 5:22); it is the proof that we are the disciples of Christ (see John 13:34-35), that we are spiritual men and not mere men. (see 1 Corinthians 3:1-3). We are to love, as Jesus has loved us. If there is one question that always has to be in the consciousness of each believer or on the mind of the believer, it is this: "How has Jesus loved me?" And the answer is this: "He gave Himself for me." (see Ephesians 5:2; Galatians 2:20).

We Ought to Lay Down Our Lives For the Brethren

Jesus' love for the world is summed up in the sacred act of GIVING Himself or laying down His life for us. Jesus Himself said, "Greater love has no one than this: to lay down one's life for one's friends." (John 15:13 NIV). After saying this, Jesus went ahead to lay down His life for us to demonstrate and teach us this greater love. Hence John writes, "BY THIS WE KNOW LOVE, because He laid down His life for us. And WE ALSO OUGHT TO LAY DOWN OUR LIVES FOR THE BRETHREN." (1 John 3:16). Indeed Jesus has left us an example of the highest degree of love. Jesus' faith and love were working together when He gave Himself and died on the cross for us. Jesus' faith or belief was that, by giving us the example of His love, believers would be bearers and sharers of His love — His selfless and unconditional kind of love — all around the world. And so He gave us a commandment to love one another, AS He HAS LOVED US. (see John 15:12). Today the greatest way we can express our love for the brethren is to give ourselves or LAY DOWN OUR LIVES for them (see 1 John 3:16), as Jesus did for us. Paul says, "For the love of Christ compels us, because we judge thus: that if One died for all, then all died; and He died for all, that those who live should live no longer for themselves, but for Him who died for them and rose again." (2 Corinthians 5:14-15). As believers, we no longer live for ourselves but for Christ, who died for us and rose again. "If we live, we live for the Lord; and if we die, we die for the Lord. So, whether we live or die, we belong to the Lord." (Romans 14:8 NIV). The way to live and die for Christ is to live and walk in love (agape). We walk in love by giving ourselves for others, as Christ did for us. Love is giving. Hence the Bible says, "it is more blessed to give than to receive." (see Acts

20:35). In other words, it is more blessed to love than to be loved. Paul said in his letter to the Corinthians that the more abundantly he loved them, the less he was loved. (see 2 Corinthians 12:15). Such is the walk of love. Love is helplessly selfless. We are to learn to be imitators of Paul, and more so "imitators of God," as beloved children, walking in love even as Christ has loved us. (see Ephesians 5:1-2). Walking in love is giving ourselves to the brethren. And one major way to do this is to **be bold and fearless in preaching the gospel everywhere**, regardless of the threat of imprisonment, stoning or death, just as Jesus did for us, and just as the early apostles did for us. Indeed, the highest and greatest expression of love is to give or lay down one's life for the brethren.

Loving Others is the Evidence that You Love Jesus

Jesus said, "He who has My commandments and keeps them, it is he who loves Me. And he who loves Me will be loved by My Father, and I will love him and manifest Myself to him…If anyone loves Me, he will keep My word; and My Father will love him, and We will come to him and make Our home with him." (John 14:21, 23). Today, if you claim to love Jesus, then prove it by keeping Jesus' commandment to love others as He has loved you. The Bible says, "Whoever claims to love God yet hates a brother or sister is a liar. For whoever does not love their brother and sister, whom they have seen, cannot love God, whom they have not seen." (1 John 4:20 NIV). Indeed, if we claim to love Jesus, then we have to love others, as Christ has loved us. And if we claim to love others, as Christ has loved us, then we have to preach the gospel of Christ to them and help them understand that "whoever calls on the name of the Lord (Jesus Christ) shall be saved." (see Romans 10:13). Paul asks, "How then shall they call on Him in whom they have not believed? And how shall they believe in Him of whom they have not heard? And how shall they hear without a preacher? And how shall they preach unless they are sent? As it is written: "How beautiful are the feet of those who preach the gospel of peace, who bring glad tidings of good things!" (Romans 10:14-15). Jesus preached the gospel because of His love for mankind, and we who walk in love today must also preach the gospel out of love, because we have been sent for this very purpose. (see Mark 16:15-16).

Beloved, love gives selflessly. Jesus said, "For God SO LOVED THE WORLD, that HE GAVE His ONLY begotten Son, that whosoever believes in Him should not perish, but have everlasting life." (John 3:16 KJV). God loved us with His great love (see Ephesians 2:4), and He loved us while we were still sinners (see Romans 5:8). Because God loved us so greatly, He DEMONSTRATED His own love toward us by GIVING His ONLY begotten Son Jesus Christ to die for us while we were still sinners. Indeed, love GIVES selflessly. Love DEMONSTRATES itself. Love is ACTION-ORIENTED; love is ACTIVE. Love is not just expressed in word or tongue, but in DEED and in TRUTH. (see 1 John 3:18). The Bible says, "In this the love of God was MANIFESTED toward us, that God has sent His only begotten Son into the world, that we might live through Him." (1 John 4:9). God loved us and manifested His love through the GIVING of His only begotten Son Jesus Christ to die for us, that we might live through Him. In this same love act of God we also see the love of Jesus or how Jesus also loved us. Jesus allowed Himself to be given to the world by God the Father; He yielded to the Father's will every step of the way (see John 4:34; John 6:38; Luke 22:42; Hebrews

10:7-10). Jesus, through the eternal Spirit, **offered Himself** without spot to God. (see Hebrews 9:14). The Book of Revelation also says that JESUS "**LOVED US** and washed us from our sins in His own blood, and has made us kings and priests to His God and Father." (see Revelation 1:5-6). Once you believe in God's love for you, once you believe and understand how Jesus has loved you, your whole life will be transformed, and you will effortlessly walk in love; you will desire to live a life that bears witness to Christ and honors and glorifies God.

God Loves You Unconditionally

The major reason many believers today are struggling to walk in love is that many churches are misrepresenting God's love by teaching that God's love for us is conditional, that He withdraws His love from us when we sin and loves us when we do right. Thus many believers tend to treat others the way they believe God is treating us; they love people based on their performance (or how they behave towards them). My friend, God is not demanding anything from you. He created you for His pleasure. (see Revelation 4:11). He created you to love you, and for you to voluntarily love Him back. Therefore, God's love for you does not depend on what you do for Him. All you have to do today is to accept God's love which is IN Christ. If you don't feel loved today, it is not God who is not loving you, it is you who is not receiving or accepting God's love which is IN Christ Jesus. As noted earlier, John 3:16 says that God so loved the world (the world of men, the world of sinners) that He gave us His only begotten Son. Romans 5:8 says Christ died for us while we were still sinners. It is man-made religion that has put conditions on God's love. Grace stops where vain Religion begins. Vain Religion says you must live a holy life, dress decently, go to church, win souls for God, pay your tithe and say the right things before God will love you. But as good as that sounds (and as much as I encourage you to do all those things), the notion that God's love for you depends somehow on whether or not you do those things, just doesn't correctly represent God's nature. God will not stop loving you, nor love you less just because you don't do those things mentioned above; nor would He love you more because you do those things. God's love for you is a constant, because it is unconditional. God remains faithful even when you are unfaithful; He cannot deny who He is. (see 2 Timothy 2:13). God is love, and so He loves you all the time. Once you know this, it will be easier for you to accept God's love which is in Christ Jesus, and to love God (see 1 John 4:19) and come to Him even when you sin; and it will also be easier for you to overcome sin and live a life that glorifies God, "for sin shall not have dominion over you, for you are not under law but under grace." (see Romans 6:14). Praise God!

In First Corinthians 13:4-8, the Bible gives us a complete and thorough description of God's kind of love, it gives us an insight into the heart of the Father, so that we can imitate Him by loving like Him. It says, "Love is patient, love is kind, it does not envy, it does not boast. It is not proud, it is not rude, it is not selfish, it is not easily angered; **it keeps no record of wrongs**. Love does not delight in evil, but rejoices in truth. It always protects, always trusts, always hopes, always perseveres. Love never fails…" (1 Corinthians 13:4-8a). Beloved, these are the characteristics of God's love. Our love should bear the same characteristics, because God's love has been poured out in our hearts by the Holy Spirit who was given to us. God's kind of love is patient or longsuffering. The Bible says, "The Lord is not slack concerning His promise, as some count slackness, but is LONGSUF-FERING (or patient) toward us, not willing that any should perish but that all should come to repentance." (2 Peter 3:9). As believers and thus children of God, we are also admonished to be longsuffering (or patient). We who are strong or mature believers are to demonstrate our patience by bearing with the failings of the weak (or babes in Christ) and building them up, as Christ did for us, rather than pleasing ourselves. (see Romans 15:1-5). Patience is a love trait that characterized the apostle Paul and his ministry. (see Hebrews 5:12-14; I Corinthians 3:1-3). As we walk in the Spirit we will also bear the fruit of love, with patience as one of its components. (see Galatians 5:22).

Another important characteristic of the God-kind of love is kindness. God's kindness is expressed to us in Christ. (see Ephesians 2:7; Titus 3:4). His lovingkindness is everlasting. (see Isaiah 54:10; Jeremiah 31:3; Psalm 89:33). The Bible says we are not to disregard or show contempt for the riches of God's kindness, forbearance and patience, but are to know or recognize that God's kindness is intended to lead us to repentance. (see Romans 2:4). As believers or God's chosen people, holy and dearly loved, we are admonished to clothe ourselves with compassion, KINDNESS, humility, gentleness and patience, bearing with one another, and forgiving one another, even as Christ forgave us. (see Colossians 3:12-13). When we walk in love by allowing the love of God to flow through us, we will be kind to others.

Yet another characteristic of the God-kind of love is that it does not envy and it does not boast. This is why Paul reproached the Corinthian Church when he learned that there was ENVY, strife divisions and boasting among them (see 1 Corinthians 3:1-4), and he admonished them to not boast in men (see 1 Corinthians 3:21). "Therefore, as it is written: "Let the one who boasts boast in the Lord." (1 Corinthians 1:31).

Love is also not easily angered. Hence the Bible exhorts us to be slow to anger. (see James 1:19). The Bible says, "Do not be quickly provoked in your spirit, for anger resides in the lap of fools." (Ecclesiastes 7:9 NIV). Being slow to anger is also an important requirement for anyone who desires to be an overseer among the flock of Christ. (see Titus 1:7). The Bible says, "The discretion of a man makes him slow to anger, and his glory is to overlook a transgression." (Proverbs 19:11). If you want to be slow to anger, use your discretion, overlook people's wrongs or offenses, for this is your glory.

Now, this brings us to the next important characteristic of the God-kind of love: "**Love keeps no record of wrongs.**" (see 1 Corinthians 13:5). We are talking about God's kind of love here, and so God does not keep record of the wrongs of those who have accepted His love which is in Christ Jesus. The Bible says "that God was reconciling the world to himself IN Christ, NOT COUNTING PEOPLE'S SINS AGAINST THEM. And He has committed to us the message of reconciliation." (2 Corinthians 5:19 NIV). Therefore if you are IN Christ today, know that God is not counting your sins against you. It is not God's nature to keep record of the sins of those who have accepted His love WHICH IS IN CHRIST JESUS. And so if you're a sincere believer today, God has promised that He will remember your sins and lawless deeds NO MORE. (see Jeremiah 31:34; Hebrews 10:17; Hebrews 8:12; Isaiah 43:25; Romans 4:8). Beloved, if God your Father is not counting your sins against you, why must you count other people's sins against them? "Be merciful, just as your Father is merciful" (Luke 6:36 NIV), because you share His nature. (see 2 Peter 1:4; Ephesians 4:24). Love does not keep record of wrongs, so walk in love by forgiving those who offend you and forgetting their wrongs. Some people often say, "I have forgiven you but I will never forget." No, that's wrong. Forgive and forget the wrongs of others, just as God has done and continues to do for you.

Indeed love is the greatest gift God has given us in Christ Jesus, because love is God Himself. The Bible says, "And now these three remain: **faith, hope** and **love**. But **the greatest** of these is **LOVE**." (1 Corinthians 13:13 NIV). Let us, therefore, hold on to love and operate in love above all other gifts. We are to FOLLOW THE WAY OF LOVE, even as we eagerly desire spiritual gifts, especially that we may prophesy. (see 1 Corinthians 14:1). We are to watch, stand fast in the faith, be brave, be strong, and do all that we do WITH LOVE. (see 1 Corinthians 16:13-14). In fact, regardless of how great the spiritual gifts you operate in, regardless of how much you prophesy and understand all mysteries and all knowledge, regardless of how much you speak in all manner of tongues (or languages), regardless of how much you exercise great faith to perform great miracles, or how you make the biggest charitable donations to the poor, and even offer yourself to be burned, if you do not have love or are not walking in love, you're nothing, and all your works will profit you nothing. (see 1 Corinthians 13:1-3). If you're not loving the brethren as yourself and using your spiritual gifts in love to edify the church, you are simply worthless, you're nothing, and you gain nothing. "Even so you, since you are zealous for spiritual gifts, let it be **for the edification of the church** that you seek to excel." (1 Corinthians 14:12). Amen.

It is Easy for the Believer to Walk in Love

Beloved, it is easy for the believer to walk in love. We have quoted repeatedly the Bible verse that says, **"THE LOVE OF GOD has been poured out in our hearts by the Holy Spirit who was given to us."** (see Romans 5:5). Notice here that it is "the love of God" that has been poured out in your heart, not the love of man. So this love in your heart came fully loaded with all the characteristics of love discussed above. When you have the revelation that "the love of God" is truly in your heart, you are seated well. Then walking in love becomes easy. You are simply to walk by letting "the love of God" which has been poured out in your heart, flow through you, instead of "trying" to love.

When we allow the love of Christ to flow through us, when we let loose the love of God that is in us, the righteous requirements of the law will be fulfilled in us without us "trying" to fulfill them. Hence, the Bible says, "Be ye therefore followers of God, as dear children; And walk in love, AS CHRIST ALSO HATH LOVED US, and hath given himself for us an offering and a sacrifice to God for a sweetsmelling savour. But fornication, and all uncleanness, or covetousness, let it not be once named among you, as becometh saints; Neither filthiness, nor foolish talking, nor jesting, which are not convenient: but rather giving of thanks." (Ephesians 5:1-4 KJV). Many (legalistic) Christians often read these verses and say, "You see, you're to love; you're not to fornicate; you're not to covet," etc. And all these are true, but they miss the whole point and the revelation which is the basis of these instructions. The truth that needs to be emphasized here again and again is that we cannot love through our self-efforts under the law. No one under the Old Covenant could keep the law that required them to love their neighbor as themselves. Under the Old Covenant, God demanded love from sinful man. And until Jesus came to fulfill the law, no man could love the way God had commanded them to. But thanks be to God, under the New Covenant, Jesus supplies us with love first, and then commands us to share it with others. We ought to be seated first in the love of God for us, which is in Christ. We ought to have the revelation in Ephesians 5:2, which actually says to "walk in love, AS CHRIST HAS ALSO LOVED US." Thus we have to first know (as we have repeatedly stated) how Christ has loved us. Paul prayed in Ephesians 3:14-19 that you may know the width, length, depth and height of the love of Christ towards you. This is the opposite of Deuteronomy 6:5 which focuses on man's power to love (or the lack thereof). First John 4:19 says, "We love Him because He first loved us."

When one walks in the love of Christ, one does not harm others nor himself by indulging in fornication, uncleanness, covetousness, filthiness, foolishness, coarse jesting, etc. It is when we leave the realm of love that we fall into the realm of selfishness and sin. But when we allow the Holy Spirit to guide us in love, our hearts will always be flooded with love, and we will not seek our own interests but the interest of others, for love does not seek its own. (See 1 Corinthians 13:4).

The realm of love is where prayers are answered. And so John writes, "My little children, let us not love in word or in tongue, but in deed and in truth. And by this we know that we are of the truth, and shall assure our hearts before Him. For if our heart condemns us, God is greater than our heart, and knows all things. Beloved, if our heart does not condemn us, we have confidence toward God. AND

Spirit Life

WHATEVER WE ASK WE RECEIVE FROM HIM, BECAUSE WE KEEP HIS COMMANDMENTS and do those things that are pleasing in His sight. AND THIS IS His COMMANDMENT: that we should **BELIEVE on the name of His Son Jesus Christ** AND **LOVE ONE ANOTHER, as He gave us commandment.**" (I John 3:18-23). What this means is that regardless of how many promises of God you plead, if you are not walking in love, your prayer life will be a failure, because your heart will condemn you before God, and thus affect your confidence or faith toward Him. Jesus said that you should first be reconciled to your brother (who has something against you), and then come and offer your gift to God. (see Matthew 5:23-24). The Psalmist says, "If I had cherished sin in my heart, the Lord would not have listened; but God has surely listened and has heard my prayer." (Psalm 66:18-19 NIV). Your prayers will not be effective if you're cherishing sin in your heart, or asking with the wrong motive (see James 4:3). Your prayers will also not be effective until you know God's will (expressed in His Word) and ask everything according to His will. (see 1 John 5:14-15; James 4:3). Beloved, if you walk in love, you will never pray with wrong motives, and your heart will never condemn you before God, and thus whatever you ask, you will receive, and your life will be a pleasing aroma of thanksgiving to God. Indeed, we can only walk in love when we give up on our self-efforts under the law, and submit to the will and control of the Holy Spirit who is in us. For those who are led by the Spirit are not under the law. (see Galatians 5:18). May you be led by the Spirit to walk worthy of your calling to love.

Today, you can rest secure in God's unfailing love. You can personalize Christ's love and experience more of His love the way John the disciple did. You can see yourself as "The disciple whom Jesus loved" (John 13:23, 20:2, 21:7, 21:20). Personalize Jesus' love, so that you can be conscious of His love and experience it afresh at all times. Today, you can call yourself "God's beloved child," and share God's love wherever you go. The Bible says, "But whoever has this world's goods, and sees his brother in need, and shuts up his heart from him, how does the love of God abide in him?" (1 John 3:17). We demonstrate our sincere love for the brethren by sharing the world's goods or our possessions (such as land, houses, money, food, clothing) with those in need. We cannot be selfish. The moment we come into Christ, love must dethrone selfishness and greed, and love must reign in our lives. We cannot cling to the world's goods and watch our brethren lack and suffer hunger. The world's goods should only be of value to us inasmuch as we are able to share them with the needy. In the early years of the Church immediately following the outpouring of the Holy Spirit on the Day of Pentecost the believers were very conscious of the love of Christ and demonstrated love for one another to a degree that still confounds many people today. The first mention of this demonstration of love is in the Second Chapter of the Book of Acts. "And with many other words he (Peter) testified and exhorted them, saying, "Be saved from this perverse generation." Then THOSE WHO GLADLY RECEIVED his WORD WERE BAPTIZED; and that day ABOUT THREE THOUSAND SOULS were added to them. And they continued steadfastly in the apostles' doctrine and FELLOWSHIP, in the breaking of bread, and in prayers. Then fear came upon every soul, and many wonders and signs were done through the apostles. Now ALL WHO BELIEVED WERE TOGETHER, AND HAD ALL THINGS IN COMMON, and SOLD THEIR POSSESSIONS AND GOODS, and DIVIDED

THEM AMONG ALL, AS ANYONE HAD NEED. So continuing daily WITH ONE ACCORD in the temple, and BREAKING BREAD FROM HOUSE TO HOUSE, THEY ATE THEIR FOOD WITH GLADNESS AND SIMPLICITY OF HEART, praising God and having favor with all the people. And the Lord added to the church daily those who were being saved." (Acts 2:40-47). Praise God! Here, we have a picture of what the new birth did to the men of the early church. After the love of God was poured out in their hearts by the Holy Spirit who was given to them, they yielded to the love of God that was in them and lived it to such impressive degree. They were all together (this is speaking of unity or togetherness), and had all things in common — they shared all things, caring for one another. Oh, how beautiful it is when believers yield to the lordship of love!

In fact, there is a second love scene recorded in the Fourth Chapter of the Book of Acts, which is also similar to the first. The Bible says, "Now THE MULTITUDE of those who believed WERE OF ONE HEART and ONE SOUL; NEITHER DID ANYONE SAY THAT ANY OF THE THINGS HE POSSESSED WAS HIS OWN, but THEY HAD ALL THINGS IN COMMON. And with great power the apostles gave witness to the resurrection of the Lord Jesus. And GREAT GRACE was upon them all. NOR WAS THERE ANYONE AMONG THEM WHO LACKED; for ALL who were POSSESSORS of lands or houses SOLD THEM, and BROUGHT THE PROCEEDS of the things that were sold, and laid them at the apostles' feet; AND THEY DISTRIBUTED TO EACH AS ANYONE HAD NEED." (Acts 4:32-35).

It is simply an amazing miracle when a multitude of people — selfish men that had lived all their lives to make money and acquire wealth and possessions for themselves, like all natural men do — suddenly give up all their possessions, sharing with others, having ALL THINGS IN COMMON, and no man saying that what he possessed was his own. It is just awesome! And no man can love this way who does not have the love of God in his heart. This is a perfect picture of what happens when the children of God let loose the love of God that has been poured out in our hearts. This early body of believers lived in manifestation of the God-kind of love. They must have recognized that God (Love) was indeed at work within them, willing and working for His good pleasure. (see Philippians 2:13). And so they yielded to Him. They must have known and believed that indeed they were overcomers, because greater is He (God, Love) who is in them, than he (Satan, Hatred and Selfishness) who is in the world. (see 1 John 4:4). Therefore they overcame selfishness. There was no selfishness whatsoever among them. It was an awesome work of God! Just beautiful!

The Curious Case of Ananias and Sapphira

But then, Satan who hates all things beautiful, plotted to destroy the work of God, just like he tried to do when Jesus began His earth ministry. You would recall that immediately after Jesus' baptism and after the Holy Spirit came upon Him, the Spirit led Him into the wilderness to be tempted by Satan (the devil), as Satan tried as hard as he could to derail Jesus from His mission here on earth and to destroy the mighty work God was to accomplish in Him. But Satan failed; Jesus would not bow or yield to Satan. (see Matthew 4). This was Satan's first failed attempt to destroy the work of God in Christ after He started His earthly ministry.

Then, when Jesus first informed His disciples about the death He was about to suffer, be buried and rise again on the third day, Satan again creeped in through the apostle Peter in an attempt to dissuade Jesus from accomplishing the new work God was to accomplish in Him. But Jesus, immediately discerning the voice of Satan in Peter, rebuked him. (see Matthew 16:21-23; Mark 8:31-33).

Here again in the early church, God had begun **a new work** of establishing **the love way of life** on earth through the Church. And Satan again sought to destroy this new work of God, because you see, without love (agape), the Christian way of life will be an empty way of life like the world's way of life. Thus Satan cunningly creeped into the midst of the believers by filling the heart of Ananias and Sapphira with selfishness and lies, in an attempt to destroy this awesome work of God, to destroy this precious gift of love that these believers had for one another. The Bible says, "But a certain man named ANANIAS, with SAPPHIRA **his wife**, SOLD A POSSESSION. And HE KEPT BACK PART OF THE PROCEEDS, HIS WIFE ALSO BEING AWARE OF IT, and BROUGHT A CERTAIN PART AND LAID IT AT THE APOSTLES' FEET. But Peter said, "Ananias, WHY HAS SATAN FILLED YOUR HEART TO LIE to the Holy Spirit AND KEEP BACK PART OF THE PRICE OF THE LAND FOR YOURSELF? While it remained, was it not your own? And after it was sold, was it not in your own control? WHY HAVE YOU CONCEIVED THIS THING IN YOUR HEART? You have not lied to men but to God." Then ANANIAS, hearing these words, FELL DOWN AND BREATHED HIS LAST. So great fear came upon all those who heard these things. And the young men arose and wrapped him up, carried him out, and BURIED HIM. Now it was about three hours later when his wife came in, not knowing what had happened. And Peter answered her, "Tell me whether you sold the land for so much?" She said, "Yes, for so much." Then Peter said to her, "HOW IS IT THAT YOU HAVE AGREED TOGETHER TO TEST the Spirit of the Lord? Look, the feet of those who have buried your husband are at the door, and they will carry you out." Then IMMEDIATELY SHE FELL DOWN AT HIS FEET AND BREATHED HER LAST. And the young men came in and FOUND HER DEAD, and carrying her out, buried her by her husband. So GREAT FEAR came upon ALL THE CHURCH and upon ALL WHO HEARD THESE THINGS." (Acts 5:1-11).

Evidently, Satan's plan failed. Peter, through the gift of the discernment of spirits, saw the spirit of hypocrisy — the lies and selfishness — Satan was trying to bring into their midst through these beloved brethren Ananias and Sapphira. And he stopped it instantly by the power of God. Peter thus judged (by the Spirit of God in Him) that it was better for Ananias and Sapphira to die than for them to corrupt the entire Church with this spirit of hypocrisy. Ananias and Sapphira had become the leaven (the hypocrisy and corrupting influence) in the church, and thus needed to be purged out so that they would not leaven (or corrupt) the entire Church. In their walk with Jesus, the apostles (including Peter) were often warned by Jesus to beware of the leaven (which is hypocrisy — the doctrine) of the Pharisees and Sadducees, and Herod. (see Matthew 16:6; Mark 8:15; Luke 12:1-3; Matthew 16:12). And so Peter, accordingly, had developed a quick discernment and strong distaste for any form of leaven, as evident from his response to Ananias and Sapphira. Paul also in writing to the Churches of Galatia warned them that "A little leaven leavens the whole lump," (see Galatians 5:9), and he called for judgment upon whoever was leavening or corrupting the churches in Galatia, whoever was persuading them or hindering them from obeying the truth. (see Galatians 5:7,10). Again, when Paul received reports that there was sexual immorality among the Corinthian Church as is not even named among the Gentiles (or unbelievers) — that a man in their church was even sleeping with his father's wife — he scolded the entire church for being puffed up rather than mourning that he who had done this deed MIGHT BE TAKEN AWAY FROM AMONG THEM. (see 1 Corinthians 5:1-3). And so Paul judged the man who had committed such abominable act, and commanded that, "In the name of our Lord Jesus Christ, when you are gathered together, along with my spirit, WITH THE POWER OF OUR LORD JESUS CHRIST, **DELIVER SUCH A ONE TO SATAN** FOR THE DESTRUCTION OF THE FLESH (body), that his spirit may be SAVED in the day of the Lord Jesus." (1 Corinthians 5:4-5). What Paul was basically saying here was that they should do to this man exactly what Peter did to Ananias and Sapphira; they should deliver him to Satan by the power of God, so that his body will be killed, and his spirit will be saved. As believers, our spirits are already saved, and so, until we commit the unpardonable sin of rejecting or denouncing Jesus Christ as our Lord and Savior and choosing instead to work for our own salvation, we remain saved, and any other sin we commit only affects our body and affects our ability to be effective witnesses for Christ. Hence, churches are commanded here to pray for the death or the destruction of the body of believers who are committing the kind of sins that hinder the work God has entrusted to us, and who are unrepentant about it. We are also to forgive them and reaffirm our love to them if they repent. (see 2 Corinthians 2:4-8; Galatians 6:1-2; Ephesians 4:32). Indeed, believers who continue in sin are a bad influence on other believers and a bad witness to Christ and for Christ. And so Peter (by the power of the Holy Spirit) gave Ananias and Sapphira over to Satan for the destruction of their body (see 1 Corinthians 5:5), but their spirits were saved, because they were believers.

The lesson in the story of Ananias and Sapphira is for believers to beware of leaven in our midst, just as Jesus repeatedly tells us in the four gospels. In that same Fifth Chapter of Paul's First letter to the Corinthians that we cited above, Paul gave to the Corinthian Church the same warning he gave to the churches in Galatia. He said, "Your glorying is not good. Do you not know that A LITTLE LEAVEN LEAVENS THE WHOLE LUMP? Therefore **PURGE OUT THE OLD LEAVEN**, THAT YOU MAY BE A NEW LUMP, since you truly are UNLEAVENED. For indeed Christ, our Passover, was sacrificed for us. Therefore let us keep the feast, not with old leaven, nor with THE LEAVEN OF MALICE and WICKEDNESS, but with the UNLEAVENED BREAD of SINCERITY and TRUTH." (1 Corinthians 5:6-8). We all as believers are to walk in the truth and conduct ourselves with all sincerity and truth, not resorting to any acts of malice and wickedness.

Now, I know someone may say, "I thought we were under grace; how could people be killed for sin?" Yes, we are under grace, but as Paul tells us in the sixth chapter of his letter to the Romans, grace is not a license to sin. Jesus, in His letter to the lukewarm church in Revelation 3:19 says, "As many as I love, I rebuke and chasten. Therefore, be zealous and **repent**." There are many believers (even preachers) who believe that preaching more grace will lead people to sin, or as they like to put it, "give people a license to sin." But the truth is that preaching the gospel of grace (which is the only gospel regardless) won't give people permission to sin, if we rightly divide the Word of truth and let believers know the consequence of sinning under grace. Even in the apostle Paul's time, there were people who raised such concerns about grace giving people a license to sin, to which Paul responded by saying, "What shall we say, then? Shall we go on sinning so that grace may increase? By no means! We died to sin; how can we live in it any longer?" (Romans 6:1-2). We Christians, as new creations (see 2 Corinthians 5:17), are no longer slaves to sin but slaves to righteousness in Christ (see Romans 6:18). As people who are born of the Spirit (see John 3:5-6), live in the Spirit (see Romans 8:9), are to be led by the Spirit and are to walk in the Spirit (see Galatians 5:18, with Romans 8:14, Galatians 5:25, Romans 7:6), we bear and demonstrate the fruit of the Spirit (see Galatians 5:22-23) and not the acts of the flesh (see Galatians 5:19-21). No believer who has truly experienced God's amazing grace and understands the price Jesus paid for our salvation will continue to live in sin (see 1 Corinthians 6:20). Sinning under grace is a mark of hypocrisy; it is a sign that you are living according to the flesh and not according to the Spirit. And the Bible warns that, "if you live according to the flesh YOU WILL DIE; but if by the Spirit you put to death the deeds of the body, you will live." (Romans 8:13). Ananias and Sapphira died when they lived according to the flesh, just as the Bible warns will happen to all who live as such. The apostle Peter also writes that, "the Lord knows how to deliver the godly out of temptations and to reserve the unjust (in this context, the false teachers and false believers) under punishment for the day of judgment, and ESPECIALLY THOSE WHO WALK ACCORDING TO THE FLESH in the lust of uncleanness and despise authority..." (see 2 Peter 2:9-10).

You may also recall that, under grace (that is, before the days of Moses through whom the Law was given), Judah's firstborn son (Er), who was judged as wicked in the sight of God, was killed; THE LORD KILLED HIM. (see Genesis 38:7). Then afterwards, when Er's wife and widow, Tamar, was given into marriage to Onan (Er's brother) so that Onan would raise up an heir for his brother, the Bible says that Onan, knowing that the heir would not be his — that is, any children he will have with Tamar will not be considered his own children, but his brother Er's children — when he went to sleep with his brother's wife, he practiced the birth control method that is known today as Coitus interruptus; Onan, to avoid having children for his brother, emitted his semen on the ground, instead of into her. (see Genesis 38:8-9). Now, mind you, all the children born along the line of Abraham, Isaac and Jacob were born to God, they were to be God's chosen people; so this malicious act committed by Onan was actually thwarting or hindering God's new work on earth of raising a people for Himself. So the Bible says, "And the thing which he (Onan) did displeased the Lord; **therefore He (the Lord) killed him also.**" (Genesis 38:10). Onan was killed by God because God had to stop or purge out the leaven (or that hypocrisy) from leavening the whole lump (or that whole family of men that the Lord had chosen). God would not allow that kind of bad precedence to go unnoticed or unpunished. And so, under grace, God purged out the leaven, just as He did with Ananias and Sapphira, and continues to do in the Church today.

Indeed, grace does not give us the license to sin. Grace elevates us and empowers us to walk in the Spirit and not according to the flesh, and when we do so, we effortlessly walk in good works which God prepared beforehand that we should walk in them. (see Ephesians 2:10). Paul in his letter to Titus says, "This is a faithful saying, and these things I want you to **affirm constantly**, that those who have believed in God should **be careful to maintain good works**. These things are good and profitable to men." (Titus 3:8). In the New Testament, Ananias and Sapphira, and the man in the Corinthian Church whose name was not given, were not the only ones who were purged out from the church for not maintaining good works. Paul again tells us in his first letter to Timothy about how he (Paul) had delivered Hymenaeus and Alexander to Satan "that they may learn not to blaspheme." (see 1 Timothy 1:19-20). Unlike Ananias and Sapphira and the man in the Corinthian Church, Hymenaeus and Alexander had even rejected the faith and blasphemed, and so their case was even worse. The Bible says, "If the righteous (that is, believers) receive their due on earth, how much more the ungodly and the sinner (that is, the unbelievers)!" (Proverbs 11:31 NIV). Whatever we do in our body here on earth, is rewarded or punished. And as believers (called to practice righteousness), we even suffer more in life for doing good, which makes it even more difficult to live a godly life; there's no way we could survive a day of the Christian walk, if not for the help of the Holy Spirit who is in us. The Bible forewarns us that "We must go through many hardships to enter the kingdom of God." (see Acts 14:22). Indeed, we must all suffer as believers. Peter says, "But **let NONE** of you **suffer as** a murderer, a thief, an evildoer, or as a busybody in other people's matters. Yet if anyone SUFFERS AS A CHRISTIAN, let him NOT BE ASHAMED, but let him GLORIFY GOD IN THIS MATTER. For THE TIME HAS COME for JUDGMENT TO BEGIN AT THE HOUSE OF GOD; and if **it begins with US FIRST**, what will be the end of those who do not obey the gospel of God? Now "If THE RIGHTEOUS ONE IS SCARCELY SAVED, where will the ungodly and the sinner appear?" Therefore let those who suffer according to the will of God commit their souls to Him in doing good, as to a faithful Creator." (1 Peter 4:15-19).

Again, Peter says, "But the end of all things is at hand; therefore be serious and watchful in your prayers. And ABOVE ALL THINGS HAVE **FERVENT LOVE** FOR ONE ANOTHER, for "LOVE WILL COVER A MULTITUDE OF SINS." Be hospitable to one another without grumbling. As each one has received a gift, minister it to one another, as good stewards of the manifold grace of God. If anyone speaks, let him speak as the oracles of God. If anyone ministers, let him do it as with the ability which God supplies, that in all things God may be glorified through Jesus Christ, to whom belong the glory and the dominion forever and ever. Amen." (1 Peter 4:7-11). Love indeed covers (or prevents) a multitude of sins. (see also Proverbs 10:12). This is a restatement of the truth that love is the fulfillment of the law.

Beloved, when we walk in love, we will not sin. It is written of our blessed Lord Jesus, "Thou hast loved righteousness, and hated iniquity; therefore God, even thy God hath anointed thee with the oil of gladness above thy fellows." (see Psalm 45:7; Hebrews 1:9 KJV). We believers, since the Spirit of Christ dwells in us, should likewise love righteousness and hate iniquity. The Bible says that those that love the Lord are to hate evil. (see Psalm 97:10). The Bible also says that, God knows every man that loves Him. (see 1 Corinthians 8:3). So we cannot deceive or mock God. The Bible says, "Do not be deceived, God is not mocked; for whatever a man sows, that he will also reap. For he who sows to his flesh will of the flesh reap corruption, but he who sows to the Spirit will of the Spirit reap everlasting life. And let us not grow weary while doing good, for in due season we shall reap if we do not lose heart. Therefore, as we have opportunity, let us do good to all, especially to those who are of the household of faith." (Galatians 6:7-10). Again, "Death and destruction lie open before the Lord — how much more do human hearts!" (Proverbs 15:11 NIV). The Lord knows the thoughts and intents of our hearts. And the Bible says that when the Lord comes, He will both bring to light the hidden things of darkness and reveal the counsels (or motives) of the hearts. (see 1 Corinthians 4:5). We cannot claim to love God and love evil at the same time. No one can serve two masters. (see Matthew 6:24). Our duty as believers, then, is to encourage one another to walk in love, and rebuke those who stray from the Way of love. The Bible commands all of us who are overseers of the flock to **rebuke those who are sinning**, in the presence of all, so that the rest may fear. It says, "Those who are **sinning**, REBUKE in the PRESENCE of all, THAT THE REST also MAY FEAR." (1 Timothy 5:20). This was what Peter did with Ananias and Sapphira. And indeed, fear came upon the Church. (see Acts 5:5,11). And I believe from that point onwards among those early believers, at least for a decent length of time, the case of Ananias and Sapphira was a cautionary tale for all, against hypocrisy. And it is a caution to all of us also who are believers today. Let us walk in love, and we will not walk in fear. The Bible says, "There is no fear in love. But perfect love drives out fear, because fear has to do with punishment. The one who fears is not made perfect in love." (1 John 4:18 NIV). Beloved, God has not given us a spirit of fear, but of power and of LOVE and of a sound mind. (see 2 Timothy 1:7). We have the Spirit of LOVE. So let everything we do be for the sake of love. (see Philemon 1:9). Let our work or labor in Christ be the labor of love. (see Hebrews 6:10; 1 Thessalonians 1:3). Let brotherly love continue. (see Hebrews 13:1). Let us love as brethren. (see 1 Peter 3:8). "And let us consider one another in order to STIR UP LOVE and GOOD WORKS, not forsaking the assembling of ourselves together, as is the manner of some, but EXHORTING ONE ANOTHER, and so much the more as you see the Day approaching." (Hebrews 10:24-25).

"Now, May the Lord direct your hearts into the love of God and into the patience of Christ." (see 2 Thessalonians 3:5). "And may the Lord make you **increase and abound in love** to one another and to all, just as we do to you, so that He may establish your hearts blameless in holiness before our God and Father at the coming of our Lord Jesus Christ with all His saints." (1 Thessalonians 3:12-13). "Mercy, peace and love be multiplied to you." (Jude 1:2). Amen.

In the next chapter, we will continue to explore how to walk in the Spirit, with emphasis on walking in the light or walking in the newness of life. I am confident that by the end of this book, you will understand and appreciate the necessity of living and walking in the Spirit as a new creation, and why you can't afford to live or walk according to the flesh (or senses). "For if you live according to the flesh you will die; but if by the Spirit you put to death the deeds of the body, you will live." (Romans 8:13).

Chapter 18

The Spirit Walk: A Walk in the Light or in the Newness of Life

You are the Light of the World

JOHN WROTE THAT, "This is the message which we have heard from Him and declare to you, that **GOD IS LIGHT** and **IN Him** is NO DARKNESS AT ALL. If we say that WE HAVE FELLOWSHIP WITH Him, and WALK in DARKNESS, WE LIE and DO NOT PRACTICE the TRUTH. But if we WALK IN THE LIGHT as He is IN THE LIGHT, we have fellowship with one another, and the blood of Jesus Christ His Son cleanses us from all sin." (1 John 1:5-7). James also wrote that God is "THE FATHER OF LIGHTS, with whom there is no variation or shadow of turning." (see James 1:17). We believers are the lights God the Father has given birth to. God is Light and the Father of lights; and we are lights and the children of Light. (see 1 Thessalonians 5:5). Jesus affirmed this when He said, "YOU ARE THE LIGHT OF THE WORLD. **A city that is set on a hill** cannot be hidden. Nor do they light a lamp and put it under a basket, but on a lampstand, and it gives light to all who are in the house. LET YOUR LIGHT SO SHINE BEFORE MEN, **that they may see YOUR GOOD WORKS** and GLORIFY YOUR FATHER

IN HEAVEN." (Matthew 5:14-16). As believers, we were created to shine in the world as LIGHT to those who walk in darkness. Each of us is a city on a hill, which cannot be hidden. The Church is the lampstand or the hill from which we all shine as light in the world to give light to all and to bring glory to God our Father. (see Revelation 1:20). We shine by loving others as Jesus has loved us, by doing good, and by testifying about the Lord Jesus to every creature under heaven. The evidence that we are shining is that others see our good works and give glory to our Father in Heaven. The Bible says that God prepared these good works beforehand for us to walk in them. (see Ephesians 2:10). This means that although the good works we do are "our good works," they are actually produced by God in us and through us by the power of the Holy Spirit. Therefore, as long as we walk in the light (or walk according to the Word of God), as long as we walk in the Spirit, these good works will manifest in our lives to the glory of God. Hence, the Bible says we are the ones that have to maintain the good works. You cannot maintain what you don't already have, and so we have the good works already, and we are commanded to maintain them. Paul in his letter to Titus wrote: "This is a faithful saying, and these things I want you to affirm constantly, that THOSE WHO HAVE BELIEVED IN GOD SHOULD BE CAREFUL TO **MAINTAIN** GOOD WORKS. These things are good and profitable to men." (Titus 3:8). We are all to learn to maintain good works, to meet urgent needs, that we may not be unfruitful. (see Titus 3:14). And we maintain good works by abiding in Christ (the Vine) and allowing Him and His words to abide in us (see John 15:4-8), just as the branches of any vine maintain their production of fruits simply by abiding in the vine.

Beloved, Jesus Christ is the Light of the world. (see John 8:12). We are also the light of the world only because we are in Christ and Christ is in us. We are the light of the world because, as Jesus is, so are we in this world. (see 1 John 4:17). Therefore, as children of Light and the children of the Day (see 1 Thessalonians 5:5), we are only able to shine by abiding or remaining in the Light and walking in the Light. Jesus Himself said, "I am the vine, you are the branches. **He who abides in Me, and I in him,** BEARS MUCH FRUIT; for **without Me you can do nothing**." (John 15:5). In other words, we produce fruits (good works) or we shine by simply abiding in Jesus Christ; and without Jesus, we can do nothing. We cannot shine or produce good works without Jesus. The Psalmist says, "For with You is the fountain of life; **in Your light we see light**." (see Psalm 36:9). Just as a light bulb produces light or shines by being plugged into the source of light (or the source of power), we also produce light or shine by being plugged into Jesus our Source of power and light. (see Ephesians 5:8). Being plugged into the Word of God is how we get plugged into Jesus, because Jesus is the Word of God. (see John 1:1, 14; Revelation 19:13). The Psalmist says, "Your word is a lamp to my feet and a light to my path." (Psalms 119:105). Indeed the Word of God is the Source of our power or ability to shine as the light of the world; it is a lamp to our feet and a light to our path. Paul, in his letter to the Romans wrote that the Gospel of Christ is THE POWER OF GOD to salvation for everyone who believes. (see Romans 1:16). When we read, meditate and act on or do the Word of Christ, we will always find and walk in the path of life (see Psalm 16:11), and we will manifest as the light of the world.

Jesus said that the blind cannot lead the blind. (see Luke 6:39). Therefore we need to have understanding (of the Word) just like our Teacher Jesus. (see Luke 6:40). Those who walk in darkness cannot lead others, or they will both be lost. It is only when we walk in the light (or understanding) of God's Word that we will know where we are going (see John 12:35) and be able to lead others as well. The Word of God is Jesus Christ Himself. (see John 1:1, 14; Revelation 19:13). Jesus Christ (the Word) gives us light (see Ephesians 5:14). We have to draw from the life of Jesus; we have to have the revelation that the Word is in us (see 1 John 2:14), that Christ is in us (see Colossians 1:27), that Life is in us (see 1 John 5:12-13), that Light is in us (see Matthew 5:14), that Power is in us (see Ephesians 1:19-20). We have to let the Word of Christ dwell in us richly in all wisdom. (see Colossians 3:16). If indeed Christ lives in us, then we have to have the revelation that Light lives in us, and there is no darkness at all in us. As anointed children of God, we can only demonstrate the same power Jesus demonstrated during His earth walk and do the same works He did and even greater works than He did (see John 14:12), when we are conformed to His character through the renewal of our mind with the Word of God, loving righteousness and hating evil. The intensity with which our light will shine before men for them to see our good works and glorify our Father in heaven thus depends on how much we DESIRE and actually FEED on the sincere milk of the Word (the Bible), as well as how much we actually DO the Word or act on the Word; it depends on how well we are plugged into Jesus who is the Word of God.

Shine By Abiding in Jesus and Allowing Him to Abide in You

Truly we cannot shine or produce light unless we have the revelation of the Word of God and walk in the knowledge, understanding and wisdom of the Word of God. Jesus Christ is the source of our power, He is the source of light; and we only walk in the light by abiding in Him, drawing from Him and allowing Him to live and shine in us and through us. (see Galatians 2:20). We cannot claim to believe or abide in Jesus Christ and venerate or bow to idols at the same time. That amounts to idolatry and a rejection or renunciation of Jesus Christ. Paul said, "Do not be unequally yoked together with unbelievers. For what fellowship has righteousness with lawlessness? And WHAT COMMUNION HAS LIGHT WITH DARKNESS? And what accord has Christ with Belial (Satan)? Or what part has a believer with an unbeliever? And **WHAT AGREEMENT HAS THE TEMPLE OF GOD WITH IDOLS**? For you are the temple of the living God. As God has said: "I will dwell in them And walk among them. I will be their God, and they shall be My people." THEREFORE "COME OUT FROM AMONG THEM AND BE SEPARATE, says the Lord. Do not touch what is unclean, And I will receive you." "I will be a Father to you, And you shall be My sons and daughters, says the Lord Almighty." (2 Corinthians 6:14-18). Indeed light has nothing to do with darkness. As believers we cannot be unequally yoked together with unbelievers, we cannot be conformed to the way of life of unbelievers. Believers have nothing to do with idols. As believers (who are also the temple of God), we can have nothing to do with idols (or carved images); we cannot venerate or use idols in worship. John said, "And we know that the Son of God has come and has given us AN UNDERSTANDING, that we may KNOW Him WHO IS TRUE;

and we are IN Him WHO IS TRUE, in His Son Jesus Christ. This is the True God and Eternal Life. Little children, **KEEP YOURSELVES FROM IDOLS**. Amen." (1 John 5:20-21). If we have truly received the understanding the Lord Jesus Christ has given us, and if we truly know the one True God and Eternal Life, then we will keep ourselves from idols. It certainly doesn't matter what name you call an idol (or a carved image); it doesn't matter even if you call it Jesus Christ or Mary, God still hates it. God says it is an abomination for you to be associated with idols, to make them, bow to them, pray to them or honor them in any way. "WHAT AGREEMENT HAS THE TEMPLE OF GOD WITH IDOLS?" He asks. "What accord has Christ with Satan?" The Bible says, "For you were once darkness, **but now you are light in the Lord**. Walk as children of light (for the fruit of the Spirit is in all goodness, righteousness, and truth), finding out what is acceptable to the Lord. And **have no fellowship with the unfruitful works of darkness**, but rather **expose** them." (Ephesians 5:8-11). We have to believe in Jesus Christ only and worship the one true God. John said, "In Him (Jesus Christ) was life, and the life was the light of men. And the light shines in the darkness, and the darkness did not comprehend it." (John 1:4-5). Those of us who sincerely believe in Jesus have His life in us (see 1 John 5:11-12), and this life is the light of men which shines in the darkness, and which the darkness does not comprehend. We have to abide or remain in Jesus and in His Word and allow Jesus and His Word to abide in us in order for His life to flow through us and for His light to shine through us in this dark world. And as we shine as light in this world, we will expose the unfruitful works of darkness.

Abiding in the Lord Jesus Christ also means surrendering our bodies, our wills and ambitions to His will and purpose for our lives, thereby allowing Him to work in us to will and to do for His good pleasure. (see Philippians 2:13). It means walking in the good works, which God prepared beforehand that we should walk in them. (see Ephesians 2:10). It means walking according to the Word of God. We have to deny ourselves or totally surrender our bodies to God for His use. Or as Paul puts it, we have to "die daily." (see 1 Corinthians 15:31). We have to present or offer our members (i.e. all parts of our body) as instruments of righteousness to God. (see Romans 6:13). After all, Christ is the Savior of our body (see Ephesians 5:23). And as Savior of the body, the body belongs to Him. And so Paul writes that the body is for the Lord, and the Lord for the body. (see 1 Corinthians 6:13). Therefore, we are to give to the Lord that which rightfully belongs to Him. Our reasonable service today is to offer our bodies as a living sacrifice, holy, acceptable to God (see Romans 12:1), because we are not our own, for we were bought at a price; therefore we are to glorify God in our body and in our spirit, which are God's. (see 1 Corinthians 6:19-20). Truly, the body is for the Lord; it is not for ourselves nor for anyone else, especially the devil. The devil has no part in us, and the Bible says that we should give no place to the devil. (see Ephesians 4:27). We should give no place to the works of the devil such as sin, sickness and disease. We should "have no fellowship with the unfruitful works of darkness, but rather **expose** them." (see Ephesians 5:11).

In fact, without "dying daily" or crucifying (by the Spirit) the deeds of the flesh, there is no experiencing or laying hold of the victory Christ has won for us. (see Romans 8:13). Paul said, "We always carry around **in our BODY the death of Jesus**, so that **the LIFE of Jesus**

may also be revealed in OUR BODY. For we who are alive are always being given over to death for Jesus' sake, so that **His life may also be revealed in our mortal body."** (2 Corinthians 4:10-11 NIV). Thus, as we walk in the Spirit and not according to the lusts of the flesh, the life of Jesus is being revealed or manifested in our mortal body. And so the only people who have genuine authority over the devil and experience in this age the fullness of the life or the victory that is in Christ Jesus, are those who choose the way of the cross and dying daily, who give no place to the devil. Paul said, "But I discipline my body and bring it into subjection, lest, when I have preached to others, I myself should become disqualified." (I Corinthians 9:27). Crucifying the flesh or disciplining your body and bringing it into subjection is not something God does for you; it is something you do for yourself (see Romans 12:1), not by willpower, but by the (help of the) Spirit. (see Romans 8:13). You have to yield to the Spirit as He empowers and strengthens you and guides or leads you in the paths of righteousness for His name's sake. You have to yield to the Spirit and follow the leading of the Spirit of God, "For as many as are led by the Spirit of God, these are sons of God." (Romans 8:14). It is also important to understand that the Holy Spirit will never lead you apart from the Word of God; He will never contradict the Word of God. This is why you have to know and understand the Word of God, so that you can discern the voice of the Spirit and heed His leading.

Also, it is by renewing your mind (with the Word of God) through the help of the Holy Spirit, that you will be transformed (in bodily conduct and from glory to glory), not conforming to this world. (see Romans 12:2). Therefore, feed on the Word of God and be renewed in your mind "until Christ is formed in you" (bodily), until the life of

Christ is revealed or manifested in your mortal body, until you come to maturity, to a complete man, to the measure of the stature of the fullness of Christ. (see Ephesians 4:13). It is to this end also, that I am sharing the Word of God with you "My little children, for whom I labor in birth again until Christ is formed in you." (Galatians 4:19).

Beloved, when you truly abide in Christ, and His Word abides in you, you can say with Paul: "I can do all things through Christ who strengthens me." (Philippians 4:13). "He must increase, but I must decrease" or "Less of me and more of you Lord" is good — for beginners. But when you can say, like Paul, that "none of me and all of you Lord," or "it is no longer I who live, but Christ lives in me," then you have arrived. Live a life that is surrendered to Christ, by offering your body as a living sacrifice, holy, acceptable to the Lord. (see Romans 12:1-2). Allow Christ to shine through you, instead of struggling to shine (through your own efforts at keeping the Law). Through false doctrines, many Christians have been taught to try to shine through their own efforts under the law, instead of by faith or reliance on the power of the Holy Spirit which has been given to us. And to such people, the apostle Paul asks, "This only I want to learn from you: Did you receive the Spirit by the WORKS OF THE LAW, or by the hearing of FAITH? Are you so foolish? Having begun in the Spirit, are you now being made perfect by the flesh?" (Galatians 3:2-3). Indeed, the Christian walk is a walk of faith. "For we walk by faith, not by sight." (II Corinthians 5:7). When, by faith, you consistently yield or surrender to the Spirit of Christ, follow Him and allow Him to work in you His own will and purpose, your light will so shine before men, that they may see your good works and glorify your Father in heaven. Indeed, you will shine wherever there is darkness, preaching the gospel to the poor, bringing healing to the brokenhearted, proclaiming liberty to the captives and recovery of sight to the blind, and setting at liberty those who are oppressed, loving others as Jesus has loved you, doing good or practicing righteousness.

Moreover, the Bible says that you shouldn't avoid or forsake the gathering of believers (see Hebrews 10:25). This is also important because the Church (the Body of Christ) is the lampstand (see Revelation 1:20) or the hill from which we all shine as light in the world to bring glory to God our Father.

Indeed it is utterly important to understand that, as a believer, you cannot walk in the same way as the unbelievers do; you cannot walk according to the flesh (or live according to the lusts or desires and passions of your body); you cannot walk in the dark dungeon of sin, because you are no longer under the dominion of Satan and sin; you have been delivered or rescued from the power of darkness, and translated or conveyed into the Kingdom of Light, into the Kingdom of God's dear Son. (see Colossians 1:13-14). You were rescued or set free so that you can live as a free man, so that you can live for freedom. (see Galatians 5:1; 1 Peter 2:16). True freedom, then, is when you allow Christ to live in you and to guide and direct your life. True freedom is when you submit to Christ and live as a slave of God, as a slave of Jesus Christ, as a slave of righteousness. Therefore, walk in the light by offering all parts of your body to God as instruments of righteousness. (see Romans 6:13). Walk in the light by walking in the truth (see 3 John 1:3-4), and by walking in good works, which God prepared beforehand that you should walk in them. (see Ephesians 2:10). Walk in the light by walking in love. (see Ephesians 5:2; 2 John 1:6). The Bible says, "Now the purpose of the commandment is LOVE from a pure heart, from a good conscience, and from sincere faith." (1 Timothy 1:5). Also, LOVE is the fulfillment of the law. (see Romans 13:10; Galatians 5:14). When you walk in love, you are walking in the light. And when you walk in the light, you do not walk in the darkness (of sin).

You are Dead to Sin, So Live For Righteousness

As new creations in Christ, the Bible says that we were baptized into the death of Christ (that is, the death He died to sin once for all); then we were buried with Him through baptism into death, "that just as Christ was raised from the dead by the glory of the Father, even so we also should walk in the newness of life." (see Romans 6:3-4). Hence we are dead to sin, but alive to God in Christ. (see Romans 6:11). Because we died to sin (with Christ), we can no longer live in sin. (see Romans 6:2). We have been raised with Christ to walk in love, to walk in the light, to walk in good works, to walk in righteousness, to walk in the newness of life, to walk in glory. Jesus Himself bore our sins in His own body on the tree, so that we, **having died to sins**, might **LIVE FOR RIGHTEOUSNESS**. (see 1 Peter 2:24). "Therefore **consider the members of your earthly body as dead to** immorality, impurity, passion, evil desire, and greed, which amounts to idolatry." (Colossians 3:5 NASB). Notice also in this verse that, in the eyes of God, idolatry is not limited to worshipping carved images and other creatures, but also includes practicing immorality, impurity, passion, evil desire, and greed. Therefore, if in this life we call ourselves believers and desire to be vessels for honor, sanctified and useful for the Master, prepared for every good work, then we have to depart from all manner of iniquity, and live a life that brings glory to God our Father. Paul in his second letter to Timothy said, "Nevertheless the solid foundation of God stands, having this seal: "The Lord knows those who are His," and, "LET EVERYONE WHO NAMES THE NAME OF CHRIST **DEPART FROM INIQUITY.**" But in a great house there are NOT only vessels of gold and silver, BUT also of wood and clay, some FOR HONOR and some FOR DISHONOR. Therefore IF ANYONE CLEANSES HIMSELF from the latter (that is, dishonor), he will be a vessel for honor, sanctified and USEFUL for the Master, PREPARED FOR EVERY GOOD WORK. Flee also youthful lusts; but PURSUE righteousness, faith, LOVE, peace with those who call on the Lord out of a pure heart." (2 Timothy 2:19-22). When we walk in love, we will not walk in selfishness, envy and pride; we will not sin, and we will flee youthful lusts — we will depart from iniquity, and make ourselves useful for the Master as vessels for honor, prepared for every good work. The Bible says, "For where envy and self-seeking exist, confusion and every evil thing are there." (James 3:16). This means that self-seeking, together with envy is the opposite of everything love stands for. Hence, the Bible says, "Owe no one anything EXCEPT TO LOVE ONE ANOTHER, for HE WHO LOVES ANOTHER HAS FULFILLED THE LAW. For the commandments, "You shall not commit adultery," "You shall not murder," "You shall not steal," "You shall not bear false witness," "You shall not covet," and if there is any other commandment, ARE ALL SUMMED UP in this saying, namely, "You shall LOVE your neighbor as yourself." Love does no harm to a neighbor; therefore LOVE IS THE FULFILLMENT OF THE LAW. And do this, knowing the time, that now it is high time to awake out of sleep; for now our salvation is nearer than when we first believed. The night is far spent, the day is at hand. Therefore let us CAST OFF THE WORKS OF DARKNESS, and LET US PUT

ON **THE ARMOR OF LIGHT**. Let us WALK PROPERLY, as IN THE DAY, not in revelry and drunkenness, not in lewdness and lust, not in strife and envy. But **PUT ON THE LORD JESUS CHRIST**, and **MAKE NO PROVISION for THE FLESH, to fulfill its lusts.**" (Romans 13:8-14).

Beloved, you cannot walk worthy of your calling in Christ or walk in the newness of life without first putting on the Lord Jesus Christ or knowing and being conscious of who you are in Christ, without first putting on the armor of light, without first knowing that you are the light of the world, without first knowing that you are a new creation created in true holiness and righteousness (see Ephesians 4:24), created in Christ Jesus for good works which God prepared beforehand that you should walk in them. (see Ephesians 2:10). Throughout the New Testament epistles, we are exhorted to rest in the reality of our NEW NATURE in Christ and to "die daily" and allow Christ to live in us. (see Galatians 2:20). We don't have to struggle to be like Jesus, because we are already as Jesus is in this world (see 1 John 4:17) — He is the Vine and we are the branches (see John 15:5); He is the Head and we are the Body. (see Colossians 1:18; 1 Corinthians 12:12, 27). We are one with the Lord in Spirit and in Body. (see 1 Corinthians 6:17; with 1 Corinthians 6:15). All we need to do then is to remain in Him and allow His life to be revealed in our body, to flow in us and through us. This is our true calling, and this is true Christianity! We are to walk in this world as the express image of the Lord Jesus Christ. We are to walk worthy of our calling (see Ephesians 4:1) — walk in love as Christ has loved us (see Ephesians 5:2); walk as children of light (see Ephesians 5:8-14); walk circumspectly, not as fools but as wise (see Ephesians 5:15); walk in newness of life (see Romans 6:4); walk in good works (see Ephesians 2:10); etc. Unfortunately believers who don't have a full revelation of who they are in Christ tend to approach each one of these instructions as a law or work to be accomplished by self-effort. But for the New Covenant believer, these are all good works that God has prepared beforehand for us to walk in them, through the power of the Holy Spirit who is in us.

In Ephesians 4:17-24, Paul tells believers: "This I say, therefore, and testify in the Lord, that you should NO LONGER WALK as the rest of the Gentiles walk, in the futility of their mind, having their understanding darkened, being alienated from the life of God, BECAUSE OF THE IGNORANCE THAT IS IN THEM, because of the BLINDNESS OF THEIR HEART; who, being past feeling, have given themselves over to lewdness, to work all uncleanness with greediness. BUT YOU have NOT so learned Christ, if indeed you have heard Him and have been taught by Him, as the truth is in Jesus: that you PUT OFF, concerning your former conduct, THE OLD MAN which grows corrupt according to the deceitful lusts, and **BE RENEWED IN THE SPIRIT OF YOUR MIND**, and that you **PUT ON THE NEW MAN** which was created according to God, in true righteousness and holiness." (Ephesians 4:17-24). The legalistic or carnal Christian, or the believer who walks "in the flesh" will read these verses and say, "You see, we must behave as Christians; we must work hard not to be lewd, unclean and greedy. This is what God requires of a Christian. We must keep the Law to be righteous and holy. If you do all of these in obedience to God, you will be blessed." Have you encountered that kind of thinking? That kind of approach would be similar to a baby trying to walk before learning how to sit!

When read in its context, however, it becomes clear from the verses that unbelievers walk in lewdness, uncleanness and greed because they DO NOT have the revelation of the gospel. Their MINDS have been DARKENED. You (the believer), however, HAVE **the revelation of the gospel**. When you believed in Jesus Christ, you became a new creation. You received a new nature in Christ — the new man. This new man is created in true righteousness and holiness (in the same nature as God). Your sinful self — called the old man has been crucified on the cross and no longer exists. Because you have this revelation, you have learned how to sit. Hence, these verses are not about a Christian trying to keep the law to try to be righteous and holy. Rather, it is about what Christ has already done — He has made you righteous and holy so that you can live a life of holiness, and practice righteousness. Therefore, your part is to know and believe (or rest in) this truth and be perpetually conscious of your holy and righteous identity. When you are conscious of your new identity in Christ, it means you have put on the NEW MAN, it means you have put on Christ. And the Holy Spirit (who is at work in you with the full power of God — see Philippians 2:13; Ephesians 3:20) will cause you to walk in your new nature — in true righteousness and holiness. This is what it means to walk in the Spirit and be "led by the Spirit." Those who keep the law to be righteous are walking "in the flesh" (or self-effort) and are not led by the Spirit. The Bible says that all of us who are led by the Spirit are not under the law (see Galatians 5:18). And because the Spirit leads us, we walk in the Spirit, and do not walk in the lusts of the flesh. (see Galatians 5:16). Galatians 5:24 emphasizes that, "**those who belong to Christ Jesus have crucified the flesh with its passions and desires.**" Thus, because we're led by the Spirit, we do not fulfill the desires and passions of the body; we walk in the fruit of the Spirit, which is LOVE, joy, peace, longsuffering, kindness, goodness, faithfulness, gentleness, self-control. (see Galatians 5:22-23). And the Bible says against the fruit of the Spirit, there is no law. In other words, there is no law against the fruit of the Spirit, there is no law against LOVE, joy, peace, longsuffering, kindness, goodness, faithfulness, gentleness, self-control; the fruit (love) is the fulfillment of the law.

As believers in Christ, our understanding is now enlightened so that we can walk circumspectly not as fools but as wise. (see Ephesians 5:15). We cannot be friends with the world (its lusts and pleasures) anymore. The Bible says that **friendship with the world is enmity with God**; and so whoever wants to be a friend of the world makes himself an enemy of God. (see James 4:4). As believers, we are in the world but not of the world (see John 15:19; John 17:16); we are of God. (see 1 John 4:4). God has put His Spirit in our hearts (see 2 Corinthians 1:22), so we have the Spirit of wisdom and revelation to open the eyes of our understanding. When we walk in the wisdom that the Spirit gives, it will reflect in our conduct. James asks, "Who is wise and understanding among you? Let him show **by good conduct** that his works are done in the meekness of wisdom." (James 3:13). Many Christians, rather than walk in the wisdom and understanding of God, try to walk in their own wisdom and understanding (that comes from self) — be it from their education, or years of life experiences. But the Bible says, "Trust in the Lord with all your heart, and **LEAN NOT on your OWN UNDERSTANDING**; In all your ways ACKNOWLEDGE Him, AND HE SHALL DIRECT YOUR PATHS. **Do NOT be wise in your OWN eyes**; Fear the Lord and DEPART FROM EVIL." (Proverbs 3:5-7). A person who trusts in his own wisdom will naturally reject the wisdom of God when God gives a new revelation or direction. Needless to say, that is a dangerous way to live. In all the wisdom of the learned Pharisees, they did not recognize Jesus as the Messiah (or the Christ). In all the wisdom of Saul (Paul), he persecuted the church of God, and he did it in all good conscience. (see Acts 22-23:1).

Before we can walk circumspectly as wise, we need to rest (or trust) in the fact that Wisdom is a person, that Jesus is our wisdom. Paul says, "But by His doing you are in Christ Jesus, who became to us WISDOM from God, and righteousness and sanctification, and redemption." (1 Corinthians 1:30 NASB). Jesus is our wisdom, and since Jesus lives in us, wisdom lives in us. The Spirit of wisdom and revelation is at work in us, and the Bible declares that we have the mind of Christ. (see 1 Corinthians 2:16). So when we rest in the reality of Christ living in us, when we depend on the Holy Spirit who is in us, we will begin to walk in true wisdom which is of God. And when we walk in the wisdom of God, we will not behave as fools by living in sin. We will walk as children of light, which we truly are. (see Ephesians 5:8-9).

A Miracle Happens When the Natural Man Comes to Christ

Today many believers struggle with sin because they're not operating by the Spirit of wisdom and revelation, and thus they haven't really caught the revelation of what happened to them when they came to Christ. Now, let's take a moment to retrace the steps that brought us to believe in Christ as our Lord and Savior and to receive the remission of our sins: If there is one thing our journeys to Christ have in common, it is the fact that it began with **repentance** (or the change of our mind) **from sin** and the empty way of life (when we heard the gospel), **to God** or to Christ and His righteousness. The Bible says, "He who covers his sins will not prosper, but whoever confesses and forsakes them will have mercy." (Proverbs 28:13). Again, the Bible says, "If we confess our sins, He is faithful and just to forgive us our sins and to cleanse us from all unrighteousness." (I John 1:9). And so, upon hearing the gospel, the Holy Spirit convicted us of sin and we repented and acknowledged or confessed that we were indeed sinners who needed mercy and forgiveness, who needed salvation. This was a necessary first step. Thus, First John 1:9 is talking about when the natural (or unregenerate) man first comes to Christ. We have explained in previous chapters of this book that the natural man (or the man who has not yet accepted Jesus Christ as his Lord and Savior, the man who is only born of the flesh and is not born of the Spirit) is a sinner and a child of the devil, regardless of how much good he has done and continues to do. In fact, he was born a sinner (see Psalm 51:5; Isaiah 48:8; Ephesians 2:3), and thus begins to sin as soon as he reaches the age where he knows the difference between right and wrong, because he has the devil working in him (see Ephesians 2:2-3). God said in Genesis 8:21 that the imagination of man's heart is evil from his youth (or childhood). When Adam fell into sin (see Genesis 3), none of us was born yet, and so we were all still in Adam's loins. Adam's name means "mankind," so when he sinned, mankind sinned. The Bible says we all became sinners through one man's (or Adam's) disobedience. (see Romans 5:18-19). By virtue of us being "in Adam," all die. (see 1 Corinthians 15:22). So sin entered the world through Adam, and death through sin, and thus death spread to all men, because all sinned. (see Romans 5:12-14). Hence, the natural man has Adam's sin nature in him, and thus sins. The natural man has no fellowship with God, which is why John is inviting him into fellowship with God. (see 1 John 1:3). The Bible says the natural man is alienated or cut off from God (see Colossians 1:21-23), and that he is BY NATURE a child of disobedience and a child of wrath. (see Ephesians 2:2-3; Colossians 3:6). Therefore when the natural man comes to Christ, he must first acknowledge that he is a sinner, and then repent of his sins. He must confess his sins or confess that he is a sinner who needs mercy and forgiveness. And when that confession is made, God is faithful and just to forgive that man his sins and to cleanse him from ALL unrighteousness. Notice that God chooses His words very carefully. He says He will cleanse that man from **ALL** unrighteousness. ALL means ALL. This is a one-time thing. When ALL is cleansed, there's NONE left to be cleansed. Even a child can understand this. And yet, Satan has blinded many people's understanding on this.

From the moment the natural man comes to Christ to confess that he is a sinner who needs forgiveness, and thus denounces sin and renounces Satan (his previous lord or master) and accepts and confesses Jesus as his (new) Lord (and Savior), that man is forgiven of ALL sins; he is eternally forgiven; he has eternal (not temporary) redemption (see Hebrews 9:12; Ephesians 1:7; Colossians 1:14; Colossians 2:13) from Satan and sin; God, who is faithful and just, fulfills His promise and cleanses him from ALL unrighteousness; he is born again, born of the Spirit, born of God, born from above (see John 3:3, 6-7) or created anew according to the true righteous and holy nature of God (see Ephesians 4:24; 2 Corinthians 5:17; 2 Peter 1:4); God Himself gives birth to him out of His own will through the Word of truth (see James 1:18; 1 Peter 1:23), and He becomes the begotten son of God (see John 1:12, James 1:18, 1 John 5:) having the very life and nature of God, having the Spirit of God, and having the power of God; he becomes **a spirit** and is no longer regarded according to the flesh because He is born of the Spirit (see John 3:6; with 2 Corinthians 5:16); he is accepted in the Beloved (see Ephesians 1:6); he becomes a member of God's Family; he becomes an heir of God and joint-heirs with Christ (see Romans 8:16-17); indeed, he becomes Jesus' brother, and Jesus is not ashamed to call him a brother. (see Hebrews 2:11).

The new birth is simply amazing and glorious! It is the most monumental and wonderful thing that can happen to a man in this life. From the moment a person comes to Christ, he is a new creation. (see 2 Corinthians 5:17). He is a partaker of the Holy Spirit (see Hebrews 6:4), and by laying hold of the great and precious promises of God in Christ, he also becomes a partaker of the divine (or God) nature, having escaped the corruption that is in the world through lust (see 2 Peter 1:4). He has the life of God. (see 1 John 5:11-12). He has eternal life. (see 1 John 5:13, John 6:47). And He has fellowship with God the Father, with His Son Jesus Christ, and with the Holy Spirit. (see 1 Corinthians 1:9; 1 John 1:3, with 2 Corinthians 13:14). He dies to Adam and his sin nature, and is made alive to God in Christ and receives His righteous nature, so that just as in Adam all die, even so in Christ, all are made alive. (see 1 Corinthians 15:22). Just as by one man's (or Adam's) disobedience many were made (or became) sinners, even so through one Man's (or Christ's) obedience, many are made (or become) righteous. (see Romans 5:19). In fact Jesus Himself is the believer's righteousness. (see 1 Corinthians 1:30). Hence, even though there are sinners in the natural world (that is, unbelievers), there are no sinners in Christ or in the Body of Christ (except the apostates or false believers, if we can include them at all — see James 4:8). In Christ, all are saints. (see 1 Corinthians 1:2; 2 Corinthians 1:1; Ephesians 2:19; Romans 1:7); all are righteous. (see Romans 5:19; 2 Corinthians 5:21). And sin cannot change that. This is why First John 3:9 says, "Whoever has been born of God does not sin, for His seed remains in him; and he CANNOT sin, because he has been born of God." This is a spiritual truth. It is a spiritual reality. This is talking about your spirit — the new man, but it can be a reality in your body also if you consistently walk according to the Spirit and not according to the flesh. That the believer does not and cannot sin, is not to be grasped by reasoning. You have to grasp it by revelation. The believer is dead to sin. God sees the believer (in the Spirit) as so righteous, so dead to sin, and so alive to God in Christ that he cannot sin. In God's eyes, as Jesus (or God) is, so are we in this world. (see 1 John 4:17). In God's eyes the believer is as righteous and sinless as Jesus. God sees the believer as His own righteousness. We are the righteousness of God in Christ Jesus. (see 2 Corinthians 5:21). Just ask yourself this question: how pure and perfect is the righteousness of God? Well, that is you, dear believer.

The believer is the righteousness of God in Christ Jesus. It is God Himself who has established the believer in righteousness, just as He promised long ago that He would do. (see Isaiah 54:14). And when God justifies, who is he that condemns? (see Romans 8:33-34). Jesus Himself is the believer's righteousness (see 1 Corinthians 1:30). The believer is indeed not under law but under grace. This is why every believer should have dominion over sin. Sin shouldn't have dominion over the believer. (see Romans 6:14). Satan is the author of sin; he has been sinning from the beginning. (see 1 John 3:8). Sin exists in Satan's kingdom (of darkness); it doesn't exist in God's Kingdom (of Light). And the Bible says that the believer has been rescued or delivered by God from the power of darkness, and has been translated or conveyed into the Kingdom of God's dear Son. (see Colossians 1:13). So Satan (and sin) has no power over the believer. Satan (and sin) used to be our lord or master before we accepted Jesus Christ as our Lord and Savior. But now, since we are in Christ, we are in the Kingdom of Light and we are seated in the heavenly realms (on the right hand of God) with Christ and in Christ (see Ephesians 2:4-6) "far above all principality and power and might and dominion, and every name that is named, not only in this age but also in that which is to come." (Ephesians 1:21). The believer is therefore a master over Satan and sin. We have transitioned from once being slaves of Satan and sin to now being Masters over Satan and sin, thanks to our Lord and Savior Jesus Christ. All believers need to catch a revelation of this truth. We need to catch the revelation that we are now IN Christ and are no longer sinners; that we are no longer unrighteous, but righteous in Christ. The Bible hammers this truth further when it says, "Do you not know that **the unrighteous will not inherit the kingdom of God**? Do not be deceived. Neither fornicators, nor idolaters, nor adulterers, nor homosexuals, nor sodomites, nor thieves, nor covetous, nor drunkards, nor revilers, nor extortioners will inherit the kingdom of God. And **SUCH WERE some of you**. BUT YOU WERE WASHED, but YOU WERE SANCTIFIED, but YOU WERE **JUSTIFIED** IN THE NAME OF THE LORD JESUS and BY the Spirit of our God." (I Corinthians 6:9-11). Beloved, when we come to Jesus, we are washed completely from all unrighteousness and we are freed from all unrighteous lifestyles; we are sanctified (or made holy, set apart to God); and we are justified (or made righteous), all in the mighty name of the Lord Jesus Christ and by the Spirit of God. (see also 2 Thessalonians 2:13-14; Romans 8:29-30; Titus 3:5-7). And not just that, we are also glorified. (see Romans 8:30). Praise God! We have been called to share in the eternal glory of our Lord Jesus Christ. (see 2 Thessalonians 2:14; 1 Peter 5:10; Colossians 1:27). This is the good news! This is the gospel!

Indeed believers are a new creation, created according to God in true holiness and righteousness. (see 2 Corinthians 5:17, with Ephesians 4:24). "Old things have passed away; behold, ALL THINGS have become NEW." Therefore we do not continue in those old unrighteous acts or lifestyles as fornicators, nor idolaters, nor adulterers, nor homosexuals, nor sodomites, nor thieves, nor covetous, nor drunkards, nor revilers, nor extortioners. We are no longer slaves to sin (of any kind), but slaves to righteousness. (see Romans 6:18-19). Sin no longer has dominion over the believer. (see Romans 6:14). As a believer, you have been made righteous in Christ so that you can practice righteousness or walk in the good works which God prepared beforehand that you should walk in them. (see Ephesians 2:10). Because righteousness is your new nature and your true nature (see Ephesians 4:24), you are expected, even required to act right or practice righteousness. This is why John says, "Little children, let no one deceive you. He WHO PRACTICES RIGHTEOUSNESS is righteous, just as He (Christ or God) is righteous." (I John 3:7). When you come to understand this, when you come to understand that, as a believer, you were washed (from all unrighteousness), and were sanctified and justified, and glorified in the name of the Lord Jesus and by the Spirit of our God, you will live a life that reflects this truth — a life that is pure, sanctified (holy; set apart to God), justified (righteous) and glorious. Praise God!

In fact, the only reason some sincere believers still live in sin is because they are ignorant; they don't know who they really are, and so they are carnal — babes in Christ. But there is hope for such believers. "There is surely a future hope for you, and your hope will not be cut off." (Proverbs 23:18 NIV). The Bible says that through knowledge shall the righteous be delivered. (see Proverbs 11:9). When the babe in Christ desires the sincere milk of the Word, renews his mind, and comes to maturity or to the knowledge and consciousness of who he truly is, when he comes to know that he truly is righteous in Christ, that is when he is empowered to live a righteous life, free of sin's dominion. The believer has to know his true identity in Christ. He has to become righteousness-conscious and not sin-conscious. He has to be "Christ-in-me-conscious." Sin-consciousness is for the unbeliever. Sin-consciousness among believers is the work of the adversary; it is not of God. Any doctrine that keeps believers in bondage to sin-consciousness is a doctrine of demons, and must be rejected.

Sadly, a major segment of the body of Christ today hasn't caught a full revelation of what Christ did and has done for us. Many are yet to catch the revelation of who we truly are in Christ. This is why so many believers are still preoccupied with sin-consciousness and are living in sin. Every time they hear someone preach about the believer's righteous identity, the only thing they think about is, "What about sin?" So many people are still in bondage to sin and sin-consciousness. But it shouldn't be this way. The blood of Jesus that washed us from our sins (see Revelation 1:5) is more powerful than sin, and the Bible says it (continually) cleanses us from all sin, as we walk in the light.

(see 1 John 1:7). This is like standing under the waterfall of Jesus' precious blood; it never stops cleansing you. Jesus Christ, who is in you, is greater than all the sin in the world (see 1 John 4:4), and He is in you to help you live a life of dominion over sin. Acknowledge Christ always; be conscious of Him, and confess Him. Look unto Jesus, the author and finisher of our faith. (see Hebrews 12:2). Christ is in you — the hope of glory. (see Colossians 1:27). Christ is the hope of the believer (see 1 Timothy 1:1), Christ is the life of the believer, and Christ is the glory of the believer. (see Colossians 3:4, with 1 John 3:2; Isaiah 60:19). That Christ lives in the believer is actually the secret of Christianity. Without the revelation and consciousness that Christ is in you, you can call yourself a believer or a Christian all you want, but you are nothing to the enemy; Satan will never be scared of you, and he will rob you and make a mockery of you. Satan is only scared of believers who truly know who they are and are conscious of Christ who is in them. Satan cannot condemn a believer who knows and continually confesses that Christ is in him; Satan cannot condemn a believer who knows and always confesses that he is the righteousness of God in Christ Jesus. Indeed, he can never condemn a believer who knows and believes and always confesses that there is now no condemnation for those who are in Christ Jesus. (see Romans 8:1). He cannot condemn a believer who knows and confesses that no one can bring a charge against God's elect (see Romans 8:33). You can be that believer. Renew your mind with the Word of God. (see Romans 12:2). And by the way, it is just stupid for a believer to live in sin. Sin is beneath the dignity of a true child of God. Sinning is submitting to Satan. (see Romans 6:16). No true child of God wants to submit to Satan by sinning, because we're masters over Satan. You just need to have this revelation also, and give no place to the devil!

Remission (and/or Forgiveness) of Sins is a Reality for the Believer in Christ

Unfortunately there are many ministers behind the pulpit today who don't have the true revelation of the gospel. They themselves don't even believe (the good news) that they have received the remission of sins through the one-time sacrifice of Jesus Christ, and so they themselves are not saved, since salvation is for only those who BELIEVE the gospel. (see Mark 16:15-16). Jesus commanded the disciples "that REPENTANCE AND REMISSION OF SINS **should be preached** in His name to all nations, beginning at Jerusalem." (see Luke 24:47). This is the core message of the gospel: REPENTANCE and REMISSION OF SINS in the NAME of Jesus. And so Peter, in response to Jesus' command preached on the day of Pentecost saying, "**REPENT**, and let every one of you be baptized in the NAME of Jesus Christ **for the REMISSION OF SINS**; and you shall receive the gift of the Holy Spirit." (Acts 2:38). "Repent" simply means change your mind, as in: change your mind from sin and Satan, to righteousness and God. In another sermon, Peter proclaims: "For Christ also hath ONCE suffered for sins, the just for the unjust, that He might bring us to God…" (1 Peter 3:18 KJV). And Paul adds, "In Him (Christ) we have redemption through His blood, THE FORGIVENESS OF SINS, IN ACCORDANCE WITH THE RICHES OF GOD'S GRACE." (Ephesians 1:7). Peter and Paul could boldly preach this gospel because THEY BELIEVED IT. They believed they had RECEIVED the REMISSION OF THEIR SINS in the name of Jesus. Thus, Peter and Paul were no hypocrites. They believed the gospel and preached it with all their might. But today, there are many preachers behind the pulpit who DON'T believe the gospel. How can you preach repentance and remission of sins to unbelievers when you yourself don't believe you have received the remission of your sins? How can you preach salvation to all nations when you yourself don't believe you're saved? Such is the HYPOCRISY and the sad state of many preachers today in our churches, and they are sadly self-deceived. They have been ordained by men, but they are certainly not ordained by God. They themselves live in sin, so all they preach about is sin, condemnation and death. Paul said such people walk as enemies of the cross of Christ (see Philippians 3:18). Jesus said, "But woe to you, scribes and Pharisees, hypocrites! For you shut up the kingdom of heaven against men; for you neither go in yourselves, nor do you allow those who are entering to go in." (Matthew 23:13). Indeed, such preachers are not saved; nor are they saving any souls.

Beloved, all true ministers of God today have been called to be ministers of the New Covenant. (see 2 Corinthians 3:6). We have been called to be ministers of the Spirit and of RIGHTEOUSNESS, and not ministers of death and condemnation. (see 2 Corinthians 3:7-9). We have been called to be ministers of reconciliation. And we are to preach the message of reconciliation, that God is no longer angry at us; that He is at peace with the world and has forgiven us all our sins because of the propitiation of the blood of Jesus Christ; and that He is calling on us all to accept His offer of reconciliation through faith in Jesus Christ. Jesus Christ was and is the culmination of God's peace project. He is the Prince of Peace, and He has brought peace between God and man. Hence, the angels who announced the birth of Jesus were joyous, praising God and saying, "Glory to God in the highest, and on earth PEACE, GOODWILL toward men!" (Luke 2:14). And Paul declares that, "having been justified by faith, WE HAVE

PEACE WITH GOD through our Lord Jesus Christ" (Romans 5:1). Paul further states that "God was in Christ reconciling the world to Himself, NOT IMPUTING THEIR TRESPASSES TO THEM, and has **committed to us the word of reconciliation.**" (II Corinthians 5:19). The word or message of reconciliation has been committed to us. Indeed the glorious gospel of the blessed God (which is the word or message of reconciliation) has been committed to our trust, to your trust and to my trust. (see 1 Timothy 1:11, with Mark 16:15). This is the message we are to preach. It is the message of reconciliation; and it is the message all the early apostles preached. John preached that Jesus Christ "Himself is the propitiation for our sins, and not for ours only but also for the whole world." (I John 2:2). Paul, in preaching the message of reconciliation also said, "Now then, we are ambassadors for Christ, as though God were pleading through us: we implore you on Christ's behalf, **be reconciled to God**. For He made Him who knew no sin to be sin for us, that we might become the righteousness of God in Him." (II Corinthians 5:20-21). Now, this sounds like good news to me! We are being implored to accept Christ's sacrifice for our sins, and in accepting it we become the righteousness of God in Christ. We are to accept that just as Christ became sin without committing any sin, we have also become righteous (through faith in Christ) without doing anything righteous. And so living in the consciousness of this truth, we can now practice righteousness. This is the good news. It is also summarized in Paul's letter to the Romans as follows: "But now apart from the law the righteousness of God has been made known, to which the Law and the Prophets testify. This righteousness **is given THROUGH FAITH** in Jesus Christ **to ALL WHO BELIEVE**. There is no difference between Jew and Gentile, for all have sinned and fall short of the glory of God, and all are JUSTIFIED (or made righteous)

FREELY by His grace THROUGH the REDEMPTION that came by Christ Jesus." (Romans 3:21-24 NIV).

Thus, the good news is not the depressing and scary fact that all have sinned and fall short of the glory of God (see Romans 3:23), and that the wages of sin is death. (see Romans 6:23). In fact, that is the bad news. But the good news, which immediately follows the bad news, is the liberating and joyful TRUTH that **ALL are justified freely** by His grace through the redemption that came by Christ Jesus (see Romans 3:24), and that the GIFT of God is eternal life through Christ Jesus our Lord. (see Romans 6:23). Hallelujah! I know, without a doubt, that many of you reading this book have been going to church for a long time, and yet, this is the first time some of you have actually heard the gospel (or the good news). The question then is, do you believe this good news? Unfortunately, many so-called Christians today still don't believe it. But this is your chance to believe it, and be saved.

Christians today just need to believe the Word of God and trust in Jesus as our Lord and Savior. There is a big problem of unbelief in the church today, which is quite unfortunate, because without faith, it is impossible to please God. (see Hebrews 11:6). Just as the message that was preached to the Israelites did not profit them (or do them any good) because it was not mixed with faith (see Hebrews 4:2), so is the gospel of Christ not benefiting many people today because they are not mixing it with faith. In fact, I find it difficult to use the word "believers" to describe all Christians, because many so-called Christians don't truly believe the gospel (or the good news) of Christ. Unless they can sense something that sounds like bad news in your preaching, they won't accept it. They just want to hear you preaching about sin, condemnation and death, about how they are all going to burn in hell if they don't stop sinning. But that is not the good news. That is not the gospel of Christ. The gospel of Christ doesn't just name the problem of sin; it offers Jesus Christ as the solution. So the truth is that sin is not the problem in the church today; faith is. You know why? Because Jesus has taken care of the sin problem already; people just don't want to believe it. People crave for something they can also do to "earn" their salvation so that they can boast in themselves. The natural man is predisposed to pride, and is driven by the lust for the pleasure of achievement through self-effort. The Bible says, "For everything in the world—the LUST of the FLESH, the LUST of the EYES, and the PRIDE of life—comes NOT from the Father but from the world." (1 John 2:16 NIV). So, No, many people don't want to accept salvation as a gift by faith. They prefer (out of pride) to work for it, so that they can boast. And that's all the problem I see in the church today, and I believe the Lord Jesus Christ sees the faith problem also, as revealed in His letters to the 7 churches. (see Revelation 2 — 3). It is only by (faith in) the blood of the Lamb, and by the Word of our testimony (or our confession) that we overcome. (see Revelation 12:11, with 1 John 5:4). The Bible says "by faith, you stand." (see 2 Corinthians 1:24). When we believe right, we will definitely live right. Knowledge of the truth of the gospel makes the believer truly free (see John 8:32) — free from every form of bondage and oppression of the devil, including the dominion of sin.

I admonish you, therefore, to believe what Jesus has accomplished for you through His death and resurrection, and be saved. And yet, I know some of you wouldn't believe or accept this message. "For the message of the cross is foolishness to those who are perishing, but to us who are being saved IT IS THE POWER OF GOD. For it is written: "I will destroy the wisdom of the wise, And bring to nothing the understanding of the prudent." Where is the wise? Where is the scribe? Where is the disputer of this age? Has not God made foolish the wisdom of this world? For since, in the wisdom of God, the world through wisdom did not know God, **it pleased God through the foolishness of the message preached to save those who believe.** For Jews request a sign, and Greeks seek after wisdom; but we preach Christ crucified, to the Jews a stumbling block and to the Greeks foolishness, but to those who are called, both Jews and Greeks, **Christ the power of God and the wisdom of God.** Because the foolishness of God is wiser than men, and the weakness of God is stronger than men." (I Corinthians 1:18-25). Indeed the message of the cross is foolishness to those who are perishing, but to us who are being saved it is the POWER of God. Hallelujah!

Jesus Christ is God's Remedy for Sin-consciousness

Jesus Christ is not only God's remedy for sin, He is also God's remedy for sin-consciousness. The Bible says, "Now if we died with Christ, we believe that we shall also live with Him, knowing that Christ, having been raised from the dead, dies no more. Death no longer has dominion over Him. For the death that He died, He DIED TO SIN ONCE FOR ALL; but the life that He lives, He LIVES TO GOD. Likewise you also, RECKON YOURSELVES TO BE **DEAD INDEED TO SIN**, but **ALIVE TO GOD** IN CHRIST Jesus our Lord." (Romans 6:8-11). Truly God has gone to great lengths to keep the believer's mind free from sin-consciousness. He has forgiven us ALL our sins (past, present, and future) through the ETERNAL redemption that came through the sacrifice of the precious blood of

Jesus Christ. (see Colossians 2:13, with Hebrews 9:12, Romans 3:24, 1 Peter 3:18, Ephesians 1:7). But He didn't stop there. He has also promised to remember our sins and lawless deeds NO MORE. (see Jeremiah 31:31-34; Hebrews 10:17-18). That would've been more than enough, but He still didn't stop there. He also says, there is now no condemnation for those who are in Christ Jesus (see Romans 8:1), and that nobody can bring a charge against God's elect — the believer. (see Romans 8:33). Then He adds that nothing (including sin) can separate the believer from the love of God which is in Christ Jesus our Lord. (see Romans 8:38-39). God could've stopped here, and this would've been way more than enough, but He still didn't stop here. He also gave us the Holy Spirit in our hearts as a seal, a guarantee, or a down-payment of our redemption or forgiveness and salvation in Christ. (see Ephesians 1:13-14; 2 Corinthians 1:21-22). And yet, sin-consciousness makes many believers still doubt their salvation. I sincerely believe that people who continually harbor doubts about their eternal salvation are perhaps not saved; they are perhaps still walking in darkness. They perhaps don't sincerely believe in Jesus Christ as their Lord and Savior.

But for those of us who sincerely believe in Him, Jesus Christ has indeed done all the work of salvation for us. This is why the Bible calls salvation the GIFT of God (see Romans 6:23) that is given by grace and must be received by faith. (see Ephesians 2:8-9). Jesus lives in the believer (see Colossians 1:27) through the Holy Spirit; He lives in us and continues His work in us. (see Galatians 2:20, with Philippians 2:13 & Colossians 1:29). He doesn't live in us to help us sin; He lives in us to help us live a life of dominion over sin and death. He has saved us completely. The Bible says, Jesus is "able to save to the uttermost those who come to God through Him, since He always lives to make intercession for them." (Hebrews 7:25). And thankfully, He has done it for me. I am not waiting to be saved; I believe and I know I am saved because I sincerely believe in Jesus Christ and confess Him as my Lord and Savior. And I know that the Lord Jesus Christ will appear a second time not to bear sin, but to bring me the salvation that is already mine. (see Hebrews 9:28). I am not the only believer who is confident of this very thing. The early disciples were all certain about their salvation in Christ. John, the disciple of Jesus, wrote to believers assuring them that they have eternal life (see 1 John 5:13); they were saved. Their salvation was secure, and not dependent on whether or not they would sin in the future. The apostle Paul also, speaking of the believer's salvation in his letter to the Romans, spoke of it in the past tense. To him, salvation was already an accomplished reality. Thus, he writes, "For we **WERE SAVED** in this hope, but hope that is seen is not hope; for why does one still hope for what he sees?" (Romans 8:24). Paul knew he was saved, together with all the believers he was writing to, including me, and perhaps you, if you believe. In fact Paul was so confident and certain of his salvation that in his letter to the Philippians, chapter 1 verses 21-25, he tells the Philippians that he was in a dilemma, as to whether to go to Christ early or to delay his departure in order to keep ministering to their needs. Every believer should have the same certainty that Paul had, that to be absent or away from the body is to be present or at home with the Lord Jesus Christ in Heaven (see 2 Corinthians 5:8).

In writing to Timothy for the second time, Paul again puts our salvation in the past tense, writing about how God "**HAS SAVED us** and called us with a holy calling, not according to our works, but according to

His own purpose and grace which was given to us in Christ Jesus before time began" (II Timothy 1:9). Evidently, Paul knew, as every believer needs to know, that Jesus Christ has by Himself accomplished the task of purifying us from our sins. (see Hebrews 1:3). The forgiveness of our sins is an accomplished work of Jesus Christ, and He wants us to sleep easy, resting in Him and believing that His sacrifice for our sins is done, never to be repeated again. The Bible says Jesus' blood has purified us of our sins so perfectly that **we should have no more consciousness of sin**. (see Hebrews 10:2). We should **no longer be continually reminded of sin** (see Hebrews 10:3), because all our sins have been taken away by Jesus' precious blood. This is the whole point that is being made in Hebrews 10:1-3. The blood of Jesus is way more powerful than sin. Hallelujah! Yet, many believers unfortunately think more about sin than they think about Jesus. They magnify sin more than they magnify Christ. They ascribe more power to sin than they ascribe to the precious blood of Jesus, and then they claim to believe in Jesus. How self-deceived such people are! They confess their sins more than they confess Jesus, who is the Apostle and High Priest of our confession. (see Hebrews 3:1). The Book of Hebrews says, "Seeing then that we have a great High Priest who has passed through the heavens, Jesus the Son of God, let us hold fast our confession." (Hebrews 4:14). Let us continually confess Jesus Christ as our great High Priest, and our Lord and Savior. Let us continually confess who the Bible says we truly are in Christ. Let us continually confess what the Bible says we have in Christ. And let us continually confess what the Bible says we can do in Christ (with and through the power or ability of the Holy Spirit that was given to us). This should be our confession continually, for we are urged to hold fast our confession. (see Hebrews 4:14). We have to continually say in agreement with God what He has already spoken to us and about us in His Word. And to be able to do this, we have to know God's Word; we have to know what Christ has done for us, we have to know who we are in Christ, what we have in Christ, and what we can do in Christ and through Christ who strengthens us. This was also Paul's prayer for the Church in Ephesus. (see Ephesians 1:15-21). We should be more conscious of He (Jesus our righteousness) that is in us than he (Satan and sin) that is in the world, because He that is in us is GREATER than he that is in the world. (see 1 John 4:4). Yes, sin is in the world, together with Satan (the author of sin); but Jesus (the greater One) is in us, so we have overcome them, and we need to be conscious of Jesus, and not sin.

Beloved, the Bible says that when Christ died (to sin) once for all, we died with Him. (see Romans 6:8). When He was raised to life to live to God, we were raised with Him (see Colossians 3:1) to live to God in Christ Jesus our Lord, and to walk in the newness of life. (see Romans 6:4). So today, instead of thinking about sin all the time and always searching your heart for sins to confess, it would be better if you didn't think about sin at all, because, as a believer, you are dead to sin and alive to God in Christ. (see Romans 6:11). Don't fix your eyes on sin. The Bible says we should fix our eyes on Jesus, the author and finisher of our faith. (see Hebrews 12:2). The more you focus on Jesus and your righteousness in Him, the more your life will reflect your righteous nature, the more you will have the power to live a life of victory and dominion over sin.

The believer is indeed dead to sin. This does not, however, mean that sin is dead; sin is still very much alive in our world today. So, in the flesh (or body), the believer might sin occasionally if he is not consistently walking in the Spirit. However, you should always renew your mind to the fact that you are dead to sin, so sin doesn't have the power to change who you are in Christ. Sin has no power over the believer. If you are truly born again, you have the nature of God (see Ephesians 4:24, with 2 Peter 1:4), you have power and dominion over sin because the seed of God is in you (see 1 John 3:9); you just have to consistently walk in the Spirit, and you will not fulfill the desires of the flesh. (see Galatians 5:16). You are a new creation. (see 2 Corinthians 5:17). Your spirit has been re-created according to God in true holiness and righteousness. (see Ephesians 4:24). Renew your mind to this truth. Also remember that you are dead to sin, and that because you are dead to sin, you don't respond to sin, you don't respond when sin calls or beckons to you. To understand this more clearly, you need to know or catch a revelation of what death looks like. Have you seen a dead person before? A dead person is dead to life as we know it in the sense realm and does not respond to life. When you are dead to sin, you also don't respond to sin. You don't fellowship with sin. You don't occupy your mind with sin. You and sin have nothing in common. Sin shouldn't be in your consciousness. (see Hebrews 10:1-3). Rather, God should be in your consciousness, because you are alive to God in Christ. Your fellowship is with Christ and with God the Father, not with sin. Your mind should be occupied with Christ and with God the Father, not with sin. You should be thinking about Christ right now, and not about sin. You should present your body as an instrument of righteousness to God (see Romans 6:12-13), because you have been made righteous in Christ. (see 2 Corinthians 5:21). You have been made alive to God in Christ. Don't wake up to sin, because you are dead to sin. Wake up to righteousness, because you are righteous in Christ. The Bible says, "Awake to righteousness, and sin not." (see 1 Corinthians 15:34). It is only by waking up to your righteousness, or being conscious of your righteous identity in Christ that you can live a life of victory over sin, and bear the fruits of righteousness. The Bible says that the fruits of righteousness are by Jesus Christ. (see Philippians 1:11). You won't bear any fruits of righteousness by living in sin-consciousness. Be Christ-conscious instead. It is only by abiding in Christ and allowing His words to abide in you (see John 15:4-7) that you can bear the fruits of righteousness. Believe what the Bible says about you and walk according to the revelation of the Word of God. When you walk according to the Word of God, you will be walking according to the will and purpose of God for your life. This is what the Bible teaches; believe the Bible; it is God's Word. The Word of God is also called the Word of His Grace (see Acts 20:32). Indeed the Bible is about the GRACE of God. No wonder Peter says that grace is multiplied to us through the knowledge of God and Jesus Christ — the Word. (see 2 Peter 1:2, with John 1:1, 14). Indeed sin shall not have dominion over us because we are not under law but under GRACE. (see Romans 6:14). Amen.

Does Grace Give Us the License to Sin?

Now, the Bible says that there is no sin in Jesus Christ (see 1 John 3:5); therefore **NO ONE who abides or remains in Him will sin**. The Bible affirms this truth in First John 3:6 which says, "Whoever **abides in Him does not sin**. Whoever sins has neither seen Him nor known Him." In fact, whoever does not have Christ is capable of committing every kind of sin. Jesus Christ is the only remedy for sin; He is God's remedy for sin. And we believers ought to be a living testimony of this truth.

Grace, therefore, does not give people the license to sin. Grace rather gives people the freedom and the power to overcome sin.

Like all true believers, I am strongly opposed to sin. I believe every believer should be able to have dominion over sin, because sin gives the devil inroads into our lives (see Romans 6:16) to attack our happiness. How to obtain this dominion over sin, however, is where I differ from many preachers. For generations, law preachers have believed that preaching more of the Ten Commandments will deter people from sin and produce holiness and the fruits of righteousness. I disagree. The Bible also disagrees. The apostle Paul in his first letter to Timothy expressed concern that some have strayed from love and turned aside to idle talk desiring to be TEACHERS OF THE LAW, understanding neither what they say nor the things which they affirm. (see 1 Timothy 1:6-7). In fact, Paul even said to the Corinthians that "the strength of sin is the law." (1 Corinthians 15:56). In other words, it is by preaching the Ten Commandments that sin is empowered or strengthened. No wonder Paul called the law "the ministry of death" (see 2 Corinthians 3:7). No wonder he called it "the law of sin and death." (see Romans 8:2). Preaching more of the Ten Commandments thus leads to more sin and more death. When the Ten Commandments were given at the foot of Mount Sinai, 3000 people died (see Exodus 32:28). Contrast this with what happened when God poured out His Holy Spirit upon all flesh on the Day of Pentecost and Peter stood up to preach the gospel of grace: 3000 people were saved. (see Acts 2:41). Notice that the law brought death, whereas grace brought salvation and life.

Thus the biblical viewpoint is that, it is the preaching of grace and more grace that breaks the dominion of sin in people's lives. You cannot claim to be under grace and continue to live in sin. This is why the Bible says in Romans 6:14 that, "sin shall not have dominion over you, for YOU'RE NOT UNDER LAW, but UNDER GRACE." In other words, sin only has dominion over those who live under the law. The power to have dominion over sin is thus imparted to believers through the preaching of grace, and more grace (not the law). The devil knows this and is not happy about it, hence he peddles deception and confusion when he hears some of us preaching grace more and more. Today there are many sincere believers who believe God wants us to keep the Law of Moses in order to obtain a relationship with Him. This is no fault of theirs because that is what Vain Religion has taught them. But the Bible says the real purpose of the law was to bring us to the knowledge of our sin and our need for God and His mercy (see Romans 3:19-20). The Law made sin and God's wrath come alive, and killed us (see Romans 7:9, with Romans 4:15). So, clearly no man can be justified by the law; the law rather brings conviction and condemns all men. It was given to show us how unholy and unrighteous we were, so that we would despair of trying to earn salvation, and just receive salvation as a gift by faith in Christ Jesus. It was given to convince us to turn from self-righteousness to a faith-righteousness that could only come through a Savior (see Romans 10:3-4). So when people are taught that God's love and blessings are dependent upon our perfect obedience to the law, that kills faith in what Jesus did for us in His crucifixion. And so the Bible says that the law is not of faith. (see Galatians 3:12). The law also magnifies sin and produces hopelessness (see Romans 7:13-25). Until Jesus came, no one could fulfill the righteous requirements of the law. (see Romans 9:31). Jesus came to fulfill the righteous requirements of the law in those of us who believe in Him and do not live according to the flesh but according to the Spirit. (see Romans 8:3-4). This is why the Bible says in Colossians 2:14 that "the handwriting of requirements" has been taken away and nailed to the cross. Consequently, we have been redeemed from the curse of the law (see Galatians 3:13).

Beloved, the law is holy and righteous, but don't count on it to make you holy and righteous, because you cannot keep the law on your own no matter how hard you try (see Romans 2:23, James 2:10, Galatians 2:16). This is why God found fault with the Old Covenant on which the law was established (see Hebrews 8:7). This is also why God gave us the New (and more glorious) Covenant of grace, which was established on better promises (see Hebrews 8:6). God has pronounced the Old Covenant of the law as obsolete (see Hebrews 8:13). Jesus Christ is the New Covenant (see Isaiah 42:6-7); He is also the Mediator and Guarantor of the New Covenant (see Hebrews 8:13, with Hebrews 7:22), for only the blood of Jesus can purify you of all sin and make you holy and righteous by faith. (see 1 John 1:7; Ephesians 1:7, with 2 Corinthians 5:21). No wonder the Old Covenant prophets prophesied about the superiority of the New Covenant when they saw it by faith. (see 1 Peter 1:10-12).

The Bible says, "The law was given through Moses, but grace and truth came through Jesus Christ" (John 1:17). This grace, which came through Jesus Christ is also the law of the Spirit who gives life and sets us free from the law of sin and death (see Romans 8:2). Romans 8:3 thus declares, "For what the law was powerless to do because it was weakened by the flesh, God did by sending His own Son in the likeness of sinful flesh to be a sin offering. And so He condemned sin in the flesh." (Romans 8:3 NIV). Christ condemned sin in the flesh (or the body). This means that sin has lost its power to control the body of the believer who lives according to the Spirit, because a greater Spirit is in the believer, giving life to his mortal body. (see Romans 8:11; 2 Corinthians 4:10-11). The re-created spirit of man is more powerful than the body and has dominion over the body of those who walk in the Spirit. As long as you're walking in the Spirit or allowing your re-created spirit to be the ruler over your body, you will walk in victory over sin. Hallelujah! This is also why the Bible says, "And **those who are Christ's** have **crucified the flesh** (or the body) with its passions and desires." (Galatians 5:24). Paul again says in his letter to the Romans "that our old self was crucified with Him (Christ) so that **the body ruled by sin might be done away with**, that we should **no longer be slaves to sin**—because anyone who has died has been set free from sin." (Romans 6:6 NIV). We who believe in Jesus Christ have been set free from sin, having died with Christ to sin. Praise God!

In Revelation 12:10-11, the devil is referred to as "the accuser of the brethren." The devil had at one point armed himself with the law to accuse and condemn God's people whenever they failed. Jesus came to change all of that and has declared through the apostle Paul, "Therefore, there is now **no condemnation for those who are in Christ Jesus**, because through Christ Jesus the law of the Spirit who gives life has set you free from the law of sin and death." (Romans 8:1-2 NIV). In other words, there is now no condemnation for the believer because there is a new law in place called the law of the Spirit, and this law gives life (and not death). This law has replaced the law of sin and death for the believer who walks in the Spirit. The spirit of the believer (which is now joined as one with the Spirit of God — see 1 Corinthians 6:17) can never be condemned, and can never die again from sin like Adam did; the believer can never taste spiritual death again — he can never be separated from God again. Jesus indeed kicked the devil out of the condemnation business. We believers have overcome the devil by the blood of the Lamb and by the Word of our testimony (not by any good deeds we have done — see Revelation 12:11). A glimpse into Heaven from the Book of Revelation further confirms this: "Then one of the elders asked me, "These in white robes—who are they, and where did they come from?" I answered, "Sir, you know." And he said, "These are they who have come out of the great tribulation; they have washed their robes and made them white in THE BLOOD OF THE LAMB. Therefore, "they are before the throne of God and serve Him day and night in His temple; and He who sits on the throne will shelter them with His presence. 'Never again will they hunger; never again will they thirst. The sun will not beat down on them,' nor any scorching heat. For the Lamb at the center of the throne will be their shepherd; 'He will lead them to springs of living water.' 'And God will wipe away every tear from their eyes.'" (Revelation 7:13-17 NIV).

Now, if you're still wondering how the life of a believer will be governed now that we're no longer under the Old Covenant of the law, God Himself has answered this question: "This is the covenant I will establish with the people of Israel after that time, declares the Lord. I WILL PUT MY LAWS IN THEIR MINDS AND WRITE THEM ON THEIR HEARTS. I will be their God, and they will be my people. No longer will they teach their neighbor, or say to one another, 'Know the Lord,' because they will all know me, from the least of them to the greatest." (Hebrews 8:10-11 NIV). As believers,

God Himself has put His laws in our minds and written His laws on our hearts to govern our conduct. This is also "the law of the Spirit" that we mentioned earlier. As the sons or children of God, God has put His own Spirit in us to guide us and to lead us. (see Romans 8:9, 14). In his letter to Titus, Paul also explains that the grace that saves also **teaches** the saved how to say no to ungodliness and live self-controlled, upright and godly lives in this present age. "For the grace of God has appeared that offers salvation to all people. **It TEACHES us to say "No" to ungodliness and worldly passions**, and **to live self-controlled, upright and godly lives in this present age**, while we wait for the blessed hope—the appearing of the glory of our great God and Savior, Jesus Christ, who gave Himself for us to redeem us from all wickedness and to purify for Himself a people that are His very own, **eager to do what is good**" (Titus 2:11-14 NIV). Living a life of purity, in essence, is our response to God's grace. It is a byproduct of salvation. The Bible says that all those who have this hope in Christ (that when Christ appears we will be like Him, having seen Him as He is), purify themselves, just as He is pure. (see 1 John 3:2-3). When you come to understand and appreciate the grace God has extended to you, the love of God will abound in your life and you won't even have the desire to sin; you will live a holy and pure life naturally. May God give you the spirit of wisdom and revelation to understand this.

Run a Good Race

Indeed, God has set a race before us, and there is a crown to be won, a crown that lasts forever. So we cannot afford to stand still! We cannot afford to just limp along! We cannot afford to carry any weight or burden that will slow us down. The Bible says, "Therefore, since we are surrounded by such a huge crowd of witnesses to the LIFE OF FAITH, let us STRIP OFF EVERY WEIGHT THAT SLOWS US DOWN, **especially the SIN that so easily trips us up**. And let us RUN WITH ENDURANCE the race God has set before us." (Hebrews 12:1 NLT). Paul tells us also that the victor's crown will be given to only those who compete according to the rules. (see 2 Timothy 2:5). The rules are the truth God has set before us to obey and to walk in. Indeed the rules are summed up in one word: FAITH. "For we walk by faith, not by sight." (II Corinthians 5:7). And we know that faith works through LOVE. (see Galatians 5:6). Thus, obedience to the faith is all that God requires of us in this race. (see Romans 1:5; 16:26). Jesus said, "To him who overcomes I will grant to sit with Me on My throne, as I also overcame and sat down with My Father on His throne." (Revelation 3:21). We overcome by FAITH. For John writes: "…And this is the victory that has overcome the world—OUR FAITH." (I John 5:4).

To the Churches of Galatia who were moving away from obedience to the faith (which is in Christ Jesus), to obedience to the Law of Moses, Paul said, "You **were** running a good race. Who cut in on you to keep you from obeying the truth?" (Galatians 5:7 NIV). Beloved, we run a good race when we obey the truth, when we walk by faith or are led by the Spirit, and do not walk according to the works of the Law, or according to the flesh. We should not allow anyone to cut in on us to keep us from obeying the truth and running a good race. Indeed, we should not allow ourselves to be entangled by false teachings or doctrines that seek to put us back in a yoke of bondage (to the Law of Moses). We ought to fight the good fight of faith, and lay hold on eternal life (see 1 Timothy 6:12), so that in the end we can say with the apostle Paul, "I have fought the good fight, I have finished the race, I have kept the faith. Now there is in store for me the crown of righteousness, which the Lord, the righteous Judge, will award to me on that day—and not only to me, but also to all who have longed for His appearing." (2 Timothy 4:7-8 NIV).

May you be strengthened in the faith by the Holy Spirit to endure to the end, "For we have become partakers of Christ if we hold the beginning of our confidence (that is, our original faith) steadfast to the end" (Hebrews 3:14). "Now may the God of peace Himself sanctify you completely; and may your whole spirit, soul, and body be preserved blameless at the coming of our Lord Jesus Christ. He who calls you is faithful, who also will do it." (I Thessalonians 5:23-24). Amen.

Be a Vessel for Honor, Sanctified and Useful for the Master

Now, as we bring this chapter to a close, let us emphasize the need for each of us to be **a vessel for honor**, sanctified and useful for the master, prepared for every good work. We know that we are all vessels in the house of God. The Bible says that "we have this treasure in EARTHEN VESSELS, that the excellence of the power may be of God and not of us." (II Corinthians 4:7). The apostle Paul in describing the different kinds of vessel in the house of God, said, "But in a great house there are not only vessels of gold and silver, but also of wood and clay, SOME FOR HONOR and SOME FOR DISHONOR. Therefore if **anyone** cleanses himself from the latter, he will be a vessel for honor, sanctified and useful for the Master, prepared for every good work." (II Timothy 2:20-21). Therefore, every believer has to decide what kind of vessel they want to be — a vessel for honor, or a vessel for dishonor. Here are two important instructions from the Bible that you are to live by, if you want to be a vessel for honor, sanctified and useful for the Master, prepared for every good work; in fact, this is just a recap of everything we have already discussed in this chapter:

First, **Put on the Lord Jesus Christ, and make no provision for the flesh, to satisfy its desires.** (see Romans 13:14). In other words, be Christ-conscious, or set your affections on Christ, and give the flesh (or the body) no place, so that you won't satisfy its lusts; subdue the flesh; crucify or put to death (by the Spirit) the deeds of the body; discipline the body and keep it under, so that the Spirit will rule over it. "For if you live according to the flesh you will die; but if BY THE Spirit you put to death the deeds of the body, you will live." (Romans 8:13).

The simple truth remains, my dear brothers and sisters, that without crucifying the deeds of the body or dying (to the flesh) daily, you cannot be a vessel for honor, sanctified and useful for the Master, prepared for every good work, you cannot experience or enjoy to the uttermost the victory which is in Christ Jesus. In fact, the only people who are able to exercise complete authority over the devil are those who choose the way of the cross and dying (to the flesh) daily. Paul said, "But I discipline my body and bring it into subjection, lest, when I have preached to others, I myself should become disqualified." (I Corinthians 9:27). Again he said, "I affirm, by the boasting in you which I have in Christ Jesus our Lord, I DIE DAILY." (I Corinthians 15:31). Indeed we are all commanded to die (to the flesh) daily, or crucify the deeds of the body.

Crucifying the deeds of the body, or disciplining your body and bringing it into subjection is not something God does for you; it is something you do for yourself. "I beseech you therefore, brethren," Paul wrote to the Church, "by the mercies of God, that ye present your bodies a living sacrifice, holy, acceptable to God…" (see Romans. 12:1 KJV). Who (according to this verse) has the responsibility to present your body? You do. Who is "you"? That's the new man, the hidden man of the heart, the man on the inside who is born again and has become a new creature. You, dear believer, are required to do something with your body in this present life while you're waiting for the Lord to return and to redeem the purchased possession (your body). If you do not do something with your body, nothing will be done with it for you. So you have the responsibility to crucify the deeds of your body, to present your body a living sacrifice, holy, acceptable to God. Indeed, you have the responsibility to offer all the different parts of your body to God as instruments of righteousness. (see Romans 6:13). And yet you cannot accomplish this by your own strength or ability. You cannot crucify the deeds of the body by self-will or willpower. You have to do it BY THE SPIRIT who is in you. (see Romans 8:13). You have to yield to the Spirit as He empowers and strengthens you and directs and guides you. You have to yield to the leading of the Holy Spirit. Therein lies your strength and power, therein lies your victory. Paul said, "I can do all things through Christ who strengthens me." Christ is in you; the Spirit of Christ is in you, strengthening you to do all things. So yield to Him.

Second, **Give no place to the Devil.** (see Ephesians 4:27). In other words, make no provision for the devil to satisfy his desires or do his works. Instead, resist the devil and enforce the victory Christ has won over him on your behalf. The Bible says that Jesus came to destroy the works of the devil. (see 1 John 3:8). So our responsibility is to keep those works of the devil (particularly sin, disease, and the fear of death and hell) destroyed by the power and authority Christ has given us. We are to walk in the good works which resulted from the destruction of the works of the devil. The Bible says that God prepared these good works beforehand for us to walk in them. Hence, all we have to do today is maintain the good works (see Titus 3:8, 14). Praise God! Oh, see how glorious this life in Christ is!

Regarding how we are to carry out the task of not giving place to the devil, the Bible says, "Therefore submit to God. RESIST THE DEVIL and he will flee from you." (James 4:7). Many people often quote the last part of this verse and ignore the first part that says "Submit to God." But the truth, as we noted in an earlier chapter, is that you cannot resist the devil without first submitting to God. To resist anything, you must first be leaning on and allowing yourself to be held by something stronger. For instance, in order for you to successfully resist a strong wind, you must be holding on to and allowing yourself to be held by a rock or an object which cannot be moved by the wind. Similarly, God, and for that matter our Lord Jesus Christ, is our Rock (see 1 Peter 2:6-8; Psalm 18:2) that we have to submit to and lean on in order to successfully resist the devil. Submitting to God and to the Lordship of our Lord Jesus Christ is accomplished by submitting to the Holy Spirit and to the Word of God — what it says about who we are in Christ, what we have in Christ, and what we can do through Christ and with the power and authority that we have in Christ. When we **believe** God's Word and **do** (or act on) **God's Word**, then have we submitted to God, then are we leaning on the immovable Rock, and so we can successfully resist every attack and every temptation of the devil. Thus, we know we have truly submitted to God when we have full assurance in our heart that Jesus has indeed defeated the devil on our behalf, just as His Word says (see Colossians 2:15; Luke 10:18; Hebrews 2:14-15; Colossians 1:13; Galatians 1:4), and has made us masters over the devil and over all his demons (see Mark 16:17-18; 1 John 4:4; Romans 8:37; 2 Corinthians 2:14; Isaiah 54:17), and that we have overcome them because He who is in us is greater than he who is in the world (see 1 John 4:4). Today, every believer can easily cast out demons, resist the devil, and trample upon all the power of the devil, in the name of the Lord Jesus Christ. Indeed, we can choose to give no place to the devil.

Thus, both of the instructions discussed above can be fulfilled by yielding or submitting to the Spirit of God who is in you, and who is working in you to will and to do for His good pleasure. (see Philippians 2:13). Someone may ask, "But how can I yield or submit to the Spirit?" By faith, for we walk by faith and not by sight. We do all things by faith. Glory to God! Set your mind and your affections on the Spirit and on the desires of the Spirit, and follow the leading of the Spirit. And He will lead you in the paths of righteousness for His name's sake, so that you will be a vessel for honor, and not for dishonor. Truly, "the solid foundation of God stands, having this seal: "The Lord knows those who are His," and, "Let everyone who names the name of Christ depart from iniquity." (see II Timothy 2:19).

In the next chapter, we will continue to explore how to walk in the Spirit, with emphasis on how to be led by the Spirit of God that is in us.

Chapter 19

The Spirit Walk: Being Led By the Spirit of God

Jesus Promised the Holy Spirit to All His Disciples

ON THE NIGHT before His crucifixion, the Lord Jesus Christ promised the Holy Spirit to His disciples in these words: "Nevertheless I tell you the truth. It is to your advantage that I go away; for if I do not go away, **the Helper** will not come to you; but if I depart, **I will send Him to you.**" (John 16:7). What Jesus was essentially saying is that having the Holy Spirit would be more beneficial to us (His disciples) than having Jesus physically present with us. How could that be? Well, as shocking as that may seem, Jesus emphasized that it's the truth. And of course it is, even though the disciples may have struggled to understand it as such. They had come to be dependent on Jesus' physical presence in their midst. Life was comfortable that way. They could just call on Jesus whenever they needed help, whenever they needed Him to multiply bread and fish, stop a turbulent storm at sea, get them money from the mouth of a fish, heal the sick, raise the dead, cast out demons or explain to them things concerning the Kingdom of God. It would be hard to imagine anything better than that. Yet, Jesus said it was better for them that He would depart, so that another Helper (the Holy Spirit) would come. Jesus also indicated that the Holy Spirit was already WITH them (an allusion to Himself — the Holy Spirit is the Spirit of Christ), but promised that the Holy Spirit would be **IN** them (see John 14:17). This is because if Jesus could complete His redemptive work on the cross, then He could come back in a different form (the Holy Spirit / the Spirit of Christ — see Romans 8:9) to live in every believer. (see Galatians 2:20; Colossians 1:27). When this happened, He would no longer be limited to being WITH us, He could and would actually be IN each one of us (believers). And thankfully, this is the reality today. (see Colossians 1:27). The Bible says we receive the Holy Spirit or the Spirit of Christ the moment we believe in Jesus Christ as our Lord and Savior. (see Ephesians 1:13). God gives us His Spirit and seals us with His Spirit as a guarantee that we belong to Him (see 2 Corinthians 1:22; Ephesians 1:13), that we are His purchased possession. (see Ephesians 1:14; with 1 Corinthians 6:19-20). When we believe in Jesus Christ, our hearts are immediately circumcised by the Holy Spirit in what is called "circumcision of the heart" (see Romans 2:29), so that we may love the Lord our God with all our heart and with all our soul, and live (see Deuteronomy 30:6); we are immediately baptized (by the Holy Spirit) into one Body — the Body of Christ) — and given the Holy Spirit to drink or to live in our hearts. (see 1 Corinthians 12:13, with 2 Corinthians 1:22). Therefore, as believers (or the children of God), not only are we all members of one household (which is, the Household of God — see Ephesians 2:19), we are all members (or parts) of one Body (which is, the Body of Christ — see Colossians 1:18), and we all share one Spirit (the Holy Spirit — the Spirit of God or the Spirit of Christ).

You Are Not An Imitation

Beloved, God did not make imitations (or copies) of the Lord Jesus Christ when He created the new humanity; He made the believer into the Original, into the Lord Jesus Christ Himself. We were created IN Him. (see Ephesians 2:10). There is one Body and one Spirit. (see Ephesians 4:4). We share one Body and one Spirit with the Lord Jesus Christ. We are members of His body, of His bone, and of His flesh. (see Ephesians 5:30). And we are joined as one with Him in Spirit. (see 1 Corinthians 6:17). So the believer is one with the Lord Jesus Christ. Of His fullness we have all received. (see John 1:16). We are complete in Him. (see Colossians 2:9-10). As He is, so are we in this world. (see 1 John 4:17). We have His life, His nature, His power, His glory. (see 1 John 5:11-13; Ephesians 4:24; 2 Peter 1:4; Ephesians 1:19-20; Acts 1:8; John 17:20; Colossians 1:27). We are kings. (Luke 22:29; Revelation 1:5-6). We are seated in Christ and with Christ on His throne (see Ephesians 2:4-6); and we are to reign in life. (see Romans 5:17). This is the consciousness we must have. Jesus is the Head, and we are His Body. (see Colossians 1:18). We share one Spirit and one Body with the Lord Jesus Christ indeed. (see 1 Corinthians 6:15, 17). His victory is our victory. His authority is our authority. His power is our power. Christianity is no child's play, my friends; it is God's ultimate project. In Christ, the believer becomes one with God. Glory to God! Don't settle for a dead Christ; reach for the resurrected, glorified, living Christ who has the keys of hell and of death. He is the triumphant One. In Him is the victory. You are in Him, and He is in you.

Never say, "Lord I can't do it but You can." That is not a mark of humility, as some people wrongly think it is; that is distancing yourself from the Lord, it is a denial of your oneness with Him, and a sign of weakness, a sign of unbelief. You are joined as one with the Lord in Spirit and in Body. So the consciousness you should rather have is, "I can do all things through Christ who strengthens me." (see Philippians 4:13). Indeed, it is not by human might, nor by human power, but by the Spirit of God. (see Zechariah 4:6). But where is the Spirit of God? He is in you, my dear believer; you are joined as one with Him. And so He is your strength; His power works in you mightily. Paul said he was striving according to "His working which works in me mightily." (see Colossians 1:29). It is God who works IN YOU both to will and to do for His good pleasure. (see Philippians 2:13). And so the Bible says God is able to do exceedingly abundantly above all that you ask or think, according to THE POWER THAT WORKS IN YOU. (see Ephesians 3:20). Don't be afraid to face any circumstance head-on and command changes, because God's power works in you. Be strong and courageous, for you are a king, and where the Word of a King is, there is power. (see Ecclesiastes 8:4). You shall decree a thing and it shall be established unto you; and the light will shine upon your ways. (see Job 22:28). Indeed, ALL THINGS ARE POSSIBLE to the one who believes. The one who believes is made strong even in weakness. Therefore, a true Christian cannot be anything less than an optimist, expectant that all things will work together for his good. (see Romans 8:28).

The Holy Spirit is Your Leader

Truly, all believers are partakers of the Holy Spirit. (see Hebrews 6:4). We all have the Spirit of God. Hence, the Bible says that we are to be led by the Spirit of God, "For AS MANY AS are LED BY the Spirit of

God, these are SONS OF GOD." (Romans 8:14). What this means is that every true son (or child) of God is led by the Spirit of God. As sons of God, we are distinguished by the fact that WE ARE LED BY THE SPIRIT OF GOD. In fact, this is not a promise; it is a present tense reality, which presupposes that those who are not led by the Spirit of God are not sons of God. And so you can determine if you are a son of God by whether or not you're being led by the Spirit of God.

Now, the Spirit of God is also known as the Holy Spirit or the Spirit of Christ, as explained earlier. Indeed, every believer has the Holy Spirit (the Spirit of God / the Spirit of Christ). In Romans 8:9, which we quoted earlier, we see that the Spirit of God and the Spirit of Christ are used interchangeably. It is also affirmed that anyone who does not have the Spirit of Christ (or the Holy Spirit) is not His. In other words, every child of God has the Holy Spirit (the Spirit of Christ, the Spirit of God). There are no exceptions. If you don't have the Holy Spirit, you are simply not a son or child of God. This is a New Covenant reality, and it is so unlike the Old Covenant where only some selected people had the Holy Spirit and were led by the Holy Spirit. Under the Old Covenant the Holy Spirit was in and upon SOME of the believers, and led SOME of the believers (including the prophets), but NOT ALL of the Israelites (or the people of the circumcision) had the Holy Spirit. The Bible says that prophecy never came by the will of man, but that it was the Holy Spirit that moved or led the holy men of God to speak (or write) them. (see 2 Peter 1:21). The Holy Spirit led or moved the holy men of God to write the Scriptures. The Bible further states that the prophets of the Old Covenant who prophesied of the grace that was to come to us through Jesus Christ, actually had

the Spirit of Christ in them (just like believers today); it is simply amazing, that the same Spirit of Christ who is in believers today was also in the Old Testament prophets, leading them and revealing things to them. (see 1 Peter 1:10-12). Thus, these prophets and holy men of God from the Old Testament had a foretaste of what is today the normal way of life of the New Covenant believer — being led by the Spirit of Christ.

Under the Old Covenant, the Holy Spirit also came ON or UPON some of the people, just as He came upon all believers at Pentecost. For instance, the Holy Spirit came upon Balaam (see Numbers 24:2), Saul (see 1 Samuel 11:6), Azariah (see 2 Chronicles 15:1-2), Othniel (see Judges 3:9-10), Gideon (see Judges 6:34), Jephthah (see Judges 11:29), and Samson (see Judges 14:6; Judges 15:14). The Holy Spirit also came upon the virgin Mary who was under the Old Covenant, and she received power to conceive Jesus Christ (the Son of God) in her womb (see Luke 1:35). The Holy Spirit came upon our Lord Jesus Christ Himself after His baptism in the Jordan, while He prayed (see Luke 3:21-22). The Holy Spirit was also upon Simeon who was under the Old Covenant (see Luke 2:25). And so, the Holy Spirit had come upon some Old Covenant folks already. But God wanted the Holy Spirit to come upon EVERY believer. So God spoke through His Prophet Joel that a time was coming when He (God) would pour out His Spirit (the Holy Spirit) on ALL PEOPLE. (see Joel 2:28). That time eventually came on the Day of Pentecost (see Acts 1:4-8; with Acts 2:1-4, 14-18), and today we are still living in that time. All of us who believe in Jesus Christ have the Holy Spirit living in us, and we can have Him upon us, when we ask.

The experience of receiving the Holy Spirit to indwell us or live in us began with the early disciples on the evening of the Lord's resurrection (see John 20:22), and ever since, every believer has had the same experience. (see 1 Corinthians 12:13; Ephesians 1:13; 2 Corinthians 1:22). Thus, when Peter preached his first sermon on the Day of Pentecost after the baptism in the Holy Spirit, he said to the people, "Repent, and let every one of you be baptized in the name of Jesus Christ for the remission of sins; and you shall receive the gift of the Holy Spirit." (see Acts 2:38). The Holy Spirit is God's gift to the believer; He is a gift only because salvation (or eternal life) is a gift (see Ephesians 2:8-9, Romans 6:23). The Bible says that as many as receive Jesus Christ (or believe in His name) are given the power or right to become the sons of God. (see John 1:12). As many as receive Jesus Christ also receive the Holy Spirit, because the Holy Spirit is the Spirit of Sonship. (see Romans 8:15, 23; Galatians 4:6). The gift of the Holy Spirit is given to us at the point when we receive Jesus Christ, to identify us as the children of God. Indeed, the Holy Spirit in us is the seal or evidence that we belong to Christ and are the children of God. Therefore the Holy Spirit will remain with us forever. (see John 14:16). The Bible says, as we noted earlier, that anyone who does not have the Holy Spirit does not belong to Christ. (see Romans 8:9). In Galatians 4:4-7 the apostle Paul says Jesus came to redeem us so that we could receive the full rights of sons, and that **because we are God's sons**, God gave us the Spirit of His Son. Indeed, the Holy Spirit has been given to us as a mark of sonship. He is in us to affirm in our hearts our true identity as children of God. He confirms to us or bears witness with our spirit that we are no longer slaves or servants but the very sons or children of God! "The Spirit Himself **bears witness with our spirit** that we are children of God" (see Romans 8:16). Hallelujah!

Unfortunately, there are many believers today who are not even aware that the Holy Spirit lives in them. They are like the disciples in Ephesus who said to Paul in Acts 19:2, "We have not so much as heard whether there is a Holy Spirit." And because of their ignorance, they are not experiencing the leading and manifestation of the Holy Spirit. There are also many believers who know about the Holy Spirit, but are not conscious of His presence in their lives. Such believers struggle to live in their own ability or strength instead of yielding to the leading and power of the Holy Spirit. Yet other believers resist the Holy Spirit and quench the Holy Spirit because they have been falsely taught that the Holy Spirit no longer manifests His gifts in believers today, that many of the gifts of the Spirit that were available to the early church have ceased and are no longer available to us. Like the people of Israel in Acts 7:51, such believers resist the Holy Spirit because they want to be in charge and do things their own way instead of allowing themselves to be controlled or led by the Holy Spirit. In fact, few believers today know and believe what the Bible really teaches about the Holy Spirit. And thus few believers walk and operate in the miraculous power or ability of the Holy Spirit. My goal in this chapter is to help believers understand what a helper, teacher, comforter, advocate, intercessor and guide we have in the Holy Spirit, and to encourage you to embrace Him and allow Him to take control of your life and lead you, so that you can live an empowered and fruitful life, because the truth is that, the Christian walk would be powerless and just impossible without the help and leading of the Holy Spirit. This is why Peter assured us in Acts 2:39 that the promised Holy Spirit (who in addition to being in the believer, was also to come upon the believer) is a gift that is "**for you and your children and for all who are far off—for all whom the Lord our God will call.**" It was not for the early disciples only. In

Luke 11:13, Jesus also affirms that God gives the Holy Spirit "to those who ask Him."

Who Exactly is the Holy Spirit?

Before we proceed any further, let us first understand and settle the issue of who the Holy Spirit really is. Simply put, the Holy Spirit is God (see Acts 5:3-4); He is the Lord (see 2 Corinthians 3:17). He is the third Person of the Godhead, and is one with the Father, and with the Son. Thus the Holy Spirit is also referred to in Romans 8:9 both as "the Spirit of God" and "the Spirit of Christ." The Holy Spirit possesses all the characteristics of God, including His omnipresence (see Psalm 139:7-8), and His omniscience (see 1 Corinthians 2:10-11). The Holy Spirit is the omnipotent power behind creation. God the Father spoke the Word, and everything was made through Jesus the Son (see John 1:3) by the power of the Holy Spirit (see Genesis 1:2). The Holy Spirit is also the power behind the resurrection of Jesus Christ and thus our redemption (see Ephesians 1:20, with Romans 8:11). He is the power behind both the first creation and the new creation.

Unfortunately, some people hold misconceptions that the Holy Spirit is just a mystical force or impersonal power. But the truth is that the Holy Spirit is a Person with a unique personality; He is God. This is why the Bible speaks of believers as the temple of God, because the Holy Spirit lives in us (see 1 Corinthians 3:16, 1 Corinthians 6:19). Jesus described the Holy Spirit as a teacher, a helper, a comforter, a counselor, an advocate, and a guide. (see John 14:16, 17, 26). These are all attributes of a Person. The early disciples also acknowledged the Holy Spirit as a Person (see Acts 5:3, Acts 5:31-32, Acts 15:28) who can be lied to (see Acts 5:3), who can be grieved (see Ephesians 4:30), who intercedes for us (see Romans 8:26-27), who bears witness (see Romans 8:16; Acts 15:28), and with whom we can have fellowship or have communion (see 2 Corinthians 13:14). Thus the Holy Spirit is real; we can talk to Him and experience His leading in our hearts.

The Holy Spirit and the Symbolism of a Dove

"And John bore witness, saying, "I saw the Spirit DESCENDING from heaven LIKE A DOVE, and He remained upon Him. I did not know Him, but He who sent me to baptize with water said to me, 'Upon whom you see the Spirit DESCENDING, and remaining on Him, this is He who baptizes with the Holy Spirit.'" (John 1:32-33).

"When He had been baptized, Jesus came up immediately from the water; and behold, the heavens were opened to Him, and He saw the Spirit of God DESCENDING LIKE A DOVE and alighting upon Him." (Matthew 3:16).

"And immediately, coming up from the water, He saw the heavens parting and the Spirit DESCENDING upon Him LIKE A DOVE." (Mark 1:10).

"And the Holy Spirit DESCENDED in bodily form LIKE A DOVE upon Him, and a voice came from heaven which said, "You are My beloved Son; in You I am well pleased." (Luke 3:22).

Based on the above Scriptures, many believers have been **wrongly** taught to believe that the Holy Spirit is like a dove in **appearance** or **form**. But a close reading of these verses (with the help of the Holy Spirit) will reveal that the Holy Spirit is **NOT** being likened to a dove in form or appearance. The image or symbolism of the dove is used in these verses ONLY to describe the **WAY** or **MANNER** in which the Holy Spirit DESCENDED upon Jesus Christ. His descent was like that of a dove. Imagine how a dove in flight descends to the earth. That is the imagery these verses of Scripture are giving us about how the Holy Spirit came down upon Jesus. Now, if you were to describe me as jumping LIKE A CAT from the floor onto the bed, I bet nobody would think for a minute that you meant to say that I look like a cat in form or appearance. And yet Satan has caused many people to think (based on the verses above) that the Holy Spirit looks like a dove. How sad! The truth is that the Holy Spirit is God, and the Bible says that man is created in the image and likeness of God, so God, and for that matter the Holy Spirit has the form or appearance of a Man, just like Jesus Christ. May you be guided by the Spirit in studying the Scriptures.

The Lordship of the Holy Spirit

The Bible says, *"When the Day of Pentecost had fully come, they (the disciples) were all with one accord in one place. And suddenly THERE CAME A SOUND FROM HEAVEN, AS OF A RUSHING MIGHTY WIND, and IT FILLED THE WHOLE HOUSE where they were sitting. Then there appeared to them divided tongues, as of fire, and one sat upon each of them. And they were all filled with the Holy Spirit and began to speak with other tongues, as the Spirit gave them utterance."* (Acts 2:1-4).

Many people have not paid careful attention to the words in this account of the outpouring of the Holy Spirit on the Day of Pentecost, and so they **wrongly** believe that the Holy Spirit came WITH a mighty rushing WIND. Some even think the Holy Spirit came AS a mighty rushing WIND. But this is far from what the Bible is saying here. The Holy Spirit rather came with A SOUND FROM HEAVEN, and this SOUND was like the sound of a rushing mighty wind, and this SOUND filled the whole house where they were sitting. Then there appeared to them divided tongues, AS OF FIRE, and one sat upon each of them. AND THEY WERE ALL FILLED WITH THE HOLY SPIRIT and began to SPEAK with other tongues, as the Spirit gave them utterance. This is what the Bible says. The Holy Spirit came with a SOUND, not with a WIND.

Again, many people have been erroneously taught to believe that the Holy Spirit is a **breath**; some say He is the breath of life. This is also due to an erroneous interpretation of John 20:22 where Jesus breathed on His disciples and said, "Receive the Holy Spirit." The Bible says, "And when He had said this, He BREATHED on them, and **SAID TO THEM**, "Receive the Holy Spirit." (John 20:22). A careful reading of this verse will also show that Jesus did not breathe the Holy Spirit on them. Rather, He breathed on them, and then **SPOKE** to them to receive the Holy Spirit. So the Holy Spirit was (as it were) SPOKEN to them; He was the WORD that was spoken, just as Jesus (God) is the WORD. (see John 1:1, 14; Revelation 19:13; John 6:63). Thus, the Holy Spirit is **not** a breath; neither is He a wind. In fact, the breath of Jesus is the breath of life, because Jesus is the Life (see John 14:6); the breath of Jesus is the breath of the Holy Spirit because Jesus and the Holy Spirit are one and the same. The breath of Jesus is **not** the Holy Spirit. The Holy Spirit is rather the Spirit of Jesus or the Spirit of Christ (see Romans 8:9; 1 Peter 1:10-11); He is the Spirit of life,

He is God, He is the Word, He is the Lord. The Bible says, "Now the Lord **IS** the **Spirit**; and where the Spirit of the Lord is, there is liberty" (2 Corinthians 3:17). Indeed the Lord is the Spirit. The Lordship of the Holy Spirit is equal to that of God the Father and God the Son.

The Blasphemy Against the Holy Spirit is the Only Sin that Will Never Be Forgiven

Now, there is a sin for which there is no forgiveness either in this age or in the age to come (see Matthew 12:30-32), a sin that leads to (eternal) death (see 1 John 5:16-17), and that sin is the BLASPHEMY AGAINST THE HOLY SPIRIT. Jesus said, "Assuredly, I say to you, all sins will be forgiven the sons of men, and whatever blasphemies they may utter; BUT HE WHO BLASPHEMES AGAINST THE HOLY SPIRIT **NEVER** HAS FORGIVENESS, but is subject to eternal condemnation" — BECAUSE they said, "He has **an unclean spirit**." (Mark 3:28-30). Beloved, you will notice from Mark 3:22 and Matthew 12:24-25 that Jesus spoke these words in response to the Pharisees and "the scribes who came down from Jerusalem" — these were unbelievers, they did not believe in Jesus and so they called the Spirit in Him (or the Holy Spirit by which Jesus performed miracles and cast out demons) **an unclean spirit**. They said, "This fellow does not cast out demons except by Beelzebub, the ruler of demons." So Jesus' statement was a direct response to the Pharisees and scribes (those who did not believe in Him). The Bible says that Jesus "knew **their** thoughts and **said to THEM**: (Mark 3:23 actually says that Jesus **called THEM to Himself and said to THEM** in parables):…He who is not with Me i**s against Me**, and he who does not gather with Me **scatters abroad**. Therefore I say to **YOU** (you the Pharisees and scribes — you unbelievers), every sin and blasphemy will be forgiven men, but THE BLASPHEMY AGAINST THE SPIRIT WILL NOT BE FORGIVEN MEN. Anyone who speaks a word against the Son of Man, it will be forgiven him; but WHOEVER SPEAKS AGAINST THE Holy Spirit, **IT WILL NOT BE FORGIVEN HIM, EITHER IN THIS AGE OR IN THE AGE TO COME.**" (see Matthew 12:25, 30-32). Mark's gospel also adds that Jesus said this to the Scribes and Pharisees "**BECAUSE** THEY SAID, "HE HAS AN UNCLEAN SPIRIT."" Thus, **calling the Holy Spirit an unclean spirit** is "the BLASPHEMY AGAINST THE HOLY SPIRIT," and it is a sin that can only be committed by unbelievers and false believers — those who are not with Christ but against Him, who do not gather with Christ but scatter abroad. In fact, Luke's gospel is the only one that does not follow the chronological sequence of Jesus' discourse regarding the blasphemy against the Holy Spirit but inserts it as though Jesus were speaking broadly to everyone. (see Luke 12:8-10). But thank God Matthew and Mark gave us clarity on the subject. The blasphemy against the Holy Spirit was also the sin John was referring to when he said, "If anyone sees his brother sinning a sin which does not lead to death, he will ask, and He (God) WILL GIVE him LIFE for those who commit sin not leading to death. **THERE IS SIN LEADING TO DEATH.** I do not say that he should pray about that. All unrighteousness is sin, and **there is sin not leading to death**." (I John 5:16-17). "Brother" as used by John in this context refers broadly to any fellow or all the people whom we have to deal with in our day-to-day business, particularly unbelievers and false believers. John is not talking about true believers in this context because true believers already have LIFE (see 1 John 5:13; John 6:47), and will therefore not need to ask God again in prayer for LIFE (zoe). In fact Jesus Himself said, "Most assuredly, I say to you, he who hears My word and BELIEVES in Him who sent Me HAS EVERLASTING LIFE, and shall not come into judgment, but HAS PASSED FROM DEATH INTO LIFE." (John 5:24). Jesus again said, "I am the resurrection and the life. He who BELIEVES in Me, though he may die, he SHALL LIVE. And whoever lives and BELIEVES in Me SHALL NEVER DIE. Do you believe this?" (John 11:25-26). Sadly, many so-called believers today don't believe this.

As stated earlier, no true believer will blaspheme against the Holy Spirit or call the Holy Spirit an unclean spirit, and so no true believer will commit the sin leading to death. No true believer will blaspheme against the Holy Spirit also because NO TRUE BELIEVER SHALL EVER DIE (see John 11:26), and yet we know that the blasphemy against the Holy Spirit is a sin THAT LEADS TO DEATH, a sin that will never be forgiven. In this context also, any so-called believer who practices idolatry is a false believer, which is why John urges us in First John 5:21 to keep ourselves from idols. Amen. Anyone who claims to believe in Jesus Christ and claims to have understanding from Him (see First John 5:20), and yet practices idolatry, has by his actions denounced and renounced Jesus Christ and the Holy Spirit with whom he was sealed for the day of redemption. Such a person, just like those who follow the law to obtain their own righteousness or who mix grace with the law and teach others to do the same, walks as an enemy of the cross of Christ: "WHOSE END IS DESTRUCTION, whose god is their belly, and whose glory is in their shame—who set their mind on earthly things." (see Philippians 3:18-19). The Bible further says of such people that "it is impossible for those who were once enlightened, and have tasted the heavenly gift, and have become partakers of the Holy Spirit, and have tasted the good word of God and the powers of the age to come, if they fall away, to renew them again to repentance, since they crucify again for themselves the Son of God, and put Him to an open shame." (Hebrews 6:4-6). And of those who fall away, the apostle John says, "They went out from us, but they did not really belong to us. For if they had belonged to us, they would have remained with us; but their going showed that none of them belonged to us." (1 John 2:19 NIV).

Now, why did Jesus say that **blasphemy or words spoken against the Son of Man will be forgiven**, but blasphemy or words spoken against the Holy Spirit will **not** be forgiven? It is because the Son of Man (Jesus Christ) came down to the level of man by becoming a Man; the Son of Man (Jesus Christ) while He walked here on earth was fully man as though He were not God; Jesus the Son of Man was in the likeness of sinful flesh (see Romans 8:3); Jesus the Son of Man made Himself of no reputation, taking the form of a bondservant and coming in the likeness of men (see Philippians 2:7), so that He would suffer and taste death for all men, and that through death He might destroy the devil who had the power of death, and release those who through fear of death were all their lifetime subject to bondage (see Hebrews 2:9-18). And so Jesus the Son of Man could be despised, rejected, oppressed, afflicted, insulted, bruised, slapped, beaten, flogged, wounded, spat on, scorned, blasphemed, even killed, and it was all forgiven. But God the Holy Spirit is no man (see Numbers 23:19); God the Holy Spirit is not at the level of man; indeed the Holy Spirit is eternally God and will never come down to the level of man like God the Son (Jesus Christ) did — who made Himself of no reputation and became Man (see John 1:1, 14; 1 Timothy 3:16). Therefore, the Holy Spirit will not accept insults or blasphemy from any man. Blasphemy against the Holy Spirit will never be forgiven. Calling the Holy Spirit an unclean spirit will never be forgiven. When a man or woman attributes the work of the Holy Spirit to the work of an unclean spirit or Satan, that person commits the sin for which there is no forgiveness, either in this world or in the world to come. Indeed, blasphemy against the Holy Spirit is dangerous. And so if you see a man of God operating in the gifts or manifestation of the Spirit and you don't understand the works of the Spirit, don't despise them and attribute the work to Satan or an unclean spirit; it is better to keep quiet.

Moreover, it is easy to discern an unclean spirit from the Holy Spirit. The Bible says, "Beloved, **do not believe every spirit**, but **TEST the spirits**, whether they are of God; because many false prophets have gone out into the world. **BY THIS** you know the Spirit of God: **EVERY SPIRIT THAT CONFESSES THAT JESUS CHRIST HAS COME IN THE FLESH IS OF GOD**, and every spirit that **does not** confess that Jesus Christ has come in the flesh **is not of God. And this is the spirit of the Antichrist**, which you have heard was coming, and is now already in the world. You are of God, little children, and have overcome them, because He who is in you is greater than he who is in the world. They are of the world. Therefore they speak as of the world, and the world hears them. We are of God. He who knows God hears us; he who is not of God does not hear us. **BY THIS WE KNOW THE SPIRIT OF TRUTH AND THE spirit OF ERROR.**" (I John 4:1-6). If you're not sure of what spirit a person is working with or performing miracles by, simply ask them (while they're in manifestation of the spirit) if Jesus Christ has come in the flesh, if Jesus Christ was manifested on earth as a Man. If the response is YES, then the

Spirit is of God; but if the response is NO, then the spirit is not of God but is the spirit of the Antichrist. The Bible further states that "no one speaking by the Spirit of God calls Jesus accursed, and no one can say that Jesus is Lord except by the Holy Spirit." (I Corinthians 12:3). Indeed if you're a true or sincere believer, you need not live in fear of blaspheming against the Holy Spirit. Amen.

Follow the Holy Spirit

Every believer must intimately know and follow this very important Leader called the Holy Spirit. I have personally come to know, love, admire and follow Him so closely. And I can say that He is a wonderful Leader with an amazing and beautiful personality. I love Him because He loved me first. And I enjoy following Him, because He is loving, gentle, kind, compassionate, merciful and faithful, and He is the most powerful Person on earth today. The Holy Spirit or the Spirit has all the attributes of the Lord, because "the Lord is the Spirit." (see 2 Corinthians 3:17).

You would remember that Jesus, while He walked on this earth, asked His disciples to follow Him. (see Matthew 4:19; Matthew 16:24). Then one day He said, "I go away to Him who sent Me." (see Matthew 16:5). "Where I am going you cannot come." (see John 13:33). Jesus also said, "Where I am going, **you cannot follow Me now, but you shall follow me afterward**" (see John 13:36). Then He pointed us to another Leader — the Holy Spirit. (see John 16:7, 12-13). Jesus promised to send the Holy Spirit to us as another Helper, another Teacher, another Leader or Guide whom we will FOLLOW.

Today, all believers are commanded to follow the Holy Spirit. He is the most important Leader here on earth. As long as you follow the Holy Spirit, you will be following Jesus Christ, because the Holy Spirit is the Spirit of Christ (see Romans 8:9; Galatians 4:6), and He is here to glorify Jesus by taking of what belongs to Jesus, and declaring it to us. (see John 16:14). The Bible says, "Now WE HAVE RECEIVED, **not the spirit of the world**, but **THE Spirit WHO IS FROM GOD**, that WE MIGHT KNOW THE THINGS THAT HAVE BEEN FREELY GIVEN TO US BY GOD." (I Corinthians 2:12). Therefore, in our own best interest, we are to follow the Holy Spirit whom we have received from God, and allow Him to lead us, so that we will know the things that have been freely given to us by God.

The Bible also says that, "For as many as ARE LED by the Spirit of God, these are sons of God." (Romans 8:14). This implies also that as many as FOLLOW the Holy Sprit, these are sons of God. The Holy Spirit is our Leader, and we must all acknowledge Him and follow Him closely. We must all have communion or fellowship with the Holy Spirit and become conscious of His everlasting presence, to the point where He is more real or tangible to us than our brother or sister or spouse or parents or best friend. The Holy Spirit indeed wants to be our closest ally in reality. And it behooves us to ally with Him — talk to Him and listen to Him. Since I came to know Him, I call Him my best Friend, my beloved Companion, my Lord, my Teacher, and my Senior Partner in Ministry, and I pray that He will become your best friend too as you acknowledge Him, follow Him, and fellowship with Him.

Do Not Grieve the Holy Spirit

The Bible commands us also not to grieve the Holy Spirit. It says, *"Let no corrupt word proceed out of your mouth, but what is good for necessary edification, that it may impart grace to the hearers.* ***And DO NOT GRIEVE the Holy Spirit of God, by whom you were sealed for the day of redemption.*** *Let all bitterness, wrath, anger, clamor, and evil speaking be put away from you, with all malice."* (Ephesians 4:29-31).

Clearly, this command was spoken to believers — true believers who were sealed with the Holy Spirit for the day of redemption. Therefore, unlike the blasphemy against the Holy Spirit which cannot be committed by a true believer, any believer can grieve the Holy Spirit, if we're not careful to consistently walk in the Spirit. And even though the Bible does not ascribe any punishment in the New Testament for grieving the Holy Spirit, it explicitly commands us not to grieve the Holy Spirit. And of course, we know from the Old Testament that grieving the Holy Spirit makes God angry. Throughout the Scriptures it is clear that "**unbelief**" grieves the Holy Spirit, especially unbelief that results in evil speaking, grumbling, bitterness, anger, wrath and clamor. Speaking concerning the children of Israel after recounting the great goodness of the Lord toward them, the prophet Isaiah says, "But they (the children of Israel) **rebelled and GRIEVED His Holy Spirit**; so He turned Himself against them as an enemy, and He fought against them." (Isaiah 63:10).

A study of the history of the Jews from the time of their deliverance from slavery in Egypt throughout their journey from the wilderness to the promised land reveals that they were a rebellious people whose unbelief is spoken of widely, who consistently were bitter and angry with one another and with their leaders; they grumbled against God, and did many other abominations against God, even to the point of worshipping foreign gods and walking as the Gentiles walk. The prophet Zechariah said, "Yes, they made their hearts like flint, **refusing to hear the law and the words which the Lord of hosts had sent by His Spirit** through the former prophets. Thus great wrath came from the Lord of hosts." (Zechariah 7:12). Indeed, the deeds of the children of Israel GRIEVED the Holy Spirit who was with them, whom God had put in their midst, and God's anger burned against them. (see Isaiah 63:10-11). The Psalmist says, "By the waters of Meribah they angered the Lord, and trouble came to Moses because of them; for they **REBELLED against the Spirit of God**, and rash words came from Moses' lips." (Psalm 106:32-33 NIV). And so when Stephen addressed the Council of the Jews in Acts 7, he said, "You stiff-necked and uncircumcised in heart and ears! You always RESIST the Holy Spirit; as your fathers did, so do you." (Acts 7:51).

Indeed, unbelief grieves the Holy Spirit. When you deny the power or words of the Holy Spirit, you grieve Him; when you refuse to hear the Word of God and refuse to do the words which He has given us by His Spirit, you grieve the Holy Spirit; when you sin willfully after you have received the knowledge of the truth (see Hebrews 10:26), you grieve the Holy Spirit; when you refuse to put off, concerning your former conduct, the old self which grows corrupt according to the deceitful lusts, and refuse to renew your mind (with the Word of God), refuse to put on the new self which was created according to God in true righteousness and holiness, and to walk worthy of the calling with which you were called, with all lowliness and gentleness, with long-suffering, bearing with one another in love, endeavoring to keep the unity of the Spirit in the bond of peace, but choose instead to give place to the devil and walk as the rest of the Gentiles walk, you grieve the Holy Spirit; when you refuse to be compassionate and kind to others, and refuse to forgive others as God in Christ forgave you, you grieve the Holy Spirit; when you steal, refuse to put away lying and refuse to speak the truth with your neighbor, when you are bitter, when you sin in your anger and allow the sun to go down on your wrath, when you engage in grumbling, clamor and evil speaking (i.e. speaking corrupt words or words that do not edify), as well as malice, you grieve the Holy Spirit, for the Holy Spirit is a Spirit of power, and **of love** and of a sound mind. (see 2 Timothy 1:7). We also know that the Kingdom of God, which has been conferred on us (see Luke 22:29) and in which we live as believers (see Colossians 1:13), is a matter of RIGHTEOUSNESS, PEACE and JOY in the Holy Spirit. (see Romans 14:17). Therefore, let us walk in the Spirit and we will never grieve the Holy Spirit; let us walk in love and we will never grieve the Holy Spirit; let us practice righteousness and holiness, and we will never grieve the Holy Spirit.

We all love the Holy Spirit, don't we? After all, He is the Lord (see 2 Corinthians 3:17), and He first loved us. (see 1 John 4:19). Therefore we shouldn't grieve the One we love. The Bible says, "Let those who love the Lord hate evil, for He guards the lives of His faithful ones and delivers them from the hand of the wicked." (Psalm 97:10 NIV). It is also written of our blessed Lord Jesus Christ, "You have loved righteousness and hated wickedness; therefore God, Your God, has set You above Your companions by anointing You with the oil of joy." (Hebrews 1:19 NIV). It is the will and purpose of God that as the Spirit of Christ dwells in us and leads us, we should likewise love righteousness and hate wickedness. Truly, the Holy Spirit is our Leader (see Romans 8:14), and He wants to lead us in the paths of righteousness for His name's sake (see Psalm 23:3); He wants to express Himself in our actions and attitudes; He wants Christ to be seen in our every word and action so that we will be effective witnesses to Christ; and all He asks is for us to cooperate with Him and yield or submit our will and our body to Him or "die daily," just like the apostle Paul, so that Christ can live in us. (see Galatians 2:20). When we do not allow the Spirit to express Himself in us and be seen in our words and actions, and choose instead to habitually do things according to the lusts of the flesh, and according to our own efforts and abilities, we put out or **quench** the Spirit (see 1 Thessalonians 5:19), which prevents us from being effective witnesses to Christ. May we all yield to the Holy Spirit as He works in us both to will and to do for His good pleasure. (see Philippians 2:13).

The Holy Spirit (or the Anointing) is In Every Believer, and He Will Be With Us Forever

The Holy Spirit, who is also called the Anointing, is in each and every believer. (see 1 John 2:20, 27). Thus every believer has the Anointing **within** them (see 2 Corinthians 1:21), but the Anointing can also be **upon** every believer through the Holy Spirit baptism. And once we have received the Holy Spirit baptism, we can walk and preach in demonstration of the Spirit and of power. (see 1 Corinthians 2:4; 1 Corinthians 4:20).

The Anointing will manifest in your life and ministry only to the extent that you have a personal, deeply private encounter with the

Spirit, desire and receive the manifestation of the Spirit or the gifts of the Spirit, and surrender completely to the Spirit as a vessel for honor, sanctified, and available for use as a witness to Jesus Christ the Master, to the praise and glory of God the Father. And it continues and grows with a fellowship and communion with the Holy Spirit that only you can develop. You can consistently walk in the fullness of the Anointing by continually studying and meditating on the Word of God, being prayerful, and especially praying in the Spirit continually, offering praises and thanksgiving to God and always being conscious of His presence. You have to devote much time to fellowshipping with the Holy Spirit — talking to Him, listening to Him, and just meditating on His presence. And finally, you have to trust the Holy Spirit. Learn to surrender like a child to the Holy Spirit. Trust Him completely and just yield to Him the way you will sit on a stable chair and yield all your weight to it without questioning its ability to support your weight. The Holy Spirit loves to use people who trust Him in a childlike way. If you will trust Him and develop your relationship with and sensitivity to the Holy Spirit, then whenever you get up anywhere and start out in faith to minister in the name of Jesus, the Anointing will manifest to the glory of God and for all to see that it is not by man's power or man's might, but by the Spirit of God.

That the Holy Spirit or the Anointing is in every believer today is a privilege which the Old Testament believers never had. In the Old Testament, God (the Holy Spirit) could not dwell in each and everyone of the people because they were sinners. The Holy Spirit or the Anointing was only in and upon a select few who were justified or declared righteous by God (by grace through faith, by the grace of God which was given in Christ before the foundation of the world — see 2

Timothy 1:9-10, with Ephesians 1:4). The Bible says that God dwelt among the children of Israel in the Holy of Holies in the Temple. No one could go into the Holy of Holies except the High Priest, and he could do so only once a year, on the Day of Atonement, and not without blood sacrifice to atone for his own sins and the sins of the nation. It would be difficult for the Old Covenant believers to fathom how the same holy God would make **each and every** New Covenant believer His temple and dwell in us. But this is the reality today. What was a mystery to them has now been revealed to us. Christ made every believer holy and righteous by the sacrifice of Himself at the cross so that God (the Holy Spirit) could dwell in every believer. Thus the Holy Spirit indwells all of us to testify to the finished work of Christ. He was sent as a direct result of Jesus' finished work in washing away our sins. The indwelling of the Holy Spirit is, therefore, the evidence that we have been made righteous and holy in Christ (see 2 Corinthians 5:21; Ephesians 4:24; 1 Corinthians 6:19). Hence, one of the primary functions of the Holy Spirit today is to convict believers that we are already righteous in Christ. This is why Jesus said of the Holy Spirit that, "And when He has come, He will convict the world of sin, **and of righteousness**, and of judgment: of sin, because they do not believe in Me; **of righteousness, because I go to My Father and you see Me no more;** of judgment, because the ruler of this world is judged." (John 16:8-11). The Holy Spirit convicts the world (unbelievers) of sin — the singular sin of not believing in Jesus Christ (see John 16:9). When we preach the gospel to unbelievers, it is the Holy Spirit who convicts them of sin so that they can repent and accept Jesus Christ as their Lord and Savior. But once we put our faith in Jesus Christ as our Lord and Savior, the Holy Spirit comes to live in us to convict us of righteousness, because Jesus has finished His redemptive work on the cross, and has gone to sit on the Father's right hand as our High Priest, Advocate and Intercessor — to uphold our righteousness in Him. (see John 16:10; Ephesians 1:20; Romans 8:34). The Holy Spirit has the duty of telling and reminding us every time that there is now no condemnation for those who are in Christ Jesus (see Romans 8:1); He bears witness with our spirit that we are children of God (see Romans 8:16). The Holy Spirit also has the function of convicting the world that the Devil and all who obey him will be judged. But that is not all. The Holy Spirit is ultimately our Helper, our Comforter. He lives in us and comes upon us **for service** to glorify Jesus Christ. (see John 16:14; Acts 1:8). He lives inside our hearts (see 2 Corinthians 1:22) and abides with us forever (see John 14:16, 17). The Holy Spirit is in each of us to help us grow in our relationship with our heavenly Father through our Lord Jesus Christ. It is **BY** the Holy Spirit that we all have **access** to God the Father through Jesus Christ our Lord. The Bible says, "For through Him (i.e. Jesus Christ) we both HAVE access **BY one Spirit** to the Father." (Ephesians 2:18). The Holy Spirit is truly one with the Father and with the Son, and is equally deserving of our recognition and worship. We can have fellowship and communion with Him (see 2 Corinthians 13:14). He is real; we can talk to Him, listen to Him, and experience His leading in our hearts. Indeed we shouldn't neglect Him, but should always be conscious of His presence and communion.

Beloved, the Holy Spirit also came **to channel the love of God into our hearts**. Romans 5:5 says that God's love has been POURED OUT in our hearts by the Holy Spirit, who has been given to us. The Holy Spirit helps us to experience the magnitude of God's love. He fills our hearts with God's love, so that we can always feel loved and share the

God-kind of love with others. He is in us to constantly encourage us and assure us of God's unconditional love, which we are also to spread around the world. He is in us to assure us that nothing can separate us from the love of God which is in Christ Jesus. (see Romans 8:38-39).

The Holy Spirit is also **our Teacher** (see John 14:26; 1 John 2:20, 27)). He is the greatest Teacher in the world, and He teaches us concerning ALL things. The Holy Spirit has no limitations on knowledge. He knows all things and is always teaching us, if only we would pay attention to His teachings and receive from Him, if only we would ask Him questions and let Him teach us. He is the Spirit of truth (see John 16:13); He is the Spirit of wisdom and revelation (see Ephesians 1:17), so He helps us to understand the truth of God's Word, and He reveals to us all that Jesus has accomplished for us, so that we can walk closely with God in a living relationship, and walk circumspectly as wise, and not as fools (see Ephesians 5:15). The Holy Spirit instructs us in our hearts since He dwells in our hearts and is joined to our spirit. First Corinthians 6:17 says, "He who is joined to the Lord is one spirit with Him." Because of this union, the Holy Spirit is able to impart His guidance and His desires into our minds and our hearts. Hebrews 8:10 says that He puts His laws in our minds and writes them on our hearts. Not only does He guide us, He also gives us the desire to walk in His will. When we are in communion with Him, we can **recognize** His promptings and we will **hear** His voice. When we are faced with difficult situations or decisions, He will point us to the best solutions and decisions, if we consult with Him. He will even tell us things to come (see John 16:8-13). Isn't it exciting and empowering to go through all of life's challenges with the help of the Person who knows all things and has all the answers? If you're in a situation today where you have tried everything but there seems to be no way out, what you need is to stop trying in your own efforts, and start asking the Holy Spirit and listening to Him for His answers. It is in experiencing the Holy Spirit as your personal Teacher and Leader, and allowing yourself to be taught and led by Him that you can know all things and live a truly fruitful and fulfilling life.

The Bible says that the Holy Spirit also **protects us** from the enemy: "So shall they fear the name of the Lord from the west, and His glory from the rising of the sun; When the **enemy** comes in like a flood, **the Spirit of the Lord will lift up a standard against him.**" (Isaiah 59:19). The Holy Spirit fights our battles for us. When the enemy comes in like a flood, he can never defeat us, because the Spirit of the Lord will defend and protect us. We should never live in fear, because victory is ours in every battle of life. "'Not by might nor by power, but by My Spirit,' says the Lord of hosts." (see Zechariah 4:6). Thank God for the Holy Spirit!

Jesus Christ is the One Who Baptizes With the Holy Spirit (the Anointing)

As a forerunner to Jesus, there were many things John the Baptist could have said about Jesus Christ, but more importantly, he spoke of Him as **the One who will baptize with the Holy Spirit**. "And he (John) preached, saying, "There comes One after me who is mightier than I, whose sandal strap I am not worthy to stoop down and loose. I indeed baptized you with water, but HE WILL BAPTIZE YOU WITH THE HOLY SPIRIT." (Mark 1:7-8). On several occasions, Jesus also spoke to His disciples about the coming Holy Spirit baptism, which He frequently referred to as "the promise of the Father" (see Luke 24:49; Acts 1:4; Luke 11:13; Luke 12:12; John 7:37-39; John 7:14-16). Indeed the Holy Spirit baptism was **promised** by the Father through the prophet Joel (see Joel 2:28-30) and also through the prophet Isaiah (see Isaiah 44:2-6), but it was to be **fulfilled** after the death and resurrection of the Lord Jesus Christ. The promised Holy Spirit was to be received after Jesus was glorified, and it was to be received by all those who would believe in Jesus Christ. (see John 7:38-39; Acts 2:39).

We learned earlier that when we accepted Jesus as our Lord and Savior, God gave us His Spirit — and sealed us with the Holy Spirit as a guarantee that we belong to Him and to the Body of Christ (see 2 Corinthians 1:22; Ephesians 1:13). Paul says, "For by one Spirit we were all baptized into one body— whether Jews or Greeks, whether slaves or free—and have all been made to drink into one Spirit." (I Corinthians 12:13). This means we all have the one (or same) Spirit of Christ, having been baptized into the Body of Christ BY the Holy Spirit. Romans 8:9 says anyone who does not have the Spirit of Christ does not belong to Christ. As believers, we have all been made to drink into one Spirit. When we believed in Jesus Christ, the Holy Spirit came to live in us to secure our salvation. It is like a fountain of water within us springing up into everlasting life (see John 4:13-14). The Holy Spirit works in us and moves in our life to give us eternal life. He helps us to know the one true God and Jesus Christ whom He has sent (see John 17:3), to experience a living relationship with God through our Lord and Savior Jesus Christ. But there is **a second experience** with the Holy Spirit where we are baptized (immersed, submerged) in the Holy Spirit BY our Lord Jesus Christ. This second experience also results in us being stirred up and **filled** with the Holy Spirit (see Acts 2:4). This is the clear teaching of the Bible. There is, however, a cross-section of believers who don't believe in this second experience with the Holy Spirit. Vain Religion has taught them that the indwelling of the Holy Spirit during the born-again experience is the only experience there is. And unfortunately, many sincere believers have bought into this false teaching and would not even allow the Bible to get in the way of what they believe. If you're one such person who wouldn't allow the Bible to get in the way of what you believe, this teaching is not for you. But if you believe in the Bible, then join me in opening our hearts and minds as the Holy Spirit unveils what the Bible really teaches on this subject.

The Spirit (or Anointing) Within Versus the Spirit (or Anointing) Upon

Let's begin with **THE EXAMPLE OF OUR FORERUNNER JESUS CHRIST, the Captain of our salvation.** The Bible says, *"How GOD ANOINTED JESUS of Nazareth WITH THE HOLY SPIRIT AND WITH POWER, who went about DOING GOOD and HEALING ALL who were oppressed by the devil, for God was with Him."* (Acts 10:38).

Now, catch this revelation and understand the parallels between the life of Jesus Christ when He walked here on earth, and the life of the New Covenant believer today. Jesus, when He first made an entrance into this world as a Man born of a woman (see Galatians 4:4), was also **born of the Holy Spirit** (see Luke 1:34-35) just like every born-again believer today (see John 3:5-6, with Titus 3:5). And so Jesus was called the Son of God (see Luke 1:35) just like every believer today. (see John 1:12; Galatians 3:26; 1 John 3:1). The Spirit of God (or the Holy Spirit) that overshadowed Mary to conceive and give birth to Jesus, remained in Him; in fact, **the Holy Spirit was His seal of Sonship**, just as He is our seal today. (see John 6:27; Galatians 4:6, with Ephesians 1:13, and 2 Corinthians 1:22). Jesus thus had the Holy Spirit **in** or **within** Him. Right from His birth Jesus was as much the Son of God as He was the Son of Man, just as all believers are today. Yet, Jesus couldn't or didn't perform a single miracle (at least, there is no record of one in the Bible), until the Holy Spirit descended (or came) **upon** Him and remained **on** Him following His water baptism by John. (see Luke 3:21-22; John 1:33). Indeed, Jesus didn't perform a single miracle until He was **anointed** by God with the Holy Spirit and with power. (see Acts 10:38). The Bible says of this anointing that the Holy Spirit descended **upon** Jesus in bodily form like a dove (WHILE He PRAYED) and remained **on** Him. (see Luke 3:21-22, with John 1:33). And from that moment, Jesus **received power**, walked **in the power of the Holy Spirit**, and went about DOING GOOD and HEALING ALL who were oppressed by the devil, for God was with Him (see Acts 10:38, with Luke 4:14); Jesus was **filled** with the Holy Spirit, and He was **led** by the Spirit. (see Luke 4:1). And yes, Jesus knew and acknowledged that the Spirit had come **upon** Him. He said, "The Spirit of the Lord IS **UPON** Me, Because He HAS ANOINTED Me TO PREACH the gospel to the poor; He has SENT Me TO HEAL the brokenhearted, TO PROCLAIM LIBERTY to the captives AND RECOVERY OF SIGHT to the blind, TO SET AT LIBERTY those who are OPPRESSED; TO PROCLAIM the acceptable year of the Lord." (Luke 4:18-19).

Thus, **after** Jesus was anointed with the Holy Spirit and with power, He began His ministry (at age 30) — see Luke 3:23). He didn't begin His ministry a minute sooner. From then, the Bible says, "And Jesus went about all Galilee, TEACHING in their synagogues, PREACHING the gospel of the kingdom, and HEALING ALL KINDS of sickness and ALL KINDS of disease AMONG THE PEOPLE." (Matthew 4:23). Jesus, **after being anointed with the Holy Spirit and with power**, went on to perform His very first miracle: changing water into wine at a wedding in Cana of Galilee. (see John 2:1-11). But until then, He walked here on earth as much a Man, as though He wasn't God. (see Philippians 2:5-8; Hebrews 4:15; Hebrews 5:7-9; Hebrews 2:9-18). The Bible says that this miracle of changing water into wine was the BEGINNING (or the first) of signs (or attesting miracles) that Jesus did. (see John 2:11). And He was able to perform this sign (or attesting miracle) only after being ANOINTED with the HOLY SPIRIT and with POWER. Thus, the Holy Spirit was the One who powered all the miracles Jesus performed while He walked here on earth as a Man as though He wasn't God.

Beloved, the Holy Spirit was the secret to Jesus' power and ministry. Jesus in His previous 29 years of existence showed no such power. The Bible only says of Him while He was growing up, that "the Child grew and became strong in spirit, filled with wisdom; and the grace of God was upon Him" (see Luke 2:40); and that, "Jesus increased in wisdom and stature, and in favor with God and men." (see Luke 2:52). He had no notable accomplishments of His own at this point in His life prior to being anointed with the Holy Spirit and with power. Jesus was only known in His hometown as Mary's Son, as the carpenter, as the carpenter's Son, and as brother of James, Joses, Judas, and Simon.

(see Mark 6:3; Matthew 13:55). He was described in very ordinary terms. But now at age 30, Jesus began His ministry with such great power that those same people in His hometown who had considered Him an ordinary Man all this while, were now puzzled; and while they still disparaged Him, they couldn't help but notice the change (or the transformation) in Him, and they expressed their bewilderment over what had become of Him; they queried if Jesus wasn't that (same) carpenter, if He wasn't that same carpenter's Son, if He wasn't that same Son of Mary whom they knew, if He wasn't the same Man whose brothers and sisters were walking around town. (see Mark 6:3; Matthew 13:55). They wondered where this same Man got these things (see Matthew 13:56) — the, power, the knowledge, and the wisdom. And so they took offense at Him. (see Matthew 13:57). "But Jesus said to them, "A prophet is not without honor **except** IN HIS OWN COUNTRY, among HIS OWN RELATIVES, and IN HIS OWN HOUSE." (Mark 6:4). How true this statement is!

Now, what made such a dramatic difference in Jesus' life? What brought such a transformation — such power — that offended people who knew Him prior to this day? I will tell you what: **it was the Holy Spirit**. When the Holy Spirit came **upon** Him and remained on Him, Jesus **received power**; He was anointed with the Holy Spirit and with POWER. (see Acts 10:38). He was **filled** with the Holy Spirit, and was **led** by the Holy Spirit. (see Luke 4:1). The Holy Spirit made all the difference. Jesus was no longer just the sinless Man and carpenter walking the streets of Nazareth of Galilee; He was now a Man anointed with the Spirit of God and the POWER of God, a Man filled with the Holy Spirit. The fullness of God was in Him bodily. He was God manifested in the flesh. The Holy Spirit had equipped

Him and strengthened Him with the power He needed for ministry or service as He represented God as a Man here on earth. And so Jesus' Words were now God's Words (see John 12:49-50); His works were God's works (see John 5:19-20; John 14:10-11). He spoke boldly, taught as one having authority (see Mark 1:22; Matthew 7:29), and performed all His deeds in the name (i.e. the authority, power and identity) of God the Father, as He went about doing God's will. (see John 6:38). Even the officers who were sent by the chief priests and Pharisees to arrest Jesus stood in awe of Him and couldn't arrest Him, returning to the chief priests and Pharisees to testify of Jesus that "No man ever spoke like this Man!" (see John 7:45-46). That is the difference the Holy Spirit makes and made in Jesus' life. And Jesus wanted His disciples (those of us who believe in Him) to have the same experience, to have the Holy Spirit come (or descend) **upon** us, remain on us, and fill us, so that we will receive power (see Acts 1:8) to be just as Himself, to be witnesses to Him, doing the same works He did and even greater works than He did (see John 14:12); so that (as Paul admonishes us) whatever we do in word or deed, we will DO ALL IN THE NAME (i.e. the authority, power and identity) OF THE LORD JESUS, giving thanks to God the Father through Him. (see Colossians 3:17). This is what it means to be a witness to Jesus. This is what Christianity is all about.

And so, before Jesus ascended into Heaven, even though He had breathed on His disciples and spoken to them to receive the Holy Spirit (see John 20:22), and thus His disciples had been born of the Spirit at that point and had the Spirit **IN** or **within** them (just like Jesus when He was originally born of the Spirit through Mary), and just like all of us when we also believed in Jesus (see 1 Corinthians

12:13; John 3:5-6; Titus 3:5), Jesus still told them not to begin their ministry yet, but to wait in Jerusalem until the Holy Spirit (the Promise of the Father) came **UPON** them and they were "ENDUED WITH POWER FROM ON HIGH." (see Luke 24:49). He said, "But YOU SHALL RECEIVE POWER when the Holy Spirit has COME **UPON** YOU; and you shall be witnesses to Me in Jerusalem, and in all Judea and Samaria, and to the end of the earth." (Acts 1:8). This became a reality for the early disciples on the Day of Pentecost.

Beloved, the Holy Spirit brought **power** to the early disciples, and they became Spirit-filled men who were so bold and powerful that (in the words of the unbelieving Jews) they "turned the world upside down." (see Acts 17:6). The Holy Spirit belongs to you also if you're a believer. The Holy Spirit is already **in** or **within** you (specifically in your heart) through the born-again experience. (see 1 Corinthians 12:13, with Galatians 4:6, and Romans 8:9). But Jesus wants Him (the Holy Spirit) to come **upon** you also, and **fill** you, so that you will be ENDUED WITH POWER from on high, and BE A WITNESS to our Lord Jesus Christ, in your immediate locality and all around the world. Jesus said that God will give the Holy Spirit to those who ask Him. (see Luke 11:13). So if the Holy Spirit hasn't come upon you yet, **ask our Heavenly Father in prayer**; and Jesus Christ who baptizes with the Holy Spirit (see Matthew 3:11; John 1:33) will send Him upon you. You can also **ask any Spirit-filled believer to lay hands on you** to receive the Holy Spirit. (see Acts 8:18). Indeed, when the Holy Spirit comes upon you and fills you, and you yield (or surrender) to Him and walk in the consciousness of His presence, exercising His power, you will never be an ordinary man; you will be a man in whom the fullness of God dwells and manifests, and to whom all things are possible. And your works will testify of you that you are truly the son of God, thus bringing glory to God the Father and to our Lord Jesus Christ.

The Example of the Early Disciples

The Bible says in Romans 10:9-10, "If you declare with your mouth, "Jesus is Lord," and believe in your heart that God raised him from the dead, you will be saved. For it is with your heart that you believe and are justified, and it is with your mouth that you profess your faith and are saved." The disciples of Jesus believed in their heart that God had raised Jesus from the dead. The Bible says Jesus presented Himself alive to the disciples "after His suffering by many infallible proofs, being seen by them during forty days and speaking of the things pertaining to the kingdom of God." (see Acts 1:3). On one occasion, Thomas even confessed Jesus as his Lord and his God (see John 20:28). All the disciples believed in Jesus and in His resurrection, so much so that Jesus Himself even called them **witnesses** of His suffering (or death) and resurrection. (see Luke 24:46-48). In fact, the disciples believed in Jesus and in His resurrection to the extent that, the Bible says, "they **worshiped Him**, and returned to Jerusalem with great joy, and were continually in the temple praising and blessing God. Amen." (see Luke 24:52-53). And so, according to Romans 10:9-10, these disciples were saved on the same day of Jesus' resurrection. On that same evening of Jesus' resurrection, because the disciples believed in Him, Jesus breathed on them and said, "Receive the Holy Spirit..." (see John 20:19, 22). Jesus was not kidding. The disciples who were present were receiving the Holy Spirit as part of their salvation experience. And so the Spirit came to dwell **in** or **within** them.

As we learned earlier, First Corinthians 12:13 says of all believers that "we were all baptized by one Spirit so as to form one body—whether Jews or Gentiles, slave or free—and we were all given the one Spirit to drink." Jesus' disciples (being a part of the Body of Christ) were also baptized by one Spirit and given the one Spirit to drink, in the same instance they believed in Jesus Christ and in His resurrection. Yet, Jesus told all of them (including Thomas) not to leave Jerusalem until they received the baptism in the Holy Spirit or until the Holy Spirit came **upon** them, which was to give them power or ability from on high (see Acts 1:4-5, 8; with Luke 24:49). The reason Jesus told them to wait in Jerusalem for the Holy Spirit to come **upon** them is that the Holy Spirit had not come **upon** them yet. This tells us that receiving the Holy Spirit **in** or **within** us at salvation IS A SEPARATE EXPERIENCE FROM receiving the THE HOLY SPIRIT **upon** us. In fact, the Bible is replete with evidence in support of this truth. We already cited the example of our Lord Jesus Christ Himself, who having been born of the Holy Spirit, already had the Holy Spirit **in** or **within** Him, and yet, did not begin His earth ministry until the Holy Spirit descended **upon** Him. (see Luke 3:21-22).

In Acts 8:14-17, there is an account of believers in Samaria who had accepted Jesus and been baptized in the name of Jesus. They were saved. According to Ephesians 1:13, they already had the Holy Spirit in them, and according to 1 Corinthians 12:13, we (including them) "were all baptized by one Spirit so as to form one body…and we were all given the one Spirit to drink." Yet, these believers in Samaria still needed to receive the baptism in the Holy Spirit. Subsequently, Peter and John went over and **laid hands on them**, and they received the Holy Spirit like the apostles did on the Day of Pentecost.

There is yet another account of believers in Ephesus who heard the gospel from Paul and believed. They received their salvation, and according to First Corinthians 12:13 and Ephesians 1:13, they received the Holy Spirit instantly. Yet, Paul did not stop there; he ministered the baptism in the Holy Spirit to them. Paul **laid his hands on them** to receive the baptism in the Spirit. The Holy Spirit came upon them and they spoke with tongues —all 12 of them. (see Acts 19:4-7).

All these examples present incontrovertible evidence that our Lord Jesus Christ, as well as all the early disciples, considered receiving the Holy Spirit **in** or **within** us at salvation as a separate experience from the baptism in the Holy Spirit when we receive Him **upon** us. The early apostles did well to preserve the faith and pass it on to us through their inspired writings. We cannot do anything contrary to what they did if we want to experience the same miraculous power of the Holy Spirit that they experienced. Today we have to live with the conviction that the Holy Spirit coming **in** or **within** us during the new birth experience is unique and separate from the experience of being baptized in the Holy Spirit or having the Holy Spirit come **upon** us. They may be separated by minutes (as I believe was the case with Cornelius in Acts 10:44-48), hours, weeks, days, months or even years; still, they are always separate experiences according to the Bible. Therefore, if you're a believer and you're not experiencing the miraculous power of the Holy Spirit in your life in the same manner as the early disciples did, it is time to desire and pray and receive the baptism in the Holy Spirit. (see Luke 11:13, with Acts 8:15). Have no doubts about the baptism in the Holy Spirit. **Those who doubt it will not experience it.** Nor will they experience the power that it brings. Peter assured us in Acts 2:39 that the promised Holy Spirit baptism is a gift that is "for you and your children and for **all** who are far off—for **all** whom the Lord our God will call." It was not for the early disciples only. In Luke 11:13, Jesus also affirms that God gives the Holy Spirit "to those who ask Him." Amazing things will happen to you when you believe in Jesus and receive the baptism in the Holy Spirit. Jesus Himself said, "And these signs will follow THOSE WHO BELIEVE: In My name they will cast out demons; THEY WILL SPEAK WITH NEW TONGUES; they will take up serpents; and if they drink anything deadly, it will by no means hurt them; they will lay hands on the sick, and they will recover." (Mark 16:17-18). This can be a reality in your life.

The Bible records that when the early disciples were baptized in the Holy Spirit on the Day of Pentecost, "THEY WERE ALL FILLED WITH THE HOLY SPIRIT and BEGAN TO SPEAK WITH OTHER TONGUES, as the Spirit gave them utterance." (see Acts 2:4). So the baptism in the Holy Spirit is an experience of the Holy Spirit falling **upon** you (see Acts 10:44), so that you are **filled** with the Holy Spirit, speak in/with other tongues, and receive power to be a witness to Christ. Thus, Acts 2:4 is the fulfillment of Acts 1:4-8. In the baptism in the Holy Spirit, or when the Holy Spirit comes upon us, God stirs up or fans to full flame for us the Spirit that is already in us, and we become FILLED with the Holy Spirit, and receive power or ability from God. Thus, the baptism in the Holy Spirit is like rivers of living water **flowing out** from our hearts (see John 7:37-39). Through this baptism, the Holy Spirit flows out from our hearts to bless others and to make our very lives a witness to Christ, as we receive the power to preach boldly and authoritatively and to perform miraculous works. This is why we should all desire the baptism in the Holy Spirit "until the Spirit is poured **upon** us from on high, and the wilderness becomes a fruitful field, and the fruitful field is counted as a forest. Then justice will dwell in the wilderness, and righteousness remain in the fruitful field." (Isaiah 32:15-16).

As we noted earlier, under the Old Covenant only few of the Old Covenant believers were chosen by God to be **filled** with the Holy Spirit for His purpose. These included Joseph (see Genesis 41:38) when he interpreted Pharaoh's dream, and Bezalel of the tribe of Judah who was given supernatural skill in designing and working the gold, silver, and bronze ornamentation for the tabernacle (see Exodus 31:2-4). John the Baptist (see Luke 1:15) as well as his parents, Zechariah and Elizabeth, were also filled with the Holy Spirit (see Luke 1:41, 1:67). The Holy Spirit also came **upon** some chosen people under the Old Covenant, as we noted earlier. Such people included Balaam (see Numbers 24:2), Saul (see 1 Samuel 11:6), Amasai (see 1 Chronicles 12:18), Azariah (see 2 Chronicles 15:1), Othniel (see Judges 3:9-10), Gideon (see Judges 6:34), Jephthah (see Judges 11:29), Samson (see Judges 14:6; Judges 15:14), Zechariah (see 2 Chronicles 24:20), Mary the Mother of Jesus (see Luke 1:35), and Simeon (see Luke 2:25). The Holy Spirit was **with** David (see 1 Samuel 16:13, 18), Moses and Joshua (see Joshua 1:5), and was also **in** all the Prophets (see 1 Peter 1:10-12). But the Holy Spirit was never made available to ALL (or every single one) of the Old Covenant folks or the people of the circumcision. The privilege we have today as New Covenant believers is that each and every one of us has the Holy Spirit **in** us, which we received during our born-again experience (see Ephesians 1:13); and we can also ask to be baptized or (completely) immersed in and filled with the Holy Spirit, so that the Holy Spirit will also be **upon** us.

(see Luke 11:13, with Acts 1:4-5, 8). And once the Holy Spirit comes **upon** us and we are filled with the Holy Spirit, we can remain continually filled by praying, praising and worshipping God both in tongues and in the known language, and in Psalms and hymns (see Acts 4:31, with Ephesians 5:18-19). In Acts 4:31, the early apostles (who had experienced the infilling of the Holy Spirit at Pentecost a few chapters earlier) prayed to the Lord and the place was shaken: "And THEY WERE FILLED with the Holy Spirit and spoke the word of God boldly." Ephesians 5:18-19 contrasts being filled with the Holy Spirit with being drunk with wine in the natural. Indeed, it is an intoxicating spiritual experience to drink the new wine of the Holy Spirit. The experience of being baptized in the Holy Spirit is not just to have the Holy Spirit in us, but to have us in Him. It is to have Him upon us, possessing us and imparting power to us and overflowing from within us. This is why Jesus commanded His disciples not to depart from Jerusalem without first receiving the baptism in the Holy Spirit (see Acts 1:4-5). It was important to Jesus that they received it, because power was to be imparted to them when they received the baptism in the Holy Spirit, and it was to make them effective witnesses to Christ.

Beloved, Jesus is telling you today that you also "shall receive POWER when the Holy Spirit has come upon you" (see Acts 1:8). And you shall be a WITNESS to Jesus. The Holy Spirit truly gives power. The Bible calls Him the Spirit of Power. (see 2 Timothy 1:7). The prophet Micah said, "But truly I am **full of power** BY the Spirit of the Lord, and of justice and might." (Micah 3:8). The Holy Spirit embodies the power and might of the Godhead. The early disciples indeed received POWER through the baptism in the Holy Spirit. All 120 disciples "began to speak in other tongues as the Spirit enabled them" (see Acts

2:4 NIV). They became bold and powerful witnesses to Christ. For example, Peter and John spoke so boldly before the Sanhedrin (that is, the rulers of the people and elders of Israel) in witness to Christ after the healing of the lame man in the name of Jesus, that the members of the Sanhedrin marveled. The Bible says, "Now WHEN THEY SAW **THE BOLDNESS** OF PETER and JOHN, and perceived that they were uneducated and untrained men, THEY MARVELED. And they realized that they had been with Jesus." (Acts 4:13). Peter was also so **full of power** after his baptism in the Holy Spirit that the sick were laid on the streets for his shadow to fall on them and heal them. (see Acts 5:15-16).

When Paul also received the baptism in the Holy Spirit after Ananias had laid his hands on him, he grew more and more powerful and baffled the Jews with his preaching about Jesus the Messiah. (see Acts 9:17-22). The Anointing on Paul was so strong that he preached the gospel persuasively and fearlessly everywhere, facing persecutions with joy. Paul was so bold and fearless that when he was preparing to go to Jerusalem and was warned about the persecution that awaited him there, as revealed by the Spirit of God, he said, "NONE of these things MOVE me; NOR DO I COUNT MY LIFE DEAR TO MYSELF, so that I may finish my race with joy, and THE MINISTRY WHICH I RECEIVED from the Lord Jesus, TO TESTIFY TO THE GOSPEL OF THE GRACE OF GOD." (Acts 20:24). Again, when some of the disciples tried to persuade Paul to cancel his trip to Jerusalem, and even wept for him, Paul said, "What do you mean by weeping and breaking my heart? For I AM READY NOT ONLY TO BE BOUND, BUT ALSO TO DIE AT JERUSALEM FOR THE NAME OF THE LORD JESUS." (see Acts 21:13). Paul was indeed full of the

Spirit and of power. The Bible says, "God did extraordinary miracles through Paul, so that even handkerchiefs and aprons that had touched him were taken to the sick, and their illnesses were cured and the evil spirits left them." (see Acts 19:12). Today, Jesus wants all believers to have that same power and become bold and fearless witnesses to Him through the baptism in the Holy Spirit.

Believers who have received the baptism in the Holy Spirit have received **power**. If you have received the baptism in the Holy Spirit, you have received power; the two are just inseparable. Jesus said you will receive power when the Holy Spirit has come upon you (see Acts 1:8); but you can't operate in this power if you don't know you have it. The first step is to know, to acknowledge and believe that you have power. You have received power. Jesus does not lie. The Bible says you have received power, and that settles it. Don't try to process it with your mind or your senses. Just believe it and be conscious of it! Don't look for any physical evidence or feelings and sensations before you become convinced that you have power. "Faith is the evidence." (see Hebrews 11:1). You may not feel that you have power, but know that you have power because the Bible says so; believe that you have power, and exercise that power! Begin to cast out demons in Jesus' name. Begin to speak in new tongues. Begin to lay hands on the sick and see them recover. You have power! Walk in that power. Walk by faith and not by sight. The power you have received also comes with the ability to speak with other tongues. So do it, as the Spirit gives you utterance! Speaking in tongues will edify you and thus help you to stir up the power that you have received.

Every Spirit-filled Believer Needs to Speak in Tongues

A careful reading of the Acts of the Apostles will reveal that SPEAKING IN TONGUES was **the common experience** of every New Covenant believer who received the baptism in the Holy Spirit. Speaking in tongues was always the confirming sign that a believer had received the baptism in the Holy Spirit. The very first instance when the baptism in the Holy Spirit was received was on the Day of Pentecost, and the Bible records that all 120 disciples (including Peter, James, John, and Mary the mother of Jesus) spoke in tongues. "And they were all filled with the Holy Spirit and **BEGAN TO SPEAK WITH OTHER TONGUES**, as the Spirit gave them utterance." (Acts 2:4). The second notable instance is in Acts chapter 10 where Peter ministered to Cornelius' household. The Bible records that while Peter was still preaching, "the Holy Spirit fell upon all those who heard the gospel. And those of the circumcision who believed (i.e. the Jewish believers) were astonished, as many as came with Peter, because the GIFT of the HOLY SPIRIT had been poured out on the **Gentiles** also. FOR THEY **HEARD** them **SPEAK WITH TONGUES** and magnify God. Then Peter answered, "Can anyone forbid water, that these should not be baptized who have received the Holy Spirit JUST AS WE HAVE?" (Acts 10:44-47). Contextually, the Jewish brethren knew that Cornelius' household had received the baptism in the Spirit, because "they heard them speak with tongues." Speaking with tongues was the conclusive evidence for Peter and all the disciples present that these Gentiles had also been baptized in the Holy Spirit. In fact, this evidence was so important that it later helped settle the big question of whether salvation was for the Gentiles (see Acts 11:15-18).

Again, in Acts 19:6, when Paul had laid hands on the believers in Ephesus to receive the baptism in the Spirit, "the Holy Spirit came upon them, and **THEY SPOKE WITH TONGUES** and prophesied" — all 12 of them. All these examples from the Acts of the Apostles support Jesus' promise in Mark 16:17 that "And these signs will follow those who believe: In My name…they will **SPEAK WITH NEW TONGUES**." This is a promise to everyone who believes. Every believer can have this wonderful experience of speaking with new tongues. It was not for the early disciples only. Once you understand this, you will have the faith to receive the baptism in the Holy Spirit, with the evidence of speaking in tongues; and if you have already received the baptism in the Holy Spirit, you will have the faith to start speaking with tongues, as the Spirit gives you utterance, because the baptism in the Holy Spirit ALWAYS comes with **the ability** to speak in tongues.

It Takes Faith to Speak with Tongues

The new prayer language of tongues is dormant in you until you pray out in faith. There are many believers today who have received the baptism in the Spirit but have not started praying in tongues. I was one such believer. I received it but did not use it because I was ignorant. I didn't understand how it worked. I thought I had to just wait for the Holy Spirit to take control of my tongue and start speaking through me. I thought I had to just ready my lips and the Spirit would take over; but as long as I spoke nothing, nothing came out. The Bible says, we are to speak with tongues; it doesn't say the Holy Spirit will speak with tongues. The Holy Spirit is a gentleman; He does not force us to speak. His role is to prompt us or give us the utterance (see Acts

2:4). If you have been baptized in the Holy Spirit, know that the Holy Spirit is always prompting you to speak with tongues; He is always giving us the utterance; we have to speak out in faith so that the Spirit can keep the utterances flowing. It takes faith to speak in tongues. When we pray in tongues, we do so by faith because we do not know what we are saying. "For if I pray in a tongue, my spirit prays, but my understanding is unfruitful." (1 Corinthians 14:14). When you speak in tongues it makes no sense to your natural mind; you do not understand what you're saying. It could even make you look stupid in the natural or sense realm, but in the spirit you speak mysteries. (see 1 Corinthians 14:2). It is the fact that speaking in tongues takes faith that makes it so powerful. When we speak in tongues, we allow the Holy Spirit to be in total control, as we trust Him to give us the words and we speak them out by faith. This helps us to exercise and activate our faith in Him. In doing so, **we build ourselves up on our most holy faith**. (see Jude 20). Today, you can take a step of faith and start praying in tongues. If you're not sure of the first word to say, just pray with friends who can encourage you. And trust me, once you say the first word you're prompted to say, the Holy Spirit will prompt you to say more. It may initially sound like stammering, but you will eventually become fluent as you keep at it. Some people cannot speak in tongues because they have magnified their intellect to the point where they will not say anything that their mind cannot grasp. It is hard to experience the reality of the Holy Spirit when we are engaged in the realm of the intellect. But when we pray in tongues, it brings us to a higher realm — beyond the mind — a realm where we experience God in a very real way through faith. It brings us into a realm where we exercise faith to speak things our mind doesn't understand.

Some believers are hesitant to pray in tongues because of confusion over the passage in **First Corinthians 12:30** where Paul asked, **"Do all speak with tongues?"** Some have misunderstood this passage and stopped short of receiving this powerful prayer language, so let us consider this verse in its proper context. "And God has appointed these **IN THE CHURCH**: first apostles, second prophets, third teachers, after that miracles, then gifts of healings, helps, administrations, varieties of tongues. Are all apostles? Are all prophets? Are all teachers? Are all workers of miracles? Do all have gifts of healings? Do all speak with tongues? Do all interpret?" (I Corinthians 12:28-30). It is important to understand that there is a difference between the PUBLIC (or Ministry Gift of) TONGUES and PRIVATE DEVOTIONAL TONGUES. First Corinthians 12:28-30 was written in the context of spiritual gifts **IN THE CHURCH** or for ministry. These are public ministry gifts given to individuals for the edification of the body of Christ or the church (see 1 Corinthians 12:7; Ephesians 4:16). Not everyone has the gift of "public ministry tongues," which is used to convey a message from the believers to God or from God to the believers, just as not all are apostles, prophets and teachers, etc. When one speaks with the gift of "public ministry tongues," the message has to be interpreted by the gift of interpretation in order to be useful (see 1 Corinthians 14:5; 1 Corinthians 14:27-28). The question "do all interpret?" comes immediately after "do all speak with tongues?" confirming that Paul was referring to the gift of "public ministry tongues." In his private devotions, Paul prayed in tongues all the time (see 1 Corinthians 14:18), yet in the church, he would rather speak five words with understanding, that he may teach others also, than ten thousand words in a tongue. (see I Corinthians 14:19). Paul emphasized that **praying in tongues is for personal edification** (see

1 Corinthians 14:4), and thus should be done in our private devotions rather than in public worship, and that **whenever it is done during public worship, it has to be interpreted in order for it to be useful** (see 1 Corinthians 14:27-28). This clearly brings out the distinction between **"private devotional tongues"** and **"public ministry tongues."** Then, of course, Paul also says that there are "diversities of tongues." (see 1 Corinthians 12:28).

Thus, in contrast to the gift of "public ministry tongues," the new prayer language of "private devotional tongues" received during the baptism in the Spirit is for our personal use, and everyone who believes can have it. (see Mark 16:17). It is a private prayer language for self-edification and for you to communicate with God. "For he who speaks in a tongue does not SPEAK to men but to GOD, for **no one understands him**; however, in the spirit he speaks **mysteries.**" (see 1 Corinthians 14:2). "He who speaks in a tongue **EDIFIES HIMSELF.**" (see 1 Corinthians 14:4). A person who first receives personal edification from God is able to operate more effectively in the gifts of the Spirit to edify others. Praying in "private devotional tongues" is, therefore, a powerful key to fan aflame or stir up the gifts of the Spirit (see 2 Timothy 1:6-7). Many anointed ministers who flow powerfully in the gifts of the Spirit attribute their success to the wonderful prayer language of tongues. No wonder the apostle Paul spoke in tongues more than all the believers in the Corinthian Church (see 1 Corinthians 14:18). He understood the benefits of speaking in tongues. You build yourself up when you speak in tongues. You edify yourself. You stir up the power that is in you. As Paul prayed in tongues, God also gave him great revelations as can be seen from his epistles. He was able to minister with such great power. We can just imagine how charged up he was! Perhaps this is why the devil is so much against speaking in tongues and keeps creating controversy around this powerful gift. Some Christians even say speaking in tongues is of the devil. By saying this, they are basically saying that all the early disciples (including Paul) who spoke in tongues were of the devil. How absurd! And is it surprising? Satan always wants to cast doubts on every good gift from God by portraying it as being of demonic origin. Even Jesus was accused of being of the devil when He cast out demons from those who were possessed. (see Matthew 12:22-32). And when Jesus preached the truth, saying to the Jews that "He who is of God hears God's words; therefore you do not hear, because you are not of God" (John 8:47), "the Jews answered and said to Him, "Do we not say rightly that **You are a Samaritan and have a demon**?" (see John 8:48). So don't let the devil's false accusations fool you or prevent you from speaking in tongues.

The Bible tells us in First Corinthians 14:39 that **we shouldn't forbid speaking in tongues**. This is a slap in the face of believers who forbid speaking in tongues. Such believers have the erroneous belief that the gift of tongues has ceased. They use First Corinthians 13:8-10 as the basis for such belief: "Love never fails. But whether there are prophecies, they will fail; whether there are tongues, they will cease; whether there is knowledge, it will vanish away. For we know in part and we prophesy in part. But when that which is perfect has come, then that which is in part will be done away." (I Corinthians 13:8-10). The problem with their belief, however, is that prophecies have not failed and knowledge has increased rather than vanish. They say "that which is perfect" in verse 10 refers to the Bible and that since we have the complete Scriptures, tongues are unnecessary. However, tongues were never used as a teaching tool like the Bible is. I believe "that which is perfect" refers to Jesus and His second coming. This is why in verse 12 Paul says, "For now we see only a reflection as in a mirror; then (when that which is perfect has come) we shall see face to face. Now I know in part; then I shall know fully, even as I am fully known." (1 Corinthians 13:12 NIV). In other words, in this present time we only see what the Bible says about the glory of Jesus and our own glory (as in a reflection or with our imagination), but then (when Jesus comes), we shall see Him face to face, and know Him and His glory (as well as our own glory) completely and fully, just as He knows us fully. Prophecy and tongues are valid gifts until then. Contextually, Paul was simply emphasizing to the Corinthian Church the point that all spiritual gifts must be used in love. For when Jesus comes and tongues and prophecies and everything else ceases, fails, or vanishes away, love will remain and will never fail. For God is Love.

The Benefits of Speaking in Tongues

Praying in tongues is a New Covenant gift for the New Covenant Believer and is received during the New Covenant experience of baptism in the Spirit. Therefore, praying in tongues is important to our New Covenant living as holy and royal priests in proclaiming the praises of Him who called us out of darkness into His marvelous light. The Old Testament believers never had the privilege of praying in tongues, but we do. Tongues were used on the Day of Pentecost to declare the wonderful works of God (see Acts 2:4, 11). Among all the benefits of tongues, **it was used first and foremost for the purpose of praise and worship**. The multitudes proclaimed, "we hear them speaking in our own tongues the WONDERFUL WORKS OF

GOD." (see Acts 2:11). In the New Covenant, it is not about the works of man but the works of God — the finished work of Christ on the cross. The Holy Spirit draws our attention from self to Christ. When Cornelius' household received the baptism in the Holy Spirit, they also spoke in tongues — **magnifying God** (see Acts 10:46). It was an expression of worship beyond the ability of their limited minds. Through speaking in tongues, the Holy Spirit thus helps us to worship God in spirit and in truth, as prophesied by Jesus in John 4:23-24. These two scenarios from the Acts of the Apostles cited above show just how important this new spiritual dimension of worship is to God. What is even more amazing is that once we start praying in tongues, it is within our control as to when to pray in tongues and when to pray in the known language. Paul said in First Corinthians 14:15, "I WILL pray with my spirit, and I WILL also pray with my understanding." It was within Paul's control whether he prayed in tongues or in the known language. The Spirit gives the utterance but it is within our control when to pray in tongues; we can pray out by faith whenever we want. Paul also indicated that we can control the public ministry gift of tongues as well; we can control when to operate in this gift (see 1 Corinthians 14:32). The Spirit does not compel someone to interrupt a service with tongues. You can keep quiet in the church if there is no interpreter, and speak to yourself and to God when you feel the Spirit prompting you to pray in tongues (see 1 Corinthians 14:28, 33).

Beloved, there are so many other benefits we can derive from speaking in tongues. We noted earlier, besides helping us to worship God in the spirit, that **praying in tongues also edifies us or builds us up.** The Bible says he who is joined to the Lord is one spirit with Him. (see

1 Corinthians 6:17). Being one spirit with the Lord means that our spirit is always in contact with the Holy Spirit. So when we pray in tongues, the Holy Spirit supplies the words and gives the utterance to our spirit (see Acts 2:4), and our spirit prays it out. In Romans 8:2, the Holy Spirit is called the Spirit of life. As the Spirit of Christ and the Spirit of God (see Romans 8:9), the Holy Spirit is the source of life. This is why Romans 8:11 says God will give life to our mortal bodies through the Holy Spirit that dwells in us. When we pray in tongues, we tap into the source of life, and words of life flow through our tongue. (see John 6:63; John 1:1-4). Hence, the Bible says, "He who speaks in a tongue EDIFIES HIMSELF." (see 1 Corinthians 14:4). A person who speaks in tongues builds himself up or charges himself up. And, of course, once you're first edified, you're also able to operate more effectively in the gifts of the Spirit to edify others.

Additionally, **praying in tongues helps us to become more sensitive to the leading of the Holy Spirit.** The Bible says those who are led by the Spirit are the children of God (see Romans 8:14), and that when we walk in the Spirit we will not gratify the desires of the flesh (see Galatians 5:16). Also, those who are led by the Spirit are not under the law. (see Galatians 5:18). When we pray in tongues, we are training our natural mind to yield to the mind of our spirit and to be more sensitive to the leading of the Holy Spirit. "For if I pray in a TONGUE, my SPIRIT PRAYS" (see 1 Corinthians 14:14). **Praying in tongues trains us to let our spirit take the lead instead of our mind.** And since our spirit receives its utterances from the Holy Spirit (see Acts 2:4), when we pray in tongues we train ourselves to be led by the Holy Spirit. We noted earlier also that it takes faith to speak in tongues. Praying in tongues seems opposed to the natural mind.

In fact, when you speak in tongues it makes no sense to your natural mind. Neither does any man understand you. Yet, in the spirit you speak mysteries. (see 1 Corinthians 14:2). It is the fact that speaking in tongues takes faith that makes it so powerful. Throughout the Bible, believers who walked in the realm of faith accomplished feats that defied logic. Peter walked on water and defied all logic until his mind started doubting. (see Matthew 14:25-31). Jesus defied logic by multiplying five loaves of bread and two fish to feed the thousands when His disciples were reasoning about their lack of money and how much money it will take to feed such multitude of people. (see John 6:1-14). Jesus performed miracles and healed the sick everywhere until the people in His hometown started reasoning that he was just a carpenter. (see Matthew 13:53-58). Today, many people are still very much engaged in the realm of the intellect. Just as in the Bible days, it is hard to experience the miraculous power of the Holy Spirit in that realm. But when we pray in tongues, it brings us to a higher realm — beyond the mind — a realm where we experience the leading of the Holy Spirit in a very real way through faith. It brings us into a realm where we exercise faith to speak things our mind doesn't understand. Almost every believer I know would like to be more sensitive to the leading of the Holy Spirit. And thankfully, God has given us the prayer language of tongues to help us accomplish this.

Speaking in tongues also helps us to receive wisdom and revelation in the knowledge of God. In Ephesians 1:17, Paul prayed for the believers in Ephesus that they may receive the Spirit of wisdom and revelation in the knowledge of God. Every believer needs the Spirit of wisdom and revelation. The Bible says, "he who speaks in a tongue does not speak to men but to God, for no one understands him; however, in the spirit he speaks mysteries." (I Corinthians 14:2). When you speak in tongues, you speak mysteries through the inspiration of the Holy Spirit. First Corinthians 2:9-16 says that the Holy Spirit knows the deep things of God, the things that God has prepared for those who love Him. These things are mysteries. They are secrets, but not to the Holy Spirit. The Holy Spirit is able to let us know these divine secrets. These secrets are spoken "not in words which man's wisdom teaches but which the Holy Spirit teaches, comparing spiritual things with spiritual." (see 1 Corinthians 2:13). When we pray in tongues, we pray in words which the Holy Spirit teaches, and the revelations of God are transmitted to our understanding, as we become more sensitive to the promptings and teachings of the Holy Spirit. When we receive the wisdom and the revelations of the Holy Spirit, our understanding grows. The passage ends by declaring, "But we have the mind of Christ." (see 1 Corinthians 2:16). The most anointed Bible teachers and ministers I have known share the same secret — they receive great revelations from the Holy Spirit through praying frequently in tongues. John 14:26 says the Holy Spirit will teach us all things. John 15:16 also says the Holy Spirit will guide us into all truth and show us things to come. Again, First John 2:27 says that the Anointing (or the Holy Spirit) which we have received abides in us and teaches us concerning all things. **Praying in tongues helps us to be sensitive to the Spirit's teachings and guidance.**

Furthermore, speaking in tongues helps us to enter spiritual rest and refreshing. It causes us to be rested and refreshed. The Bible considers speaking in tongues not as work, but as rest. Isaiah prophesied, "For with stammering lips and another tongue He will speak to this people, To whom He said, "This is the rest with which You may cause the weary to rest," And, "This is the refreshing" (see Isaiah 28:11-12). The rest and refreshing this passage is referring to is "speaking in other tongues!" Well, how do we know? We know from First Corinthians 14:20-22 where the apostle Paul quotes and uses this same passage from Isaiah in the context of praying in tongues. He writes, "Brethren, do not be children in understanding; however, in malice be babes, but in understanding be mature. In the law it is written: "With men of other tongues and other lips I will speak to this people; And yet, for all that, they will not hear Me," says the Lord. Therefore tongues are for a sign, not to those who believe but to unbelievers" (see I Corinthians 14:20-22). Quite often, tongues can sound like stammering lips. It could also be a fluent language, or it may sound like groaning in the spirit. But it is common for people who receive the baptism in the Spirit to start off with tongues that sound like stammering. Indeed, we do not despise the simple things of God, for they are powerful. Since tongues is a New Covenant prayer language that was given to us as a result of the finished work of Christ, when we pray in tongues, we are resting in the grace of God and in the finished work of Christ; we are resting in a position of victory as we depend on the power of the Holy Spirit to effect change. As we rest through praying in tongues, God starts to work on our behalf. Clearly, the New Covenant is about entering the rest of God (see Hebrews 4:11). Many believers (myself included) testify about experiencing rest and refreshing in our souls and physical bodies when we pray in tongues. There are also many testimonies of wonderful miracles that happen when people start to pray in tongues.

Also, **speaking in tongues helps us to pray in God's perfect will**. This is why the apostle Paul decided that he will not only pray and sing with his understanding, but also with his spirit. (see 1 Corinthians 14:15). With our natural mind, we do not know God's perfect will in every situation, so we are limited when we only pray with our own mind (or understanding). But the Bible says we have the mind of Christ. (see 1 Corinthians 2:16). It is our spirit that has the mind of Christ. It is also our spirit that prays in tongues (see 1 Corinthians 14:14). So when we pray in tongues, we pray from the mind of Christ, and thus pray according to the perfect will of God. Moreover, it is the Holy Spirit that gives us the utterance when we pray in tongues (see Acts 2:4). And as we learned earlier from First Corinthians 2:9-16, the Holy Spirit knows the deep things of God, the things that God has prepared for those who love Him. So when we pray in tongues, the Spirit always gives us words to pray according to the perfect will of God. The apostle Paul affirms this in Romans 8:27 where he declares that the Spirit intercedes for us **according to the will of God.**

Last but not the least, **praying in tongues is a powerful weapon in our spiritual warfare.** The Bible says, "we do not wrestle against flesh and blood, but against principalities, against powers, against the rulers of the darkness of this age, against spiritual hosts of wickedness in the heavenly places." (see Ephesians 6:12). So we are to put on the whole armor of God. (see Ephesians 6:13). All the pieces of the armor of God mentioned in Ephesians 6:13-18 point to the Person of Jesus Christ. As Paul points out in Romans 13:14, we are to clothe ourselves with the Lord Jesus Christ. After putting on the whole armor of God by establishing our lives in the revelation, knowledge and consciousness of Jesus Christ, we are ready for battle to take and possess the victory that Jesus has already won for us. The Bible says we are to stand against the devil and take the victory in spiritual warfare by **"praying always**

with all prayer and supplication IN THE SPIRIT" (see Ephesians 6:18). In other words, we are to pray always in tongues, as we also pray with our understanding from the Word of God.

Beloved, the prayer language of tongues is a powerful gift that is important to our New Covenant living as holy and royal priests. It is not a status symbol, as it is received freely by any believer who asks for it. And it has no benefits when it is not used. But when it is frequently used, all the benefits discussed here and more will be reaped. I encourage you to tap into the full potential of this prayer language so that you can walk in the same miraculous power that the early disciples experienced, as recorded in the Book of Acts. Many believers only think of praying when they need something, but **praying in tongues enables us to simply spend time in the presence of God**. I pray that you will desire and receive the baptism in the Holy Spirit (with the evidence of speaking in tongues) so that you will receive power to be a witness to Christ. If you have not yet received the baptism in the Spirit with the new prayer language of tongues and you desire to do so, you can ask believers who minister in this area to pray for you and lay hands on you. (see Acts 8:15-18). Alternatively, you could pray by faith to receive from Jesus your Baptizer. Say the following prayer from your heart:

Almighty Father, I desire to be baptized in the Holy Spirit so that I will be filled with the Holy Spirit and receive power to become a witness to Jesus. Lord Jesus, the Bible says that You are the Baptizer in the Holy Spirit. I receive the baptism in the Holy Spirit now by faith. I receive the ability to pray in new tongues. I thank You Father, in Jesus' name. Amen.

If you prayed this prayer by faith, believe that you have received the baptism in the Holy Spirit, and you would sense a gentle flow of the Spirit from within you. As the rivers of the Spirit flow out, you would sense the prompting to pray in new tongues. Just respond in faith by praying aloud as the Spirit gives you utterance. This new prayer language is dormant in you until you pray out in faith. Your next step is simply to pray aloud. God gives us good things because He loves us. Enjoy yours!

Understanding the Leading of the Holy Spirit

Now, when Jesus promised that He would send the Holy Spirit to us, He also told us what the purpose or function of the Holy Spirit would be. Therefore, we can understand how the Holy Spirit leads us by understanding His purpose or function in our lives. Jesus said, "And I will pray the Father, and He will give you **another HELPER**, that He may abide with you **forever**— the Spirit of truth, whom THE WORLD CANNOT RECEIVE, because it neither sees Him nor knows Him; but you know Him, for He dwells with you and WILL BE IN YOU. I will not leave you orphans; **I will come to you**. But the HELPER, the Holy Spirit, whom the Father will send in My name, **He WILL TEACH YOU ALL THINGS**, and **BRING TO YOUR REMEMBRANCE ALL THINGS THAT I SAID TO YOU.**" (John 14:16-18, 26). "When He, the Spirit of truth, has come, **HE WILL GUIDE YOU into ALL TRUTH**; for He will not speak on His own authority, but whatever He hears **He WILL SPEAK**; and **He WILL TELL YOU THINGS TO COME.**" (see John 16:13). From these verses, it is clear what purpose or function the Holy Spirit serves in the life of a believer: He serves the purpose of HELPER (or COMFORTER) — GUIDE, TEACHER OF ALL THINGS, FACILITATOR OF MEMORY regarding all the teachings of Jesus, and REVEALER OF THINGS TO COME. According to Acts 1:8, Jesus also added that the (ultimate) result of the Holy Spirit coming upon believers is that **we will receive POWER** (or ability from God) to be WITNESSES to Jesus. The Holy Spirit is the Spirit of power. (see 2 Timothy 1:7). In fact, the Holy Spirit not only makes us bold witnesses to Jesus Christ, but He Himself being the Spirit of truth, also bears witness of Jesus (see John 15:26); and He bears His witness in us and through us (believers). The Holy Spirit also bears witness with us that we are children of God. The Bible says, "The Spirit Himself bears witness with our spirit that we are children of God." (see Romans 8:16). It is, therefore, very important for every believer to be baptized in the Holy Spirit, and to experience **the twofold witnessing of the Holy Spirit** — bearing witness with our spirit that we are children of God; and bearing witness of Jesus (in and through us).

We will explore further in this section how the Holy Spirit leads us to be effective witnesses to Christ. And we will learn from the example of the early disciples by examining how they yielded to the leading of the Holy Spirit and thus became such bold, fearless and powerful witnesses to Christ, who were able to preach the gospel to the whole world and to every creature under heaven. (see Colossians 1:6, 23). The Book of Acts is basically an account of how the Holy Spirit empowered and led the early disciples to be witnesses to Christ. In fact, it is obvious (from Acts 1:2) that **the Holy Spirit started leading the early disciples immediately after Jesus breathed on them on the night of His resurrection and said, "Receive the Holy Spirit."** (see John 20:22). The Bible says that, until the day Jesus was taken up (or ascended to Heaven), it was THROUGH THE HOLY SPIRIT that Jesus GAVE COMMANDMENTS to the apostles whom He had chosen. (see Acts 1:2). And so the Holy Spirit was already at work before the Day of Pentecost, actively leading the apostles — instructing them or GIVING them COMMANDMENTS. In essence, the Holy Spirit put the commandments of Christ in the minds of the apostles, and wrote them in their hearts, just as He did for us when we also believed in Jesus. (see Acts 1:2 with Hebrews 8:10).

The Holy Spirit's leading of the disciples was, however, to expand, and did expand into another dimension on the Day of Pentecost when the Spirit came **upon** them. The Bible records that, filled with the Holy Spirit, all 120 disciples "began to SPEAK with other tongues, AS THE SPIRIT GAVE THEM UTTERANCE." (see Acts 2:4). This is clearly the second recorded instance in the Book of Acts, of the Holy Spirit leading the disciples. And this time, He did not give them commandments, but instead, **He led them to SPEAK with other tongues, giving them the utterance**, as they proclaimed the wonderful works of God. We will discuss this second instance in greater detail later in this book. But for now, let us discuss the first instance a little further.

The Holy Spirit Instructs Us or Gives Us Commandments

Beloved it is apparent that one of the key ways the Holy Spirit leads us is by instructing us or giving us commandments (or things to do). We have already made reference to this truth as spelled out in the introductory part of the Book of Acts where Luke writes: "The former account I made, O Theophilus, of all that JESUS BEGAN both to do and TEACH, UNTIL THE DAY in which He was taken up,

AFTER He **THROUGH THE HOLY SPIRIT** had GIVEN COMMANDMENTS to the apostles whom He had chosen" (Acts 1:1-2). What Luke is saying here is that, before He was taken up (to Heaven), Jesus gave commandments to the apostles whom He had chosen; and He gave these commandments **THROUGH THE HOLY SPIRIT**. This is right in line with the promise God made through the prophet Jeremiah concerning the New Covenant, saying, "But this is the covenant that I will make with the house of Israel after those days, says the Lord: I WILL PUT MY LAW IN THEIR MINDS, AND WRITE IT ON THEIR HEARTS; and I will be their God, and they shall be My people. No more shall every man teach his neighbor, and every man his brother, saying, 'Know the Lord,' for they all shall know Me, from the least of them to the greatest of them, says the Lord. For I will forgive their iniquity, and their sin I will remember no more." (Jeremiah 31:33-34. See also Hebrews 8:10-12).

Under the Old Covenant, God wrote His law on tablets of stones. The stones were cold, lifeless and non-interactive. But in the New Covenant, God puts His law (or His Commandments) in our minds and writes it on our hearts through His Spirit that is in us, so that we no longer live life trying to follow laws written on stones, but rather following the leading of the Spirit who lives in our hearts and fellowships with us. The Bible says, "For **the law of the Spirit of life** in Christ Jesus has made me free from the law of sin and death." (Romans 8:2). Thus, God, not desiring us to try to keep His laws externally or hypocritically, has put His Spirit in our hearts to transform us from within and guide us in His ways. No longer do people have to tell us what to do, because the Spirit Himself leads us in the paths of righteousness for His name's sake, as we yield or submit to Him.

Galatians 5:18 says, "But if you are led by the Spirit, you are not under the law." This means that following the law written on stones is opposed to following the Spirit (who is in our hearts). Therefore, we have to cease striving to follow the law written on stones, and yield to the leading or promptings of the Spirit who is in us, trusting Him completely. Romans 7:6 thus contrasts following the written code of the law with following the promptings of the Spirit. It says, "But now we are **DISCHARGED from the Law** and having **TERMINATED all intercourse with it**, having died to what once restrained us and held us captive. So now we serve not under [obedience to] the old code of written regulations, but [under obedience to the promptings] of the Spirit in newness [of life]." (Romans 7:6, AMP). Hallelujah! This is the new way of life under the New Covenant. We are to yield to the guidance and instructions of the Holy Spirit as He leads us; and when we do so, we will be experiencing a living relationship and communion with God the Father, and with His Son Jesus Christ.

The Holy Spirit Speaks to Us

It is also clear from the Acts of the Apostles that the Holy Spirit is not only in us to give us commandments and help us obey them, but He is in us to also guide us in a real relationship or fellowship with God, with the goal of accomplishing the plans and purposes of God on earth through us, especially in regard to the propagation of the gospel and the salvation of souls. Our role and obligation then, is to always be attentive to His voice and yield to the leading of the Holy Spirit. We have to trust and obey the direction the Spirit gives us. The Bible says that the Spirit speaks to us, and I believe He loves to speak to us, because I hear Him all the time. Our Lord Jesus Christ promised that the Spirit will speak to us. He said, "**I still have many things to say to you, but you cannot bear them now**. However, when He, **the Spirit of truth**, has come, He will guide you into all truth; for He will not SPEAK on His own authority, but WHATEVER HE HEARS **He will SPEAK; and He WILL TELL YOU THINGS TO COME.**" (John 16:12-13). Indeed, the Spirit speaks. He tells us things to come and gives us direction. The prophet Isaiah said of our day that, "Your ears shall hear a word behind you, saying, 'This is the way, walk in it,' whenever you turn to the right hand or whenever you turn to the left." (Isaiah 30:21). This is obviously a reference to the voice of the Holy Spirit and to His guidance and direction. The Holy Spirit speaks to us, and He often speaks to us from within our hearts, because He lives in our hearts. It is the ears of our spirit that often hear His voice. His voice is often an inward voice, and not so much of an audible voice (from without), although He can and does sometimes speak in an audible (thunderous, or still small) voice also (as He is not limited in His mode of operation).

The inward voice of the Holy Spirit is like a still small voice within us. It may be in the form of a thought that comes to our mind from our spirit — like an inner knowing, a spiritual intuition or perception. Or it may simply be a desire that comes to our heart from the Holy Spirit (as in feeling led in your spirit to do something or go somewhere). The apostle Paul must be singled out here as one disciple whose ability to perceive is reported extensively in the Acts of the Apostles. Paul's ability to perceive saved him from death (on a number of occasions) — for instance, when he was arrested in Jerusalem and brought before the council (the Sanhedrin). The Bible says, "But when Paul PERCEIVED that one part were Sadducees and the other Pharisees, he cried out in the council, "Men and brethren, I am a Pharisee, the son of a Pharisee; concerning the hope and resurrection of the dead I am being judged! And when he had said this, a dissension arose between the Pharisees and the Sadducees; and the assembly was divided. Now when there arose a great dissension, the commander, fearing lest Paul might be pulled to pieces by them, commanded the soldiers to go down and take him by force from among them, and bring him into the barracks." (Acts 23:6-7, 10). Later, when Paul was being transported as a prisoner on a voyage from Jerusalem to Rome, he again PERCEIVED that the voyage would end in a shipwreck, and it did when they didn't heed his advice. The Bible says, "Now when much time had been spent, and sailing was now dangerous because the Fast was already over, Paul advised them, saying, "Men, I PERCEIVE that this voyage will end with disaster and much loss, not only of the cargo and ship, but also our lives." (Acts 27:9-10). Paul indeed made good use of his ability to perceive. But how did He perceive these things? He was attentive to the inward voice of the Spirit.

In the Acts of the Apostles, we have many examples of the Spirit speaking to the disciples in diverse ways. We are told, for instance, that the Spirit **spoke** to Philip. When the Ethiopian Eunuch was sitting in his chariot reading the Book of Isaiah, the Spirit TOLD Philip to go to him. The Bible says, "Then the Spirit SAID TO PHILIP, "Go near and overtake this chariot." So Philip ran to him, and heard him reading the prophet Isaiah, and said, "Do you understand what you are reading?" (Acts 8:29-30). We all have to learn, like Philip, to listen and hear the voice of the Spirit, and obey Him. Jesus said, "My sheep hear my voice, and I know them, and they follow me." (John 10:27). The voice of the Holy Spirit is the voice of Jesus Christ, because the

Holy Spirit is the Spirit of Christ. (see Romans 8:9; Galatians 4:6). And so if we are truly the sheep or disciples of Jesus, then we must listen and hear His voice, whether it is a still small voice or an audible voice; we must be able to recognize His voice and follow Him. Hearing the voice of the Spirit is one distinguishing characteristic of a disciple of Christ. All the early disciples knew and heard the voice of the Spirit, and followed Him. Philip was not the only disciple whom the Spirit spoke to; He spoke to all the disciples, and still speaks to us today. In his sermon on the Day of Pentecost after the Holy Spirit had come upon all the disciples, Peter quoted from the Old Testament prophet Joel, explaining that in the last days, the Holy Spirit will be poured out on all people with accompanying signs that include prophecy, dreams and visions (see Acts 2:17). And so visions (or angelic/divine visitations) and trances (or dreams) were also commonplace among the early disciples. (see Acts 5:19-21; Acts 8:26; Acts 12:7-8; Acts 9:10-17; Acts 10:3-7; Acts 10:9-20; Acts 16:9-10; Acts 18:9-11; Acts 22:17-21; 2 Corinthians 12:1-4). The Spirit spoke to them all the time, oftentimes giving them direction, as in when He spoke to Peter to go to Cornelius' house. The Bible says, "While Peter thought about the vision, THE SPIRIT SAID TO HIM, "Behold, three men are seeking you. Arise therefore, go down and go with them, doubting nothing; for I have sent them." (Acts 10:19-20). Later when Peter recounted this incident to the other disciples, he said, "Then THE SPIRIT TOLD ME TO GO WITH THEM, doubting nothing…" (see Acts 11:12).

The Holy Spirit was always LEADING and directing the disciples — speaking to them. On one occasion, the Bible says, "As they ministered to the Lord and fasted, THE HOLY SPIRIT SAID, "Now separate to

Me Barnabas and Saul for the work to which I have called them." (Acts 13:2). Here, the Spirit spoke to all the disciples (i.e. the prophets and teachers in the Church at Antioch), as they ministered to the Lord and fasted. And evidently, the disciples yielded to the leading of the Holy Spirit. The Bible says, "Then, having fasted and prayed, and laid hands on them, they sent them (i.e. Paul and Barnabas) away." (Acts 13:3). They did exactly as the Spirit had commanded. The Holy Spirit was so real to the early disciples that they attributed many of their actions to Him. "So, being SENT OUT BY THE HOLY SPIRIT, they (Paul and Barnabas) went down to Seleucia, and from there they sailed to Cyprus." (Acts 13:4). Thus, Paul and Barnabas were sent out BY the Holy Spirit. On another occasion, when the apostles made a decision regarding whether or not the Gentiles should be required to keep the law of Moses, they wrote this letter to the Gentiles, saying: "For IT SEEMED GOOD TO THE HOLY SPIRIT, **and to us**, to lay upon you no greater burden than these necessary things: that you abstain from things offered to idols, from blood, from things strangled, and from sexual immorality. If you keep yourselves from these, you will do well. Farewell." (Acts 15:28-29). Here again, they attributed the decision to the Holy Spirit foremost (and called it a joint decision between themselves and the Holy Spirit). Also, when Peter testified before the council in Acts 5:31-32, he said that they were witnesses of Jesus' resurrection, and SO WAS THE HOLY SPIRIT.

You Must Be Filled With the Holy Spirit

Beloved, to hear frequently and clearly from the Holy Spirit and follow His leading as the early disciples did, **you have to be full of the Holy Spirit and of faith.** This is why the early apostles always looked for believers who were full of the Holy Spirit and of faith whenever they needed people to fill various positions and perform various roles in the church, such as when they needed people to serve tables or oversee the daily distribution of their joint possessions (see Acts 6:3). Stephen was one of the seven men they appointed for this role, and the Bible says that he was full of the Holy Spirit and of faith. (see Acts 6:5). And because he was full of the Holy Spirit and of faith, Stephen was very attentive to the voice of the Holy Spirit, such that when he spoke, his detractors could not resist the wisdom and the Spirit with which he spoke. The Bible says that some from the Synagogue of the Freedmen plotted against Stephen, upset over the fact that when they disputed with him, **"they were not able to resist the wisdom and the Spirit by which he spoke."** (see Acts 6:10).

Another man chosen together with Stephen to serve tables was Philip, who was also full of faith and of the Holy Spirit. It was this Philip who later became the evangelist that was sent by the Holy Spirit to minister the Word to the Ethiopian Eunuch. (see Acts 8:29-30). Philip also baptized the Ethiopian Eunuch. And the Bible says that "when they came up out of the water, **THE SPIRIT OF THE LORD CAUGHT PHILIP AWAY**, so that the eunuch SAW HIM NO MORE; and he went on his way rejoicing. But PHILIP WAS FOUND AT AZOTUS. And passing through, he PREACHED in all the cities till he came to Caesarea." (Acts 8:39-40). Thus, Philip was transported or carried by the Spirit from the road in the desert which goes down from Jerusalem to Gaza, and brought all the way to AZOTUS. The Holy Spirit was in that moment Philip's personal means of transportation. That is what the Holy Spirit can do with, and be for a person who is full of faith and of the Holy Spirit. May you be that person.

To be full of the Holy Spirit, you have to be baptized in the Holy Spirit, and you have to study and meditate on the Word of God continually for the Word to dwell in you richly in all wisdom, because the Word is Spirit (see John 6:63); you have to also **pray continually** both with your spirit and with your understanding. People who are filled with the Holy Spirit continually worship the Lord with thanksgiving, singing and making music in their heart to the Lord; they speak to one another in Psalms, hymns and songs from the Spirit, "giving thanks always for all things to God the Father in the name of our Lord Jesus Christ, submitting to one another in the fear of God." (see Ephesians 5:18-21). In Acts 4:31, the early apostles (who had experienced the infilling of the Holy Spirit at Pentecost a few chapters earlier) **prayed to the Lord** and the place was shaken: "And THEY WERE FILLED with the Holy Spirit and spoke the Word of God boldly." Prayer opens us up to be filled with the Holy Spirit. Hallelujah!

To be full of faith also, you have to continually study (or hear) the Word of God, because "faith comes by hearing, and hearing by the Word of God." (see Romans 10:17). Stephen was obviously full of faith because he had studied and meditated on the Word of God, as is evident in his address to the council in Acts chapter 7. The same can be said of Philip as evident in his ability to explain the Scriptures to the Ethiopian Eunuch, and to preach the gospel as an evangelist. May you take time to also study and meditate on the Word of God to understand it and build up your faith. As Paul said to Timothy, "**Study** to shew thyself approved unto God, a workman that needeth not to be ashamed, rightly dividing the word of truth." (2 Timothy 2:15 KJV). You have the Holy Spirit as your Teacher to help you in this regard (see 1 John 2:20, 27), but it behooves you to show up for class and be taught.

The Holy Spirit Speaks Through Us

Not only does the Holy Spirit speak **to** us, He also gives us the utterance to speak — be it with the known tongue (or language) or with other tongues (or languages). Regarding the Holy Spirit's work of giving us utterance in **the KNOWN TONGUE,** or speaking through us, Jesus said, "You will be brought before governors and kings for My sake, as a testimony to them and to the Gentiles. But when they deliver you up, do not worry about how or what you should speak. For IT WILL BE GIVEN TO YOU IN THAT HOUR WHAT YOU SHOULD SPEAK; for it is NOT you who speak, **but THE SPIRIT OF YOUR FATHER (or the Holy Spirit) who SPEAKS in you.**" (Matthew 10:18-20; See also Mark 13:11; Luke 12:11-12). It was definitely not Stephen who was speaking when those people from the Synagogue of the Freedmen disputed with him, for "they were not able to resist the wisdom and the Spirit by which he spoke." (see Acts 6:10). The Holy Spirit gave Stephen the utterance at that very hour when he spoke before the Council in Acts 7. And Stephen, filled with the Holy Spirit, spoke so boldly to the Council that they couldn't stand him, and therefore stoned him to death. Peter in his first epistle also tells us that those who preached the gospel to us preached **BY the Holy Spirit sent from heaven.** (see 1 Peter 1:12). When you also preach the gospel, it has to be the Holy Spirit in you doing the preaching; you must acknowledge Him and submit to Him, and resist the temptation to preach on your own authority or from your own understanding. Jesus said, "The words that I speak to you I do not speak on My own authority; but the Father who dwells in Me does the works." (see John 14:10).

As mentioned earlier, the Holy Spirit also gives us utterance to speak in **OTHER TONGUES**. The Bible says that, when the Holy Spirit came upon the disciples on the Day of Pentecost, "they were all filled with the Holy Spirit and began to SPEAK with OTHER TONGUES, as the Spirit gave them utterance." (Acts 2:4). The Holy Spirit led the disciples or prompted them to speak in other tongues; He supplied the words they spoke. Whenever we are filled with the Holy Spirit, the most common form of manifestation is for us to **SPEAK**. Sometimes we would speak with other tongues when we are filled with the Holy Spirit. But other times, a person filled with the Holy Spirit will PROPHESY or speak with the known tongue (known language). The crux of the matter is that, when we are filled with the Holy Spirit, more often than not, we SPEAK, as the Spirit gives us utterance. The Holy Spirit leads us to speak boldly and with wisdom. It is reported in Acts 4:8 that Peter, FILLED WITH THE HOLY SPIRIT, spoke (to the rulers of the people and elders of Israel), and he spoke with such BOLDNESS that the people marveled. (see Acts 4:13). The Holy Spirit is a Spirit of boldness, and so when He leads us, He leads us to act or speak boldly and powerfully, soundly and lovingly. "For God has not given us a spirit of fear, but of power and of love and of a sound mind." (2 Timothy 1:7).

Beloved, **the Holy Spirit loves to express Himself through us when we are full of the Spirit**. There are so many other examples to support this truth. Even under the Old Covenant, when Elizabeth was filled with the Holy Spirit, she also prophesied or spoke out to Mary the Mother of Jesus. The Bible says, "And it happened, when Elizabeth heard the greeting of Mary, that the babe leaped in her womb; and ELIZABETH WAS FILLED WITH THE HOLY SPIRIT. Then **SHE SPOKE OUT with a loud voice** and said, "Blessed are you among women, and blessed is the fruit of your womb!" (Luke 1:41-42). When zacharias (Elizabeth's husband, and the father of John the Baptist) was also filled with the Holy Spirit, he spoke and prophesied. The Bible says, "Now his father Zacharias was **filled with the Holy Spirit**, and **PROPHESIED,…**" (Luke 1:67). May you also be filled with the Holy Spirit and allow Him to express Himself through you to PROPHESY and to speak in new tongues. The Bible says, as we quoted earlier: "And do not be drunk with wine, in which is dissipation; but BE FILLED WITH THE SPIRIT" (Ephesians 5:18). This means that **it is your responsibility to be continually filled with the Holy Spirit;** it is within your control. And we have already discussed how this can be achieved. It is by being filled with the Spirit that we receive deep revelations from God. Today we all have the Holy Scriptures (or the Bible) because some holy men of God were filled with the Spirit, and allowed the Spirit to express Himself through them, "For prophecy never came by the will of man, but holy men of God SPOKE as they were MOVED BY THE HOLY SPIRIT." (2 Peter 1:21). It was the Holy Spirit who spoke through all the writers of the Scriptures, including the Prophet Isaiah. (see Acts 28:25), and King David (see Acts 1:16; 4:25). The Spirit of Christ who is in us today was also in the Old Testament Prophets. The Bible says, "Of this salvation **the prophets** have inquired and searched carefully, **who prophesied of the grace that would come to you**, searching what, or what manner of time, THE SPIRIT OF CHRIST **WHO WAS IN THEM** was indicating when He testified beforehand the sufferings of Christ and the glories that would follow. TO THEM IT WAS

REVEALED that, not to themselves, but to us they were ministering the things which now have been reported to you through those who have PREACHED THE GOSPEL to you BY THE HOLY SPIRIT SENT FROM HEAVEN —things which angels desire to look into." (1 Peter 1:10-12). Today, it is that same Spirit of Christ (or the Holy Spirit) in us that moves or leads us to preach the gospel. I preach the gospel to you BY the Holy Spirit sent from Heaven. (see 1 Peter 1:12). Hallelujah! It is the Holy Spirit who helps us to know and understand the things that have been freely given to us by God. (see 1 Corinthians 2:12).

The Holy Spirit Loves to Lead Us

Indeed the Holy Spirit loves to lead us and to be in charge of our affairs. The early disciples knew this, and they understood that as children of God they were supposed to be led by the Spirit of God; and so they yielded to the leading of the Spirit. In fact, the early disciples made no decisions without consulting the Holy Spirit. Some people often claim that because the disciples cast lots to elect Matthias as an apostle to replace Judas Iscariot, they were at that point not being led by the Holy Spirit, and that the Holy Spirit only started to lead them after He came upon them on the Day of Pentecost. But from everything we have learned thus far from the Bible, it is obvious that this assertion is just NOT true. The Holy Spirit was leading the apostles all along from the moment Jesus breathed on them on the evening of His resurrection and said, "Receive the Holy Spirit." (see John 20:22). In fact, it was the Holy Spirit who led the disciples to cast lots in the first place. The apostles were just following the Scriptures or the Word of God and were fulfilling what the Scripture says in Psalm 109:8. You see, the Holy Spirit doesn't lead us independent of the Scriptures. Because He inspired the Scriptures and knows the Scriptures, **the Holy Spirit never leads us to do anything contrary to the Scriptures.** Therefore, whenever you hear a voice speaking to you, one way to determine whether it is the voice of the Holy Spirit or the voice of Satan is to verify it from the Scriptures — to see whether the statement is contrary to the Scriptures or in harmony with the Scriptures. As we know, Jesus had already opened the minds of the disciples to understand the Scriptures (see Luke 24:45), so they knew what they were doing when they cast lots to elect Matthias as an apostle; and they were acting with the wisdom of the Holy Spirit.

Now, concerning the casting of lots to elect an apostle to replace Judas Iscariot, the Bible says, "And in those days Peter stood up in the midst of the disciples (altogether the number of names was about a hundred and twenty), and said, "Men and brethren, this SCRIPTURE had to be fulfilled, WHICH THE HOLY SPIRIT SPOKE before by the mouth of David concerning Judas, who became a guide to those who arrested Jesus; for he was numbered with us and obtained a part in this ministry." "Therefore, of these men who have accompanied us all the time that the Lord Jesus went in and out among us, beginning from the baptism of John to that day when He was taken up from us, ONE OF THESE MUST BECOME A WITNESS WITH US OF His resurrection." And they proposed two: Joseph called Barsabas, who was surnamed Justus, and Matthias. And THEY PRAYED and said, "You, O Lord, who know the hearts of all, SHOW WHICH OF THESE TWO You HAVE CHOSEN to take part in this ministry and apostleship from which Judas by transgression fell, that he might go to his own place." And THEY CAST THEIR LOTS, and the lot fell on MATTHIAS. And he was numbered with the eleven apostles." (Acts 1:15-17, 21-26). It will be sad to suggest that the prayer of the disciples was not answered by God, in the same way as it would be tragic to suggest that the Holy Spirit was not privy to the choice of Matthias to be numbered with the eleven apostles as a replacement for Judas Iscariot. Besides, it was the same or similar method the apostles used after the Day of Pentecost to choose seven men to serve the tables or oversee the daily distribution. When the twelve apostles summoned the multitude of the disciples and asked them to seek out from among themselves seven men of good reputation, full of the Holy Spirit and wisdom, whom the apostles may appoint over the business of serving tables, the Bible says, "And the saying pleased the whole multitude. And THEY CHOSE Stephen, a man full of faith and the Holy Spirit, and Philip, Prochorus, Nicanor, Timon, Parmenas, and Nicolas, a proselyte from Antioch, whom they set before the apostles; and when they had prayed, they laid hands on them." (Acts 6:5-6). Now, how did the multitude of disciples choose these seven men? Did the Holy Spirit send a list from Heaven? NO. They followed whatever wisdom the Holy Spirit gave them. The truth is that the Holy Spirit leads us from within, because He lives in us. And so the apostles did what the Holy Spirit told them (from within) to do in electing or choosing Matthias, in the same way as they did what He told them (from within) to do in electing or choosing those seven men to serve tables. In both instances, the disciples were the ones who chose the people through prayer and faith. And that is just how the Holy Spirit leads us in such matters.

God wants us to ask Him for counsel and direction in every plan we make or every step we take. And we do this through prayer, and faith that is founded on knowledge of the Word of God. In the Old Testament God rebuked the children of Israel for not asking Him for counsel and direction: "Woe to the rebellious children," says the Lord, "Who TAKE COUNSEL, BUT NOT of Me, And who DEVISE PLANS, BUT NOT of My Spirit, that they may add sin to sin; who walk to go down to Egypt, and HAVE NOT ASKED My ADVICE, to strengthen themselves in the strength of Pharaoh, and to trust in the shadow of Egypt!" (Isaiah 30:1-2). God takes His leading of His children seriously, and He leads us by His Spirit. "For as many as are led by the Spirit of God, these are the sons of God." (Romans 8:14). All children of God are led by the Spirit of God. Jesus was led by the Spirit of God. (see Matthew 4:1; Luke 4:1; Luke 4:14). The early disciples were also led by the Spirit of God. And so must we.

The Spirit tells us things to come and gives us direction. As we noted earlier, the prophet Isaiah said of our day that, "Your ears shall hear a word behind you, saying, "This is the way, walk in it," whenever you turn to the right hand or whenever you turn to the left." (Isaiah 30:21). May you hear the voice of the Spirit and follow it. The early disciples always heard and followed the voice and leading of the Spirit. They were directed by the Spirit throughout their ministry, sometimes being **compelled** to go to certain places or do certain things, and other times being **forbidden** from going to certain places. For instance, the Bible says, "When Silas and Timothy had come from Macedonia, Paul WAS **COMPELLED** BY THE SPIRIT, and testified to the Jews that Jesus is the Christ." (Acts 18:5). In another instance, the Bible says, "Now when they had gone through Phrygia and the region of Galatia, THEY WERE **FORBIDDEN** BY THE HOLY SPIRIT to preach the word in Asia. After they had come to Mysia, they tried to go into Bithynia, but THE SPIRIT DID NOT PERMIT THEM." (Acts 16:6-7). The Holy Spirit also testified when there was looming danger; He told them about things to come, just as Jesus had promised. For example, the Bible says, "Then one of them, named Agabus, stood up and SHOWED BY THE SPIRIT that there was going to be a GREAT FAMINE throughout all the world, which also happened in the days of Claudius Caesar." (Acts 11:28). On another occasion, Luke reports of the prophet Agabus that, "When he had come to us, he took Paul's belt, bound his own hands and feet, and said, "THUS SAYS THE HOLY SPIRIT, 'So shall the Jews at Jerusalem BIND the man who owns this belt, and DELIVER him INTO THE HANDS OF THE GENTILES.'" (Acts 21:11). Paul is also quoted as saying, "And see, now I go bound (or compelled) in the spirit to Jerusalem, not knowing the things that will happen to me there, except that THE HOLY SPIRIT TESTIFIES IN EVERY CITY, SAYING that CHAINS AND TRIBULATIONS AWAIT ME." (Acts 20:22-23). Also, Luke tells us that, in Tyre, they found some disciples there, "And finding disciples, we stayed there seven days. THEY TOLD Paul THROUGH THE SPIRIT not to go up to Jerusalem." (Acts 21:4). Those disciples in Tyre told Paul through the Spirit not to go to Jerusalem. And so the Spirit was leading the disciples in every way — teaching them, speaking boldly through them, speaking to them, performing miracles in and through them, guiding their every move, helping them and comforting them, revealing to them things to come and protecting them from danger. Indeed, the early disciples walked in the COMFORT or encouragement of the Holy Spirit. The Holy Spirit was truly their Comforter. The Bible says, "Then the churches throughout all Judea, Galilee, and Samaria had peace and were edified. And WALKING in the fear of the Lord and IN THE COMFORT

OF THE HOLY SPIRIT, they were multiplied." (Acts 9:31). Beloved, may you also be led by the Holy Spirit and walk in the comfort of the Holy Spirit.

The Holy Spirit lives in you, so you can talk to Him anytime and anywhere. Consult Him regarding any decision, plan or action you desire to take. Never doubt the leading of the Holy Spirit. He is more interested in the affairs of your life than you can imagine, so listen to His leading in your heart. The Holy Spirit will always bear witness with your spirit. (see Romans 8:16). Therefore, you can be sure of His leading, your conscience also bearing you witness IN the Holy Spirit. (see Romans 9:1). You can continually enjoy His tangible presence and His leading by always being conscious of His presence, acknowledging Him and talking to Him not only in worship and in prayer but in every undertaking. In my daily devotions, I always ask the Holy Spirit to help me to pray and worship the Lord, because just as Romans 8:26 states, I don't always know what to pray for as I ought. But the Spirit knows. And thankfully, every time I ask Him to help me, my prayer is filled with His presence and is very smooth and effortless. I also talk to the Holy Spirit all the time, thanking Him, telling Him how much I love Him and how much I appreciate His love, His help, His comfort, His teachings, His guidance, His protection, His strengthening, His power, His communion, and the fact that He is always with me and will never leave nor forsake me. I always ask the Holy Spirit for explanation when I don't understand something in Scripture or just anything, and He always responds. When I am going to a meeting, I would ask the Holy Spirit if there is anything I need to be aware of about the people I am meeting. It is always comforting to talk to the Holy Spirit and to hear Him talk back. He will actively engage you in conversation if you will allow Him to. May you enjoy communion or fellowship with the Holy Spirit. "The grace of the Lord Jesus Christ, and the love of God, and the COMMUNION OF THE HOLY SPIRIT be with you all. Amen." (2 Corinthians 13:14).

Be Turned into Another Man

Now, let's conclude this chapter with this amazing passage from the Old Testament regarding the impact of the Holy Spirit upon a man: *"Then the Spirit of the Lord will COME UPON YOU, and you will **prophesy** with them and **BE TURNED INTO ANOTHER MAN**. And let it be, when these signs come to you, that you do as the occasion demands; for God is with you." (I Samuel 10:6-7).*

The words above were spoken to King Saul in the Old Testament. Now, imagine the Spirit of God upon a man turning him into ANOTHER MAN, a super man. Beloved you will cease to be a mere man when the Spirit of God comes upon you. Get baptized in the Holy Spirit and begin to walk in power. Paul said, "For our gospel DID NOT come to you IN WORD ONLY, but also **IN POWER**, and **IN THE Holy Spirit** and in much assurance, as you know WHAT KIND OF MEN WE WERE among you for your sake." (1 Thessalonians 1:5). Indeed there are many kinds of men, but you can be the kind that has the Spirit of God upon him. Be the kind of man that walks in demonstration of the Spirit, and of power. When the Spirit of God came upon Jesus Christ and He was walking in power, commanding the sea and the winds to be still, "The men marveled, saying, **WHAT MANNER OF MAN IS THIS**, that even the winds and the sea obey

Him!" (Matthew 8:27 KJV). He was the manner of Man who had the Spirit of God upon Him.

The Holy Spirit, when He came upon the early disciples at Pentecost, also brought them power, and they became Spirit-filled men who were so bold and powerful that (in the words of the unbelieving Jews) they "turned the world upside down." (see Acts 17:6). The Holy Spirit belongs to you also if you're a believer. The Holy Spirit is already in you through the born-again experience. But Jesus wants Him (the Holy Spirit) to come upon you also, and fill you, so that you will be ENDUED WITH POWER from on high, and BE A WITNESS to our Lord Jesus Christ, in your immediate locality and all around the world. Jesus said that God will give the Holy Spirit to those who ask Him. (see Luke 11:13). So if the Holy Spirit hasn't come upon you yet, ask our Heavenly Father in prayer; and Jesus Christ who baptizes with the Holy Spirit (see Matthew 3:11; John 1:33) will send Him upon you. You can also ask any Spirit-filled believer to lay hands on you to receive the Holy Spirit. (see Acts 8:18). If you have already been baptized in the Holy Spirit, then know this: **the secret to walking in power as a Spirit-baptized Christian is to BELIEVE that you have received the same Spirit and power that was upon the Lord Jesus Christ when He walked here on earth.** When you believe this and then act in faith, you will be indomitable, commanding circumstances and situations, and trampling upon serpents and scorpions and all the power of the devil; nothing will be impossible to you.

Indeed, when the Holy Spirit comes upon you and fills you, and you yield (or surrender) to Him and walk in the consciousness of His presence, exercising His power, you will never be an ordinary man; you will be turned into another man — a man in whom the fullness of God dwells and manifests, a man anointed with the Spirit of God and the power of God, a man to whom all things are possible. And your works will testify of you that you are truly the son of God, thus bringing glory to God the Father and to our Lord Jesus Christ. May this be a reality in your life.

In the final and concluding chapter of this book (which is coming up next), we will identify and discuss the three different kinds or categories of people in this world, and emphasize the need for each of us to grow into spiritual men and women.

Chapter 20

Unleash the Spiritual Man Inside of You

THE BIBLE IDENTIFIES three categories of people in this world. There is the NATURAL MAN, the CARNAL MAN, and the SPIRITUAL MAN. If you've been reading this book from the beginning to this point, you must already know the differences between these three categories of people. The NATURAL MAN is the person who has not yet accepted Jesus Christ as his Lord and Savior. Such a person is not born again (or born of the Spirit of God) and, therefore, lives a life that is dominated by his fleshly desires or the lusts of his body. His body (or flesh) rules over his soul and spirit, because he is spiritually dead or dead to God, alienated from the life of God. (see Ephesians 4:18). Every man born of Adam (or born of the flesh) is a NATURAL MAN and a sinner, until he comes to believe in Jesus Christ as his Lord and Savior and is born of the Spirit, so that he becomes a spirit or a spiritual man (see John 3:6; 1 Corinthians 3:1; 1 Corinthians 15:45-49). Prior to accepting Jesus Christ, every one of us was living in the flesh (or according to our senses); we were living after (the desires of) the flesh (the body), and our mind was dominated by the flesh (or the desires of the senses), and thus, we had what the Bible calls the mind of the flesh, which is death. (see Romans 8:6). And when you're in the flesh, your primary concern and preoccupation is what you're going to eat, drink and wear. Your life is dominated by your fleshly needs; your mind is occupied by what your body needs, as opposed to what your spirit needs. The Bible says, "The mind governed by the flesh is hostile to God; it does not submit to God's law, nor can it do so. Those who are in the realm of the flesh cannot please God" (Romans 8:7-8 NIV). In other words, the natural man does not, and cannot live a life that is pleasing to God. Thus the Bible emphasizes the distinction between the NATURAL MAN and the SPIRITUAL MAN, in these words: "But the NATURAL MAN does not receive the things of the Spirit of God, for they are foolishness to him; nor can he know them, because they are spiritually discerned. But HE WHO IS SPIRITUAL judges all things, yet he himself is rightly judged by no one." (1 Corinthians 2:14-15). Indeed the natural man does not receive the things of the Spirit of God, because he neither SEES nor KNOWS the Spirit of God; and of course, he also cannot receive the Spirit of God. (see John 14:17). And so everything that is from the Spirit of God is foolishness to the natural man. The Bible says that the message of the cross is foolishness to the natural man who is perishing. (see 1 Corinthians 1:18). Again, the natural man is not able to judge the spiritual man rightly, but the spiritual man judges all things. (see 1 Corinthians 2:14-15). When Paul preached Jesus and the resurrection to those Epicurean and Stoic philosophers in Athens, these natural men judged Paul (the spiritual man) wrongly as a "babbler" and "a proclaimer of foreign gods" (see Acts 17:18), whereas Paul judged them rightly as ignorant (see Acts 17:29-30). Paul's preaching about the cross and the resurrection was foolishness to those who were perishing, and they even mocked Paul (see Acts 17:32), but to those of them who were being saved (see Acts 17:34), the message of the cross was, and still is, the power of God. (see 1 Corinthians 1:18). Hallelujah!

My dear friend, if you believe in Jesus Christ, or if you accept Him right now as your Lord and Savior, you are a new creation (see 2 Corinthians 5:17), and you're no longer a natural man. The Bible says that as new creations in Christ we have been blessed with every spiritual blessing in the heavenly realms in Christ Jesus. (see Ephesians 1:3). So our responsibility today is to take possession or lay hold of all the blessings that belong to us. We have to KNOW all the things that have been freely given to us of God (see 1 Corinthians 2:12), and then LAY HOLD OF THEM, "giving thanks to the Father who has qualified us to be partakers of the inheritance of the saints in the light." (see Colossians 1:12). Purpose in your heart today that you're going to enjoy or lay hold on your share of the inheritance of the saints in the light. This is important because becoming a new creation, or being born into God's Family does not automatically give you full access to your inheritance in Christ. You cannot enjoy your full rights of sonship until you come to maturity in Christ. Yes, you are still an heir of God and joint-heirs with Christ (see Romans 8:17), but "What I am saying is that AS LONG AS an heir is UNDERAGE, he is NO DIFFERENT FROM A SLAVE, although he OWNS THE WHOLE ESTATE." (Galatians 4:1 NIV). This thus brings us to the remaining two categories of people in this world, both of which are believers or Christians.

As a Christian or a new creation in Christ, you fall into one of two categories: you're either a BABY (an underage son), or a MATURE son of God. You are either a CARNAL man, or a SPIRITUAL man. The CARNAL MAN is the BABY CHRISTIAN, or the new creation man who has not grown or come into full maturity and so does not yet fully know what belongs to him, and consequently does not enjoy his full share of the inheritance of the saints in light. Such a man is governed by his senses (or what he can see, feel and hear, taste and smell), rather than by his spirit. The apostle Paul makes mention of the CARNAL Christian in his first epistle to the Corinthians, where he writes, "And I, brethren, could not speak to you as to SPIRITUAL people but as to CARNAL, as to BABES in Christ. I fed you with milk and not with solid food; for until now you were not able to receive it, and even now you are still not able; for you are still CARNAL. For where there are envy, strife, and divisions among you, are you not carnal and BEHAVING LIKE MERE MEN?" (I Corinthians 3:1-3). The carnal Christian behaves like a mere man, and walks like the (natural) men of the world, like the rest of the Gentiles walk. The Bible says he is unskilled in the word of righteousness (in other words, he does not fully understand the Word of God and its teachings regarding the righteous identity of the believer and how to practice righteousness), because he is a baby (see Hebrews 5:13); he has not learned to walk in love, and so is riddled with envy, strife, and selfishness. (see 1 Corinthians 3:3). He has not renewed his mind with the Word of God to know that God has poured His love into the heart of the believer through the Holy Spirit that is in us (see Romans 5:5). He has not caught a revelation of how much Christ has loved him, and so is yet to learn to walk according to the law of love. (see John 13:34-35; John 15:12). He has not yet learned to be an imitator of God, as a beloved child, walking in love even as Christ has loved him. (see Ephesians 5:1-2). In short, the Carnal or baby Christian is the Christian whose mind is not yet renewed. Peter tells us in his first epistle about how such a Christian can grow. He says,

"Therefore, laying aside all malice, all deceit, hypocrisy, envy, and all evil speaking, AS NEWBORN BABES, DESIRE THE PURE MILK OF THE WORD, that you may GROW thereby, if indeed you have tasted that the Lord is gracious." (I Peter 2:1-3).

In fact, almost every believer goes through the Carnal or babyhood stage. But we're not supposed to remain babies or carnally minded forever or for too long, "For to be carnally minded is death, but to be spiritually minded is life and peace." (Romans 8:6). By reason of time, we are to grow and come to maturity and become spiritually minded, and even become teachers. (see Hebrews 5:12-14). All that the baby or Carnal Christian needs to do to develop and come to maturity is to put on the spirit man (or the new man) by renewing his mind with the inspired Word of God. (see Romans 12:1-2; Ephesians 4:24; Colossians 3:10). Feeding on the pure Word of God is how we grow up to become spiritually minded, to become Spiritual men and women. And thankfully, God has given us the Holy Spirit (see 1 John 2:27), as well as pastors, apostles, prophets, teachers, and so forth, to help us in this regard. Thus Paul wrote that God "Himself gave some to be apostles, some prophets, some evangelists, and some pastors and teachers, for the equipping of the saints for the work of ministry, for the edifying of the body of Christ, till we all come to the unity of the faith and of the knowledge of the Son of God, **to a perfect man, to the measure of the stature of the fullness of Christ**" (Ephesians 4:11-13). Let everyone of us, therefore, take full advantage of all the resources God has made available to the Church for its edification and growth.

Now, the SPIRITUAL MAN is the new creation man who, through a continuous and committed study of the Word of God (with the help of the Holy Spirit), has renewed his mind and come to maturity as a complete man, to the measure of the stature of the fullness of Christ. He is the believer who is skilled in the Word of righteousness, who walks in love, who is continually filled with the Spirit and consistently walks in the Spirit, and who is not governed by his senses, and so is not governed by natural laws. He has developed in the things of God (through the renewal of his mind with the Word of God) to a point where his spirit has gained the ascendancy over his intellect and his senses. He is not limited by natural laws, because He operates by a different law called "the law of faith." (see Romans 3:27). He is governed by the Word of God, by the law of faith. And with that comes endless possibilities. In fact, you cannot limit the Spiritual man, because all things are possible to him. Jesus Christ, throughout His earth walk, was a perfect example of the Spiritual man, and He was the One who made the astounding statement that "all things are possible to him who believes." (see Mark 9:23). Jesus Himself functioned on this earth by "the law of faith." He defied all the natural laws. He walked on water as easily as He did on solid ground. (see Matthew 14:22-33). He bypassed the laws of nature by changing tasteless water into the finest wine. (see John 2:1-11). He defied the law of scarcity by feeding 5000 men with five loaves of bread and two fish. (Matthew 14:13-21; John 6:1-14). He defied the laws of medical science by healing all diseases, including diseases that science had classified as incurable. (see Matthew 4:23; Matthew 9:35). He even defied death by raising the dead back to life. (see John 11:41-44; Matthew 9:25 Mark 5:21-42). He defied the forces of nature, commanding the wind to be still and the storm to be calm. (see Mark 4:35-41). He defied the laws of banking by withdrawing money from the mouth of a fish — turning it into the first ever ATM machine. (see Matthew

17:24-27). Jesus was a wonder to the natural man. He inspired such an awe that made Pilate proclaim: "Behold the Man!" (see John 19:5). He was indeed the Man! Jesus was the ultimate Spiritual Man. He was everything the New Creation man is in the spirit, and is capable of being in the soul and body.

Beloved you are a new creation in Christ, so you are a giant in the spirit realm. The Bible says that as Jesus is, so are you in this world. (see 1 John 4:17). This means that in your spirit, you are as perfect and powerful as Jesus Christ. You are complete in Christ. (see Colossians 2:10). You are a spiritual giant. You bear the image of the heavenly Man Jesus Christ. You have His glory. (see John 17:22; Romans 8:30). But you have to manifest that glory; you have to unleash that giant that you are in the spirit realm into the physical realm; you have to allow the life of Jesus that is in your spirit to manifest or be revealed in your body, by renewing your mind with the Word of God and walking in the Spirit and not according to the flesh. You have to allow the Word of God to abide in you to a point where the Word gains ascendancy over your mind and body. You have to become one with the Word, and walk according to the Word, being in harmony with the will of God for this age. That is how you can lay hold on all that belongs to you as a child of God. May you begin this journey today, if you haven't already. May you know all the things that have been freely given to us by God. May you know that you have been freely given the gift of righteousness in Christ (see 2 Corinthians 5:21; Romans 5:17), that you are the righteousness of God in Christ Jesus, which not only means that you can effortlessly practice righteousness, but also, that you have the ability to stand before God in fellowship, without any sense of guilt, condemnation or inferiority. May you know that you have been freely given the measure of faith. (see Romans 12:3). May you know that you have been given grace (see Ephesians 4:7), and that you stand (permanently) in grace (see Romans 5:2); you are highly favored, you are surrounded with favor as with a shield (see Psalm 5:12), because you are righteous and are accepted in the Beloved (see Ephesians 1:6). May you know that you have been freely given peace and joy and love (see Romans 5:1; Ephesians 2:14; John 15:11; Romans 5:5). May you know that you have been given the kingdom, the power, and the glory (see Luke 22:29; Ephesians 1:19-20; Acts 1:8; John 17:22). May you know that God's divine power has given to you all things that pertain to life and godliness (see 2 Peter 1:3). May you know that you have overcome the world because you are born of God. (see 1 John 5:4-5). May you know that you have overcome Satan and his antichrist spirit, because He who is in you is greater than he who is in the world (see 1 John 4:4). May you know that the spirits are subject to you, and that your name is written in the Book of Life. (see Luke 10:20). May you know that you are complete in Christ. (Colossians 2:9-10). May you know that you are a partaker of God's Spirit (see Hebrews 6:4) and a partaker of the divine (or God) nature. (see 2 Peter 1:4). And may you walk according to all that knowledge. May you be an imitator of God, as a beloved child, walking in love even as Christ has loved you. (see Ephesians 5:1-2). "And whatever you do in word or deed, DO ALL IN THE NAME OF THE LORD JESUS, giving thanks to God the Father through Him." (Colossians 3:17).

Indeed, **the Spiritual man walks in Christ Jesus**; the Spiritual man speaks and does everything IN THE NAME OF THE LORD JESUS. The name of the Lord Jesus is the Name above all names; it is the NAME at the mention of which every knee should bow — of those in heaven, on earth, and under the earth. (see Philippians 2:9-10). And so this excellent name of the Lord Jesus represents His authority, power, might, and the fullness of His being. Hence, the spiritual man heeds to the Bible's admonition to believers that we speak and do all things in the Name (i.e. in the authority, power and identity) of the Lord Jesus. (see Colossians 3:17). In other words, the spiritual man does not do anything in his own name or in his own "human" capacity and ability, but in the ability and capacity of the Lord Jesus (who lives in him). The spiritual man understands and heeds "the word of the LORD to Zerubbabel: 'Not by might nor by power, but by my Spirit,' says the LORD Almighty." (see Zechariah 4:6 NIV). The Spiritual man does not walk or do anything by the might of man or by the power of man, but by the Spirit of God. The spiritual man preaches the gospel by the Holy Spirit. (see 1 Peter 1:12). The spiritual man demonstrates the Spirit and power of God. (see 1 Corinthians 2:4-5). We all have to grow in our Christian walk to the point where we consistently yield to the Spirit and power of God that is at work in us (see Philippians 2:13; Ephesians 3:20), and speak and do all things as though Jesus Himself were the one speaking and doing it. This calls for an acute awareness on our part that Jesus truly lives in us, that the Spirit of Christ lives in us, that He that is in us is greater than he that is in the world. (see 1 John 4:4). Even Jesus, while He walked on this earth as a Man said, "I can of Mine own self do nothing." (see John 5:30 KJV). And He didn't have to do anything of His own self, for He had the Father in Him, and He was conscious of the Father in Him. It was the Father in Him who did the works. (see John 14:10). Therefore, to us also, Jesus said, "without Me you can do nothing." (see John 15:5). And thankfully we are not without Him, for He is in us, Christ is in us (see Colossians 1:27), which is why Paul, living in the consciousness of Christ in Him, could say, "I can do all things through Christ who strengthens me." (see Philippians 4:13). When you're acting in the name (or authority and power) of the Lord Jesus, you can do all things — all things will be possible to you. Jesus said that all things are possible to the one who believes. (see Mark 9:23). Beloved, if you believe in the name of the Lord Jesus, and do all things in that NAME, all things will be possible to you.

Wherever you stand to speak or act today and always, do so as though Jesus Himself were doing it. After all, you have clothed yourself with Jesus Christ (see Galatians 3:27); it is no longer you who lives, but Christ lives in you. (see Galatians 2:20). Thus, you represent Jesus on this earth, as He lives in and through you. You are Christ's ambassador. (see 2 Corinthians 5:20). You are the express image of His being. Have this consciousness then, that when you show up anywhere, Jesus shows up; when you speak, Jesus speaks; when you do something, Jesus does it. This is only true when you believe it and act in the name of the Lord Jesus, conscious of the presence of Christ in you, and of the authority He has given you to live in His name and act in His name. The spiritual man lives this truth. And you can be that man. You can be the man who says as his mantra: "I am to speak and do all things in the name of the Lord Jesus. I am to take His place, and act with His authority or in His capacity, just as an ambassador of a country will act in the name (authority and capacity) of his president and country. I am to do all things as though the Lord Jesus were the one doing it, because He is in me with His ability, His working works in me mightily, I am joined as one with Him in spirit and body, and I have His authority to act in His Name. He that is in me is greater than he that is in the world. Jesus lives in me and through me to exercise

His authority and His power through my words and my deeds. I can do all things through Christ who strengthens me. He has given me the power of attorney (that empowers me) to speak and do everything in His Name. I am to fully assume and exercise the authority of Jesus in all my undertakings, giving thanks to God the Father through Him. Praise God!"

Beloved, I encourage you to grow in the Lord and manifest your true identity as a spiritual man, if you're not doing so already. Don't settle for the babyhood stage of Christianity. Delight yourself in the Lord; get into the Word of God — study it, meditate on it and do the Word — and see yourself mature into a spiritual man or woman, "to the measure of the stature of the fullness of Christ" (Ephesians 4:13). And do not neglect to pray continually also both with your spirit and with your understanding. When you live and walk as a spiritual man, nothing will be impossible to you; you will not have any unanswered prayers. The Bible says, "**Delight yourself also in the Lord**, and **He shall give you the desires of your heart**. Commit your way to the Lord, **trust also in Him**, and **He shall bring it to pass**." (Psalm 37:4-5).

Somebody asked me the other day: "**Can Satan thwart or withstand the answer to our prayer under the New Covenant**, as he did to Daniel (see Daniel 10:12-13) under the Old Covenant?" And my answer was NO — not if you're a spiritual man (or a mature believer who knows and believes the Word, and trusts in the Lord). You see, Satan can influence anything you do as a believer, including your prayer life, if you are a baby, if you don't know who you are, or if you don't know or believe your rights and privileges (or your inheritance in Christ). Indeed, **prayer in the New Covenant is very different**

from the Old Covenant, but you have to understand it. Under the Old Covenant, the glories that were to follow the sufferings of Jesus Christ were not available to the believers (see 1 Peter 1:10-12), so Satan still had power to influence many things, including their prayers, an example of which is recorded in Daniel 10:12-13. Still, Satan could not win over the believers, because the Lord was with them. Moreover, under the Old Covenant they did not pray in the (wonderful and excellent) NAME of Jesus.

The Bible calls Satan "the prince (or ruler) of the power (or kingdom) of the air." (see Ephesians 2:2). And so "the prince of the kingdom of Persia" in Daniel 10:12-13 is a reference to Satan. Satan had the power in the past to withstand or fight against the answer to the prayers of believers (even mature believers like Daniel), even though Satan always lost the battle. But today, under the New Covenant, Satan does not have any such power to withstand or thwart the answer to our prayers, because Jesus has defeated Satan (on our behalf) and we are living in that victory. The Bible says, "He (God) has delivered us from the power of darkness (or the power of Satan) and conveyed us into the kingdom of the Son of His love" (see Colossians 1:13). And of course, we have to live in the consciousness of this truth. Jesus died on the cross on our behalf (and the Bible says that we died with Him — see Romans 6:8; and then He was buried (and the Bible says that we were buried with Him — see Romans 6:4). Thus we were still with Him when He went to hell on our behalf, and defeated Satan on our behalf, and so we were raised with Him in His resurrection into newness of life (see Romans 6:4-11; Ephesians 2:6), into a life of glory. So the victory Jesus won over Satan is our victory. In that battle, Jesus disarmed Satan. He entered Satan the strong man's house, tied him up, and plundered his house. (see Mark 3:27). The Bible says Jesus disarmed the rulers and authorities (i.e. Satan and his demons); then He made a public spectacle of them, triumphing over them in it. (see Colossians 2:15). Jesus paralyzed Satan; He destroyed him; He rendered Satan powerless. (see Hebrews 2:14). And that victory is our victory. (see 1 John 4:4; 1 John 5:4-5; 1 Corinthians 15:57; 2 Corinthians 2:14).

The Bible says that after Jesus defeated Satan in hell and was raised from the dead, He stood before His disciples and declared that all authority has been given to Him in heaven and on earth. (see Matthew 28:18). Then, Jesus gave that authority to us (His disciples), commanding us to go in **His Name** and make disciples of all nations, baptizing them in the name of the Father, of the Son, and of the Holy Spirit. He said anyone who believes and is baptized will be saved. Then He added, an amazing statement, saying, "And these signs will follow those who believe: **In My Name** THEY WILL CAST OUT DEMONS; they will speak with new tongues; they will take up serpents; and if they drink anything deadly, it will by no means hurt them; they will lay hands on the sick, and they will recover." (Mark 16:17-18. See also Luke 10:17-19). It is just amazing that Jesus gave all believers authority over demons, and over Satan. But sadly, many believers are not laying hold on that authority. Jesus said that **in His name**, we will cast out demons, we will trample upon serpents and scorpions and upon all the power of the devil. The spirits are subject to us in the Name of Jesus. (see Luke 10:20). Today, we who are born of God (i.e. all believers) have overcome the world and its god or ruler, who is Satan (see 2 Corinthians 4:4); and **this is the victory** that has overcome the world—**our FAITH**. (see 1 John 5:4). And so the

Bible declares that "You are of God, little children, and have overcome them (i.e. Satan and his antichrist spirit), because He who is in you is greater than he who is in the world." (see 1 John 4:4). Hallelujah! Today, all you need to do is believe these truths and act on them. All you need to do to reign (as a king) in life is to receive abundance of grace and the gift of righteousness that is in Christ Jesus; accept all that Jesus has already accomplished for you, as revealed in the Bible. The Bible says, "For if by the one man's offense death reigned through the one, much more THOSE WHO RECEIVE **abundance of grace** and of **the GIFT of righteousness** WILL **REIGN IN LIFE** through the One, Jesus Christ." (Romans 5:17).

Indeed, the New Covenant is a superior Covenant with better promises. (see Hebrews 8:6). In the New Covenant, God has made every believer righteous (see 2 Corinthians 5:21; Romans 3:22; Romans 5:17; 1 Corinthians 1:30), and God has made every believer a partaker of the divine nature. God Himself lives in the believer. The body of the New Covenant believer is the temple of God. (see 1 Corinthians 3:16; 1 Corinthians 6:19). And so, because God Himself lives in us, the Bible says God (with His mighty power) **works in us** both to will and to do for His good pleasure (see Philippians 2:13). Therefore, our prayers are answered right from within us. The answer to our prayer doesn't even have to come from Heaven, since God lives in us and His power is within us. Hence, the Bible says that God "is able to do immeasurably MORE than ALL WE ASK or imagine, **ACCORDING TO HIS POWER THAT IS AT WORK WITHIN US**" (see Ephesians 3:20 NIV). The answer to our prayers, therefore, cannot be thwarted or withstood by Satan. The Bible says, "The prayer of a righteous person is powerful and effective." (see James 5:16 NIV). The believer is the righteous person this verse is referring to. Jesus Himself is our righteousness. (see 1 Corinthians 1:30). Therefore, because we are righteous, our prayer is powerful and effective. The Bible again says that, "the eyes of the Lord are on the righteous and His ears are attentive to their prayer..." (see 1 Peter 3:12 NIV). Today the only thing that can withstand the answer to our prayers is UNBELIEF, and not Satan. Jesus said, "Therefore I say to you, whatever things you ask **when you pray**, BELIEVE THAT YOU RECEIVE them, AND YOU WILL HAVE them." (Mark 11:24). Then the Spirit, speaking through James, also adds that we are to "ask in FAITH, with NO DOUBTING, for HE WHO DOUBTS is like a wave of the sea driven and tossed by the wind. For LET NOT THAT MAN SUPPOSE THAT HE WILL RECEIVE ANYTHING from the Lord" (James 1:6-7). John also adds in his epistle: "Now this is the CONFIDENCE that we have in Him, that IF WE ASK ANYTHING according to His will, **He hears us**. And **if we know that He hears us**, WHATEVER WE ASK, WE KNOW THAT **WE HAVE THE PETITIONS THAT WE HAVE ASKED OF HIM.**" (1 John 5:14-15). Asking according to His will in this context simply means asking with the right motive (see James 4:3), and in the manner in which Jesus taught us to ask. Jesus said we should ASK THE FATHER in the NAME of Jesus. We are NOT to pray to Jesus when we need something; we are to pray to the Father in the NAME of Jesus. (see John 16:23-24). Once we have prayed with the right motive, and in the manner Jesus asked us to, we are to believe and know that whatever we have asked for, we have received. This is faith. And this is what the Bible teaches.

Thus, FAITH is the single most important factor in getting our prayers answered. The Bible says, as we noted earlier, that, as believers we are already blessed with every spiritual blessing in the heavenly realms in Christ Jesus. (see Ephesians 1:3). ALL THINGS are ours. (see 1 Corinthians 3:21-23). Therefore, when we pray, we are just bringing into the physical realm that which is already ours in the spiritual realm. FAITH is therefore the key that releases the answer to our prayer from the spiritual realm into the physical realm. FAITH is like the ATM card that withdraws money from our bank account. The money is already ours; but we can't receive it in our hand at the ATM, without asking with the ATM card. The Bible says, "Now faith is the substance of things hoped for, the evidence of things not seen" (Hebrews 11:1). It is your faith that gives substance to your prayer; it brings the answer God has already given to your prayer, into its physical manifestation. God gives the answer to you in the spirit immediately when you pray; then faith brings it into the physical realm. This is why the Bible emphasizes that whenever you pray, you have to **believe** that something has happened beyond what your five senses can perceive; you have to believe that the answer has been given. If you don't believe it, you won't receive anything from God. (see James 1:6-7). It is as simple as that. And this also explains why some believers get their prayers answered, and others don't. It is simply the truth that some believers are spiritual, and others are carnal, even though the ideal is for all believers to be Spiritual men and women. Spiritual men immediately receive (by faith) the answer to their prayer, whereas Carnal Christians often argue in favor of Satan having power to thwart or withstand the answer to their prayers. But just think about it: the Bible says you have to believe you receive (at the very moment) when you pray. So where does Satan come into the equation?

Beloved, the only way Satan can fight against your prayer or withstand the answer to your prayer under the New Covenant, is to fight against YOUR FAITH. If Satan can take control over your mind and fill your heart with doubt, or cause you to doubt that God has answered your prayer, then he has succeeded in thwarting or withstanding the answer to your prayer. And so the Bible says we should give no place to the devil. (see Ephesians 4:27). We are to submit to God, resist the devil, and he will flee from us. (see James 4:7). Paul said, "The weapons we fight with are not the weapons of the world. On the contrary, they have divine power to demolish strongholds. We demolish arguments and every pretension that sets itself up against the knowledge of God, and we take captive every thought to make it obedient to Christ." (2 Corinthians 10:4-5 NIV). The strongholds Paul is talking about here are the arguments and claims Satan throws into our mind (through people and circumstances), to try to cause us to doubt the Word (or knowledge) of God. And the weapons of our warfare that we are to use to withstand Satan and lay hold on our victory are also listed in Ephesians 6:10-18. We demolish the strongholds of Satan the enemy with the shield of FAITH. The Bible says, "In all circumstances take up **the shield of faith**, with which you can **extinguish all the flaming darts of the evil one**" (Ephesians 6:16). FAITH is the key to getting answers to our prayers. We should all be steadfast in faith like our father Abraham. (see Romans 4:19-20). This is what spiritual men do. Also, spiritual men do not cherish sin in our heart. When we cherish sin in our heart it affects our confidence toward God; it makes us wonder about or doubt if we are good enough to receive from the Lord. And of course, if our heart condemns us, then we are condemned, our doubts will prevent us from receiving the answer to our prayer. This is why the Psalmist says, "If I had cherished sin in my heart, the Lord would not have listened; but God has surely listened and has heard my prayer." (Psalm 66:18-19 NIV). Because the Psalmist did not cherish sin in his heart, he had confidence toward God that He had **surely** listened and heard his prayer. Spiritual men walk in love, and when we walk in love, we will not cherish sin in our heart, and so we will have confidence toward God that He has surely heard and answered our prayers. The realm of love is where prayers are answered. Thus the apostle John writes: "My little children, let us not love in word or in tongue, but in deed and in truth. And **by this** we know that we are of the truth, and **shall assure our hearts before Him**. For if our heart condemns us, God is greater than our heart, and knows all things. Beloved, **if our heart does not condemn us, we have confidence toward God.** And WHATEVER WE ASK WE RECEIVE from Him, BECAUSE we KEEP His COMMANDMENTS and do those things that are PLEASING in His sight. And this is **His commandment**: that we should **BELIEVE** on the **name** of His Son Jesus Christ and **LOVE** one another, as He gave us commandment." (I John 3:18-23).

I pray in the name of our Lord Jesus Christ, that you may have a strong desire for the pure milk of the Word, so that your faith will be strengthened, as you read the Word, meditate on the Word and do the Word, even as you grow and come to maturity in Christ, to a complete man, "to the measure of the stature of the fullness of Christ" (Ephesians 4:13). I also encourage you to read the entire book again and again, until it sinks in, until it fills your heart and saturates your spirit, soul and body, until you are enlightened and empowered to walk consistently in the Spirit, so that you will not fulfill the lusts of the flesh. "For if you live according to the flesh **you will die**; but if by the Spirit you put to death the deeds of the body, **you will live**." (Romans 8:13). Remain blessed.

If this book has blessed you in an extraordinary way and you would like to share your testimony with us, please write to: vincentboatengministries@gmail.com

You are encouraged to also share the good news in this book with others; recommend the book to everyone, especially to every pastor or teacher of the Bible. If you can, get copies of this book for your relatives, friends and neighbors who need to hear this glorious message of the gospel of Christ.

You are also invited to follow Apostle Vincent Boateng on:

Twitter: @ApostleVincentB

Facebook: https://www.facebook.com/The-New-Covenant_Believer-767055796659881/

and

www.facebook.com/SpiritLifeBook/

About the Author

Vincent Boateng is an apostle and minister of the New Covenant, a bondservant of Jesus Christ, a preacher and a teacher appointed by the Lord Jesus Christ Himself to be an overseer among all the flock, to shepherd the Church of God which He purchased with His own blood. Vincent was called by our Lord Jesus Christ Himself through the Spirit to be an apostle and minister of reconciliation, "to preach peace in My name" and teach all men in faith and truth. Before his miraculous rebirth or conversion to True Christianity and his calling into ministry, Vincent was a zealous Roman Catholic, and was educated in college as a teacher of Social Studies. Vincent was also a poet and a relationship coach. His poetry collections include "A Toast to Utopia," "If You Should Ask Me Why I Love You," "The Jesus I Know," and "Fishing For a Poem." He also authored the relationship advice book "How Aliens Fall in Love: A Practical Manual For the Serious Marriage-seeking Woman." By the grace of God, Vincent, today, is a gifted preacher and teacher of the pure Gospel of Grace, having himself been well-taught by the Holy Spirit, the greatest Teacher on earth. Vincent leads a growing Online Ministry called "The New Covenant Believer" where he teaches the pure Word of God to many hungry and thirsty souls. The focus of Vincent's ministry is to point people to Jesus, to debunk false teachings, beliefs and doctrines, and to commend the brethren to God and to the Word of His grace, which is able to build them up and give them an inheritance among all those who are sanctified. The testimonies from the adherents to his teachings are astounding, and the move of the Holy Spirit through this anointed man of God is palpable. Vincent indeed has been given a gift of unparalleled depth and magnitude since the Pauline era, in unveiling the deep mysteries of the Kingdom of God. He unveils with ease and simplicity the truth vain religion doesn't have and can never give. "Spirit Life" is a testimony to God's marvelous work in Vincent, and His amazing gift to him as a teacher of the pure Word of His Grace.

May God confirm His Word with signs, wonders, miracles, and gifts of the Holy Spirit in your life as you read this book in faith, and may this book be a blessing to you and all the people you will recommend it to, in the Mighty Name of Jesus. Amen.

Glory be to God!